The Brighton Line

Three Bridges looking south towards the station from the vantage point of the Down Fast home signals. The Down sidings, a hive of activity in this photograph, were the home for numerous LB&SCR rail chairs (*below*) right up to the early 1980s when the sidings were finally taken out of use. The photograph also vividly shows how the 1907 quadrupling of the lines was carried out by widening the existing double track on both sides. The resulting 'kinks' in the distance reveal that the Up Fast line was once the Down line and the Down Slow once the Up line.
13th August 1929, The Edward Wallis Collection

Brighton on the cusp of change: in a week's time all the semaphore signals seen here were to have been swept away and the new power signalling brought into work. Amidst a sea of escaping steam, 'L' Class 'Baltic Tank' No. 332 awaits departure with the 09.20 to London Bridge. *10th October 1932, H.C. Casserley*

THE BRIGHTON LINE
BRIGHTON TO COULSDON NORTH
A SIGNALLING PERSPECTIVE

CHRIS DURRANT

Lightmoor Press

This book is dedicated to five fine railwaymen and signal engineers, all 'Brighton Line' devotees:

John Collins, John Rodriguez, Peter Jackson, Brian Hymas and the late Peter Scott.

Also to the late Wyndham 'Bob' Tubb, without whose foresight this journey would not have happened.

To my father Jack, who made that extra journey from the Traction Inspector's office at Brighton to arrive unannounced at the Signal Engineer's Department in New England Road, when he could have just gone back to work, and the enlightened Traction Inspector who suggested giving the S&T a try when he could have just said "sorry". Sadly, I never knew who he was.

This book is also dedicated to my three wonderful children: Mark, Emma and Claire; indeed the whole family, who have put up with their father's preoccupation with railways, including enduring numerous excursions to signal boxes, stations and disused railway lines when they thought they were meant to be on holiday!

As this manuscript went to press, I heard the news of the passing of two gentlemen who were a tremendous help in providing material for inclusion in this book.

John Scrace was a career railwayman whose passion was taking photographs of everything Southern. He photographed steam to diesel to electric, stations to signal boxes, and just about anything else in between that took his fancy. I first came across him through a signalman at Haywards Heath, who lived close to John in Horsham and therefore had a number of John's images amongst his own vast collection. John was my photographic hero and in my early exploration of railway photography I always tried to think of how John would have composed an image; I aspired to his perfectionism, timing and flair for composition. John and I met in the late 1970s and we became good friends. One thing that always amused him was my 'following in his footsteps' when revisiting locations, a closed station for example, where I would take a photograph from the same place where he had stood a number of years previously, my scene of desolation set against his pristine image of yesteryear.

Laurie Marshall was a collector possessing a large number of photographic albums featuring his beloved LB&SCR; if a photograph was taken after 1923, he wasn't interested. Steam was his real passion and each volume featured different images of a particular type of locomotive – although, thankfully for me, three volumes were entitled 'Miscellany'. Amongst these are some of the photographs reproduced in this book, as Laurie, with typical generosity, allowed me to take home and scan whatever I wished.

This book would be much the poorer without their input and they both took a keen interest in its progress. Although I am unable to present them each with a copy of the finished product as intended, I would like to recognise here their significant contribution to the endeavour.

© Chris Durrant and Lightmoor Press 2021
Designed by Nigel Nicholson
British Library Cataloguing-in-Publication Data. A catalogue record for this book is available from the British Library
ISBN 9781 911038 96 2
All rights reserved. No part of this publication may be reproduced, stored in a retrieval system or transmitted in any form or by any means, electronic, mechanical, photocopying, recording or otherwise, without the written permission of the publisher

LIGHTMOOR PRESS

Unit 144B, Lydney Trading Estate, Harbour Road, Lydney, Gloucestershire GL15 4EJ

www.lightmoor.co.uk

Lightmoor Press is an imprint of Black Dwarf Lightmoor Publications Ltd
Printed in Poland; www.lfbookservices.co.uk

Contents

Foreword 7
Preface 8
Acknowledgements 9
Introduction 11
A Brief History 13

The Line

1. Brighton 15
2. Lovers Walk Junction 51
3. Brighton Upper Goods 53
4. Preston Park 59
5. Patcham 75
6. Brapool Cutting 79
7. Clayton Cutting 81
8. Hassocks 87
9. Burgess Hill 97
10. Keymer Junction 103
11. Keymer Crossing 111
12. Wivelsfield 117
13. Folly Hill 121
14. Haywards Heath 125
15. Copyhold 139
16. Ouse Viaduct 147
17. Stone Hall 151
18. Balcombe 153
19. Balcombe Intermediate 160
20. Balcombe Tunnel 161
21. Three Bridges 169
22. Tinsley Green 197
23. Gatwick 199
24. Horley 219
25. Salfords 231
26. Earlswood 237
27. Redhill 249
28. Holmethorpe 267
29. Merstham 271
30. Star Bridge 277
31. Coulsdon South 281
32. Worsted Green 283
33. Quarry Intermediate 285
34. Star Lane 289
35. Cane Hill 295
36. Coulsdon North 297

Appendices

1. Instructions to Signalmen and Others 315
2. Westinghouse Brake & Saxby Signal Co. Ltd 320
3. Six Anxious Hours 344
4. Early Trials with Axle Counters on the Southern Railway 346
5. Signal Sighting 352
6. Main Line Quadrupling 355
7. The Thirteen Signal Box Scheme 356
8. Westinghouse Signals 358

Bibliography 360

The array of signals controlling moves from the Down Main and Local lines towards the Brighton 'throat', with the next gantry or 'girder stage' signals giving the driver his final destination. Lovers Walk signal box No. 60 Up distant signal is mounted on the right-hand 'doll'. Above the second LM&SR wagon can be seen the equivalent signals for trains coming off the London Road viaduct. Note also the ground mounted miniature arm shunt signals adjacent to the buffer stops. *August 1932, K.R.M.*

BELOW: A few metres in the rear of where the mechanical signals once stood, the new colour lights now control all routes directly into the platforms. *November 1932, K.R.M.*

Foreword

The literature of railway signalling has been growing over the past thirty years as traditional mechanical signalling continues to be gradually phased out. Interest in its history has increased following the publication in 2011 of the Network Rail plan to eliminate it completely within the foreseeable future. In response to the plan, I prepared a report for English Heritage, for which I was then working, which identified the surviving signal boxes that ought to be considered for retention for their architectural or historical interest, the vast majority of which were subsequently listed.

Chris Durrant has looked at a much earlier major resignalling scheme, that of the Brighton main line in 1932-3 in connection with its electrification, and at its subsequent history. While a number of signal boxes were closed following the scheme, many more were retained and it is this mix of the modern, in the form of colour light signals, and the traditional, with some of the surviving boxes dating back to the 1860s, that adds interest to the subject.

The book is perhaps the most detailed survey of the signalling of a main line to be published for an amateur readership and also illustrates much of the infrastructure of the Brighton line. Written by a professional signal engineer, it leavens what has to be, at times, precise technical description with an engaging sense of humour. Chris was often in the right place at the right time and, through his professional position, was able to capture subjects that would have been denied to an outsider. Working for the railway also meant that he knew many of the signalmen involved and so there is a human element here which is often missing in many accounts of signalling.

John Minnis

The author taking track circuit readings at Hassocks in 1981.

Preface

It had been in the back of my mind ever since I retired, some time ago now, that I should one day sit down and write a book, the perennial problem being of course, actually getting round to it.

Many railwaymen have written books, possibly the majority being former footplatemen who came through the classic career path of cleaner, passed cleaner, fireman, passed fireman and up through the various driving links. Indeed during the latter years of my career I had the privilege of spending many happy hours in drivers' cabs talking to Top Link men on journeys to various parts of the country who had come through that very path and were approaching fifty years' service, something which is virtually impossible to achieve these days. Their books would invariably be in the 'auto-biographical' style, charting the author's life on the railway including fascinating reminiscences and 'tales of the line'. The other railway profession which turned railwaymen into authors seemed to be signalmen and operators, again recounting a career path and describing anecdotes, historical facts and various occurrences along the way. I am not sure, however, that many books have been written by a former signal engineer (other than books on the science of signalling itself, maybe) so for anyone with an interest in this subject, and on this particular piece of railway, I sincerely hope that this book will appeal. But this is not a serious history book, as many eminent railway historians have already written copious tomes on the London, Brighton & South Coast Railway and on the Brighton line in particular. Neither is it an in-depth history of 'Brighton' signalling equipment: you will not find here the intricate workings of Harper's block instruments or the complexities of Sykes 'Lock and Block', though undoubtedly one day that book will be written.

Instead, what I hope to contribute is a snapshot of the southern end of the Brighton line, detailing its history as it emerged from the Southern Railway's resignalling and electrification of the early 1930s and into the 1980s Three Bridges power box era, charting the changing layouts and the many signal boxes that disappeared as a result. When earlier material has been made available, I have included that too, where it is of interest. I have also used many photographs I took myself during this time while working on this line, along with photographs and extracts of signalling plans and notices from my own collection. I was always badgering signalmen and S&T[1] linemen of the older generation to search out photographs that they may have taken or been given, and some gems turned up this way. One of my biggest 'scoops' was when the landlord of the Liverpool Arms Hotel in Haywards Heath (the pub now sadly under the car park) unearthed a collection of photographs his father had taken of the station being rebuilt in conjunction with the electrification/resignalling works of 1932. I would take all these back home and copy them on my parents' kitchen table using two 60 watt standard lamps either side of the photograph, my camera mounted on a tripod with extension rings on the lens to get close to the picture to enable it to be 'framed', taking two or three exposures at different shutter speeds and apertures. Normally something eventually emerged that became usable. Oh, for a flatbed scanner back then!

My father always had an interest in photography and used to develop his own 2¼ inch negatives from his early Voigtlander bellows camera. My first efforts were taken on this and Dad taught me how to wind the film into the developing reel, place that in the tank and then, using the process of developer, stop bath and fixer, produce a roll of twelve negatives. His next camera (after I trod on his precious Voigtlander whilst attempting to take some photographs in Cinder Hill Tunnel just below Sheffield Park) was a Russian Zenith 35mm SLR[2] model, built like the proverbial tank. I started using this, but with mixed results as the light meter was unpredictable to say the least. By this time I had built my own dark room in my parents' loft and could now not only start developing my own 35mm negatives, but print them as well. With a regular wage, I could upgrade to the camera of my dreams, a Canon AE-1 SLR in black, a whopping £206 back then, which I still have to this day.

The book is structured geographically, covering each station and pre-1932 signal box in turn from Brighton to Coulsdon North. For each location it chronologically charts developments from the 1932 resignalling through to the inception of the Three Bridges power signal box in 1983. For completeness I have also covered the 'Old Road' via Redhill even though it stayed, in signalling terms, in the dark ages until 1985. Concerning the captioning of photographs where any form of traction is involved, one thing that will become readily apparent to the informed reader is my lack of in-depth knowledge regarding rolling stock. Those in the know, who can spot a Stroudley 4-wheel Brake Third from a Billinton Composite at a hundred paces, will have to forgive me when I refer to anything with carriages as a 'passenger train'; likewise, anything with wagons will be a 'mixed goods'. My expertise with anything steam follows a similar vein, as a 'D4' looks very similar to a 'Gladstone' which looks very similar to everything else! I have aimed for accuracy, but can only apologise for any inadvertent errors.

Chris Durrant,
East Peckham, Kent.

---

1. S&T: Signal and Telegraph – now Signalling and Telecommunications.

2. SLR: Single Lens Reflex.

Acknowledgements

All photographs have been taken by the author unless otherwise stated. Photographs stated as being from my collection have either been obtained in the manner mentioned earlier, or donated by like-minded railwaymen over the years and I can only apologise if no due credit is offered.

My thanks also go to other railwaymen, friends and colleagues for freely allowing me access to their collections and searching out material on my behalf; individual credits are given to each photograph where applicable (sadly some have passed on since this book was started). One of the joys of researching material is how one contact can lead to another and it is truly humbling to be welcomed by complete strangers into their homes. The majority of the historical photographs have come from private collections or established archives and, as such, some of the photographs, owing to the paucity of images available, have been published before. At the time of railway privatisation in 1994, many offices were being cleared out and I was given a number of official British Rail archival signalling-related photographs that probably would otherwise have been destroyed. Where these have been included, I have credited them to British Rail.

Extracts from the signalling track plans, 'Yellow' signalling notices, promotional booklets and various other plans and drawings are from my own collection, and I know of no copyright that exists for these.

For help in the provision of material for this book my thanks go, in no particular order, to:

Brian Hymas, Roger Resch, John Hemsley, Nick Catford (who runs the excellent www.disused-stations.org.uk), Derek Osborne, Tony Manktelow, David Postle of the Kidderminster Railway Museum, Lens of Sutton, Richard Spencer, Edwin Wilmshurst, Alan Grove, Steve Wilkins, Ron Razzell, Brian Read for provision of his 'Control' drawings, Jim Jenkins, Ian Nolan, Margaret Casserley, Marjorie Mason, Kevin Robertson, Martin Elms, Michael Harvey, John Turner of 53A Models of Hull, Pete Jackson, the late James Aston, Ken Bacon and the late John Scrace. Also to Roger Cruse, Roger Price and Tony Hillman from the Bluebell Railway. An enormous debt of gratitude goes to John Minnis and the late Laurie Marshall from the Brighton Circle.

For anyone interested in signalling, I can heartily recommend The Signalling Record Society, whose journal and archive material are second to none (see www.s-r-s.org.uk for more information). I am grateful to them for permission to use drawings from the John Wagstaff Collection of books of signal box layouts and copies from their SR & BR(S) Signal Diagrams and Notices; they have been unfailingly helpful and courteous. Also to John Creed from the Signalling Record Society for permission to use his narrative 'The Early Use of Axle Counters'. Likewise for students of the LB&SCR, The Brighton Circle exists to further knowledge of that company and certain snippets of information used in the compilation of this book have come from correspondence gleaned from their journal *The Brighton Circular* (see www.lbscr.org for more details). Another website well worth a visit comes from the Brighton Branch of ASLEF[1] and my thanks go to Paul Edwards for his help (see thebrightonbranchofaslef.yolasite.com). The National Library of Scotland provides mapping (ongoing at the time of writing) for the whole of the country dating back to the late 19th century (see http://maps.nls.uk for more fascinating information). My thanks to them also.

Lastly, I have been extremely fortunate to have been given access to the Wallis Collection of photographs, a number of which have been included here. Edward Wallis was a signal engineer himself and was, by 1922, taking a camera to work with him, albeit one having a fastest shutter speed of $\frac{1}{60}$th of a second and capable of taking just twelve quarter plate glass negatives before having to be reloaded. Some of his images are therefore not of the quality that can be achieved today, but have been included here where relevant; we should be wholly grateful that people like Edward had the foresight to record events before they were lost forever and I like to think that he would have been pleased with this offering. Coincidentally, Edward's plates were developed and printed by a Horsham signalman, Jesse Jupp, whose two sons, Alby and Wally, I worked with at Three Bridges.

I would like to thank my wife Judy for proof reading, help and suggestions on the text. She has taken what she kindly calls my *'talking to friends down the pub'* style of prose and turned it into something that is eminently more conducive! Thanks also to my brother Peter for his help and guidance and Brian Hymas for suggestions and corrections.

John Minnis has given freely of his exhaustive knowledge and experience and has contributed additional material and suggestions, along with the foreword, for which I am most grateful.

As with all these things though, while acknowledging help and guidance from friends and colleagues, any errors are my own.

The author on the occasion of his retirement on 17th April 2009 with Bob Tubb, ex Area Signal Manager at Brighton, the man who started it all.

---

1. ASLEF: Associated Society of Locomotive Engineers & Firemen

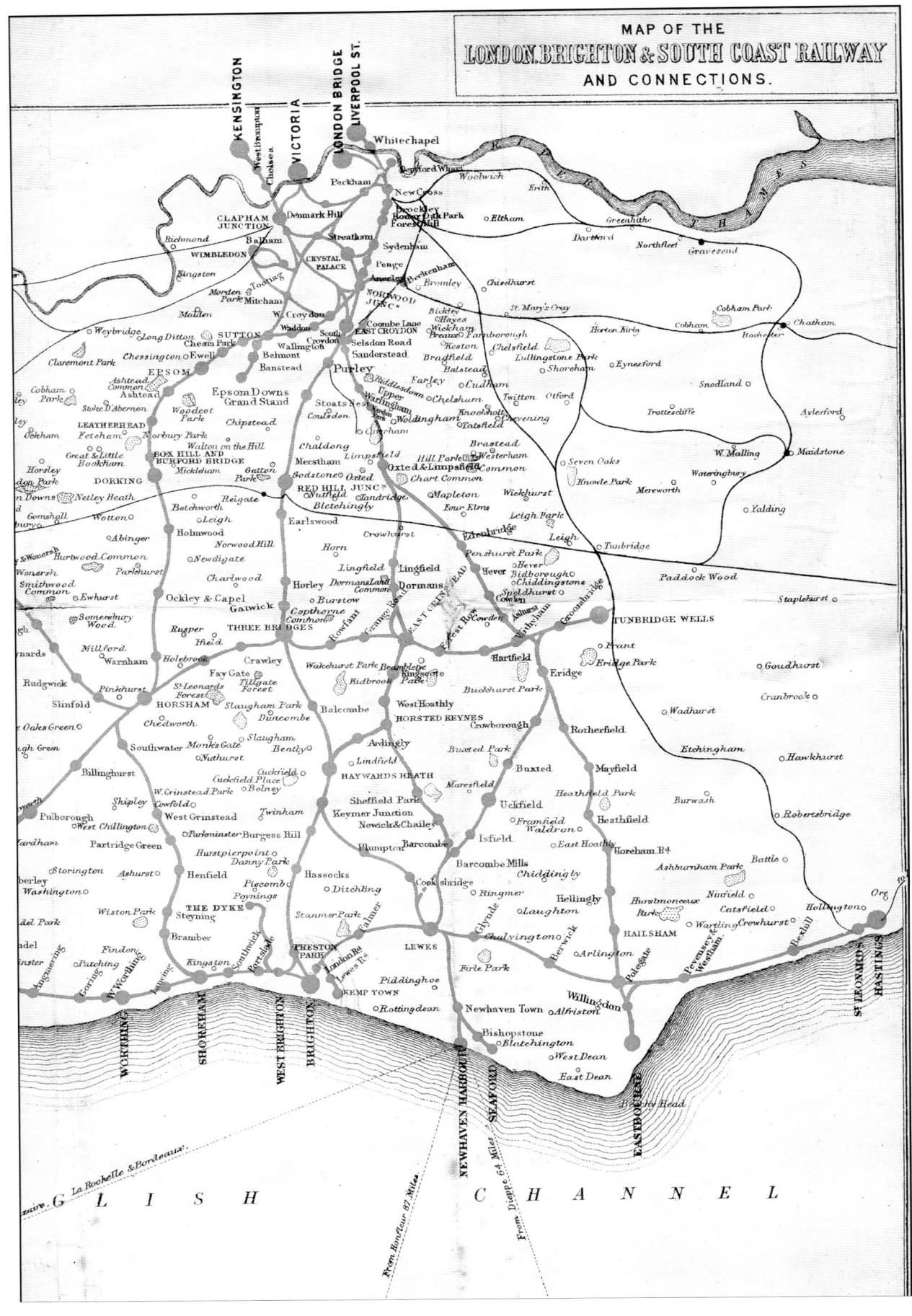

Introduction

It was the Geordie folk/rock band Lindisfarne that started it all.

I had emerged from the Fifth Form at Oakmeeds County Secondary School in Burgess Hill, Sussex, with seven CSE grades and not the first idea of what I wanted to do in life. Somehow I managed to gain a place in the Lower Sixth Form (normally a place for students who had achieved their GCE grades and were going on to 'A' Levels) to try my hand at gaining some GCE 'O' Levels. This I managed to achieve with a scraped pass in Maths and English Language – sadly not so successful with English Literature and Physics. What to do next though? Unbelievably I somehow managed to blag my way into the newly created Upper Sixth Form and spent yet another year at school achieving absolutely nothing in the way of academic achievement, but having the time of my life, mainly helping out the Physical Education department in taking the first and second years for games and P.E.

But time stands still for no man, and approaching the summer of 1972 I was out on my own. The school careers officer found me a job with a one-woman printing firm and I started my first job as her assistant. These were the days of photocopying as a 'wet' process, dye line printing of architectural and industrial drawing negatives using light sensitive paper, Gestetner duplicating from typewritten sheets of stencil paper and 'offset' printing which entailed a water versus printing ink combination. The only saving grace was that one of the architects we dealt with owned an former Atlantic racing yacht which he kept at Bosham Harbour, where I'd help out at weekends with restoration; for this he would pay me more for a couple of days' work than I earnt in a week. Printing-wise, I was useless. After six months of this hell, I had to get out. Parents, however, being the ever sensible adults, stated that I could not hand in my resignation until I had another job to go to.

Being a 'child of the 60s' and into the early 1970s, music ruled my life and by now, aged 18, I was regularly going to gigs in London and to various other venues. Some friends at school were huge Lindisfarne fans and we found that the band were playing at the Top Rank Suite in Brighton. We bought our tickets and on the evening of 27th September 1972 we caught a train down to Brighton and walked the reasonably short distance down to the sea front. There were two support acts: a singer called Rab Noakes (who did actually go on to greater things) and a supposedly up and coming 'prog rock' band called Genesis. Any memory of the first act has completely vanished but I acutely remember Genesis being, to my mind anyhow, quite awful. Their singer (Peter Gabriel of course) dressed up in the most outlandish costumes and I seem to remember their guitarist (Steve Hackett) playing sitting down with his back to the audience. Their volume was such that they also managed to blow the sound limiter during the gig, which cut the power supply to the stage leaving only Phil Collins' drums audible.

We had a beer in the interval. Lindisfarne came on eventually and were utterly brilliant, so much so that they played encore after encore. One of the best things about being young is the lack of any semblance of responsibility; time passed and it was obvious that we'd missed our last train home. If any of us had had any sense, of course, we would have foregone the last few encores and trotted back up to catch the last train but no, we did not want to miss anything. Back up at the station after the gig at something after midnight, the only option was for one of my friends to ring his father and get him to come and collect us. As you do. There is not a great deal you can do on a railway station at that time of night with a wait of half an hour or more, other than go for a wander around. And there, leaning up against a door, was a blackboard proclaiming the message in chalk, *'Traction Trainees required, apply within'*. I did not have the first idea as to what a traction trainee was, but it seemed like a possible job opportunity and the chance to escape from that wretched printing firm.

Over breakfast the following morning I related to my father what I had seen and, as he worked down on the London Road in Brighton in the shadow of the London Road viaduct, he said he would make the walk up the hill to the station to see what he could find out. He duly knocked on the door to discover that traction trainees were trainee drivers, who at that time required A1 vision. I, of course, wore glasses. The whole encounter could have ended at that point but the enlightened Driver Manager (as we now know them) asked father what sort of thing his son was interested in. *"Mending radios"* he replied, *"taking old televisions to bits and building circuits, anything to do with electricity really"*. *"Well, you could try the Signal Engineers over the road"*, he said, *"they may be taking people on"*. Taking the directions, Dad made the short trek to the Combined Engineering Depot and sought out anyone he could possibly talk to. He was directed into the office of Bob Tubb, the Area Signal Manager, and duly pleaded his case. *"We're not actively recruiting"*, Bob said, *"but bring him along and we'll have a look at him"*.

On the afternoon of the 15th November, I was ushered into the ASM's office for an interview. What on earth Bob saw in me I do not know but, on condition of a medical, he offered me a post with a six-month probationary period. I was issued a free ticket to Southern House in East Croydon for the medical which thankfully did not show up any undue problems. Being 18 years of age I was too old to undertake an apprenticeship but, on the 5th December 1972, I caught the 07.32 train from Burgess Hill to Brighton and started work in the Signal Engineers Department of the Southern Region of British Rail as a Junior Railman, the lowest grade B.R. could offer anyone.

Thus started a career path that would last until 17th April 2009.

FACING PAGE: An extract of an LB&SCR map taken from a Brighton Directory of 1898. Note the absence of the Quarry Line, which was still being constructed as the directory went to press.

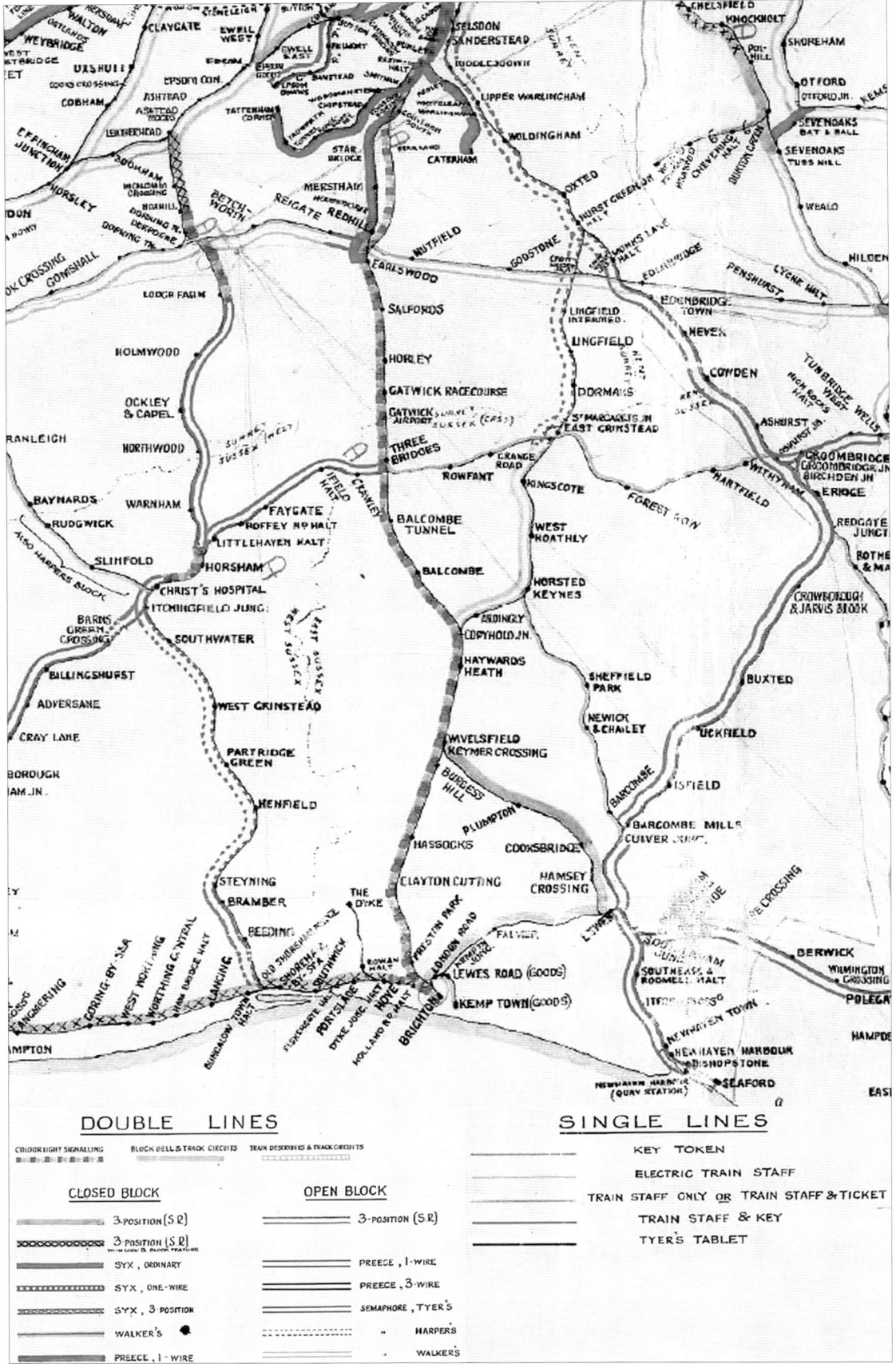

An extract from the Southern Railway Block Diagram dating from the early 1930s which, in its entirety, shows the complete system and the method of block signalling employed on each line. In this portion of the plan, just the Brighton main line along with short stretches of line through Horsham and Dorking are shown as 'Colour Light Signalling'. Horsham and Dorking's new 'glasshouse' signal boxes opened in 1938.

A Brief History

Even though a lot of the following is outside the scope of this book, a very brief overview of the history of the Brighton Line would be in order to give an oversight of how the whole line came into being.

On 15th July 1837, Royal Assent was given for the construction of the London & Brighton Railway (L&BR) to the design of Sir John Rennie, being the more direct line to the coast than those proposed by others via either the Adur gap or Oxted.

The London & Croydon Railway had been in existence since 1839 between London Bridge and its terminus at West Croydon, and it was with this line that a junction was made in the vicinity of Norwood, leaving a little under 42 miles to what would become the terminus at Brighton. Haywards Heath was reached on 12th July 1841 and Brighton on 21st September that same year. However, due to various political machinations involving the South Eastern Railway (SER), the L&BR were forced to sell the section of line between Coulsdon and Redhill to the SER (who then went on to complete their main line to Dover via Tonbridge) leaving the L&BR, although with running powers, at the mercy of their rival company. In 1846 the London & Brighton Railway amalgamated with the London & Croydon Railway to form the London, Brighton & South Coast Railway (LB&SCR), the title of which it was to hold until the 'Big Four' grouping of 1923.

Many suburban routes were now being developed. Following the success of Joseph Paxton's 'Crystal Palace' being dismantled and transported from the Great Exhibition of 1851 in Hyde Park to a site in Sydenham (purchased from Leo Schuster, the LB&SCR Deputy Chairman), the London, Brighton & South Coast Railway became the major shareholder in the new West End of London & Crystal Palace Railway, eventually with a West End terminal station in Pimlico, south of the River Thames. This hugely successful venture, transporting many tens of thousands to view this wonderful structure, gave impetus to the construction of further lines including a new route from Norwood Junction to Crystal Palace (as it was now named). In 1860 this station, somewhat inconveniently situated, was closed and a new station named Victoria opened on the rapidly expanding north bank of the river. The next two years saw the opening of the more direct route via Wandsworth Common and Clapham Junction, thus giving the 'Main Line' we know today. The final piece of the jigsaw was the LB&SCR finally running out of patience with the power struggles at Redhill; after decades of delays, quarrels over revenue, operating difficulties and outright hostility at the hand of their deadly rival, they obtained powers to bypass the junction and construct what we now known as the Quarry Line. This 6½ mile 'avoiding line' left the route at Coulsdon to the west of the existing line before swinging over the Redhill line (which then became rather affectionately known as the 'Old Road') on a skew girder bridge in the Cane Hill area. This hugely expensive piece of civil engineering with deep cuttings and two tunnels of 2,113yds (Quarry Tunnel) and 649yds (Sand Tunnel) eventually emerged at Earlswood Junction having finally burrowed under the SER's Redhill to Tonbridge line. This section of line opened for passenger traffic on 1st April 1900 and at last gave the Brighton company a clear run to the capital.

With burgeoning traffic, capacity was becoming a problem and so various widening projects came into force. Preston Park towards Brighton was quadrupled in 1883 (which considerably eased operating problems for traffic through the Cliftonville tunnel towards Hove) and later the same year from Copyhold Junction to Haywards Heath in conjunction with the branch line to Horsted Keynes, itself part of the new Lewes & East Grinstead Railway. One project which is discussed later was the building of a proposed flyover at Keymer Junction. In 1881 this was projected to have cost in the region of £35,000 and the scheme was authorised the following year. If this had come to fruition it would have given an improved turn-out to the Down Lewes line with the Up[1] branch being carried over the main lines on a flyover, culminating in a new junction just north of where Wivelsfield station is today. Sadly, due to the generally unfavourable economic climate of the time, this came to nothing and the powers granted for the development were abandoned. Returning to the Quarry Line: a natural continuation of what was now effectively a four-track main line from Coulsdon to Earlswood Junction would be the quadrupling of the remainder of the line southwards towards Brighton; by the turn of the century plans had been put in place, at the enormous estimate of in excess of £1¼ million, to complete these works to Preston Park. Four-tracking to Three Bridges was achieved by 1907 and to the north end of Balcombe Tunnel (where the widening work can still be seen to this day) by May 1910. At this point, however, the Directors baulked; faced with the cost of duplicating tunnels at Balcombe, Haywards Heath, Clayton and Patcham, plus a parallel Ouse Valley Viaduct, the plans were quietly dropped and the remaining works have stayed as nothing but a dream.

Although all traffic at this time was still steam hauled, the LB&SCR had been at the forefront of suburban electrification, introducing their 6,700V ac overhead system in 1909 on the South London Line to huge commercial success. The system expanded throughout the inner London area, was interrupted by the outbreak of the First World War, but then continued on the Brighton Line reaching Balham and eventually Coulsdon North on 1st April 1925, by then firmly under control of the newly formed Southern Railway.

The Southern Railway (SR) came into being on 1st January 1923 as Britain's railways were grouped into four companies, the SR being formed by the merger of the London, Brighton & South Coast Railway, London & South Western Railway (L&SWR), South Eastern Railway and the London, Chatham & Dover Railway – although since 1899 a Managing Committee (SE&CR)

---

1. Down: to Brighton London; Up: to London.

had run the latter two companies as a single entity. The General Manager of the L&SWR, Herbert Walker, was chosen as General Manager of the newly formed Southern Railway and on 10th October 1929 he laid out before his Directors his plan to continue electrification from Coulsdon to Brighton: *"Gentlemen, I have decided to electrify to Brighton."* Previously, as the Brighton company had been electrifying their system using the aforementioned overhead electrification, so the L&SWR had been expanding their own suburban empire using the 660V dc 'third rail' system. For consistency something had to give and, perhaps inevitably owing to the L&SWR's predominance, it was the third rail system that was chosen in preference. By 1929 electrification of the main line to Coulsdon North had been converted from overhead (after an existence of a mere 4½ years) to third rail, leaving the remaining 36 miles of electrification to the South Coast to complete. The cost for this, to include new electric stock and resignalling (absolutely necessary to reap the benefits of the new rolling stock and vastly improved traffic frequency), was to be £2,700,660, and annual mileage was estimated to rise from 1,972,000 to 4,921,000, a considerable increase. Subsequently electric services reached Three Bridges on 17th July 1932, and through to Brighton and West Worthing on 1st January the following year.

The contract for the resignalling was let to the Westinghouse Brake & Saxby Signalling Company Ltd and their booklet produced to commemorate and publicise their work is reproduced in full in this book (see Appendix 2). I will not, therefore, duplicate their narrative here other than to say that the preparation to enable each commissioning to happen as it did must have been meticulous to say the least. The ex-SER line via Redhill was excluded from the resignalling and had to wait another fifty-three years for modernisation.

Thus the installation – with various renewals, rationalisations and improvements along the way – continued into the early 1980s, but with the lack of what were by then considered signalling basics in the way of AWS (Automatic Warning System) and signal lamp 'proving', resignalling was long overdue. Three Bridges, being reasonably central and with available land, was chosen to be the site of the new control centre and so construction of the enormous signalling centre and various remote relay rooms began. Solid State Interlocking (first trialled at Leamington Spa in 1985) was on the horizon but this was firmly a relay interlocking scheme utilising either freewire circuitry or Westinghouse's own geographical 'Westpac' system', according to circumstances. Thus to house the endless racks of relays, power supplies, telecommunication and remote control systems, not to mention the huge control panel at Three Bridges, everything was large. As work proceeded between 1982 and 1985, the new signal box gradually expanded its empire to take eventual control from north of Selhurst and Norwood Junction down to Brighton, including West Croydon, the Tattenham Corner/Caterham lines and fringing on the various branches towards Reigate, Tonbridge, Lewes and the East and West Coastway routes from Brighton. This signal box's importance will slowly diminish, where control will eventually be transferred across to the new Three Bridges Regional Operating Centre (ROC). It is truly amazing to see the banks of monitors working traffic centres many miles away, where a relay room the size of those at Brighton or East Croydon can be controlled from what is essentially something akin to a home computer, as technology marches on.

A fine view looking out over Brighton Yard and the London Road viaduct, with the rolling farm lands of the South Downs in the distance. Brighton Yard signal box is in the centre with the paint shops on the left and the works to the right. *Laurie Marshall Collection*

1 – Brighton

The above and following photographs show the early Saxby & Farmer installation at Brighton dating from 1862. Brighton North signal box (later to become Montpelier Junction) is seen above, depicting the rudimentary signalling that shows how drivers had to cope with the barest minimum of information.
Laurie Marshall Collection

ABOVE AND RIGHT: Two wonderful manufacturers' photographs of the 1862 Brighton Yard signal box. *E.T.H. Zurich*

A fascinating 1881 photograph shows the transition from the old Saxby & Farmer boxes to the soon to be commissioned brick-built structures. The new South (with siding running beneath) and West signal boxes can be seen towards the left of the photograph. *Laurie Marshall Collection*

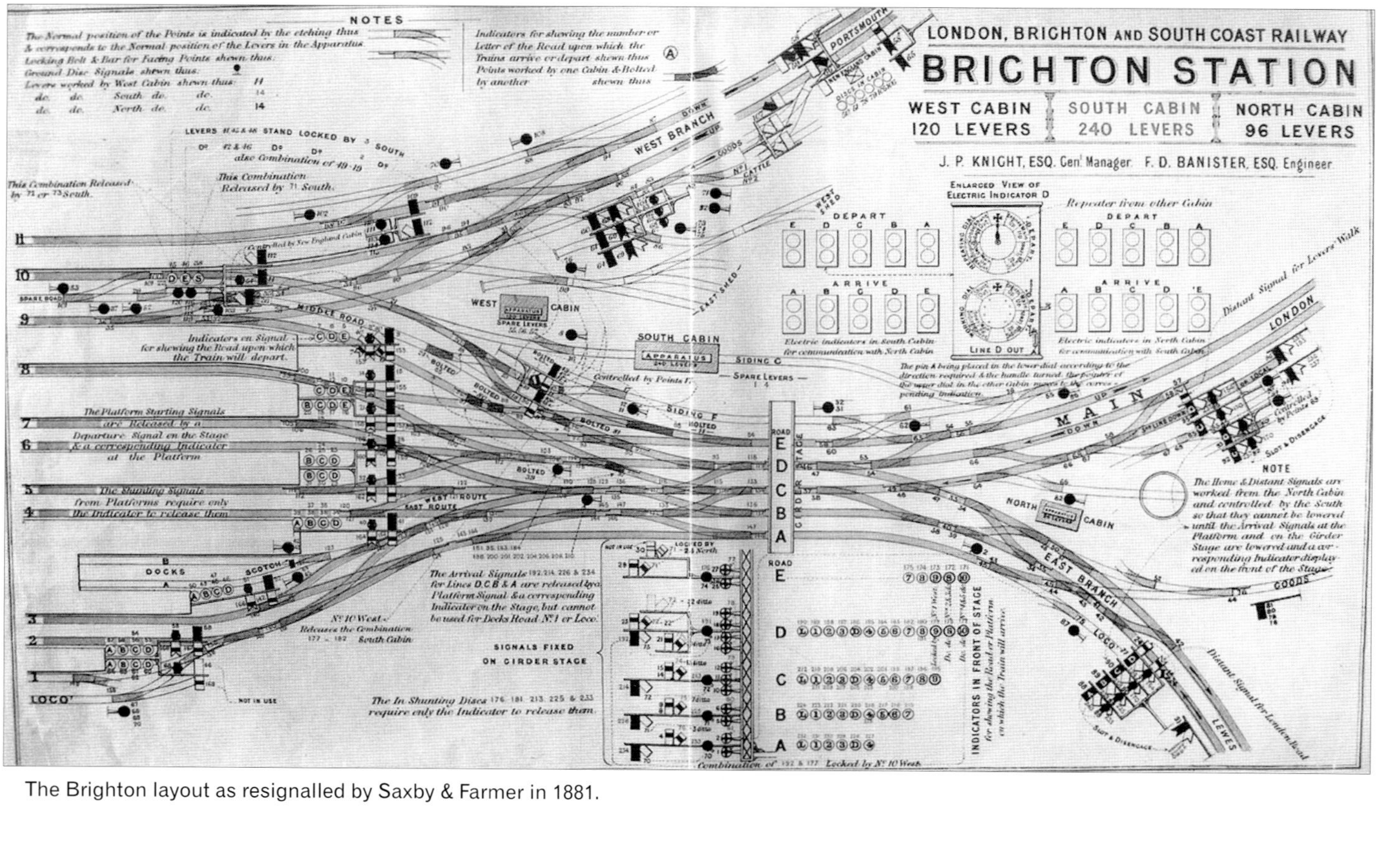

The Brighton layout as resignalled by Saxby & Farmer in 1881.

The enormous structure that was Brighton South signal box was built on arches of 1ft 11ins brickwork to accommodate 'Section G' siding which runs beneath. It dealt wholly with the station movements as far as Line 8 and then, in conjunction with West box, traffic movements appertaining to Lines 9 and 10. The rectangular patches of light on the near return wall and signal box steps supports, which also appear in the photograph of Brighton West, would appear to be the sun shining through the signal box steps creating patterns of light on the timber and brickwork. The function of the small building that just fits underneath the signal box steps, looking almost like an early tobacconist's booth, is open to conjecture. Early photographs of the Brighton concourse, as below, show a very similar looking structure (although with top appendage) that served as a baggage check-in kiosk and one could well have been moved here to act as an engine number taker's hut or something similar. The three Brighton signal boxes – South, West and North – were brought into work in 1881, replacing the former Saxby & Farmer (S&F) wooden structures that had the controlling signals integral to the structure, a feature of early S&F signalling and of the Brighton line in its formative years. *Above: 1932, K.R.M.; Below: Laurie Marshall Collection*

Facing Page Top: The interior of Brighton South signal box (internal dimensions 18 feet by 113 feet) from a Saxby & Farmer official photograph. Seemingly yet to be brought into work, the frame was supported by a massive 'H' girder running from end to end of the cabin and intermediately supported by supplementary castings and cross girders, the locking supported by a second longitudinal iron girder. *Laurie Marshall Collection*

Facing Page Bottom: An excellent view of the rear of the frame showing the 'grid iron' locking to good effect; also the Tyers describing instruments sending and receiving from Montpelier Junction, one for each of the five line 'sections'. *K.R.M.*

Above: Another view of the somewhat spartan interior of Brighton South signal box, showing the Saxby & Farmer 240-lever frame. A whole range of clutter is arrayed on the rear wall along with the signal box clock (long before almost every clock had its face repainted with the inevitable 'John Walker, 1 South Molton Street' legend), signalmen's coats and caps. Staff comfort is not necessarily the highest priority.
The majority of levers at the front end of the frame have two horizontal bands (probably painted yellow) under their catch handles showing that these are 'indicator' levers. These worked circular discs under the platform starting signals showing the driver the road (Section A to E) upon which his train would depart. Even more indicator levers existed at the end of the frame, working indicator discs on the girder stage (incoming signals) showing the driver his final line destination. When these indicator discs were abolished (they must have been a maintenance headache!) the levers were still required to maintain the locking. In the foreground, indicator lever No. 5 is reversed along with 'shunt out' signal No. 8, thus indicating a shunting movement from No. 8 platform out via Line E. *1932, K.R.M.*

As to the working of the frame, we gain fascinating insights from an article published in the *Railway Magazine* for November 1910 thus:
> The locking gear is of the order known as the 'spring catch', that is to say, before any movement whatever of the lever can take place, all the requisite locking is accomplished by the actuation of the catch handle, while, at the same time the levers to be released are held until the 'releasing' lever itself is fixed by the notch in the completely reversed position. Thus the interlocking is actuated by the grasp of the signalman's hand, and his intention to move the lever, as expressed by the grasp of the spring catch, is made to interlock all levers which should be so locked, while there is no possibility of error, or chance of straining the mechanism. Working in conjunction with each catch handle is a rocker, which has the appearance, upon the interior of the South Cabin, of an ordinary quadrant; but a closer inspection will reveal not only the rocker with its fulcrum, but also a slot link cut in the rocker itself. The catch rod carries a stud, upon which is a block which carries along the slot mentioned. Normally, the front end of the rocker is down, in harmony with the natural position of the catch rod; but when the lever has travelled over, the catch rod falls into the opposite notch, and the rocker is now tilted in the opposite direction. In advance of the rocker is a jaw carrying a universal jointed link, which actuates a crank at the end of a spindle. The latter is so arranged that the locking bars can travel above it, but directly a spring catch rod is raised the oblong spindle partially revolves, and thus blocks the passage of the locking bars above it. The system described, albeit in itself very efficient, and formerly, indeed, probably the most efficient, is no longer the 'standard' interlocking of the London, Brighton & South Coast Railway, the ubiquitous 'tappet' locking now supplanting, as upon many railways, the methods of other days. It will, however, be observed upon the interior of the South Cabin that the interlocking itself is above the floor.

You can only admire a photographer who is willing to lug his heavy plate glass camera up to heights such as this. Taken at the only shutter speed available to him, 1/60th of a second, this is the panoramic view of Brighton taken from the station roof looking north. The engine sheds dominate the left background with the massive locomotive works filling the right; West box sits in the immediate foreground, with South box in the centre; the complexity of the layout is seen to good advantage. *1924, The Edward Wallis Collection*

BELOW: A fine array of 'Brighton' lower quadrant semaphore signals. The platform starting signals – i.e. those with their arms to the left of the posts (outer pair) or 'dolls' (inner pair) as we look – require the relevant route to be set, departure signals on the girder stage ahead lowered and the corresponding indicator lever (or route locking or proving lever) reversed before these themselves can be pulled 'off' (see the internal photograph of South box, above). Note though that the 'Section' indicator mechanisms had been removed by the time this photograph was taken. Brighton West and South boxes dominate the centre of the photograph, from left to right respectively, whilst the new power box can just be glimpsed on the far right, ingeniously set into the works buildings. The incoming home and distant 'platform clear' signals (with their arms to the right, as before) give the driver the state of the platform ahead: stop arm lowered and distant 'on' means the platform is partially occupied, both arms 'off' means the road is clear to the buffers. Sometime around 1920, electric fouling bars (EFBs) were installed along the platform roads (one can just be seen below the buffer beam of the locomotive alongside the 6ft rail of the opposite platform road). 'Rule 55' (or the LB&SCR equivalent) diamond signs, which would have been installed along with the EFBs, can be seen on the signal posts. The 'gongs' (exhibiting a five-point star), hanging from their elaborate brackets, showed drivers their stopping points to ensure that the fouling bars were actuated, these positioned to try and cover all likely positions of standing rolling stock. The following extract from an accident report, where the driver of an incoming train misjudged his approach and collided with a stationary train in the platform, not only explains how the platform entry signals worked but also shows that the human element can never be ruled out. *1932, K.R.M.*

Extract of MOT Accident Report, Brighton 7th March 1926, collision between two trains in platform 2 (east side):
There are two of these signals for each road, the upper one being of the stop signal type and the lower one of the distant signal type. The arrangement of this signalling is that when the whole of the platform road is clear both stop and distant signals are lowered. When, however, the latter half of the road at the terminal end is occupied the lever operating the distant type signal is locked and the train is signalled in under the stop arm only. This locking is effected by means of electric treadles of which there are two adjacent to one another near the terminus, one 9 feet from the buffer stops 17 feet long the other 5 feet away from the first, being 35 feet long. At a distance of 257 feet from the buffer stops there is another treadle 35 feet long, the occupation of which locks both the stop and the distant type signal arms. The effect of this arrangement therefore, is that when any portion of the platform road up to a maximum of 257 feet is occupied, the incoming train is warned by the holding of the distant type signal in the danger position. When more than 257 feet of the platform road is occupied, both running type signal arms are locked and movements are allowed in under a shunt signal (these being on the girder stage). The total length of the five coaches standing against the buffer stops was 255 feet 6 inches, and the last wheel of these coaches was therefore within a few feet of the centre platform treadle.

The investigating officer concluded that the staff involved should have known how the signalling worked and did not make any recommendations! Under the 1932 resignalling, electric fouling bars were installed at the buffer stops even when the platform roads had been track circuited. A 'light' engine that may have pulled stock into the platform, ending up hard to the buffers, could not be relied upon to operate the track circuit where the rails would be contaminated by drips from locomotives and where the rails would be rarely run over, likewise it was not unheard of to have vans or wagons left on the stops to service the station infrastructure.

BRIGHTON SOUTH.—After a Shunt Signal has been lowered for a Train or Engine, it must not be put to Danger until the Train or Engine for which it was given has come to a stand or passed the Signal in advance of the Shunt Signal.

All Passenger Trains must be described on Tyer's Train Describers before the Slot is given, and the man receiving the descriptive Signal must satisfy himself that the Slot given corresponds. Under no circumstances must a Train be given a signal to move when there is a discrepancy between the Describer and the Slots given.

BRIGHTON WEST.—Instructions respecting working of Shunt Signals (shown under Brighton South) also apply at this Box.

Line Clear Signal must not be given to New England unless a Road is clear in the Station.

LEFT: An extract from LB&SCR 'Regulations for Train Signalling together with Instructions and Information for the Guidance of Signalmen', dated 1917.

Facing Page: An early view of the east side of the station with electrification still to arrive. The function of the indicator levers, seen in the earlier photograph of the interior of the South signal box, is shown to good effect here, with the platform 11 starting signal lowered and the indicator disc telling the driver that he is to depart via Section A (the starting arms have their relevant platform number, not line number as for incoming trains, painted on the arms themselves). From platforms 10 and 11, only four sections were available through which to depart (A to D inclusive), thus the four corresponding return weights can be clearly seen with, in this case, the 'A' section weight raised. The star sign, which again was seen earlier, can now be seen to be exhibiting the initials 'E.F.B.' (Electrical Fouling Bar), with its white diamond sign, conveniently mounted on the indicator housing, telling the driver that the signalman is aware of his presence. The platform 10 EFB can be seen on the immediate left and a pair of rotating ground signals can be seen in the distance. Platform 11 was not long enough to require an incoming 'distant' signal, thus only a platform-entry home signal is warranted. Access to Brighton Works was available from the loco siding on the extreme right, but with room for not much more than a light engine. *K.R.M.*

Photographs can always throw up conundrums. The earlier photograph of the starting signal from platform 11 had the 'Section' departure indicators working, the one taken from platform 8 has them removed, whereas this photograph has the indicators and associated mechanisms still in position, yet not working. This is an excellent photograph, though, showing 'King Arthur' Class No. 802 *Sir Durnore* preparing to leave with a passenger train. As can be seen from the platform 7 starting signals, the starting arms have their relevant platform number (not line number as for incoming trains) painted on the arms themselves. Notice also the notch cut out of the shunt ahead arm for platform 6 (No. 27 lever) to enable it to drop to its fullest extent despite the railing being in the way: ingenuity will always win out! *March 1932, K.R.M.*

Above: The girder stage nears the end of its life as a signal gantry, as the commissioning of the new signalling cannot be far away. Here, a train has been signalled from Line B towards the East Coast Branch. Under normal conditions, no incoming train would ever be brought to a halt here, as these signals were pre-set by the relevant platform entry signals. Taking this a stage further, both sets of home signals (including the main line signals seen to the left of Montpelier Junction signal box in the distance) could only be lowered once the relevant signal here had been lowered. Suffice to say that once a home signal had been cleared, the driver would know he had the road into a platform but with further information to come. Complex 'slotting' was a way of life back then. Originally these incoming signals had indicators fitted (probably removed at some point between 1920 and 1924), which gave the driver his final 'Line' (not platform) destination and it was this lever, once the route had been set, that released the signal. Considering that No. 192 signal (third from left) and its associated 'shunt in' signal No. 191 below it (controlling movements from Line D towards the platforms) had between them no fewer than thirteen indicators in four group mechanisms, the complexity can be imagined. The three outgoing signals (counting from the right) controlled movements from Lines A-C departing to the East Branch: Line D was the only line which could signal trains towards either the East Branch or the Up Main, hence the splitting signals third and fourth from left with the lower arm applying to the branch. This leaves Line E (second from left) which applied to the Up Main only. The trestles sitting atop the stage would almost certainly be in place to effect a quick removal of the signal arms come the changeover which, remarkably, was achieved in approximately 6 ½ hours.

Something which is never given much thought is the amount of scrap material that emanates from a resignalling scheme such as this, although no doubt a fair proportion would have been kept for strategic spares. Even back then, metal would be sent back to be melted down for reuse (the Southern Railway almost seemed to have had a vendetta against LB&SCR cast iron trespass notices for example) so nothing would be wasted. With timber signal posts, either there were enormous bonfires, Brighton Loco commandeered it for fire raising, or the staff had plenty of kindling wood for a considerable period of time. *1932, K.R.M.*

Facing Page Bottom: A pre-grouping view of Brighton station shows clearly the platform entry and departure signals and the rear of the indicators; electrical fouling bars were yet to be installed. This is where it gets complicated, as 'Line' numbers were directly opposite to platform numbers, thus line 11 (furthest west) applied to platform 1 and Line 11 (furthest east) to platform 1. Only a railway company could invent that one, but it was a system prevalent to the LB&SCR. The indicators on the girder stage would have told the driver of the incoming train his final destination line and this number is repeated on the white rectangle on the face of the platform entry signal arm itself. The entry signals on the far left are for entering platform 9 (Line 3). The line numbers of the signals in view are then, from right to left, 9, 8, 7, 6, 5 and 3, with 2 and 1 on the 'T' structure in the left background. The necessity of the complex destination indicators on the girder stage could be called into question, where the final destination has already been given to the driver by these signals on show. The lack of visible signal wires and cranks is due to the fact that the wire runs went down to the 'tunnel' below, a photograph of which is depicted in the Westinghouse signalling brochure (see Appendix 2). At platforms where water columns were provided, it was considered ideal that *'Starting signals should, wherever practicable, be placed in such a position beyond the water column as will enable an engine (65 feet in length) to take water without having to pass the signal at danger'*, which probably was not the case here as there was not room. *1906, Laurie Marshall Collection*

ABOVE: Taken from a window in South signal box, the girder stage with its array of lower quadrants commands the photograph. It must have taken some imagination to envisage that a new signal box could be inserted into the front elevation of the Works rather than finding spare land where it could have been built as a free-standing structure, and it is a matter of speculation as to what internal alterations were necessary to allow this to happen. A train has been signalled along Line B round to the Lewes Branch as, just visible in the background, the signalman in Montpelier Junction signal box has lowered his No. 24 signal (with London Road's distant beneath also lowered), thus clearing the route over the London Road viaduct. *29th July 1924, The Edward Wallis Collection*

Left: Brighton West signal box warrants inclusion in this book by virtue of the fact that it could signal trains to and from the main line via platforms 2 and 3. Home to another Saxby & Farmer rocker frame of 120 levers (brought into service in 1881), it worked to Brighton South, next door, and New England box a mere couple of hundred yards away around the West Branch, also controlling what must have been an almost constant procession of engine moves from the adjacent shed. With the resignalling in full flow and with bespoke point fittings to produce, three portable forges can be seen and you can imagine the fitters coming back and forth asking the blacksmiths for another ¼inch set in whatever drive or detection rod they were fitting. Carbide lamps are trackside in the centre of the photograph, enabling work to continue around the clock. *August 1932, K.R.M.*

Above: The interior of Brighton West signal box (internal dimensions 59ft 4ins by 13ft 2ins) with a 120-lever Saxby & Farmer grid iron rocker frame, the vertical rods (and what look very similar to early carriage racks) behind the frame working the mechanical request discs operated by the adjacent signal boxes' 'asking levers'. I like to think that the unevenness of the signalman's tread board running along the front of the frame is purely down to 51 years' wear, the more well-used levers eliciting the deeper grooves in the wood. You would have had to be reasonably fit to hold down a signalman's job in signal boxes such as this. The fireplace at the far end, with the signalman's teapot and mug on the mantelpiece, would not look out of place in a stately home. *1932, K.R.M.*

Left: An LB&SCR mechanical request disc, as mentioned above, originating from Hailsham and now requisitioned by the Bluebell Railway, is shown here propped up in a vice, better to reveal the workings, the crank worked by the relevant 'asking lever' in the adjacent signal box. *Brian Hymas*

Poetry in motion: two Westinghouse 'M3' machines drive a 3-way point layout. With the rear switches reverse (33 points) you are routed from Section C to Section B, whilst 100 points reverse route towards Section D, either move completed by way of a bewildering array of bell cranks. The left-hand machine drives the front switches and both sets of points are locked and detected in conjunction with combined 4ft detectors. The rear pair of stretcher bars are of a very early type, but a layout like this emphasises why there were portable forges outside West box in the photograph opposite. The preparation for installing machines whilst the points were still mechanically operated would be considerable and the method of achieving this may never be known. Long timbers (bearers) with insulated sole plates would have been laid in to support the new machines. Then, either, prior to the commissioning and under possession, the new rodding would be connected up so that the points could be rehearsed before returning them to mechanical working, or, more likely, temporary controllers would have been fitted to the point levers and the points electrically worked from the old frame. Whichever method was used, the old timbers in view here bear the scars of their previous mechanical workings. The new Brighton box had been in work for a few weeks when this photograph was taken, but it would appear that some stock and switch track circuit bonding was being caught up with, as a lone chap drills away with his 'hurdy gurdy' hand drilling machine. Note the early health and safety initiative, with the ends of the conductor wing rails painted white. *November 1932, K.R.M.*

If the interior of Brighton South looked spartan, then Brighton North (Montpelier Junction) looks even more so, in fact you could almost be forgiven for thinking that it had already been taken out of service. However, for a photograph dated August 1932, its 96-lever frame still had a few weeks of life left. These must have been cold places to work in the depths of winter, with the wind whistling up through the levers and window frames, and whatever heat a coal fire could provide disappearing up through the uninsulated roof. In 1920, it was estimated that about 430 trains and light engines (not counting shunt moves) were signalled by this box during a 24-hour spell. Montpelier Junction worked to Lovers Walk signal box by Sykes 'Lock and Block' (and likewise to London Road) but by Tyers instruments to the South box. Tyers train describing instruments were also used between these two signal boxes and a drawing of one of these is shown on the 1881 track layout diagram. *K.R.M.*

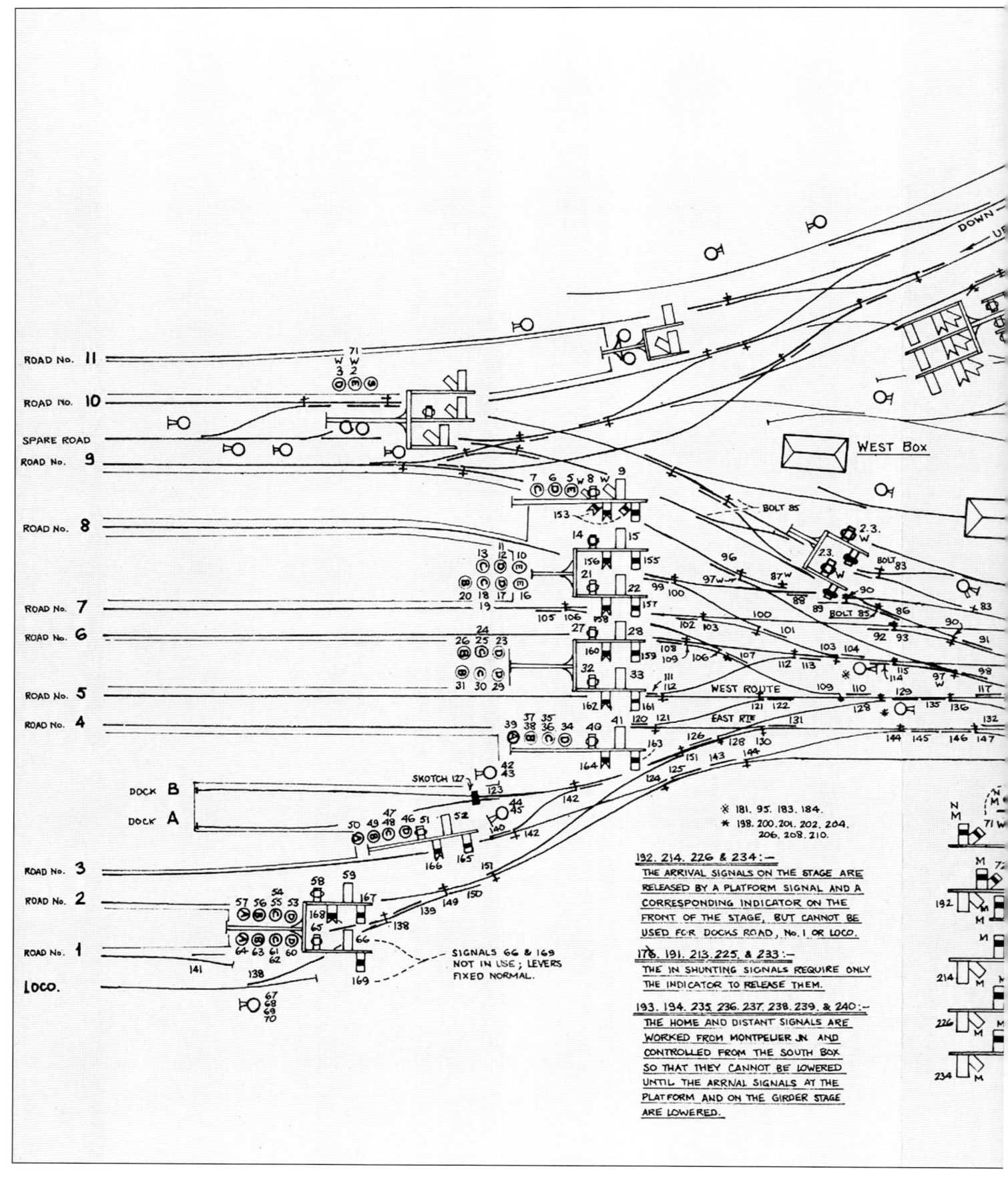

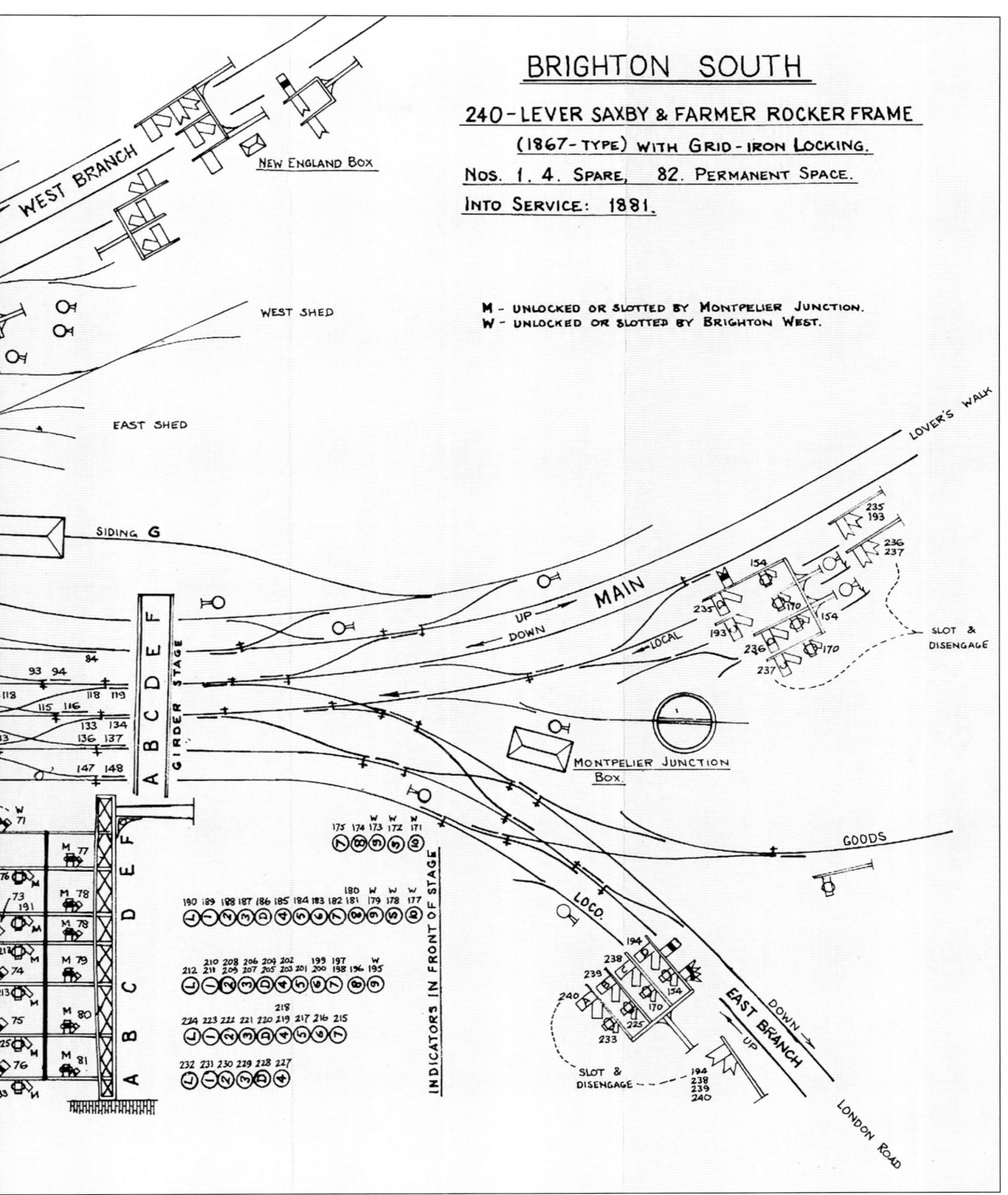

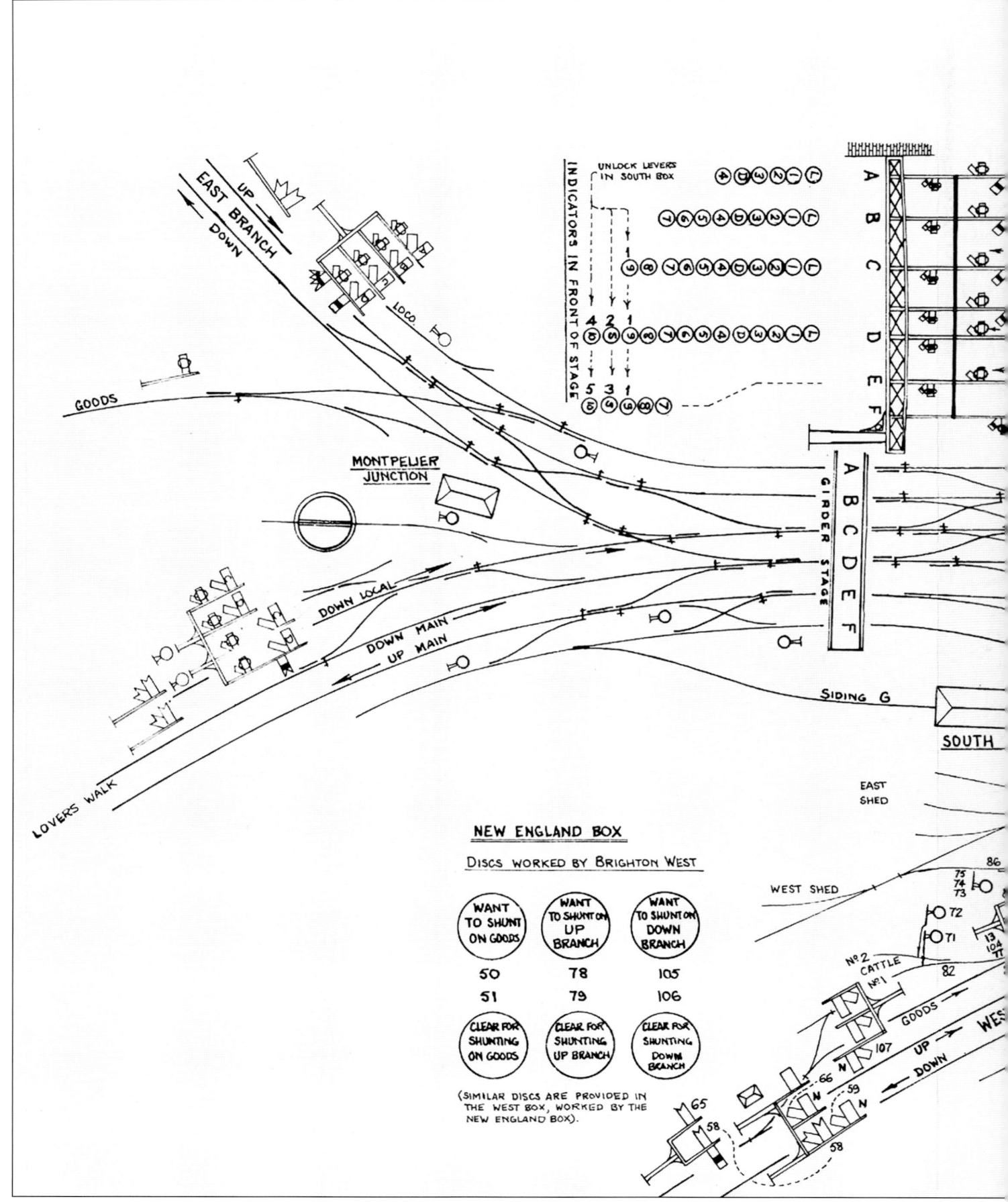

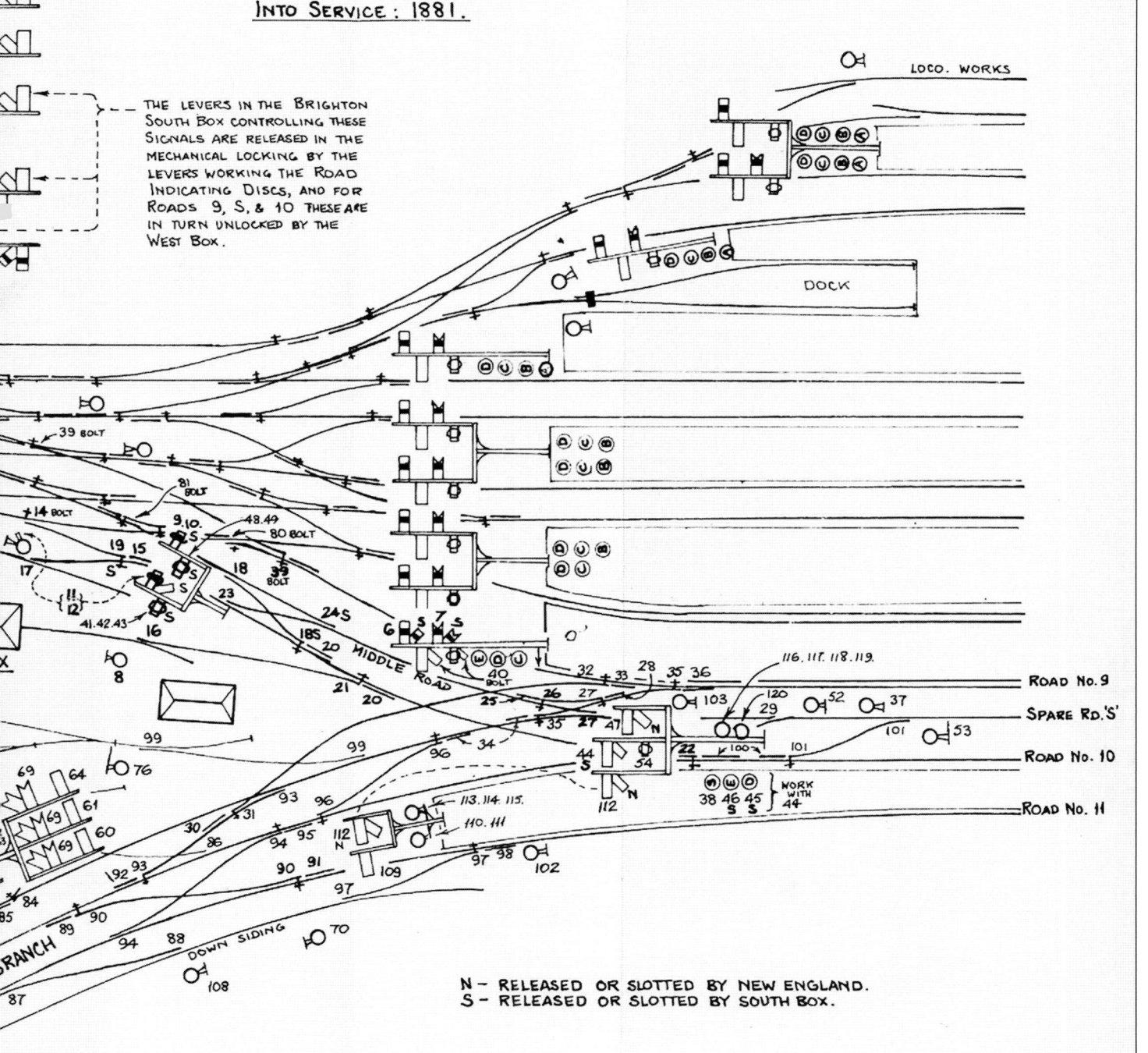

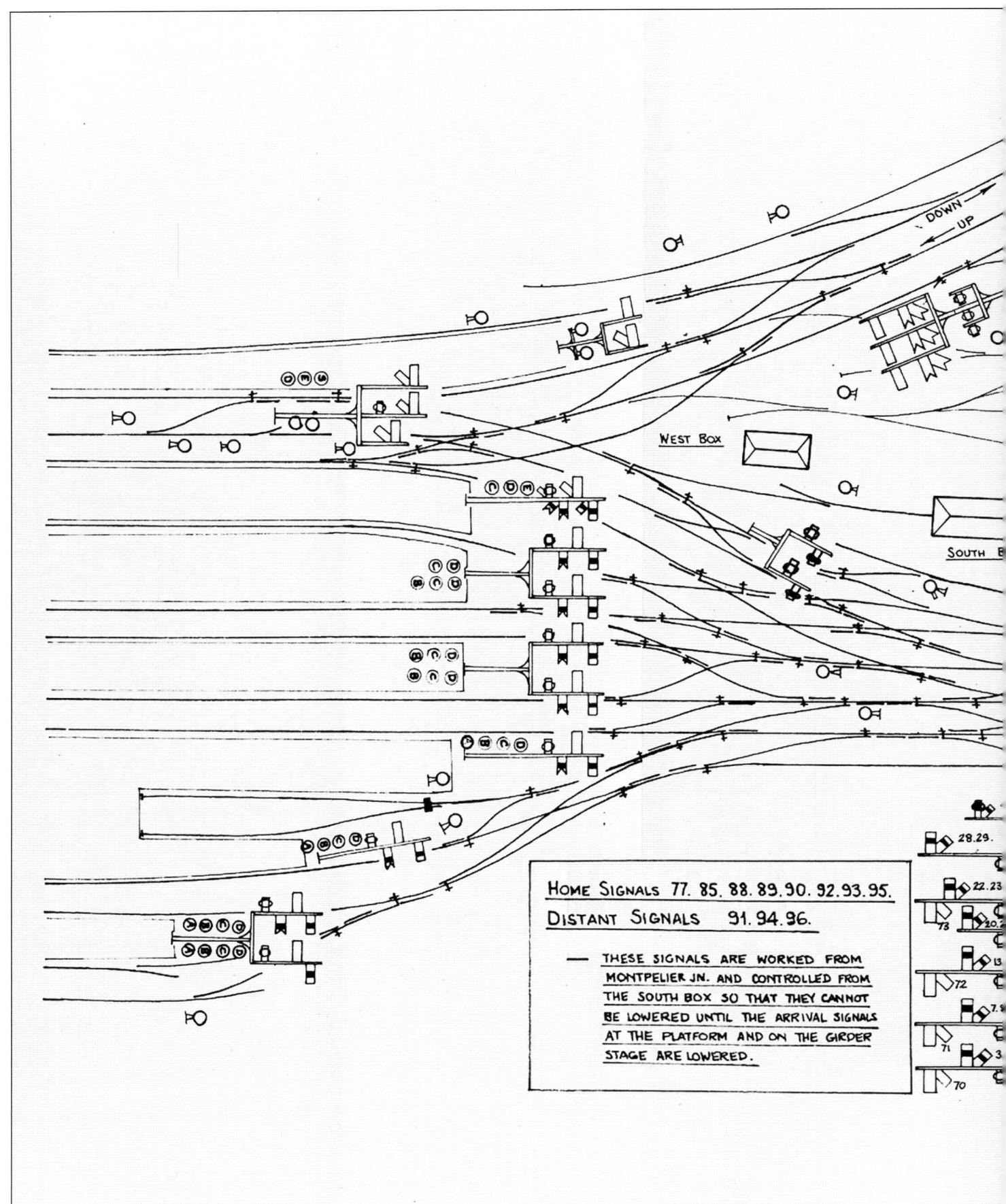

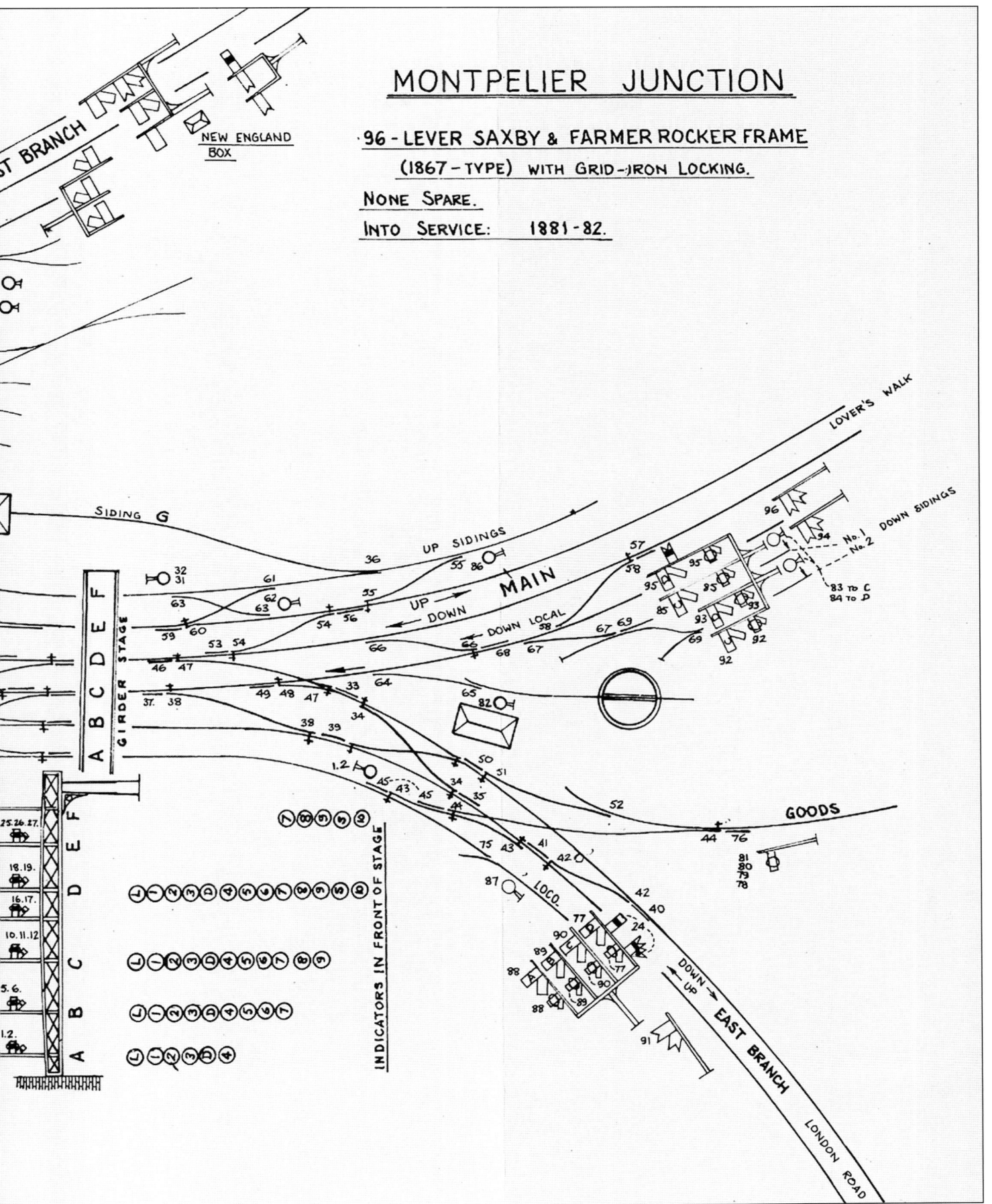

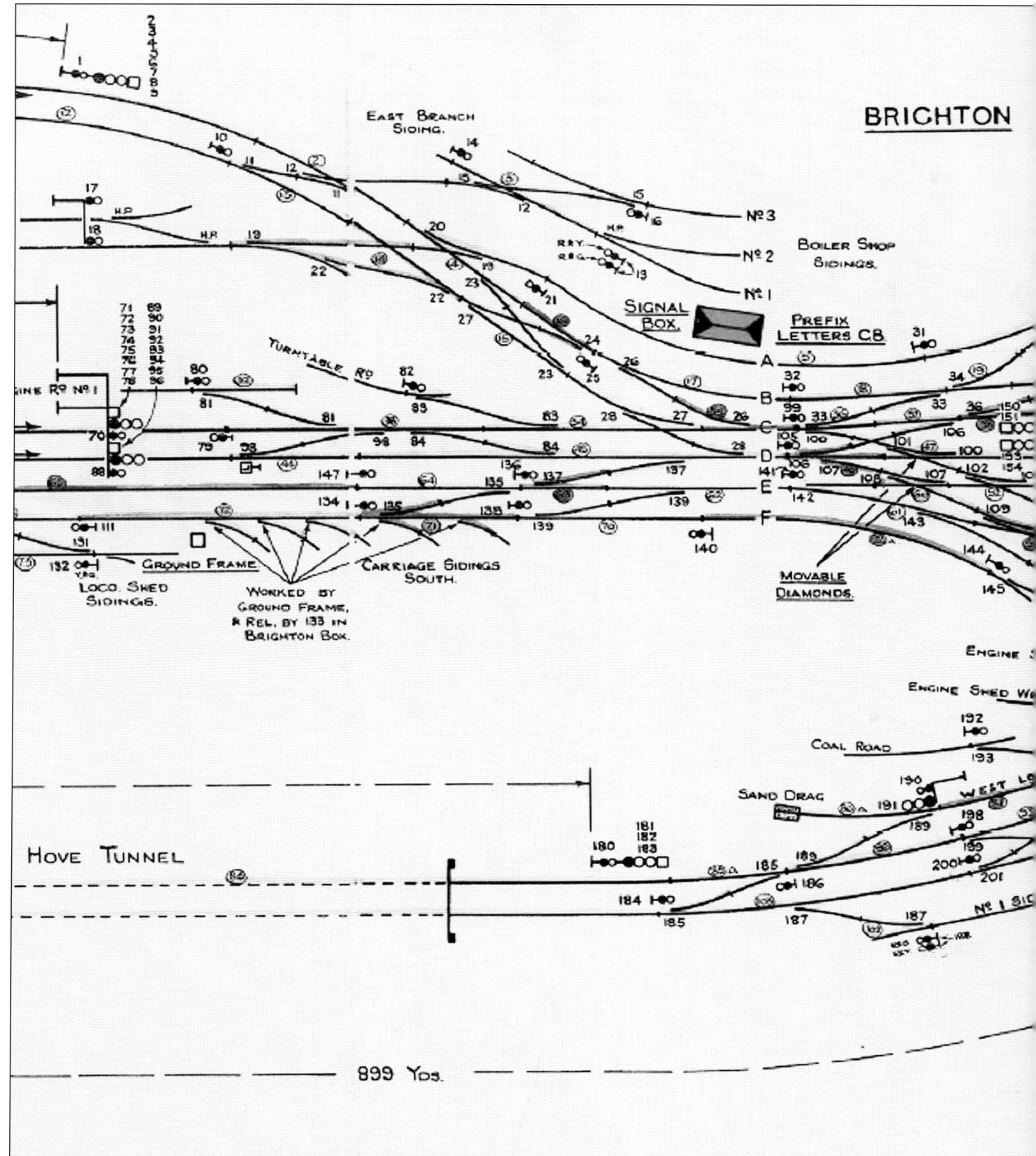

Brighton station layout as resignalled in 1932. The single arrival platform 8 has been filled in and platform 11 abolished, with the platform numbering altered accordingly. Note the Electrical Fouling Bars at the buffer stops.

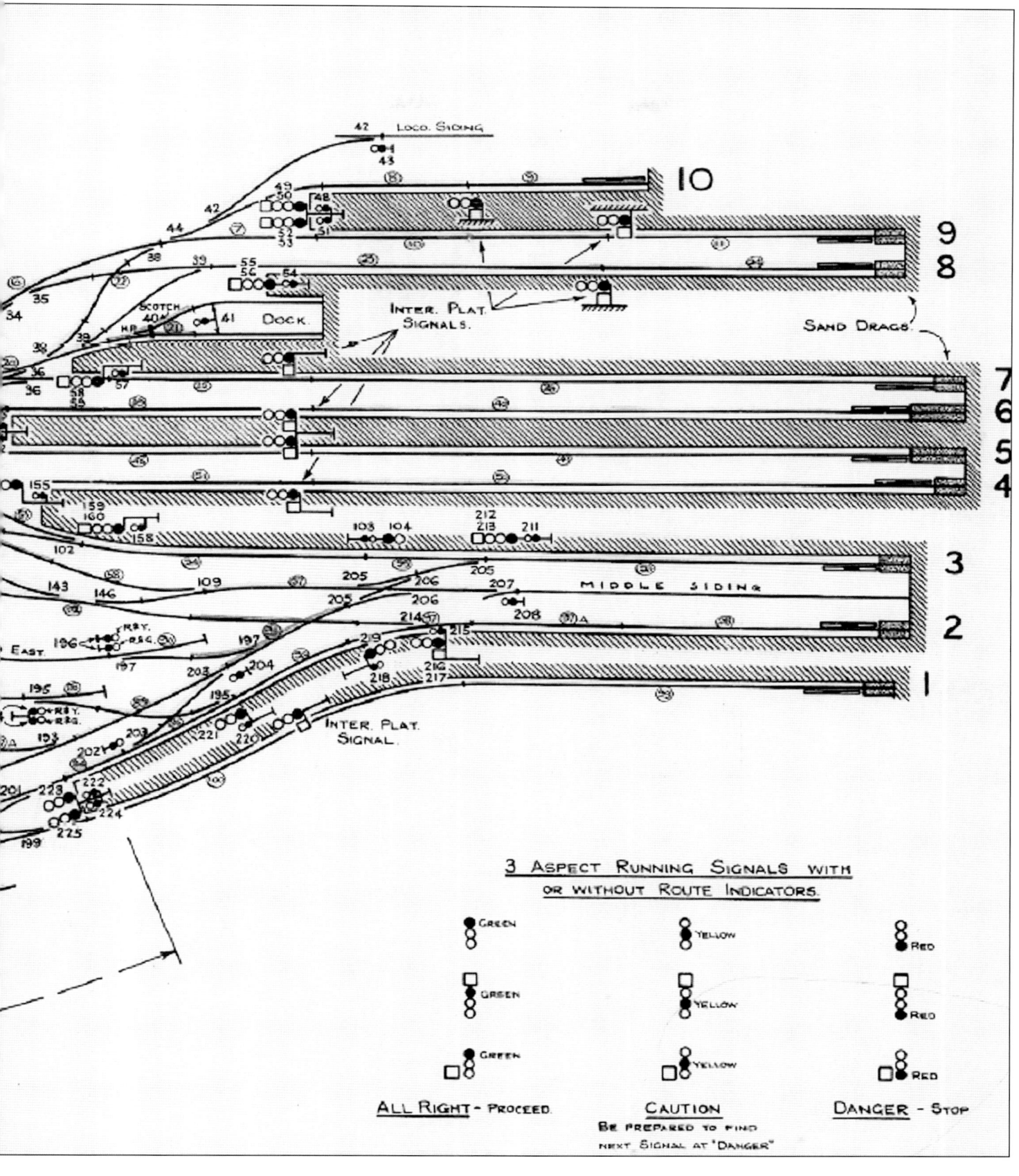

A pristine view of the brand new 225-lever Brighton signal box in 1932, ready to provide an unbroken 53 years' service. The parquet-floored room houses this Westinghouse 'L' style miniature lever frame which was a step up from the 'K' frames that preceded it (Charing Cross and London Bridge, for example) as the lever-to-lever interlocking was effected by electrical locks as opposed to its predecessor's mechanical locking. The interlocking lever bands can be seen through the glass panels at the front of the frame whilst the selection bands are at the rear, the basic working of the frame is described in the Westinghouse brochure (see Appendix 2). The large duplicated Southern Railway diagram has the standard track circuit indications of the day, where an unoccupied track circuit shows a single white light which extinguishes when occupied (no diagram 'Power Off' light required); this remained until the very early 1970s when it was converted to the more modern and recognisable red lozenge (alight when occupied) type. Walkers rotary train describers work to Upper Goods and Hove East respectively, with standard 3-position block to Kemp Town Junction. In the centre of the main line frame (and under the rather splendid Gents of Leicester 'Pul-syn-etic' clock) is an early Siemens train describer transmitter to Preston Park with two magazine-type receivers above. *1932, British Rail*

SOUTHERN RAILWAY.

Signal Instruction No. 40, 1932.

INSTRUCTIONS TO ALL CONCERNED
AS TO THE

INTRODUCTION OF COLOUR LIGHT SIGNALS
(In place of existing Semaphore Signals)

BETWEEN PRESTON PARK, HOVE AND BRIGHTON, INCLUDING LONDON ROAD;

BRINGING INTO USE NEW SIGNAL BOX AT BRIGHTON;

ABOLITION OF EXISTING PRESTON PARK NORTH, LOVERS WALK, MONTPELIER JUNCTION, BRIGHTON SOUTH AND WEST, NEW ENGLAND AND HOLLAND ROAD SIGNAL BOXES;

AND

RE-NAMING OF LINES BETWEEN PRESTON PARK AND BRIGHTON; PRESTON PARK AND HOVE, AND BRIGHTON AND HOVE,

ON SUNDAY, 16th OCTOBER, 1932.

Rules 70, 71 and 72 to be observed. Drivers to keep a good look-out for hand signals.

Commencing at 12.5 a.m. on Sunday, 16th October, the existing semaphore running signals between Preston Park North signal box and Brighton; Preston Park South signal box and Hove East signal box; Brighton and Hove East signal box, and Brighton and London Road signal box, will be abolished, and colour light signals installed in lieu thereof.

The existing Preston Park North, Lovers Walk, Montpelier Junction, Brighton South and West, New England and Holland Road signal boxes will be abolished. A new power worked signal box, to be known as Brighton, will be provided outside "A" Section at Brighton; the points at present worked from Lovers Walk, Montpelier Junction, Brighton South and West, New England and Holland Road signal boxes will be operated from the new Brighton signal box. Certain points and ground signals at present worked from Preston Park North box will be operated from Preston Park South box, which will be known, in future, as Preston Park.

The running lines will be re-named as follows :—

Existing Name.	New Name.
PRESTON PARK STATION.	
Down loop.	Down local.
Up branch.	Up local.
BETWEEN PRESTON PARK AND BRIGHTON.	
Down local.	(*No alteration*).
Down main.	Down through.
Up main.	Up through.
BETWEEN PRESTON PARK AND HOVE.	
Down spur.	Down branch.
Up spur.	Up branch.
BETWEEN BRIGHTON AND HOVE.	
Down main.	Down west branch.
Up main.	Up west branch.

On and from the date of introduction of the new colour light signals, the new Train Signalling Regulations dated April, 1932, for the sections of line between Coulsdon North No. 2 Box and Brighton; Preston Park and Hove East; and Brighton and Hove East must be worked to throughout.

Signalling notice No. 40 detailing the introduction of the new signalling on 16th October 1932, brought into work in approximately six and a half hours.

38 THE BRIGHTON LINE: BRIGHTON TO COULSDON NORTH – A SIGNALLING PERSPECTIVE

Facing Page Top: Brighton signal box had been in use for 25 years when this internal view was taken, but apart from the lighting not much seems to have changed. Presumably a visit from a local school or technical college is taking place, with three interested students taking in proceedings whilst a master looks on. With the time at 16.40, it would have been after studies had finished for the day. The signalman nearest the camera is 'pegging' a description to Hove East on the Walkers rotary describer and the service will soon be ramping up for the evening peak. For signalmen transferring from the draughty, labour intensive, basic environments of the old mechanical boxes, this must have seemed like another world. *14th September 1957, K.R.M.*

Facing Page Bottom: The interior of Brighton signal box with barely a couple of years of its life left shows that wooden fronts to access the lever bands had replaced the original glass fronts during the war as an air raid precaution. Access to the internal workings were via the end panels, where steps led down to a 'well' in which you could virtually stand upright. It was from here that the lineman would be able to effect a back-lock release if a signalman had, say, cleared a signal for a movement but for whatever reason the train was unable to proceed. As the requirements for the interlocking had not been fulfilled, the signalman would be unable to replace the lever in the frame to release the route so a 'back-lock' would have to be given by the lineman and the relevant details entered into the train register. More easily, yet probably less officially, this could also be carried out by lifting out the sloping panels above the rear lever bands behind the frame, giving access to the selection locks that way. Amazingly, the wooden telephone concentrators still survive, as do the old Southern Railway diagram frames (renewed with one illuminated diagram for each frame), but the original parquet floor has succumbed to a covering of good old-fashioned linoleum. *30th October 1983*

Above: The end rack within Brighton relay room, with PDRs (point detection relays) on the left, and track and track circuit repeater relays on the right. One $20\mu F$ (track circuit) condenser can also be seen, whilst signal and signal stick relays are along the end wall. The wire used for the relay room wiring was PBJ (PolyButyl Jute) insulated copper wire with a red-brown woven sheath containing a solid copper conductor which required an 'eye' to be formed and terminated, some 115 miles of it being used. This work was carried out by Westinghouse themselves. Brighton relay room and the wiring to the 'L' frame were rewired in the period 1969 to 1973 (selection circuits only – the interlocking was left well alone) with contractors running the wires and the Brighton Minor Works team effecting the changeovers and testing. The author spent his very first day on the railway, 5th December 1972, up a ladder at the far end rack on the left, being taught how to lace wire trees using plastic lacing twine! *1932, British Rail*

Facing Page: Brighton East frame diagram complete with Walkers rotary train describer transmitter to Lovers Walk below – note the winding key hanging on the side. It was normal practice to allow the hand to complete a full 360° before pegging the destination to alert the receiving signalman to the fact that a description was being sent. The corresponding receiving instrument, just out of picture to the left, still bore descriptions for 'Loco Coal' and 'Kemp Town Goods or Cattle'. By this time, 'Section A' in front of the signal box had been taken out of use.
3rd October 1983, Derek Osborne

Although we are heading through Brighton in a 'time orderly' fashion I thought it judicious to include a comparison photograph to the one below. This is undated, but with point machines in place and what seems to be the vast majority of the conductor rail laid in (although no sign of the new colour light signals at the platform ends), this was possibly taken around early 1932. Edward had obviously alerted the signalman in South box, who strains out of the window to get in the shot. *The Edward Wallis Collection*

The Brighton 'throat', still a complex piece of permanent way with a number of short conductor rail lengths to prevent 'gapping' by short-formed electric units or light engines. The trusty Westinghouse 'M3' machine powers everything point wise but the row of four machines off to the middle right of the photograph have their corresponding switches often three roads away; bespoke point rodding indeed. On the extreme left, the outer face of what was once platform 11 (mainly serving the Kemp Town Branch) can still be discerned, but the once mighty Brighton Works complex has had the ignominy of being reduced to a car park. *August 1979*

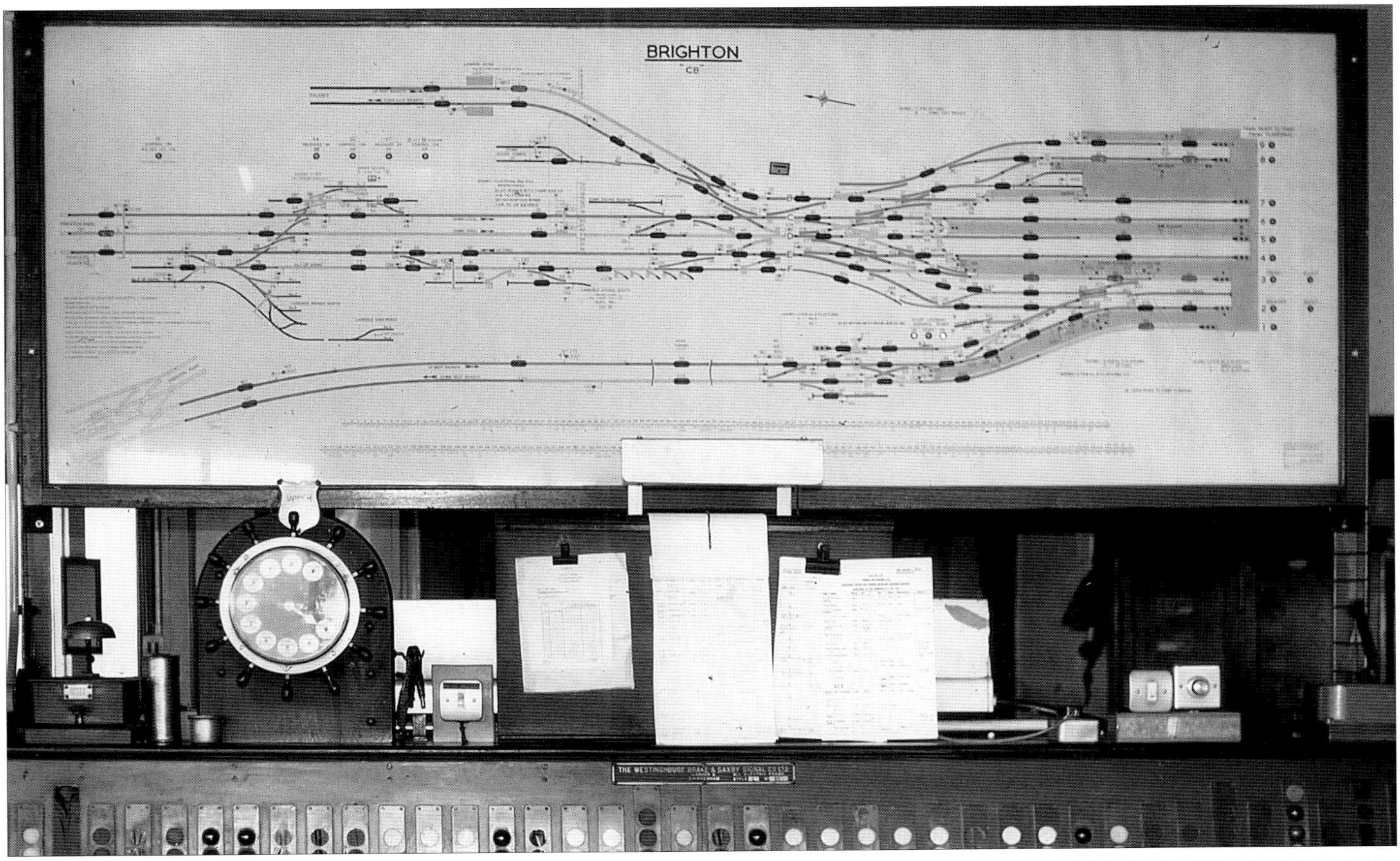

Brighton signal box on 30th October 1983 with the old girder stage now fulfilling a different function altogether. To the right are the very last vestiges of the old Brighton Works into which the signal box was built, along with the steps of the official walking route up to the operating floor. At some point the enamel nameboard must have been deemed unsafe from its original position set into the brickwork, as it now resides on the ground. To the left is the nemesis of so many signal boxes as the new relay room starts to takes shape. This, significantly, was at the time of the 'Brighton Bombing' of the Conservative Party Conference at the Metropole Hotel, so this structure was allegedly built to be bomb proof. The S&T roster technicians had their mess room at the rear of the signal box via a short passage from the operating floor, but their official entrance and exit route was using the spiral staircase seen in the far corner. The S&T mechanical gang had to make do with a basic lobby on the ground floor set behind the brickwork on the right. However, with all the signalmen and S&T staff on duty, the signal box housed just a single toilet!

An unusual visitor to Brighton (Cl;ass '9F' 2-10-0 No. 92220 *Evening Star*, designed at Brighton) is moved into the station by the local shunting engine in conjunction with an open day to commemorate the closure of the Kemp Town Branch. Note the beautifully constructed wooden trunking housing the positive traction cables with, where necessary, the 'hook switch' (for enabling local isolations) number screwed to the top. At least five non-combined point machines with remote 'four foot' lock and detection mechanisms can be seen incorporated into the double and single slips on view. The ladder to the girder stage was added after the mechanical signals had been removed, to give access to the new signal box from track level. The base of the old Montpelier Junction signal box remains in the vee of the junction. *26th June 1971, Edwin Wilmshurst*

The classic overall view of the Brighton throat has been beloved of photographers from the Victorian age onwards. The magnificent London Road viaduct dominates the rear background, where a 4-car train can be seen approaching from the Lewes direction. In the middle foreground can be seen the bane of many an S&T department in the form of permanent way TSR (temporary speed restriction) boards: warning boards to the right. commencement (C) and termination (T) boards to the left. These almost always had to be electrically lit with the power for the 60W incandescent lamps provided by the S&T. It was the Permanent Way's (P-Way's) responsibility to run out the (drop) twin cable to the nearest signalling location case (the cable quite often being completely inadequate for the task, with many joints or in several pieces) – run, literally, along the cess and often to a lineside apparatus case devoid of a supply as they were not to know. It was then down to us to connect it to the 110V signalling supply. This we would do with a temporary connection on to the 110V bus-bar via a 3-amp fuse, although sensibly, an instruction was eventually issued that the connection should be made via an isolating (1:1) transformer to decouple the signalling supply from any potential earthing problems. This then meant that we had to carry up to three heavy transformers to wherever the permanent way slack was, usually in the middle of nowhere. Such unsatisfactory and fragile arrangements were always going to be prone to failures; call outs to attend speed boards which had 'gone out' were numerous. You would always hope it would be the lamp that had failed, but more often than not it was the cable. The importance of these markers was tragically highlighted by the Nuneaton accident on 6th June 1975 where a warning board (albeit gas lit) had extinguished and the train entered a TSR of 20mph at an estimated 80mph with devasting consequences. *23rd March 1979*

The ingenious use of a cantilever brings CB159 signal head the correct side of the track circuit joint at the tips of 102 facing points which are actually inside platform 3 (although the signalling plan show these two signals as separate structures). With the route set for the branch towards Lewes, CB159 would exhibit a 'B' in the theatre indicator, whilst with lever 160 reversed and the route set for the Up Through line towards London a 'T' would be exhibited. Two routes were available from each signal, although the driver would be unaware of which way he was being sent. The observant will notice a lamp out on the bottom left 'B' in the indicator of CB151 signal on platform 6; the signalling could suffer a number of these outages before the signal would fail to change aspect. The makeup of figures in an indicator such as this would be carefully configured so that if a number of lamps failed, its degraded state could not be interpreted as another letter or numeral. A mop and bucket are leaning up against the structure leg for drivers to give their windscreens a quick wash before departure; note also the TRTS (Train Ready to Start) plungers mounted on the upright. The outline of the old works roof can clearly be seen on the side of the signal box. *30th October 1983*

Looking north from the ex-girder stage, the Brighton steam crane with its auxiliary coaches sits in the carriage sidings adjacent to the sheds but the base of the old Montpelier Junction signal box has now been replaced by a humble shed. The staff foot crossing adjacent to the crane is devoid of any warning lights and just requires staff to keep a sharp lookout while crossing. A number of 'running shunts' can be seen for which the 1932 signalling notice states: *'Drivers of trains whose movement has been authorised by a running signal are not required to observe the position of the relevant shunt signal. It may, however, happen in an emergency that a shunt signal applicable to the direction and line on which the train is travelling has been placed at Danger by the signalman and, in these circumstances, if this this signal is noticed by the driver he should bring his train to a stand.'* So 'keep an eye on them anyway' was the message. The spare land to the right once gave access to Brighton Works and was also the site where on one occasion we tried burning the redundant wire removed from the relay room to reduce it to bare copper for the scrap man. With swathes of black smoke drifting over the running lines, and following complaints from drivers, we abandoned the practice!
August 1979

Left: This undated photograph gives a comparison to the above image, with Montpelier Junction signal box seen in the centre background. I also much like the fact that with this and the earlier pair of pictures from this vantage point, Edward and I stood in very similar positions, some 47 years apart.
The Edward Wallis Collection

Taken from the top of the pair of signals controlling the exit from Down sidings No's 1 and 2 (seen to the right of the signal box in the previous picture), this wonderfully atmospheric photograph really brings home the difference between working conditions of that era compared with the sanitised railway we have nowadays. This view towards the station also gives a rare view of the entrance into the works to the left and if I knew anything about wagons I could have a field day! General clutter abounds as various workmen go about their daily duties; none of them seem to be aware that they are about to be recorded for posterity. *The Edward Wallis Collection*

Looking over Brighton's second 60ft turntable (the other being to the east of the engine sheds), the re-roofed bottom half of the signal box during the early 1970s acted as the mess room for the Brighton Minor Works S&T technicians who were busily involved with the Brighton signal box rewiring. It is safe to say now that coal was 'borrowed' from the supply allocated to the Brighton steam crane and carried across the adjacent foot crossing to be reduced in size and added to any scrap wood that would have been found lying around to get the fire going on a cold morning. *1939, John Minnis Collection*

Taking advantage of a nearby lighting pole, this is looking towards Brighton station on 30th October 1983. CB71 and CB89 signals positioned on the cantilever in the centre of the photograph give the final platform destination for the Down Local and Down Through lines respectively, although these are both three aspect signals. When commissioned it was SR practice (as seen before with the equivalent mechanical signalling) to give a green aspect if the line was clear to the buffer stops and a yellow aspect if the platform splitting track circuit was occupied. If both tracks were occupied then a miniature red/green shunt signal would show a green aspect for an attaching engine or similar. By this time the controls would have been altered (after the Moorgate accident of 1975) to allow only a yellow aspect to the buffer stops. A 2-position white light 'calling on' signal can be seen to the right of each main signal head to give the driver authority to enter an already occupied platform, this after the train had been brought virtually to a stand. Although plated as mentioned above, both of these signals are controlled by no fewer than eight levers in numerical sequence (71-78 and 89-96) to give access to platforms 3-10 inclusive (although only nine platforms when this particular photograph was taken).

Having turned his camera through 180 degrees from the earlier photograph of Montpelier Junction, this picture of Edward's leads us nicely towards the next chapter as the close proximity of Lovers Walk and Upper Goods signal boxes can be seen in the distance. We finish with the following photographs as Brighton enters its period of 1980s modernisation.
The Edward Wallis Collection

On 12th April 1985, the face of Brighton is changing forever with the signal box in its final death throes and the throat layout changing to something distinctly simpler. Trains are still running, however, as a 4-car can be seen heading towards London Road viaduct and the Lewes direction, achieved by clipping and scotching the required points and flagging trains in and out so as to keep a basic service running on the East Coast route whilst the Central section was blocked. The Brighton signal box fire of 1st October 1984 had hastened the work here as only a very basic signalling system had been brought back into work. After the passage of the 21.48 to Victoria, signalled out of platform 4, the signal box closed forever on the 30th March 1985. *Derek Osborne*

Fast forward nine days and the signal box has succumbed some more (apparently it gave the demolition contractors a real headache) whilst the rebuilt platforms are taking shape. The new platform starting signals are in position and it will not be too long before signal corresponding and point rehearsals start taking place, controlled from the Westinghouse Mark 4A 'Westpac' geographical interlocking in the relay room off to the left, all controls and indications linked to the new Three Bridges signal box via a Time Division Multiplex (TDM 69) system. Platforms 1-3 for the west coast route in the foreground had already been commissioned (on 17th March), controlled by Three Bridges signal box, so part of the interlocking had already been brought into use. Brighton bound trains from the main line therefore had access via the Cliftonville Spur, with reversal at Hove. *21st April 1985, Derek Osborne*

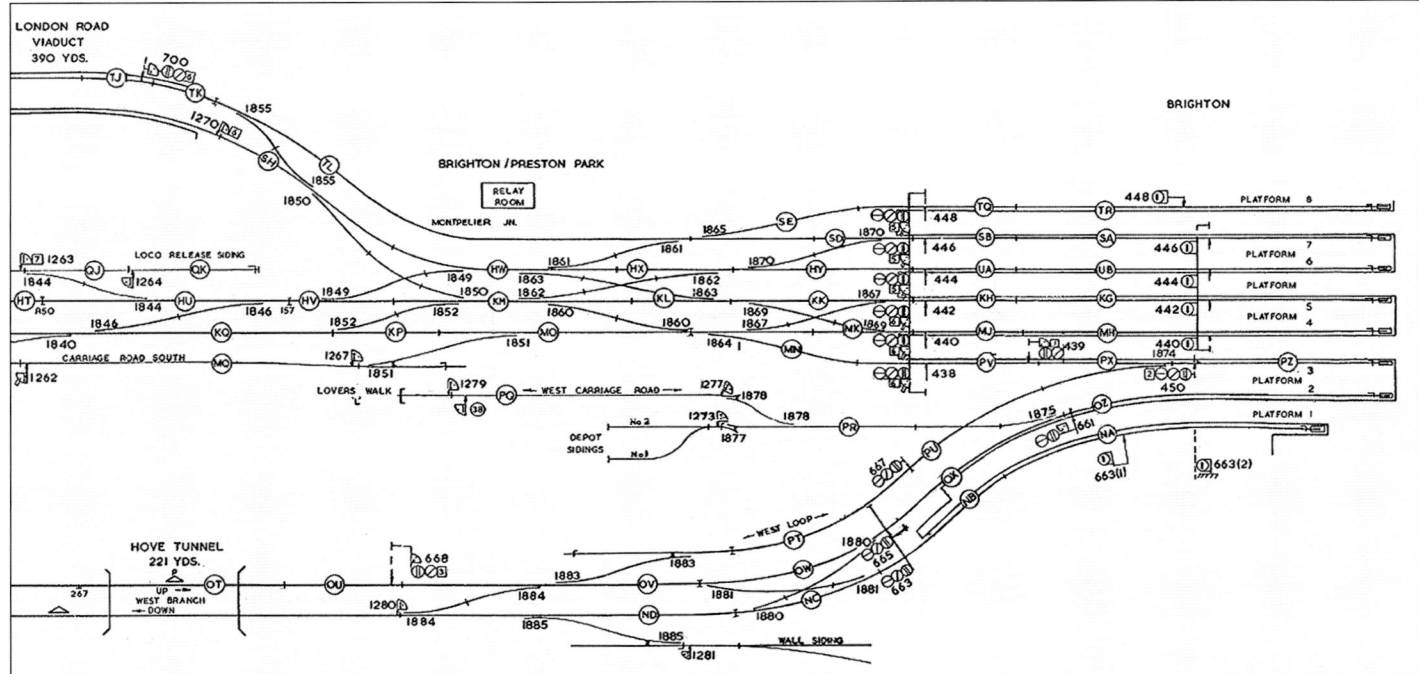

The fully remodelled Brighton layout was opened to traffic on 29th April 1985. Compare this to the 1933 track plan extract and marvel as to *'How the mighty are fallen'*. The number of platforms has been reduced to eight, the middle siding and dock roads have gone and access from platform 2 to the Up Main is no longer available, platform 3 being the only interchange between the Main and East Coast routes. With standard permanent way design, standard components and point fittings throughout, no portable forges were necessary to facilitate the installation this time.

2 Lovers Walk Junction

This well-known photograph depicts the 1862 Lovers Walk signal box in what must be the last few weeks of its life, showing the building materials lying in the cess by the lead-away of the new box. The new signal box steps would be constructed with a typical veranda once the old structure had been demolished. If only the photographer had panned to the left a bit more to get the new signal box into the picture as well – obviously the engine was deemed to be more important! *Lens of Sutton Collection*

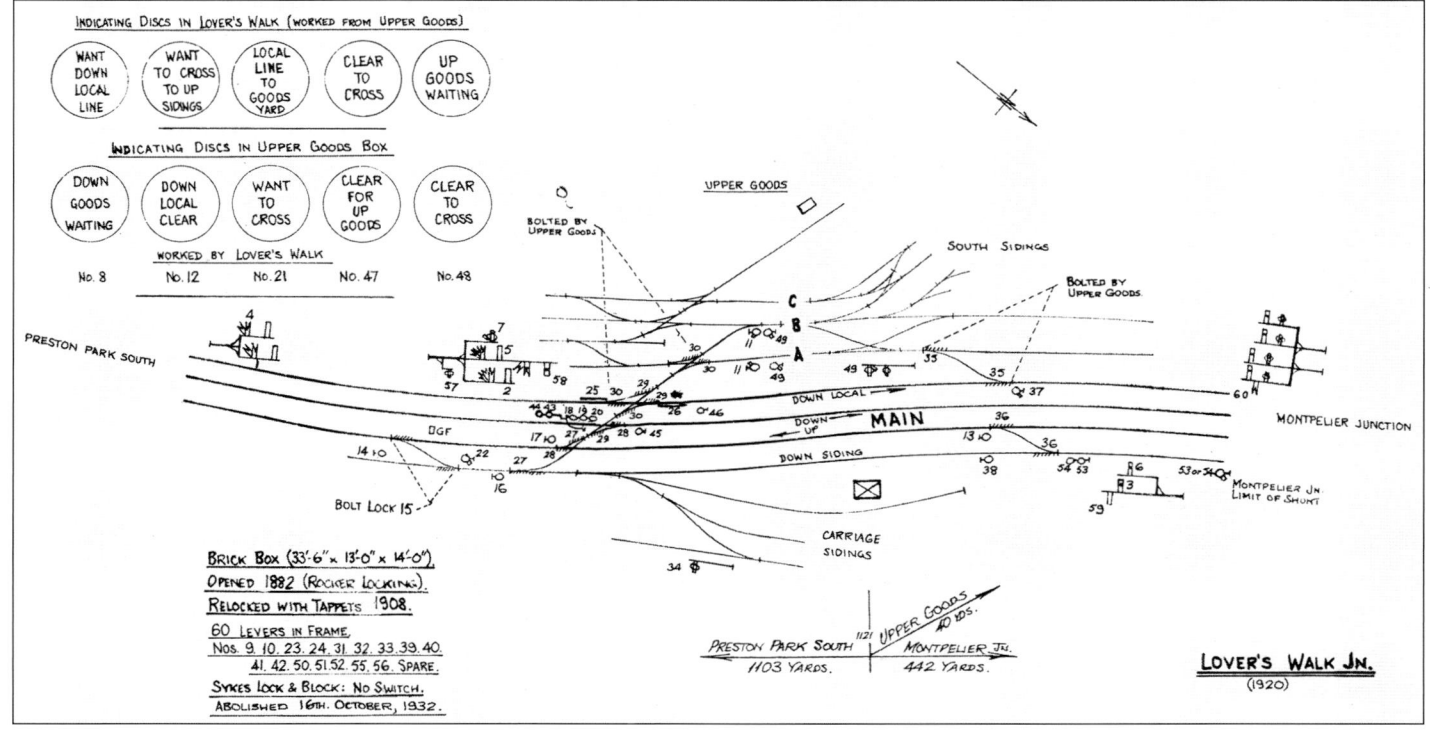

Lovers Walk Junction signal box layout in 1920.

Although not an image of the best quality, Lovers Walk signal box is seen here in the mid 1920s with a 3-SUB unit for the South Eastern Electrification scheme standing alongside. These units were converted from ex-L&SWR steam stock, their painting and trimming taking place at Lancing Works, from whence the units were steam hauled to Lovers Walk where the electrical equipment was installed. Lovers Walk signal box was a block post which opened in 1882 containing a 60-lever frame and working to Montpelier Junction to the south and Preston Park South to the north. As with the Brighton station signal boxes, this also had indicating discs working to Upper Goods, almost opposite, for requesting moves between the two.
Andrea Thorne Collection, courtesy thebrightonbranchofaslef.yolasite.com

The LB&SCR record card for William Godley, who ended his impressive 49 years' service as a signalman at Lovers Walk. Born on 27th February 1862, he began his profession as a platelayer in 1878 before joining the Operating Department the following year. His career subsequently encompassed spells at Henfield, Chichester, Billingshurst, Crawley, Kemp Town Junction, Havant and Preston Park before becoming signalman at Lovers Walk. Retiring on 31st December 1927, his wages had risen from 16 shillings per week to 60 shillings. His otherwise unblemished 'Service Record' (*right*) on the rear bears this stark stamp.

3 – Brighton Upper Goods

The 'Brighton Belle' in its post-1969 blue and grey livery, passing Brighton Upper Yard around four and a half months before it was withdrawn from service. Lovers Walk carriage sidings, sheds and shunters cabin (all points in the yard being hand operated) are on the right, with a staff walkway crossing all tracks towards Upper Goods beneath the last coach of the train. The fan of sidings in the distance holds a number of parcel vans and wagons whilst the line down towards Lower Goods, descending on a gradient of 1:53, can be seen beyond the signal box and pair of mechanical signals in the distance. In a diversion from railways, the enormous building that is St. Bartholomew's church, with its tall gabled roof (135ft from ground level to the ridge) can be seen towards the top right-hand corner of the photograph, built, according to urban legend, to the dimensions of Noah's Ark! *11th December 1971, Edwin Wilmshurst*

Right: Brighton Upper Goods shunt box was never a block post and was not operated by a signalman but by a 'pointsman', so called as the signal box did not preside over any passenger traffic. A splendid relic of the past exists in the form of an original LB&SCR wooden signal post (complete with suitably embossed post cap) now housing a mechanical shunt (Upper Goods No. 7) signal. Standing on top of the ladder whilst wielding an oil can or attempting to change the lamp in the floodlight was a somewhat precarious occupation! CB66 shunt signal, with its back to the camera and released by Upper Goods No. 33 lever, was the exit shunt from Upper Goods, showing yellow as its most restrictive aspect (applying to No. 1 goods siding and therefore allowed to be passed at will) and a green aspect when exiting Upper Goods for the Down Local line. It is astonishing to think that when opened in 1932, Brighton signal box controlled no fewer than eighty-three shunt signals, which gives some idea of the vast number of moves that were once available; the 1985 layout provided just seventeen. What was once the staff crossing from Lovers Walk is now piled up in a heap of timber. Upper Goods box closed on Saturday 30th June 1984. *30th October 1983*

BRIGHTON UPPER GOODS

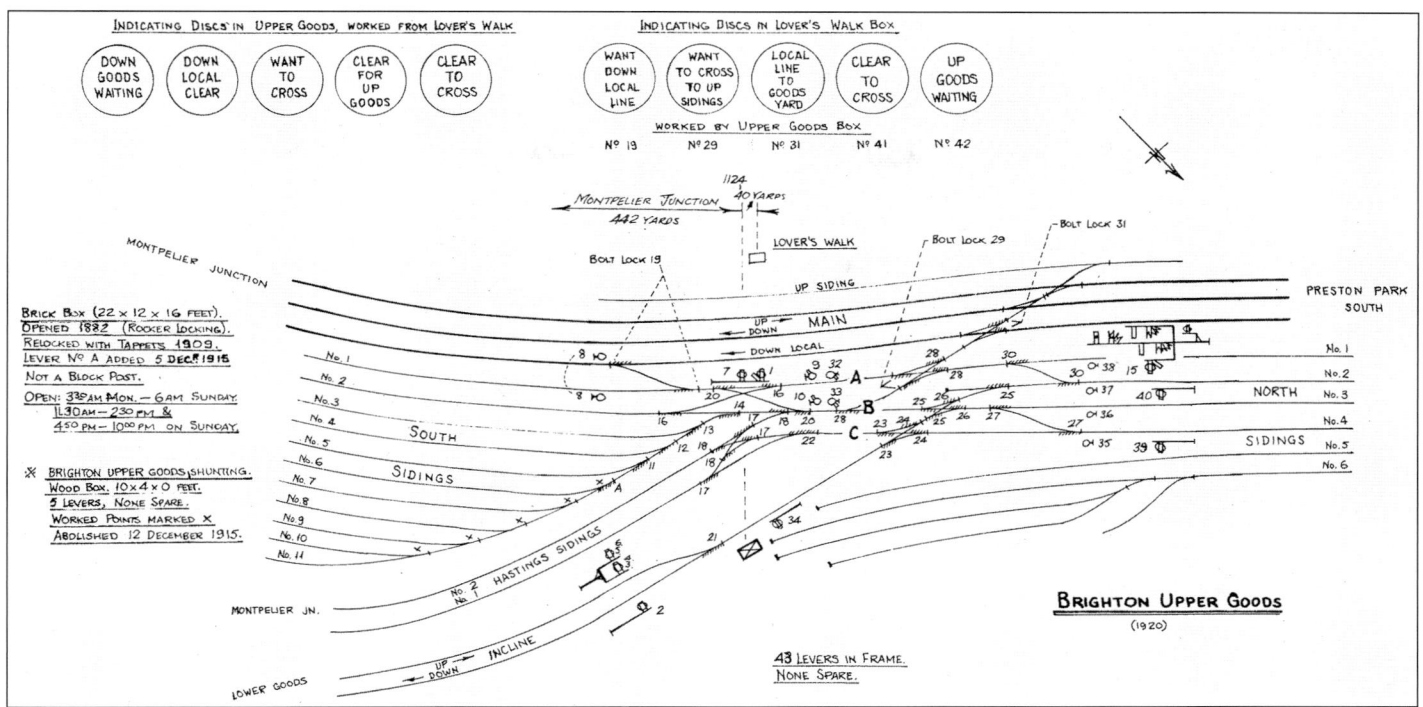

Brighton Upper Goods is shown at the bottom of the drawing, Lovers Walk signal box can be seen at the top.

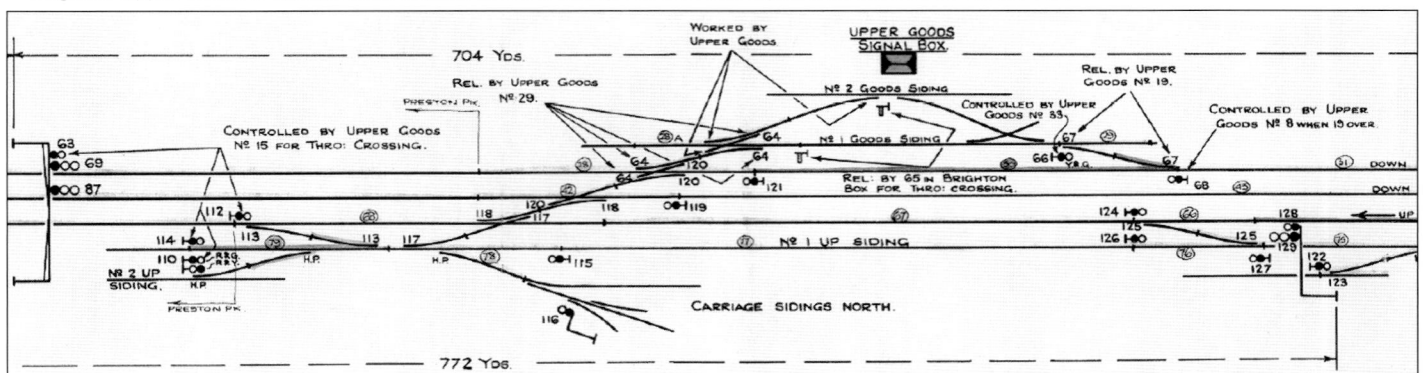

ABOVE: Moving north from the previous Brighton track plan (*pages 34/35*): Upper Goods signal box in 1933 with Lovers Walk carriage sidings below.

FACING PAGE: The interior of Brighton Upper Goods signal box taken on a bright morning in January 1980. All the levers are working mechanical apparatus bar three (No's 15, 18 and 30 points) which have had the top four inches of the lever sawn off, showing that they are motor operated points. The first lever is labelled 'A' (access to No. 6 south siding which was added late in December 1915), No. 1 lever being next and the rest of the frame in correct numerical order from there. A number of signal lamp burners can be seen on the shelf over the end of the frame, some of which are alight so it must have been 'lamping day' when lamp maintenance took place. The Walkers rotary train describer receiver from Brighton suspends incongruously from a piece of wire attached to the vertical upright separating the sliding sash windows. *Courtesy 53A Models of Hull*

RIGHT: Upper Goods Walker's train describer transmitter was still, as seen earlier in Brighton cabin, capable of the most unlikely transmissions for this late date. *13th May 1977, Derek Osborne*

Rebuilt Bullied 'West Country' Class 'Pacific' No. 34108 *Wincanton* passes Upper Goods with a southbound Southern Counties Touring Society 'Southern Rambler' rail tour on 19th March 1967. *Bluebell Railway Museum Archive, Joe Kent Collection*

Looking north from the bridge seen in the background of the 'Southern Rambler' rail tour photograph earlier, this is the newly relaid formation between Preston Park and Brighton with just an Up and Down main line left. The Lovers Walk carriage washer is seen on the left with the old Pullman Works (now demolished) beyond. *16th September 1984, Derek Osborne*

Above: Upper Goods had a happy ending, however, as it was saved by the Bluebell Railway to reinvent itself as the new signal box for Kingscote station. Here the timber structure is being lifted from its brick base to be placed onto a low loader for its early morning journey through the Sussex countryside towards its new home. *6th April 1986, Alan Grove*

Above Right: The remains of the signal box awaiting demolition after the top had been lifted. *6th April 1986, Alan Grove*

Right: On the same morning, the convoy carrying the top of the signal box negotiates its way through the picturesque village of Cuckfield, no doubt to the astonishment of residents. *6th April 1986, Alan Grove*

Below: Resplendent in Southern colours, the refurbished structure is lowered on to its newly constructed base at the north end of Kingscote station on the Bluebell Railway. Commissioning of this new, award-winning signalling, now utilising a Westinghouse miniature lever 'L' frame, finally took place during early 2017.
30th August 1996, Alan Grove

4 – Preston Park

A lovely panoramic view of Preston Park station with its enormous 'bedhead' running-in board and ornamental shrubs decorating the platform. The foliage was no problem in sighting the Up starting signals due to the height of the arms. Preston Park North signal box is visible amidst the sea of lower quadrant semaphore signals. *Lens of Sutton Collection*

From a similar angle but from further back up the hill, a rare shot of Preston Park South box in its original all-timber form as a London-bound train makes its way up the main line. The advertising hoardings, just to the right of the signal box, are propped up with long baulks of timber at the top of the embankment. Possibly a photograph taken on a Monday, judging by the washing hanging out in the back gardens of the houses at bottom left. *Derek Osborne Collection*

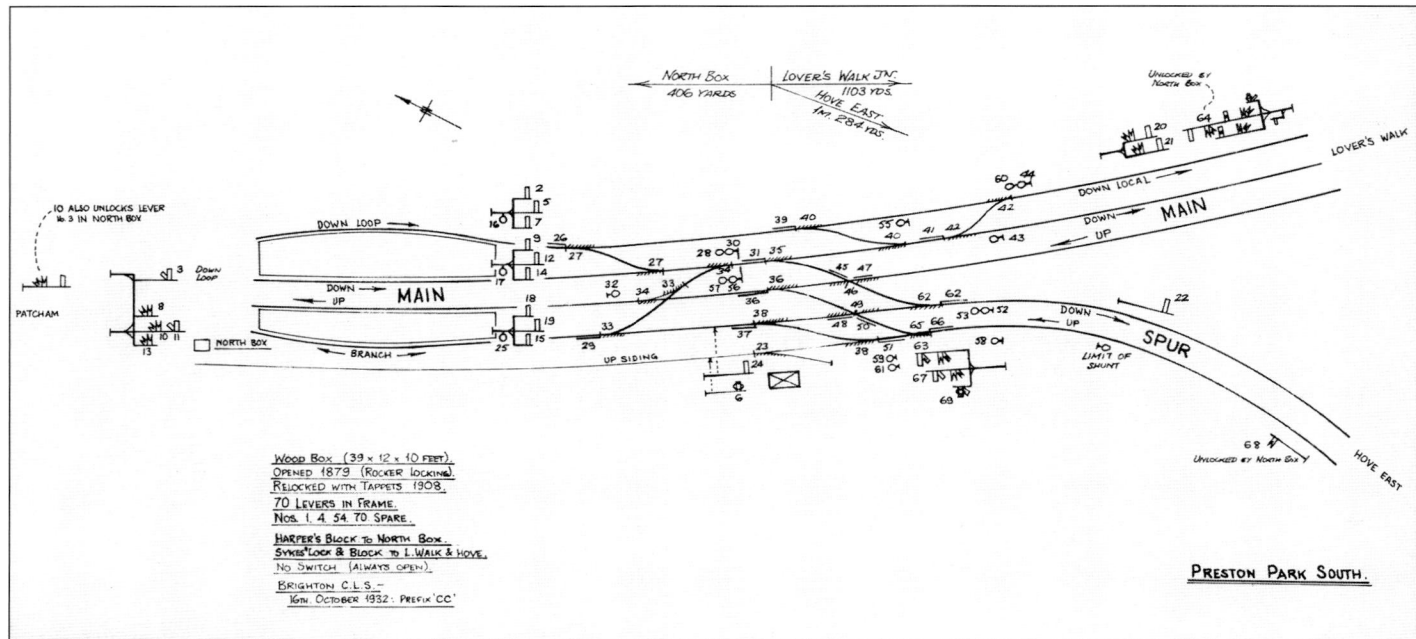

Preston Park South is seen here in 1920. As ever with the close proximity of signal boxes, slotting abounded and the maximum route information provided for the driver was admirable, as distant signals were provided for every route both north and south of the station and to and from the Cliftonville Spur towards Hove. These were the days before individual speed signage for 'turnouts' (diverging routes at points) was widespread. Permanent speed indicators did exist back then and two types of indicators were in use *'at selected places'*: a white triangular sign on a black background depicting the point where the restriction commenced, with a similar 'T' where the restriction terminated. These were also illuminated at night but ultimately it was the driver's route knowledge that enabled him to control his train. A Southern Railway 'Permanent Speed Restrictions' booklet from August 1945, under the heading *'General Speed Restrictions Applicable To Junctions Etc.'*, relates that:

> The speed of trains must not exceed **20 miles per hour** through all junctions diverging from the line on which a train is running, or converging to the line on which the train is to run, unless otherwise advised in the [following] special speed notices. The speed of trains must not exceed **15 miles per hour** when crossing from one line to another.

The section in the booklet giving all relevant speed restrictions in excess of this on the Brighton line finishes at Haywards Heath, thus inferring that everything south of there is subject to the above paragraph. Nowadays with colour light signalling, the signalling system itself (to a large degree) controls the speed of the train with regard to junctions and you certainly would not have continuous green aspects from line-speed leading to a 15mph junction, as is effectively the case in these semaphore days (naturally subject to any individual signal box instructions). Strangely, there is no connection from the Up Main to the Up Loop platform (or Branch as it is called here) although this was rectified with the 1932 resignalling, when an additional slip connection was installed opposite the single slip, No's 33 and 34 points.

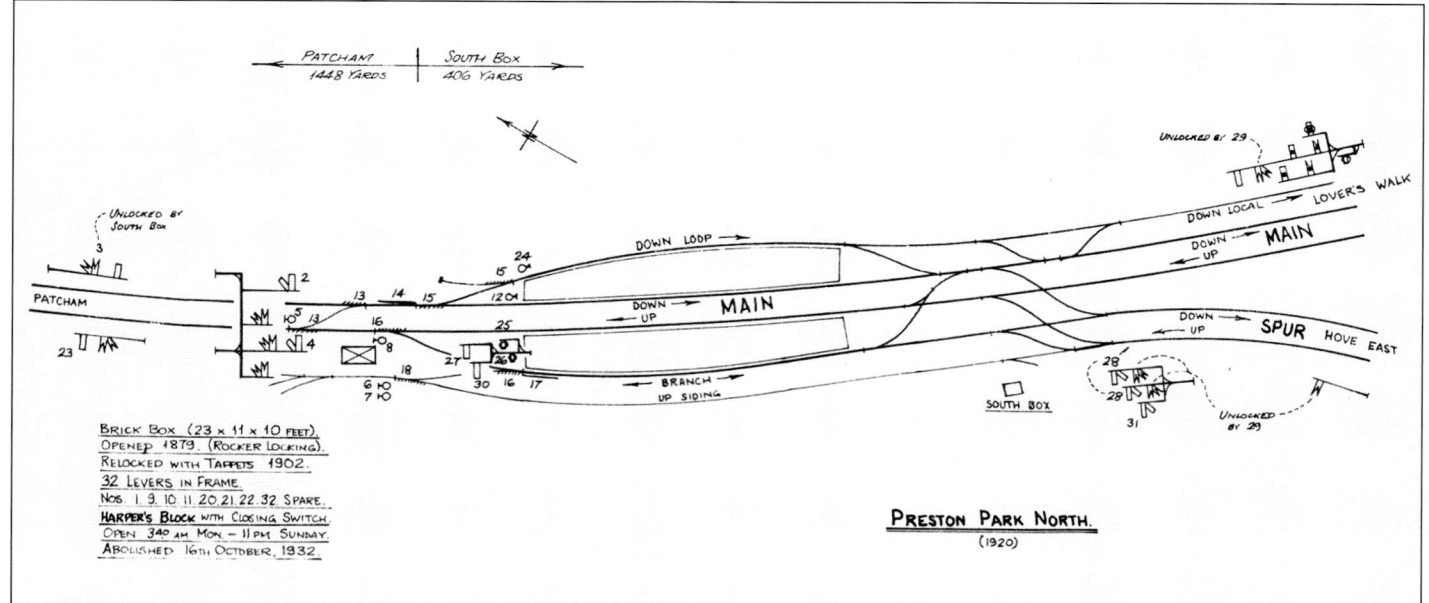

Preston Park North signal box's area of control in 1920.

Preston Park North signal box was of Saxby & Farmer manufacture and contained a 32-lever frame; it worked to Preston Park South in the Brighton direction and Patcham Intermediate to the north and is seen here in 1926. *Derek Osborne Collection*

Preston Park looking towards Brighton from the high vantage point of North signal box's Down home signals. The third rail is in position and the new elevated signalling cable route can be seen adjacent to the Down road. A lone worker seems to be taking a great deal of interest in the concrete portion as it curves behind the buffer stops. The machine for what will become 10B points (for moves into the Down Local platform) can be seen in the 6ft opposite the signal box but there is nothing for the crossover in the foreground, as that was due to disappear under the resignalling. *The Edward Wallis Collection*

The rear three coaches, about to form a Worthing service, are 'slipped' (i.e. parted at speed) approaching Preston Park (try getting a safety case for this procedure nowadays!). The guard will bring them safely to a stand in the platform where a waiting engine will then attach and take the three coaches forward, the front portion of the train running straight through to Brighton. The practice of *'slipping carriages from trains in speed'* was discontinued from Saturday 30th April 1932. Occupying the site adjacent to where the new sub-station was later built is Preston Park North's No. 23 Up advance starting signal with Patcham's Up outer distant (No. 1) below, situated between the two sidings, the only space available.
John Minnis Collection

RIGHT: There are just two years and three months to go before this area will be electrified and resignalled, yet there is no apparent preparatory work under way. The facing crossover seen beyond the Down local signals on the left was removed prior to the resignalling, thus all trains bound for the Cliftonville spur after that time had to be routed along the Down Through platform. The tall 3-doll signal post in the distance is for moves off the Up spur, whilst the two signals seen to the right of the signal box control movements towards the Down spur and from the Up siding respectively. All three starting signals were replaced by colour light signals with the same profile.
24th July 1930, John Minnis Collection

FACING PAGE TOP LEFT: A closer view of the Up Spur signals seen in the above picture, with the replacement signals for trains coming off the Cliftonville Spur in the foreground. It must have been assumed that maintenance personnel were professional contortionists considering the agility required to attend to the left-hand signal head, perhaps hooking a knee over the ladder hoop before leaning out over the abyss below. The installers would have had the luxury of making off the signal cables while the assembly was horizontal; once it was up it was somebody else's problem!
The Edward Wallis Collection

FACING PAGE TOP RIGHT: Taken from a Southern Railway document entitled 'Preston Park & Brighton – Bases & Posts for Colour Light Signals' (covering every signal structure for this area and presumably given to Westinghouse for construction purposes), this extract, shown as No. 14 of 27, is for the centre and right-hand signal posts shown in the following photograph, hence the note for two posts. A caveat at the bottom states *'Heights of red lights to be as shown except where posts & fittings will not clear gauge'*. It was obviously someone else's job to check that then, although in this particular case, with the red aspects at 15 feet above rail level, clearances would not have been a problem.

FACING PAGE BOTTOM: This shows such a clean environment that you would hardly think that a major resignalling had just taken, or was taking place; contrast this with a similar situation today where location cases and disconnection boxes would abound in a sea of orange pipe. The four 'dog kennel' locations on the left (cast in the Westinghouse foundry at Chippenham) house track circuit equipment for the 'double to double' a.c. track circuits (feed and relay impedance bonds respectively) in the Down Local and the parallel 'double to single' in the Down Through. The photograph poses a bit of a mystery as it is dated November 1932, i.e. around a month after this section was commissioned on 16th October, yet all the aspects are unlit and even the ladder is missing on the Down Through starters. It may have been taken during the commissioning itself, although even then any activity is notorious by its absence. One signal per route was the order of the day, so on the Down Through line the driver would pass two red aspects (three counting the red/green shunt signal) whilst obeying the third. The Down Through signals were re-sighted onto a cantilever structure at a later date. The scuffed area on the platform in the near foreground is where the support post for the three-doll semaphore structure that preceded these signals would have been removed. *K.R.M.*

2'-6"
2'-6"
15'-0"
C.C. 9/12/14/17.
C.C. 15/18/19/26.
2 POSTS.

CC.2
CC.5
CC.16
CC.9
CC.12
CC.14
CC.17
DANGER
DON'T TOUCH
CONDUCTOR RAILS

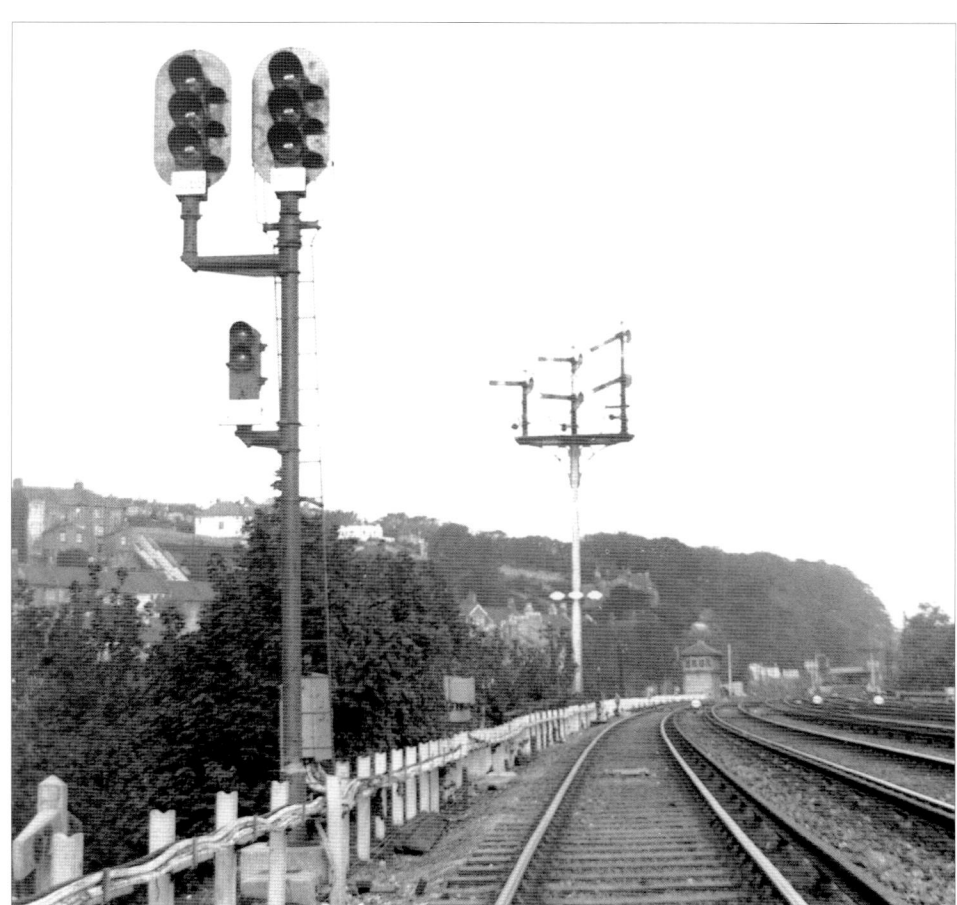

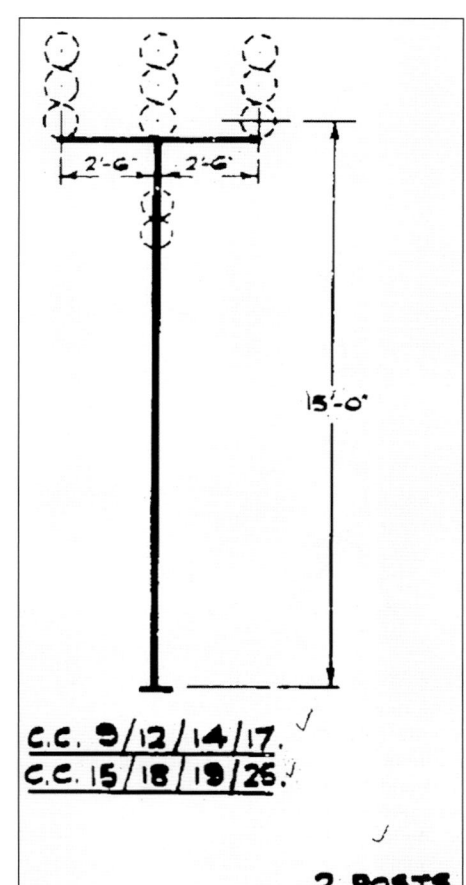

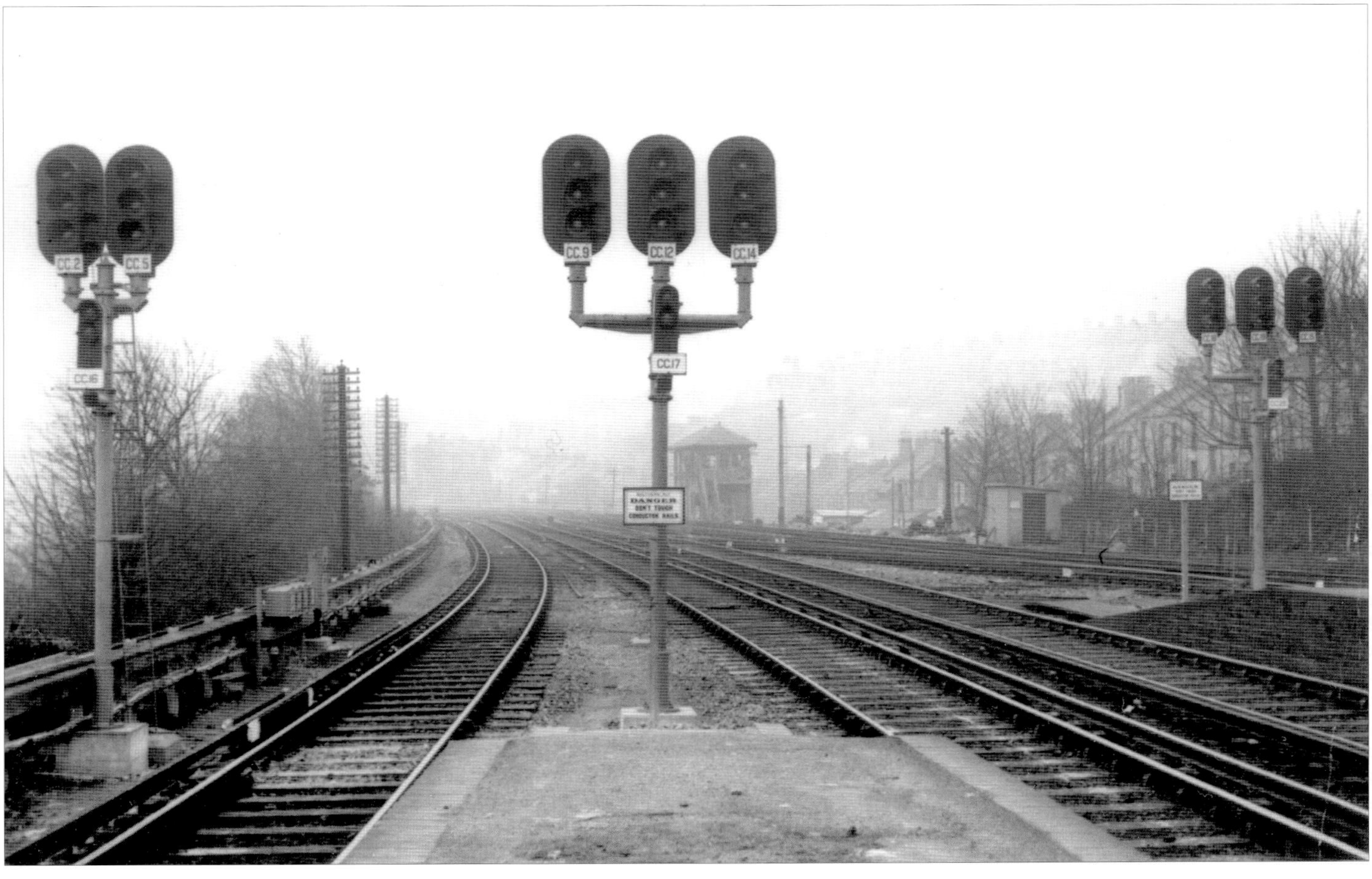

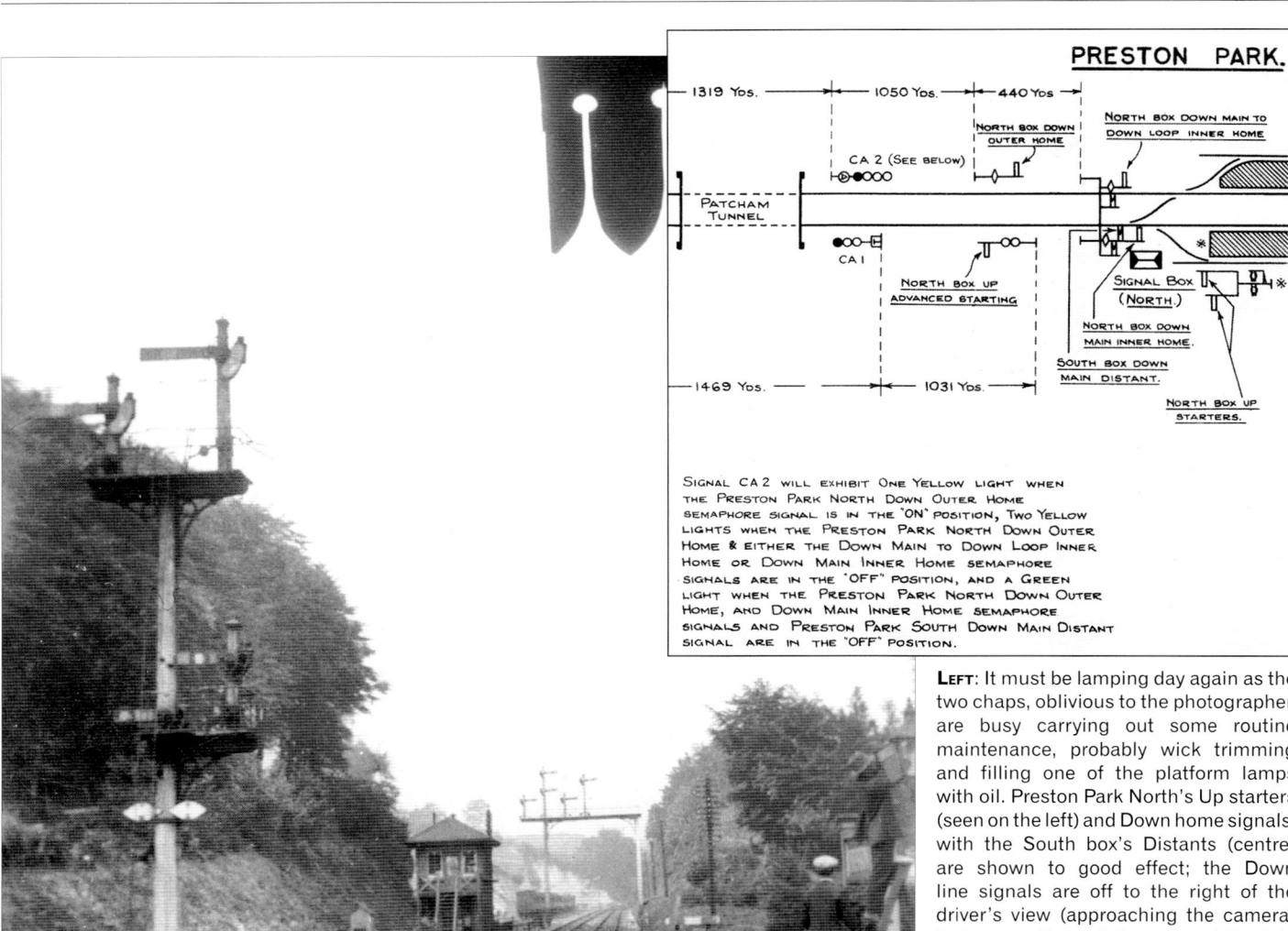

LEFT: It must be lamping day again as the two chaps, oblivious to the photographer, are busy carrying out some routine maintenance, probably wick trimming and filling one of the platform lamps with oil. Preston Park North's Up starters (seen on the left) and Down home signals, with the South box's Distants (centre) are shown to good effect; the Down line signals are off to the right of the driver's view (approaching the camera) to improve the sighting around the left-hand curve on approach. Just peeping over the top of the Down platform ramp can be seen No. 12 shunt signal. It would appear that No. 13 crossover, seen beyond, was out of work at this stage as the crossings seem to have been plain lined and the returning shunt signal, No. 5, cannot be seen. Certainly the crossover did not survive the resignalling, with No. 12 being replaced by a Limit of Shunt. *24th July 1930. E.R. Lacey, John Minnis Collection*

RIGHT: Engineer Townsend's copy of signalling notice No. 36 detailing the filling in of the remaining mechanically signalled 'islands' left after the Haywards Heath area and Coulsdon North to Balcombe Tunnel commissionings. After the success of these, the Traffic Department must have had complete faith in the Signal Engineering function as Balcombe Tunnel to Stone Hall was commissioned during the early hours of Monday 3rd October with Folly Hill to Patcham following on Thursday 6th October. Preston Park North was abolished as part of the Brighton commissioning on 16th October, just ten days later.

FACING PAGE TOP RIGHT: Extract from Signalling Instruction No. 36 from 1932, *'On a date to be advised'*, showing the alterations required at Preston Park to enable the new colour light signalling (already brought into work northwards) to work to the existing mechanical signalling. This was undoubtedly complex work, with new circuit closures being fitted to the existing mechanical arms, followed by some thorough aspect sequence testing on completion.

FACING PAGE BOTTOM: Preston Park track plan extract from 15th November 1933 showing that South signal box was the sole survivor after the 1932 resignalling. No. 32 track circuit on the Up road was the first track indication for potentially four signal boxes, although Keymer Crossing was the only one permanently in use. Signal CA1 was provided with a telephone as it protected Patcham Tunnel and CA2 was provided with an 'A' light. This was a separate indication below the red aspect (on automatic signals) which, in a failure condition, showed an illuminated 'A' and gave the driver permission to pass the signal at danger as stated in the signalling notice, thus:

232040

SOUTHERN RAILWAY.

Signal Instruction No. 36, 1932.

INSTRUCTIONS TO ALL CONCERNED
AS TO THE
INTRODUCTION OF COLOUR LIGHT SIGNALS
(In place of existing Semaphore Signals)
BETWEEN BALCOMBE TUNNEL AND HAYWARDS HEATH
ALSO
BETWEEN HAYWARDS HEATH AND PRESTON PARK NORTH
AND
ABOLITION OF EXISTING BALCOMBE INTERMEDIATE, STONE HALL, FOLLY HILL, WIVELSFIELD, KEYMER JUNCTION, BRAPOOL AND PATCHAM SIGNAL BOXES

ON A DATE TO BE ADVISED.

Rules 70, 71 and 72 to be observed. Drivers to keep a good look out for hand signals.

The existing semaphore running signals between Balcombe Tunnel and Stone Hall signal boxes, inclusive, and between Folly Hill and Preston Park North signal boxes will be abolished and colour light signals installed in lieu thereof.

The existing Balcombe Intermediate, Stone Hall, Folly Hill, Wivelsfield, Keymer Junction, Brapool and Patcham signal boxes will be abolished.

On and from the date of introduction of the new colour light signals, the new Train Signalling Regulations dated April, 1932, for the sections of line between Coulsdon North No. 2 Box and Brighton ; Preston Park and Hove East ; and Brighton and Hove East must be worked to throughout as between Coulsdon North No. 2 and Preston Park North Boxes.

A diagram showing the new signals and their types, locations and meanings, together with the existing signals between Stone Hall and Folly Hill is attached to this notice. The signals are prefixed by letters to denote from which box they are worked, the relative prefix letters being indicated against each signal box. The signals prefixed by the letters "C.A." are automatic signals.

Balcombe Station, Burgess Hill, Hassocks, and Clayton Cutting signal boxes will be switched out of circuit for certain periods, and during the time these signal boxes are so closed the running signals will work automatically.

Plates bearing the appropriate prefix letters and the number of the signal will be fixed to each colour light running signal post.

The new colour light running signals will show three or four aspects and will be known as automatic, semi-automatic or controlled signals, viz. :—

(a) Automatic signals are those which will not be worked from a signal box but which will be controlled by track circuit only.

(b) Semi-automatic signals are those which will be controlled from one or more signal boxes when such boxes are open, but which, when the boxes are closed, will work automatically and be controlled by track circuit only.

(c) Controlled signals are those which will always be worked from a signal box.

The aspects of the new colour light signals will be the same by day as by night.

Colour light running signals will be fitted with small side lights repeating the aspects exhibited by the signals, to assist drivers of trains drawn close up to such signals.

Back lights will not be provided in the colour light signals.

The height of the centre of the red light of the new colour light running signals will vary between 10½ feet and 17½ feet above rail level.

TRACK CIRCUITS.

Track circuits have been installed throughout the area covered by the colour light signals, and all running signals and certain shunt signals worked from Balcombe, Keymer Crossing, Burgess Hill and Hassocks boxes will be controlled by the track circuits.

Track circuits will also control the automatic signals.

A driver on stopping at a signal in obedience to the danger aspect, must, if the aspect of the signal does not change in the interval and PROVIDED THE SIGNAL EXHIBITS AN ILLUMINATED LETTER 'A', 'wait' thereat three minutes, give one long whistle and then 'proceed' cautiously at a speed not exceeding 5 MILES AN HOUR as far as the line is clear or as far as the next signal, being prepared to stop clear of any obstruction.

Above: Preston Park interior just after mid-day at an unknown date in the 1950s with Signalman Spink on duty, complete with his regulation-issue trousers and braces. Gas lamps were still the order of the day and the splendid vaulted timber roof can be seen to good effect; sadly, the exterior of this would be on view within the next three decades or so. The single original Southern Railway diagram dating from the 1932 resignalling is still in place and two Siemens train describers are also on view. *Derek Osborne Collection*

Facing Page Top: Taken from the top of the signal box steps, Brighton Shed's (75A) own 'K' Class 2-6-0 No. 32339 passes through Preston Park early on a sunny morning. Looking at the three Down Through starting signals seen above the tender of the locomotive, it is clear how the sighting was improved around the slight left-hand curve on approach by repositioning them on a cantilever structure although, as mentioned before, when this was done is unclear. The three signals on the left were for turn back moves from the Up Local platform only. Round point rodding was still in use at this time. *1956, Derek Osborne*

Facing Page Bottom: This was the sight that greeted the early-turn signalman reporting for duty on a beautiful Friday morning on 13th May 1966 – fortunately for us, he paused to capture it for posterity. Manfred Mann's 'Pretty Flamingo' was No. 1 in the charts on this side of the Atlantic with the Mamas and the Papas 'Monday, Monday' topping the Billboard Hot 100 on the other. It would be a mere 78 days before England football captain Bobby Moore lifted the Jules Rimet World Cup. CC60, exhibiting a red aspect at the end of the Up Through platform, infers that a train has not long passed through – so not a single passenger, commuter or indeed customer is in sight. Green enamel proliferates by way of totems (two on every Exmouth Junction concrete works lamp post). The valancing on the downside canopy has been removed at both ends to facilitate the sighting of the original signals, which were mounted three abreast on a straight post. *Derek Osborne*

Above: Preston Park's Up home signals, CC67 and CC69 (coming off the Up Branch on the left) and CC63 and CC43 (applying to the Up Through in the centre) have both left-hand heads signalling the route towards the Up Local platform. In CC69 and CC43 signals the green aspect has been taken out of use and blanked off, leaving a single yellow aspect, thus cautioning the driver for the turnouts into the Up Local platform. A chippings bin lies derelict in the foreground whilst a less than pristine coasting board leans inwards just beyond; the short stub of what must have been an old gas lamp can be seen between those and the signals. Evidence of the resignalling exists in the form of new concrete cable troughing being laid in the left middle distance, whilst the short wooden posts in the bottom left-hand corner would almost certainly be for 'pegging out' new signal positions or location cases. *30th October 1983*

Below and Facing Page Bottom: Preston Park (South) signal box was a Saxby & Farmer type opening on 25th May 1879, containing a 70-lever S&F frame. All the points in the vicinity of the signal box were mechanically worked right up to the Brighton Line resignalling of the 1980s. Appearances can be deceptive as this was an all timber construction when constructed (a lighter structure being built on an embankment) with the brick 'blast wall' added as a wartime precaution similar to Balcombe Tunnel Junction, the original timber frame being very much in evidence when venturing below the operating floor. The S&T had a mess room and small workshop excavated into the chalk embankment beneath the ground floor which was entered via a trap door and down a ladder. Nothing much has changed between the two photographs, although the 1966 view *(below)* still shows the original nameboard. In the later view *(right)*, Signalman Derek Osborne surveys his domain; the signal box mop remains in its traditional place at the top of the steps!
Below, Derek Osborne. Right, August 1979

JUNCTION INDICATORS.

A new feature in connection with this colour light signalling scheme is the introduction of an indicator, known as the "Junction Indicator," to work in conjunction with colour light signals applicable to movements over junctions and facing crossings. The object of the junction indicator is to avoid providing a separate signal post or doll for each diverging route at a junction or facing crossing, and the indicator will consist of a row of three lunar white lights arranged to denote by its angle with the main signal the extent of divergence intended, viz., an angle of 45 degrees for a diverting movement to the right or left, as the case may be, with a further movement of 45 degrees for every additional divergence in the same direction. No junction indication will be exhibited when the signal is at Danger or when the signal is off for a movement along the straight or main road.

Left: Preston Park's Down Through platform starting signals shortly to be converted to a single signal head with Position 1 and 4 position light junction indicators ('feathers') giving the required route information for the Down Local (Position 1 to the left) or the Down Branch (Cliftonville Spur), towards Hove (Position 4 to the right). The original Brighton Line junction signalling of 'one head per route', a direct descendant of mechanical signalling, was gradually being abolished, as junction indicators had been around for a while, eliminating the process of passing a red aspect. The first recorded instance of their use on the Southern appears to be for the Waterloo 'B' to Clapham Junction resignalling of 17th May 1936 as shown below. Five lamp indicators were obviously deemed to be fine here despite the Up Local turn-back signals seen on the right, which had been converted back in April 1962, using the three-lamp style. The Down Local signals on the left are about to receive the same treatment, as evidenced by the tip of the Position 4 indicator just visible, mounted over the left-hand signal of the pair. The author just about remembers being part of the team which carried out the changeovers on a weekend overtime night turn during early November 1973, with a flagman in attendance. The shunt signal seen in the early photograph (CC17) has been abolished and also, to improve sighting, the signals are now mounted on a cantilever structure manufactured partly from old bullhead rails. This would appear to have been a conversion prior to 1949 and no doubt improved the sighting considerably, the structure almost certainly constructed within the Southern Railway's own workshops. The Down Local line and platform succumbed to the Brighton Line resignalling and rationalisation and were taken out of use on 28th August 1984.
28th October 1973, Derek Osborne

Left Centre: An extract from the Southern Railway Signalling Instruction No. 18, Waterloo 'B' to Clapham Junction resignalling as mentioned above.
Courtesy Jim Gibbons

A fine view of the new Preston Park Down home signals clearly showing the 'pigs ears' (12V 4W lamps) to the right of the main heads enabling the driver to draw up as close as possible to the signal. The term 'defensive driving' was still a few decades away from becoming railway terminology, where the driver is encouraged to stop a coach length or so from a red signal. The pygmy lamps were accessed from within the signal head and to change the lamp you had to pull the whole lamp holder out, renew the lamp and replace the holder in situ, this in the days before the angled 'hot strips' on the outer lens became the norm. A driver could, if the main aspect was out but the side light was showing an aspect other than red, pass the signal (having first brought his train to a stand), proceeding cautiously to the next signal and reporting the circumstances to the signalman at the earliest opportunity. The only thing missing? The signal post cap remains on top of the telephone case, possibly as it would not fit between the pair of back blinds, so the post awaits its final crowning. The new sub-station has been built in almost the same spot as the signals seen earlier in the 'slip coach' photograph. *March 1933, K.R.M.*

S&T linemen Harry Marley and Fred Prince, wearing the dress code for the era, pose by No. 35 points alongside a Westinghouse combined facing point lock (FPL) (No. 31) and 4ft detector. Two rocker arms connect to the point switches via short rods to the oversails which can be seen bolted to both the lock stretcher and the tips of the points. Another mammoth task would have been to insulate every stretcher (as seen in the foreground) and soleplate upon which the front slide chairs rest, to enable track circuits to be installed through every item of pointwork, from Brighton to Coulsdon North. *18th July 1954, Derek Osborne*

The beautifully kept interior of Preston Park signal box, with spare levers still in single figures and a reasonably even mix of both mechanical and electrically operated levers. A false ceiling has been installed to try and retain some heat. The signal repeaters for the controlled signals are mounted behind the levers rather than on the front of the block shelf, which was often the more favoured position. Two illuminated diagrams are now in place to cover both ends of the frame in lieu of the single large Southern Railway diagram seen earlier.
August 1979

Above: Preston Park diagram with the familiar two-lamp 'red lozenges' indicating the presence of a train. The indications for the Down line commence with No. 10 track circuit (all track circuits at this time still bore numerals as opposed to letters which are used today), through Burgess Hill ground frame, continuing through Hassocks (switched in as required) and both Clayton and Patcham tunnels to reach Preston Park station. Two not particularly professional patches to the left of the diagram blank off what used to show Clayton Cutting signal box and its associated crossover. The consecutive run of Central Automatic (CA) signals (from right to left) ends here, as what was Clayton's CD8 signal had to be renumbered CA168 (a spare number) when that box was abolished. The diagram then continues through the mass of pointwork to Brighton (CB) and round towards Hove where a Down train can be seen exiting Cliftonville Tunnel. Back to the left-hand end of the diagram, and it was at CA4 signal where, shortly before 23.20 on the evening of 19th December 1978, the 21.50 Victoria to Brighton train was brought to a stand some 506 yards north of Patcham Tunnel, due to an earlier incident at Brighton where the traction current had been isolated and the Preston Park signalman had replaced CA4 to danger. A few minutes later it was struck violently in the rear by the 21.40 Victoria to Littlehampton train running out of course due to earlier problems at Victoria. The driver of this train had received a single yellow aspect at signal CA164, just over 1½ miles in the rear of CA4 signal, but the train's speed had not been significantly reduced by the time it passed the next signal, CA6. This signal, which should have been exhibiting a red aspect and thus protecting the rear of the 21.50 train, was unlit as the 21.40 train passed it. The train continued at speed until the driver made an emergency brake application on sighting the red blinds of the stationary train ahead. The brake application had little time to take effect and it is estimated that the train was still travelling at between 45 and 50 mph when it ran into the back of Brighton train. The reason for CA6 signal not displaying a red aspect was found to be a high resistance contact between one of the lamp springs within the holder and the solder base of the lamp itself, an SL17 type where both the main and auxiliary filaments should be alight simultaneously. It is worth remembering that this was signalling as installed 46 years previously with no AWS (automatic warning system) and no lamp proving, whereas the failure of a signal lamp now would automatically replace the signal in the rear to danger. The required sighting distances for the signals concerned were all found to be correct, as were the braking distances (calculated from the sighting distance as opposed to 'post to post' as of today), but the red lamp in CA6 may have failed and subsequently gone undetected for days or even weeks before the incident. *August 1979*

Facing Page Top: This image from underneath Preston Park signal box in 1982 shows how the bottom floor was adapted to become the relay room, the wooden racks constructed out of the most beautiful teak. Signal stick relays on the top right-hand shelf and track circuit relays (with their associated record cards peeking out) can be seen whilst the everyday minutiae of the S&T technician (fuses, a couple of boxes of lamps, a roll of solder, diagrams and whatever was in the 'Giant Size' tin of Marvel powdered milk) are nearest the camera. *Derek Osborne Collection*

Facing Page Centre Left: Demolition 1980s style showing the inevitable end for one of so many similar proud structures. Trains were still running (a lookoutman has been appointed but is out of view to the right) and the method employed seems to be to turn the building into a giant skip, filling it up from above. The last few sliding sash windows have been positioned to add extra support as removal of the roof nears completion. 1985, *Derek Osborne*

Facing Page Centre Right: Taken from a similar angle as the photograph above, pretty much the only thing that can be said of this scene of devastation is that the original timber framed construction of the signal box now becomes visible, and the exterior lapped cladding just be seen inside the later external brickwork. The internal wiring seen in the trunking at the far end is the original 1932 PBJ (PolyButyl Jute) that was used in Brighton relay room and elsewhere, where existing signal boxes were adapted for the conversion to colour light signalling. *Derek Osborne Collection*

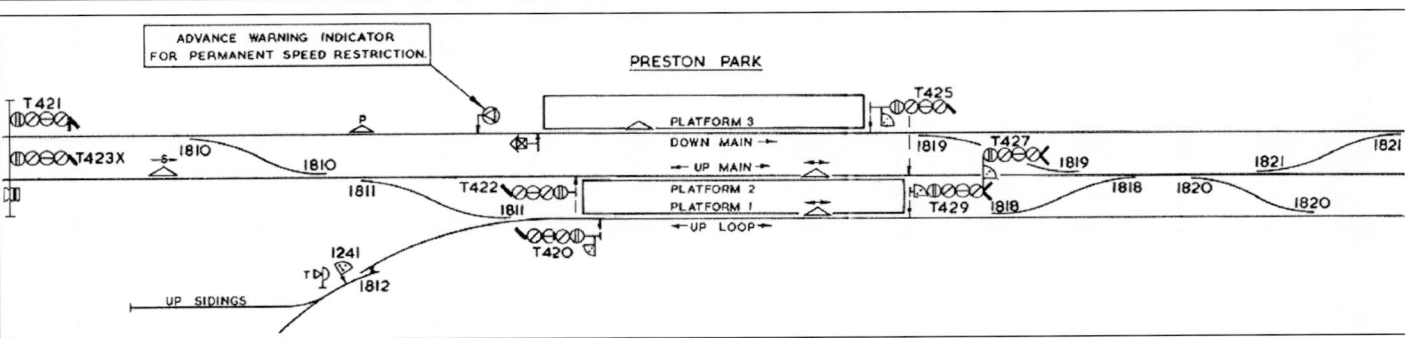

Finally, Preston Park is shown as commissioned on to Three Bridges signal box on 29th April 1985, again showing the simplicity compared with the original layout. The Down Local line and platform have gone, with both the Up Main and Up Loop becoming reversible; additionally, the approach and departure roads towards Brighton have been reduced from three to just Up Main and Down Main. The junction for the Cliftonville Spur is just off the page to the right.

Above: Just over a decade earlier, the same fate had befallen the lovely Preston Park station, seen here mid-demolition on 24th September 1972. *Derek Osborne*

Below: Depicting the basic amenities that replaced it, this is Preston Park in August 1979, lacking any architectural flair whatsoever.

5 – Patcham

Patcham Intermediate signal box opened in 1868 and is seen here at an unrecorded date with its immaculately attired signalman posing proudly for the camera. It was situated on the Down side of the line just under a quarter of a mile south of Patcham Tunnel, working to Brapool Cutting to the north and Preston Park North signal box to the south, housing a 6-lever frame and no spares. With a measuring 'yardage' recorded on the front of the box and the new cable route in place it cannot be far off its last rites. One oddity was its inner distant below its Up home (No. 2) signal but worked by No. 3 Up starting signal. As Patcham Tunnel is approached on a rising gradient on a left-hand curve and in a deep cutting, the tunnel was protected by what would have been a not particularly well sighted No. 3 signal. If a train left Preston Park with No. 1 distant 'on', it would have been helpful to confirm No. 3 was 'off' by providing an inner 'hurry up' distant under No. 2 signal to give the driver confidence to 'open up' and this was achieved by operating both arms from the same No. 3 lever. Quite possibly, due to driver concerns, this was a later addition to what had been installed originally and was carried out in this manner as no spare levers were available. The access to underneath the frame is visible by a somewhat rudimentary door positioned at the front of the signal box. *The Edward Wallis Collection*

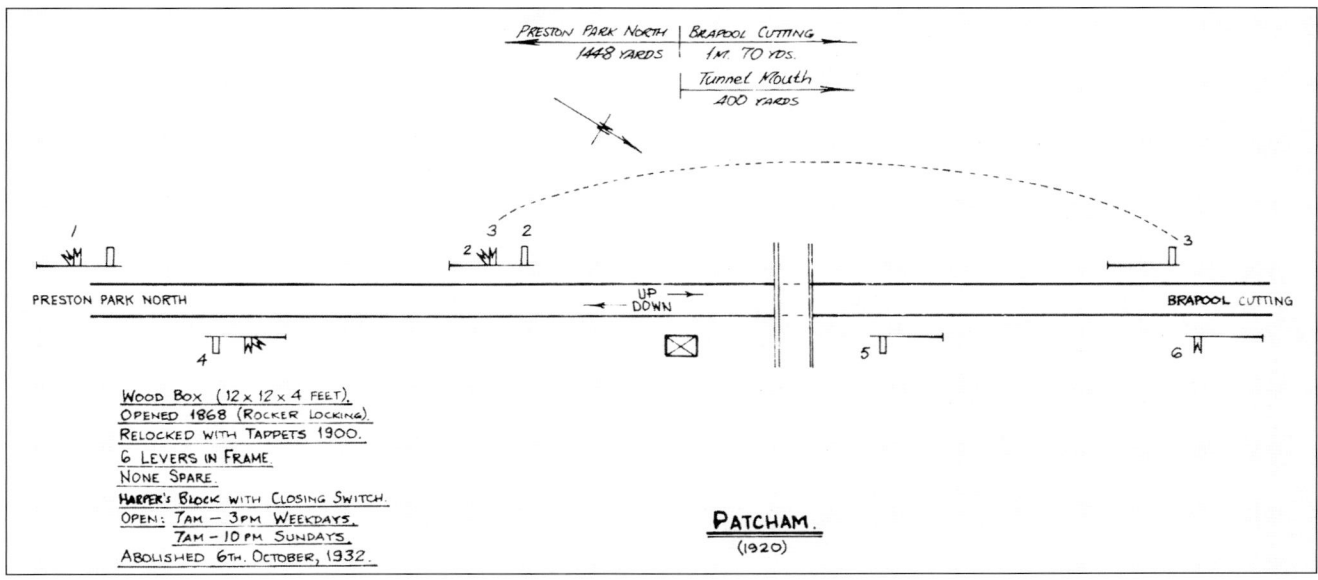

Patcham signal box layout in 1920.

Entitled by Edward as the 'Late replacement of Preston Down distant signal', the photograph allegedly records the impossible. The distant arm, however, is electrically operated (the motor can be seen attached to the post below the signal's spectacle plate) and Edward has caught the moment the stop arm has been replaced but the distant arm motor has not disengaged. This ambiguous display is not uncommon when the camera shutter catches the moment the naturally sluggish response of the motor has not caught up with reality.
The Edward Wallis Collection

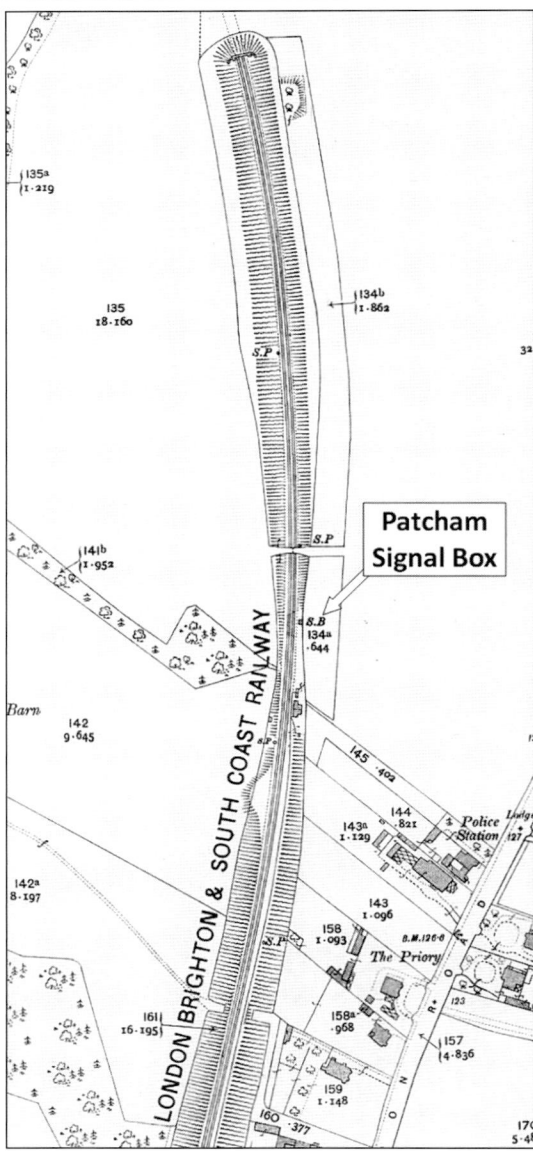

Facing Page Top: LB&SCR 'C3' Class 0-6-0 No. 300 passes through with a Norwood to Brighton coal train on 5th October 1912. *Author's Collection*

Right: Looking north from the top of Patcham Intermediate's No. 4 signal, the staff cottages and signal box are all visible in the distance as the line curves to the left on its approach to Patcham Tunnel; the fogging hut for Preston Park North's distant signal stands in the foreground. *The Edward Wallis Collection*

Facing Page: 1911 map showing Patcham signal box with the railway cottages seen just below. The southern end of Patcham Tunnel can be seen at the top. *Reproduced by permission of the National Library of Scotland*

Not long before they were demolished, the substantial signalmen's cottages are seen here in September 1982 with their windows boarded up and exterior looking somewhat the worse for wear. During their occupancy the inhabitants presumably got used to the noise and vibration of passing trains! Resignalling is getting closer as evidenced by the new lineside location case and the large (and monstrously heavy) bi-directional 'suppressor' AWS magnet sitting in the 6ft waiting to be installed. The first Up road 'Brighton Automatic' – CA1 (C for Central) – is facing us (*above*) whilst the back of CA2 is nearer the new gantry with the two signals visible heralding the arrival, and increased flexibility, of bi-directional working.

Left: 0-4-2 'Gladstone' Class No. 199 *Samuel Laing* emerges from the north portal of Patcham Tunnel and over the bridge beneath which Mill Road rises up towards the South Downs. Patcham's magnificent No. 6 Down distant signal is visible on the left, housing a standard lower quadrant spectacle plate but still bearing a red arm. It is almost as if the fireman is expecting the photographer to be in position as he leans out of the cab to make sure he gets in the shot.
Bluebell Railway Museum Archive, M.P. Bennett Collection

The late John Scrace was a good friend of mine and he gave me complete freedom to use whatever I liked from his extensive photographic collection. *"I like to think that I had an eye for a photograph"* was a phrase he often used, as confirmed by this lovely composition taken adjacent to the north portal of Patcham Tunnel as the 14.28 London Victoria to Brighton passes close to the spot where the previous photograph was taken. The railway cottages date from circa 1850. *27th April 1967, John Scrace*

6 – Brapool Cutting

Brapool Cutting signal box was situated on the Up side of the line, 902 yards north of Patcham Tunnel, working to Clayton Cutting to the north and Patcham Intermediate to the south. Brapool was a later addition, opening in 1910 as a block post to improve capacity on the southern half of the line, therefore eleven years after the opening of the Quarry Line did the same for the northern section. Circa 1910, LB&SCR Class 'B4' No. 71 is seen passing Brapool's No. 8 Down home signal. The signal box housed a 9-lever tappet frame working just one distant, home and starting signal in each direction (six working levers) as possibly a crossover was planned to be installed at a later date. The signal box closed on 6th October 1932. *Lens of Sutton Collection*

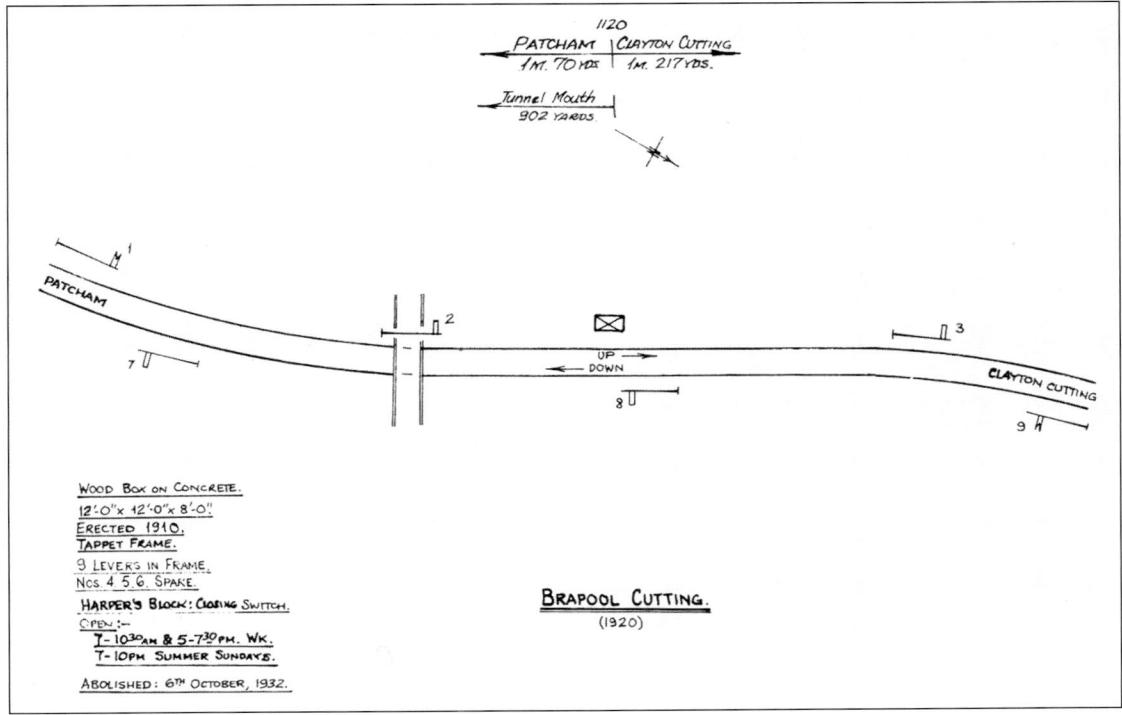

Brapool signal box layout in 1920.

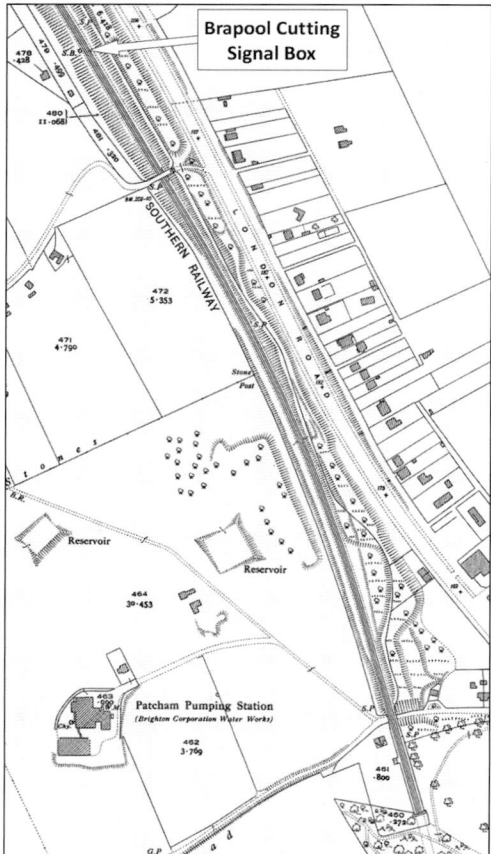

Above: The Down 'Pullman Ltd' passes the signal box hauled by an unidentified Class 'H2' 'Atlantic'. Including four Pullman cars in its rake (*Maud*, *Victoria*, *Beatrice* and *Louise*), the service commenced on 5th December 1881 leaving Victoria at 10am and 3.50pm, and returning from Brighton at 12.30pm and 5.45pm. *E.R. Morton, copyright C.M. & J.M. Bentley*

Left: Brapool Cutting signal box can be seen at the top of this 1930 map, with the north end of Patcham Tunnel at the bottom. The London Road runs parallel to the railway line. *Reproduced by permission of the National Library of Scotland*

7 – Clayton Cutting

A wonderful view of the deep cutting south of Clayton Tunnel amply depicting what manpower alone can achieve. The Clayton Cutting signalman was in no hurry to put his Down distant signal back 'on' (right-hand mounted to improve the sighting around the left-hand curve exiting the tunnel) as No. 333 *Ventnor* trundles south with a mixed bag of rolling stock. Clayton's No. 3 Up advance signal is visible on the left and it looks like some resleepering is taking place along with some rerailing as a number of 30ft lengths sit in the 6ft. Some element of care must have been entertained during inclement weather when descending the steps to the tunnel mouth seen in the background.
Bluebell Railway Museum Archive, M.P. Bennett Collection

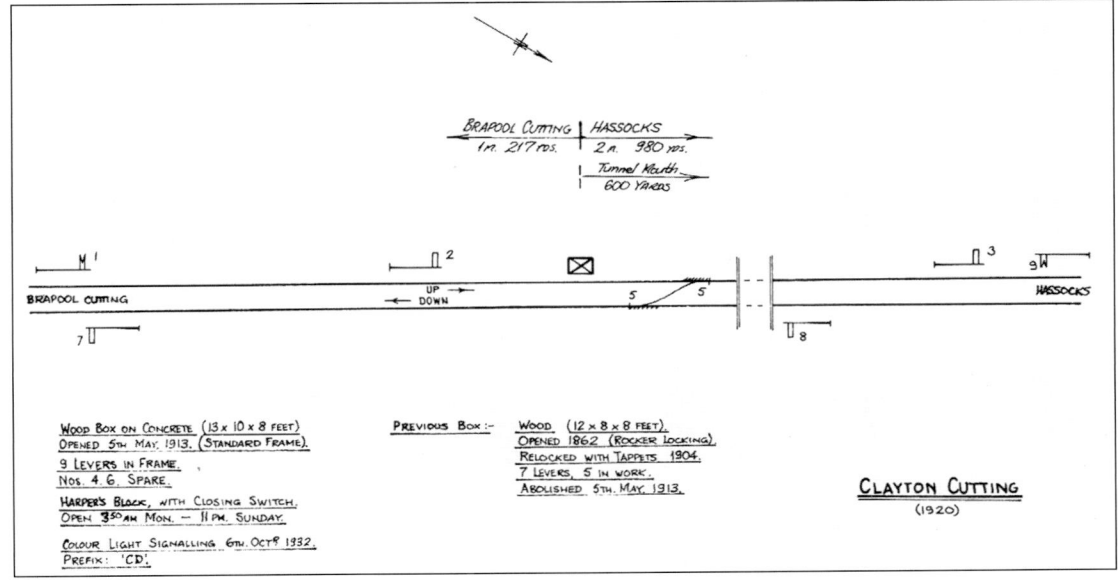

Clayton Cutting signal box layout in 1920.

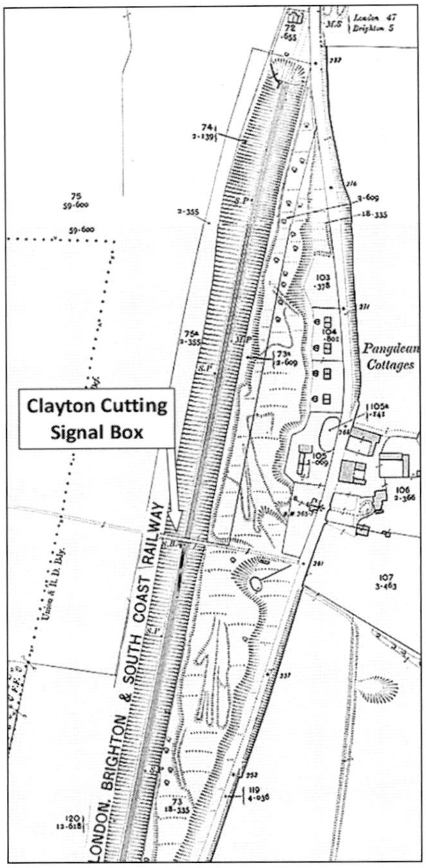

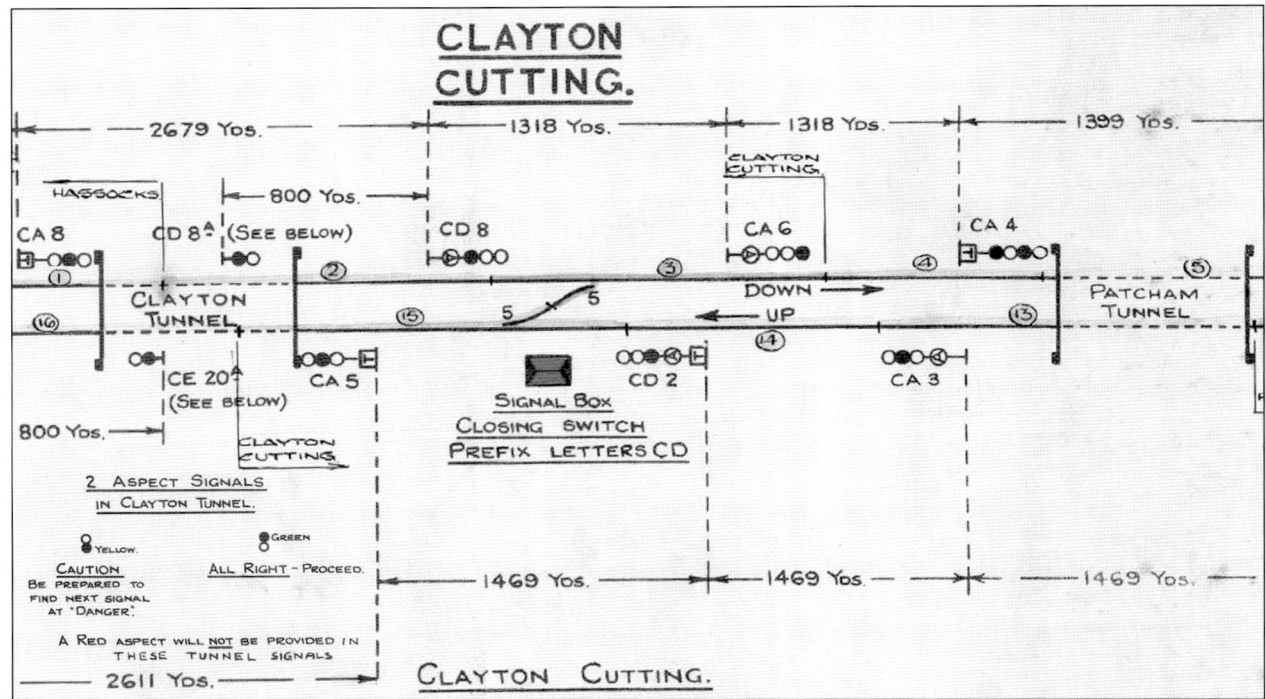

Above Left: Clayton Cutting signal box nestles below the tall, three-arch overbridge from which Maurice Bennett took the photograph seen at the beginning of this chapter. The south end of Clayton Tunnel is visible at the top of this map. *Reproduced by permission of the National Library of Scotland*

The track plan extract for Clayton Cutting with the enviably regular signal spacing on both roads, spoilt only by the proximity of Clayton Tunnel. The explanation for the two-aspect green/yellow repeater signals on each road located within the tunnel itself (this in the days before the most cautionary aspect was placed uppermost) is shown on the diagram. The automatic signals protecting both tunnels were fitted with telephones, as was Clayton's CD2, the rest fitted with 'A' lights. Note also that the track circuit numbering has started again with No. 1 track circuit (Preston Park and Clayton Cutting's first indication) approaching Clayton Tunnel on the Down road.

Facing Page Top Right: Clayton Cutting signal box with the Area Traffic Inspector Ken Roberts, pointing out the problems with chalk falls in this area of the deep cutting. Clayton Cutting signal box opened in 1913 and worked to Brapool Cutting to the south and Hassocks to the north. It survived the resignalling, normally switched out of use, until it closed on 30th November 1972, being demolished the following year. The crossover had been disconnected from the signal box on 9th October 1972 and some of the point stools with their rodding wheels can be seen discarded in the cess. The 'A' end switch (the 'A' point end being the end nearest to the signal box or relay room) is just visible in the bottom left-hand corner of the photograph. Clipped, scotched and padlocked in position, it remained *'available for use in an emergency and/or in connection with Engineering Work'* according to the signalling notice. This too was removed in April 1978. Emergency tools are in the locker at the side and the fire bucket brackets are still in position on the signal box steps (maybe LBSCR embossed?). *Derek Osborne*

Top Right: A young British Rail S&T apprentice does what he is asked by the photographer and points at the diagram, amazingly still the Southern Railway original complete with its 'eyeball' track circuit indications. Containing a 9-lever 'Brighton' frame when opened in 1913, it was replaced by the Westinghouse version seen here (date of installation and type not known) containing the same number of levers and presumably in the same position. No. 1 was the Up line king lever and No. 2 the Up home signal with its indication showing yellow. No. 5 lever, visible in the centre of the frame and correctly painted black, works the trailing crossover, shunt signals never having been provided. No. 8, Down home signal lever is reverse and again out of sight behind our friend, although its indication can just be seen exhibiting another yellow aspect. No. 9 was the Down line king lever. The locking chart hangs below the block shelf at the rear of the frame.
14th December 1971, Derek Osborne

Right: The Clayton Cutting signal box clock was an 8ins dial, weight-driven longcase regulator, supplied by Richard Webster of 74 Cornhill, London. Similar clocks to this were supplied by Webster to the LB&SCR in 1866 so it is almost certain that this was not its original home; it was probably just transferred from the original signal box. Although the dial is original, the 'L.B.&S.C.R.' initials that would have adorned it have disappeared (or been deliberately erased) although its number, 245, can be seen behind the minute hand along with its later SR branding of 245B ('B' for Brighton) below. I wonder if it survived? As not uncommon with signal box clocks of this nature, different generations of signalmen have signed their names on the inside of the door, two of the latter being familiar to the author. The original label is still in position reading *'London, Brighton & South Coast Railway, Instructions for Regulating Clocks. Turn Screw at Bottom of Pendulum Half Round to <u>RIGHT</u> to <u>GAIN</u> 1 minute per day; or Half round to <u>LEFT</u> to <u>LOSE</u> 1 minute per day. BY ORDER'*. A throwback to the original pole route exists with the glass fuses and surge arrestors (which would have protected the block circuits and telegraph/telephones) seen behind the glass frame to the right of the clock. Below is a card listing all the various railway departments' contact details should they be needed. *14th December 1971, Derek Osborne*

LEFT: With the signal box door open, we are looking south towards Preston Park with the row of telephones adorning the wall. The BR dial telephone is on the left with the ubiquitous Pyrene fire extinguisher hanging on the door frame below it. In a continually manned box this would be highly polished but appears to be somewhat neglected here. Immediately above the telephone concentrator is the electrification phone connecting to Three Bridges Electrical Control Room and to its right, the Control phone connecting to Redhill Control. A pair of Omnibus phones are next, the one on the left being direct to Brighton cabin, with the right-hand being on No. 108 circuit. Even at this late date, the interior of the signal box still bore its original SR colours of green and cream. This is a glimpse into a bygone world.
14th December 1971, Derek Osborne

RIGHT: The Omnibus telephone codes for No. 108 Circuit.

BRITISH RAILWAYS (SOUTHERN REGION)
Central Section Telephone Circuit No.108
Between Haywards Heath Box and Preston Park Box.

Telephone at	No. of Rings.
Haywards Heath Box	2 - 1
Signal CH.1/2	3 *
Signal CA.14	1 - 4 *
Signal CA.13	3 - 1 *
Signal CA.12	1 - 5 *
Signal CA.11	5 - 1 *
Signal CG.19	2 *
Signal CA. 9	3 - 2 *
Signal CG.17/18	2 - 5 *
Keymer Crossing Box	1 long (key down)
Signal CG. 8	1 - 2 - 3 *
Signal CF. 3	4 - 1 *
Burgess Hill Box	7
Signal CF.29	1 - 3 - 2 *
Signal CA.10	2 - 3 - 1 *
Signal CA. 7	2 - 1 - 2 *
Signal CE.14	3 - 3 *
Signal CE.19	4 - 2 *
Signal CE.15	1 - 2 - 1 *
Hassocks Box	1 - 3
Signal CE.20	3 - 4 *
Signal CA. 8	4 - 3 *
Signal CA. 5	4 - 4 *
Ganger responsible between 45M. 70chs. to 48M. 10chs.	4 Special
Signal CD. 8	1 - 2 - 2 *
Clayton Cutting Box	5
Signal CD. 2	2 - 2 - 2 *
Signal CA. 6	2 - 2 - 1 *
Signal CA. 4	2 - 3 - 2 *
Signal CA. 3	3 - 2 - 1 *
Signal CA. 2	3 - 1 - 2 *
Signal CA. 1	2 - 4 *
Signal CC3/11	2 - 2 *
Preston Park Box	1 - 2
Ganger responsible between 48M. 10chns. to 49M. 40chs.	6 Special

Note: * Switches to circuit when telephone cupboard door open.
C.2450/79.R2.
To operate from 8.0am Sunday 17th August 1958.
EACH CALL SIGNAL TO BE ACKNOWLEDGED BY BEING REPEATED BEFORE THE CONVERSATION IS COMMENCED.

BELOW: Extract from the Weekly Operating Notice from the last week in November 1972

CLAYTON CUTTING.—The signal box has been abolished. Signals CD2 and CD8 have been converted to automatic signals and renumbered CA163 and CA164 respectively.
(P/EW 49 C.D., 1972)

In complete contrast to the following two photographs, LB&SCR Class 'B4' No. 44 makes a spectacular exit from Clayton Tunnel with an Up passenger train. Directly above the left tower, the first of eleven air shafts that pierce the chalk ridge can be seen. Quoting from Gordon Biddle's *Britain's Historic Railway Buildings*:

Clayton is among those early tunnels that have a plain portal at one end and a highly decorative entrance at the other; in this case in the form of a medieval castle gateway at the north end. In yellow brick with stone dressings, a great pointed two-tier arch rears up from broad splayed buttresses which form the bases of two hexagonal towers, arrow slitted, dentilled, and crenellated; a powerful composition in the best Victorian romantic manner. More arrow-slits adorn the deep parapet, which beyond the towers continues along wide wing walls to terminate in a small square turret at each side. A little brick cottage crouches incongruously behind the parapet.

1 mile 499 yards long and on the ruling gradient of 1:264 rising southwards, the trackbed is 270 feet down at its deepest point. *Bluebell Railway Museum Archive, M.P. Bennett Collection*

It was thirty-six years since the line had been resignalled and electrified, yet this photograph could almost have been taken within a few months of that event. Signal CA8 remains in its original condition with the row of cast iron 'dog kennels' housing the relevant relays for the signal, track circuits and track circuit condensers (to use the term then used for capacitors) seen beyond. The pole route takes its wires up and over the South Downs to rejoin the line on the other side of the tunnel whilst the 17.28 Brighton to London Victoria emerges from the gloom and into the immaculately manicured cutting. The 11th-century parish church of St. John the Baptist, Clayton can be seen at top left.
31st May 1968, John Scrace

The classic façade of the north end of Clayton Tunnel with a semi-fast Brighton to Victoria (via Redhill) train emerging. The early stages of the Brighton line resignalling are obvious, with new concrete cable troughing in the Up cess ready to be laid in. It was a sight to behold when the Clough Smith civil engineering contractors man-handled these great lumps of concrete around, happily putting them (and larger troughs) on their shoulders and crossing multiple lines including 'juice' rails! Access to the track here was through a gate from the main road and across what was effectively the back garden of the cottage above the tunnel mouth, before descending steps to track level just to the right of the train. The owners of the cottage at the time kept an exceedingly aggressive dog whose lead was affixed to a ring attached to a wire rope that paralleled the length of the path (at just a safe enough distance) between the road and the gate leading to the steps. For the duration of that walk therefore, the hound's teeth were altogether a bit too close for comfort. The cutting sides are clearly not quite so well-tended as they were in the previous photographs. *May 1981*

8 – Hassocks

After a magnificent view of the south end of Clayton Tunnel earlier, it is only right that we should see the opposite side and what better than this. An unidentified passenger train approaches Hassocks' No. 21 Up distant signal (still with its Coligny-Welch lamp giving the illuminated chevron shape to the side of the lamp), with the glorious panorama of the South Downs in the background. Above the tunnel mouth with its castellated turrets, the roof of Clayton Tunnel cottage can just be seen over the road bridge in the distance. In the centre of the photograph is what was then the Matsfield Arms Beer House (shown on early maps as BH). Now named the Jack & Jill, the windmills after which it is named are just out of shot to the left of the Hassocks to Pyecombe road, which very obviously bisects the South Downs in a distinctive vee shape. The quarries of Clayton Lime Works can be seen scarring the landscape whilst the telegraph pole route can be seen snaking up the hillside paralleling the road. A short distance away on the approach to the signal, the fog-signalman's hut nestles into the shallow cutting side with the top of the stove chimney just peeping out. What a lonely vigil that must have been in a pea-souper of a fog! The four stay wires attached to the top of the post maintain some structural integrity, with the ladder rising up on the approach side of the signal. *Laurie Marshall Collection*

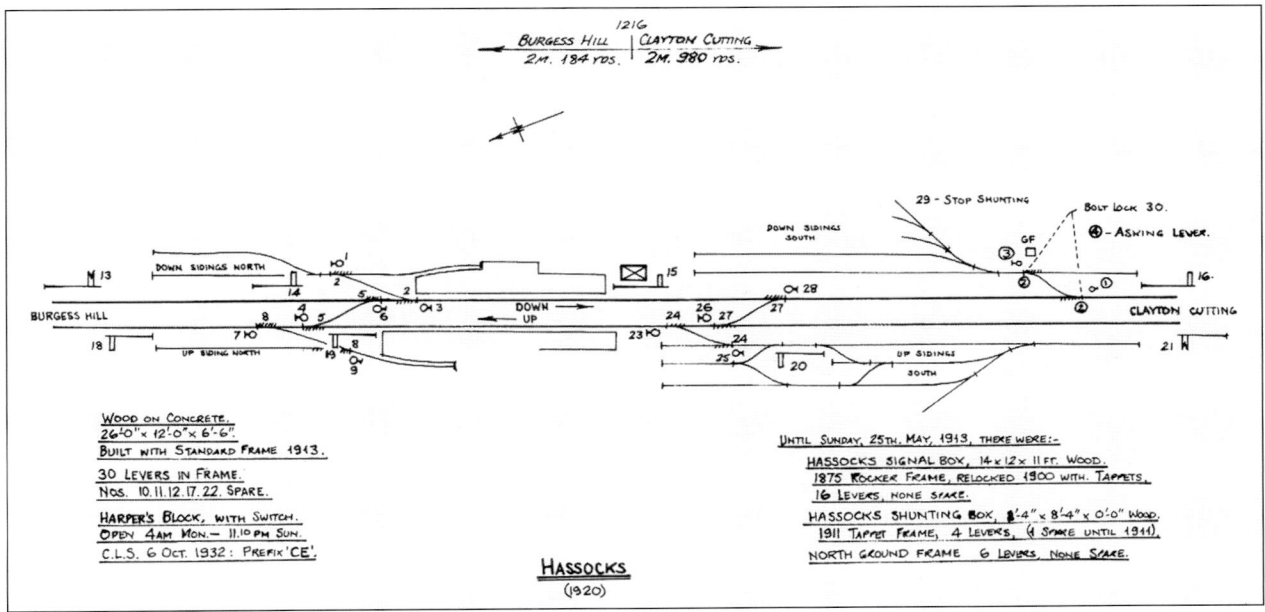

The Hassocks pre-electrification layout, giving some detail to the original signal box which once existed on the Down platform.

Until 25th May 1913, the 16-lever Saxby & Farmer signal box seen in this postcard was situated on the Down platform. The platforms cross the bridge (No. 127) carrying the Stonepound Crossroads to Keymer road below.
*A.H. Homewood,
John Minnis Collection*

Hassocks station photographed from the top of No. 20 Up home signal. The original goods shed seen centre left is the only building that survives today, whilst the roof of its replacement, dating from the rebuilding of the station in 1880-81, is in the foreground. The local gas works, which also provided lighting for the station and signal box, can be seen on the left. *21st June 1930, The Edward Wallis Collection*

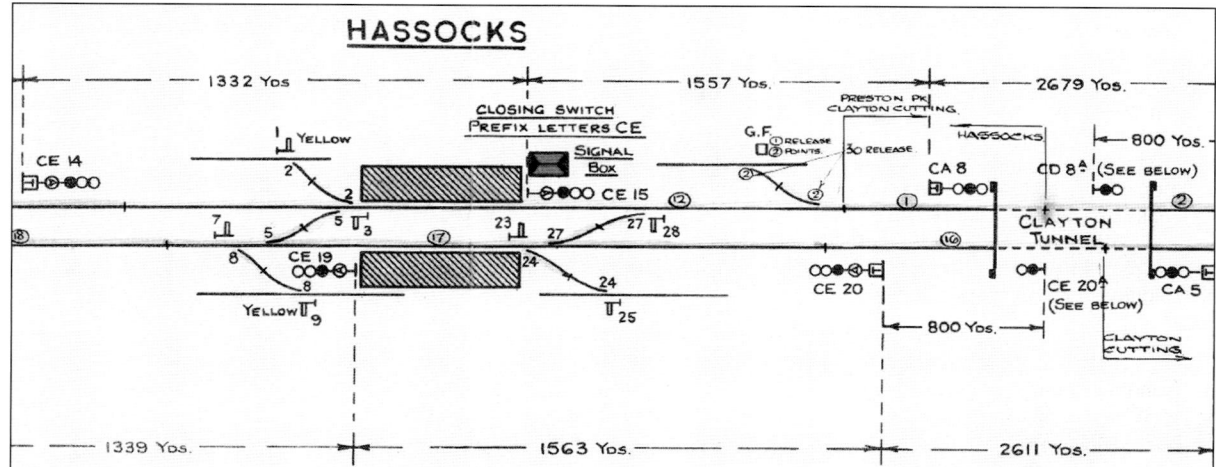

Hassocks signal box was brought into work just twenty days after Clayton Cutting had opened and is seen here on 21st June 1930. Judging by the shadow of the goods shed roof creeping up the front of the structure it must be early evening. The late turn signalman, E. Walton, makes sure he is included in the photograph. *21st June 1930, The Edward Wallis Collection*

Thirty-one years later the signal box is only opened as required and here, with both the box door and window open, it seems to be just such a day. Signal CE15, the word 'Semi' in the lower panel of the prefix plate denoting the fact that the signal works as an automatic whenever the box is switched out, is worked from the same lever as its mechanical predecessor, but since it was commissioned it has gained a telephone and lost its 'A' light. During the Second World War, long hoods were provided over signal aspects to try and prevent them from being seen from the air by enemy aircraft who could use a railway line as a direct guide to its target, and these are still fitted. The points are yet to be converted to motor operation and remain mechanically worked. The Down sidings at Hassocks were used to accommodate condemned stock and these iconic Pullman carriages await that fate – but, diverting us from that depressing aspect of the view, the famous South Downs landmark of the Jack and Jill windmills can be seen above the nearest carriage. In the previous chapter I mused over whether the fire bucket brackets on the signal box steps at Clayton Cutting were LBSCR embossed; the brackets supporting the signal box balcony seen here most definitely were. *7th September 1961, Denis Cullum, Lens of Sutton Collection*

FACING PAGE BOTTOM: The impressive Hassocks layout was not to last. Up Sidings North (via No. 8 points) was the first to go on 19th June 1960, with Down Sidings North (via No. 2 points) following on 29th September 1962. The ground frame south of the station was abolished on Sunday 24th November 1968 and the country-end crossover in August 1975. The signal box was downgraded to a ground frame (released from Keymer Crossing) on 7th August 1982 as part of stage-works in conjunction with the resignalling, working just No. 5 crossover and associated shunt signals. A further stage on 17th March 1985 saw the crossover *'clipped and padlocked pending abolition'* and Hassocks signal box was no more. It was hoped to save the structure but its condition was such that it was demolished. A ground frame was brought into use to control the remaining siding points.

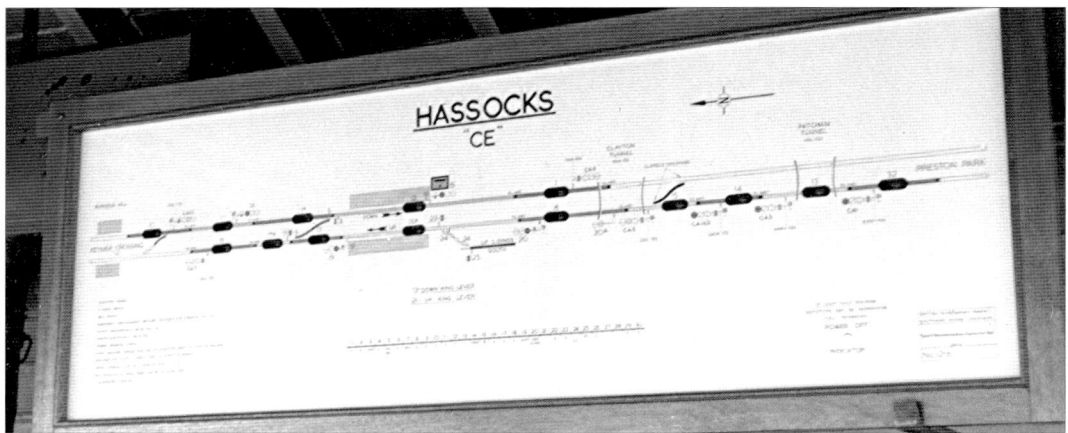

Above: The interior of Hassocks signal box, gas lit to the end. Sadly, by this time the levers out of work exceeded the number of levers in use, but it was always immaculately kept. The locking chart is in the wooden frame to the left and I only wish I had taken more interest in the original clock (seen below the diagram) and the hand-lamp on the shelf at the end – either a 'Brighton' lamp or a common S.R. or B.R. type, probably the latter. The two king levers in the LB&SCR frame can be seen reversed either side of the four running signals with the block bells and plungers to Keymer Crossing and Preston Park visible on the block shelf above. The shunt signals have now been replaced by the 'position light' type and the points motorised, hence the cut-down levers. The closing switch can be seen just to the left of the Preston Park bell plunger whilst the two auto-replacement switches at the end were for returning the protecting signals approaching Patcham Tunnel (CA1) and Clayton Tunnel (CA5) to danger in case of an emergency, these also replicated at Keymer Crossing. The telephone concentrator with its individual rocker switches (press down to ring, up to speak) sits on the metal cabinet on the right. We opened the signal box most months for maintenance purposes such as points testing, with the early or late turn porter/signalman at Hassocks liking nothing more than a telephone call from us requesting his services to escape from his booking office and other platform duties for a while. He would stand on the frame and, with both arms outstretched, give 5-5-5 bells concurrently to both boxes either side to signify the signal box opening. As Hassocks was not equipped with train describers it gave both the Preston Park and Keymer signalmen a little more to do, as descriptions were now sent by block bell, each movement carefully recorded in the train register. When he had finished, 7-5-5 on the bells returned Hassocks signal box to slumber mode.

FACING PAGE TOP: Hassocks signal box diagram on 22nd November 1976. By this time all the sidings other than the Up Siding South had been removed, along with the country end crossover, but the relevant shunt signals remained mechanically worked. This diagram would have been renewed some five years earlier as Clayton Cutting signal box has been abolished but the emergency crossover was still in situ, clipped and padlocked. If a train was approaching CE20 (Hassocks' Up home) signal at red, the driver would encounter consecutive single yellows on the approach. CE20 signal was not visible from within the tunnel, necessitating the repeater (20R) to give the driver advance information as to the state of the road ahead, the same situation occurring on the Down road exiting the tunnel towards Preston Park. The 'Power Off' light in the bottom right-hand corner burns brightly to show the signalman that the indications are working correctly (the lamps behind the indication lozenges being duplicated). As mentioned previously, this was not necessary with the old Southern Railway diagrams where the track circuit indications were shown as normally alight, thus self-proving.
Derek Osborne

RIGHT: Porter Signalman George Tasker (a fine railwayman and true gentleman) communicates with Keymer Crossing via the block bell. Many signalmen would use the palm of their hand to send bell codes, but George was a 'thumb' man.
Derek Osborne

Facing Page Top: On the day that the Soviet Union launched its first woman cosmonaut into space, Class '5' 4-6-0 No. 45253 heads northwards through Hassocks with an excursion train. The fireman leans out to get in the shot and might be mildly relieved that as it is a Sunday, so the filth emitting from his chimney will not be sullying any washing hanging in the gardens behind the coaches in the Down sidings! The green enamel running in board on the Up platform is framed by the goods shed (still extant today), unusually almost at right angles to the track. A row of monuments (early datum plates of tapering concrete blocks dug into the ballast between the sleepers with a metal bar set into the top) can be seen in the 4ft of the Down road. A slot was cut into the top of the metal plate from which measurements would be taken to indicate the correct level or position of the track. Experienced permanent way men made shovelling ballast look as easy as turning soil in the garden; when it came to the turn of us young S&T chaps to excavate a hole to drop in an impedance bond or the like, we would borrow a shovel or fork and the P.Way men would stand back and watch as the tools bounced off the stone, jarring wrists and emitting sparks in the process.
16th June 1963, Edwin Wilmshurst

Facing Page Centre: At the dawn of the 1920s, Class 'B4' No. 48 brings a passenger train into the Down platform. For any unwary passengers who may *'Alight here for Hurstpierpoint College'* though, this would involve a walk of just over two miles. No. 8 starting signal stands proud at the end of the Up platform with Up Siding North just visible beyond. *H. Gordon Tidy, Laurie Marshall Collection*

Facing Page Bottom: A fine overall view of Hassocks goods yard with the goods shed, station and the roof of the signal box seen in the distance. E6059 brings a London Bridge to Brighton van train past the sub-station with the Down siding ground frame visible on the right.
31st June 1968, John Scrace

Above: Its work done, the remains of the 2-lever ground frame are seen here on 23rd November 1976. *Derek Osborne*

Looking south from under the Down platform canopy, a row of 'Suggs' gas lamps can be seen alongside the glorious support columns and decorated spandrels. All this to be swept away in the name of modernity. *21st May 1972, John Scrace*

Two photographs of Hassocks station from very similar positions. It remained gas lit until everything seen here was summarily demolished, even more indefensible being the wanton destruction of the original David Mocatta building (which opened as Hassocks Gate in 1841), seen here on the right in both photographs. In the bottom view, as at Preston Park, the canopy valancing has been cut back to facilitate sighting of the Down starting signal, CE15. Allegedly, the screen seen at the far end of the Up platform was erected after an incident where the driver of an Up service, in the dark, had looked back along his train for his guard's hand signal and, seeing the green aspect of CA8 (Down road automatic) in the distance, mistook this as his permission to start. What the consequences were we will never know but, if this was the case, it was serious enough for action to be taken.
Above: Lens of Sutton Collection. Below: 21st May 1972, John Scrace

Above: Hassocks station Down-side buildings; even the exterior lamps were gas lit. *21st May 1972, John Scrace*

Below: The Up-side buildings at Hassocks were far more grandiose than their Down-side counterparts, even though that side led directly to the town. The Clayton Park Hotel is just visible on the left, with a single car outside; the commuters' cars parked in the foreground would certainly now be considered of the 'Classic' variety. *7th September 1961, Denis Cullum, Lens of Sutton Collection*

'It is a building designed by committee: all they have been able to agree on is that it should be rectangular, have windows, and not fall over.'
(Max Barry, Architect)
He was not talking about Hassocks, but it is an extremely accurate portrayal of the brutalist structures that replaced the impressive J.L. Myres designed buildings that were once Hassocks station. *May 1981*

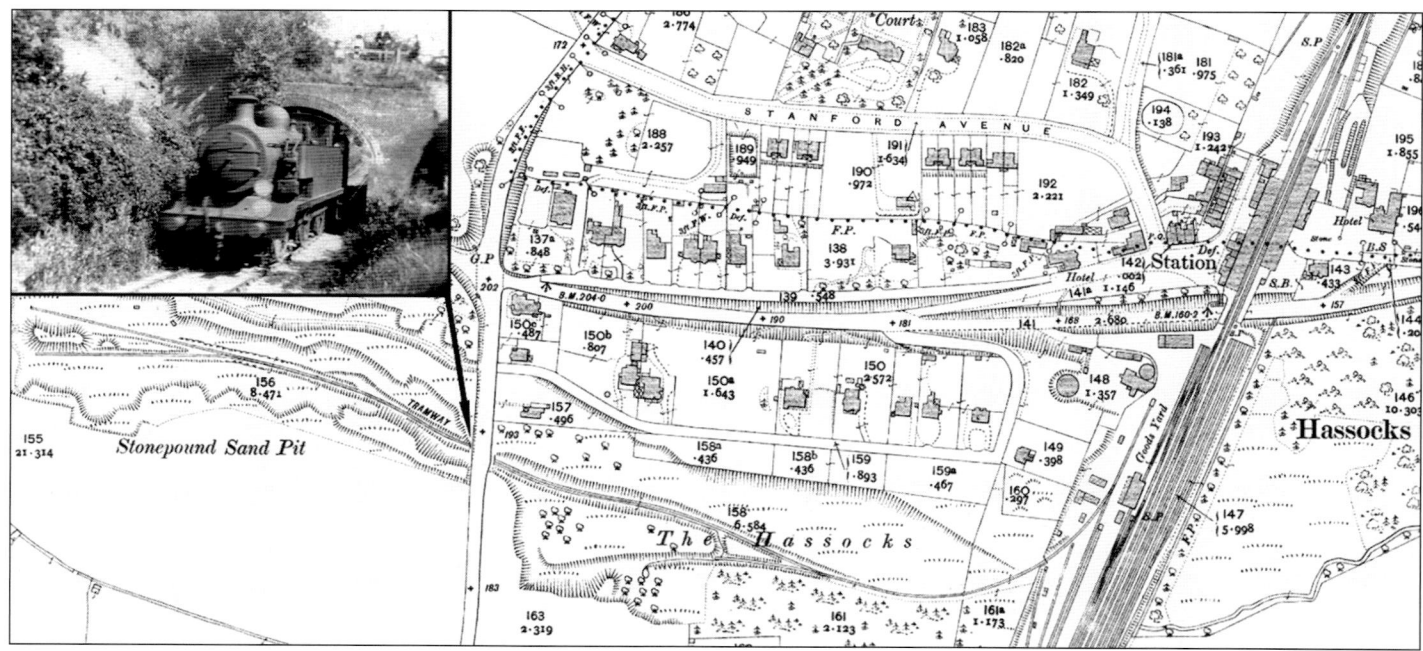

One lesser-known part of Hassocks' railway history is this tramway that ran from the Up sidings to sandpits west of the Brighton road. In existence from the 1870s through to the late 1920s, Hudson's Sand Pits provided high quality red sand for the building trade as this extract from a Sussex Industrial Archaeology Society Newsletter states:

The motive power was supplied by the engine (usually one of the small tank variety) which came up from Brighton to shunt a number of open wagons to the point where the red sand was being excavated, then bring back the full ones that were put there previously. The number varied but was usually six or nine, each wagon carrying a nine-ton load. The bulk of the sand was dug out before 1914, but after that, the remains went to Hampden Park, Eastbourne, which had started to develop, the Hassocks sand being highly thought of by the building trade.

Quite probably the only photograph in existence is reproduced here, showing LB&SCR Class 'E2' locomotive No. 109 passing through the impossibly tight clearances (I wonder how often the local P.Way department carried out gauging checks?) of the bridge just south of Stonepound Crossroads on its way to the pits. I like to think that maybe that is the photographer's family looking on, Gordon interrupting the afternoon stroll on a summer's day in 1921 to nip down and take a quick photograph.
1910 map reproduced by permission of the National Library of Scotland. Inset Gordon Hector, John Minnis Collection

9 – Burgess Hill

London, Brighton & South Coast Railway 'B4' Class 4-4-0 No. 60 *Kimberley* passes Burgess Hill's Saxby & Farmer signal box with an Up passenger train. This signal box, straddling the Up siding, entered service in 1875 and housed a 22-lever frame (extended from its original 17 levers in 1889) working to Hassocks to the south and Keymer Junction, less than three quarters of a mile away, to the north. Interestingly, situated at the end of the dock platform is a supporting post with straining wires anchored across to the operating floor of the building, maybe added at a later date to try to stabilise an ageing structure. The advertising hoardings are just beyond, sadly just unreadable, also the structure gauge supported from the underside of the signal box to ensure that all loads were within the allowed gauge for exiting the Up siding towards the Down road. The hipped roof tapers up to a finial whilst the signal box bell can be seen at the nearest angle, to be rung vigorously to warn the platform staff of an approaching train. The signalman's toilet facilities are positioned within the angle beneath the signal box steps. This box's imperious position came to an end on 7th November 1926 when the new Southern Railway signal box, situated at the country end of the Down platform, was brought into work. *Bluebell Railway Museum Archive, M.P. Bennett Collection*

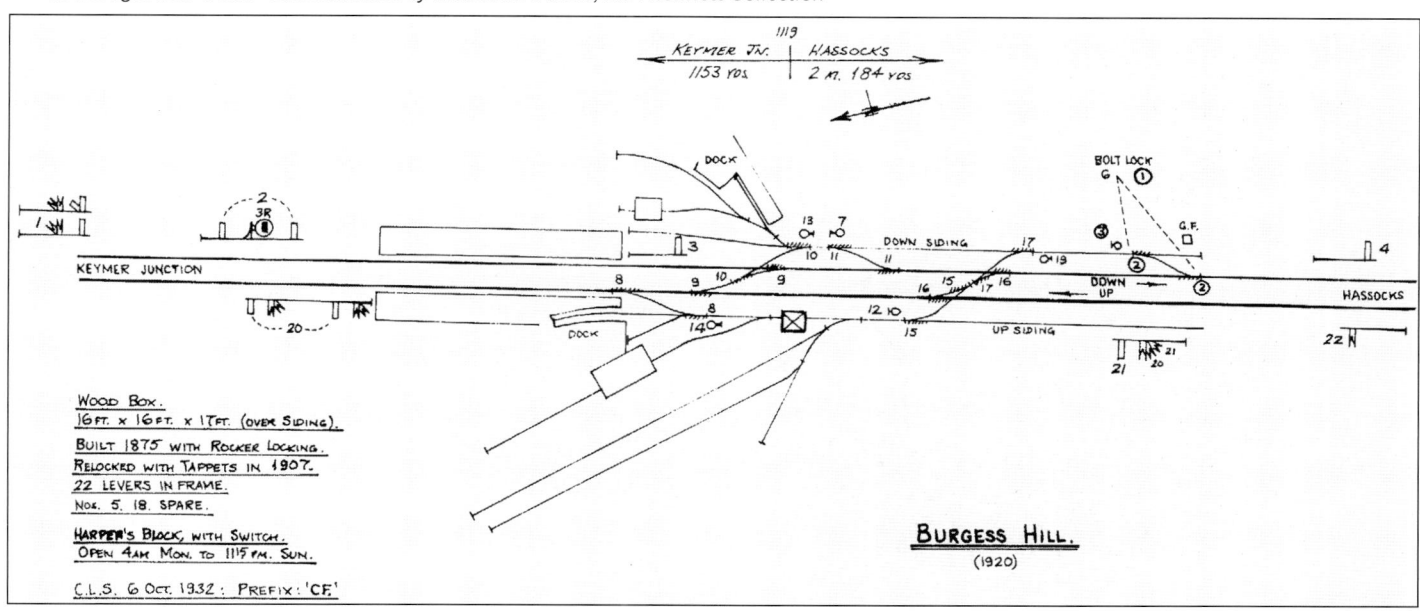

Burgess Hill signal box layout in 1920 when still controlled from the elevated signal box over the Up siding.

It was a brave man who scaled heights such as these while carrying the necessary equipment to carry out maintenance on the signal mechanisms and lamps, a far cry from today's regulations where working on anything over 2.5m demands wearing a harness; even the basic luxury of ladder hoops is absent. The posts were almost certainly imported from abroad and constructed from pitch pine: if that much timber was above ground, how much was below? In the left-hand photograph, facing the camera on the left is Burgess Hill's No. 2 Down home signal, the circular banner repeater repeating No. 3 Down starting signal at the end of the platform. The stop arms on the right are Burgess Hill's No. 20 Up starting signals with Keymer Junction's inner distants below, all with co-acting arms. The Down signal's top arm is 'blind', i.e. was not provided with a spectacle plate nor, therefore, a lamp, whereas all the arms on the Up line signals would have required the regular visit of a lamp man. The right-hand photograph shows the same signals facing London, the extraordinary height of the Up-road signal was for long range sighting over the station buildings. *21st June 1930, The Edward Wallis Collection*

Left: To steady a heavy plate glass camera at heights such as these, the bold photographer must have picked a still day. The smoke-blackened bridge parapets can be seen bracketed out from the bridge to provide a pavement up the hill towards Hoadley's Corner, while two ancient taxis await their next fare. The signal box sits at the far end of the Down platform, showing how relatively short the platforms were; when these were extended the short portions beneath the bridge (just visible in the shadow) were demolished with the necessary lengths added to the country end. Anyone who has printed their own photographs using an enlarger will be well aware of the curse of Newton's rings, and these can be seen in this photograph, emanating from the station chimney like a ghostly fan.
*21st June 1930,
The Edward Wallis Collection*

BURGESS HILL

The station is still proudly gas-lit in this 1950s view looking south from the end of the Up platform. There were no fewer than three platform-to-platform staff foot crossings: the two seen here and one more at the end of the platform ramp behind the photographer. These were once an everyday scene at almost every station in the country, seeing porters, with just a cursory glance up and down the line to make sure it was safe to cross, scuttling back and forth with parcels and correspondence. *Lens of Sutton Collection*

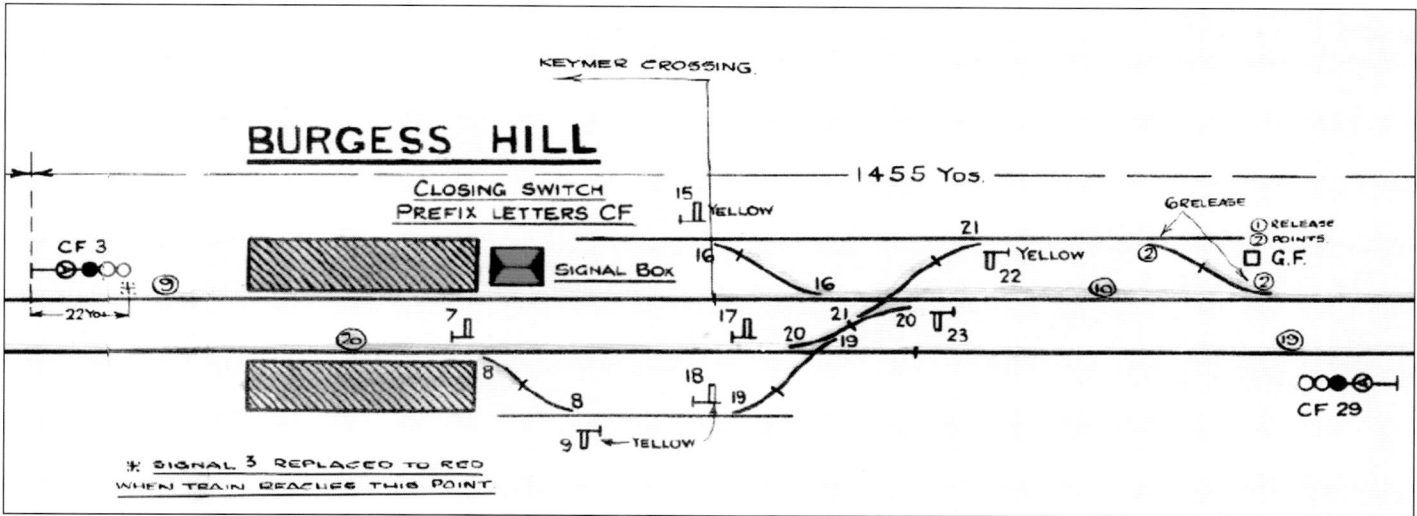

This extract from the 1933 signalling track plan shows the Burgess Hill layout with the signal box barely seven years old – again, as with all the other locations, showing what extensive facilities were retained to accommodate the still substantial freight traffic. What the plan does not show is the 'split' track circuits. Consider No. 9 track circuit through Burgess Hill on the Down road where CF3 signal is replaced to red just 22 yards ahead of the signal. This would have consisted of two separate circuits being a pair of 'double to double' a.c. track circuits labelled to the signal engineer as 9A and 9B, but being only one to the signalman, this particular situation returning CF3 to danger as soon as a train had passed this signal to prevent any possible 'read through' from a train standing in Wivelsfield station. Likewise No's 10 and 20 track circuits would have been split 'single rail' (through the point-work) and 'double rail' (plain section) track circuits. If any of these circuits failed then it would be the S&T's first job to ascertain which portion had failed and then to investigate further. Four 'yellow shunts' control both Up and Down siding exits enabling a train to shunt up and down all day long passing these signals in the 'on' position, and only when they were 'off' were they set towards the main lines. No's 18 and 22 shunt signals were taken out of work in February 1963 when the layout was simplified and a new trailing crossover and slip connection to the Up sidings was installed further to country, this then becoming the ground frame 'D' layout when Burgess Hill box was abolished. The Down Line ground frame at the country end of the station and the Down sidings were finally abolished in June of that year.

This early photograph of Burgess Hill signal box may have been taken around the time of the resignalling, judging by the elevated cable route over the lead-away. Opened in 1926 as a fully functioning signal box, it took over the working of the old box seen earlier and survived the 1932 resignalling, kept like many others to be opened as required. It housed a 30-lever frame but by the time it closed on 31st August 1963 only six were left in work: two protecting signals, two ground frame releases and the inevitable king levers, one for each direction. Two ground frames took over what remained of the layout when the box closed.
Author's Collection

LEFT: Burgess Hill signal box was built to an attractive design (designated as Southern Railway 'Type 11B', as was Haywards Heath) and is seen here at a later date. The 41½ mile post is just to the left in the top picture whereas in this photograph it has been moved to the right, maybe because some remeasuring took place. As I was always told, mileposts were only as good as the person who put them there in the first place. I wonder if the original LB&SCR signal box nameplate survived, notorious by its absence in the lower photograph. Sacks of coal in Corrall's yard are piled up on the right of the cabin.
Lens of Sutton Collection

RIGHT: This closure notice spelt the end of Burgess Hill signal box after a relatively short life in permanent use (from 7th November 1926 to 8th October 1932), but remaining opened as required until 31st August 1963.

BURGESS HILL AND KEYMER CROSSING

To be carried out on Saturday 31st August, commencing at 10.0 pm until completed on Sunday 1st September.

Burgess Hill signal box will be abolished and all signals at present operated therefrom will in future be controlled by Keymer Crossing signal box, together with the electrical control of the existing ground frames 'C' and 'D'. The telephones provided at ground frames 'C' and 'D' will be connected to and provide direct communication with Keymer Crossing signal box.

Keymer Crossing signal box will in future be in electrical communication with Hassocks signal box.

The following signals will be pre-fixed as under:—

Old Prefix (Burgess Hill)	New Prefix (Keymer Crossing)	Description
CF.3	CG.20	Down Main Starting
CF.29	CG.23	Up Main Outer Home
CA.7 Automatic (Situated 1339 yards the approach side of CF.29 signal).	CG.24	Up Main 2nd Outer Home.

(P/EW 32, C.D. 1963)

FACING PAGE BOTTOM: The original Keymer Crossing ground frame 'D' diagram was positioned over the frame with the indications (all two of them) activated by a switch at the front. We would open this from time to time (especially if permanent way works were imminent or single line working was due to be implemented) to check all was well. Ground Frame 'C' (abolished on 17th January 1975) was far less interesting as it simply comprised a release lever and one set of points. The diagram is dated 27th August 1963, three days before Burgess Hill signal box closed, and the two protecting signals are now plated as Keymer Crossing (CG) signals. Ground Frame 'D' survived its near neighbour by less than a month as it went the same way on 10th February. This, however, was not the end of the story as a new ground frame was provided (this time somewhat luxuriously housed within a prefabricated concrete hut), operating the crossover and associated shunt signals only. The 'roof' outlines over the two shunt signals No's 4 and 5 in the diagram depict that they electrically illuminated.

Above: A superb overall view looking south from a window of the covered footbridge that led from the ticket office at road level to the steps down to the platforms.
17th September 1961, Ian D. Nolan

Center Left: Rod Laver was the current Wimbledon tennis champion as 'Battle of Britain' Class No. 34083 *605 Squadron* hauls a mixed rake of seemingly ancient rolling stock past the dormant Burgess Hill signal box with an inter-regional special. The trailing connection into the goods yard is shown to good effect with the rear of No. 9 yellow shunt, for moves on to the Up Main line, visible to the right. More of the sidings are shown here than were shown on the signalling plan, as that only depicted 'signalled lines' rather than the intricacies of the yard itself. The structure gauge seen suspended from the foreshown 'signal box on stilts' has now been relocated over the Down sidings to cater for wagon loads exiting in either direction.
*29th July 1961,
Bluebell Railway Museum
Archive, Joe Kent Collection*

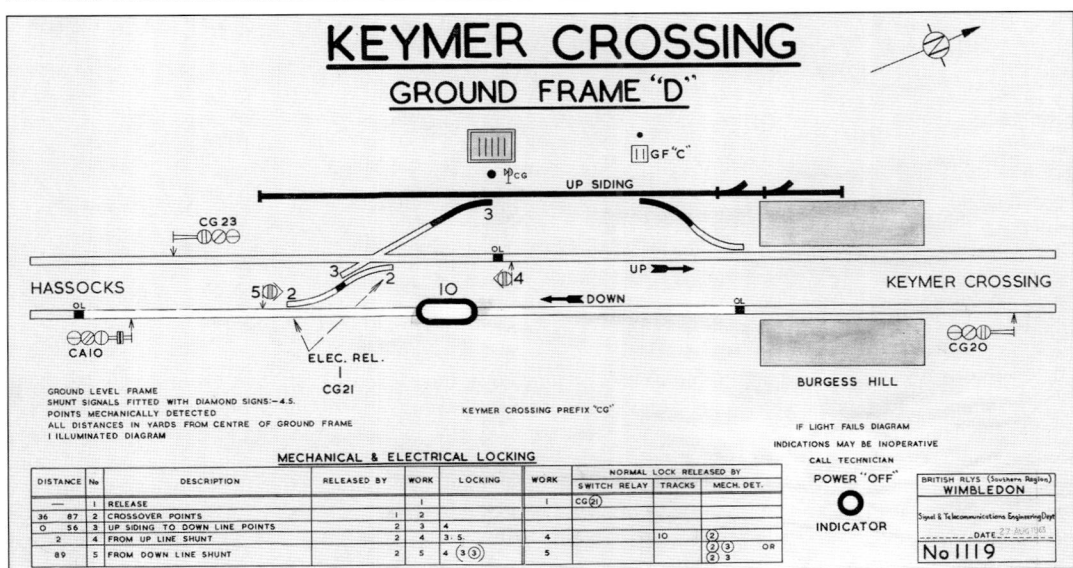

Burgess Hill station in March 1978 showing the four different Up-side platform heights in the distance. The station lighting is still of the Southern Railway concrete 'Exmouth Junction' type whilst the 41½ milepost (seen in the shadow on the right) has been raised to platform level, giving an indication of where the signal box once stood.

Left: The original 1840s station building (now serving as a Corrall's coal office) was rendered redundant when the new 1877 station straddling the railway at street level was built. It was demolished during the mid-1980s. *March 1978*

Right: Moving away from signalling for a moment, this was the magnificent Burgess Hill station clock situated on the Up-side platform. Clocks like this were provided countrywide due to Board of Trade requirements that drivers must be able to note the time when passing certain stations. The number is 209B, the 'B' denoting an ex-LB&SCR timepiece. It was supplied by Webster of Cornhill in December 1861 for £18 (which must have been a small fortune then; in real terms, in 2020 this would have been £2,191) and remained in the same place for all of its working life. For the benefit of any horologists reading, it boasted a 30ins dial and had a weight-driven part regulator movement, so was of excellent quality. Worthy of note is that the SR clock registers show that the Southern Region of British Railways eventually owned some 6,500 clocks (Lyman, 2004). One of the Burgess Hill porters had told me that its days were numbered, so I took the photograph to record it for posterity; where it went from there I know not, presumably Collectors' Corner in Euston. It came up in a specialist antique auction house sale in July 2003 where the hammer price was £4,200, with buyers' premium and VAT increasing this to £4,940: an impressive percentage over the years. As Ian Lyman commented, the lucky bidder must have had help moving it and an understanding family! *(Clock details courtesy of the late Ian P. Lyman), 21st May 1980*

10 – Keymer Junction

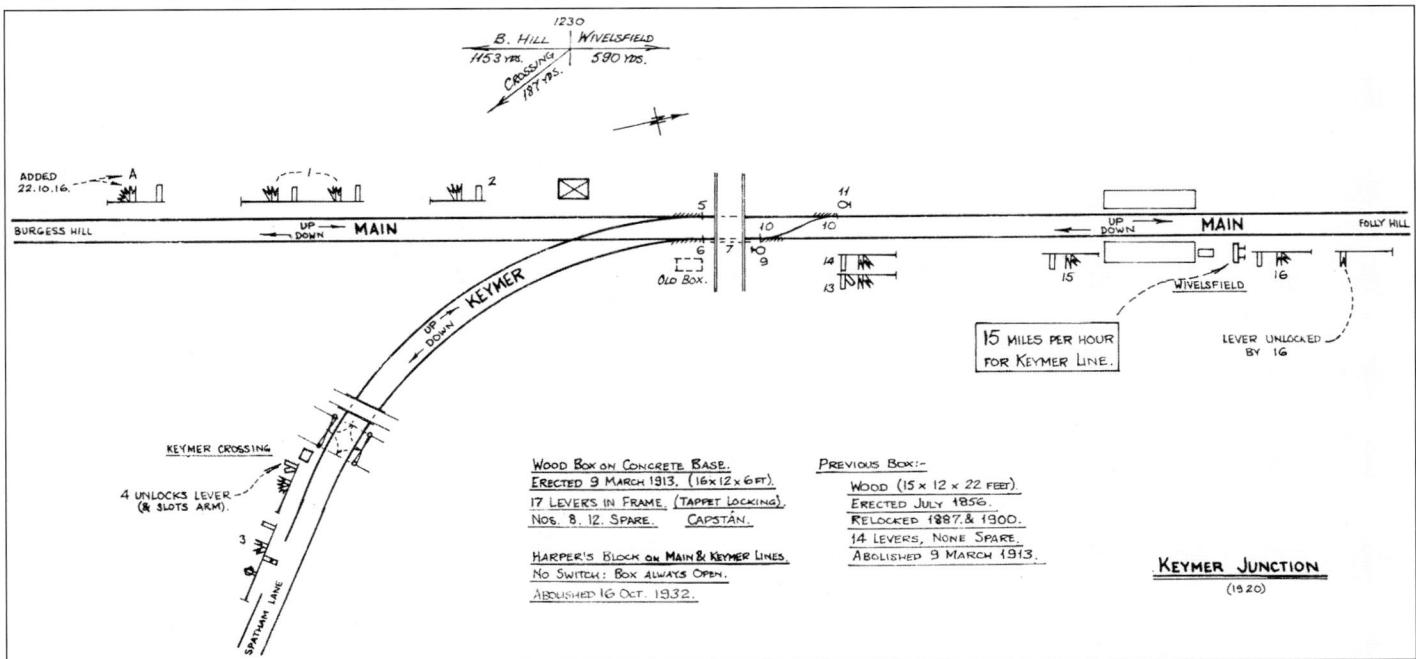

Giving the signalman a commanding view of the area under his control, from the operating floor 22ft (6.7m) above rail level, this signal box of a design so beloved of the LB&SCR housed a 14-lever frame. The photograph was almost certainly taken in early 1913, right at the end of its life, as the point rodding leading to the new replacement box just to the left of the photographer can be seen running along the Up cess ready for the changeover. On what must have been a beautiful sunny day we again have the delightful chequered effect on the vertical timbers as the signalman keeps an eye on proceedings from his lofty perch. *John Minnis Collection*

Keymer Junction's area of control in 1920 shows the extra lever 'A' added as an outer distant signal south of Burgess Hill. With four consecutive distant signals on the Down road and three on the Up, drivers could not have been better informed as to the state of the road ahead. The Down facing (No. 6) points' normal lie is purposefully directed to the branch, so as to divert any train that passed the Down home signals at danger away from a collision course with a train travelling on the Up Branch, a standard practice that still exists today.

Delving back in time, Keymer Junction is captured in this beautifully posed photograph taken in 1886. Keymer Junction station was originally situated on the Lewes Branch between the junction and the level crossing but was repositioned on its present site on 1st August of that year. It was renamed Wivelsfield in 1896. As part of the works a new station signal box was built at the south end of the Down platform which, it was hoped, would also control the junction and allow for the demolition of the box seen here, ironically only opened some three or four years previously. The 'junction' was to be relocated in the vicinity of the new signal box with interlaced track from there to the point of divergence just south of the overbridge. However, the Board of Trade had different ideas. It considered that visibility of signals and trains from the new station cabin (346 yards from the junction) would be severely diminished and therefore would not sanction its opening as a replacement. In concequence, the LB&SCR agreed to work the new cabin as a *station* signal box, thus granting the original junction box a further lease of life. In a selective enlargement of the photograph *(left)* the new station signal box can be seen clearly, along with the interlaced track being laid in, which was never to see a train.
Laurie Marshall Collection

Looking north from the overbridge that spans the main line at this point, a Down train approaches the junction having been signalled for the branch, the driver no doubt heeding the speed restriction sign situated at the north end of the station and bringing his train down to the requisite 15mph for the turnout towards Lewes. The splendid junction signals are prominent at the top of the bank and the signal wires are seen snaking their way up the cutting side. Not for the faint hearted, the signal ladder goes up the centre of the structure to the somewhat flimsy looking platform with two separate access ladders angling up from there. To the left of the locomotive there seems to be a problem with the Up road going out of alignment as two baulks of timber are wedged between cast concrete blocks set into the bank and a pair of the Up Main sleepers, obviously to keep things in true. Very sensibly, the LB&SCR seemed to like their shunt signals positioned in the cess providing a safe place for maintenance. Their SR mechanical replacements and the later solenoid shunt signals that were installed when the Keymer panel took control were placed in the 6ft, thus prey to dirt and general filth, especially when the de-icer trains were running.
Bluebell Railway Museum Archive, M.P. Bennett Collection

Two very similar views taken from the bridge spanning the junction. In the above photograph we have an excellent southwards panorama showing the 1862 signal box along with Keymer Junction's Up home and Wivelsfield's Up distant signals, the very ones the driver missed that led to the Wivelsfield station accident that occurred in 1899. As shown previously, baulks of timber are counteracting the sideways thrust caused by trains coming off the branch. The signalmen would have taken their well-worn path on a daily basis leading from the vee of the junction to their railway-owned cottages. In the later photograph a short passenger train is caught passing the 1913 signal box which seems to have obliterated the very neat allotment seen in the Up cess in the above picture. If that had been maintained by the previous signalman, he would have been a fit chap in tending to this between trains! *Above: Laurie Marshall Collection. Below: Lens of Sutton Collection*

Above: A wisp of steam visible in the distance heralds the approach of an Up train just leaving Burgess Hill station but Edward had plenty of time to take this fine photograph of Keymer Junction before moving his camera and tripod to a place of safety. The pole seen at this end of the signal box acts as a spur off the main pole route, connecting the signal box's functions to the main route running adjacent to the Down Road. I can safely say that I never had the dubious pleasure of ascending one: when I first started on the railway in 1972, Brighton still had a pole gang but it was not too long before it was abolished. *21st June 1930, The Edward Wallis Collection*

Below: Turning his camera round, Edward captures this nicely framed photograph looking north towards Wivelsfield station. A Permanent Way hut can be seen just the other side of the bridge; it was taken for granted for men to use basic messing facilities such as this, where they would gather themselves for a day's work on their 'length', eat their lunch and have their tea breaks. *The Edward Wallis Collection*

Above: The John Saxby manufactured 16-lever Keymer Junction signal box was increased to 17 levers on 22nd October 1916, when an 'A' lever was added. It was brought into work on 9th March 1913 upon the closure of the iconic 'box on stilts' shown earlier, itself closing on 6th October 1932 when its functions were transferred to Keymer Crossing signal box. *The Edward Wallis Collection*

Below: Climbing to the top of the Down home signals, Edward pointed his camera south to produce this wonderfully atmospheric photograph encompassing Keymer Crossing to the left with the junction in the foreground. It might be expected that, by now, urban growth would have encroached up to the western boundary of the railway line, but even today it remains as open space. *The Edward Wallis Collection*

Photographer Edward Wallis was himself a signal engineer and was involved with the 1932 resignalling, perhaps supervising this smart team of installers. It must be remembered that, except from Brighton signal box, which was a purely Westinghouse installation, all of the signalling equipment for the scheme was provided by the Westinghouse company but installed by the Southern Railway's own staff. Gangs must have been brought in from all over the system, with various depots set up at key locations to store the equipment which, for the larger items anyhow, would have been trolleyed out at night. All of the staff travelled everywhere by train and messing facilities (and basic hygiene) must have been minimal to say the least. This fine group of men are wiring up this suite of locations at Keymer Junction with a number of the relays visible, although there do not appear to be any wiring diagrams on show. The end case on the left houses the 440/110V 1KVA transformer taking the 440V supply from the sub-station and transforming it down to the signalling supply. The gentleman kneeling appears to be making off the power cable to feed the transformer (stripping it back to the cable cores); the third rail very obviously not live at this point! The workers' coats and caps are lined up on the other side of the bridge where the P. Way hut (seen in the earlier photograph) once stood. *The Edward Wallis Collection*

ABOVE: 'H2' Class No. 32424 *Beachy Head* brings the 10.20am Hastings to Sheffield Victoria train through Keymer Junction on 4th August 1956, the ghost of the old junction signal box existing merely as an indentation in the shallow cutting side to the right of the train. Burgess Hill station can just be seen in the distance whilst Keymer Junction sub-station, built for the 1932 electrification, is just beyond the railway cottages: how different this view would have been had the much anticipated flyover been built. Four rows of round point rodding can clearly be seen working the two sets of junction points (plus the facing point lock for No. 6 points) and the crossover situated between the bridge where the photographer is standing and Wivelsfield station. On 19th June 1960 a staff warning light was provided in the 'vee' of the junction (approximately behind the coupling of the first and second coaches) to give notice to staff working on the junction of an approaching branch line train. It was installed as normally 'out' (i.e. lit for an approaching train) but was altered to fail-safe mode (normally alight) under the 1983 resignalling. *K.R.M*

Land West of the Railway

Network Rail (NR) is in the final stages of the purchasing the land to the west of the railway from British Rail Body (Residual) (BRBR).

NR is planning to introduce an extra line of railway track in the vicinity of the Keymer Junction Bridge. This new section of track would begin to the South of the Keymer Junction passing under the bridge. The line would include a new set of points back onto the mainline just north of the bridge and a passing loop that would run behind Wivelsfield Station.

LEFT: This planning proposal was submitted by Network Rail in early 2013 to increase capacity at the junction, although whether this will come to fruition is, at the time of writing, still open to question.

11 – Keymer Crossing

The interior of Keymer Crossing signal box with its area of control, after the abolition of the junction signal box, now extended. The Saxby & Farmer lever frame, dating from the opening of the signal box in 1884, was accordingly increased from 17 to 22 levers to cope with the extra workload. The magnificent Southern Railway 'bullseye' diagram dominates the photograph and shows the limits of its working to good effect. *1932, K.R.M*

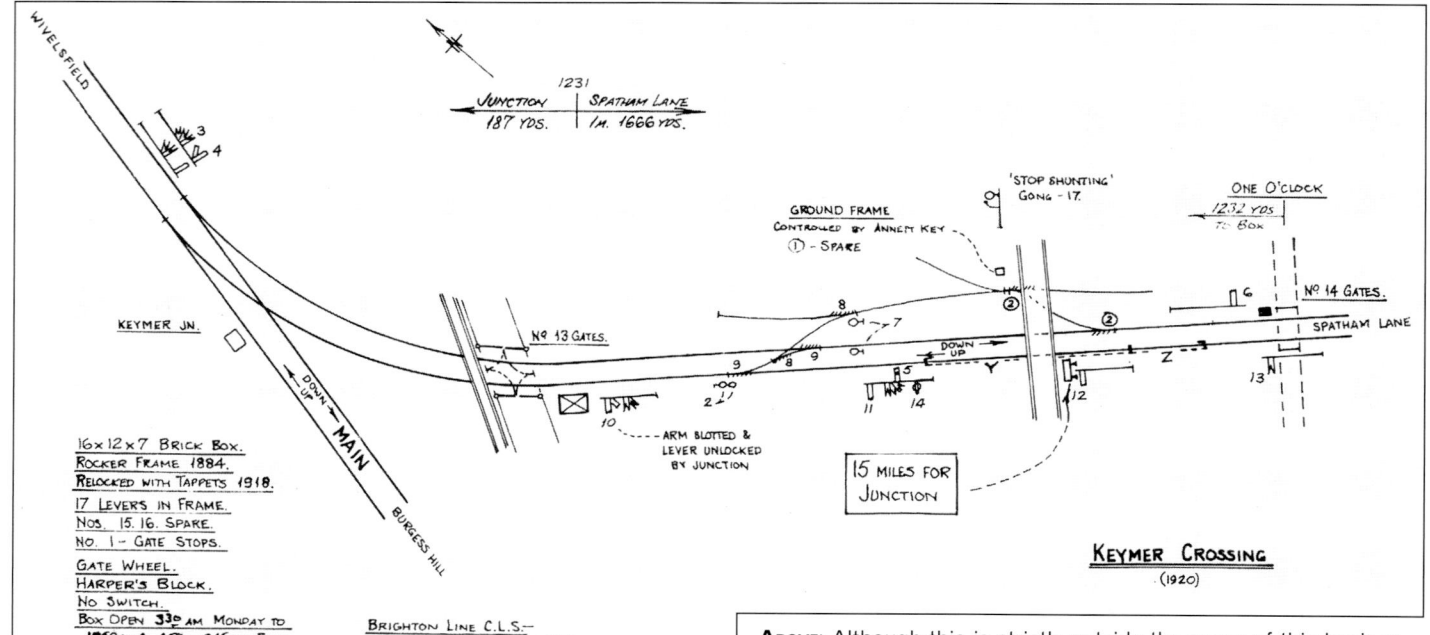

ABOVE: Although this is strictly outside the scope of this book as Keymer Crossing, apart from No's 3 and 4 signals, had no bearing on the main line until after the 1932 resignalling, this diagram is included for completeness.

LEFT: A view dating from the early 1950s with the SR diagram still in use; the LB&SCR booking desk and stool stand by the window. The same items of furniture were retained at Haywards Heath signal box until its closure in 1983, the pull handle on the drawer proudly proclaiming the company initials to the end. *Author's Collection*

BELOW: The extract from the November 1933 track plan shows that with the crossing signal box now boasting a 22-lever frame, only two levers, 9 and 11, were spare, No. 1 lever being the gate stops and not shown. Everything apart from the four new colour light signals on the main line remained mechanically worked, including the junction points which must have needed some pulling around the sharp curve, the diagram not showing anything close to the actual tight radius.

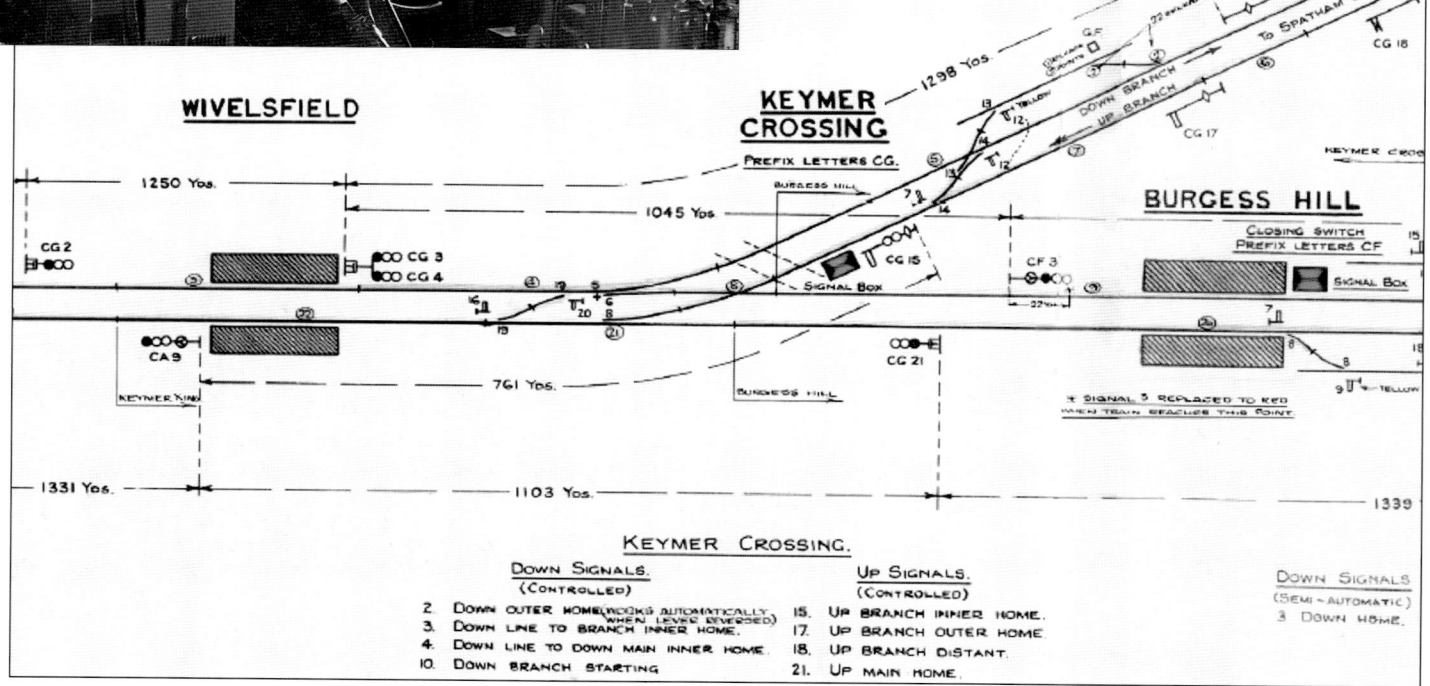

The beautifully clean lines of the Westinghouse-built Keymer Crossing OCS (one control switch) panel in a photograph taken just twenty days before being brought into work. Installed at the back of the signal box opposite the frame, this controlled the same area as the lever frame had, from north of Clayton Tunnel on the Up line to south of Haywards Heath Tunnel on the Down line. The next signal box around the branch towards Lewes was Spatham Lane Crossing, with the three-position block instrument working to there cleverly incorporated into the panel and seen above the block-bell plungers for Burgess Hill, Haywards Heath, Spatham Lane and the Wivelsfield platform bell. The carpenters were obviously still at work as the old signal box door is still in position in the far back corner behind the Haywards Heath train describer transmitter. Just to the left of the panel can be seen the block emergency release mechanism provided to restore the branch block instrument to normal in the event of a 'line clear' having been given where, for whatever reason, the train did not run. Akin to using a desk mounted pencil sharpener, the signalman would stand there winding interminably until the 'N' in the viewing glass reappeared to reset everything to normal, the whole exercise providing valuable thinking time. The reason for the Burgess Hill ground frames becoming 'C' and 'D' now becomes apparent as the 'A' and 'B' ground frames were installed first for the Keymer Brick & Tile Works sidings and can be seen, with their releases, adjacent to the Down Branch. Unusually, the facing points at the junction were given the nomenclature of 'M' and 'B' (Main and Branch instead of the usual 'Normal' and 'Reverse') whilst the crossover points followed suit with 'M' and 'C' (Main and Crossover). The junction trailing points were altered to spring operated working on 25th August 1957 (preparatory works for the introduction of the panel), with the normal lie being for the main line, the wheels of trains off the branch thereby forcing the switches over. In latter days, however, the tips had more of a habit of remaining somewhere in the middle! Maintenance of this entirely unsatisfactory affair lay (thankfully) solely with the local Permanent Way Department and the points remained that way until they were converted to motor operation on 31st January 1982 as part of the resignalling. The junction signals at the country end of Wivelsfield station are shown as two separate signals, which they were at this juncture. The signal aspects were ingeniously repeated on the panel by a very early type of fibre optic, namely a length of square profile perspex (covered in a muslin type material) running from the relevant indication lamps behind their green/yellow/red diffusers, the three 'tubes' then joining as one at the panel face behind the indication aperture. This was early days for route setting panels and was too much for some signalmen who had spent their whole railway lives 'setting the road' via the relevant point levers and bolting them where required with facing point locks before pulling off the necessary signals, watching the passage of every train and not giving 'out of section' until the tail lamp had been correctly observed. With the onset of signalling panels, where you could signal trains you could not see, and where the actuation of one switch (or the pressing of an entrance button followed by an exit) could do the same work, it is not surprising that some may have found it difficult to adjust to the new mind-set.
3rd March 1958, British Rail

RIGHT: Keymer Crossing signal box, still carrying its original LB&SCR nameboard, showing where the entrance door was situated before the 1958 alterations.
Author's Collection

RIGHT CENTRE AND BOTTOM: A number of changes had taken place by June 1978: signal replacement switches were provided for Wivelsfield's Up starting signal plus two to protect both Patcham and Clayton tunnels. The red 'switch actuated' lamp shone through the tops of the switches themselves when turned. Spatham Lane signal box was abolished on Wednesday 5th May 1965 and was replaced by automatic half barriers, the absolute block section then being extended to Plumpton. With Burgess Hill signal box long gone, the signals either side of the station have been added to Keymer Crossing's care whilst the sole remaining ground frame, 'D', remains to work a crossover only. Care and attention to panel face alterations are more than evident; the removal of the Keymer Brick & Tile point-work and associated ground frame equipment is invisibly erased in distinct contrast to the ugly patches that cover later alterations to other parts of the facia. In the bottom left-hand corner, under the bell plungers (altered to accommodate the abolition of both Spatham Lane and Burgess Hill boxes), has been added a brass slider to act as a reminder to the signalman as to the state of the one remaining intermediate signal box, Hassocks. A slider labelled 'Inter Box' reads 'Closed' to the left and, when slid across, 'Open' to the right, the latter being a nudge to the signalman that he is now (whilst still describing to Preston Park) sending and receiving train descriptions to Hassocks using block-bells. Another alteration of note is the Down junction signal at the end of Wivelsfield station, which has been altered to a single signal head with a Position 1 junction route indicator as opposed to the two separate heads from the earlier photograph, the panel face being altered accordingly. The signal box retained its manual crossing gates during these alterations (a challenge to wind, with a mere 5 to 6 turns to open and close them). A new knee frame was also installed containing the gate stops, gate locks and a detonator placer for each of the Up and Down branches, the gate wheel being moved to the opposite corner. Lifting barriers were finally installed, much to the relief of the signalmen, on 18th March 1979.

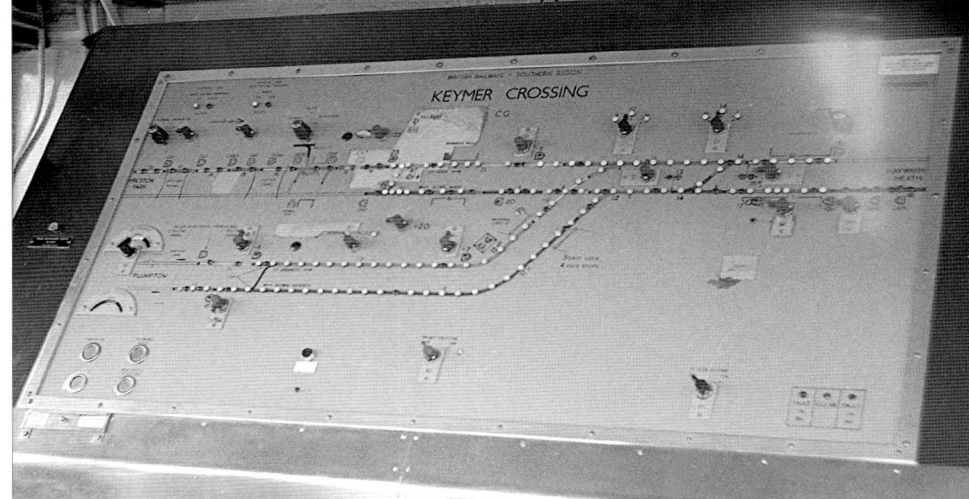

ABOVE: This later photograph reveals a mini kitchen area incorporated where the old door used to be, although the signalman still had to brave the elements to reach it. By 1978 the whole landing had been covered in but the use of the very basic privy (just out of shot to the left) still entailed a trip into the open. The ground floor windows have been bricked up, the railway cottage demolished, the crossing gates renewed and, with electric heaters now installed, a chimney is no longer required. The large wooden box under the balcony contains the Minerva fire detection equipment, installed when the 1958 panel was introduced and the ground floor adapted to house the relay room. Smoke detectors were installed and to prevent the system from being activated when venturing underneath, the correct procedure was to remove the front panel (seen wedged shut in the photograph) and insert a large 'key' (or metal flag) into an aperture that prevented massive weights dropping, thereby preventing the system being set off and engulfing the whole area in carbon dioxide.   *28th April 1971, John Scrace*

```
               BRITISH RAILWAYS (SOUTHERN REGION)
               Central Section Circuit No.92.
                     Directory Prefix 'J'
            Between Keymer Crossing Box and Brighton
                          Switchboard.
     ─────────────────────────────────────────────────
      Telephone at                        Code Ring
     ─────────────────────────────────────────────────
      Keymer Crossing Box                   2 - 3
      Burgess Hill Station Master         2 - 1 - 2
    **Burgess Hill Booking Office             4
     †Burgess Hill Box                        7
      Hassocks Station Master             1 - 3 - 1
      Hassocks Down Booking Office            3
     †Hassocks Box                          1 - 3
     †Clayton Cutting Box                     5
      Preston Park Box                      1 - 2
     +Signal CC.43/63                      3 - 1
     +Signal CC.70                            2
      Brighton Upper Goods
          Weybridge Inspector               1 - 4
      Brighton Upper Goods Box            1 - 2 - 1
      Brighton Box                       1 long (3 Secs)
      Brighton Inspector's Office
          (West Side)                       6 - 1
      Brighton Platform
          Nos.4 & 5 (South End)             4 - 1
      Brighton Switchboard                1 (Spl.Key).

     † Switch to Electrification Circuit No.21.
     * By switch
     + Switch to Circuit when telephone cupboard
       door opened.

     The Telephone outside Preston Park Substation
     can switch on to this circuit when required.
     C.2450/79.R2.
           To operate from 8.0am on Sunday 17th
                        August, 1958.
     EACH CALL SIGNAL TO BE ACKNOWLEDGED BY BEING
     REPEATED BEFORE THE CONVERSATION IS COMMENCED.
```

ABOVE: The Keymer Crossing to Brighton telephone circuit notice, dating nearly five months after the opening of the new panel.
BELOW LEFT: The Keymer Crossing to Three Bridges telephone circuit notice.
BELOW RIGHT: The instructions on how to deal with signal post telephones where a signal box within your area of control (that would normally be closed out) could be open.

```
              BRITISH RAILWAYS (SOUTHERN REGION)
              Central Section Telephone Circuit No.90.
              Between Three Bridges Station Inspector's
                   Office and Keymer Crossing Box.
    ─────────────────────────────────────────────────────────
    Telephone At.                          No.of Rings.
    ─────────────────────────────────────────────────────────
    Three Bridges Station Inspector
       (Middle Platform)                       1 - 4
    Three Bridges Up Local Platform            1 - 3
    Three Bridges Down Through platform        3 - 3
    Three Bridges Box                            4
    Signal C.L.67                 *            5 - 1
    Signal C.L.86                 *            1 - 5
    Signal C.A.22                 *            3 - 1
    Signal C.A.24                 *          1 - 2 - 2
    Signal C.A.21                 *            3 - 4
    Signal C.A.23                 *            4 - 3
    Signal C.K.18                 *            5 - 2
    Signal C.K.20                 *            2 - 5
    Balcombe Tunnel Junction Box  †              2
    Signal C.I.16                 *              5
    Signal C.J.15                 *              3
    Balcombe Station Box          †            1 - 2
    Signal C.J. 7                            1 - 2 - 1
    Signal C.A.18                 *          2 - 1 - 2
    Signal C.A.17                 *          1 - 3 - 2
    Signal C.A.16                 *          2 - 3 - 1
    Signal C.A.15                 *          1 - 2 - 3
    Signal C.H.54/59              *            4 - 1
    Signal C.H.23                 *            2 - 2
    Signal C.H.60                 *            3 - 2
    Signal C.H.13/15/20/21        *            4 - 2
    Signal C.H.46/53/57           *            2 - 4
    Wickham Road Bridge                          6
    Haywards Heath Box            †            2 - 1
    Haywards Heath Station Foreman           2 - 2 - 2
    Haywards Heath Up Platform               2 - 2 - 1
    Wivelsfield Office                         6 - 1
    Keymer Crossing Box                   1 long (key down)

    *  Switches on to Circuit when telephone cupboard door opened.
    †  Switch to Electrification Circuit No.21.
    NOTE  The telephone outside Ouse Valley Sub-Station can switch on
          to this circuit when required.
          Type of Telephone.
          Res.of Relays.
    C.2450/79.R.2.
              To operate from 8.0am on Sunday 17th August, 1958.
    EACH CALL SIGNAL TO BE ACKNOWLEDGED BY BEING REPEATED BEFORE
               THE CONVERSATION IS COMMENCED.
```

BRITISH RAILWAYS (Southern Region)   Form "XX"

TELEPHONES AT SIGNALS

INSTRUCTIONS TO SIGNALMAN AT.. **KEYMER CROSSING** ..SIGNAL BOX.

The instructions and code calling indications in the telephone cabinets at the undermentioned signals provide for your signal box being called, in the first instance, by a Trainman of a train detained at any of these signals. When a Trainman communicates with you by telephone announce the name of your signal box.

You must satisfy yourself in all cases that you are certain from which signal telephone a Trainman is calling, the description of his train, and exactly where it is standing.

You will be responsible for putting a Trainman calling from one of the undermentioned signals into contact by telephone with the Signalman controlling, or having jurisdiction over the passing of, such signal. For example, when you receive a call from a Trainman detained at a signal shown in column 'A' and at that time the signal box shown in column 'C' is open, you are required to ring the Signalman at that box by the code call shown in column 'D' and request him to speak to the Trainman, satisfying yourself that he does so. If the signal box shown in column 'C' is not open you will be responsible for giving the Trainman appropriate instructions.

(A) Signal number or description	(B) Telephone at signal		(C) Signal box to which Trainman should be referred if open	(D) Code call of signal box referred to in column (C)
	Circuit No.	Code Call		
UP LINE				
CA.1	C.108	2-4	Clayton Cutting	5
CA.3	C.108	3-2-1	Clayton Cutting	5
CD.2	C.108	2-2-2	Clayton Cutting	5
CA.5	C.108	4-4	Hassocks	1-3
CE.20	C.108	3-4	Hassocks	1-3
CE.19	C.108	4-2	Hassocks	1-3
CA.7	C.108	2-1-2	Burgess Hill	7
CF.29	C.108	1-3-2	Burgess Hill	7

Above: An Ore to London Victoria train passes over Keymer (Junction Road) level crossing, the author as photographer standing in a position that most certainly would not be designated as a 'place of safety' today! As mentioned above, Keymer gates required constant maintenance and one safety measure we could put in place when working on the them during normal hours was to remove a designated link on one of the signal relays under the signal box, ensuring that CG17 signal could only display a yellow, cautionary aspect. Gate stops were mechanisms in the centre of the road which rose as the gates were being wound to prevent them from travelling beyond where they should. Just before the gates reached their maximum extent and hit the stops, they travelled over 'tumblers' which were then locked by the gate lock lever in the signal box to prevent them swinging back. One of the less pleasant aspects of maintaining manual crossing gates was keeping the gate pits (the recesses in the centre of the road housing the contrivances) clean as they filled with detritus from the road. Junction Road was a busy thoroughfare taking traffic from the top of the town down to the 'Worlds End' neighbourhood (allegedly given its name after the Wivelsfield accident) of Burgess Hill, so carrying out such a task during the day would have been too hazardous. So it was that every few months, this would be done on an overtime turn of duty, either a Friday or Saturday night. Since the gate locks would be disconnected and thus the signalling affected, a flagman would be booked on with us, although as this was normally carried out after the passage of the last train, he was more usefully employed ensuring we were not mown down by passing cars as, kneeling in the centre of the road with only Tilley lamps for lighting, we spooned out buckets-worth of 'muck'! These days, of course, the road would either be closed or temporary traffic lights installed, but there were no such luxuries back then. *September 1977*

Left: Keymer Crossing signal box closed on 25th June 1983 with all controls, including controlling the crossing by CCTV, passing to Three Bridges. The inevitable final act is seen here. *Author's Collection*

12 – Wivelsfield

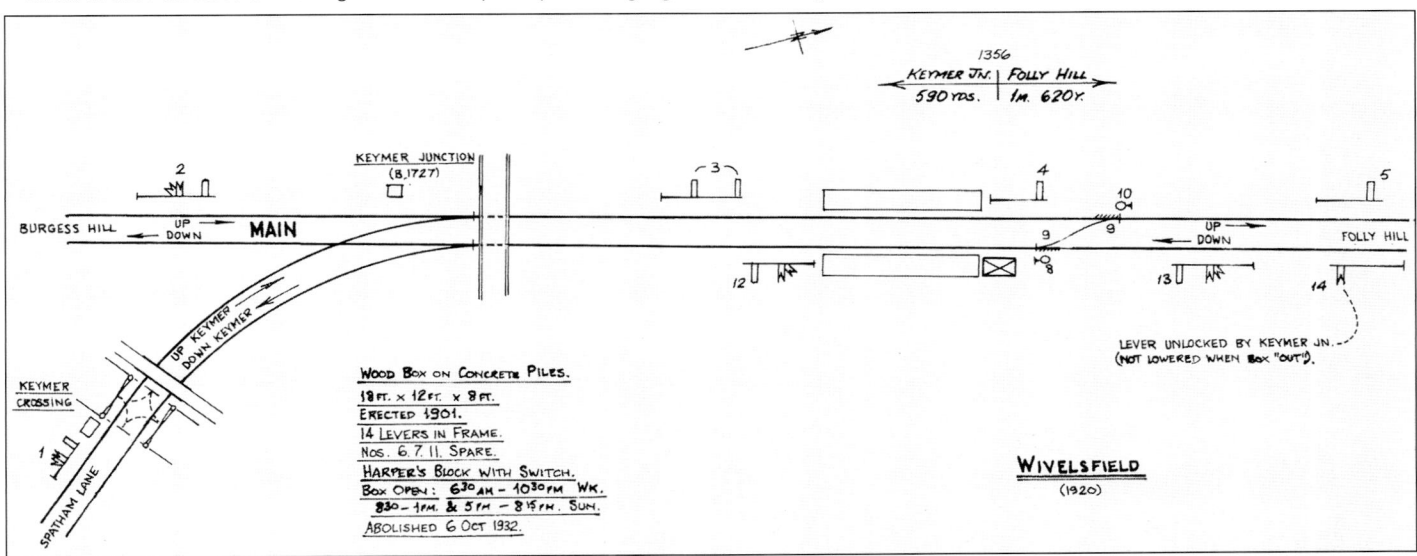

Wivelsfield station signal box opened in 1901 as a direct result of the Wivelsfield station accident on 23rd December 1899, where a late running Up Main Pullman train ran into the rear of a Newhaven boat train that had just started away from Wivelsfield's Up platform starting signal, the driver of the Pullman train having missed the Up line protecting signals in thick fog. *Author's Collection*

Wivelsfield station signal box's area of control is seen here in 1920. The signal box was constructed of wood built on concrete piles, necessary as it was situated on the top of a high embankment where known slippages had occurred. During heavy rain in the autumn of 1886, a portion of the Up platform disappeared down the embankment, a further section following in 1913. The result of the inspecting officer's report into the 1899 accident (of which more shortly) can be seen with co-acting signals now protecting the Up platform and Wivelsfield's Up distant situated below Keymer Junction's Up home signal.

'B2' Class 4-4-0 No. 206 *Smeaton*, of the Pullman train mentioned previously, lying on its side across the Down line about 44 yards north of the point of collision. As well as highlighting the non-supply of fog-signalmen, amongst other things the inspecting officer was critical of the position of the signal box at the south end of the platform with its close proximity to the junction box:

> In conclusion, I would recommend the Company to make some alteration in their signalling arrangements at Wivelsfield. I cannot think it satisfactory that the section between Keymer Junction and Wivelsfield should be considered as a separate block section, and yet should have no separate Up signals. The station might be treated as an intermediate station in a section between two block signal cabins, having only signals worked from the platform for the protection of trains standing thereat, or if a block signal cabin be necessary there should be an Up home signal from Wivelsfield, with an Up distant signal on the Keymer Junction Up home signal post. The signal cabin would probably be better placed at the north end of the station, and the existing main line crossover road, now worked from it, might be moved forward, or back to be worked from the Junction cabin. Another matter worth the attention of the Company is in reference to their high signals. It is the practice upon some lines to provide duplicate low arms upon all signal posts over a certain height, in one case fixed at 45 feet. It is possible that, although the driver of the Pullman train missed seeing the Keymer Junction Up distant signal lamp, only 14 feet above rail level, he might have caught sight of a low signal lamp on the Keymer Junction Up home signal if there had been one.

Colonel Marindin's report was published on 18th January (they moved quickly in those days) and the LB&SCR obviously accepted the good Colonel's recommendations as the new signal box (to a standard design containing a 14-lever frame) opened at the north end of Wivelsfield's Down platform in 1901. Keymer Junction retained its crossover, another was provided here and the signalling was altered to adhere to the report's findings. Along with the junction cabin, Wivelsfield station signal box succumbed on 6th October 1932.
Photograph and accident report courtesy of thebrightonbranchofaslef.yolasite.com

Looking south from Wivelsfield station towards Keymer Junction sees the co-acting signals protecting the station as recommended by Colonel Marindin in his report into the 1899 accident. The top 'blind' arm would provide better sighting in natural light as opposed to the lower arm which could become lost in the background – although that, naturally, carries the signal lamp. A train is signalled on the Down Main and one must be due on the Up, as Keymer Junction has lowered its home signal but Wivelsfield station has yet to react. An impressive twelve arms exist on the pole route atop the cutting side and, as ever for a photograph of this vintage, the lineside maintenance is a credit to the local length gang. *The Edward Wallis Collection*

Facing Page Centre: Brighton-built Standard Class '4' No. 80015 leaves the station and is about to pass the remains of the 1886 signal box, the lead-away still visible.
*11th June 1955,
Bluebell Railway Museum Archive, J.J. Smith Collection*

Facing Page Bottom: Brighton 'Atlantic' No. 32422 *North Foreland* (with approximately 2½ years of its life left) brings the 10.51 Hastings to Leicester through Wivelsfield. The station still exudes 'Southern charm', complete with splendid barley twist lamp-posts with their swan necks, gas lamps, Wivelsfield 'targets' and running in board. Keymer Crossing's CG3 and CG4 signals, still worked from the lever frame, are off the bottom of the platform ramp, while the base of the former 1886 signal box can be seen beyond the platform having been converted, it would seem, into a permanent way hut.
*28th August 1954,
Bluebell Railway Museum Archive, J.J. Smith Collection*

Above: Signal CG4 at the far end of the platform gives a green aspect to the driver entering Wivelsfield station with a Brighton-bound train. Signal CA9, with its back to the camera, still has its 'A' light whilst its associated signal post telephone (not shown on the 1933 track plan) is very sensibly mounted on the fence at the bottom of the platform ramp. *24th April 1937, H.C. Casserley*

Class '33' No. 6558, running light engine, enters the station on 30th April 1971. The Down inner home signals have moved 100 yards further south, the original pair of signals replaced by a single head with a three-light Position 1 junction route indicator. Along with this work, carried out on Sunday 11th September 1960 in conjunction with the platform extensions, Burgess Hill's CF3 signal moved forward accordingly. The signal is plated as CG17 although, as it is now worked from the panel, the 'One Control Switch' could be moved two ways: moving the switch upwards set the route along the Down main (shown as CG18 on the panel) while downwards was the route for the branch (CG17). Unusually for a colour light signal, it is mounted on a pair of old bullhead rails. *John Scrace*

Left: A pair of 'then and now' images of Wivelsfield station, probably taken not much more than seventy or so years apart. In the intervening years not a huge amount has changed – although the Up platform has been reduced in width, the wooden boarding survived into the 1980s. The station exists on a transition between embankment (considered by the engineer John Rastrick to be the heaviest on the line) and cutting, resulting in a three-tier entrance up from Leylands Road below. As a result, the booking office resides within the middle section, with steps up to it from road level and up from it to the Down platform (via a subway and steps to the Up platform). In the upper photograph the posts of Wivelsfield's Up starter and Down home are visible but their arms are lost in the sky. The Up starting signal CA9 is visible in the lower photograph; it required a banner repeater when the 1980s resignalling took place. Both roads are now signalled for bi-directional working.
(Upper) Lens of Sutton Collection
(Lower) 23rd March 1979

13 – Folly Hill

The first Folly Hill signal box was situated on the Up side of the line just north of Folly Bridge, opening in 1863 and taking its name from the adjacent farm of the same title. At the same height as the very similar Keymer Junction signal box, with its operating floor at 22 feet above rail level, the signalman had a graceful ascent to his place of work, whereas the signal lineman had to make do with a metal ladder to attend to his maintenance of the various mechanisms below the lever frame. The number of levers this contained is not known, but it can be safely said that it would have been hard pushed to reach double figures. It is likely that the platform extending towards the bank over the rudimentary toilet facilities was the signalman's official access to the cabin, via a route from Folly Bridge situated a short distance to the south. *John Minnis Collection*

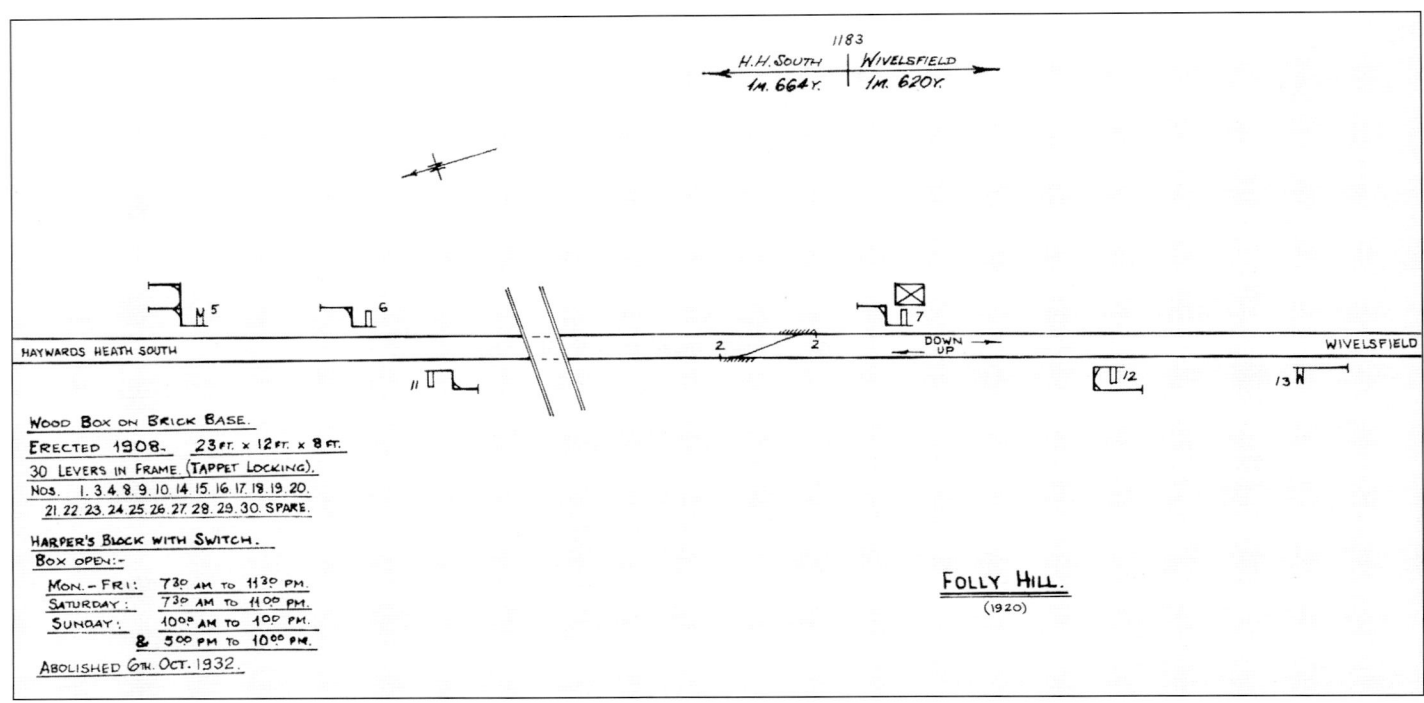

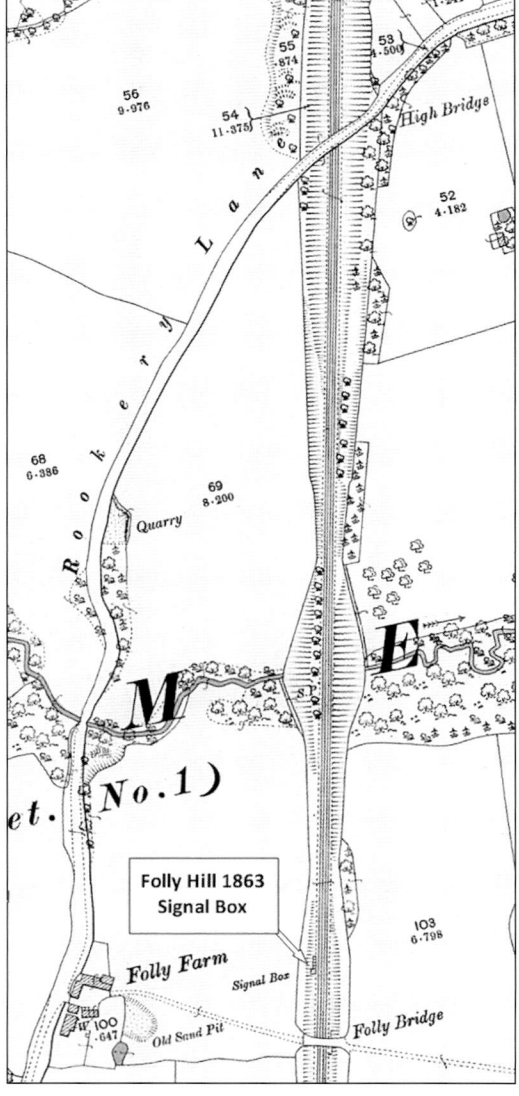

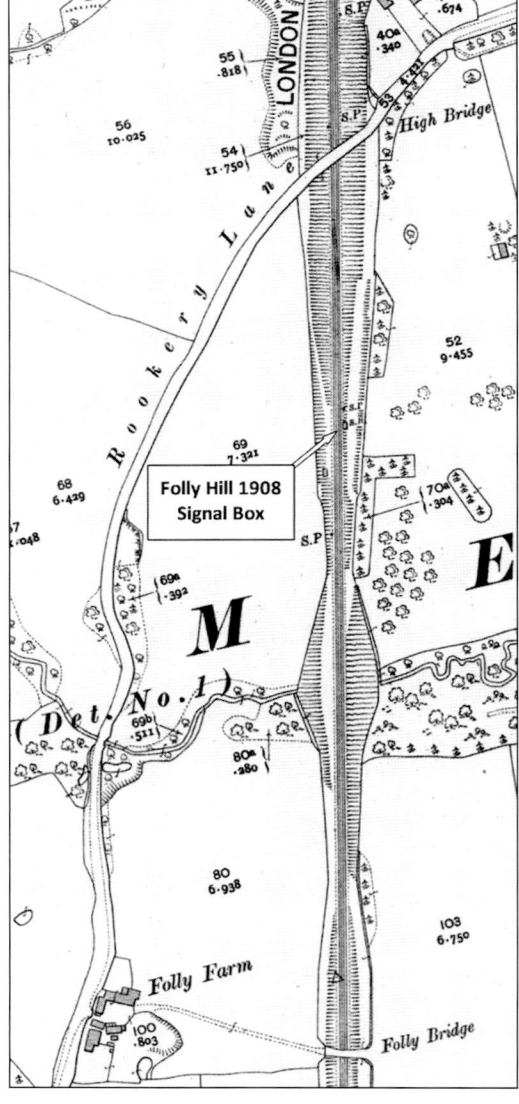

Above: Folly Hill signal box's area of control in 1920. It appears overly extravagant that all of the signals, except the Up distant, are on cantilever brackets with No. 12 being of a 'gallows' type. Understandably, signals No's 7 and 11 are so mounted for sighting through the arches of the tall Rocky (Rookery) Lane three-arch bridge, and possibly No. 5 Down distant for the approach view from within Haywards Heath Tunnel, but, as the line through here is completely straight, it is not clear why the others (with the additional expense incurred) were positioned as such. One possible reason is that the majority of the line through here is in deep cutting and having the arms projected further inwards puts them more against the sky line and thus gives greater visibility.

Left: Location of the 1863 signal box.
Reproduced by permission of the National Library of Scotland

Right: Location of the 1908 signal box.
Reproduced by permission of the National Library of Scotland

ABOVE: Folly Hill signal box, pictured here during the First World War, opened on 1st June 1908, replacing the signal box seen at the beginning of this chapter. Its position can be seen in the 1910 map opposite.
John Minnis Collection

When researching photographs for publications such as this it never ceases to amaze me as to the range of scenes that were recorded for the postcards of the day. Pictured here is a crisp northwards view showing Folly Hill's No's 7 and 11 signals (along with their relative wire runs and pulleys), Rookery Lane bridge, a telegraph pole and not a great deal else. In the far distance is Ashenground Bridge where, in the early 1900s, the local council petitioned the company for a halt to be constructed. Needless to say, nothing came of the proposal.
Laurie Marshall Collection

The 1908 Folly Hill signal box (situated some 300 metres north of the original cabin) is seen looking towards Haywards Heath with the tall Rookery Lane bridge in the background and clear signals on the Down road. Quite why a 30-lever frame was installed here when a mere seven levers were required will probably forever remain a mystery. Heralding its demise, new cable routes and conductor rails are in situ and the two-aspect approach light signal (required for the temporary transition from mechanical to colour light signalling prior to this box being swept away) can be seen below No. 11 signal just north of the overbridge. The brick base of the structure (converted at some point into a Permanent Way hut) still survives at the time of writing although Rocky Lane, as it became, has since been by-passed by a new Haywards Heath southern ring road passing over the line between the signal box and the bridge. *The Edward Wallis Collection*

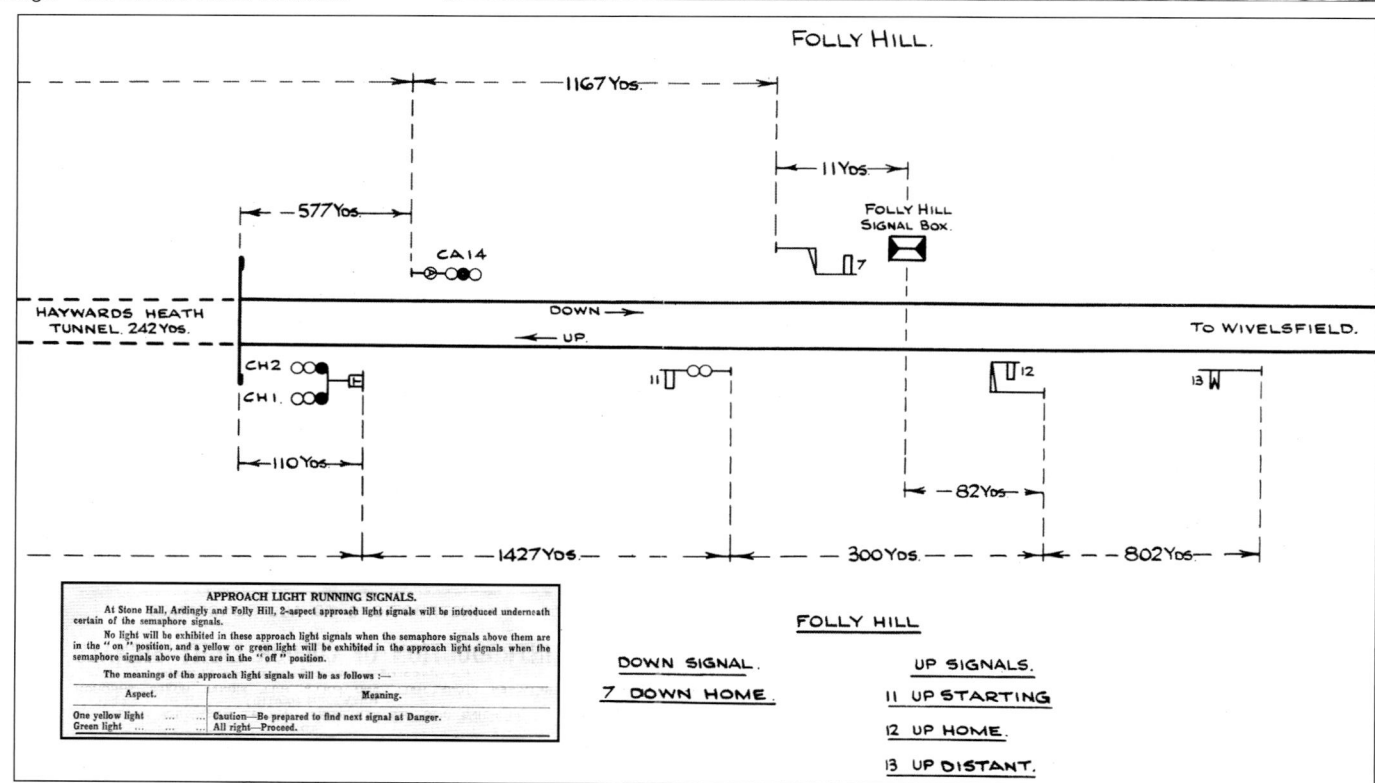

ABOVE: When the new Haywards Heath signal box was brought into work on 12th June 1932, the limit of that commissioning stage was just south of Haywards Heath Tunnel. This extract from Signalling Instruction No. 23 shows the stage-works required at Folly Hill, with an extract from the notice overlaid showing the working of the approach light beneath No. 11 signal at the interface to the new CH1 and CH2 signals. All the Up road mechanical signals were to survive for a bit longer but No's 5 and 6 signals on the Down have disappeared forever.

LEFT: These mouldering remains of the signal box were photographed during March 2018.

14 – Haywards Heath

Two similar views of Haywards Heath both warranted inclusion due to the wealth of detail they contain. South signal box is prominent in both photographs but North box is better seen in the lower. The Down home signal bracket and the tall Up advance starting signal beyond can be seen in the photograph below, the latter reckoned to be approaching some 60 feet in height and one of the tallest on the system. The rural nature of the area is evident where the town, as with so many other villages in the country, has built up following the coming of the railway, thus sounding the death knell for the coaching routes that once ran through the neighbouring villages of Cuckfield and Lindfield. In the first few years alone, passenger journeys increased from three quarters of a million in 1845 to seven and a quarter million in 1857, with season ticket receipts increasing by some 200 per cent: impressive figures and music to the ears of the company and their shareholders. Besides passengers, the station also dealt with commodities such as bricks, dung, lime, salt, coal and fullers earth (any of which would be in the wagons shown in the photographs), along with livestock. *Above: Laurie Marshall Collection. Below: Lens of Sutton Collection*

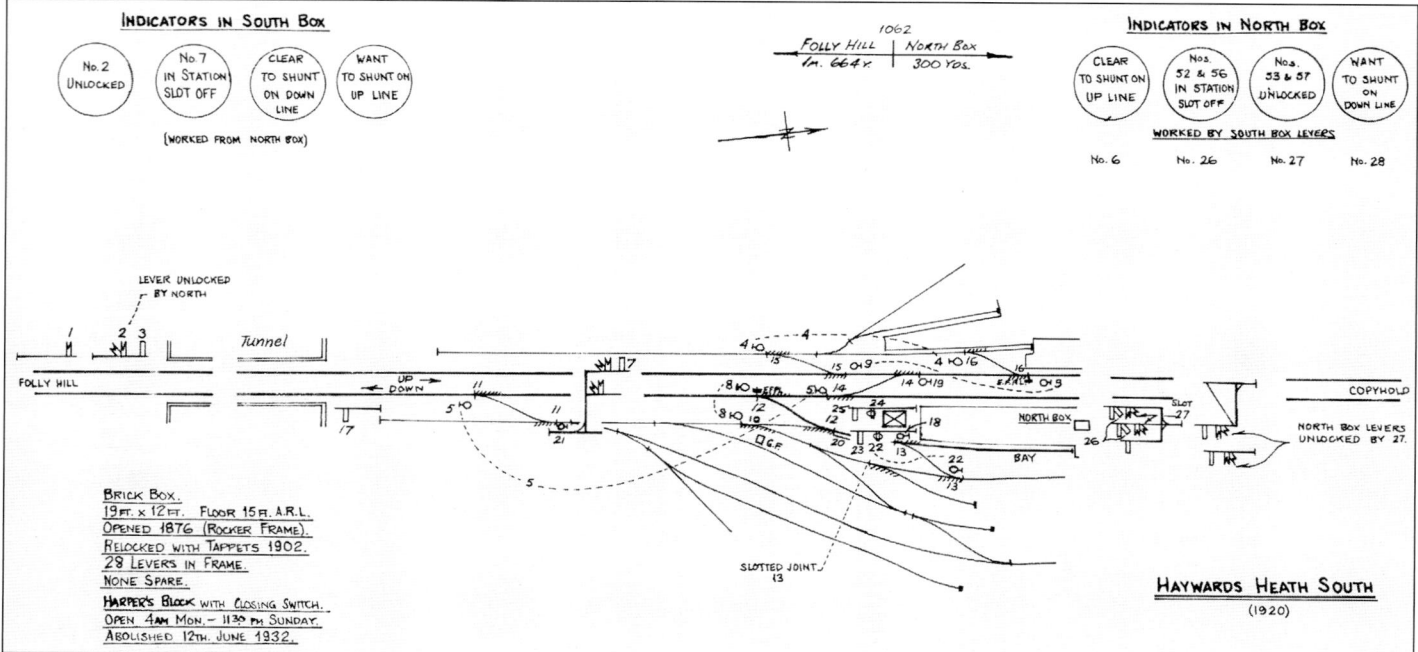

Haywards Heath South signal box layout in 1920. Two sets of main line trailing points (No's 12 and 16) were operated with an Economical Facing Point Lock, shown as 'EFPL' on the diagram; to watch one of these in motion was to see mechanical engineering at its most brilliant.

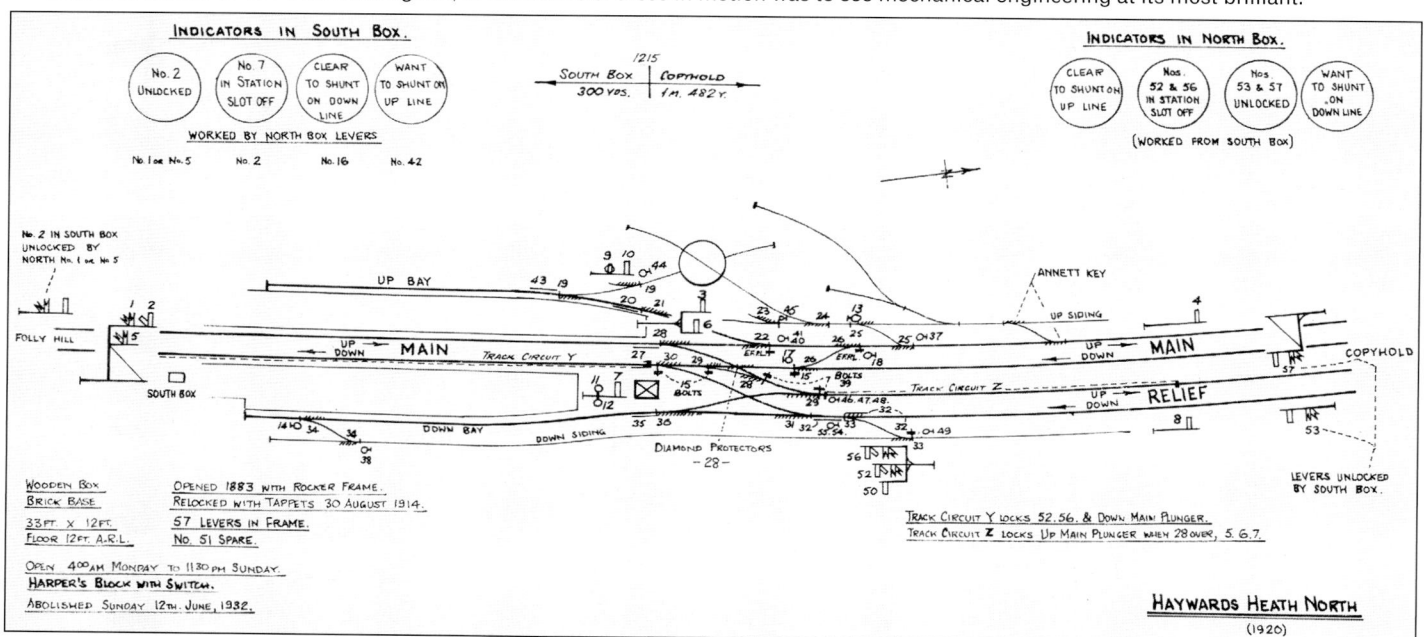

Above and Right: Haywards Heath North signal box layout in 1920. Of interest are the 'diamond protectors' on No. 28 'angles' on the Down Main, fitted as there had been problems with modern bogie vehicles crossing the diamonds. These were also fitted at Brighton and a contemporary explanation described their working as follows:

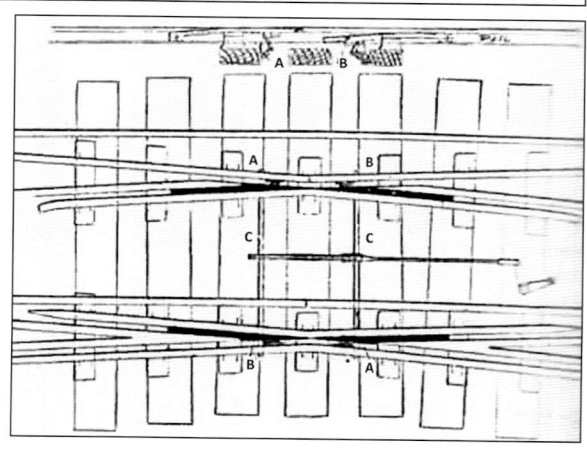

At 'A' (top left & bottom right) are two steel treadles, or wedges, which are up flush with the running rail while 'B' (top right & bottom left) are down clear of the wheels and vice versa. The wedges are raised or depressed by the rocking shafts 'C' (centre) which are actuated from the signal box by the same lever that operates the switches connecting with the diamond crossing. These wedges fill up the spaces between the elbow and the point, and absolutely prevent the wheel flanges from either striking the point or running upon the wrong side of it. The wheel pressure comes on the sides, not upon the top, of the wedges, which transmits it to the wing rails.

Above: From a similar, but slightly lower viewpoint from the earlier photographs, Unit No. 7036 leaves Haywards Heath station with the 11.00am Selhurst to Brighton, shortly to enter Haywards Heath Tunnel.
7th September 1965, John Scrace

A slightly different viewpoint sees a diesel multiple unit (almost certainly on its way to St. Leonards Depot) about to enter Haywards Heath Tunnel during September 1980. The 249 yard tunnel was always notoriously wet (as evident by the gleaming patches on the tunnel walls and sleepers) and provided problems for the contractors. Three men were killed during its construction on 2nd January 1841. Permanent speed restriction boards are in place for both leaving and entering the tunnel.

Haywards Heath station looking south in 1898, showing the Up and Down main lines along with the north end bay platforms. The crossover and associated shunt signal seen here were abolished sometime prior to 1920 as they are not shown on North signal box's 1920 layout drawing. The gable end of the Liverpool Hotel with its oriel window, along with the roofs of the company's cottages (demolished sometime during the late 1970s to make room for the station car park) can be seen above the R.J. Billinton designed Class 'D3' tank engine sitting in the Down siding. The 26-lever Haywards Heath South signal box is in the distance. *O.J. Morris, Laurie Marshall Collection*

The first signal box at this location was a Saxby & Farmer wooden affair, opening in 1863/64 but only lasting until 1876. Haywards Heath South signal box, shown here, replaced it during 1876 and was the sole structure until after the station rebuilding of 1880/81, when North box was introduced. South box contained a Saxby & Farmer 'rocker' frame of 28 levers, extended to 30 sometime after 1920. Like its near neighbour it succumbed to the resignalling, closing on 6th June 1932. No. 24 signal has been lowered for a shunt move while the water column dribbles away.
The Edward Wallis Collection

In this pre-electrification view of the old station, a London-bound train cannot be far away as a goodly number of passengers occupy the Up platform, probably having bought their reading material (maybe even a copy of *The Family Herald*) from Hampton's bookstall seen in the centre. A light engine sits in the Up Bay platform in the distance whilst in the foreground No. 9 shunt signal controls movements back over South box's No. 16 points. These are a method of working points incorporating the aforementioned Economical Facing Point Lock where the FPL is withdrawn from the lock stretcher, the points moved across and the FPL replaced, all in one lever movement. *Laurie Marshall Collection*

Right: Extract from LB&SCR 'Regulations for Train Signalling', June 1917, sensibly protecting the Down Bay against any over-run of the Down home signals.

HAYWARDS HEATH NORTH.—Line Clear Signal must not be given to Copyhold on the Down Relief Line unless the Down Bay Platform Line is clear or the Junction Points are set for the Main Line and that Line is clear.

Right: Haywards Heath North signal box, housing a 57-lever Saxby & Farmer frame, opened in 1883 and closed, along with South box, on 12th June 1932 when the new Southern Railway 60-lever signal box opened. John Saxby was born near Hurstpierpoint in 1821 and was originally employed as a carpenter and joiner with the LB&SCR. He left railway service in 1862 to form his own signalling business (with his first premises near to Haywards Heath), before being joined by John Farmer. The pair of them then went on to become pioneers of railway signalling across the world, eventually employing some 2,000 people from their premises in Canterbury Road, Kilburn.
The Edward Wallis Collection

Above: Haywards Heath station is shown here looking towards London, prior to electrification and rebuilding. The first station opened with the line in 1841 for *'Conveyance of passengers, parcels, horses and carriages'* according to the press announcement, but, as a temporary terminus, a coach service provided onward travel to Brighton. The station was rebuilt into the form seen here around 1880, with the roof over the south bay platform bearing a similarity to that at Three Bridges. Cattle pens are seen to the left of the photograph. *The Edward Wallis Collection*

Above: A smartly dressed company surveyor with his theodolite poses for the camera along with his assistant (holding his 'levelling rod') as we look towards North signal box, the Up Bay platform in the process of being converted to what will become the new Up Local platform. The Up Main starting signals are on the left for routes towards the Up Main and Up Relief lines respectively, while the ones seen on the right are for departing northwards towards Copyhold Junction from the Down Bay platform. *Author's Collection*

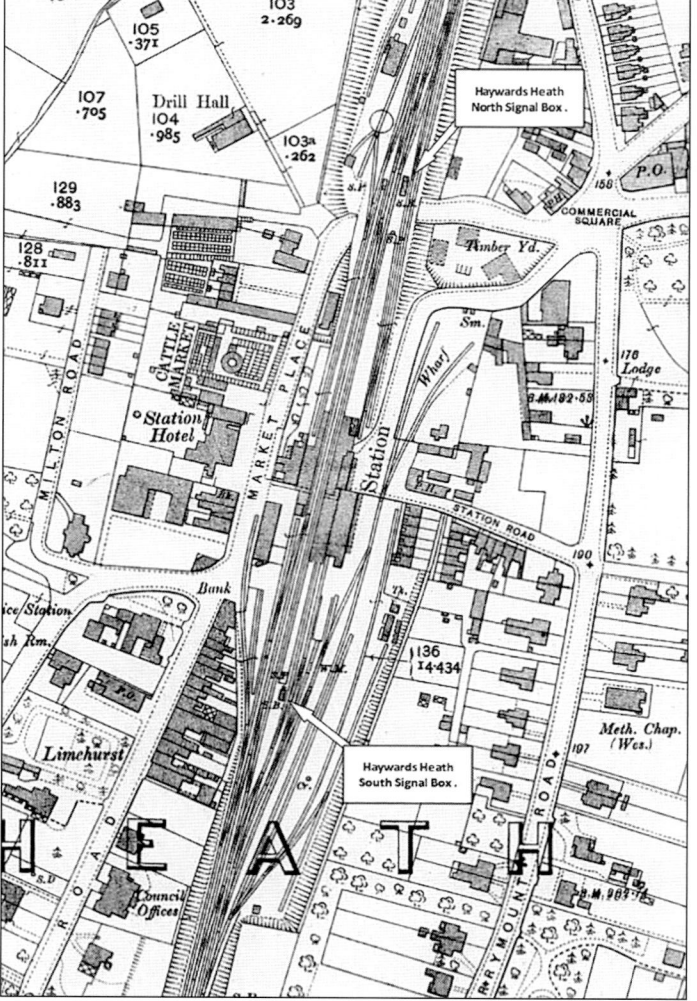

Left: Haywards Heath from a 1910 map. The Station Hotel can be seen opposite the Up-side station entrance whilst the Liverpool Hotel (shown as 'PH' at the bottom of Station Road on the Down side) had an LB&SCR boundary plaque set into the wall up until its untimely demise. To complete the trio of local hostelries, the Burrell Arms is situated just off Commercial Square which, in the days when all public houses closed their doors at 2.30pm, stayed open until 4.00pm on Tuesday afternoons as it was Haywards Heath market day (note the cattle pens in the earlier photograph). The row of LB&SCR terraced cottages are located across the road from the Liverpool Hotel and the position of the hand crane (safe working load 7 tons 10cwt) is shown as CR in the centre of the Down sidings. Both North and South signal boxes are highlighted.
Reproduced by permission of the National Library of Scotland

The 1932 station offered a rather more spacious layout with its pair of 800ft island platforms seen here in this view taken at 11.05am on 11th August 1979. Even at this relatively late stage the rebuilt goods shed was still handling a considerable amount of parcels traffic from the Red Star offices situated next to the booking office in the station forecourt. A slightly worrying 'wet spot' (where voids form below the track bed and water seeps in mixing with clay which then 'pumps' its way to the surface as trains pass over) can be seen developing in the Up Fast line which would shortly require the attention of the P.Way. Digging out between the sleepers to get to the root of the cause (with reballasting) was the only option, possibly even requiring a temporary speed restriction while the work was being carried out if the situation was bad enough.

Left: Looking north again, here is proof that trains kept running whilst rebuilding work progressed as the signalman has pulled off for an Up Main train plus a shunt move from the Down Bay platform. Lighting is provided in the interim to give some illumination over the temporarily very narrow Up Main platform. A steam crane simmers away behind the borrowed LM&SR wagon whilst the worker in the light-coloured trousers appears to be standing on some footings that could well be the base for the new Up Local platform face. Cloth caps are being worn by everyone except for the chap doing some digging on the left, who is sporting a very natty trilby – not a hard hat in sight!
Author's Collection

Right: Looking across the main lines towards the piles of rubble that were once the Down-side buildings, the railway cottages are on the left and the Liverpool Hotel, a Nalder & Collyer's Entire house (Croydon brewery) dominates the centre. Becoming the Liverpool Arms later in life (although a glass panelled door within the bar still proudly proclaimed its origins to the very end) this worthy establishment sadly closed in 1990 and was demolished some five years later.
Author's Collection

The old Up-side station buildings have been demolished, the new signal box is in position and the skeleton of what will become the new platform canopy, following a standard S.R. pattern for the period, has been erected. What will become the new Up Local platform continues to be dug out by hand, with the wooden cross, acting as a handy clothes peg, depicting where the new passenger subway will pass beneath. *Author's Collection*

A Southern Railway porter, or even a station foreman, poses amidst the rebuilding works. The old North signal box is still in work and can just be glimpsed in the right background, with the new box evident on the left. A single remnant of the old station remains, as a solitary pillar can be glimpsed adjacent to the Up platform, but the Down-side canopy and platform works appear to be complete. *Author's Collection*

Two rail-mounted steam cranes prepare to lift in the new east-side bridge parapet over Market Place Road whilst two gentlemen in the North signal box take a keen interest in proceedings from the top of the box steps. The bridge here required widening to accommodate the new Up and Down local lines, and with the newly built brick wing walls in place the new parapet could be lifted from the bolster wagon and lowered into place. Horsehay Ironworks Co. Ltd, Makers, Shropshire were obviously not shy in advertising their wares. *Author's Collection*

SOUTHERN RAILWAY.

Signal Instruction No. 23, 1932.

INSTRUCTIONS TO ALL CONCERNED
AS TO THE
INTRODUCTION OF COLOUR LIGHT SIGNALS
(In place of existing Semaphore Signals)

BETWEEN STONE HALL AND FOLLY HILL SIGNAL BOXES (THROUGH HAYWARDS HEATH);

BRINGING INTO USE NEW SIGNAL BOX AT HAYWARDS HEATH

AND

ABOLITION OF EXISTING COPYHOLD JUNCTION AND HAYWARDS HEATH NORTH AND SOUTH SIGNAL BOXES;

ALSO

REVERSAL OF LINES BETWEEN COPYHOLD JUNCTION AND HAYWARDS HEATH

On SUNDAY, 12th JUNE, 1932.

Rules 70, 71 and 72 to be observed. Drivers to keep a good look out for hand signals.

Commencing at 1.0 a.m. on Sunday, 12th June, the existing semaphore running signals at Copyhold Junction and Haywards Heath will be abolished, and 3-aspect colour light signals installed in lieu thereof.

The existing Copyhold Junction and Haywards Heath North and South signal boxes will be abolished. A new signal box, to be known as Haywards Heath, will be provided on the up side of the line at Haywards Heath Station; the points and signals at Copyhold Junction will also be operated from this box.

On and from 12th June the new Train Signalling Regulations dated April, 1932, for the sections of line between Coulsdon North No. 2 box and Brighton, Preston Park and Hove East; and Brighton and Hove East must be worked to as between Stone Hall, Haywards Heath and Folly Hill signal boxes.

The up relief line between Haywards Heath North and Copyhold Junction will become the down through line and the down main line between those points will become the up through line.

The running lines between Copyhold Junction and Haywards Heath will be re-named as follows:—

Existing Name.	New Name.
Down relief.	Down local.
Up relief.	Down through.
Down main.	Up through.
Up main.	Up local.

A diagram showing the new layout also the new signals and their location is attached to this notice; the signals, operated from Haywards Heath box are prefixed by the letters C.H. and will be known as controlled signals.

Automatic signals are prefixed by the letters C.A. and will be controlled by track circuit only.

Plates bearing the relevant prefix letters and the number of the signal will be fixed to each running signal post.

Each 3-aspect running signal will consist of a group of three lamps, and the aspect exhibited at any one time will be (a) a red, or (b) one yellow, or (c) a green light.

The aspects of the new colour light signals will be the same by day as by night.

Colour light running signals will be fitted with small side lights repeating the aspects exhibited by the signals to assist Drivers of trains drawn close up to such signals.

Back lights will not be provided in any of the colour light signals.

The meanings of the new colour light signals will be as follows:—

THREE-ASPECT RUNNING SIGNALS.

Aspect.	Meaning.
Red Light	Danger—Stop.
One Yellow Light	Caution—Be prepared to find next signal at Danger.
Green Light	All right—Proceed.

230907—1.

The signalling notice detailing the introduction of the new Haywards Heath signal box. It is easy to read the text now and smile at the lines that read *'Aspects of the new colour light signals will be the same by day as of night'* and that *'Back lights will not be provided'*, but for many drivers back then, mechanical working would be the only form of signalling they would have come across and this was the dawn of a brave new era.

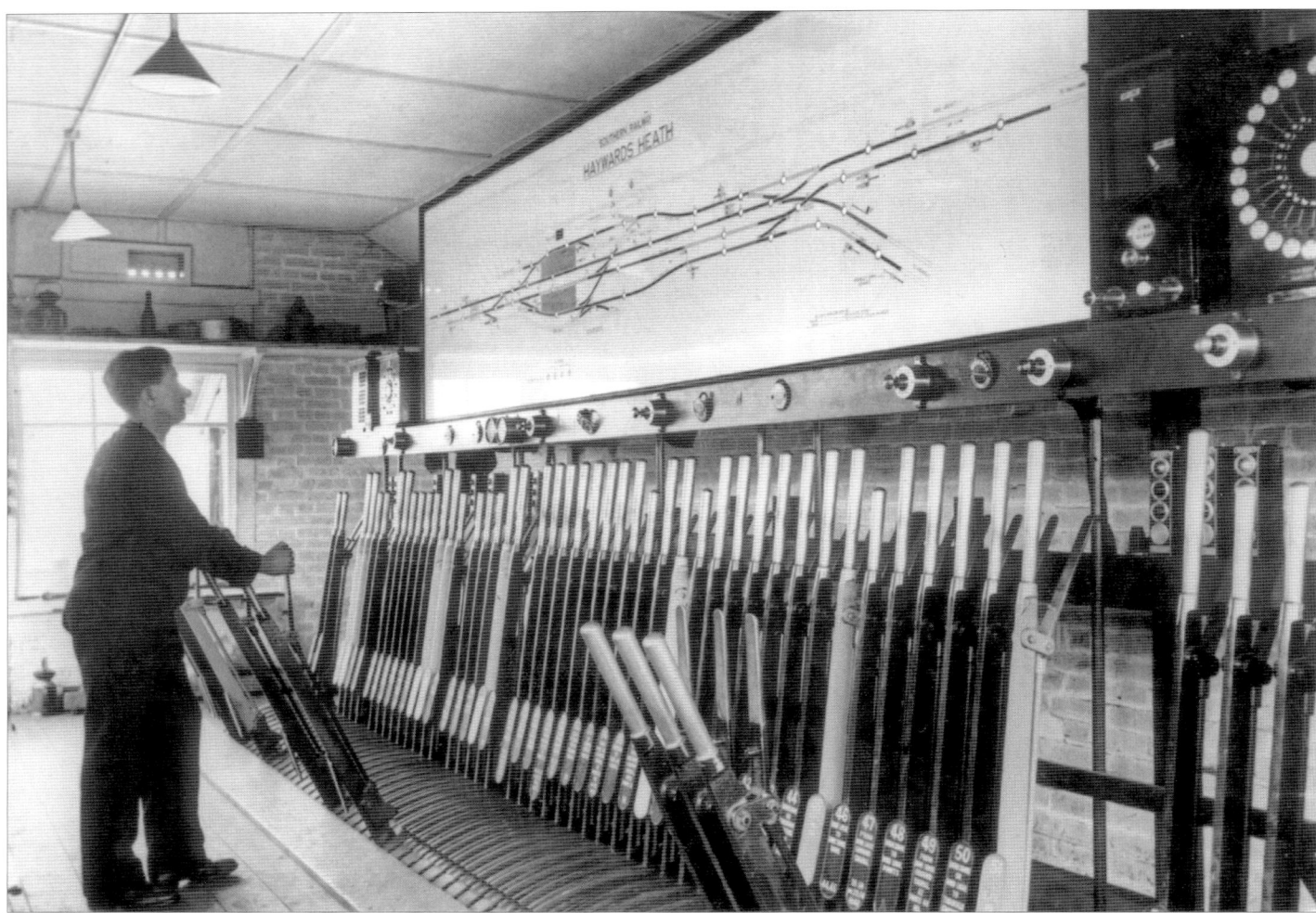

Above: The interior of Haywards Heath signal box, as commissioned, showing the 60-lever 'A2' Westinghouse frame and the enormous Southern Railway illuminated 'bullseye' diagram to good effect. Siemens rotary train describers work to Keymer Crossing at the far end of the frame and Balcombe Tunnel Junction nearest the camera, with the wonderful Harper's instrument controlling the block section towards Ardingly. An interesting point here is that after the arrival of a train from the branch, the signalman would have to give 'train out of section' to Ardingly – but, from his position in the box, he would not be able to observe the tail light (thus ascertaining that the train had arrived complete), nor was continuous track circuiting in place from Copyhold Junction. It was probably a designated task for a member of the station staff to notify the signalman that the train had arrived intact. All the points and shunt signals within the station area were mechanically operated with only the points at Copyhold Junction controlled by machines; the starting signal towards Ardingly (CH23) was a semaphore signal, albeit motor worked. *K.R.M.*

Facing Page Bottom: Haywards Heath signal box photographed during August 1979. Opening on 12th June 1932 it controlled the remodelled layout brought about by the station rebuilding, thus consigning the previous North and South signal boxes to history. The relay room was behind the blind wall to the left of the window in the single storey extension at the end which also housed the S&T mess room, workshop and stores. The window at the far end of the signal box was the regular meeting point between station supervisor and signalman where conversations about train routing and general day-to-day running matters would take place. Bert West was one of the station foremen and was unconditionally adored by his regular commuters. No robotic autonomous train announcing back then: Bert would sally forth for every train with style and wit and ran his Up-side platforms during the morning peak with the finesse and precision of a military manoeuvre. When trains ran out of course he would begin his announcement with something akin to, *"Will all passengers on platforms three and four **please** listen carefully to what I'm about to say because if you don't, you'll end up getting on the wrong train, ending up somewhere you don't want to go and be blaming me for it in the morning"*. His description of an Up stopping train, *"The next train from platform three will call at Balcombe, Three Bridges, Gatwick Airport, Horleysalfordsearlswoodredhill, Merstham, Coulsdonsouthpurley, East Croydon, Clapham Junction and Victoria"*, became the stuff of legend. Every moving train departing from either platform was watched with an eagle eye and any door seen left on the catch was summarily slammed shut with a well-aimed boot!

This is not a book of reminisces but I will just mention a couple:
- The freezing cold night when I was waiting for the Permanent Way to finish some rail welding (for which I had extracted the relevant track circuit fuse) and, retiring to the mess room, thought I'd warm it up by turning the gas oven and all the rings up to full and then falling asleep. Awaking coughing and spluttering with what little oxygen was left in the room I hastily flung open the door and staggered outside.
- And the occasion I did a power changeover during the morning peak (not the cleverest of ideas but there had been power supply problems during the previous night), was momentarily distracted and managed to extract the wrong fuse first, thus plunging the whole of the Haywards Heath operating area into signalling darkness. I can still recall the hefty 'clunk' as every relay de-energised as one, the ensuing deathly silence shattered only by the expletives from the operating floor! I seem to recall that the inevitable failure form contained that immortal railway phrase, *"admitted and regretted"*.

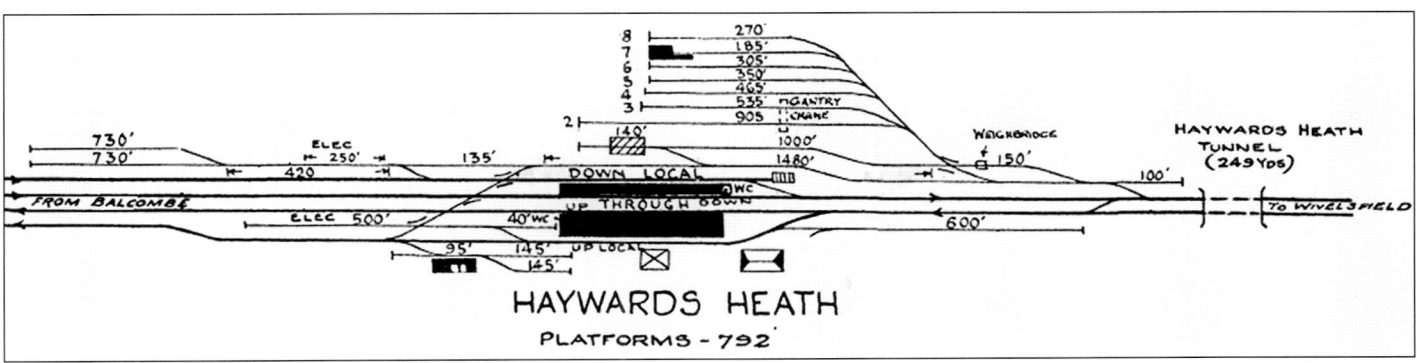

Above: The Haywards Heath control diagram.

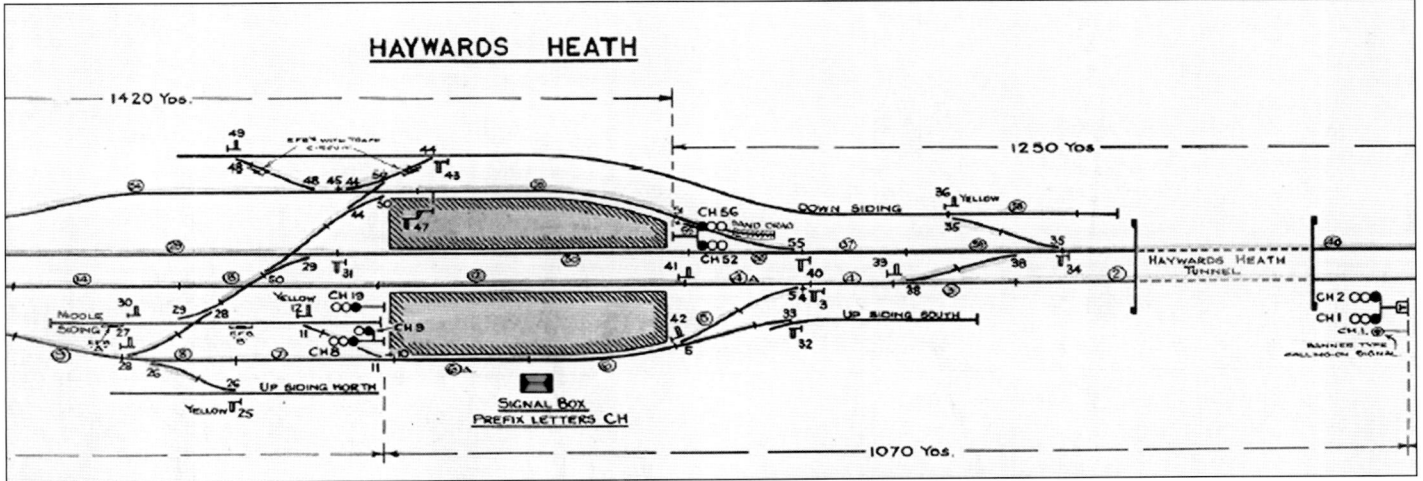

Above: Haywards Heath as resignalled in 1932. Up Siding South was abolished on 26th January 1972, otherwise, apart from points conversion to motor working and mechanical shunt signals to position lights, the layout remained the same up to the Brighton Line resignalling. Quite why CH8 signal at the end of the Up Local platform was positioned on the right-hand side will remain a mystery (possibly to avoid the need for an 'Off' indicator), as the approach sighting was poor to say the least. As early as 1959, CH1 was changed to a two-aspect head (R/Y) so a single yellow was the highest aspect a driver would see. Note the split track circuits in the Up Local platform to cater for joining trains, the 'banner type calling on signal' coming 'off' when 6A track circuit was occupied and No. 1 lever reversed.

Left: Haywards Heath looking south from a high vantage point sees an Up Ore to London Victoria train running in. An impressive number of parcels vans are stabled in the Down sidings whilst some 'British Rail Utility Trolley Equipment' (or Brutes as they were more widely known) are nearest the camera, the one on the Up Local platform being manhandled towards the lift shaft. *October 1977*

Below: The same train leaves the station via the Up Main, the photograph showing the north end layout with the long crossover beneath the train and the middle siding between that and the Up Local. The inner home signal gantry seen in the distance was a later addition, being brought into work on Sunday 22nd July 1962 to give an extra signal section between Copyhold Junction and the station. When the 1932 resignalling and new station were introduced, the running lines here altered from the former Up and Down Relief lines (to and from the Ardingly Branch) on the right and Up and Down Main lines on the left to 'paired by direction', i.e. Down Main/Down Local to the right and Up Local/Up Main on the left. The dock to the centre left of the picture was mainly used for tamping machines by this point (hence the stockpiling of hydraulic fluid seen within the cage) and the local Permanent Way gang's 'mess and tool' lorry can be seen in the bottom left-hand corner. The S&T's British Leyland van is parked close by: an unadulterated luxury, as before this arrived all travel for maintenance activities around the branch from Keymer Junction had to be undertaken by the local Southdown bus services (as there were no stopping services outside of the peaks), the Senior Technician using a book of specially provided tickets. The transport for emergencies or failures on that same stretch of line was by taxi, although what the cab drivers thought of three men getting into their cars in overalls with a large, heavy and none too clean tool bag in the boot, I never found out. Access everywhere else was by train and foot (notwithstanding the occasional 'drop off' from a friendly driver). *October 1977*

The portion from the signal box diagram showing the layout at the north end of the station. Note that even as late as 1972 two electric fouling bars still exist within the middle siding, in the same places as they were when installed in 1932 and indicated as a track circuit would be. The extra signal gantry (added in July 1962) can be seen housing CH52 and CH56 along with the shunt signal CH46. It was this shunt signal (when it was in its original position adjacent to CH57 on the cantilever structure in the rear – see the Copyhold Junction diagram) that a driver took as the main signal aspect, mistakenly thinking he was being routed straight along the Down Local, resulting in the 1945 tragedy recounted below. The following extracts are selected from inspecting officer Colonel A.C. Trench's report:

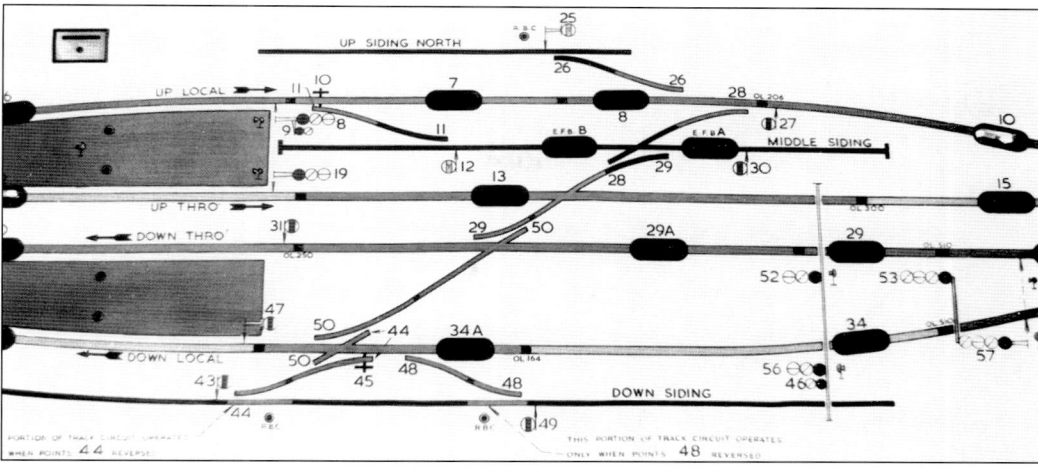

On 2nd September 1945, the 2.50 am. special empty coach train, Streatham to Newhaven, which should have come to a stand in the Down siding, prior to reversing across to the Up line, over which single line working was in operation, failed to stop and collided at high speed with the buffer stops at the south end of this siding, and with the face wall of the tunnel portal immediately beyond these buffer stops. Both Enginemen, Driver Scrase and Fireman Bartlett from Stewart's Lane depot, Battersea, were killed and the guard suffered from bruises and shock. The speed limit prescribed through the Copyhold Crossover to the Down Local is 40 m.p.h., and through crossover 44 to the Down siding, 15 m.p.h. The intention was the train, which had crossed over to the Down Local at Copyhold Junction, should traverse points No.44 into the Down siding, and come to a stand there, prior to being propelled backwards across all tracks to the Up Local, and going forward along this line under the single line working arrangements in force. The train was too long to use the Down Local line for this reversal as coming to standing at the starting signal, its rear end could not have been clear of the track circuiting holding the crossover over which it was to be propelled.

This regrettable accident must be attributed to the coincidence of two factors:
  (a) Scrase must apparently have misinterpreted the green aspect of the subsidiary signal CH46, directing movement into the Down siding, and,
  (b) Neither Driver Scrase nor Guard Prince was aware of the single line working arrangement.

Considering (b) first, it is clear that Scrase had not taken a copy of the Weekly Notice, and no copy was found in his kit bag on the engine after the accident; moreover, I think that Guard Prince is probably correct in his opinion that Scrase would have mentioned the single line working to him if he had been aware of it. At the same time Prince had failed to see the copy of the Weekly Notice which was available for inspection in the Inspector's Office at Clapham when he booked on, in addition to which the clerk responsible for the preparation of the Special Train Notice had failed to appreciate the single line working and to embody this in the notice.

Explanation of (a) is more speculative. Scrase had encountered two yellow signals and in obedience thereto he had duly slowed down through Copyhold crossover on to the local line; before this, he would have seen about 1/2 mile ahead, the two red signals 57 and 53 for the local and through lines respectively. It is a reasonable assumption that about the time he passed through the crossover he would have been able to pick up the subsidiary signal 46 alongside the Down Local signal, and that about the same time the sub signal may have changed from red to green but, both from a distance and from close up, the indication of this signal is definitely less conspicuous and different from ordinary running signals, and it is difficult to understand why this difference was not appreciated.

It would also appear reasonable to assume that Scrase thought he was going to pass through the station on the Down Local line, rejoining the Down line at the South end of the station but in such it becomes difficult to understand why he failed to notice the violent shock which the engine must have sustained when passing through crossover 44 at a speed much in excess of what was permitted. It is even more difficult to understand why, if he thought he was on the Down Local line he failed to pay attention to the red light of the Down Local starting signal at the South end of the platform, which, as noted above, with an immediate brake application, there would have been sufficient distance to come almost to stand before striking the buffer stops. A possible explanation of these latter questions is that, in passing through crossover 44, the violent jolt may have caused Scrase to strike his head against the side of the cab with the result that he was momentary dazed; this is, of course pure speculation, but it would explain such surprising dual failure on the part of a reliable driver, and in the short period available and in the dark the Fireman would hardly have notice anything wrong with his driver.

The possibility of some defect having developed on the engine, which might have distracted the Driver's attention, cannot be disproved, owing to damage to all footplate fittings in the collision, but this is rather discounted by the Fireman being found with a tea can in his hand and by other circumstances, and no indication of any such defect has been found.

I cannot but conclude, therefore, that all available evidence points to the primary responsibility for this accident being attributed to Driver Scrase in that he failed to obey the indications displayed to him by the signals. In lesser degree neither he nor the Guard Prince can be absolved from some share of the blame for their failure to study the weekly notice containing the intimation of single line working. It is to be regretted also that Prince failed to observe the aspect of signals 57 and 46, but having regard to the "Blackout" limitation of vision from his lookout windows, I hesitate seriously to criticise this failure. A minor contributory factor was the unfortunate omission from the special train timing notice of the stop and reversal at Haywards Heath.

As a postscript to this, readers will note the name of Driver Scrase, bearing the same sounding surname as John Scrace whose photographs appear in this book. John recounted to me that early the same morning of the accident, he, as a young lad, and his mother were catching a train from Horsham where they lived to visit some relatives. On arriving at the station and finding that services were disrupted, they learnt of the accident at Haywards Heath. John's father was a Horsham based driver and had been working the previous night shift and was yet to return home. John remembers his mother asking a member of the station staff if they knew the name of the driver involved and, upon being told, seeing the colour drain from his mother's face. Thankfully for them it was pure co-incidence as 'Scrace'/'Scrase' was not an uncommon 'railway name' and there was no family connection.   *Photograph, 21st September 1972, Author's Collection. Accident report courtesy of thebrightonbranchofaslef.yolasite.com*

Left: Another internal view, this taken in August 1979. Here an Up train has been signalled via the Up Local platform then back on to the Up Main line at Copyhold Junction; at the far end of the frame a Down train has been routed straight along the Down Through line. By now the diagram has been changed to a 'miniature illuminated' along with the upgrading of the train describers to the 'magazine' type; note though the enormous VDU depicting trains described from Three Bridges, almost 'cutting edge technology' back then. Hanging on the right-hand side of the diagram (just about visible as a dark shadow) is the 'one engine in steam' train staff for the Ardingly freight trains, merely a cut-down piece of broom handle with a brass plate showing 'Ardingly Branch' screwed on. Not very 'cutting edge' at all!

Right: Having provided sterling service for almost 51½ years, Haywards Heath signal box closed on 25th June 1983 with this being the sight that greeted the photographer a few months later. On a personal note, I was based here on a day turn of duty (maintenance and fault finding from a district that encompassed Balcombe Tunnel to Clayton Tunnel and around the Lewes Branch to Hamsey) from June 1974 to the summer of 1978, when the depot was closed and we transferred to shift work at Three Bridges. I have fond memories of this box, working it (unofficially of course) on many occasions and dealing with some fine signalmen along the way. All was not lost, as some of the redundant locks and controllers, seen accumulated at the far end, found their way to the Bluebell Railway for use in Horsted Keynes signal box. A sad view nonetheless.

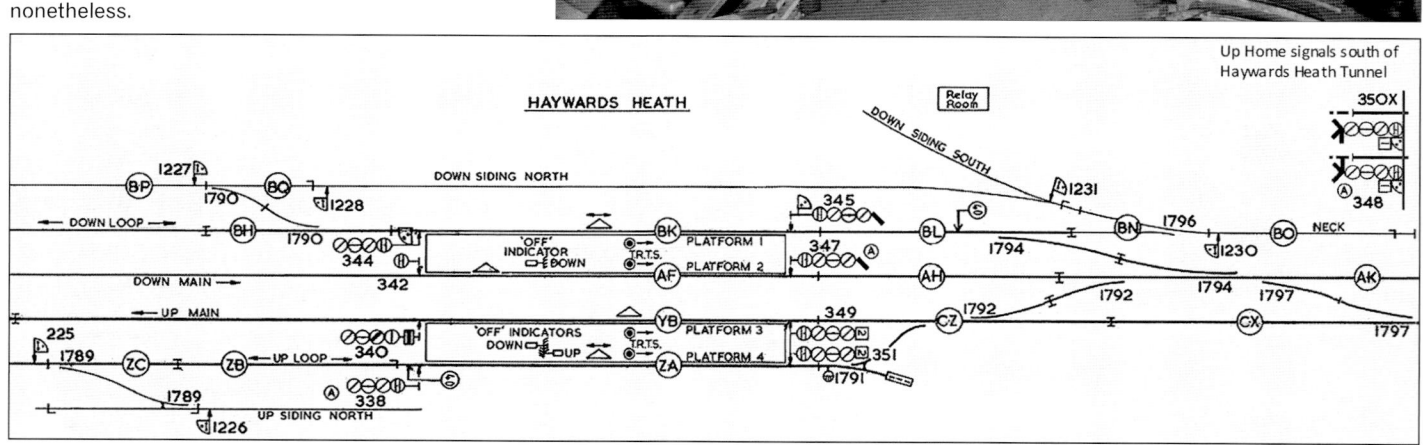

Haywards Heath as commissioned on to the Three Bridges panel with the inevitable rationalisation brought about by the resignalling. This saw the Up and Down local lines being renamed 'Loops' and signalled for reversible working, thus increasing the flexibility of the layout; the Down Main platform could also accept a terminating train 'wrong road'. As with the rest of the Brighton Line resignalling, all the new work was contracted out to Westinghouse Signals, with stage works (the art of integrating new and altered signalling into the existing control centre before the transferring of all controls to the new operating centre) and testing carried out 'in house' by British Rail's own signal engineers.

15 – Copyhold

Above: Taken from the ideal viewpoint of Copyhold Lane overbridge, the Ardingly Branch tails in from the right as 'B4' Class No. 58 brings a south-bound train along the Down Main line. The fearfully tall 'wrong road' signal seen at the rear of the train is the Up distant signal for Ouse Viaduct signal box, which opened in 1863 and was situated at the south end of that structure. Copyhold signal box did not exist at this juncture and Haywards Heath North worked direct to Ouse Viaduct. *Bluebell Railway Museum Archive, M.P. Bennett Collection*

Below: 'H1' Class No. 39 works a Down passenger train past the brand new Copyhold signal box. Erected in June 1912 and yet to control a junction, at this time the two pairs of lines ran parallel to Haywards Heath North signal box. To gain an extra block section and thus improve traffic flow, Copyhold and Stone Hall (south of Balcombe) cabins opened within a month of each other, acting purely as intermediate signal boxes but now providing three block sections between Balcombe station and Haywards Heath, as opposed to the previous two. With this new arrangement in place, Ouse Valley signal box closed the following month. Copyhold contained a 32-lever frame but with only six working. Although other signal boxes like Folly Hill and Stone Hall were given frames well in excess of the capacity needed; it must have been considered here that at some point in the future it would control a junction. This duly came about four years later. *John Minnis Collection*

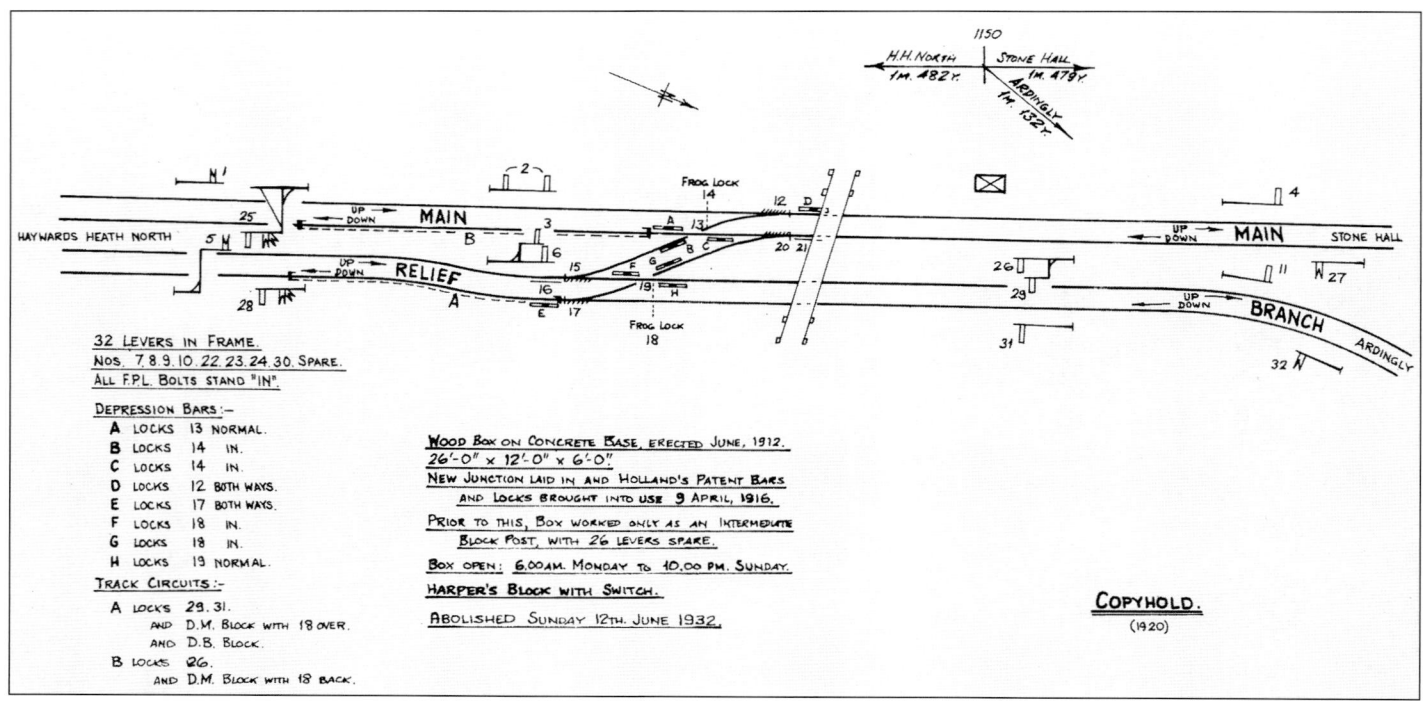

Copyhold signal box layout in 1920.

Copyhold Junction's Up home signals, reading from left to right, No's 2, 3 and 6, the higher arm of No. 2 signal having a 'blind arm'. In the foreground are the fogging repeaters for the fog signalman whose hut would have been behind the photographer; the rodding led from a detonator placer lever and would operate the detonator placers – detonators on the top of the rail would explode to warn the driver if the signal was 'on', with all personnel keeping well clear of any flying fragments. All signals could be 'fogged', depending on staff availability, but distant signals would always be given priority. The double-arch bridge carrying Copyhold Lane, whence the name originates, is seen in the background. *The Edward Wallis Collection*

The new junction was brought into work on 9th April 1916, thus reducing the number of spare levers in Copyhold signal box to just eight. The box closed on 12th June 1932 when the new Haywards Heath signal box took control; the remote relay room that assumed the work of its manual predecessor is just visible on the extreme right. Lying in the foreground is a wooden frame for holding a temporary speed restriction board. *The Edward Wallis Collection*

Looking from the bottom of the signal box steps a train disappears into the distance towards Haywards Heath. Copyhold Lane bridge dominates the scene and the vertical join in the brickwork is evident from when the bridge was extended in conjunction with the line opening to Horsted Keynes in 1883, just 40 years before this photograph was taken. *3rd March 1923, The Edward Wallis Collection*

Above: Passing Copyhold Junction's No. 26 signal in the 'off' position and thus signifying the route straight along the Down Main line, Maunsell designed 'U' Class 2-6-0 No. 794 brings an Eastbourne bound train past the signal box during the summer of 1928. *Author's Collection*

Below: Some 35 years later, a '2-BIL' unit passes through Copyhold with a Down train bound for Horsted Keynes, the foundations of the old signal box still evident. *31st March 1963, Ian D. Nolan*

Above: To complete the set, this is a much later view, where a forest obscures almost everything. Copyhold's brick-built relay room can be seen adjacent to where the signal box once existed, the controlling relays housed in a small room accessed through the door seen nearest the camera. At the rear was the dark, damp room housing the point batteries which used to consume distilled water as if it was going out of fashion. We had to roll large five gallon 'carboys' (rigid cylindrical containers housing the water) down the slope from the bridge and manhandle them into the battery room to decant into smaller vessels to feed their inexhaustible appetite. The line to Horsted Keynes closed to passenger traffic on 28th October 1963 and the remaining Down line was reduced to a siding, however it saw a considerable amount of traffic to the road-stone rail head constructed on the old station site at Ardingly. The items of maintenance left for us were CH60 signal (seen with its back to us bringing trains off the branch) and a telephone used for communication between the rail head and Haywards Heath signal box. Even this was not straight forward; the telephone wires had remained on the original overhead telegraph pole route but, being copper, were prey to thieves as we found one morning when called out to see why it was not working. The 'drop twin' cable we ran along the cess to take its place was a constant source of trouble for years afterwards. *March 1978*

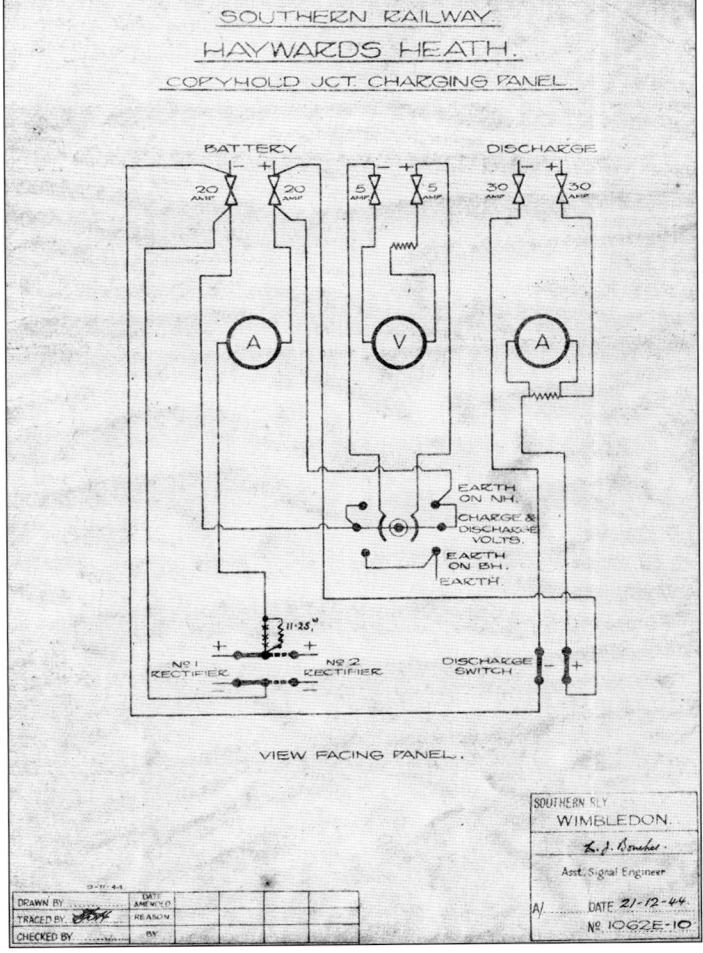

Right: The SR point battery charging diagram dating from 1944, which was displayed in its wooden frame to the very end.

Above: Looking south from Copyhold Lane bridge, the original junction layout is still extant as the fledgling Bluebell Railway's 'Spring Belle' heads towards Haywards Heath with ex-LB&SCR 'E4' Class No. 473 *Birch Grove* at the head of the train and ex-L&SWR 4-4-2T No. 488 providing assistance at the rear. The elevated notice to the right of the trailing points in the foreground is to warn staff that they are spring-operated 'self-acting' points and therefore any movement over them in the facing direction requires them to be clipped and scotched before it can take place. *31st March 1963, Ian D. Nolan*

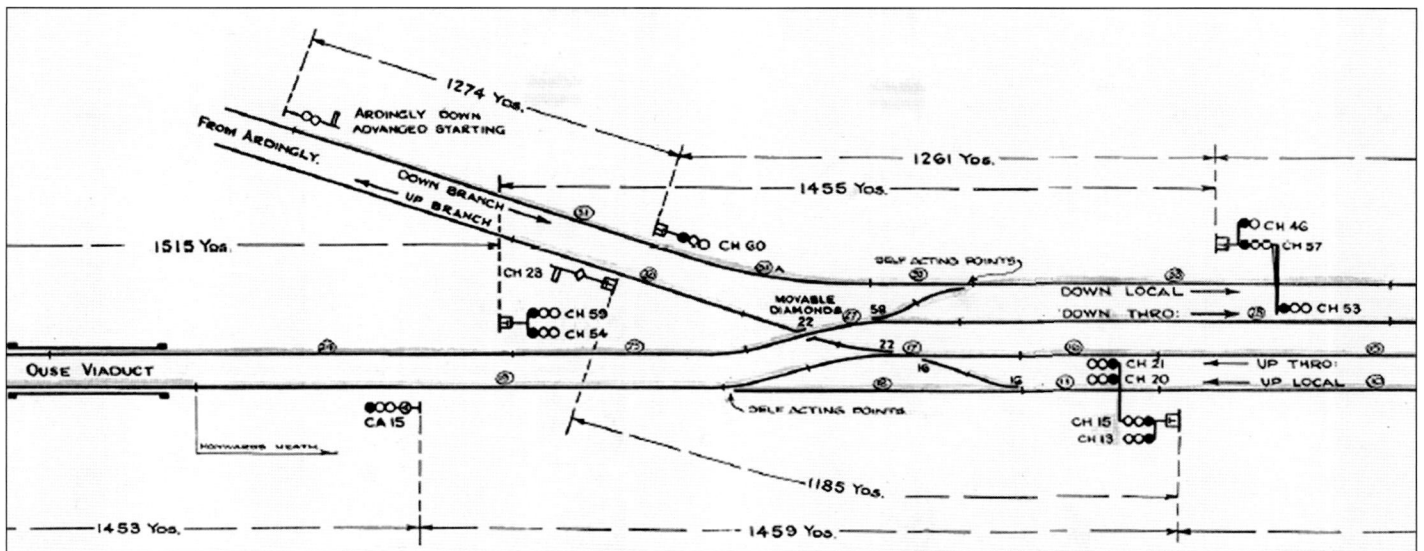

Copyhold Junction as resignalled in 1932 shows the running lines now paired by direction and all controls now on the new Haywards Heath signal box. Two point machines have been saved by utilising 'self-acting points' (spring worked) on both sets of trailers on the Up and Down Local lines respectively. The Down home signals CH54 and CH59 remained as separate three-aspect signals until the additional inner home signals were added between Copyhold and Haywards Heath, a position one feather then introduced in conjunction with a single four-aspect head. CH46 shunt signal (involved in the 1945 accident described earlier, where the driver apparently took it as the main aspect) can be seen in its original position. The mechanical signal CH23 was motor worked until it was renewed as a colour light, also acting as Ardingly's Up distant, during December 1953. The layout depicted here remained largely unchanged until the line to Horsted Keynes closed in 1963, when a much simplified arrangement was brought into work.

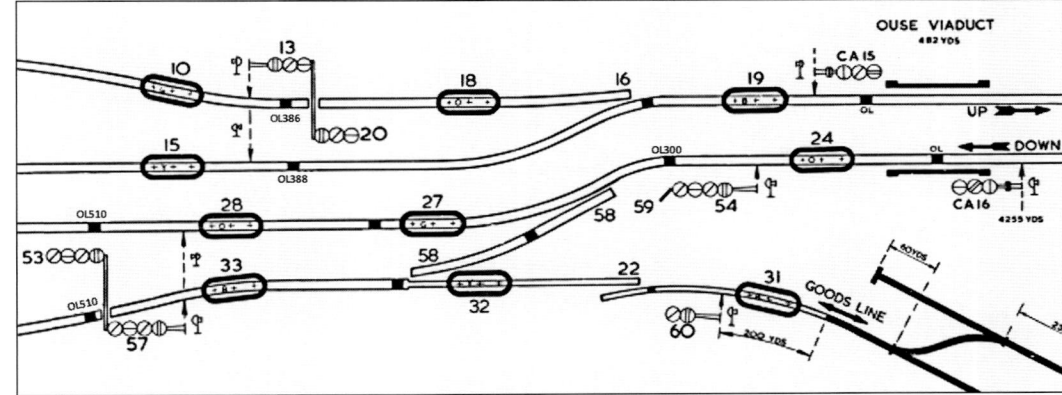

Right: An extract from the Haywards Heath signal box diagram showing the remodelled Copyhold Junction brought about by the closure of the branch to Horsted Keynes and the reduction of the remaining section to a goods line.

Facing Page Bottom: The simplified Copyhold Junction looking south in December 1980 with the tell-tale signs of the resignalling visible in the form of new concrete cable routes taking shape and troughs littering the route. The elevated structure at centre left is Copyhold T.P. (track paralleling) Hut, situated midway between Haywards Heath and Ouse Valley sub-stations.

On Saturday 16th December 1972 at around 22.00 a collision occurred between two passenger trains, thankfully with no casualties. Lieutenant Colonel I.K. McNaughton was the Inspecting Officer and the following is a summary from his report:

The 21.28 electric multiple-unit (EMU) stopping passenger train from Brighton to Victoria formed of 8 coaches, having passed CH13 (the signal protecting the converging junction with the Up Through line) at danger, was on the junction points when it was struck at the sixth vehicle by the 12-coach 21.45 Brighton to Victoria EMU express passenger train running under clear signals on the Up Through line.

Upon leaving Haywards Heath, on account of a gentle left hand curve, the Up Through line signal CH20 comes into view first at a distance of 572 yards followed by CH13 at 528 yards, a continuous full view of both signals is obtained from the Up Local line over a distance of 506 yards. In looking for a reason for this signal being passed at danger, I am satisfied that neither the siting (sic) of the signal, which was unmistakably positioned with respect to the line to which it applied, nor the prevailing weather conditions of patchy fog which was not thick enough to prevent the clear reading of colour light signals, nor the pattern of train working which was in accordance with an instruction that had been in force over 5 years, can be held in any way responsible. I can only assume that Drivers' failure to see the signal or to comprehend its message was the result of his allowing his concentration to wander from his job at the critical time as he approached it to the extent that he just did not react to a well-sited (sic) colour-light signal which was displaying a red aspect as he approached and passed it. The Automatic Warning System (AWS) of train control, by which a driver is warned on his approach to a signal at Caution or Danger by a horn sounding in his cab, which warning must be acknowledged, in default of which the brakes are automatically applied, might well have prevented this accident, and the fact that AWS is not provided on this important line cannot be allowed to pass without comment. This accident could have also been possibly averted had Signals CH13 and CH20 been provided with separate berth and overlap track circuits because the occupation of the overlap track circuit of Signal CH13 by the Slow train would have resulted in Signal CH20 changing from Green to Red when the Fast train was some 300 yards on the approach side of it, at which juncture an emergency brake application could have prevented a collision.

Accident report courtesy 'thebrightonbranchofaslef.yolasite.com'.

Left: The accident site showing the Up fast train on the left with the Up stopping train on the right. *Derek Osborne Collection*

Above: The aftermath showing both sets of points plain lined to enable a limited service to reopen. The line was not fully restored until 21st January. *Derek Osborne*

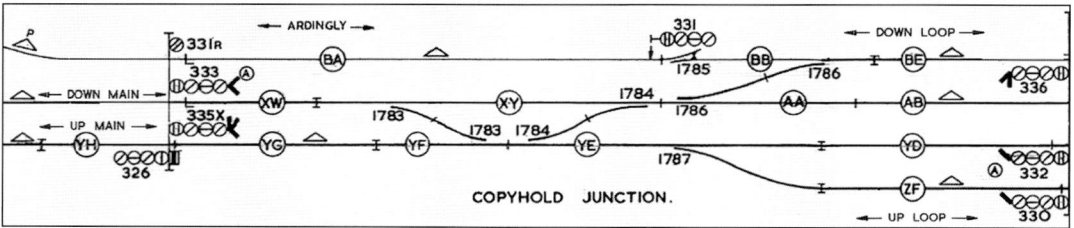

Left: As part of the Brighton Line resignalling, Copyhold Junction was remodelled further towards Haywards Heath and the final layout is seen here as controlled from Three Bridges.

Although not strictly within the remit of this book, it is worth briefly examining the ill-fated Ouse Valley Railway. During the railway boom of the mid-1860s with the rival South Eastern and London, Chatham & Dover railways proposing new lines towards Eastbourne and Brighton, the LB&SCR gained approval for a new 20-mile 'blocking line', to leave the Brighton main line just south of Ouse Valley Viaduct and continue towards Uckfield and Hailsham. By virtue of two triangular junctions on the Polegate to Redgate Mill Junction 'Cuckoo Line', it was ultimately intended to reach St. Leonards, an extra 18 miles. This would have provided a marginally quicker journey to Eastbourne and Hastings than via Keymer Junction and Lewes, but at huge cost. Construction of the line began in 1866, but with the collapse of the Overend & Gurney Bank, financiers of many major railway projects at the time, all work stopped in February 1867 and never resumed, probably to the relief of all the companies concerned but certainly not of the contractor who had 400 to 500 men employed on the scheme when he received the telegram to stop work. The left-hand photograph shows the abutments of what would have been the start of the line at Skew Bridge, with Copyhold Lane Bridge in the far distance; on the immediate right we have CA15 signal with its back to us with the new gantry carrying Copyhold Junction's soon to be outer home signals, T327 and T335R. The right-hand photograph shows a considerable length of embankment constructed at Kenward's Farm near Lindfield; further earthworks and abandoned brickwork can still be seen on its would-be journey towards Uckfield. *Left; February 1982. Right; September 1979*

16 – Ouse Viaduct

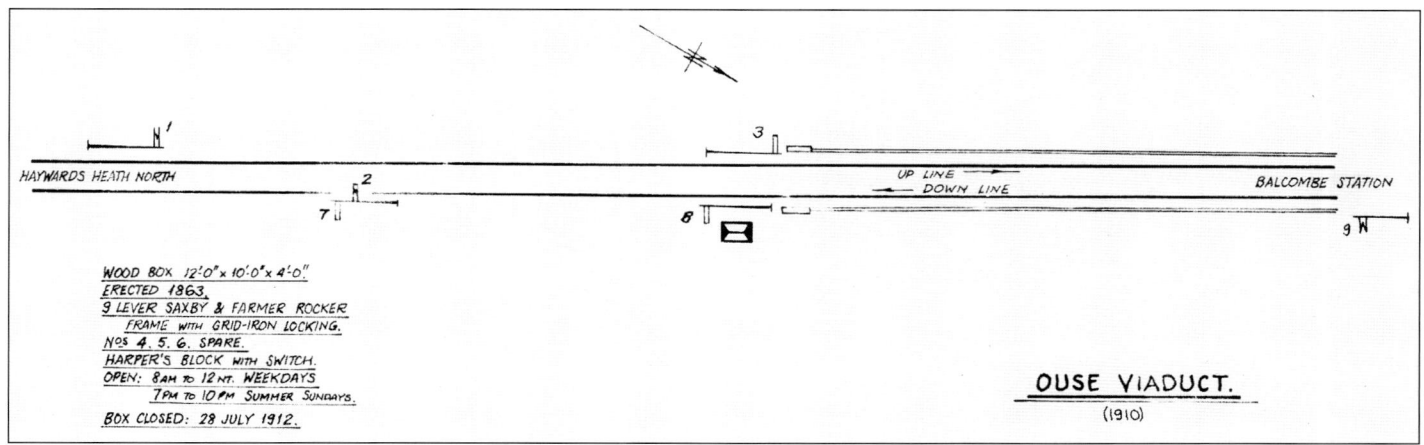

Courtesy Cuckfield Museum / Laurie Marshall Collection

Ouse Viaduct signal box layout in 1910 had just three signals in each direction. The Up home, No. 2, is mounted on the same post as the Down starting signal for better sighting around the left-hand curve on approach. When opened, Ouse Viaduct worked to Haywards Heath North to the south and Balcombe station signal box to the north, and was equipped with a Saxby & Farmer rocker frame with grid iron locking. With the Brighton company's drive to improve their train service, Copyhold and Stone Hall cabins (either side) were opened in 1912 to provide an extra block section, thus rendering this redundant. It closed in July 1912 and, as far as I am aware, no photograph exists. One anomaly is that No. 1 Up distant is shown to the left of the Up line whereas contemporary maps of the period and the photograph taken from Copyhold Bridge in the previous chapter showed it positioned on the right.

I make no excuse for including another photograph of a signalling location as it was installations like this that were the backbone of the 1932 resignalling. Quite simply mounted on old bullhead rails with cross members to take the enclosures, these were a common sight to all signal engineers working on this stretch of line until inevitable renewals saw them gradually replaced by more modern location cases. Not enough praise can be heaped on the Westinghouse Brake & Signal Company for providing the safety critical equipment that sat out in a raw environment such as this, experiencing temperature extremes from well below freezing to heatwaves, housed in metal boxes. WB&SCo. could, and did, make everything, and the plan of their extensive works (included in the Appendix) is well worth studying to appreciate the scope of what they could manufacture. (No computer aided design available then!) As mentioned previously, all installation was carried out by the Southern Railway's own installation teams, and also, it is probably safe to say, tested by them as well in the absence of separate teams of testing and commissioning staff. O.S. Nock, in his book *A Hundred Years of Speed with Safety* (a history of the W.B.&.S.Co), with reference to the later Waterloo area resignalling, writes:

The installation staff of the Southern Railway working to standard circuits and standard equipment, had by that time become so familiar with the various techniques that major 'openings' [his term for what we now call 'commissionings'] *were taken completely as a matter of course. I well remember the weekend of June 27-8 1936, on which the outermost section of the Waterloo job, to Hampton Court Junction, was brought into service, not because I was personally involved in the signalling, but because I was riding up from Portsmouth on the footplate of one of the non-stop expresses, then steam-hauled. At 11.00am on a Sunday morning one might perhaps have expected some slight technical 'hangovers' from the night of the changeover; but no. Running on time we entered the newly finished colour light area at 77mph and ran with clear signals to Clapham Junction.*

This seamless practice would have been developed during the Brighton Line resignalling scheme. CA15 was the first automatic signal past Copyhold on the 'Up' with its track circuit beyond the overlap and running over the Ouse Valley Viaduct, the above photograph depicting a typical installation for an automatic signal. With the neatly stencilled nomenclature on the lids, from left to right are: the IR (Inner Relay) which changed the signal aspect from yellow to green; the HR (Yellow Relay) changing from red to yellow (given the right conditions of course); CA15 track circuit relay, normally energised but de-energised when occupied by a train; the track circuit 20µF relay capacitor, and the power supplies as described in the Keymer Junction chapter. The lids were heavy in themselves and you had to watch your fingers when replacing them; you also learnt very quickly not to rest a hand on any of the metalwork when you were working amongst the terminals! The installer's standard test meter is sitting on the trunking on the left.

The Edward Wallis Collection

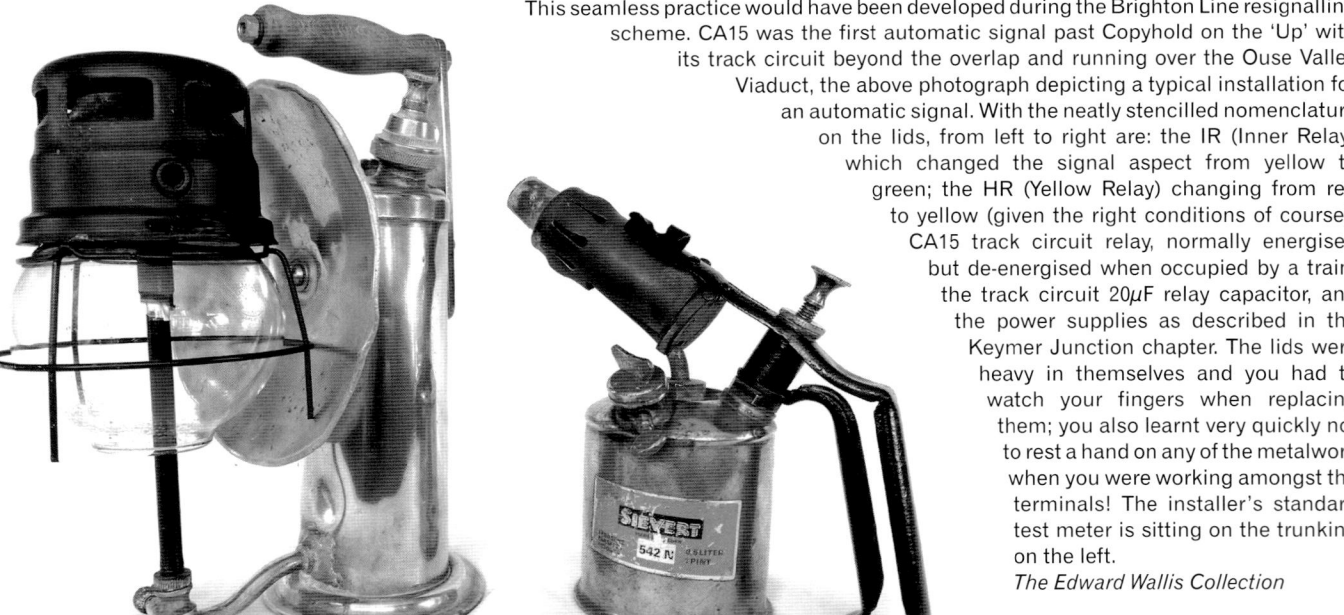

Left: A Tilley lamp and blowlamp, once everyday items of equipment.

Permanent way renewals 1970s style were an arduous process. During a 52-hour possession the S&T Department would be the first on the scene on the Friday night to remove all signalling equipment, cross cables etc. that would be in the way of the dig. The Permanent Way would then take over and start by cutting the old rails into lengths which would be lifted out bodily, complete with sleepers, and loaded onto flat wagons. The diggers would now come in to excavate the old ballast (on the Up road in this case) before depositing it into empty wagons positioned on the adjacent Down line. Once the correct depth had been reached, a membrane would be laid and ballast wagons run with the diggers taking out the requisite amount and laying a level stretch to ready the new formation (or solum). New sleepers carrying 'service rails' in 60ft lengths were next laid on to the fresh ballast, the rails fish-plated together and cad-welded to maintain an electrical path for the dc return (and signalling) currents. At this point we would be focused on reinstating the signalling equipment before the hoppers ran to cover everything with new ballast. The tamper would now run, the signalling would be tested and the line handed back to traffic with a speed limit imposed. A week later when the new track had bedded in, the service rails would be removed, continuous welded rail laid in and normal working would resume.
Both photos, October 1977

'The Railway' (and the Permanent Way in particular) were very good at looking after staff who, maybe through a work-related accident or poor health, were reassigned to 'light duties'. This could mean anything from becoming a 'runner' between offices carrying correspondence (easily done back then with a staff 'all stations duty pass'), to providing, literally, buckets of tea to the workforce in the middle of a permanent way job. For a mere 10p, a bucket of tea and mugs would appear and your given receptacle would be scooped into the brown liquid to provide your very own personal brew. An optional extra was a teaspoon of condensed milk.

In the top photograph a string of incandescent light bulbs provides a modicum of illumination at night. Tilley lamps were the only other method of lighting your way and, for that period in time, provided the best form of lighting possible. An S&T depot would have a goodly number of these whereas any P. Way depot would have many dozens to cater for night shifts on relaying/welding or any of the other myriad tasks that were carried out at night. Lighting the lamps, prior to carrying them out to site, was a task to be carried out in advance and could not be hurried. The reservoir would be filled with paraffin and a clamp of wadding material, kept in a 'gob pot' full of methylated spirit, positioned on the vapouriser tube below the mantle. Ensuring the valve feeding the burner was turned 'off', after a few pumps to build up pressure the wadding would be lit and the heating process would begin. After some lapse in time (estimated by experience) the valve could be turned to the 'on' position, thus feeding vapourised paraffin to the mantle. This would then 'pop' and if you got it right, the mantle would light with a gentle yellow glow. Extra strokes to build up more pressure could be applied, the mantle would turn bright white, and you were up and running. Get it wrong, however, and the whole thing would explode into a ball of flame. As 'health and safety' was pretty minimal back then, protestations from the inexperienced would just be met with *'Make sure you do it properly next time, then'*.

Another device that was used on a regular basis by departments such as the S&T, and could have similar consequences, was the blowlamp. Used out on the track and also in the workshop for making up bonding leads for stock and switch renewals etc., lighting one of these followed a similar process to the Tilley lamp. Patience and experience were again key as lighting the nozzle before the paraffin had vapourised could send a 10ft jet of burning fuel shooting through the air!

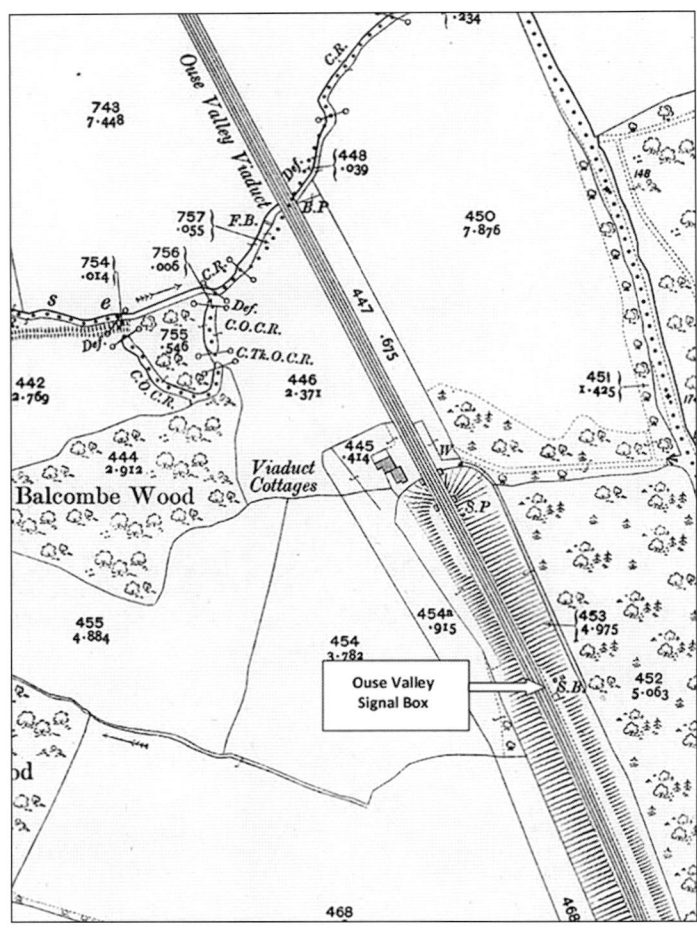

An extract from a 1910 map showing the south end of Ouse Valley Viaduct and the position of the signal box, with cottages provided for the signalmen.
Reproduced by permission of the National Library of Scotland

An unusual view of the Ouse Viaduct that shows to exceptional effect the sheer brilliance of the Victorian bricklayer. Necessitated by strict adherence to the 1 in 264 gradient, the structure is 492yds long, 96ft high and consists of 37 brick arches of 30ft span. Each of the tapering piers, varying in height from 40ft at the ends to 96ft in the centre, is pierced by rounded relieving arches (through which we are looking), each of differing heights. *October 1977*

Left: Looking along the west elevation, this is a structure that arguably enhances, rather than imposes upon, the landscape. All the materials for the construction were brought by barge up the River Ouse which was then navigable, something that is difficult to envisage today, where here it is little more than a stream. The Caen stone balustrades and pairs of Italianate pavilions at either end add that extra touch of class. Somewhere, close to where the cows are grazing, is the point where I lost a ring spanner. I was undoing a reticent bolt to take the lid off an impedance bond when my spanner flew from my hand, spun through the balustrading without touching the sides and descended to the valley floor. As far as I know, it is still there! *October 1977*

17 – Stone Hall

Stone Hall was purely an intermediate cabin to gain another block section. It contained a Brighton 30-lever standard frame with spare levers outnumbering the working ones by a ratio of 4:1. It worked to Balcombe station to the north and Copyhold to the south, closing on 3rd October 1932, probably not long after this photograph was taken. Signalman Bradford, seen at the window, may well be contemplating his career progression. *The Edward Wallis Collection*

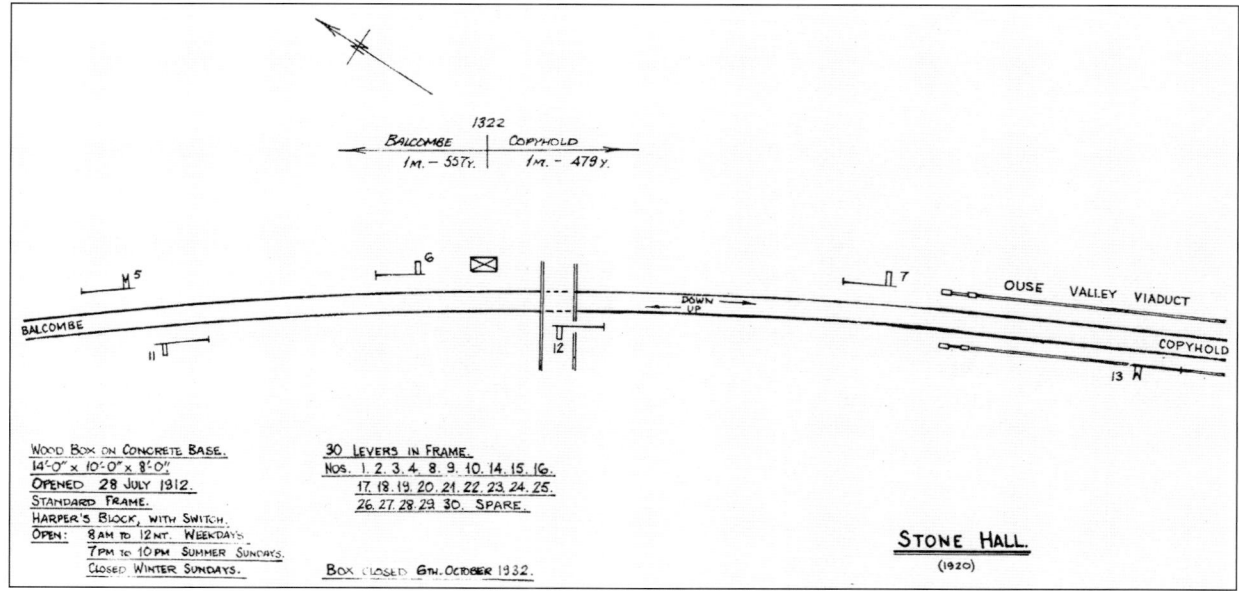

Stone Hall signal box layout in 1920. Intriguingly, the Up distant was situated on the viaduct, which must have made for an interesting climb for lamp changing or other maintenance activities. Stone Hall takes its name from the Dower House of the nearby Balcombe Place Estate.

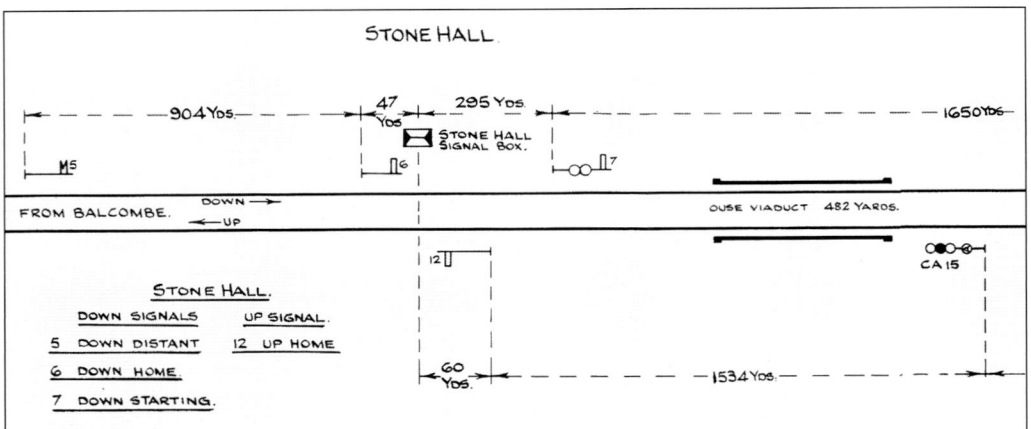

Left: Stone Hall signal box control area taken from the signalling notice for the opening of the new Haywards Heath signal box on Sunday 12th June 1932. This was to remain as a fringe box for barely four months before it, too, would be demolished. Approach lights take the driver from mechanical signalling on to a colour light area (in this case No. 7 towards CH54/CH59 signals) just as seen at Folly Hill earlier. CA15 signal worked as an automatic up to Stone Hall's No. 12 signal and No. 11 signal has been dispensed with. Note the discrepancy in the length of the Ouse Viaduct compared with the official measurement 492 yards.

Looking north from the adjacent overbridge seen in the previous map, No. 6 signal is 'off' indicating that a Down train must be imminent. The soon to be commissioned Ouse Valley sub-station can just be glimpsed in the distance; as with other early photographs of the third rail electrification, it seems that the preferred position of the conductor rail was on the outside of the running lines. The signalman's normal access to his place of work has been rudely interrupted but at least a plank of wood has been provided to help him clamber over the new cable routes. Length gangs may have been labour intensive but their maintenance was immaculate; you could have ridden your bicycle along the Up cess!
The Edward Wallis Collection

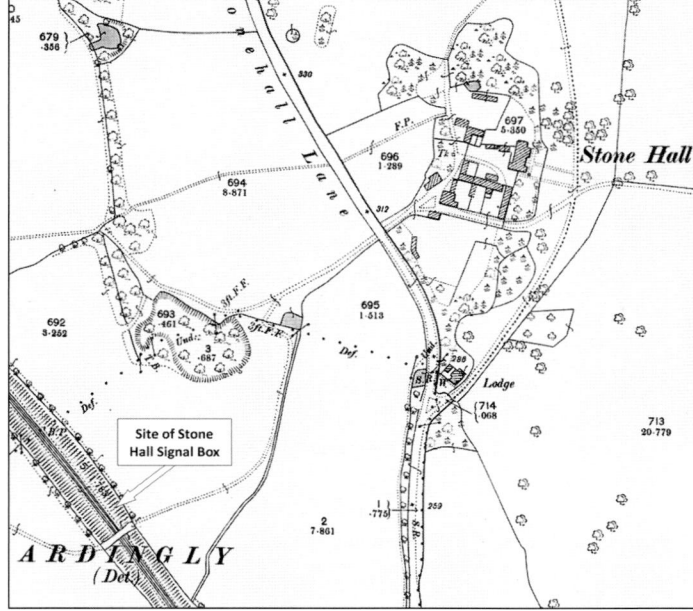

Above: The site of the 1912 Stone Hall signal box is still clearly visible in this March 2018 photograph.
Left: Stone Hall from an 1897 map, before the signal box was installed, with its eventual position marked. Balcombe Place is just north of Stone Hall.
Reproduced by permission of the National Library of Scotland

18 – Balcombe

Looking towards London from south of the station, this is a view of the tall signals so beloved of the LB&SCR, both the Down starter and the Up home signals having duplicate arms. No. 2 crossover, with its right-hand mounted shunt signals, can be seen along with the short section between the Down starting signal and the Down advance starting. Some serious tree clearance is taking place along the Up-side bank.
Laurie Marshall Collection

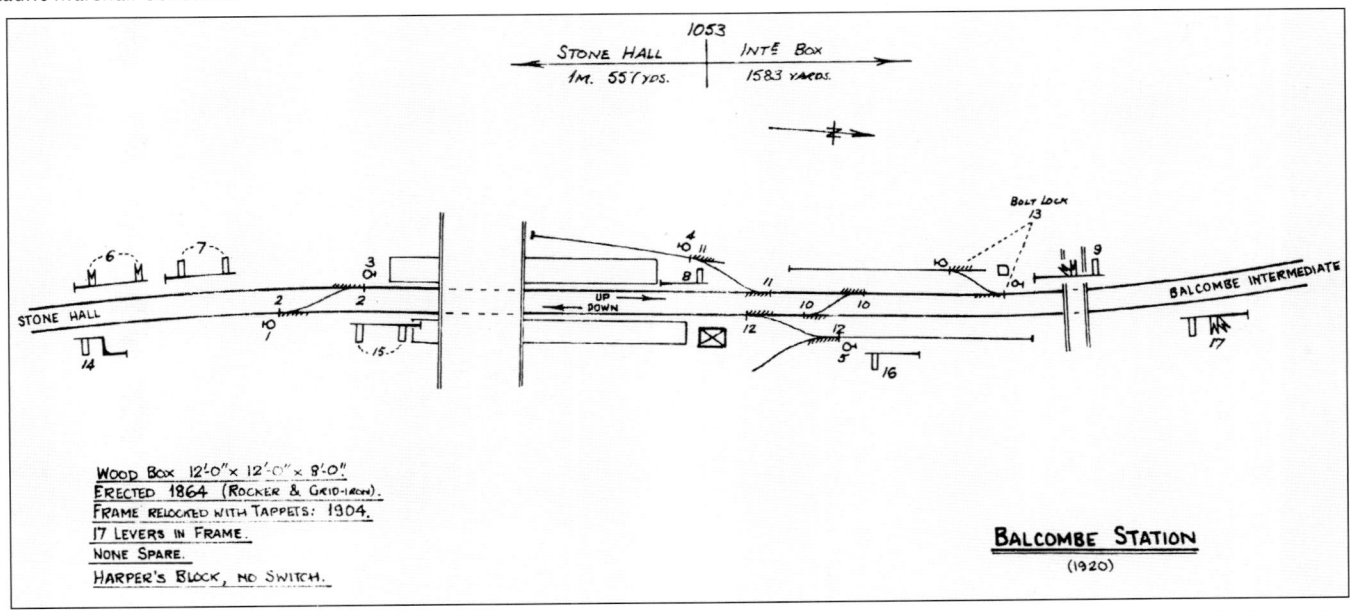

Balcombe Station signal box layout in 1920, working to Stone Hall to the south and Balcombe Intermediate to the north. Due to the short section from Balcombe Intermediate (less than a mile), Balcombe's Down distant was positioned beneath the Intermediate box's Down starting signal. Likewise Intermediate's Up distant was below Balcombe's Up advance starter.

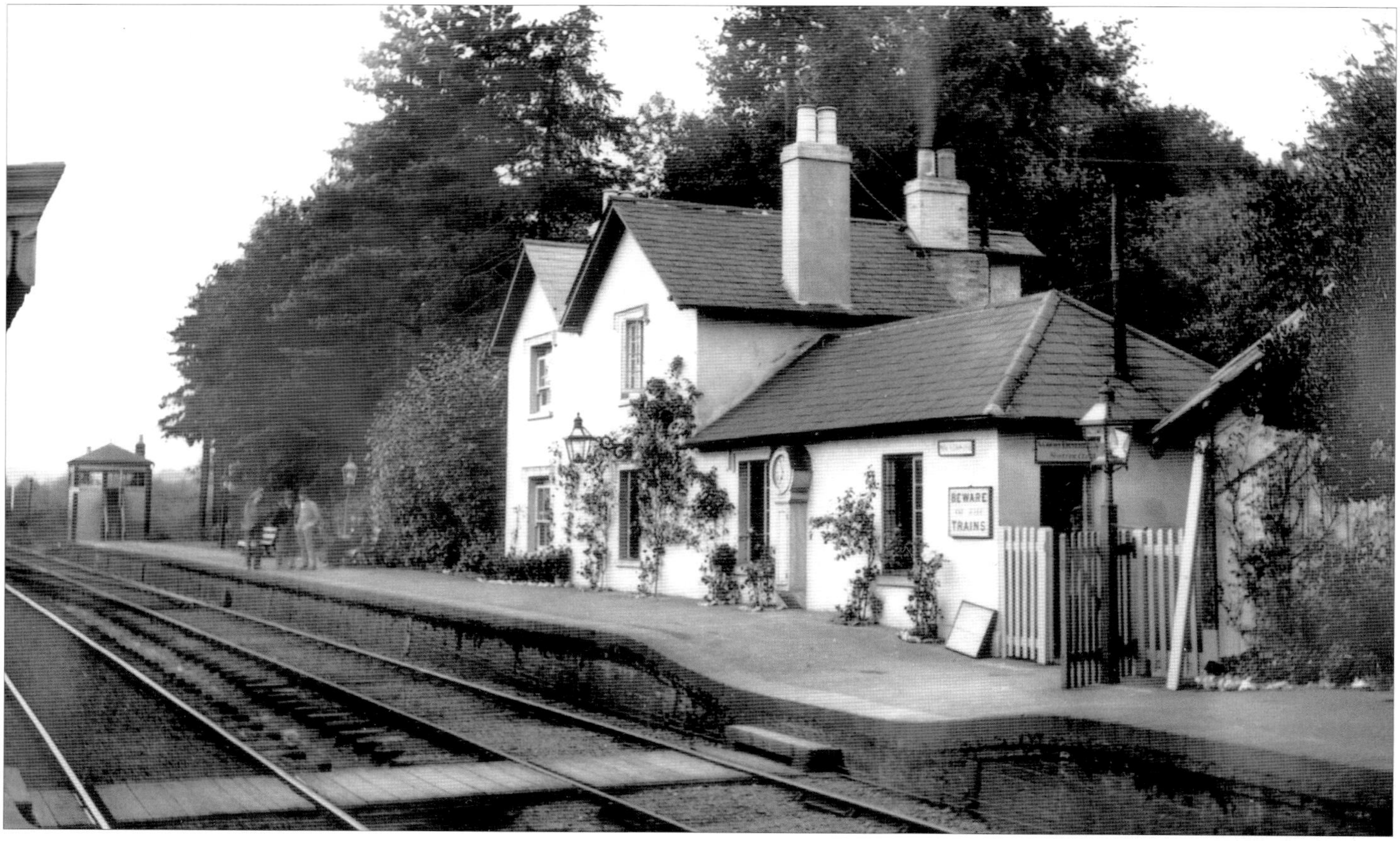
BEWARE
TRAINS

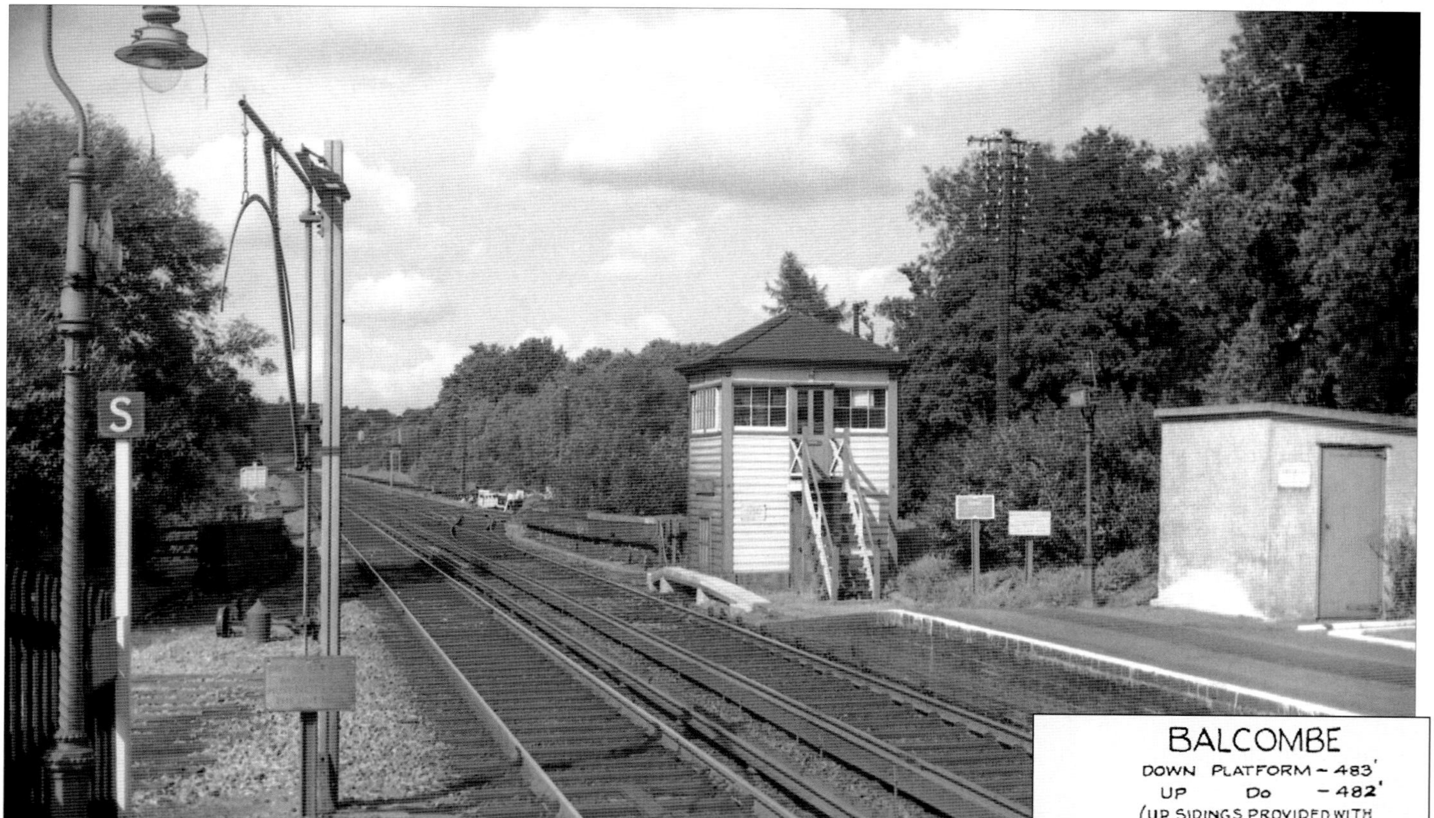
S

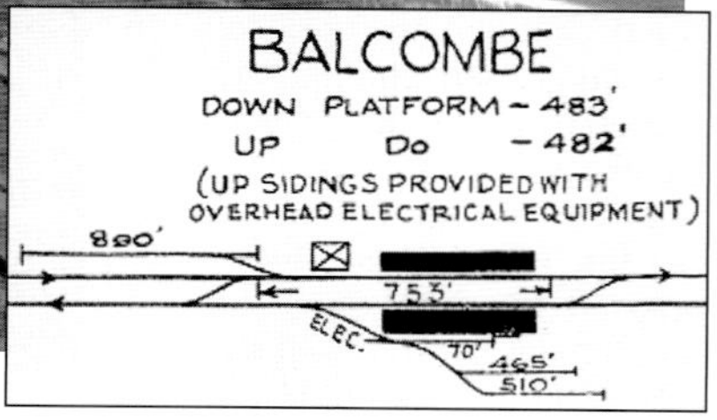
BALCOMBE
DOWN PLATFORM – 483'
UP Do – 482'
(UP SIDINGS PROVIDED WITH OVERHEAD ELECTRICAL EQUIPMENT)
890'
753'
ELEC.
70'
465'
510'

Right: Extract from the SR control diagram showing the electrified Up siding.

FACING PAGE TOP: With such a bucolic view, this could be a country station residing on almost any branch line in Sussex rather than the busy main line it sits on. With the trees in full leaf, the photograph appears to have been taken in summer so maybe it was a chilly morning as smoke from the chimney rises lazily from the open fire within the Balcombe station master's house. For the benefit of the station user, the name of the station clerk – *'Albert Ernest ...'* – is displayed over his office door. Before a footbridge was provided, the only means of crossing the line was by means of the lowered platform and foot crossing, although it makes you wonder how many sprained ankles there may have been from passengers caught out by the platform being not quite where they expected it to be! The 1864-built signal box nestles at the London end of the Down platform. *Laurie Marshall Collection*

FACING PAGE BOTTOM: Before the platform was lengthened, the original site of the Up siding can be seen trailing in behind the Up platform, the out-of-work loading gauge still extant with its bracket to stop the arm swinging out on to the main line atop the post. This siding had been electrified with an overhead catenary at 650V DC and used by Class '70' and '71' electric locomotives – the system was used in a number of yards and sidings on the Southern network where it was deemed dangerous to have staff coupling and uncoupling trains at ground level with a live third rail. The siding, which apparently dealt mainly with timber traffic from Balcombe Forest, was abolished on 6th August 1961, one month before this photograph was taken. *Denis Cullum, Lens of Sutton Collection*

ABOVE: A classic view of Balcombe station; time was running out for the signal box as it was to close the following year. Note the porter crossing between platforms.
28th June 1962, Ian D. Nolan

RIGHT: Looking north from the road bridge, the lattice iron footbridge led straight into the covered steps that connected the roadway above with the Down platform below. The stanchions in the Up sidings which once carried the 650V overhead line equipment are still in place.
28th June 1962, Ian D. Nolan

Above: In conjunction with the installation of the new footbridge (a SR 'Exmouth Junction Concrete Works' type rescued from the 1935 Gatwick Airport station which had closed in 1958), the access to the platforms from the road above was moved from the enclosed wooden staircase seen in the previous photograph to an extension of this bridge with steps leading up to the pavement. In conjunction with this the station house was demolished, retaining part of the building as facilities for the station staff. The Up-side canopy was shortened and the roof modified but the remaining structure was still an attractive feature. The 13.25 Victoria to Littlehampton passes through on 30th May 1968. *John Scrace*

Above: The end is nigh, as the concrete panels that will form the new Down platform extension are piled up in readiness for the signal box's demolition. The original connection to the Down siding has already been lifted. The extension had to cross the minor road that runs beneath the line here; the parapets of this can be seen just beyond the box and temporary speed restriction board.
Author's collection

Right: The method of constructing the platform extension can be seen from this photograph taken from the lane that runs below the station, the concrete sections cantilevered out onto a steel joist.
10th June 1978

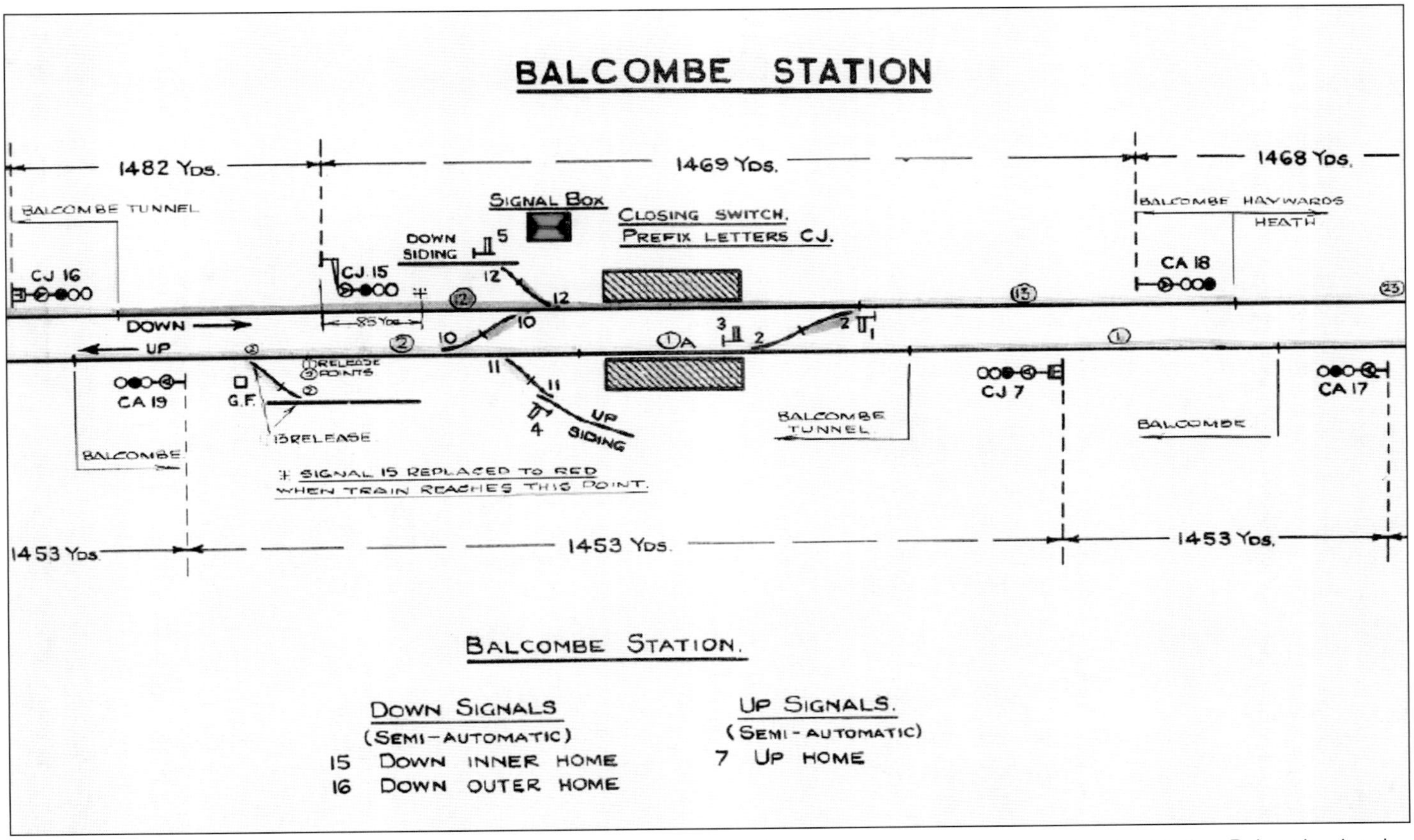

Above: Balcombe Station shown at the height of its powers, this extract taken from the signalling track plan of 1933. By this time Balcombe signal box was only opened 'as required' for freight working, maintenance, renewals or emergencies, the controlled signals working automatically when the box was closed. The crossover at the country end of the platform was abolished on 1st June 1963, the signal box following on Sunday 6th October.

Facing Page Bottom: Balcombe station in September 1977. The Haywards Heath Permanent Way gang attend to some work in the 4ft while their lookout keeps a watchful eye out for approaching trains.

Above: With both platforms now extended, Unit No. 2955 enters the station on a beautiful late spring day with the 14.12pm London Bridge to Brighton stopping service. The roses in the immaculately kept flower beds on the Down platform have been pruned back to encourage their summer growth while the sun casts shadows of the 'totem' signs on the Up platform. A lone worker strolls casually along with his jacket over his shoulder, still a while before any type of 'high visibility' jackets will be introduced. The ground frame that replaced the signal box is just out of sight off the end of the Up platform, but the crossover and Down siding have been relaid in their new position.
31st May 1968, John Scrace

Right: A later freight train derailment reduced the Down side extension to not much more than a pile of rubble; it was never rebuilt.
John Fowler

Below: The 'Office Copy' of the Balcombe signal box diagram almost at closure. Only five levers are left in work (two of them being king levers for opening and closing the box) with all the remaining points clipped and padlocked pending their transfer to the ground frame that was installed in its place to maintain basic functions. The Down siding (moved northwards along with the crossover to allow the platform extensions to be built) lasted long enough to be controlled from the ground frame but was abolished on 28th October 1973.

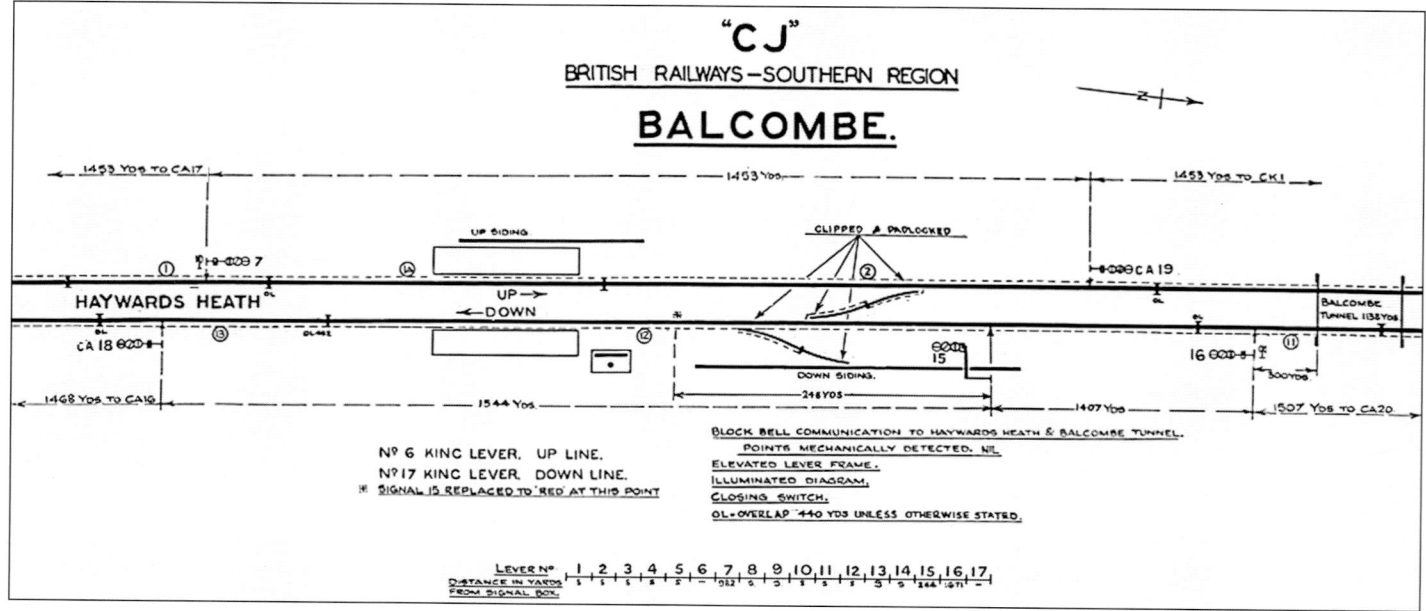

ABOVE: As built, both platforms ran through the short tunnel at the south end of the station, but after lengthening they were truncated at the entrances seen above. After the freight train derailment, however, the Down platform had a short extension added to the London end and the section through the bridge was reinstated with the relevant notices regarding limited clearances displayed. Just to the north of the bridge on the Down platform is an inscription carved into the soft sandstone rock *"W.F.C. The Strike of the LBSCR Engine Drivers Tuesday 26 March 1867"*, WFC thought to be the initials of a driver detained at Balcombe during the ASLEF dispute with the company that year.
Denis Cullum, Lens of Sutton Collection

RIGHT: The entry in the Weekly Operating Notice for October 1963 detailing the signal box's demise.

BALCOMBE TUNNEL AND BALCOMBE
BALCOMBE

To be carried out on Sunday, 6th October, commencing at 12.5 am.

Balcombe signal box will be abolished and all signals at present operated therefrom will in future be controlled from Balcombe Tunnel signal box.

Haywards Heath signal box will in future be in electrical communication with Balcombe Tunnel signal box.

BALCOMBE TUNNEL

The following signals will be re-prefixed as under:—

Old Prefix (Balcombe)	New Prefix (Balcombe Tunnel)	Description
CJ 7	CK 1	Balcombe Intermediate Up Home
CJ 16	CK 19	Balcombe Intermediate Down Outer Home
CJ 15	CK 18	Balcombe Intermediate Down Inner Home
(Balcombe Tunnel) CK 1	(Balcombe Tunnel) CK 2	Up Outer Home
CK 2	CK 3	Up line to Up Local Inner Home
CK 18	CK 21	Down Through Home

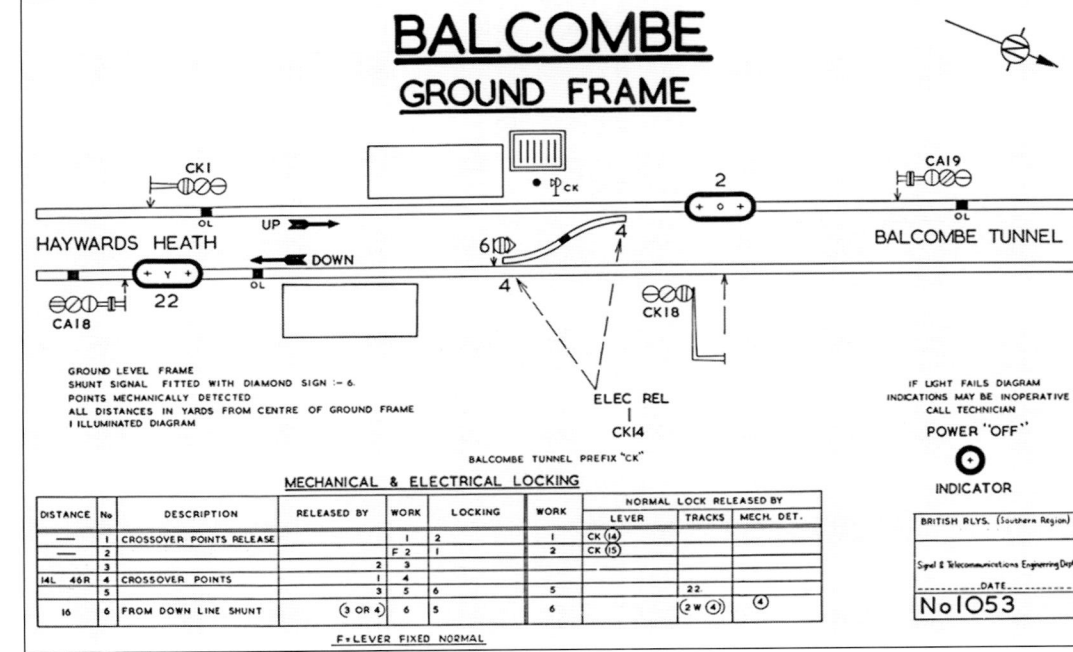

Balcombe ground frame, now with just a mere crossover and a single shunt signal. At this point it was still released from Balcombe Tunnel signal box, but when that was abolished during October 1978, the release was transferred to Three Bridges and the signals were renumbered accordingly. CK18 signal, still mounted on a cantilever structure over a non-existent siding, was transferred on to a straight post in October 1975. The crossover was taken out of use on 24th June 1983, pending removal as part of the Brighton Line resignalling, the ground frame following forthwith.

19 – Balcombe Intermediate

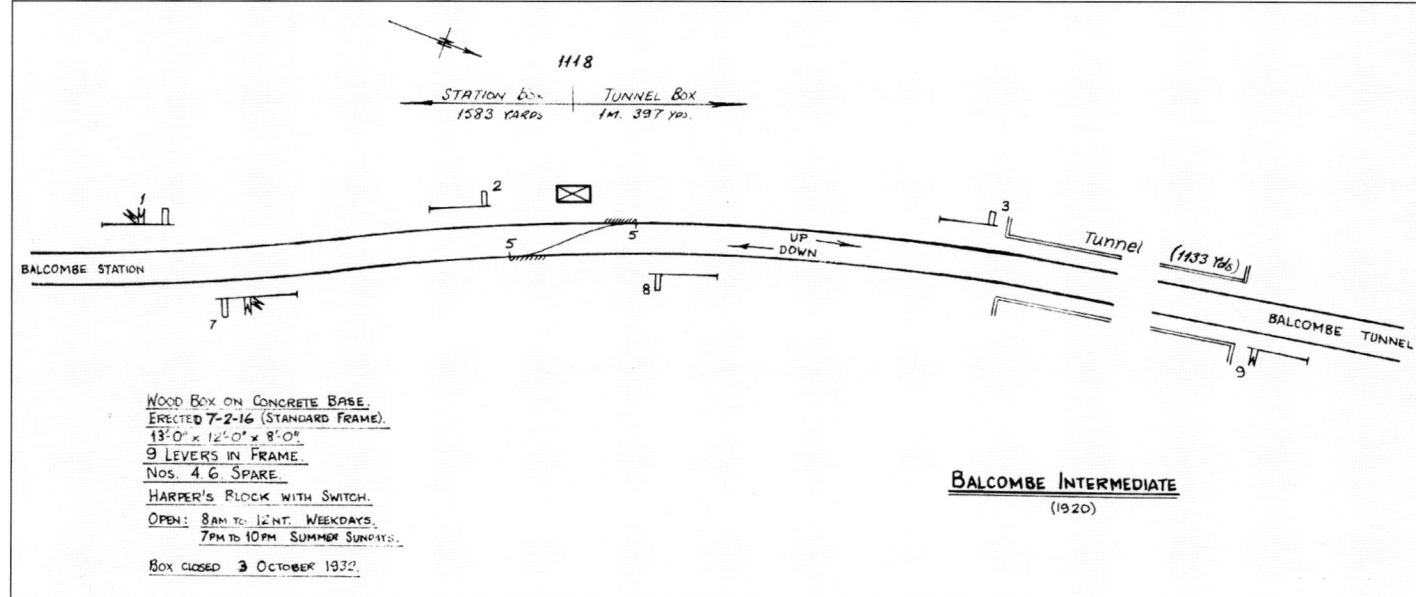

Balcombe Intermediate (similar in style to Clayton Cutting) was situated adjacent to the Up road in the cutting approaching the tunnel and must have been a lonely spot for the signalman during the dark winter months. Replacing a hut that was originally erected in 1906, this was another cabin opened in 1916 to split up the section between Balcombe Tunnel Junction and Balcombe station. The author is unaware of any photographs existing, but the following record card, dating back to its opening, has come to light. Maintenance areas did not change much, as the south end of Balcombe Tunnel was our maintenance extremity (northwards) when I was at Haywards Heath in the early 1970s.

20 – Balcombe Tunnel

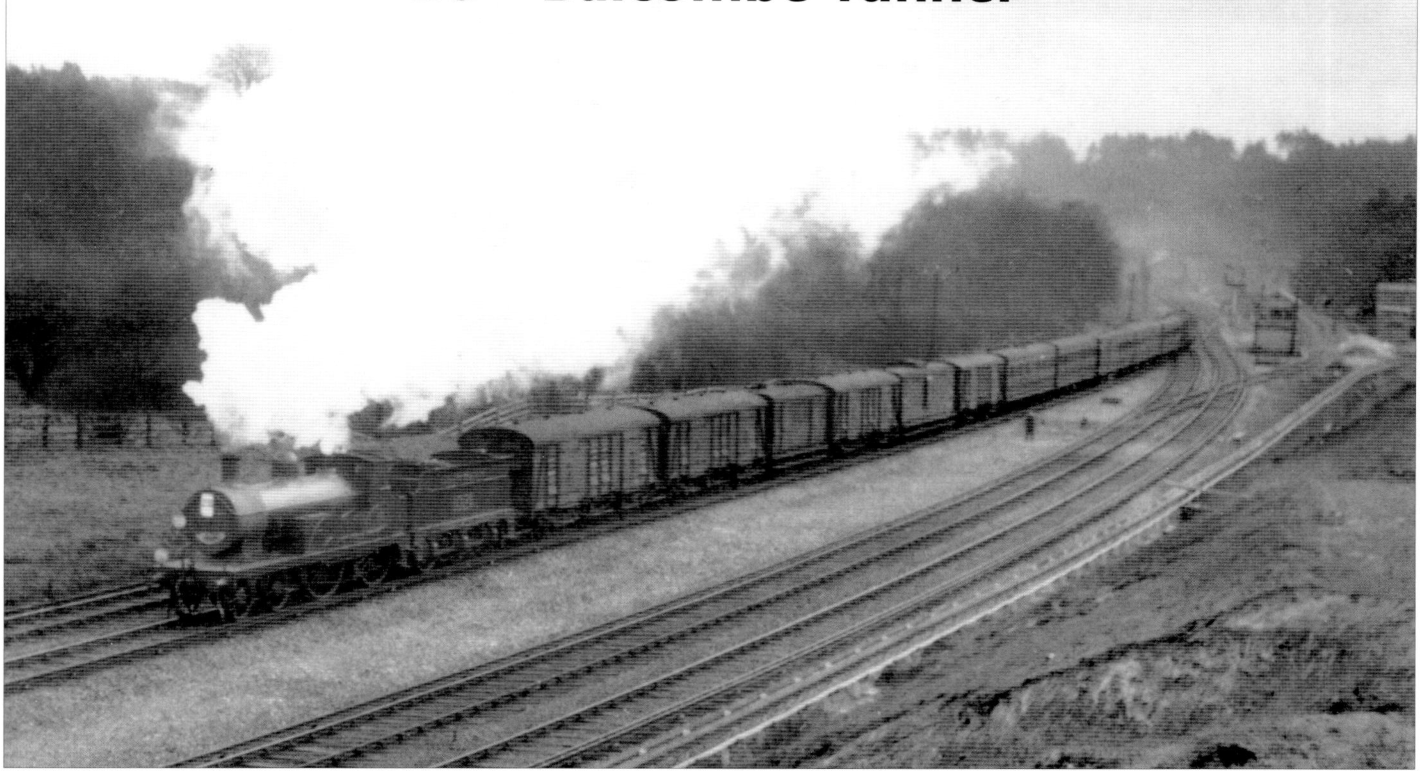

Above: This and the following two photographs are from similar positions but were taken some 51 years apart. Here, SR 'B1' Class 4-4-0 No. 1021 is bringing a train of mixed stock past the all-timber signal box in the dying days of mechanical signalling; the Up road splitting signals, No's 2 and 5, are visible in the middle distance. With all the trappings of electrification seen in place – the new sub-station in position and the third rail laid in – the formal opening of electric services to Brighton would begin on 30th December, with the public timetable starting on 1st January. *March 1932, KRM*

Right: A record card depicting the particulars of the signal box on 7th June 1966.

TS.18

BRITISH RAILWAYS - SOUTHERN REGION
DIVISIONAL SIGNAL ENGINEER'S (CTL.) OFFICE, CROYDON
SIGNAL BOXES AND GATE BOXES ON THE CTL. DIVISION

1. Place:- Balcombe Tunl Box.
2. Type of structure. Brick base - Wood Superstructure
3. Approx. dimensions (int.) 14'6" x 11'0"
4. Condition of S. box structure. Appears Good
5. Method of illumination a) Operating floor Electric.
   b) Ground floor
6. Type of lever frame. Mechanical LB&SC Frame.
7. " " " " support. Wood.
8. ~~Method of gate operation.~~
9. ~~Gate stops a) Road stops~~
   ~~b) Rail stops~~
10. ~~Type of C.B. battery.~~
11. ~~C.B. battery housed. Internal/external.~~
12. Leadaway a) External. ~~Timber~~/Metal plate.
    b) Internal. Timber/~~Metal~~ plate.
13. Date when particulars taken. 7 June 1966
14. Voltage of electric supply and where from. 110 Volts. Signal Engineer's (off Sub Station)
15. ~~15~~ tele. circuits in box. No 21-90-140-634.
16. Unusual features. Signed...................... District Inspector

per

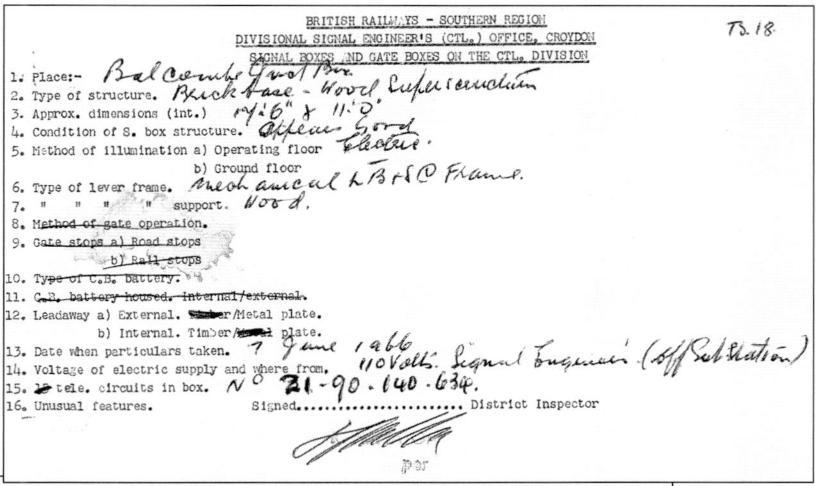

Below: Balcombe Tunnel's area of control in 1920, when the Up splitting distant signals were north of the tunnel; also No. 17 Down starting signal is positioned in the Up cess to improve the sighting around the left-hand curve on approach. The facing points to the 'Overshoot Road' were abolished on 15th November 1959, with the siding renamed 'Sub Station Siding' and the connection realigned to the Up Local line. This arrangement lasted until October 1972 when the points were taken off the lever frame to remain clipped and padlocked for 'use as required'.

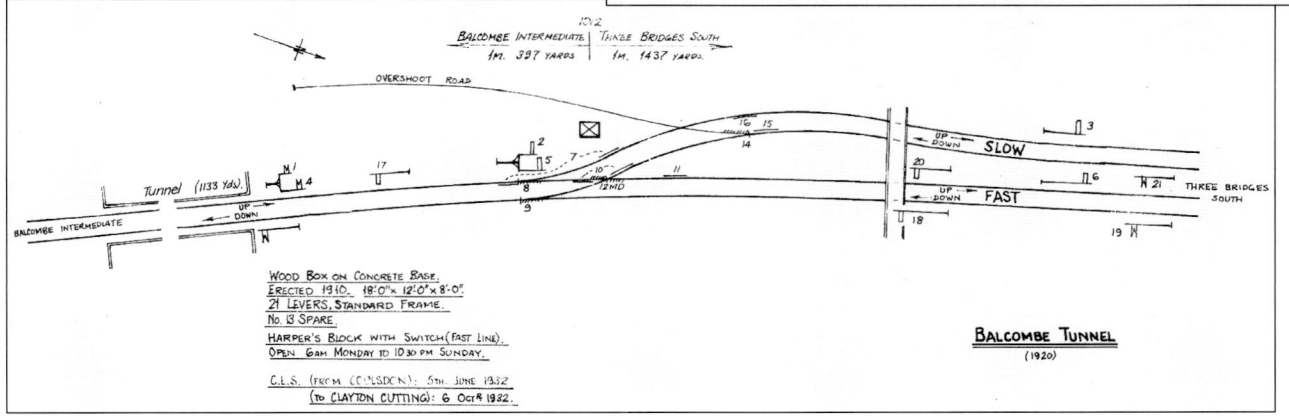

SOUTHERN RAILWAY.

Signal Instruction No. 17, 1932.

INSTRUCTIONS TO ALL CONCERNED
AS TO THE

INTRODUCTION OF COLOUR LIGHT SIGNALS
(In place of existing Semaphore Signals)

BETWEEN COULSDON NORTH No. 2 AND BALCOMBE TUNNEL SIGNAL BOXES
(VIA QUARRY LINE);

AND

ABOLITION OF EXISTING CANE HILL, QUARRY, WORSTED GREEN, EARLSWOOD STATION, TINSLEY GREEN, AND THREE BRIDGES NORTH AND SOUTH SIGNAL BOXES;

ALSO

RE-NAMING OF LINES BETWEEN EARLSWOOD JUNCTION AND BALCOMBE TUNNEL

ON A DATE TO BE ADVISED.

Rules 70, 71 and 72 to be observed. Drivers to keep a good look out for hand signals.

The existing semaphore running signals on the down and up Quarry lines between Coulsdon North No. 2 and Earlswood Junction signal boxes, and on all lines between Earlswood Junction and Balcombe Tunnel signal boxes, will be abolished, and colour light signals installed in lieu thereof.

The existing Cane Hill, Quarry, Worsted Green, Earlswood Station, Tinsley Green and Three Bridges North and South signal boxes will be abolished. Earlswood Junction and Three Bridges Central signal boxes will be known in future as Earlswood and Three Bridges respectively.

The running lines between Earlswood Junction and Balcombe Tunnel will be re-named as follows :—

Existing Name.	New Name.
Down fast.	Down through.
Up fast.	Up through.
Down slow.	Down local.
Up slow.	Up local.

A diagram showing the new signals and their location is attached to this notice, the signals being prefixed by letters to denote from which box the signals are worked, as follows :—

Prefix letters.	Signal box from which signals are operated.
C.T.	Coulsdon North No. 2.
C.S.	Star Lane.
C.R.	Earlswood.
C.Q.	Salfords (local lines only).
C.P.	Horley North.
C.N.	Horley South.
C.M.	Gatwick.
C.L.	Three Bridges.
C.K.	Balcombe Tunnel.

NOTE.—Star Lane, Salfords, Horley North, Horley South and Gatwick signal boxes will be switched out of circuit for certain periods and during the time these signal boxes are so closed the running signals will work automatically.

Automatic signals will be prefixed by the letters C.A.

Plates bearing these prefix letters and the number of the signal will be fixed to each signal post carrying running signals.

The new colour light running signals will show three, four or two aspects and will be known as automatic, semi-automatic or controlled signals, viz. :—

(a) Automatic signals are those which will not be worked from a signal box but which will be controlled by track circuit only.

(b) Semi-automatic signals are those which will be controlled from one or more signal boxes when such boxes are open, but which, when the boxes are closed, will work automatically and be controlled by track circuit only.

(c) Controlled signals are those which will always be worked from a signal box.

In certain cases 2-aspect colour light shunt signals will be provided.

Each 3-aspect running signal will consist of a group of three lamps, and the aspect exhibited at any one time will be (a) a red, or (b) one yellow, or (c) a green light.

Each 4-aspect running signal will consist of a group of four lamps, and the aspect exhibited at any one time will be (a) a red, or (b) one yellow, or (c) two yellow, or (d) a green light.

Each 2-aspect running signal (except those in tunnels) will consist of two lamps, and the aspect exhibited at any one time will be either (a) a red or (b) one yellow light.

Each 2-aspect Tunnel signal will consist of two lamps and the aspect exhibited at any one time will be either (a) one yellow or (b) a green light. (NOTE.—A red aspect will NOT be provided in Tunnel signals).

230009—1

The front page of the signalling notice for the substantial commissioning that took place over the Sunday morning of 5th June 1932. The logistics for such an event must have been extraordinary, with extra staff brought in from all parts of the system, needing mess facilities and probably accommodation in vans or coaching stock. The railway was brought successfully back into work within the mere six-hour timescale allowed by the operators. See Appendix 3 for an eyewitness account of the resignalling of 48 track miles of main line railway, from a 1932 Southern Railway publication.

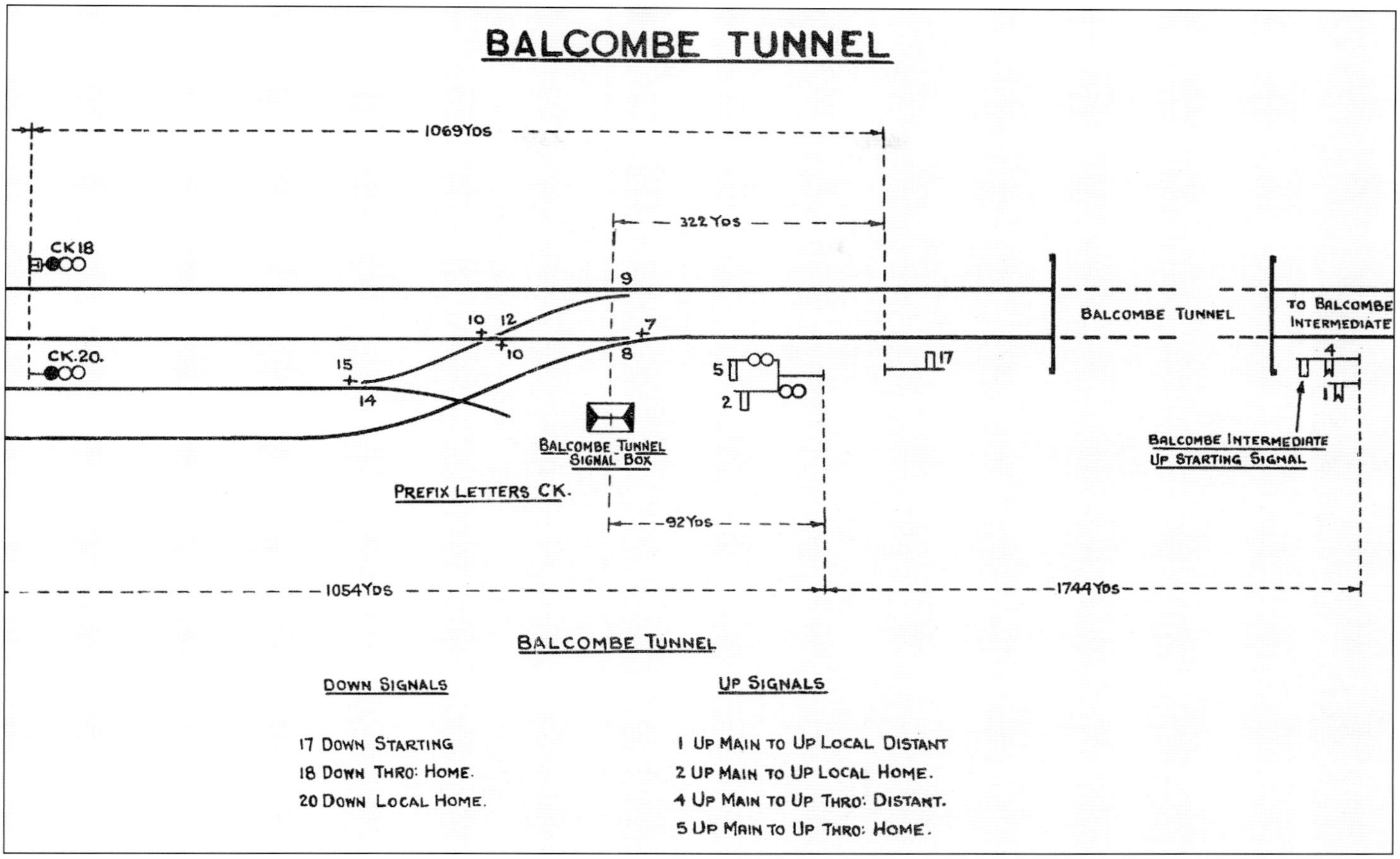

BALCOMBE TUNNEL

Down Signals
- 17 Down Starting
- 18 Down Thro: Home.
- 20 Down Local Home.

Up Signals
- 1 Up Main to Up Local Distant
- 2 Up Main to Up Local Home.
- 4 Up Main to Up Thro: Distant.
- 5 Up Main to Up Thro: Home.

Above: This extract, taken from the 1932 signalling notice, shows Balcombe Tunnel between commissionings. Colour light signalling was introduced from Coulsdon North to here on 5th June 1932, with the route southwards to Copyhold following on 6th October. The Up distant signals have been relocated south of the tunnel (with Balcombe Intermediate's Up starting signal above) while temporary approach lights below Balcombe Tunnel's Up home signals lead in to the new colour light area.

Below: Balcombe Tunnel signal box's area of control immediately after the resignalling worked to Three Bridges to the north and, during normal operating conditions, Haywards Heath to the south. All the points have remained mechanically worked, the crosses adjacent to the point numbers denoting the facing points locks. An interesting comparison can be made between this drawing and the 1920 layout as the number of spare levers has increased from one to eight.

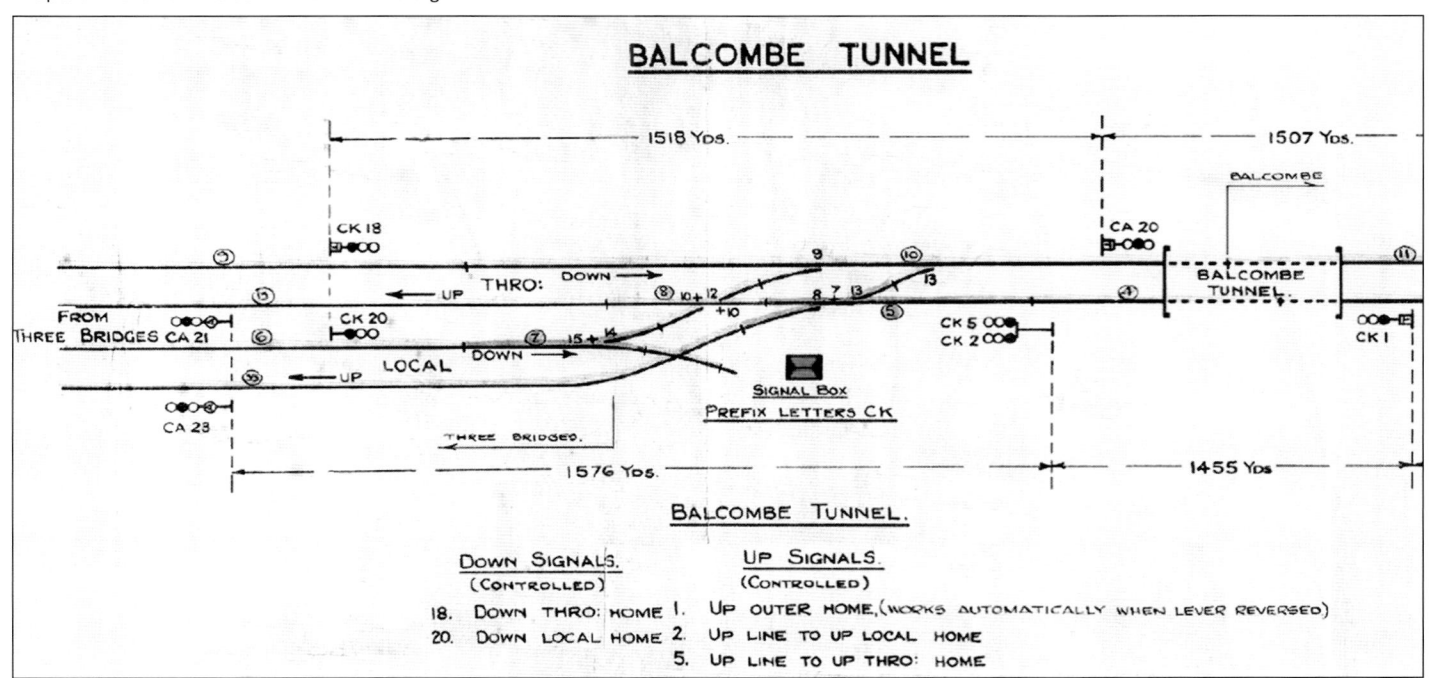

BALCOMBE TUNNEL.

Down Signals. (Controlled)
- 18. Down Thro: Home
- 20. Down Local Home

Up Signals. (Controlled)
- 1. Up Outer Home, (works automatically when lever reversed)
- 2. Up Line to Up Local Home
- 5. Up Line to Up Thro: Home

Left Top: Two services pass each other during June 1978, the only real change in the layout (reference the photograph on p. 161) being that the Up siding connection has switched allegiance to the Up Local line.

Left Center: Fast forward to 1983 and all is swept away. With the new junction now positioned further to the north, the 17.24 Brighton to Gatwick Airport passes the recently lifted track bed of the old local lines, with just the long siding to the sub-station for company.
16th July 1983, John Scrace

Left Bottom: Still bearing the original LB&SCR nameboard, this is Balcombe Tunnel Junction signal box on 15th July 1969. Replacing a structure that first existed five chains further south, the new box was brought into work in conjunction with the quadrupling that opened to here on 22nd May 1910. Balcombe Tunnel was the name of the first cabin that had opened in the early 1860s (the suffix 'Junction' was not added until 1873) so the nameboard may have been transferred over.
Edwin Wilmshurst

Facing Page Bottom: Looking northwards from the tips of No. 8 Up Local/Up Through points (normal for the Up Through), the expanse of Balcombe Forest is evident in the background and highlights the remoteness of this signal box. A relic of the steam age still exists in the form of a circular enamel sign, facing the camera adjacent to the 50 PSR, which warns enginemen that they are entering a *'zone of specially high fire risk'* and therefore not to shovel out hot ashes! This sign took the form of a black conifer silhouetted on a yellow background, the one on the right (exit from zone) being a black vertical band against the same colour. A trusty Westinghouse 'M3' point machine is seen in the foreground with its back detector (to ensure the 'heel' of the points are closed) beyond, its back-drive snaking up the 6ft. Under the Brighton Line resignalling the junction moved north of Parish Lane overbridge in the background and on to the straight section of track approaching Three Bridges. *June 1978*

Right: Looking through an open window, this is a glimpse of the inside of the signal box showing the 21-lever Brighton standard frame, the letters LBSCR embossed on the 'drop box' at the bottom of every lever. The signalman has pulled off for trains on both the Up and Down through lines, the Up train making its presence known by occupying the first track circuit on the diagram. The splendid block bell is from Haywards Heath, whereas the Up Through and Local lines from Three Bridges must make do with slightly more mundane gongs. At the far end of the block shelf is the emergency replacement switch for CA20 signal, protecting the tunnel on the Down Road. *October 1977*

Above: The signalman has 'pulled off' for an approaching train to take the route along the Up Local line as CK3 signal on the left exhibits a green aspect. After some forty-six years in service the original 1932 Westinghouse signal heads are still in place along with their 'pigs' ears' for close-up viewing. The signal prefix plates have taken on the new form for controlled signals (white letters on a black background) and a signal post telephone (SPT) has also been added to give direct communication with the signal box. The rudimentary wooden walkway can be seen for the driver to access the SPT, the third rail correctly boarded in the vicinity of his stopping point. *June 1978*

Having just emerged from the tunnel, a Class '33' runs light engine towards the junction. The photograph again shows the considerable works that took place in anticipation of the continuation of the quadrupling through here, not just the earthworks but also the five-arch overbridge built to accommodate the extra tracks that were never to be. The hut in the foreground was where the Permanent Way staff kept Tilley lamps and paraffin for their daily patrols through the tunnel.
Derek Osborne Collection

The north portal of Balcombe Tunnel taken through the cab window on a snowy April morning in 1937. The telegraph pole route cuts a swathe through the trees (another job for the local Permanent Way gang was keeping it clear), whilst a warning board adjacent to CA20 signal cautions drivers that a speed restriction of 15mph is in place a mile further ahead. The third rail switches to the 6ft here to enable anyone working within the tunnel to find a safe recess without having to clamber over it. The diamond sign facing the Up road is a coasting board enabling motormen to shut off power whilst still maintaining a constant speed. *H.C. Casserley*

Right: Looking through the tunnel in June 1978 a couple of reminders of the past still remain. Over the top left of the tunnel arch, the remnants of the whitewashed brickwork that would once have given a more definitive background to Balcombe Intermediate's Down distant signal can just about be seen, also the old pole route clearing through the trees over the top is just discernible. Although approached by curves at both ends, the tunnel itself is straight.

Facing Page Bottom: Taken northwards from the accommodation overbridge seen in the photograph of the Class '33' above (shown as 'Rastrick' in the BR Bridge Book), West Country Class No. 34108 *Wincanton* brings a Southern Counties Touring Society rail tour through Balcombe Junction on 19th March 1967. The photograph shows to good effect the widening of the cutting here which would have formed the continuation of the quadrupling should it have been carried out, now boasting no more than the path that leads from the signal box to the tunnel mouth. Access to the junction was from the A23 at Pease Pottage and down Parish Lane, a meandering and rutted track through the forest that was mostly impassable to motor vehicles during winter months, necessitating a long walk; not so good with a heavy tool-bag when you were meant to be attending a failure. The nearest telegraph pole has now become a terminal pole where the wires have been brought down to a termination box to transfer their functions on to a multi-core cable for the route through the tunnel, doing away with the original route over the tunnel itself. *John Scrace*

The closure notice for Balcombe Tunnel signal box taken from the Weekly Operating Notice of October 1978.

> **SUNDAY, 22 OCTOBER – BETWEEN THREE BRIDGES AND HAYWARDS HEATH.** – Balcombe Tunnel signal box will be abolished and all points and signals worked therefrom will be transferred to the control of Three Bridges.
>
> At Balcombe Tunnel the crossover, at present secured out of use, will be connected to a new 3-lever Balcombe Tunnel ground frame which will be released from Three Bridges signal box. A telephone giving communication with the signal box will be provided at the ground frame. A position light shunting signal will be provided to control movements from Down Main line to Up Local or Up Through line.
>
> At Balcombe station the ground frame will in future be released from Three Bridges signal box.
>
> Certain signals will be re-numbered as follows:—
>
> | Line | Location | Existing No. | New No. |
> |---|---|---|---|
> | Down Through | Three Bridges side of Balcombe Tunnel Junction | CK.21 | CL.48 |
> | Down Local | Three Bridges side of Balcombe Tunnel Junction | CK.20 | CL.42 |
> | Down Main | Between Balcombe tunnel and Balcombe station | CK.152 | CL.152 |
> | Up Main | Haywards Heath side of Balcombe Station | CK.151 | CL151 |
> | Up Main | Between Balcombe tunnel and Balcombe Tunnel Junction | CK.3 | CL.34 |
>
> All telephones giving communications with Balcomne Tunnel signal box will in future be connected to Three Bridges signal box. The signal post telephones concerned extend as far as CL.152 on the Down line and commence at signal CA17 on the Up line.

Left: The ignominious end of Balcombe Tunnel signal box after some 68 years in service, the unremarkable REB (Relocatable Equipment Building) visible to the left of the wagons now housing the relay interlocking worked from the lever frame at Three Bridges. *March 1979*

In 1932, Balcombe Junction was the fringe between commissionings and was to fulfil this function again, as can be seen in this extract from the signalling notice dated 26th/27th March 1982. The two signals positioned in the tunnel have smaller heads to fit within the restricted structure gauge and have their yellow aspects placed at the top and at the bottom to maximise the distance, and so accentuate the double yellow aspect. AWS is provided for the new signalling whereas the existing signalling remains without.

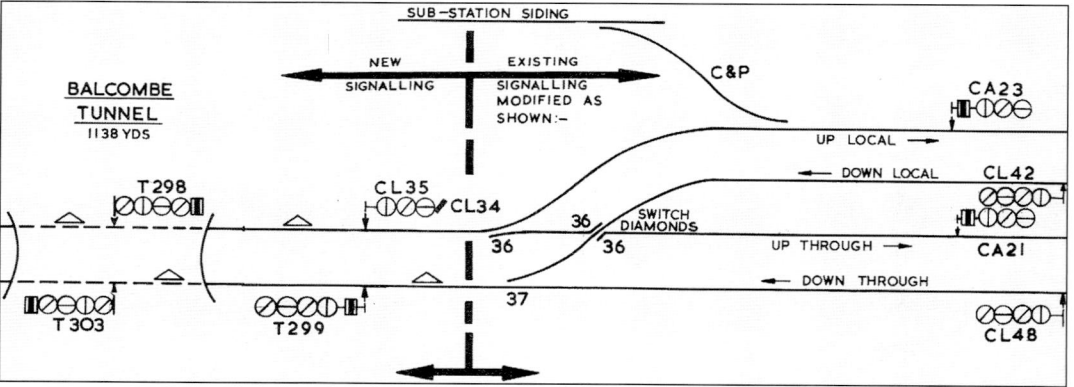

The final layout is controlled from the new Three Bridges panel, commissioned during June/July 1983. Crossovers for reversible working are in place with the sub-station siding still in situ, clipped and padlocked

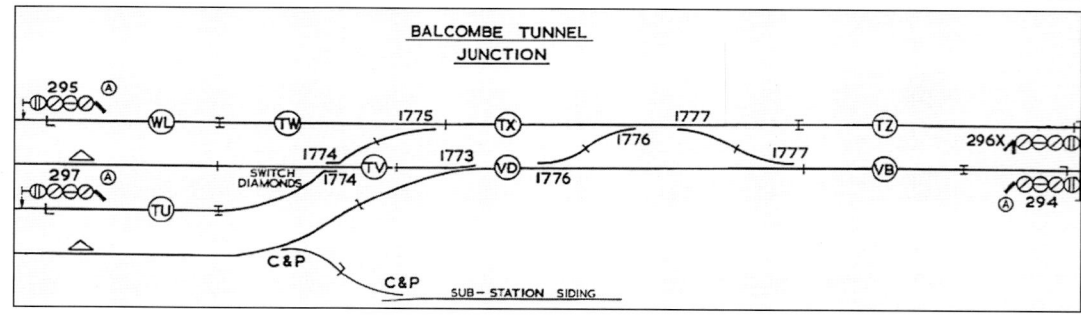

21 – Three Bridges

Taken from the new station forecourt this is a fine shot of the Fox Hotel, built by the railway company and conveniently situated directly opposite the front of the new Three Bridges station entrance. Another Nalder & Collyer's establishment (as was the Liverpool Hotel in Haywards Heath), it was demolished in 1989 when the road was converted into a dual-carriageway necessitating the complete rebuilding of the underbridges seen here. This was not quite the end for the venerable public house since, as part of the redevelopment in association with the new road building, the Fox was rebuilt as the 'Snooty Fox' slightly further to the north than its predecessor. The old North signal box sits in the centre near to the end of its life, with the estate offices of A. Eversley Hardwick (Land Surveyors and Estate Valuers) on the extreme left. Perhaps it is the photographer's car in front of the bridge, enhancing the composition of the picture. *Roger Resch Collection*

Class 'B1' 0-4-2 No. 177 *Southsea*, designed by William Stroudley and built at Brighton, brings a Down passenger train past the first Three Bridges North signal box, probably at around the turn of the century. Above the locomotive is the starting signal for the Up Fast platform, while behind the imposing water tower is the signal for starting away from the Up Loop line, this photograph taken before the quadrupling.
Roger Resch Collection

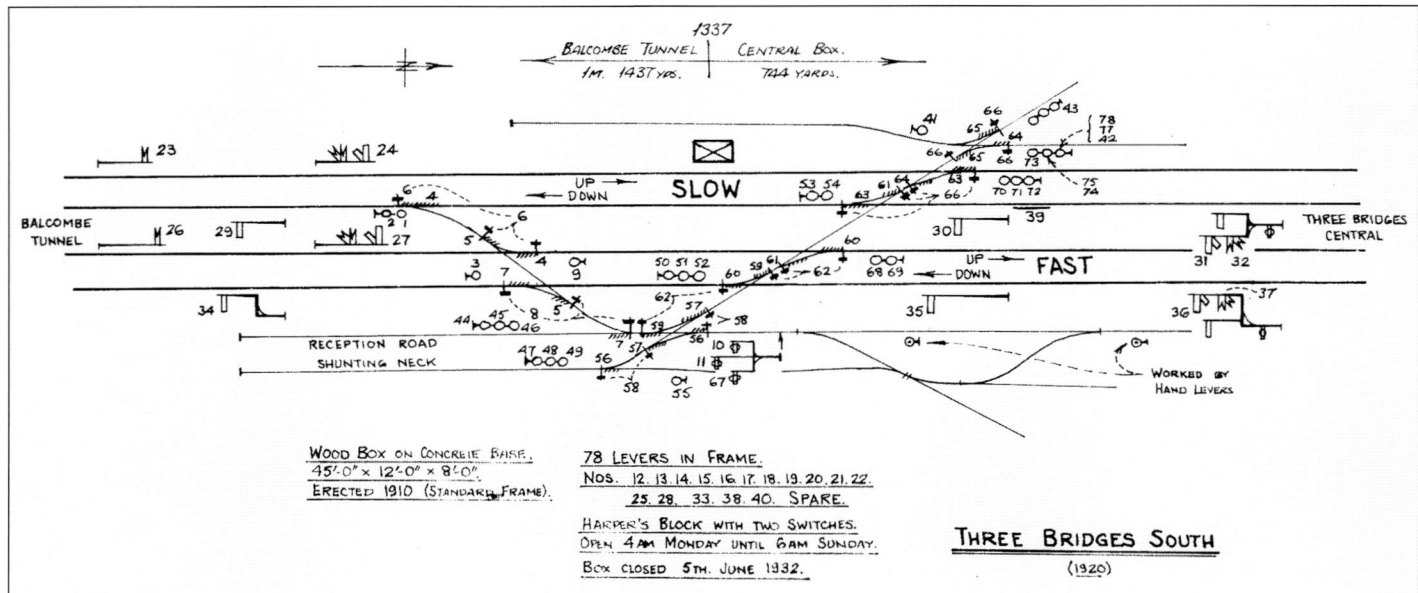

Three Bridges South signal box's area of control in 1920. A mere 744 yards from Central box, this opened on 22nd May 1910 when the line south of the station was quadrupled, necessitating the renaming of the then South signal box at the country end of the station as 'Central'. The splitting signals on the far right of the diagram are the platform starting signals. This signal box seems to be another one that escaped the photographer's lens.

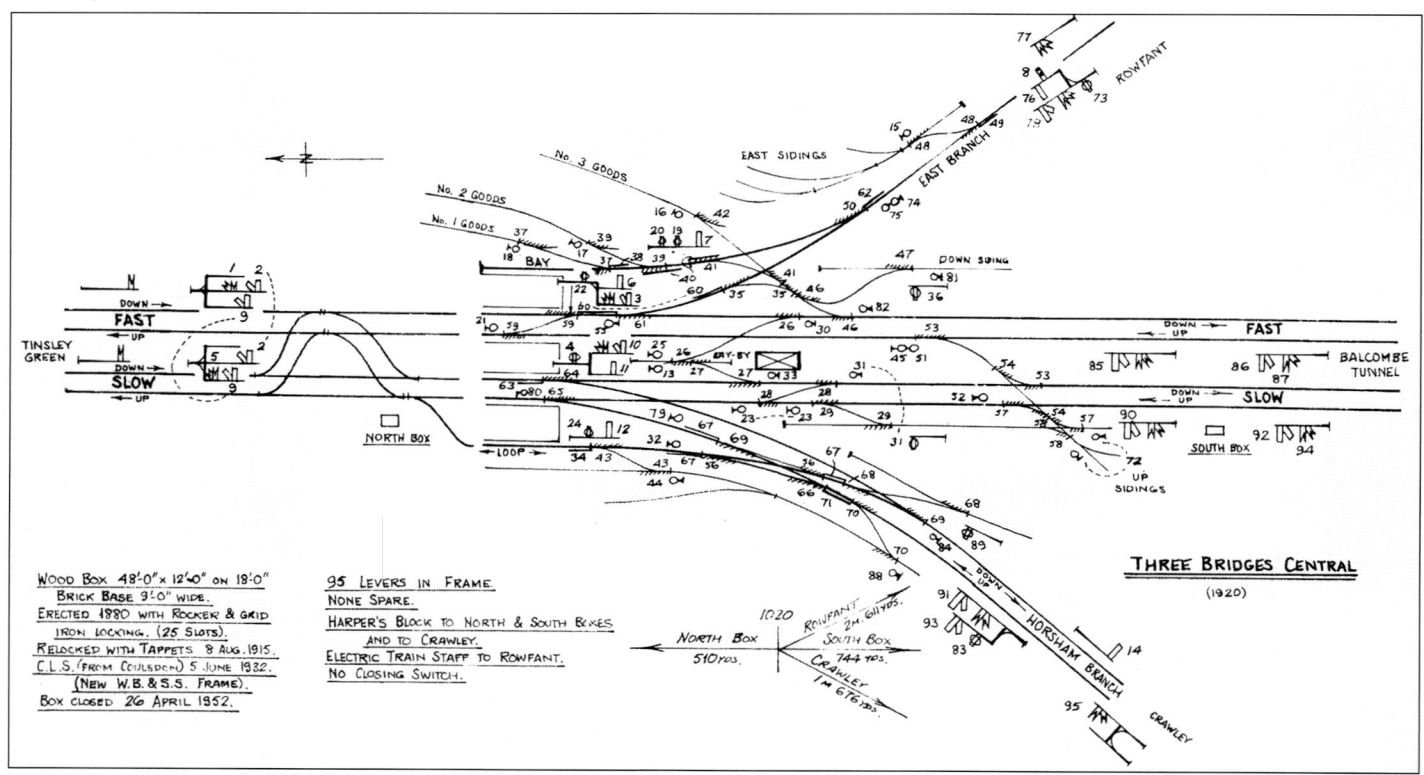

Above: Three Bridges Central signal box's area of control in 1920. At the London end of the station the lever frame is fully utilised necessitating a pair of levers being saved by operating four signal slots from two levers, the correct signal selection operating through the relevant point selector.

Facing Page Bottom: Two maps of Three Bridges. On the left is the layout from 1897, before widening of the line, with the right-hand map from 1911 showing the station area post quadrupling, although there still appears some work to do. The later map also shows both north signal boxes in place although the south signal box remains constant. The row of LB&SCR cottages situated on the original station approach road date from around 1850 and can be seen just to the south of the main road at the top of the maps. The more recent map also shows an extra siding added to serve the corn mill on the east side of the line. After widening in 1911, the old passenger entrance in the main station building on the Down side of the line was moved to the west of the line, accessed from the main road. This is not shown on the later map but the new subway is visible, which will connect with the approach ramp up from the new frontage. *Reproduced by permission of the National Library of Scotland*

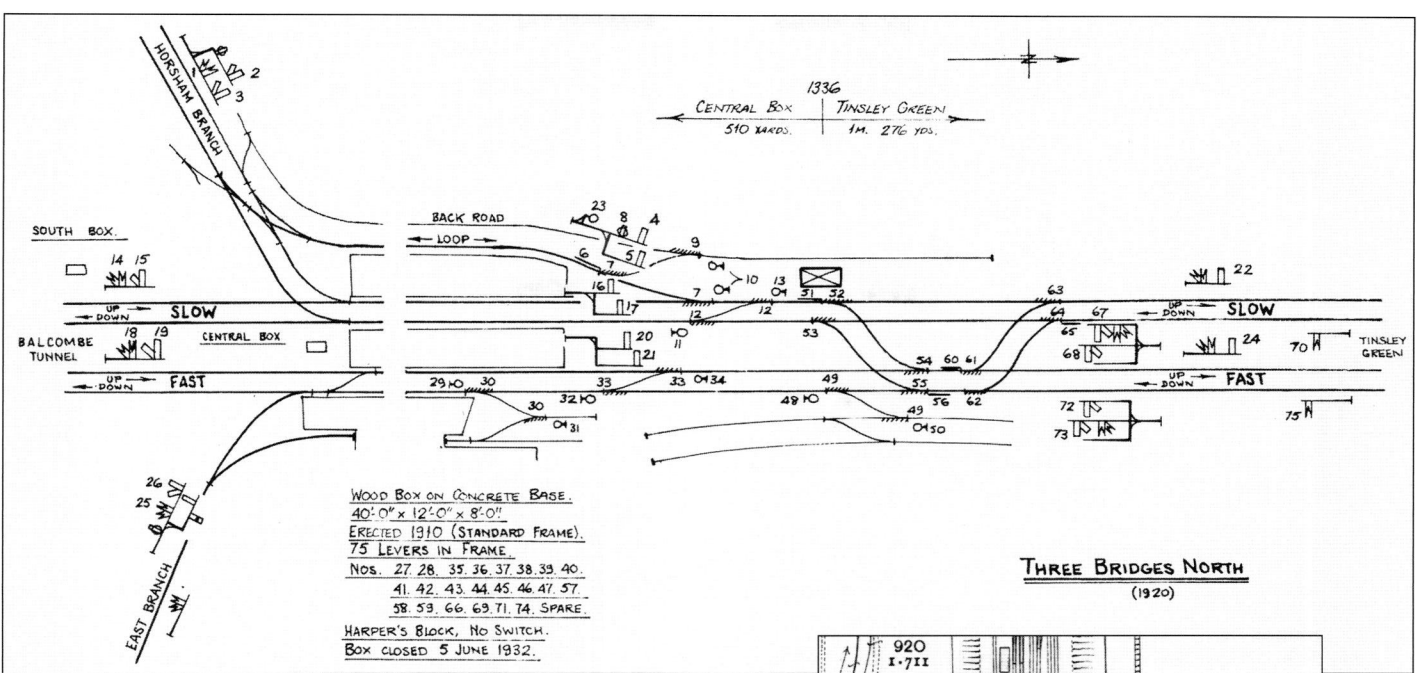

Above: The 1920 layout for Three Bridges North signal box.

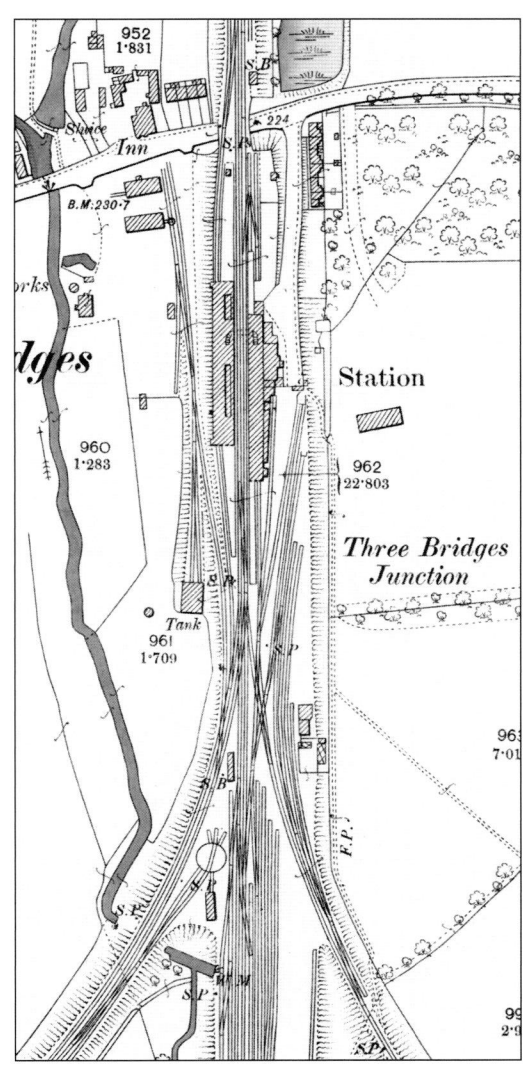

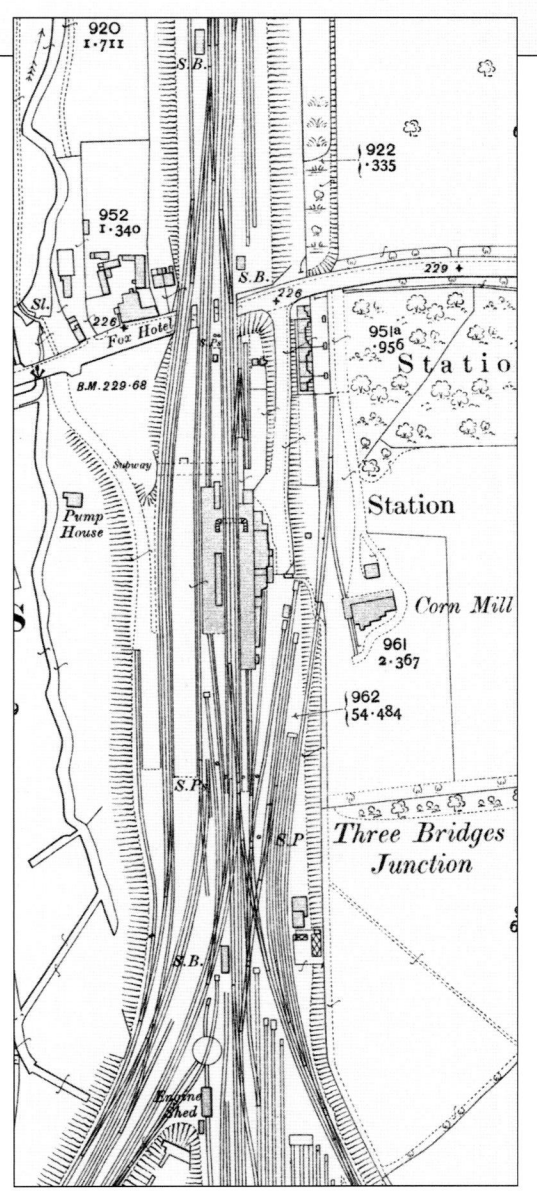

This and the following photograph are pre-quadrupling views of Three Bridges station, taken from the window of what was then the South signal box. The outer arms of the three preposterously high signals refer to the east and west branch lines respectively, with the main line signal top arm just out of view in the centre but repeated below. Short ladders exist for maintaining the shunt signals midway up the posts but access to the cross platform, and thus the top arms, is by what looks like a somewhat flimsy method of ascent. East Grinstead trains departed from the Down Bay on the right, whilst Horsham-bound services mainly used the covered loop line platform on the left where the light engine sits.
Laurie Marshall Collection

The original engine shed is on the immediate left with two goods sheds beyond, the nearest one connected to the steep inclined siding by a wagon turntable. The original 38-lever North signal box is obscured by drifting smoke in the first photograph, but can just be seen at the end of the Down platform in this view. Opening in 1874, it survived until 1910 when a new cabin was opened to deal with the enlarged layout brought about by the quadrupling. Looking at both photographs gives some idea of the vast amount of spoil that must have used to provide the new embankment for the extra roads when the line was quadrupled. *The Edward Wallis Collection*

Quadrupling reached Three Bridges in 1907 and was extended on to Balcombe Junction on 22nd May 1910. The new enlarged station with its six platforms, again taken from the signal box window, is seen here in 1928 with the signals repositioned in rather more sensible proportions. *The Edward Wallis Collection*

BELOW: Electric services reached Three Bridges via the 'Old Road' through Redhill and the Quarry Line on 17th July 1932. Mirroring the previous photograph, the station is seen here during the afternoon of 31st December 1932, the last day before full electrification was extended to Brighton and West Worthing. The new frame in the remaining signal box is now doing its work (brought into use overnight on 4th/5th June 1932) although the by now redundant North cabin can still be seen. 'King Arthur' Class No. 798 *Sir Hectimere* sits in the Down Slow platform opposite a new electric unit which would provide unparalleled cleanliness, comfort and efficiency. *O.J. Morris, Laurie Marshall Collection*

This is one of the author's favourite photographs in the book, deemed worthy of a page to itself. In the early days of the Southern Railway, looking off the bottom of the ramp of the Up Slow platform, with the East Grinstead line branching off to the left and the line to Horsham on the right, the ganger in his suit and tie cocks a quizzical eye towards the cameraman. He appears to be standing next to a portable forge, as a range of irons are leaning up against the anvil along with two hammers; a standard LB&SCR wooden tool chest is adjacent so perhaps some alterations or renewals to the point rodding are taking place. A fine array of signals is on view, including Central box's Up home signals with North box's distants below. The chap standing in the diamond crossing is presumably the lookout, maybe clutching his warning horn in his right hand with his flags under his left arm. South signal box can just be glimpsed on the middle far-right of the photograph.
O.J. Morris, Laurie Marshall Collection

Looking south from the Up Fast platform circa 1910, Central box sits in the centre of the photograph framed by the Down platform starting signals. The Down Fast signals on the left have the starter towards East Grinstead on the left while the Down Slow signals have the starter towards Crawley and Horsham on the right. In both cases the main line signals have South box's distants below the main arms, but all are slotted from South box as can be seen by the three weight arms on show in both cases. The distant signals still have their Coligny Welch reflectors. The signalman has pulled off No. 20 'shunt ahead' signal for a move out of either No. 1 or 2 goods sidings.
Laurie Marshall Collection

Right at the end of their lives: the semaphore signals still hold sway, although their far less grandiose replacements are waiting in the wings. By this point the distant arms have been altered to standard spectacle plates. The third rail is in place (along with the new Three Bridges sub-station) which unusually, for a short distance anyhow, runs up the inside face of the Up Fast platform to cater for the crossover. In the far distance a train has clear signals along the Up Fast. Due to the poor quality of the photograph, South box can hardly be seen, even though less than half a mile away. The practice of the day was not to provide hoods over the new colour light signals, so when testing was taking place, the signal lamps must have been inserted and then removed afterwards, or links slipped at the terminating end of the tail cable.
1932, E.R. Lacey, John Minnis Collection

No. A790 brings the 17.12 Eastbourne to London Victoria (SO) along the Up Fast platform at Three Bridges. The signalmen have pulled 'off' for trains for both the Down Fast and Down Slow lines, as both South signal box's distant signals are lowered and Central box's Down starters are South box's outer homes. The signalman in Central cabin can just be seen leaning forward towards his block shelf, possibly giving 'In Section' to North box. In the days before enamel targets and totems, the lamp tablet suspended below the gas lamp underneath the canopy on the left illuminated the station name.
19th July 1930, H.C. Casserley

An almost symmetrical view looking southwards off the country end of the centre island platform. The contents of the chippings bin would be wheel-barrowed out to wherever required, to fill voids under sleepers (termed 'lifting and packing'), and it had recently been (rather generously) filled. Central cabin had only disappeared some eleven years earlier and its site can be seen beyond the buffer stops. All the points at this end were still mechanically operated and, whereas larger centres like Brighton had a separate mechanical gang, Three Bridges S&T were billed as 'Dual Duties' and covered everything, electrical and mechanical. *21st July 1963, Ian D. Nolan*

With just a couple of months left for Three Bridges North signal box (seen in the distance) and its associated semaphore signals, this is the scene looking north from the Down Slow platform. The new colour light signals are in place, by this time almost certainly tested and ready to go at the changeover. Notice the mix of mechanical structures with an original all timber affair (post, dolls and the requisite cap) on the right compared with the lattice and 'open cruciform' finials assembly on the left. *K.R.M. April 1932*

Again looking north, and from a very similar position from the previous photograph, a Class '33' enters the Down Local platform with a track testing train. The Up Through platform starting signals on the right have not changed, whereas the Up Local signals have had their aspects raised and moved further north in conjunction with the platform extensions that have encroached over the road bridge. The starting signals from the Loop platform, although still in their original position, have been placed out on a cantilever structure to improve sighting around the curve of the platform – a very similar situation to Preston Park with its Down Through platform starters. *July 1978*

As explained earlier, Three Bridges North signal box came into being on 22nd May 1910, replacing the original cabin that sat at the north end of the old Down platform. An all-timber affair, it housed a 75-lever 'Brighton' standard frame with 22 levers spare. When this photograph was taken it had but seven weeks left before it, too, would be swept away under the modernisation. Two Westinghouse 'M3' point machines can be seen, no doubt already rehearsed and ready to be connected up, although it is quite possible that they were already working from this lever frame temporarily. If that had been the case, the changeover would only have involved removing the temporary control cable from the old signal box and putting links through (in the relevant apparatus case) to connect it to the new frame in the Central signal box. This was probably standard practice for most of the scheme. The enamel Southern Railway 'Electrification Notice' is affixed to the front of the signal box; it will not be there for long but already it is warning staff of the inherent dangers of working too close to a 650V live rail. The standard LB&SCR signal box nameboard is seen here: 6ins high letters mounted on a 9ins single wooden board. *19th April 1932, The Edward Wallis Collection*

No. E803 on the 17.35 Victoria to Brighton brings its rake of passenger stock into the Down Fast platform. No. 73 signal is still 'off' in its wake, although a clear road has not been granted as the distant arm below remains resolutely 'on'. The 1910 North signal box is visible and a train must be due on the Up Fast as the signalman has pulled 'off' in preparation; one also approaches on the Down Slow. The quadrupling of the line was carried out by widening on both sides of what was the existing double track, so the old Down line took the alignment of the Up Fast (and the Up Fast became the Down Slow) on the approach to the station. This is shown to great effect by the resulting 'kink' in the realigned track, distinctly obvious in the distance. A fine example of a 'Brighton' revolving shunt signal (No. 29) can be seen in the foreground controlling movements back over No. 30 crossover (the tips of which can just be seen under the leading wheels of the locomotive) and into the Dock behind the station nameboard. *15th July 1930, H.C. Casserley*

Taken from almost the same spot as where Henry Casserley stood in the previous photograph, the 'Brighton Belle' runs through Three Bridges in a very different era. The original nameboard has been over-plated by a standard green enamel sign (with a suffix added below) and, similar to the previous image, CL83 signal shows a green aspect for a train to proceed along the Up Fast line. The use of the 'horn' seen over the running in board is open to conjecture although it could, possibly, have been linked to the signal box for signalmen to ask drivers to 'go to the phone'.
1st Sept 1964, John Scrace

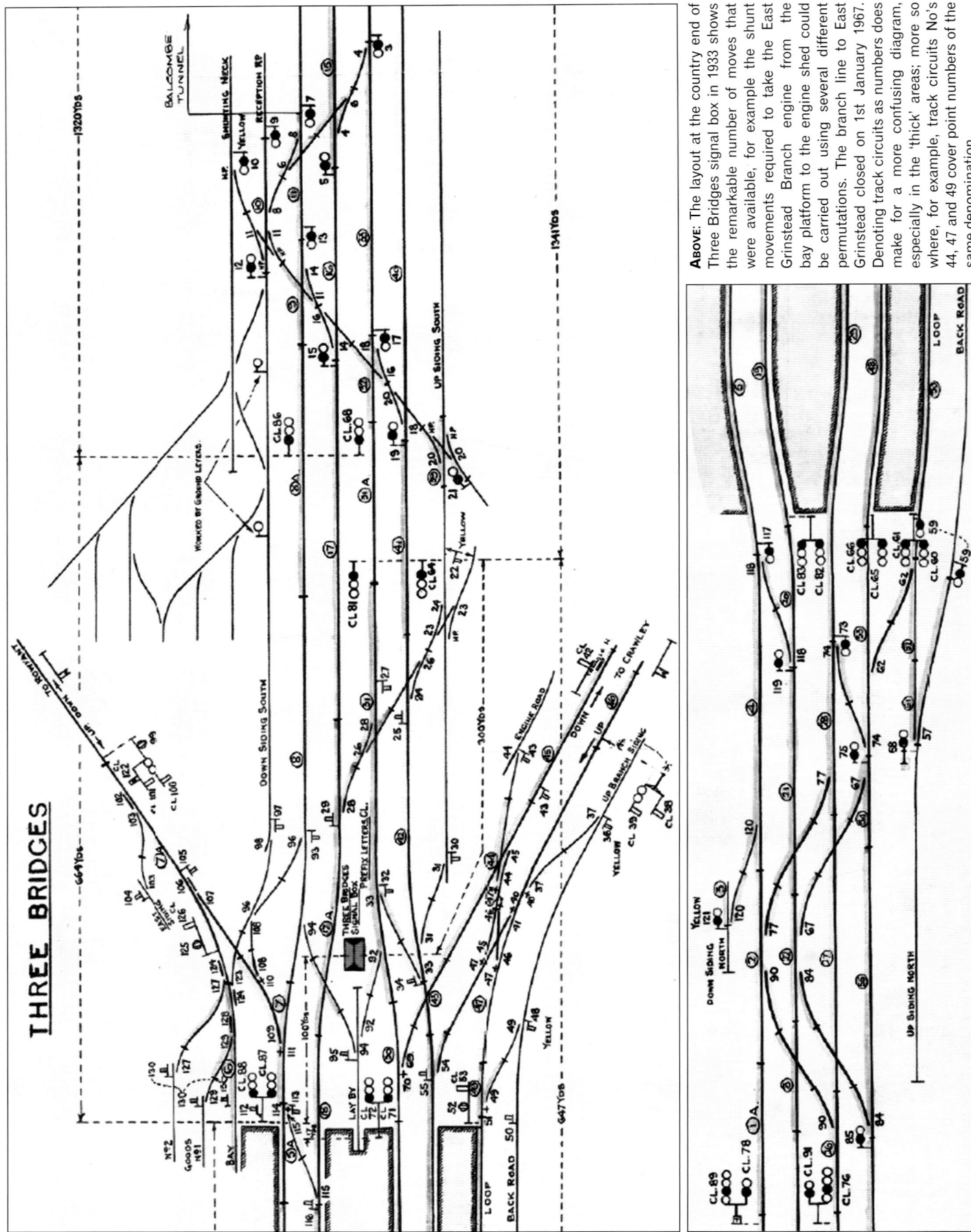

Above: The layout at the country end of Three Bridges signal box in 1933 shows the remarkable number of moves that were available, for example the shunt movements required to take the East Grinstead Branch engine from the bay platform to the engine shed could be carried out using several different permutations. The branch line to East Grinstead closed on 1st January 1967. Denoting track circuits as numbers does make for a more confusing diagram, especially in the 'thick' areas; more so where, for example, track circuits No's 44, 47 and 49 cover point numbers of the same denomination.

THREE BRIDGES

BETWEEN ASHURST JUNCTION AND THREE BRIDGES.—Monday, 2nd January. The single line between the above points, including the lines between East Grinstead 'A' and 'B' signal boxes, will be taken out of use. The facing points in the Up line at Ashurst Junction will be disconnected from the signal box and clipped and padlocked in the reverse position. Buffer stops will be provided adjacent to the Up East Branch Distant signal at Three Bridges.

Facing Page Bottom: The north end of Three Bridges as controlled from the new frame in the old Central signal box. The fast line platforms are incorrectly shown as having curved faces where they are actually straight, this to keep the running lines parallel and create more room at the south and more complex end of the station. No. 59 shunt signal exiting the Loop and Back Road shares the same lever (thus saving one), the correct selection being carried out through No. 57 points detection.

Right: In 1933 there was no access from the Down Slow in to the Loop platform and this was not corrected until March 1958, six years after the new signal box had opened, when a new facing crossover (No. 58) was provided. At the same time the Down home signals were renewed with their red aspects at the bottom and position light route indicators provided. Unfortunately 180 degrees out of phase with the other drawings, this diagram extract from the north end of Three Bridges dates from March 1958.

Below: The Three Bridges control diagram, showing such delights as the Mill and Blacksmith sidings trailing in off the East Grinstead Branch. The Main Control Station is probably better known as the Electrical Control Room which monitored and controlled the third rail supply.

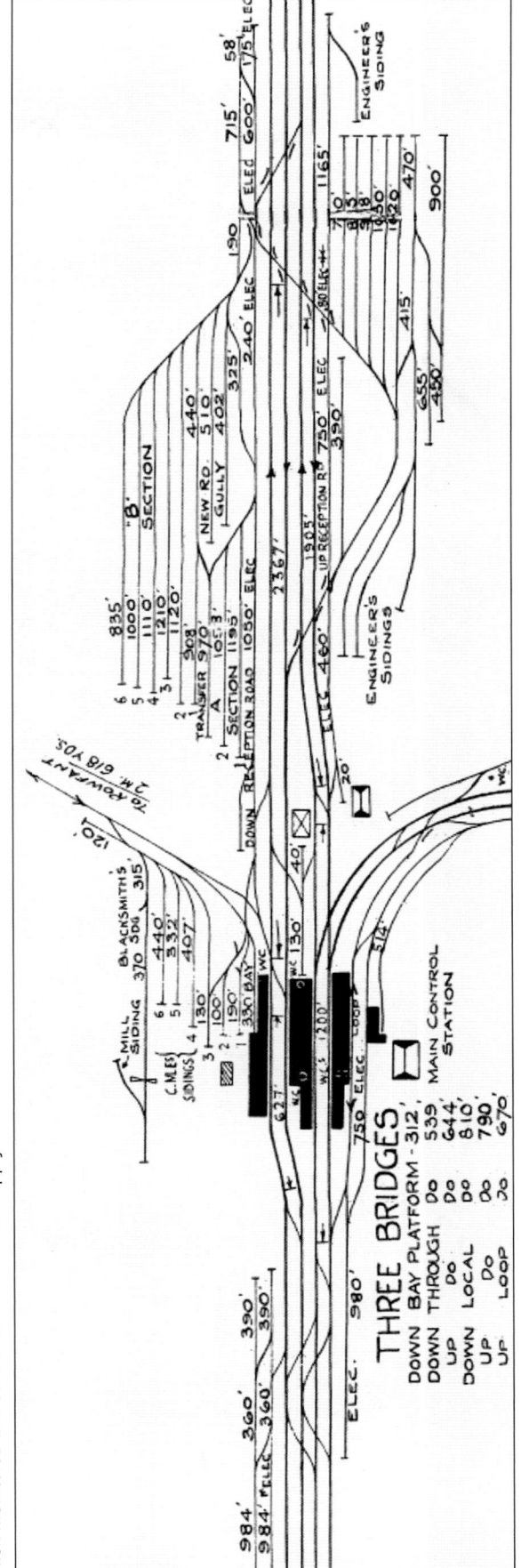

Once Three Bridges South signal box, this became Central on 22nd May 1910 with the opening of new South box, then purely Three Bridges on 5th June 1932 when both North and South signal boxes closed under the resignalling. A Saxby & Farmer structure, it opened in 1880 and is seen here in 1928. Due to space constraints under the operating floor, batteries are housed in wooden enclosures and mounted on the external wall of the signal box.
The Edward Wallis Collection

With the advent of the new colour light signalling, it was found to be impractical to adapt the 94-lever frame in Central box (originally rocker and grid iron locking but relocked with tappets in August 1915) to work the area, bearing in mind also that the one remaining signal box was now taking the place of three. The decision was taken to install a new 130-lever Westinghouse 'A2' frame opposite the original, the result of which can be seen in the above photograph, in decidedly cramped circumstances. The days are numbered for the old frame with its levers at different stroke, Harpers instruments and rows of plungers. Presumably the bulk of the installation would have been carried out during quieter periods, perhaps even at night, and hopefully the relationship between the signalmen and the installers was, at the very least, cordial. The new frame can be seen on the right-hand side with the new illuminated diagram, Siemen's magazine describers and signal repeaters all in position. *April 1932*

Still immaculately kept and looking as though it had been there forever, this is an internal view of the old Three Bridges signal box with four days left before it, too, would pass into history. Not all was wasted, as 40 levers found their way to Newhaven Town to replace the old frame. When that was replaced by a panel in 2013, the Bluebell Railway requisitioned levers and various other parts for future use at Sheffield Park; recycling at its very best. Supporting scaffold poles encroach on to the operating floor. *23rd April 1952, British Rail*

After 72 years of being buffeted by trains passing either side, by the time this photograph was taken in April 1952 it was propped up with scaffolding. The two-storey building at the end was home to the S&T Department and the relay room. The signal box closed on 27th April 1952 when the new 'glasshouse' signal box opened almost opposite. *British Rail*

Towards the end of the 1940s it was becoming obvious that the old Central box had a very limited future, mainly due to its deteriorating structural condition. The decision was thus taken to provide a brand new signal box in the Southern Region's 'glasshouse' style and a 142-lever 'A3' frame was duly ordered from Westinghouse in December 1948. Opened on 27th April 1952, it is seen here four days before assuming control of its near neighbour's duties. The relay room (with air vents) can be seen at the far end of the building whilst nearest the camera are, from left to right, the door to the operating floor plus window, window for the S&T workshop, door to the S&T mess room and window for same. The door on the far right was for the office of the Chief Lineman, a coveted position in those days. *23rd April 1952, British Rail*

This internal view of the new signal box shows train describers and the block instrument to Crawley sandwiched between the pair of illuminated diagrams. As with the old cabin, all points within the immediate vicinity of the signal box remained mechanically operated. The loud-hailer by the nearest diagram is obviously for bawling at anyone within close proximity: drivers, track-side workers or platform staff. *April 1952, K.R.M*

As the signalling diagram in the photograph below is somewhat bleached, it is worth including this image with Tinsley sidings at the extreme right-hand side of the diagram. During the 1970s it was home to a Kellogg's (cereal) depot and the author well remembers boxes of cornflakes and related products piled up in the storage buildings there. The staff and shunters maybe were not as adept in their handling prowess as they should have been, resulting in broken boxes with their contents strewn everywhere, which would crunch underfoot on your way along the sidings. The local wildlife population had a field day though! At the time of writing the sidings are still in use as an aggregate depot.
Author's Collection

Westinghouse 'A' frames came in bays, or sections, comprising either six or eight levers – the frame here coming in bays of eight. In 1958 the frame at Three Bridges received an extra eight levers, of which six were working with two spare; this was to accommodate Tinsley Green sidings (also known as Crawley New Yard) built between here and Gatwick Airport, and opened during April 1958 to cater for the burgeoning Crawley New Town, the freight facilities at Three Bridges and Crawley deemed not sufficient enough to deal with the expanding growth. The photograph above shows the frame at its maximum 150-lever extent. The old Siemens train describers have given way to a more modern type, to Balcombe Tunnel and Earlswood, and the block instrument to Crawley to a standard three-position type. The signalmen's kitchen area was behind the screen seen beyond the end of the frame. *Author's Collection*

Above: The original Down-side Three Bridges station building with its handsome Italianate features was designed by David Mocatta and opened with the line in 1841. Originally a single-storey structure, it received its upper floor during 1860. It is pictured here in May 1980.

Left: Two quite wonderful views of a backwater off a busy main line junction station, showing the Mill Siding seen in the control diagram. The first looks towards the main road and what would have been the head-shunt, and the second looks southwards to the gate separating the private siding from the main railway. Hand points control the single set of points.
24th March 1963, Ian D. Nolan

Facing Page Bottom: Looking across the long crossover that spanned all four main lines connecting the Up and Down sidings. No. 9 Points are in the foreground working double slips with their 4ft combined lock and detectors. Note also the welded zig-zag strips on the top of the rails, to ensure a better connection with the wheels of rolling stock and thus the correct functioning of the track circuit on rails that saw infrequent traffic.
6th May 1979

A busy scene taken from the window of Three Bridges signal box as the local S&T Department carry out some point maintenance under their lookout's watchful eye. A fair number of passengers occupy the platforms, including some schoolchildren, so this could be an early morning view as they wait for their train; a father and son on the Up Slow platform take a keen interest in proceedings. The canopy on the Down Fast platform affords some shelter for anyone taking the branch train towards East Grinstead which sits ready for the off, the roof and chimneys of the old station building visible above. Steam still exists on the main line as well, as evident from the water column on the Down Slow platform, dating this photograph to the early to mid-1960s.
Author's Collection

A similar view taken during March 1978, but with barely a handful of passengers on show. With the closure of the East Grinstead Branch, the canopy on the Down Fast platform was shortened, revealing more of the handsome station house, sadly demolished to make way for a W.H. Smith distribution depot. The green enamel station totem signs have given way to B.R. corporate black and white, but there is evidence of where the base of the water column once existed. The points remain mechanically worked with the facing point lock for No. 73 points clearly visible while S&T technician Bo Adams, hopefully having ascertained that no trains

were approaching, changes the red lamp in CL75 signal, using a rag as they got extremely hot. The new base near the top of the platform ramp was for a new post to carry a single signal head with a position light route indicator, although this was not carried out until January 1979.

With the photographer balancing precariously on top of a ballast hopper wagon, this is the view looking northwards towards Three Bridges station, taken adjacent to where the South signal box was once situated. Up Sidings South was a busy area as can be seen by the mix of wagons on view. *6th May 1979*

Looking south from the top of a convenient lamp post, Three Bridges sub-station is in the foreground, whilst beyond to the right is a new crossover unit being prefabricated in the Permanent Way yard. The Down sidings contain wagons loaded with concrete cable troughing to be delivered to site and also a cable train with drums loaded; it is early days but the resignalling is underway. At the extreme top left are a pair of Relocatable Equipment Rooms (or remote relay rooms), also ready to be transported to their relevant sites, these having been pre-wired in the Westinghouse factory in Chippenham. *6th May 1979.*

Just veering off the main line for a moment, this splendid photograph looks out over the rural isolation surrounding the branch towards Horsham. The diminutive three-road Three Bridges Motive Power Depot (MPD), closed to steam in 1964 but lingering on for mixed traction until 1969, can be seen in the centre of the picture. With electrification arriving at Three Bridges, a new motorman's depot was opened.
The Edward Wallis Collection

Taken on 12th December 1980, this is a similar scene but from a little further forward. The land which once housed the MPD (coded 75E by BR) has been expanded and taken over by the Permanent Way with their offices in the centre of the photograph and the tamper maintenance building seen beyond that. The approach road that accesses the site runs below the line and emerges into daylight behind the sub-station fence; the same bridge is visible to the right of the ornate lamp in the previous photograph.

Looking through the pair of Up home signals (CL68 and CL87), the prefabricated building in the middle distance was home for the British Rail New Works Department for the onset of the resignalling. The Three Bridges shunting engine sits outside the sub-station, whilst in the far distance, what looks suspiciously like a jumbo jet comes in to land at Gatwick Airport. *6th May 1979*

Left: Gatwick Airport station was rapidly expanding during the 1970s and the area where the signal box sat on the centre island platform was required for further improvements. Plans were therefore put in place to transfer the functions of the signal box to a new panel housed within Three Bridges signal box. Although not the most brilliant of photographs, this is the new signalling panel being installed by staff of M.L. Engineering (Plymouth) Ltd, one of the first signalling contracts awarded to that company by British Rail. To enable the installation of the panel, the lever frame had to be reduced from 150 to 126 levers, meaning that Tinsley New Yard (which had been worked by lever No's 143-146) had to be relocated to a temporary switch panel which can be seen on the left between the heads of the signalman and signalling inspector. A new relay room was built at Gatwick to house the interlocking using a Westinghouse '69' TDM (Time Divisional Multiplex) system to transmit the controls and receive the indications. *March 1978*

The new N.X. (**en**trance–**ex**it) panel was brought into work on Thursday 27th April 1978 during a normal train service (as things were done back then) and Tinsley New Yard can be seen incorporated on the left-hand side of the panel diagram. Signalman Brian Anderson patiently explains the fine art of route-setting to the author's sister! *June 1980*

An internal photograph of Three Bridges showing the reduced frame made necessary by the introduction of the Gatwick panel. The large VDUs (visual display units) in the centre of the block shelf show the train descriptions from Haywards Heath and Earlswood respectively. *May 1980*

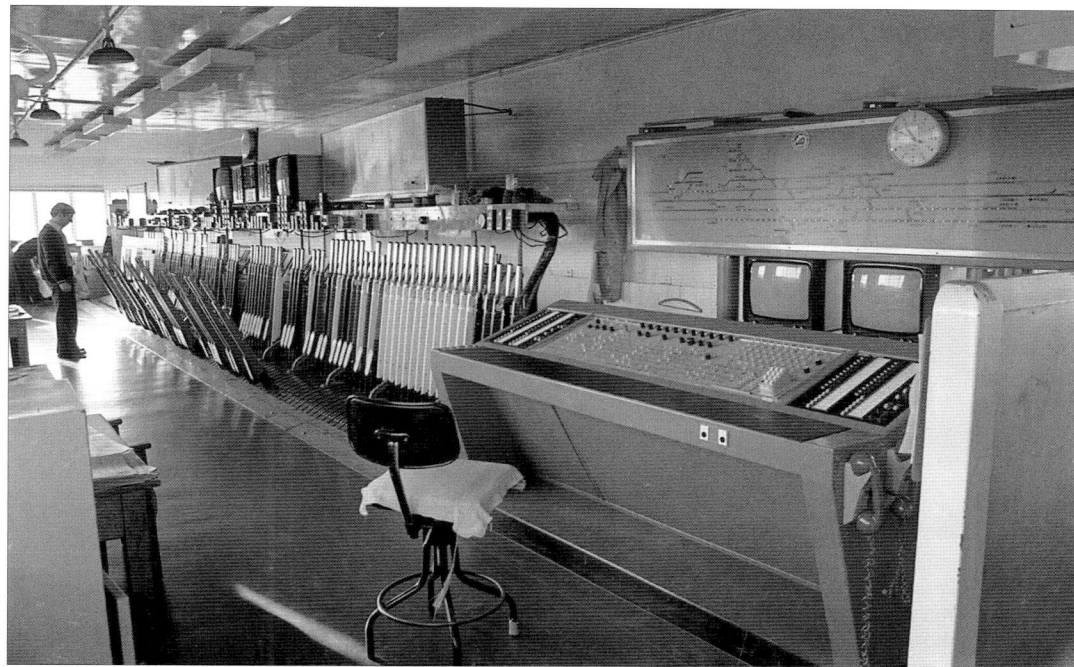

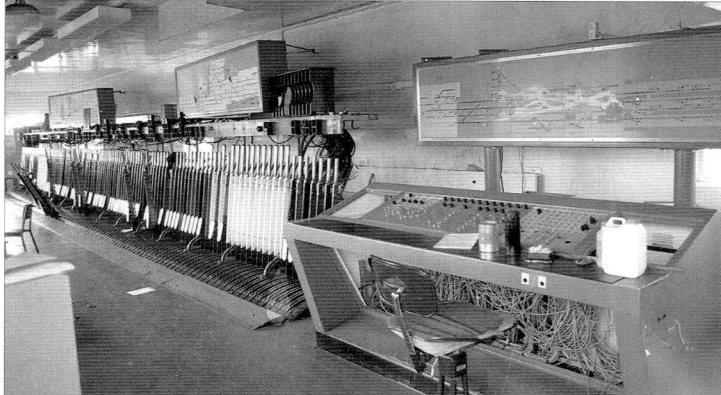

Left: Stripped of anything of any value, this was the end, although the refurbished panel was to find a new home at Chichester from 1985 until 1992. *July 1983*

Below: An unusual photograph of the locking trays underneath Three Bridges signal box, ready to be dismantled having provided 31 years of safe service. Mechanical locking is an art form unto itself and watching locking fitters at work was an endlessly fascinating business. *July 1983*

Top: The Meccano-style structure of the new operating centre is nearly complete and can be seen here before the bricklayers got to work. The middle lay-by siding has been relaced by a new cable route and the only relic from the 1932 resignalling is the Down Fast starter, CL93, which still boasts its original head. Its partner that once sat beside it is long gone. On the dock to the left of the signal box can be seen the S&T 'Faulting and Maintenance' van, and parked in the back road a 4-car set that also used to berth there late at night and destroy whatever television picture (with an aerial hanging out the window) we used to be able to get in the mess room on a night turn of duty. Not that television sets were allowed anywhere near railway premises of course. *March 1981*

Right: What would become the new operating floor, seen in the days when a photographer could climb all over construction sites without getting himself arrested! *July 1982*

Above: Not the most aesthetic creation to emerge from the Southern Region Architect's Office, but at least they used a decent brick and far worse signalling centres were constructed around the country. James Longley were the building contractors and, to BR's credit, were a local firm from Crawley, founded in 1863 and involved in many railway projects during their lifetime. (Not to either of the aforementioned companies' credit, however, was the 1973 atrocity that was the rebuilt Hassocks station.) *September 1982*

Above: The new signalling panel takes shape.
17th January 1983, British Rail

Left: Perhaps a self-indulgent photograph, but as Brighton relay room was included at the beginning of the book, I think I can be forgiven for including this. The beautifully constructed 1932-style teak relay racks have given way to regimented metal-plated versions with the bases for the plug-in '930' Style relays seen here in place. Each relay (with its unique pin code to ensure that only the correct relay will fit into its own base) will shortly be introduced so that testing of the interlocking can begin. This is one of the many racks comprising the freewire interlocking for Three Bridges.
17th January 1983, British Rail

ABOVE: The official British Rail photograph showing the new signalling panel at Three Bridges. Brighton is on the extreme right with the East and West Coastway lines leading off to the top and bottom. The main line continues towards Keymer Junction on the second row down, before dropping to Haywards Heath centre right. Three Bridges, with the Horsham Branch, can be seen just above the head of the gentleman sat on the outer right, with Gatwick Airport visible above the two empty chairs. Redhill is in the centre, with the lines leading to Tonbridge (top) and Reigate (below), the Quarry Line joining at Earlswood just to the right. Purley is to the left of the gentleman in the light-coloured shirt; the terminating branches are to Caterham (top) and Tattenham Corner (bottom). South Croydon has the line towards Oxted branching off to the top whilst the complex junctions at Gloucester Road, Windmill Bridge, etc. can be seen towards the left, with the lines splitting to London Bridge (top) and Victoria (below). Finally the West Croydon line is seen above the two gentlemen on the extreme left.
British Rail

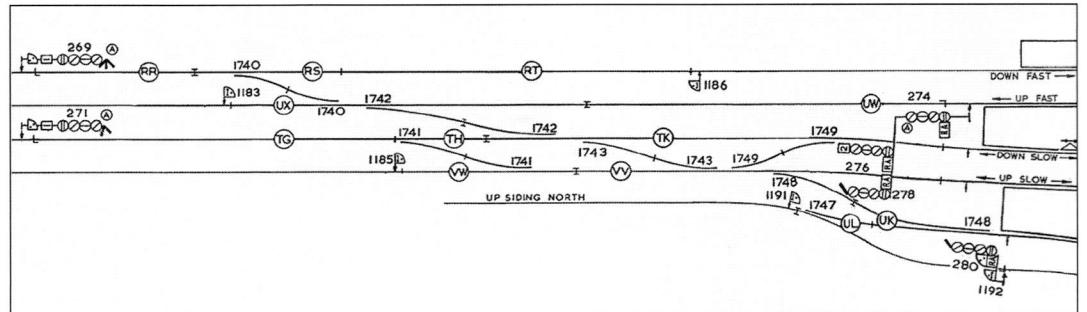

Below: Three Bridges (*south end below, north end facing page*) as commissioned on to the new panel signal box. As seen before, simplification of the layout is everything but the advent of reversible working through the station area provided so much more flexibility. With the diagram below, though, it is reassuring that even then, a siding off the Down Crawley Branch could still be called 'Engine Road'.

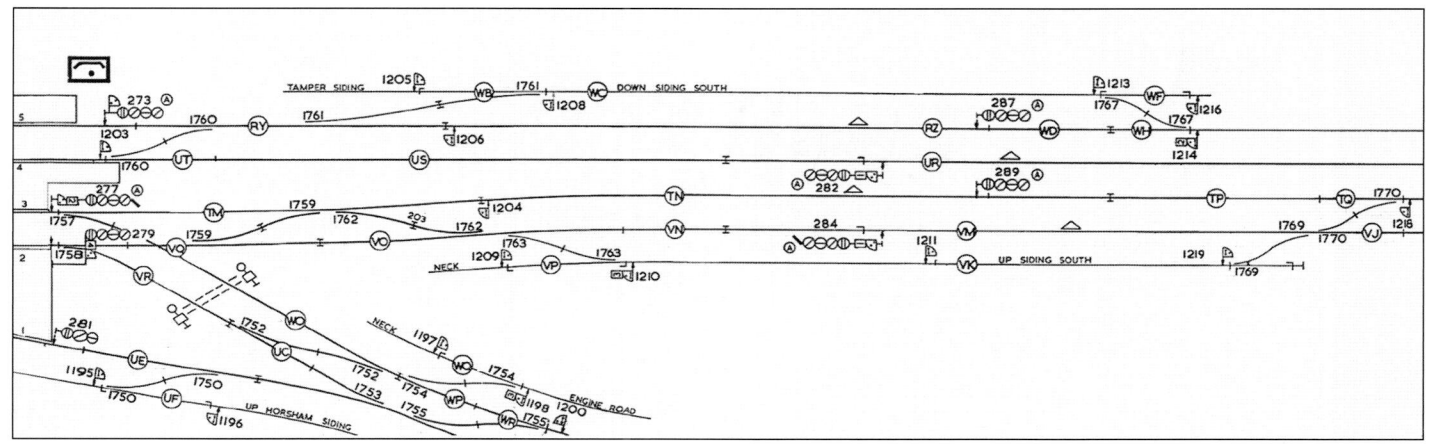

Three Bridges looking south from the top of the new signalling centre, a scene unrecognizable today where the new Thameslink Train Depot and Regional Operating Centre now dominate the scene. It was a hive of activity in July 1982 as the Brighton Line resignalling was well under way, with this being the hub. As seen before, the nearest prefabricated office was the home of BR's own New Works Department, whereas the extra building to the left was for Westinghouse's own staff who by now were out in force, connecting up all the new lineside equipment and wiring in the relay rooms. As the maintenance technicians caught up in all of this, we got on well with the Westinghouse installers although we did, on occasions, try to blame them if we were called to a failure when they were working in the vicinity. They were obviously working on 'dead' equipment so were actually blameless, whereas our own New Works staff, on probably more occasions, maybe were not so innocent. It was not that unusual to be called to a failure in an area where they were working only to find it had miraculously self-rectified, the requisite failure form stating: *'No cause found, all equipment tested and left working correctly, New Works staff working in the area.'*

22 – Tinsley Green

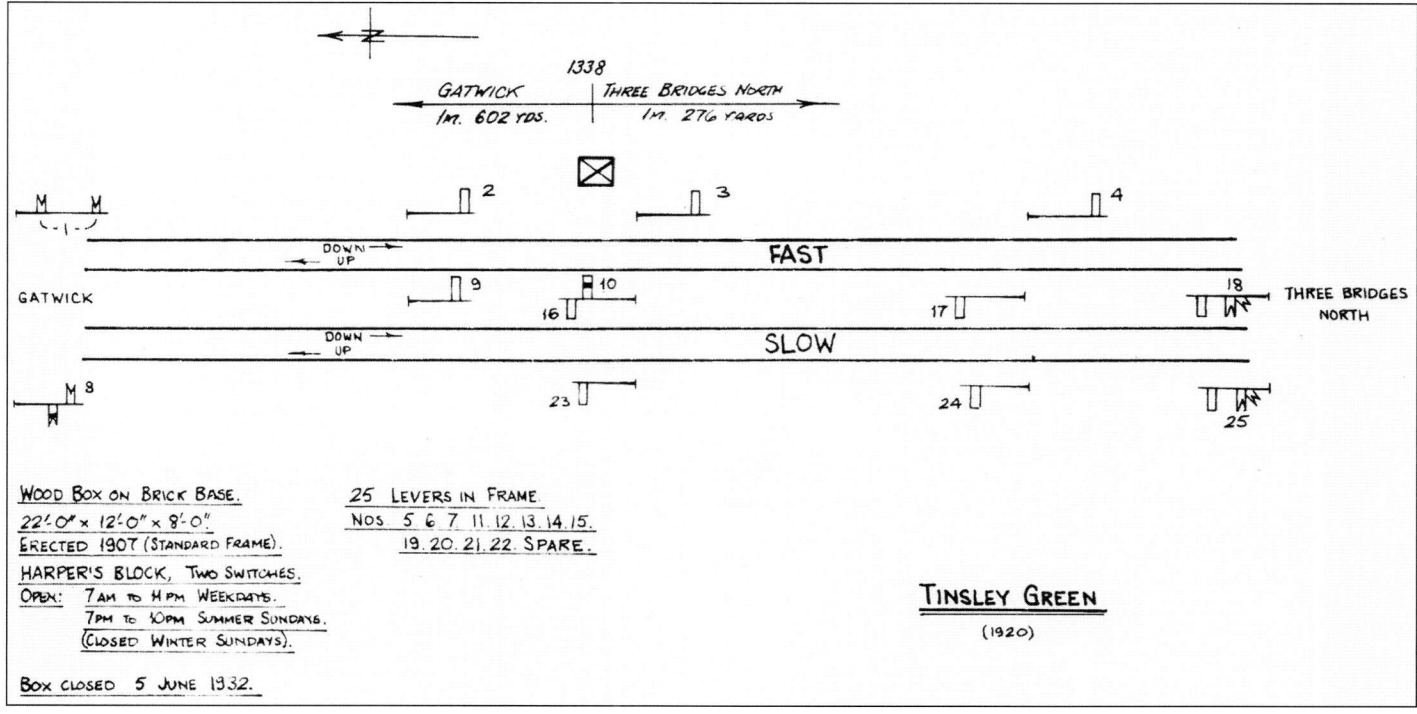

Tinsley Green signal box is pictured here on 19th April 1932. Another generously proportioned 25-lever 'standard' frame, 12 of which were spare, it worked purely as a break section box until it, too, was abolished with the advent of colour light signalling on 5th June 1932. The structure appears to have been constructed over a parallel ditch or drain, given the timber bridge accessing the signal box steps and entrance to below the cabin. As in the photograph of Three Bridges North, a conductor rail warning sign is in position and the signalman, resplendent in his white shirt and tie, stands at the window. *The Edward Wallis Collection*

Tinsley Green signal box layout in 1920. The Down Fast line has distant (with co-actor), home, starter and advanced starter whereas the other three lines have distants, home and starters only. The Down Slow starter shares its post with the Up Fast. Both Up distant signals are slotted beneath Three Bridges Up advance starting signals but it is not clear why No. 8 (Down Slow distant) shares the post with Gatwick's Up Slow distant (positioned in the Up Slow cess) as the line is virtually straight here so there is no advantage in sighting. Perhaps it just saved a post.

Above: Looking south on the same day as the photograph at the beginning of this chapter, and with a train due on every road except the Up Fast, this is a fine study of three LB&SCR wooden post signals.
The Edward Wallis Collection

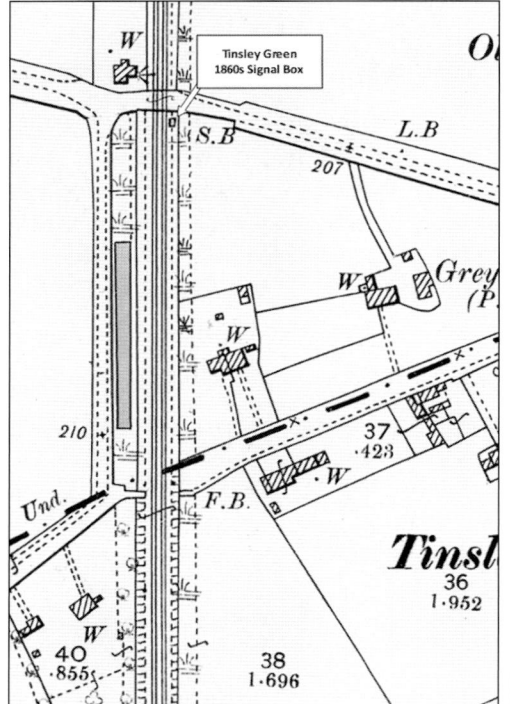

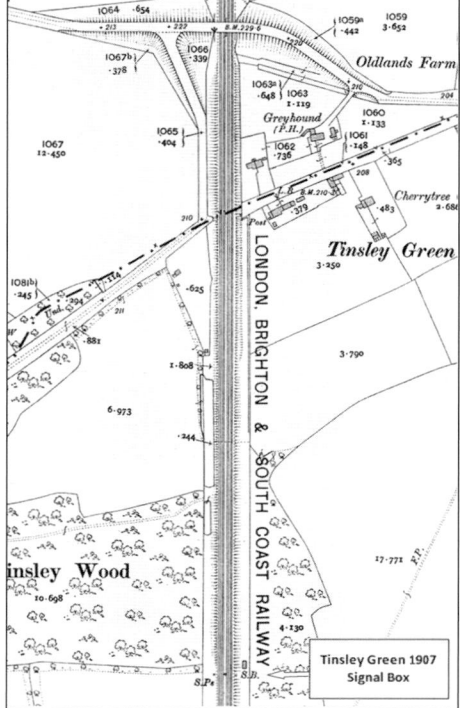

Left: The first signal box here opened in the early 1860s and controlled the level crossing seen in the 1898 map (*far left*). When the line was quadrupled in 1907, an overbridge was built slightly to the north of the crossing (thus rendering it redundant) and a new signal box was opened, again on the Down side but further to the south. This is seen in the later 1913 map (*near left*).The Greyhound public house is evident in both maps and is worthy of a mention as it has been home to the British and World Marbles Championships (individual and team events) since 1932, with such worthy winners as Big Bert Botting in 1935. Even a Southern Railway team attained the runners-up spot the following year, sadly losing to the Crawley Busmen in the final. A foretaste of railway privatisation perhaps…
Reproduced by permission of the National Library of Scotland

Right: Probably the only photograph that exists of the 1862 Saxby signal box that controlled the level crossing seen in the 1898 map. Quadrupling is underway, the new overbridge and approach embankments appear to be complete except for a few capping stones, and the signal box and crossing will close in 1907, the signal box disappearing under what will become the new Down Fast line. The LB&SCR wagon is somewhat incongruously perched on what will become the new Radford Road; it is probably safe to assume that a temporary siding was laid in to facilitate tipping the spoil that formed the new roadway. *Reproduced from* The Railway Engineer, *John Minnis Collection*

23 – Gatwick

Tinsley Green station, opened in September 1935, was brought into use for air passengers on Sunday 17th May 1936 and renamed Gatwick Airport on 1st June. Prior to this, hundreds of workmen engaged in the construction of the airport had used the station during the winter months. It was officially opened on 6th June and the Southern Railway magazine for July 1936 states that: *'The new station, which is conducted on up-to-date lines, has been designed in keeping with the Airport Buildings, and is connected with the aerodrome by an underground tunnel so that the Air passengers are under cover the whole way from the Continent to London.'* The construction of the station (barely three quarters of a mile south of the Gatwick station of 1891 which served the racecourse) had no effect on the signalling and sat nicely with Gatwick's Up home signals, CM52 (Up Fast, with its back to the camera) and CM58 (Up Local) effectively acting as the Up platform starters. A proliferation of green enamel Southern Railway station 'target' signs exist (one on every lamp post and on hanging brackets under the canopies), with 'Gatwick' in the main panel and 'Airport' in the lower quadrant. I was on early turn one morning at Three Bridges when a retired lineman came into the mess-room for a cup of tea and a chat; I did not know him but it was just after Gatwick signal box had been abolished, with the structure still standing. He mentioned that years before he had hidden one of these signs in a cubby hole on one of the floors beneath the lever frame. The next day I searched the place from top to bottom getting filthier and filthier by the minute – so exciting, but all to no avail! The station closed on 28th May 1958 but the platforms and the kink in the local lines remained until 1978, when the island platform was finally demolished and the lines were straightened out to their original alignment. *11th August 1956, J.H. Aston*

Left: 'N' Class No. 1812 brings a hotchpotch of wagons along the Down Through line past Gatwick Airport station and under Tinsley Green bridge. It was this bridge that replaced the level crossing that existed here prior to the quadrupling. Signals CA26 (which the train is passing) and CA 28 have their backs to the camera and still retain their 'A' lights along with their enormous telephone cabinets. The simple signal construction shows how easy it was to maintain these, as when working on whichever aspect required attention, you simply stood on the ladder rung that was comfortable for your height whilst leaning back against the hoop; balancing a meter was not quite so straightforward!
4th June 1946, H.C. Casserley

Above: Gatwick Airport station exterior on 12th August 1956.
Bluebell Railway Museum Archive, J.J. Smith Collection

Right: Gatwick Airport station looking north shows the covered concrete footbridge, one half of which eventually found its way to Balcombe station to replace the original footbridge there.
10th August 1956, John Scrace

Taken from the bridge seen in the photograph at the bottom of the previous page, this is a view looking north towards the airport station. In 1938, Airwork General Trading, whose hangers are seen on the Up side, moved from Heston Aerodrome in Middlesex (infamous as the airfield to which Neville Chamberlain returned after his talks with Adolf Hitler, brandishing his 'peace in our time' paper) to the new airport to expand their manufacturing business. At the outbreak of the Second World War, Gatwick Airport was requisitioned by the Air Ministry to become a satellite airfield to RAF Kenley. It subsequently became an essential part of the war effort in aircraft repair, maintenance and parts manufacturing, whilst also providing initial training for pilots. *Lens of Sutton Collection*

RIGHT: The remains of the Up-side platform building in June 1978.

ABOVE: Looking north from approximately the same position as the photograph opposite, but some three feet lower. This was taken shortly after the island platform was demolished, the Up Fast being the first track to be straightened, with the Up Local line following shortly after. This would eventually become the site for Tinsley Green Junction.
June 1978

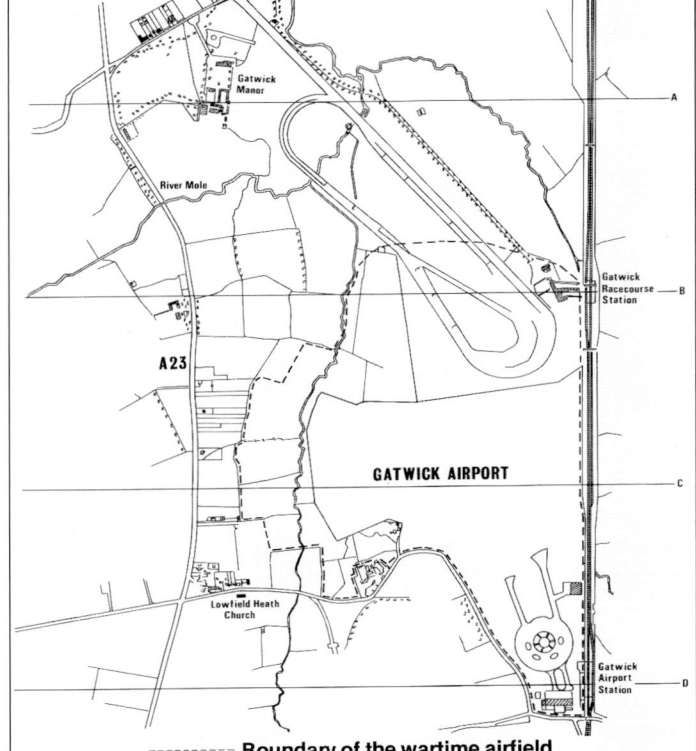

RIGHT: A 1936 map showing the layout of the racecourse and later airport, and illustrating the extent to which the Air Ministry appropriated extra land for the war effort. Gatwick station has by this time been renamed Gatwick Racecourse, with the newer Gatwick Airport station shown to the south. The original course of the A23 can be seen, also the River Mole which had to be diverted through a culvert under the new runway when it was built. Gatwick Manor (from which the name originates) can be seen top left and Lowfield church, near the foot of the map, is still a landmark when taking off or landing.
Reproduced from The Gatwick Express *(G. Tait & Associates Ltd)*

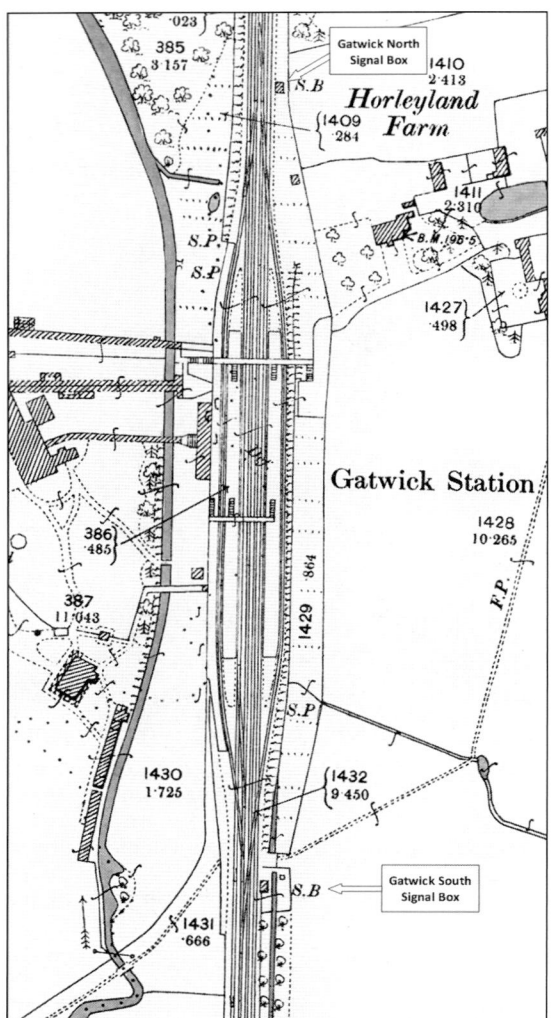

LEFT: Opened on 1st October 1891 and constructed with through lines within the island platforms, Gatwick station is seen on this 1896 map showing the pair of Saxby & Farmer signal boxes dating from the opening of the station. These were both closed during 1907 when the line was quadrupled either side of here, although an additional line (Up Local) had been constructed between Gatwick and Horley in 1892. Covered footpaths from the station are shown leading to the racecourse.
Reproduced by permission of the National Library of Scotland

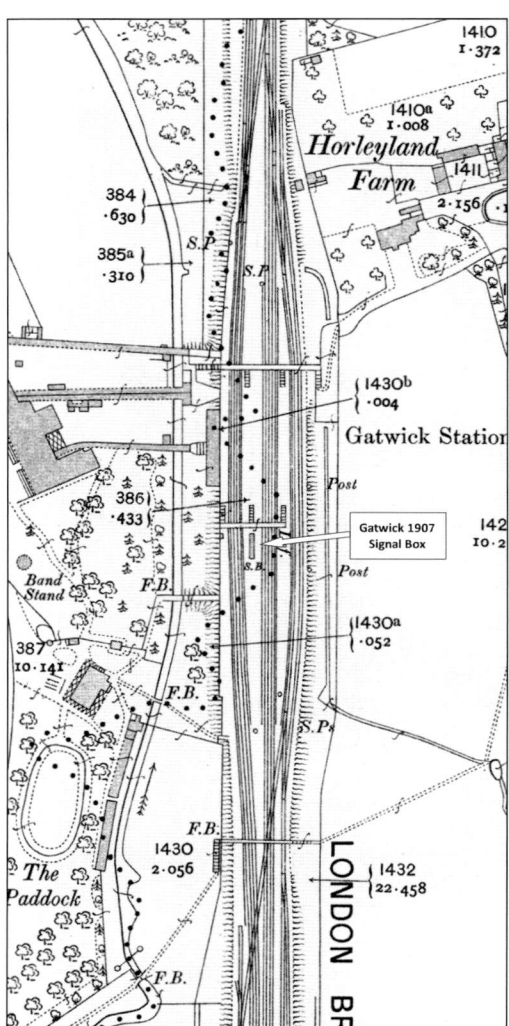

RIGHT: Post quadrupling of the line, this is an extract from a 1913 map showing the new signal box positioned in the middle of the widened Up island platform. Contributing to Gatwick's status as a premier racecourse for London rivalling Ascot, later embellishments to the surrounding area can be seen in the form of a bandstand and a paddock, described at the time to be *'the biggest and best in the country'*.
Reproduced by permission of the National Library of Scotland

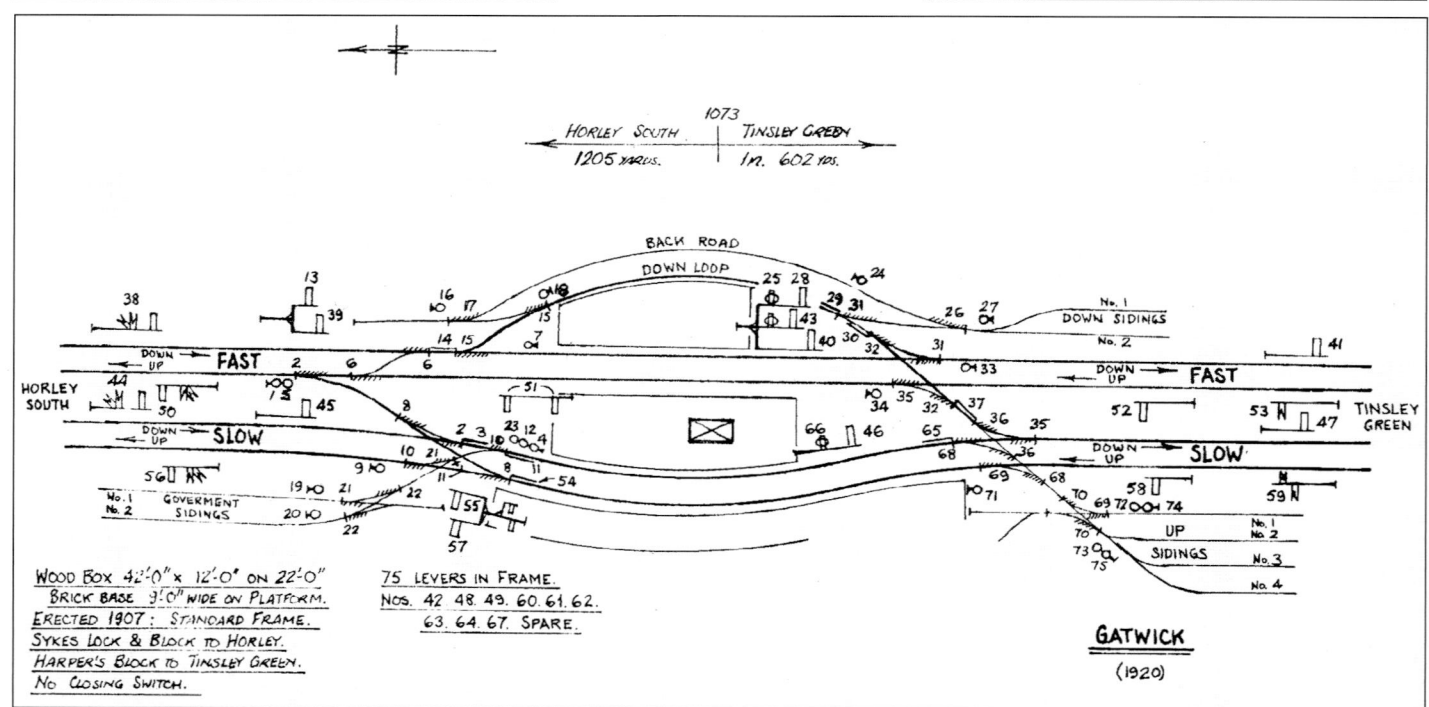

Gatwick signal box layout in 1920. Note the absence of a closing switch as it was not until the 1932 resignalling that the signal box became 'opened as required'.

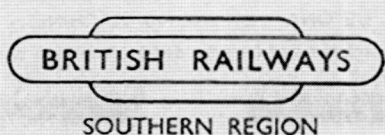

BRITISH RAILWAYS

SOUTHERN REGION

Signal Instruction No. 1, 1958

Instructions to all concerned as to

BRINGING INTO USE AN ADDITIONAL RUNNING LINE AND ALTERED SIGNALLING ARRANGEMENTS AT

GATWICK AIRPORT
(Previously known as Gatwick Racecourse.)

On SUNDAY, 25th MAY, 1958.

Rules 77, 78, 79 and 80 to be observed. Drivers to keep a good look out for hand signals.

Commencing at 11.0 p.m. on Saturday, 24th May, additional facilities will be provided which will include the provision of an additional running line through the station to be known as up local line. The existing up local line through the station will become a reversible line for trains in both directions. Gatwick Racecourse signal box will be renamed Gatwick Airport.

All points at present clipped and padlocked in the normal or reverse positions, will be connected to, and worked from, the signal box.

Additional running and shunting signals will be provided as follows:—

Running Signals.

CM.46 Down local inner home, 3-aspect, with junction indicator 45° upper quadrant right.
CM.55 Reversible road to up through starting (provision of junction indicator 45° upper quadrant right on CM.57).
CM.59 Up local starting. 3-aspect.
CM.72 Reversible road to down local starting. 3-aspect.
CM.62 Up local home (provision of junction indicator 45° upper quadrant left on CM.63).

Auxiliary Signals.

CM.64 From up local calling-on (situated below CM.63).

Shunting signals

CM.16 Down siding to down loop (yellow arm)
CM.18 Down loop to down siding or back on down loop.
CM.56 Up local to up sidings.
CM.71 Reversible road to up sidings.

The existing down local outer home 4-aspect colour light signal (CM.45), which is at present working as a 3-aspect signal (the top aspect being obliterated) will, in future, work as a 4-aspect colour light signal.

The existing down through home 4-aspect colour light signal (CM.39), which is at present working as a 3-aspect signal (the top aspect being obliterated) will, in future, work as a down through automatic 4-aspect signal (CA.46).

Full details of the new layout and signalling are shown on the diagram enclosed with this Notice.

The lights of all the 4-aspect running signals will be as shown on the diagram and not as appearing on page 4 of the General Appendix to the Working Time Tables.

The new colour light running signals will be fitted with small side lights repeating the aspects exhibited by the signals to assist Drivers of trains drawn up close to such signals.

A plate bearing prefix letters and the new number of the signal will be fixed to each colour light signal post.

JUNCTION INDICATORS.

Junction indicators will be provided at certain signals as shown on the diagram, and will apply as provided for in Rule 35, Clause (e).

TELEPHONES.

Telephones will be provided at or adjacent to certain signals as indicated on the diagram.

SIGNALLING DURING FOG OR FALLING SNOW.

Fogsignalmen will NOT be provided at any of the colour light signals controlled by GATWICK AIRPORT signal box.

The title page of the 1958 signalling notice detailing the arrangements for the new Gatwick Airport station.

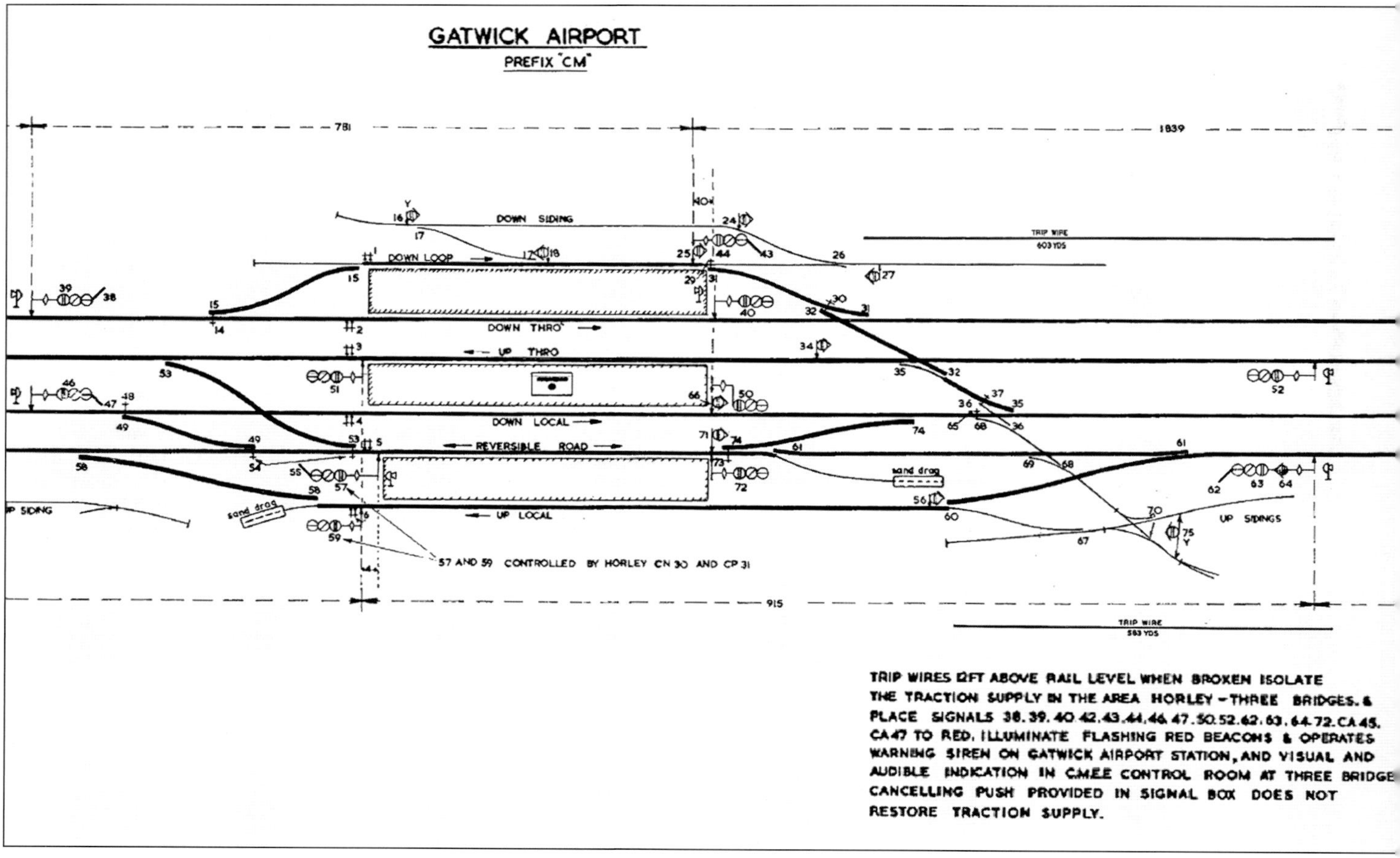
GATWICK AIRPORT
PREFIX "CM"
781
1839
DOWN SIDING
DOWN LOOP
TRIP WIRE 603 YDS
DOWN THRO
UP THRO
DOWN LOCAL
REVERSIBLE ROAD
UP LOCAL
UP SIDING
UP SIDINGS
sand drag
57 AND 59 CONTROLLED BY HORLEY CN 30 AND CP 31
915
TRIP WIRE 583 YDS
TRIP WIRES 12FT ABOVE RAIL LEVEL WHEN BROKEN ISOLATE THE TRACTION SUPPLY IN THE AREA HORLEY - THREE BRIDGES. & PLACE SIGNALS 38. 39. 40. 42. 43. 44. 46. 47. 50. 52. 62. 63. 64. 72. CA45. CA47 TO RED. ILLUMINATE FLASHING RED BEACONS & OPERATES WARNING SIREN ON GATWICK AIRPORT STATION, AND VISUAL AND AUDIBLE INDICATION IN C.M.E.E CONTROL ROOM AT THREE BRIDGE
CANCELLING PUSH PROVIDED IN SIGNAL BOX DOES NOT RESTORE TRACTION SUPPLY.

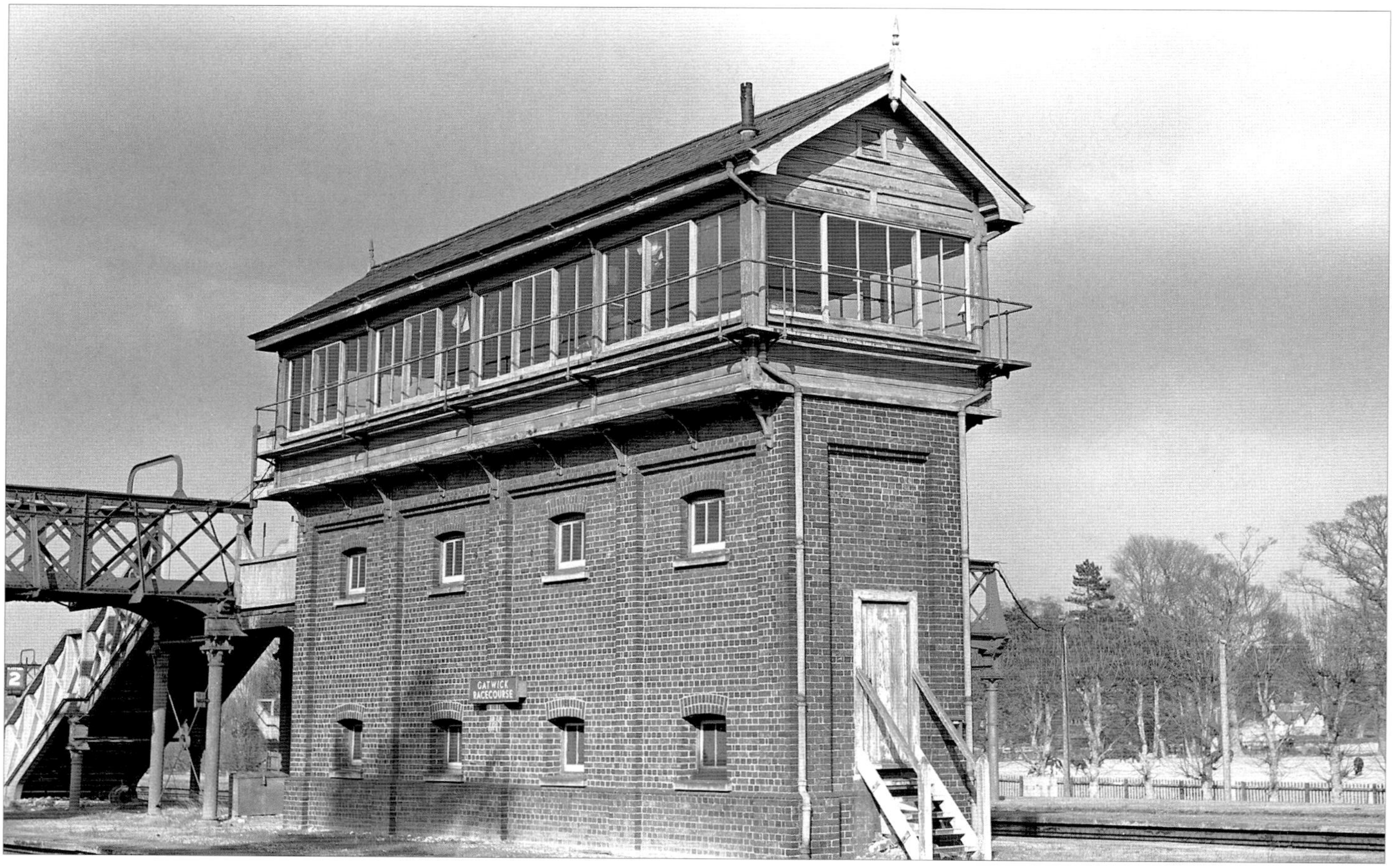
GATWICK RACECOURSE

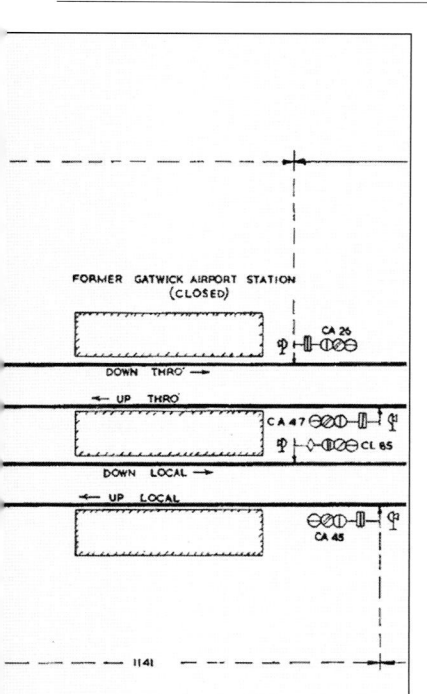

Left: An extract from the Gatwick Airport signalling notice dated 25th May 1958 showing the layout as remodelled for the newly opened airport station. Here it can be seen that the pair of signals that were once positioned at the north end of the old airport station (1933 track plan) have moved forward to now control moves towards the Up Though (CM52 as before) and Reversible Road or new Up Local (CM62/CM63), with a new signal section added for each road in the rear. The trip wire spanned the width of the airport runway on both sides of the line to the south of the station to protect the railway in the event of an aircraft incident and had to be tested on the last Sunday night shift of every month. This entailed liaising with the signalman, the Electrical Control Room operator and Gatwick Airport control tower (who also had to liaise with the emergency services) to find a slot between trains and, of course, aeroplanes. Usually getting the go-ahead somewhere between 2 and 3am on the Monday morning, it was quite satisfying to hear the sirens sound out and see flashing red beacons illuminate. The footnote inserted from the signal box diagram details the outcome should the wire be broken.

Facing Page Bottom: Gatwick signal box opened in 1907 and replaced the two cabins that were previously situated at either end of the station prior to the quadrupling. It housed a 75-lever standard frame and is seen here as Gatwick Racecourse, the name it gained on 1st June 1936 when the new Tinsley Green station further to the south was altered to Gatwick Airport. With the advent of the 1932 resignalling, it joined the list of 'opened as required' signal boxes until 25th May 1958, when it became fully functioning again and was renamed, for the final time, as Gatwick Airport.
17th March 1956. Bluebell Railway Museum Archive, J.J. Smith Collection

Below: With the expanding station infrastructure encroaching ever nearer, the main steps to the operating floor had to be moved to the south end when the new lift shaft was constructed. The 1950s-built relay room is nearest the camera. *11th September 1968, John Scrace*

Using what available land was left, the racecourse at Gatwick held its last point-to-point meeting in April 1948. As seen earlier, at the outbreak of the Second World War the Air Ministry had taken over the old airfield further south whilst also expanding its operations on to parts of the racecourse. At the cessation of hostilities, the government maintained control of the site and in 1952 decided that the location would become the new airport for London. The racecourse station officially closed in March 1956 and this photograph, taken from a moving train and at a relatively slow shutter speed, shows the transformation in progress to a modern airport interchange. The new relay room for the expanded station layout is complete, while the new passenger terminal building is well under way. Unusually for a station, the conductor rail runs along both platform faces of the fast lines as the twelve rows of point rodding occupy the 6ft, the mitigation being that the live rail is boarded for the duration. *19th October 1957, Lens of Sutton Collection*

Taken just a month after it opened on 28th May 1958, this panorama shows the newly reconstructed station. Enamel 'running in' boards are provided, but the station name (in green lettering) is now emblazoned on either side of the perspex covers housing the fluorescent tubes on every lamp post. The new airport was officially opened by Her Majesty the Queen on 9th June. *29th June 1958, John Scrace*

The new station looking from the footbridge that spans all lines south of the station. As part of the remodelling, the old Up Local platform was shortened at the country end and converted into an island with the new Up Local line realigned around it, the original line then forming a reversible platform. The Down Local starting signal has now been cantilevered out to provide better sighting around the signal box, with a banner repeater also provided. *29th June 1958, John Scrace*

During July 1978, viewing from an identical position, the layout has changed again in conjunction with the abolition of the signal box. The Down starting signal for the reversible line has been cantilevered out to become a left-hand signal to drivers while the Down Local signal has reverted to a straight post. In March of this year the Up Local/Reversible platform was widened, as evidenced by the clean ballast in the realigned track on the left, as it was to become the principal platform for airport passengers. The new line became the Up Platform Loop and the Reversible changed back to the Up Local. All three platforms were signalled for reversible working.

Apart from the permanent feature of the footbridge, it is difficult to tell these two photographs are of the same place. The top picture gives another view of the Racecourse station, but this time from the country end, while the lower shows the Airport station from virtually the same viewpoint but now controlled from Three Bridges. *Above: 11th August 1956, J.H. Aston; Below: 26th September 1982*

In January 1972 construction work started on Junction 7 to 8 (Hooley to the M25), at the northern end of what would become the M23 motorway; February of the same year saw work starting on Junction 8 to 11 (M25 to Pease Pottage). The contract was awarded to W.C. French and in association with this, a new private siding was brought into work on 4th June 1972 at the north end of Gatwick to cater for the huge amount of aggregate that would be brought in by train. Discharge facilities were provided within the temporary site to transfer the stone to road lorries. New mechanical shunt signals were provided to access and exit the siding, with No. 15 points lever even bearing the legend 'French's Siding Points'. Although starting a motorway at Junction 7 may seem slightly odd, it should be explained that the extension northwards towards the South Circular road had been planned (which would have been Junction 1) but was never authorised. Part of the route was intended to slice a swathe through a housing estate south of Mitcham and carve its way through woodland before crossing the Chipstead Valley on what would have been an enormous concrete viaduct. From there, it was to parallel the Brighton main line to Hooley where the motorway now starts. It is no wonder that it never happened: logistics aside, the South Circular road alone was in no shape to take the additional traffic that would have been thrust upon it. The construction of the motorway east of Three Bridges was useful to us railwaymen, as we were able to access it for a while as an easier route to Balcombe Junction – no one seemed to mind! The photographs below show a bit more detail.

Class '47' No. 1682 over the French's sidings drops on 3rd March 1973. *John Scrace*

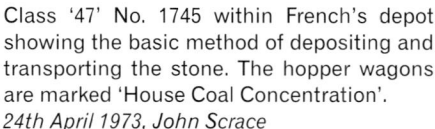

Class '47' No. 1745 within French's depot showing the basic method of depositing and transporting the stone. The hopper wagons are marked 'House Coal Concentration'. *24th April 1973, John Scrace*

Class '47' No. 1685 leaves the sidings with its empties on 26th April 1973. The motorway bridge carrying the M23 extension into the airport is still under construction in the background. *John Scrace*

Above: Class '47' No. 1959 at Gatwick on 26th April 1973, the airport still in an almost rural setting. *John Scrace*

Right: The motorway construction siding was abolished in July 1978 and the abandoned track bed can be seen here later the same year. *Richard Spencer*

Taken from the end of the Up Local platform a Class '33' locomotive approaches the station with a long van train, once an everyday occurrence. The long siding (which used to extend through to Horley) is visible to the left and houses an electrical multiple unit which could only have been propelled into its position as the siding is not electrified. The area covered by the trees to the left of the siding became the site of the new relay room in 1978. The barrow crossing, for the vast amount of passenger baggage that was trolleyed across to the airport, was provided with lifting barriers until the platform was widened in March 1978, when the barriers were abolished and the crossing was protected by white lights. The bridge carrying the M23 extension towards the airport can be seen in the background, whilst an abandoned barrow sits in the foreground awaiting its next turn of duty. There is a detonator machine (shown as S5 in the 1958 signal box diagram) just to the right of the large telephone cabinet in the centre of the photograph. *Richard Spencer*

Looking from the footbridge south of the station towards the long crossover and the sidings that were initially provided to house race-day specials, the Up 'Brighton Belle' approaches the Airport station on 9th June 1963. The long crossover survived until Sunday 1st May 1977 when it was abolished, leaving just the connection from the Down Loop to the Down Through line and the connection from the Up sidings to the Up Local. A long line of chippings bins (for lifting and packing purposes) are provided along the 10ft. *John Scrace*

Taken from the top of the signal box steps looking out over the roof of the relay room, a steam hauled freight crosses from the Down Loop towards the Up sidings. You can just imagine the signalman praying that he will get his points back to 'normal' after a move like this! The 'Beehive' terminal building from the original airport can just be seen in the background with the British United Airways building on the right. The A23 (with all of four cars on view) can be seen on the right. *George Farmer*

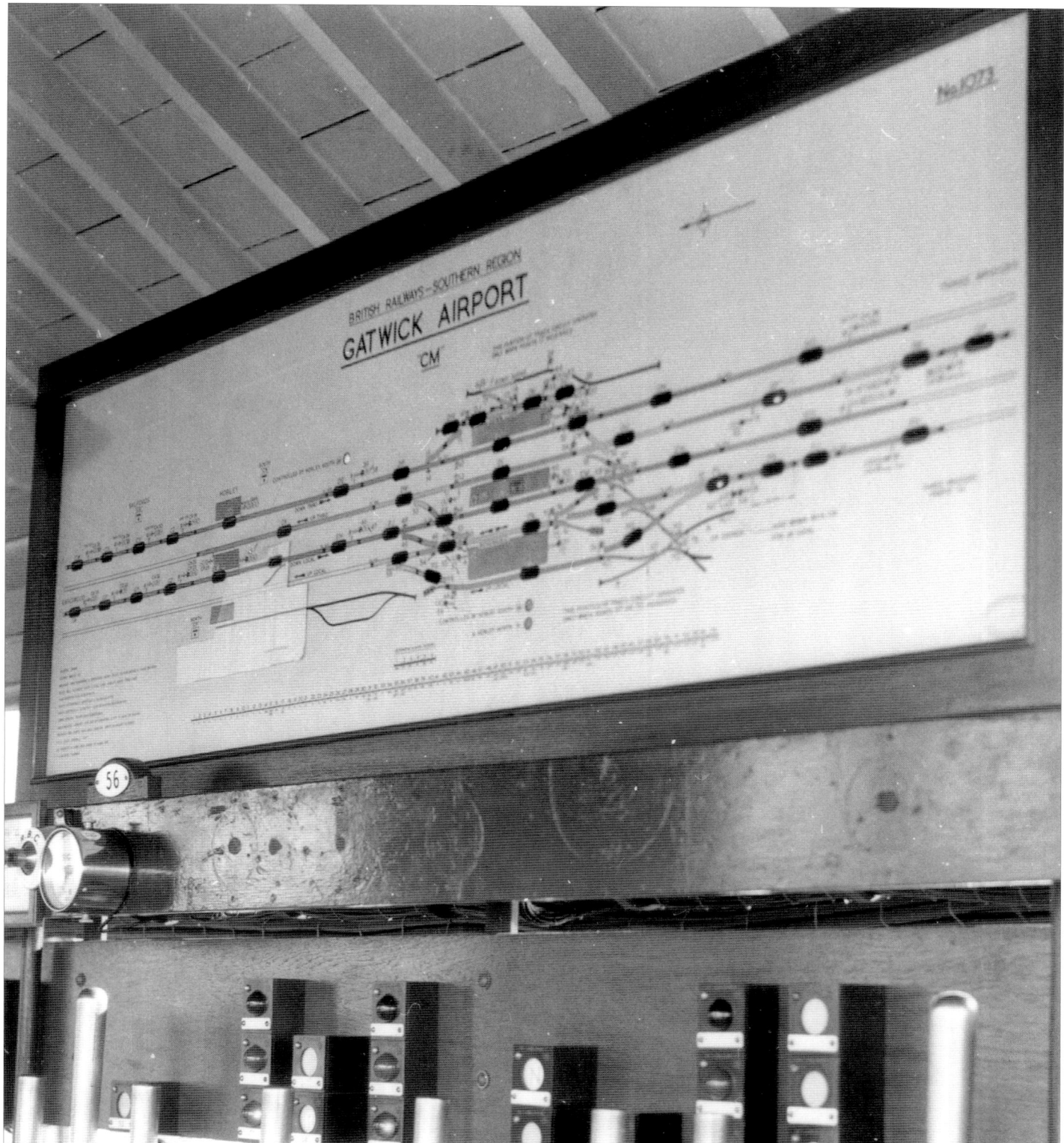

Above: Gatwick illuminated diagram showing the long siding extending through to Horley, although the connection back on to the Up Local line has been severed. Horley's two signal boxes are still in situ. The block shelf bears the scars of previous instruments. *George Farmer*

Facing Page Top: A late 1960s view of the frame in Gatwick signal box, showing to good effect the length of lever travel; due to this, one of the signalmen I knew here used to walk along the quadrant pulling the levers behind him as he went! The train register is open on the sloping shelf (no box boy here) whilst the original clock records the time as 10.31. *George Farmer*

Facing Page Bottom: A late 1977 internal view of Gatwick signal box with its pair of illuminated diagrams and banks of magazine train describers working to Earlswood and Three Bridges. Although the first lever on view starts at No. 19, there is an impressive number still in work. Two signal design office staff involved with the abolition of the signal box can be seen in the foreground. *Richard Spencer*

British Rail

Signal Instruction No. 15 C.D.

SOUTHERN REGION—CENTRAL DIVISION

ALTERATIONS TO SIGNALLING AND PERMANENT WAY BETWEEN HORLEY AND THREE BRIDGES ON FRIDAY, 28 APRIL AND SATURDAY, 29 APRIL, 1978

DRIVERS TO KEEP A GOOD LOOK-OUT FOR HAND SIGNALS

The area under the control of Three Bridges signal box will be extended to include the area controlled by Gatwick Airport signal box, which will be abolished.

All signals at present controlled from Gatwick Airport signal box will be renumbered. Automatic signals will retain their numbers except for Down Through line signal CA46, which will become a controlled signal, CL201.

Certain signals will be repositioned, some three aspect signals will be converted to four aspect operation and new draw-ahead and position light shunting signals will be provided.

Attention is drawn to the amended applications of the junction indicators above Down Local line signal CL207.

At Gatwick Airport the following platform lines will be renamed:—

Line	New name
Down Loop	Down Platform Loop
Reversible	Up Local
Up Local	Up Platform Loop

The following lines at Gatwick Airport will be signalled for reversible working:
  Down Local
  Up Local
  Up Platform Loop

Lamps which flash with a white light to call the attention of the Technician will be fixed to certain apparatus cases in the area.

Full details are shown on the diagram enclosed with this notice.

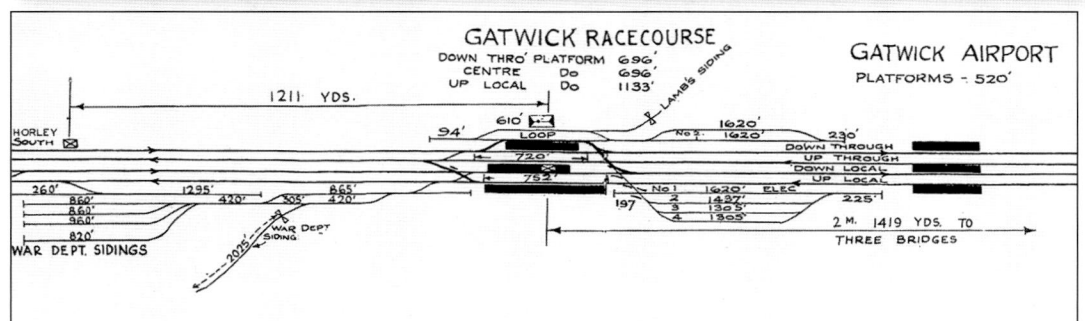

LEFT: The title page of the 1978 signalling notice detailing the arrangements for abolition of Gatwick Airport signal box and the transfer of control to Three Bridges. The note *'Drivers to keep a good look out for hand signals'* was common to most signalling notices of the time when so much work was being carried out during a normal train service.

FACING PAGE CENTRE: An extract from the 'Yellow Peril' signalling notice for 28th April 1978 when Gatwick signal box was abolished and the new panel in Three Bridges signal box assumed control. Note that the signals have taken on the Three Bridges 'CL' prefix. The plans on these two pages are at polar opposites, with north to the left of the control diagram (*below left*) and south to the left of the signalling diagram (*right*).

FACING PAGE BOTTOM: Taken from the top of CL220 signal, this shows the extra road that was brought into work on Friday 11th May 1979 to form a new Up Loop Line. Comparing this with the earlier signalling notice, it can be seen that the former No. 1 Up siding was sacrificed to make the space, the sidings being renumbered accordingly. Behind the row of lamp-posts on the left are the tops of three of the poles carrying the Up side trip wire, their galvanised metal caps glinting in the sunshine, with the last one just this side of the footbridge. *September 1982*

LEFT: The control diagram for Gatwick.

This is the way to demolish a signal box – just park the spoil wagons either side and run the train service around it. I had hoped to get here a bit earlier but arrived just in time to photograph the one corner left standing. This was the end on 21st October 1978, although, as the new signalling panel at Three Bridges that replaced it was to provide unblemished service for another five years, the advertisement on the left seems apposite: *'Times change, values don't.'* The hard hats are on site, but maybe not where they should be!

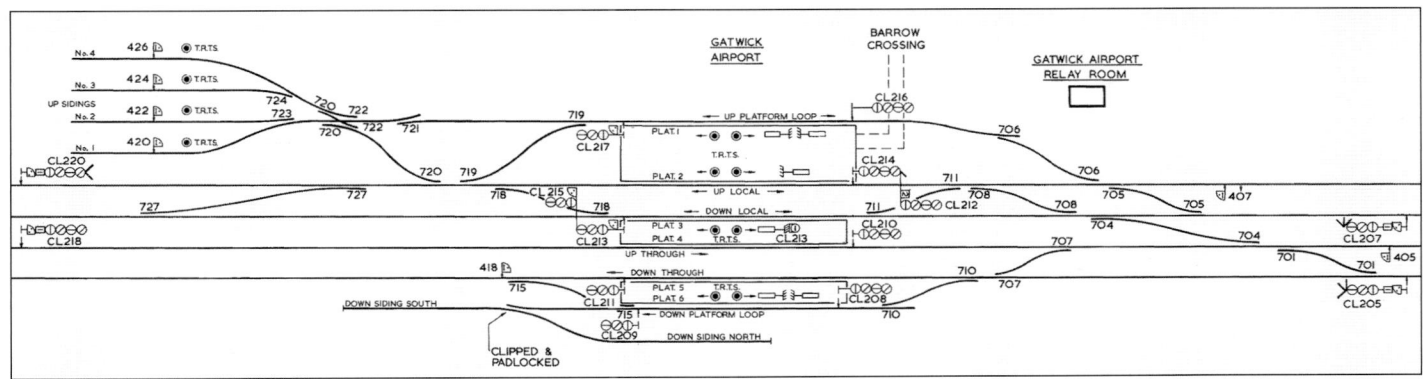

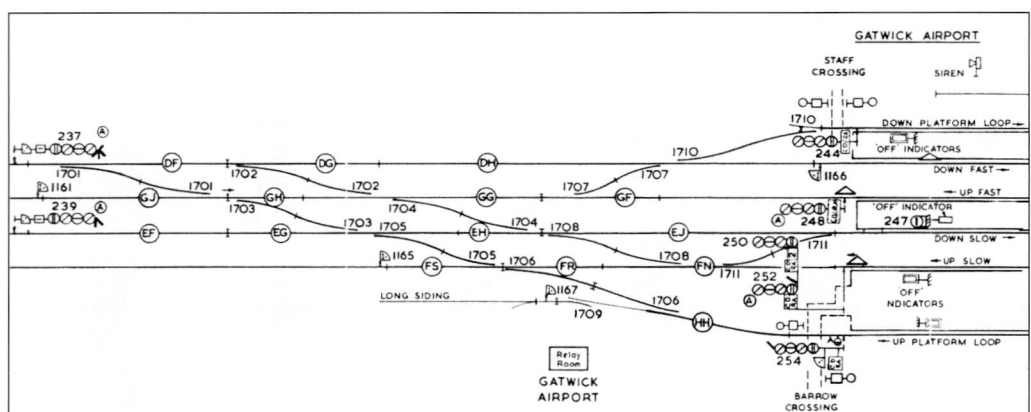

Left: The north end of Gatwick Airport as commissioned on to the new Three Bridges panel in July 1983. Note the siren at top right, activated when the trip wire is broken.

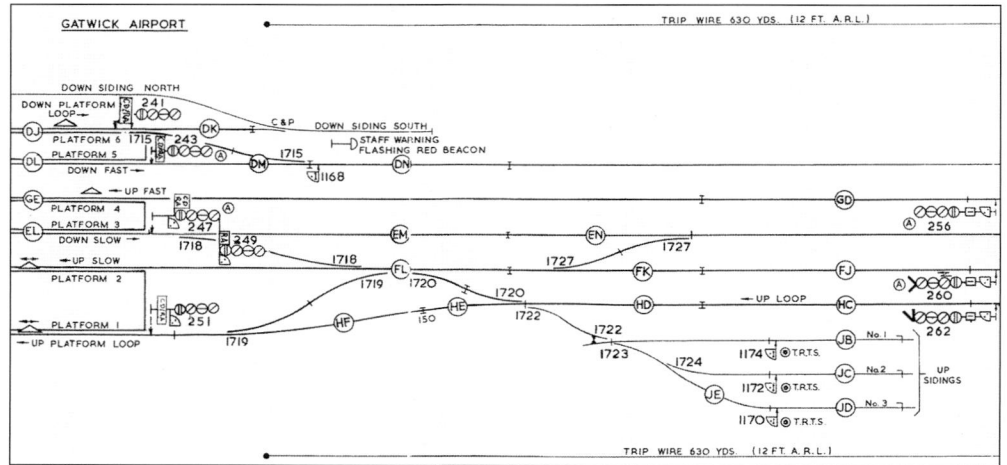

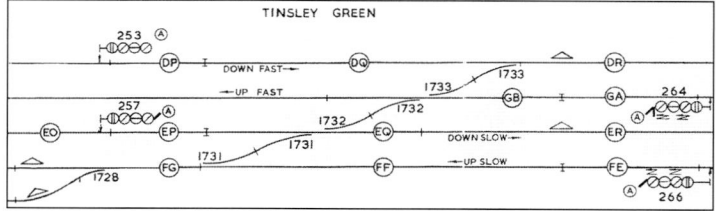

Centre and Right: The south end of Gatwick Airport as commissioned on to the new Three Bridges panel in July 1983. The lower panel shows the ladder crossovers installed during July 1980 in the vicinity of the old airport station some three quarters of a mile to the south, whilst 1728 points are the turnout into the Up Loop line. The 'Z' arrows adjacent to T260, T264 and T266 signals denote flashing yellow aspects.

Below: The last photograph in this section is a reminder that Gatwick serves the second busiest airport in the country. *June 1978*

24 – Horley

Two superb views of Horley station dating from the early 1890s. The first Horley station opened with the line in 1841 and was enlarged into this form around 1883, before being completely rebuilt at its present site in 1905. The top view is looking north towards Station Road and shows to good effect the Brighton lower quadrant (Down starting) signals of the type employing separate lamps, prior to the use of spectacle plates. A revolving mechanism within the lamp put the correct coloured glass (red or green) in front of the internal burner for sighting at night and was worked by a crank, seen emanating below the lamp housing. However, due to an instance where a crank rod broke giving a permanently clear aspect with the signal arm at danger, the whole mechanism was redesigned to give the now familiar 'outside arm' with coloured spectacle plates and fixed lamp behind. When Horley station was first built, it was seen as the perfect place for the Company's workshops and carriage sheds as it was almost at the midway point between London and Brighton, with the line at ground level and with a plentiful source of water from the River Mole. Facilities were provided on the Up side of the line but were not to last, as Brighton was to become the focal point of activity. The bottom view shows the handsome station building on the Down side (which survived as staff accommodation into the 1960s) with Victoria Road level crossing in the distance, the enormous water tower also evident in both views. The stationmaster beams at the cameraman and poses along with some members of his staff and two immaculately attired and well-behaved children, perhaps destined to become company servants.
John Minnis Collection

Horley South signal box layout in 1920.

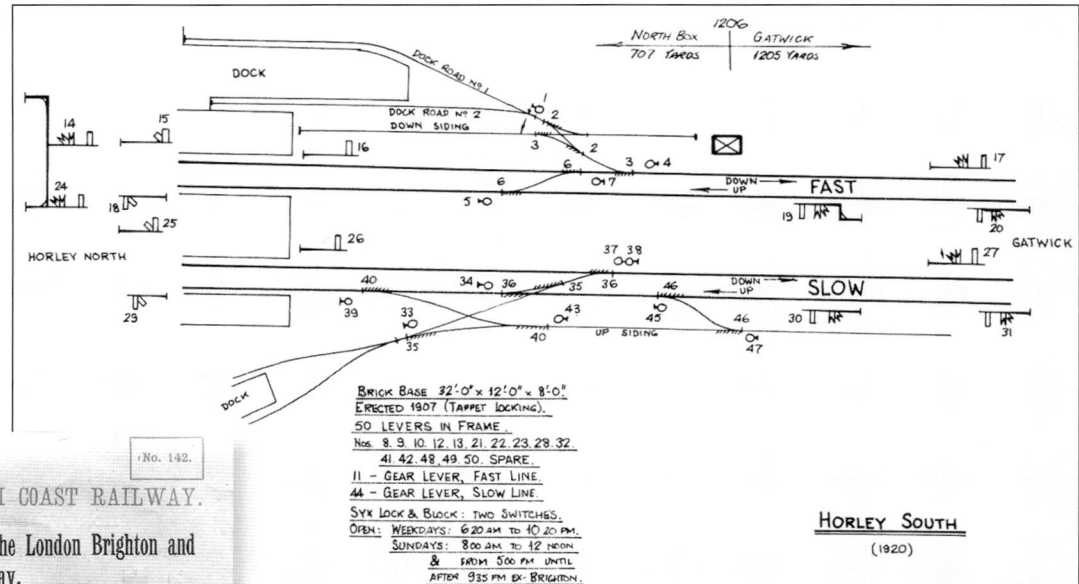

LONDON BRIGHTON AND SOUTH COAST RAILWAY.

Notice to the Officers and Servants of the London Brighton and South Coast Railway.

HORLEY.

OPENING OF NEW PASSENGER STATION.

Commencing with the first Passenger Train on Sunday, December 31st, the New Passenger Station, Platforms and Approaches, will be opened for Passenger and Parcels Traffic.

On and from the same date, all Passenger Trains booked to call at Horley must do so at the respective New Platforms.

SLIPPING CARRIAGES AT HORLEY.—The opening of the New Station will not alter the present arrangement for the Slipping of Carriages at Horley.

The East Grinstead slip part of the 5.5 p.m. Train from London Bridge, must be brought to a stand at the same place as hitherto, where the Engine will be attached and the Train drawn **ON THE DOWN MAIN LINE** to the Down Platform at the New Station at Horley for Passengers to alight.

Left: An extract from the opening notice for the new Horley station dated 27th December 1899.

Below: Horley South signal box contained a standard 23-lever frame and opened in 1883. It controlled Victoria Road level crossing and closed in December 1905 when the road was diverted over a new bridge further to the south, upon which the new station buildings were constructed. *Lens of Sutton Collection*

Right: The 30-lever Horley North signal box controlling Station Road level crossing opened in 1883, replacing a Saxby & Farmer structure dating from 1864. With the LB&SCR's policy to abolish all level crossings on the line, it closed prior to the widening works in December 1905.
Lens of Sutton Collection

Left: Henry Young (H. Young & Co.) opened his foundry in Pimlico in 1871 and supplied the LB&SCR with this handsome footbridge, seen (*upper left*) in June 1890, at a cost of £240. The Horley Supply Stores (est. 1859) dominates the background and was still in evidence, although in a different guise, in December 1980 when the later photograph (*lower left*) was taken. The replacement footbridge does not quite have the charm of the earlier structure.
(Upper left) Author's Collection

Horley North signal box layout in 1920 with an impressive 51 levers in work, although this would reduce to 39 in 1932 with the advent of colour light signalling.

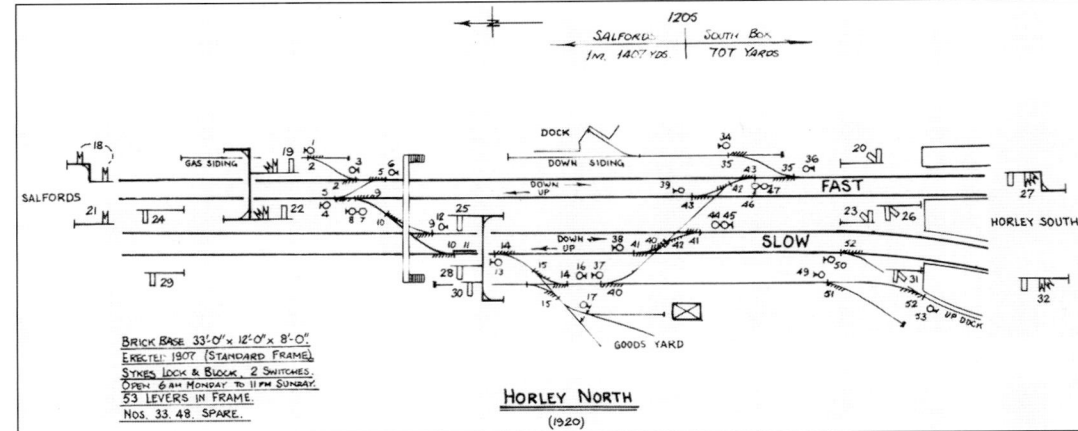

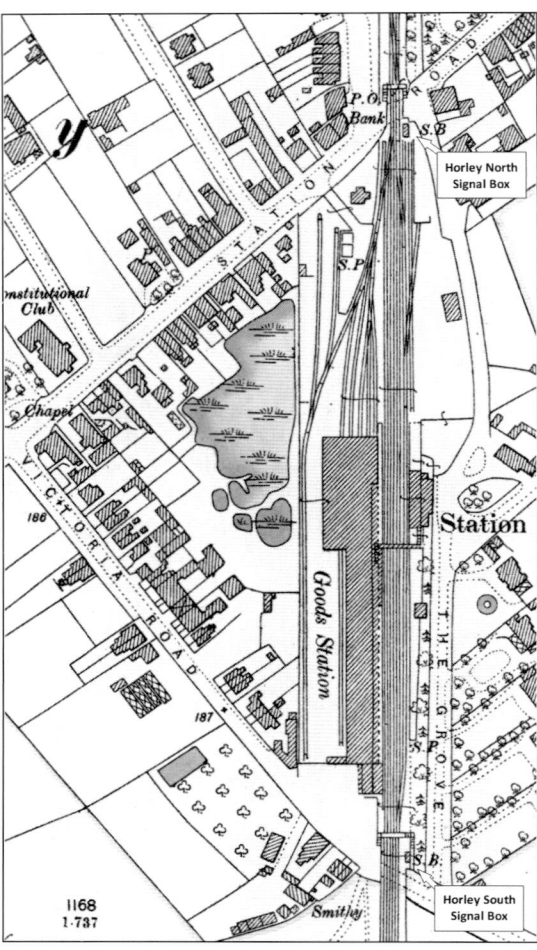

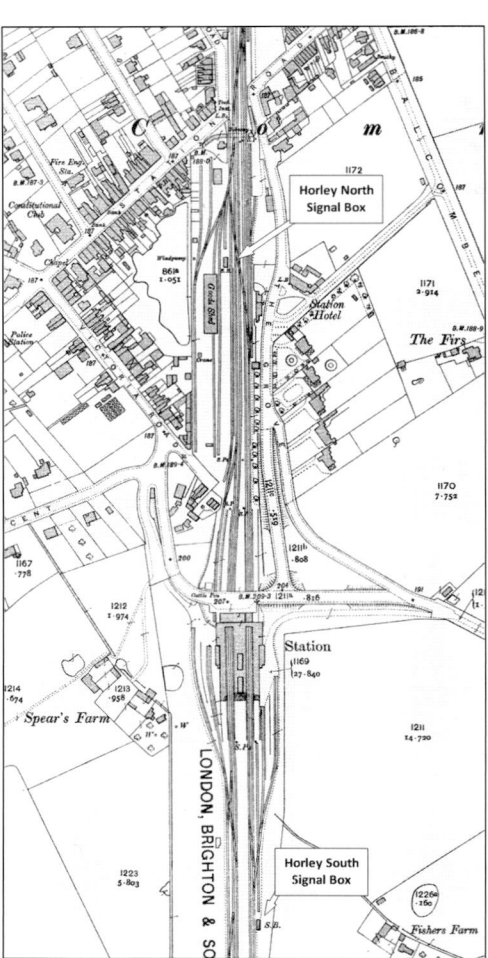

LEFT: The original Horley station site from an 1896 map showing the two signal boxes that controlled Station Road level crossing to the north and Victoria Road crossing to the south.
Reproduced by permission of the National Library of Scotland

RIGHT: The reconstructed station site from a 1913 map showing both the new station and the changes to the road layout required to abolish both Station Road and Victoria Road level crossings that had once existed at either end. The two replacement 1905 signal boxes are marked.
Reproduced by permission of the National Library of Scotland

BELOW: Horley South signal box opened in December 1905 containing a 50-lever standard frame. Renamed Horley 'B' in May 1959, it was the first to go, closing its doors on 23rd September 1960.
John Minnis Collection

A Down passenger train with one Pullman car in tow approaches the signal box circa 1930. *John Minnis Collection*

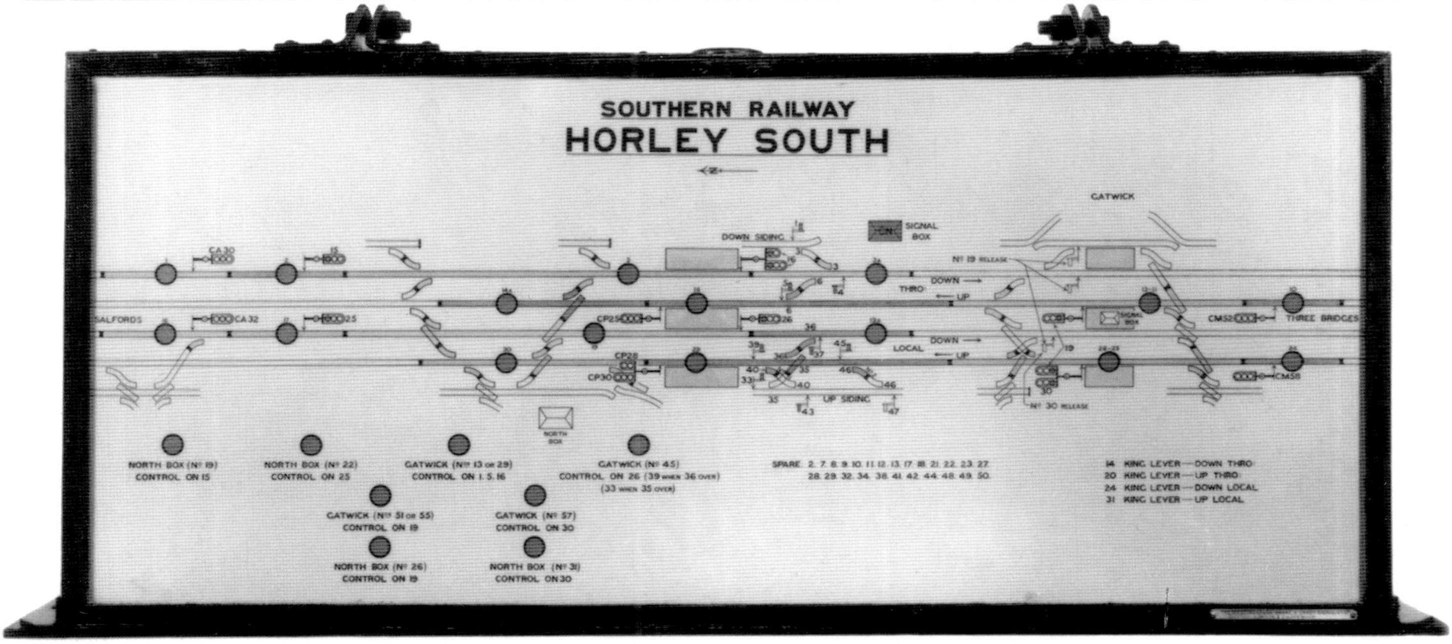

HORLEY 'B'

To be carried out on Friday, 23rd September, commencing at 9.0 am

Horley 'B' Signal Box will be abolished and all points and connections operated therefrom will be put out of use, the points being clipped and padlocked in the 'normal' position.

All Shunt signals operated by the Signal box will be removed.

(P/EW 35, LCD, 1960)

HORLEY

To be carried out on Monday, 26th September, commencing at 9.0 am.

The points and connections previously operated from the former Horley 'B' signal box, all of which are at present clipped and padlocked out of use, will be abolished.

(P/EW 36, L.C.D. 1960)

Above: The manufacturer's official photograph for the new Horley South box diagram. The *'Westinghouse Brake & Saxby Signal Co. Ltd., London & Chippenham'* brass plate is affixed to the bottom right corner of the frame. *K.R.M.*

Left: Closure notice for Horley 'B' signal box, 23rd September 1960.

Below: The later Horley control diagram, the layout already showing signs of rationalisation.

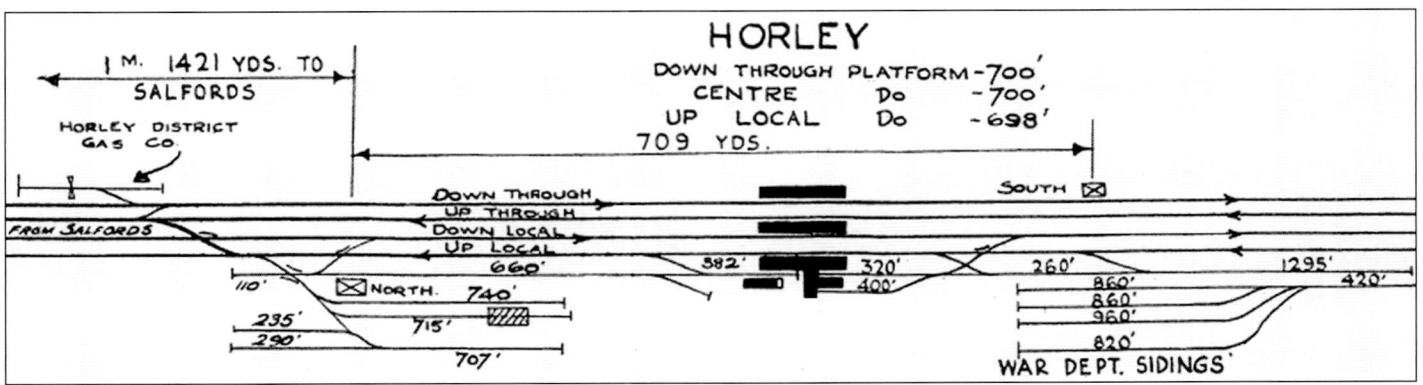

Above: Looking north from the island platform of the new Horley station, with the old station buildings just visible above the carriages; four slip coaches are being brought into the Down Fast platform, probably to form a service on towards East Grinstead or Horsham. Happily there is a good view of the London end of the station with the Up Fast starting and Down home signals prominent. I would hazard a guess that a Great Northern Railway signal engineer (whose somersault signal arms in the 'Off' position bordered on the vertical) would not have been particularly impressed with South box's No. 15 signal arm, struggling to attain 30° below horizontal. *Laurie Marshall Collection*

Below: Taken from a very similar position five or more decades later, the 16.00 London Bridge to Brighton (via the Quarry Line) heads south through Horley station. The complexities of the semaphores and their associated slotting are long gone and only Horley North's three-aspect CP25 signal is on view. *23rd September 1968, John Scrace*

A pre-electrification view looking south from the footbridge adjacent to what was once Station Road level crossing. The subway that was built to compensate for the loss of a flat crossing is still in use today. The old station has all but disappeared, with just the main station building on the Down side still in situ and visible to the immediate left of the Up Fast signal No. 25. North signal box can be glimpsed between No's 28 and 30 signals and the goods shed, today a listed building and fulfilling a different purpose as a retail outlet, can be seen to the right of it. The bare outline of where the original Horley North signal box once stood can just be discerned in front of the curved subway roof on the left, whilst the Up-side subway emerges to the right of the guards' brake parked in the Up-side siding. *John Minnis Collection*

The reliveried 'Brighton Belle' passes through Horley on 15th July 1969. Horley signal box, seen on the right, presides over virtually nothing and within another nine months will have passed into history. The ghosts of what were once the lovely buildings of the old station are lost in the trees on the left and cars are encroaching on to the land once occupied by Up sidings. *John Scrace*

A fine photograph of the SR Signal Works gang posing in the 4ft of the Up Fast line with Horley North's Up advance starting signals in the background. They are in the process of installing the new a.c. track circuits and have dug out the ballast in the 10ft ready for the tail cables to come across from the elevated cable route over in the Up Slow cess. Half of the gang are wearing ties but, resplendent in his double breasted jacket, the Lineman, Arthur Razzell, wears the cap. The seated gentleman in the centre of the group is sitting on a newly installed impedance bond. The pair of contrivances seen behind the seated group would appear to be bond lifting mechanisms.

The $9/32$ins holes for the track circuit connections (two per lead with the copper track leads soldered to the bonding wire inserted in the holes using a 'mox' iron) would have been drilled using a chain driven 'hurdy gurdy' machine, whilst the $7/8$ins holes for the traction side-leads would almost certainly have been drilled using a 'ratchet and clamp' (twenty minutes per hole, as I know from bitter experience). A 'Merx' (or mox) iron, Illustrated below, was an extremely useful device for making soldered connections out on the track. A 'briquette', a cylindrical cartridge filled with magnesium with a central hole covered with a thin foil, was placed in the receptacle and the tip of one of the matches pushed through the foil and into the powder. With the lid closed and fastened, a second, lighted match, was now pushed through to ignite the ignition powder which in turn fired the magnesium. It was best to look away now as a sheet of white flame and sparks would shoot skywards before the process settled down to a happy gurgling sound. After a short time (the temperature reaching some 5,000°F), the soldering tip would be hot enough for perhaps five minutes of work so you had to be quick, thereon repeating the procedure as required. The groove seen on the tip was used for exactly the procedure described above, heating the bonding wire to make the soldered connections. *31st October 1931, Ron Razzell Collection*

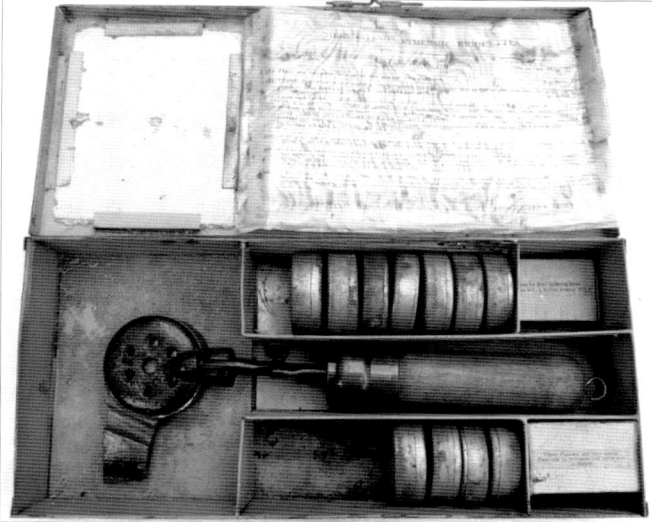

A Mox Iron kit (*left*) along with a box of Flamers (matches) (*above*). *Courtesy of* Blowlamp News

Above: A wonderful study of Horley North's Down Fast distant signal (No. 18) with a top 'blind' arm. Just visible on the lower arm between the chevron and the post is a mercury switch, indicating that the arm is 'on', as part of the requirement for Horley North giving a 'line clear' and accepting a train from Salfords. Although on occasion I have questioned the Company's delight in providing vertigo-inducing signal posts, their worth was certainly proved here as the Down home signals rise majestically beyond the overbridge in the distance, giving the driver excellent approach viewing. The gas works, once a common sight in any large town and here commanding its own siding, provides a distinctive landmark.
3rd July 1930, The Edward Wallis Collection

Top Right: Looking north, the same signal can be seen along with its partner applying to the Down Slow. Originally, both would have been of wooden post construction but No. 21 has been renewed at some point with an unusual tapering lattice structure, more modern fittings and a cruciform finial. The battery boxes for the repeater circuits can be seen at the base of both signal posts. Note the fogging huts, the Down Fast being redundant as the hut positioned in the 10ft has a pair of detonator placer levers to work both roads. Seen ahead is what will become CA29 signal.

Right: Lineman Arthur Razzell claims the structure as his own.
Top Right and Right, Ron Razzell Collection

ABOVE: As the sliding sash windows and box door are open to allow some air into its interior, on what must have been a warm summer's day, an Up mixed freight passes Horley North signal box. Opening at the same time as its near neighbour at the south end of the station, Horley North had three more levers than its counterpart, containing 53 in another standard LB&SCR frame. Along with the South cabin it enjoyed some twenty-seven years in regular service but post-1932 was only opened as required; it did, however, manage to last nearly a decade longer than its partner, closing on the 8th March 1970. It was renamed Horley 'A' in May 1959 and plain Horley when 'B' 'box closed in 1960.
John Minnis Collection

LEFT: The extract from the Weekly Operating Notice for March 1970 (*top*) details the demise of the sole remaining signal box at Horley. The signal box layout had been gradually reduced as detailed in the other entries from the mid-1960s.

HORLEY—Sunday, 8th March.—The signal box will be abolished and the colour light signals at present operated therefrom will in future be automatically controlled by track circuits only and be re-numbered as follows:—

Old Number	New Number	Description
CP25	CA27	Up Through Home (Platform starting)
CP30	CA49	Up Local Inner Home (Platform Starting)
CP19	CA28	Down Through Home
CP22	CA48	Down Local Home

Gatwick Airport signal box will in future be in electrical communication with Salfords signal box on the Local lines and Earlswood signal box on the Through lines.

(P/EW 10 C.D. 1970)

HORLEY

To be carried out on Sunday, 22nd November commencing at 00 05

The facing connection in the Up Local line 170 yards Earlswood side of signal box leading to Up Through line will be abolished.

The trailing points in the Up Local line 133 yards Earlswood side of signal box leading from Up Siding, together with the trap points in the siding and slip connection 90 yards Earlswood side of signal box leading from Goods Yard will be abolished.

The Up Local to Up Through inner home signal situated 262 yards Gatwick Airport side of signal box (CP.28) will be removed.

The shunting signal 136 yards Earlswood side of signal box controlling movements back on Up Local line or from Up Local line to Up Siding or Goods Yard will be removed.

The shunting signal 78 yards Earlswood side of signal box controlling movements along Up Siding northwards or from Up Siding to Up Local or Through lines will in future only apply for movements along Up Siding.

The shunting signal 78 yards Earlswood side of signal box controlling movements from Goods Yard to Up Siding, Up Local or Up Through lines will in future only apply for movements from Goods Yard to Up Siding.

The shunting signal 277 yards Earlswood side of signal box controlling movements from Up to Down Through lines or from Up Through line to Down Local or Up Local lines will not in future apply for movements from Up Through to Up Local lines.

(P/EW 44, C.D. 1964)

HORLEY

To be carried out on Tuesday, 18th May, commencing at 10 00.

All points operated from the signal box will be put out of use, being disconnected from the signal box and clipped and padlocked in the normal position, pending abolition.

All shunting signals will be removed.

(P/EW 18, C.D. 1965)

HORLEY

To be carried out on Saturday, 19th June, commencing at 23 00, until completed on Sunday 20th June.

The trailing points in the Up Local line, 189 yards Gatwick Airport side of signal box, leading from Up Siding, together with the trap points in the siding will be abolished.

The trailing connection between Up Local and Down Local, and the slip points leading from Up Siding 7 yards and 12 yards Earlswood side of signal box respectively, together with the Up Siding and trap points therein will be abolished.

The trailing points in the Down Local line, 176 yards Earlswood side of signal box, leading from Up Through line will be abolished.

(P/EW 22, C.D. 1965)

HORLEY—Thursday, 3rd August.—The trailing points in the Down Through line, 245 yards Salfords side of the signal box, leading from former Gas Siding, previously clipped and padlocked out of use, have been abolished.

The trailing crossover between Down and Up Through lines, 244 yards Salfords side of the signal box, previously clipped and padlocked out of use, have been abolished.

(P/EW 28, C.D. 1967)

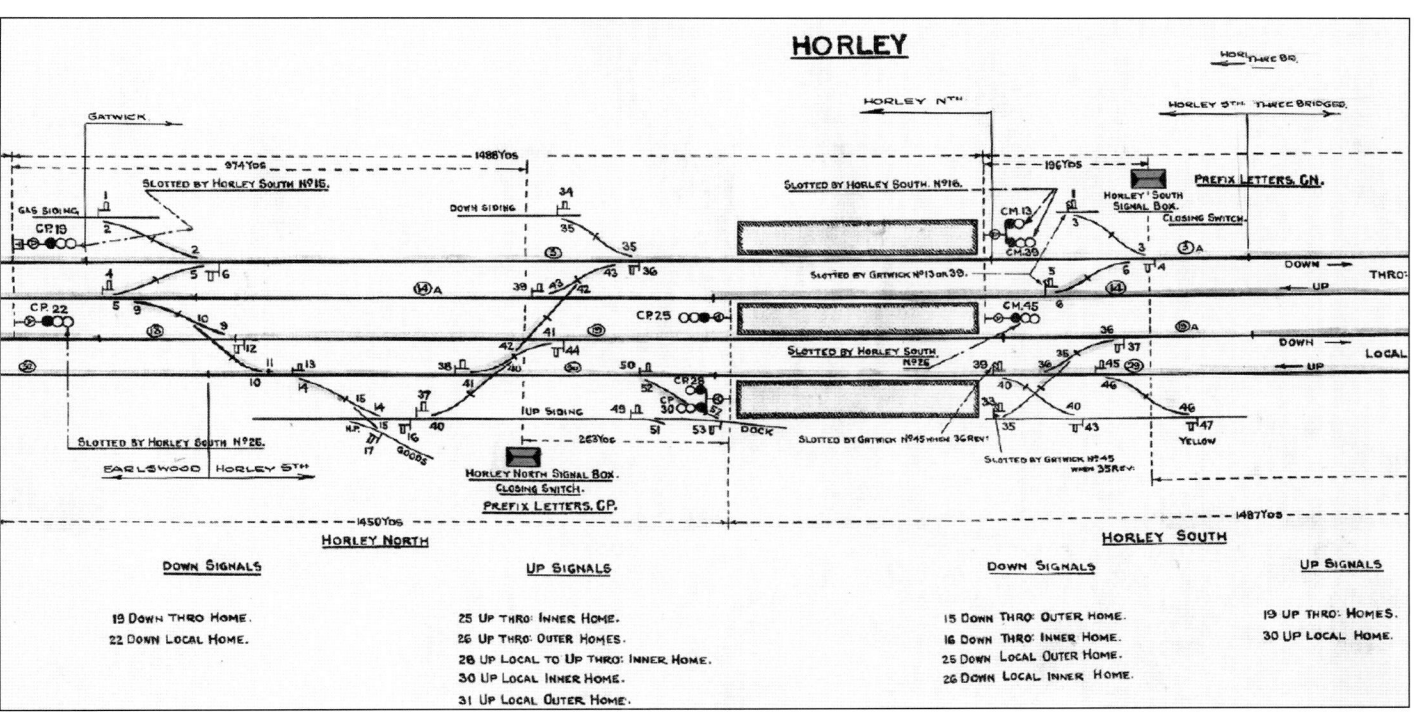

ABOVE: Horley station from the 1933 track plan showing the remarkable layout that was controlled, as and when required, from either the North or South signal boxes. The Down platform starting signals belong to Gatwick (slotted by Horley South) with CM13 leading to Gatwick's Down Loop. It must be remembered that at this time all four signal boxes between Earlswood and Three Bridges were normally switched out of use, hence every main running signal on show is fitted with an 'A' light. The Railway Clearing House 'Official Handbook of Stations' for 1938 lists the amenities for the station to include the carriage of: *'Furniture Vans, Carriages, Motor Cars, Portable Engines & Machines on Wheels, Live Stock, Horse Boxes & Prize Cattle Vans'*. Carriages and motor cars could also be conveyed on passenger trains. The fixed crane power was 5 tons. South signal box was the first to go in 1960 with North box following suit ten years later. It is almost too embarrassing to include the drastically simplified current situation, below.

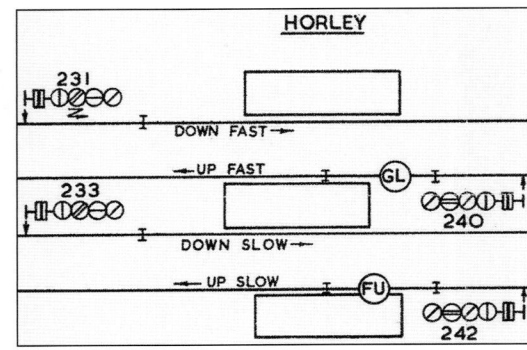

LEFT: Cable laying on the Up Slow line north of Horley station in preparation for the 1932 electrification. The three cables are being laid into the CM&EE (Chief Mechanical & Electrification Engineer) route, the signalling route being the one nearest the track. Apart from the motive power provided, the principle has not changed to this day.
31st October 1931, Ron Razzell Collection

Above: A late 1950s view of Horley station, unaltered from when it was built with generous canopies for each platform. Note the conductor rail protection boards at the bottom of the platform ramp as that is where staff were expected to cross; how times have changed!
Lens of Sutton Collection

Below: With British Rail reducing their maintenance overheads, this was the scene in September 1984. The Down Fast platform canopies have gone completely and the nearest platform building on the island platform is in the process of being demolished; the Up Slow platform canopy has also been shortened. The pile of timber seen here did not go to waste though (it can be safely revealed now), as van loads found their way back to the author's parents' house to be used in the construction of his first dark room in their loft.

25 – Salfords

Salfords signal box opened with the widening of the line in 1907, replacing an 1891 cabin that had once existed further to the south. It contained a 44-lever standard frame, 20 of which were spare prior to the resignalling but rising to 30 thereafter. On the same day that Cliff Richard's 'Living Doll' topped the charts, ex-LM&SR No. 45426 brings a holiday special from Eastbourne to Manchester (via Brighton) past the signal box. 22nd August 1959. Bluebell Railway Museum Archive, J.J. Smith Collection

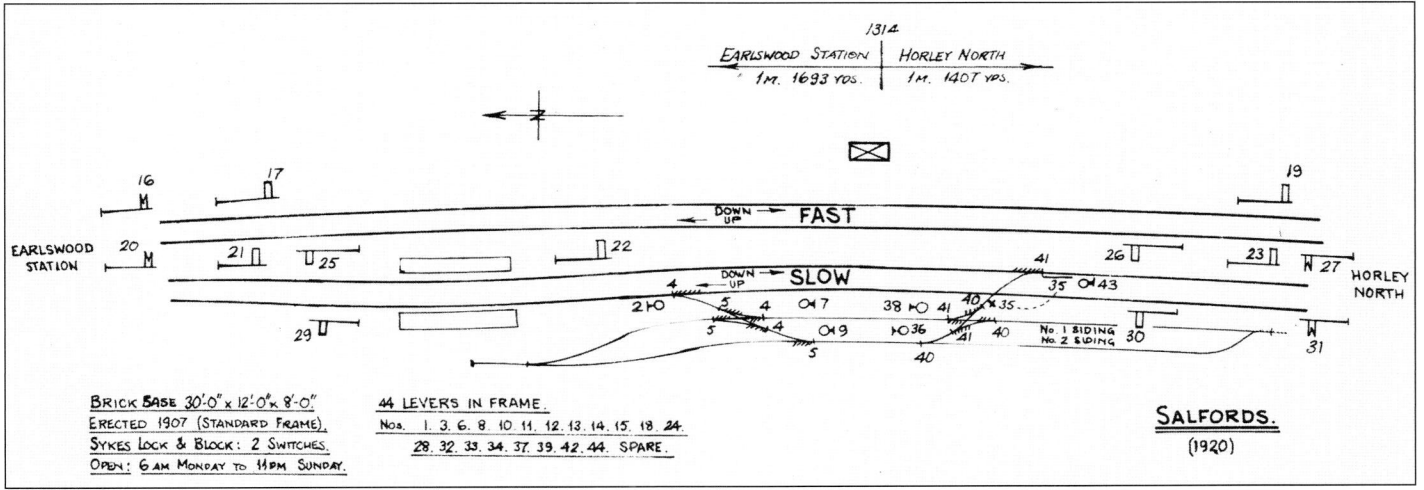

ABOVE: Salfords layout in 1920 with the standard distant, home and starter for all roads except the Down Slow, which has an additional platform starting signal to protect moves from the Up sidings.

RIGHT: The Salfords track plan extract from 1933 showing that after the resignalling the signal box controlled the Local lines only. The two controlled signals ('CQ' prefix) were fitted with 'A' lights as they would be working automatically for the vast majority of the time.

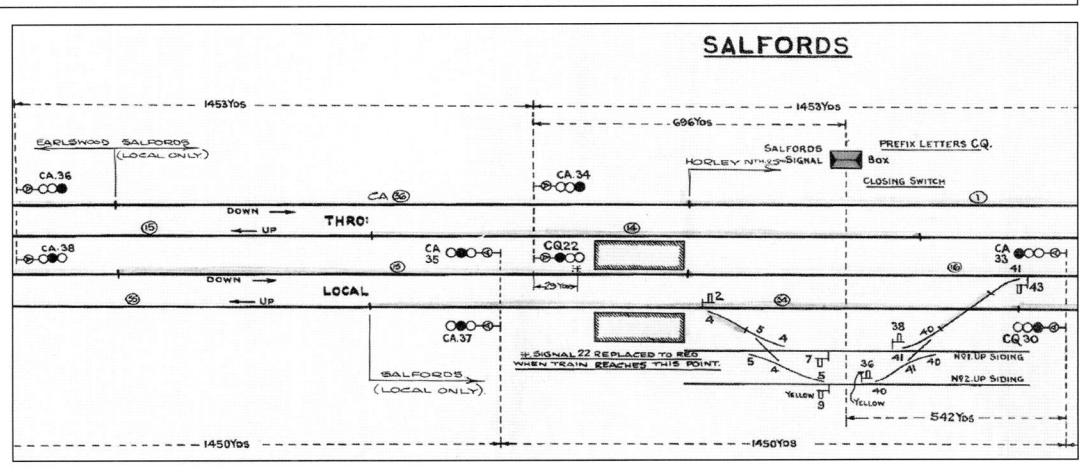

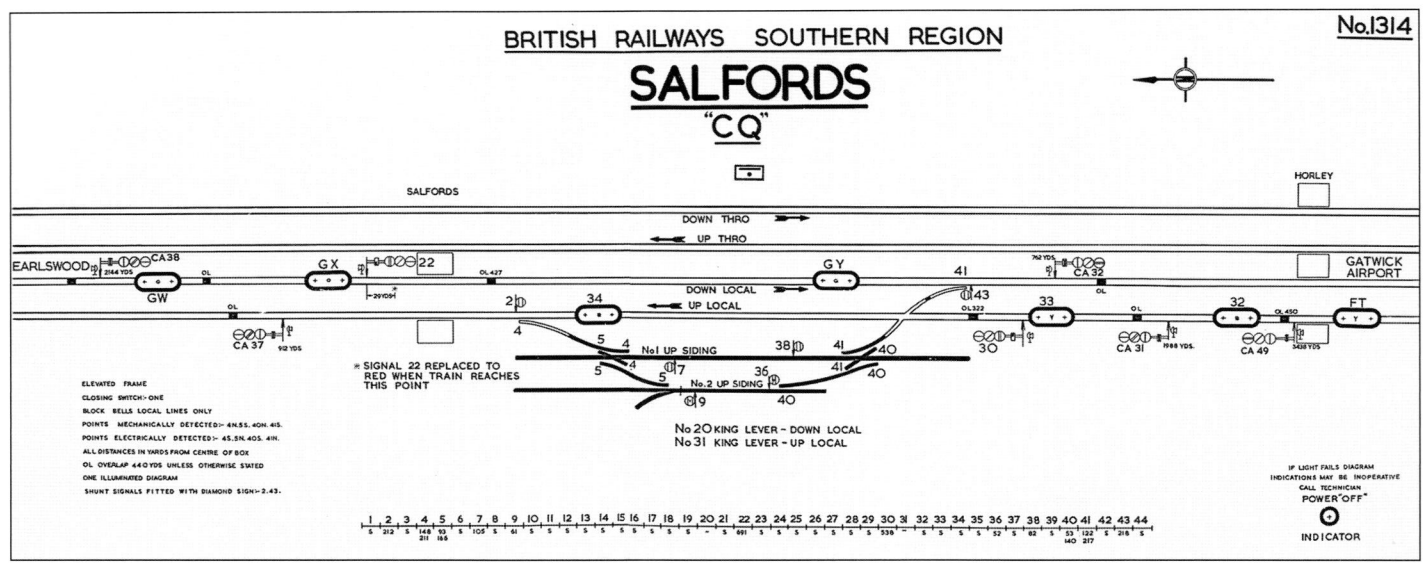

Above: Salfords' signal box diagram dated 25th March 1971. Both Horley boxes had gone by this time, so Salfords, when opened, fringed to Gatwick Airport and Earlswood respectively.

Left: Salfords' Up Fast distant signal (with an unusually decorative 'fish-tail'), waits to be returned to the 'on' position as a short passenger train disappears into the distance, shortly to pass the signal box itself. As was typical for a 'Brighton' signal, the ladder ascends to the front and, having climbed some forty rungs to a painfully small landing with a single grasp rail positioned to the left, it must have been assumed that all maintenance personnel who worked at these heights were right handed!
3rd July 1930, The Edward Wallis Collection

Facing Page Centre: Salfords signal box retained its original nameboard until the end and is seen here on 4th August 1967. *John Scrace*

Facing Page Bottom: With the sliding sash windows open at either end, the signal box was seeing some use and, although there is not a soul in sight, it would appear that the signalman had just finished some washing up as his ceramic bowl is upturned on the veranda to dry. Maybe some wagons were being prepared in the sidings as a pair of tail lamps can be seen at the bottom of the box steps, along with a paraffin container and a pourer. Official access to the signal box was via the steps down the bank. The Calor gas containers providing the heating had just one more winter to contend with, as Salfords signal box closed on 27th April the following year.
6th April 1974, Edwin Wilmshurst

Right: The extract from the control diagram shows the extent of the sidings, Salfords' sub-station being depicted in the vee of the sidings.

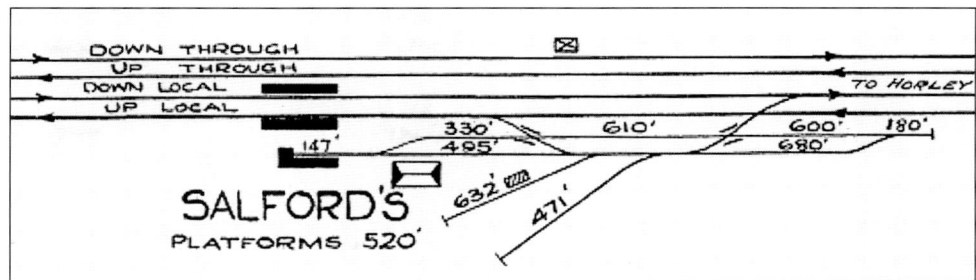

Salfords, not opening until 8th October 1915, was the last station to be built on the main line although there had been some pressure to provide one here as early as 1896. Platforms were built serving the slow lines only and it was first used for workers to access local factories such as the Monotype Corporation and Mullards (to whom the author applied unsuccessfully for an apprenticeship!) before entering the public timetable. *Lens of Sutton Collection*

The closure notice for Salfords signal box from the Weekly Operating Notice. The slip connections had been taken out of work earlier in the month and – with the remaining points converted to motor operation and the mechanical shunts to position lights – the 'dark art' of the Signal Engineer seamlessly transferred control of the area on to the Earlswood lever frame.

Sunday, 27 April – Salfords.–The signal box will be abolished. The trailing connection between the Up Local line and Up Siding No. 1 and the trailing connection between the Down Local and Up Siding No. 1 will be operated from Earlswood.

The under mentioned semi-automatic signals will be controlled from Earlswood, re-numbered as shown:–

DESCRIPTION & EXISTING NUMBER	SITUATED	NEW NUMBER
Down Local line signal CQ 22	Earlswood side of station	CR 35
Up Local line signal CQ 30	Gatwick Airport side of station	CR 59

The telephone at Down Local line signal CA32 situated Gatwick Airport side of the station will give direct communication with the Gatwick Airport Signalman.

All other signal telephones which, at present, give direct communication with Salfords signal box, will, in future, communicate direct with Earlswood signal box.

Left: Proving that not an awful lot had changed in the interim, this is a similar view to the one opposite, taken in November 1979.

Below: The 16.50 Victoria to Ore passes the signal box on 7th June 1969, the structure gauge standing guard over the empty sidings. *John Scrace*

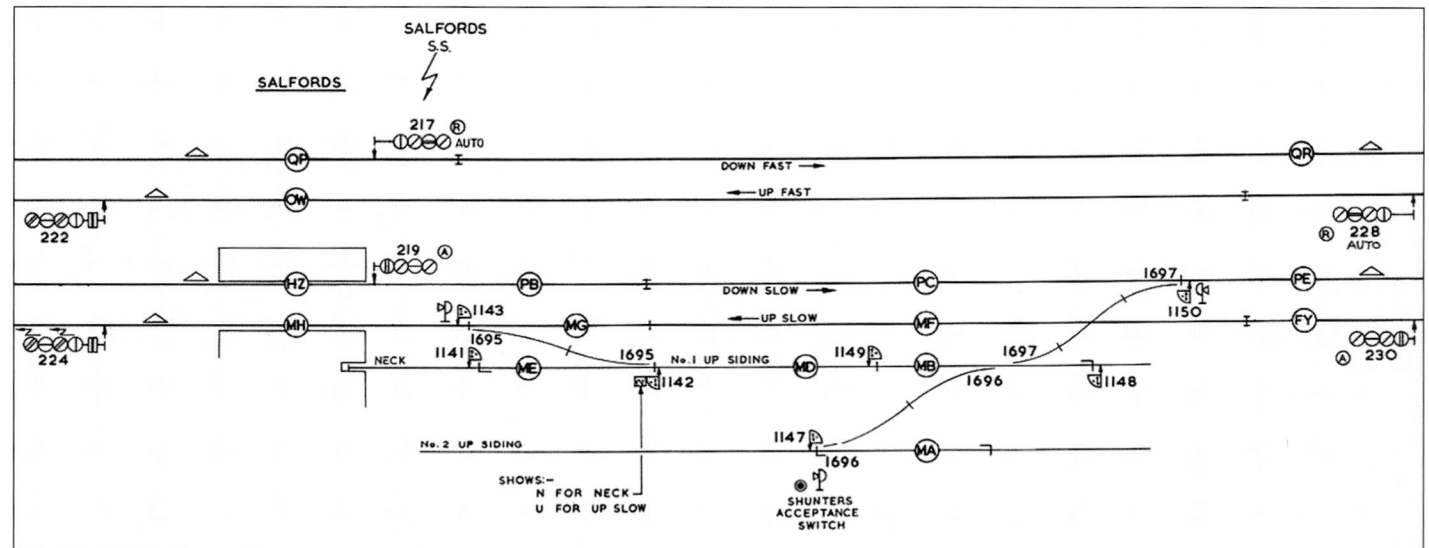

Looking south from the station footbridge, a healthy number of passengers waits for a Down train. The signal box is still extant and can just be glimpsed, along with its access steps down the bank, through the mist in the far distance. In the days before dedicated pipelines, Salfords was a major depot for aviation fuel and a number of enormous holding tanks can be seen to the right of the sub-station. Aggregates are beginning to take hold though, as some hopper wagons also occupy the sidings. The fast lines pass by untroubled.
27th June 1972, Denis Cullum, Lens of Sutton Collection

Salfords suffered far less than many of its compatriots. It is seen here as commissioned on to the Three Bridges panel and except for the removal of two pairs of double slips, the layout has not changed much from 1933.

26 – Earlswood

ABOVE: A goods train with a rake of empty wagons sits in the middle siding at Earlswood station waiting for an Up train to pass through on the Fast Line. Earlswood station signal box (seen here at the country end of the Up Local platform) opened in 1906, contained a 41-lever standard Brighton frame and controlled the south end signals and entrances to the east, west and middle sidings. *M.P. Bennett Collection, Courtesy Bluebell Railway Archives*

RIGHT: Earlswood and its environs enjoyed a complicated history regarding its signal boxes. Initially two had been provided: one in 1863 just south of St. Johns Road bridge, with another, Redhill Goods, a little later in 1869. Both are highlighted in this 1874 edition map. At this time Earlswood worked to Earlswood Common signal box (opened in 1863), providing a break section between there and Salfords. In 1899, with the opening of the new Quarry Line, both Earlswood and Redhill Goods were replaced by new structures as detailed in the opening notice (*overleaf*); Redhill Goods (41 levers) to a position in the vee of the new junction and Earlswood (50 levers) to a site at the north end of the newly reconstructed station. This must have been a busy time for Brighton's signal engineering department as both of these lasted a mere six years. Earlswood Junction (reverting to plain Earlswood in 1932 and which was to have to have the greatest longevity of all) opened during November 1905, with a new signal box opening at the south end of the station the following year. All of this enabled both aforementioned short-lived cabins, plus Earlswood Common, to be abolished.
Reproduced by permission of the National Library of Scotland

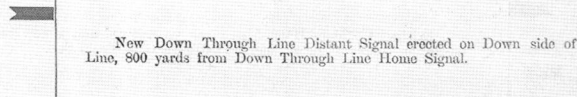
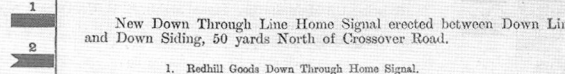

ABOVE AND FACING PAGE: The title page and selected inside pages to the now rather grubby opening notice for the quadrupling of the line from South Croydon to Coulsdon North and the new Quarry Line on to Earlswood. The new line opened for goods traffic on 5th November 1899 and to passenger traffic on 1st April the following year. The arrangements for South Croydon continue but are outside the scope of this book.

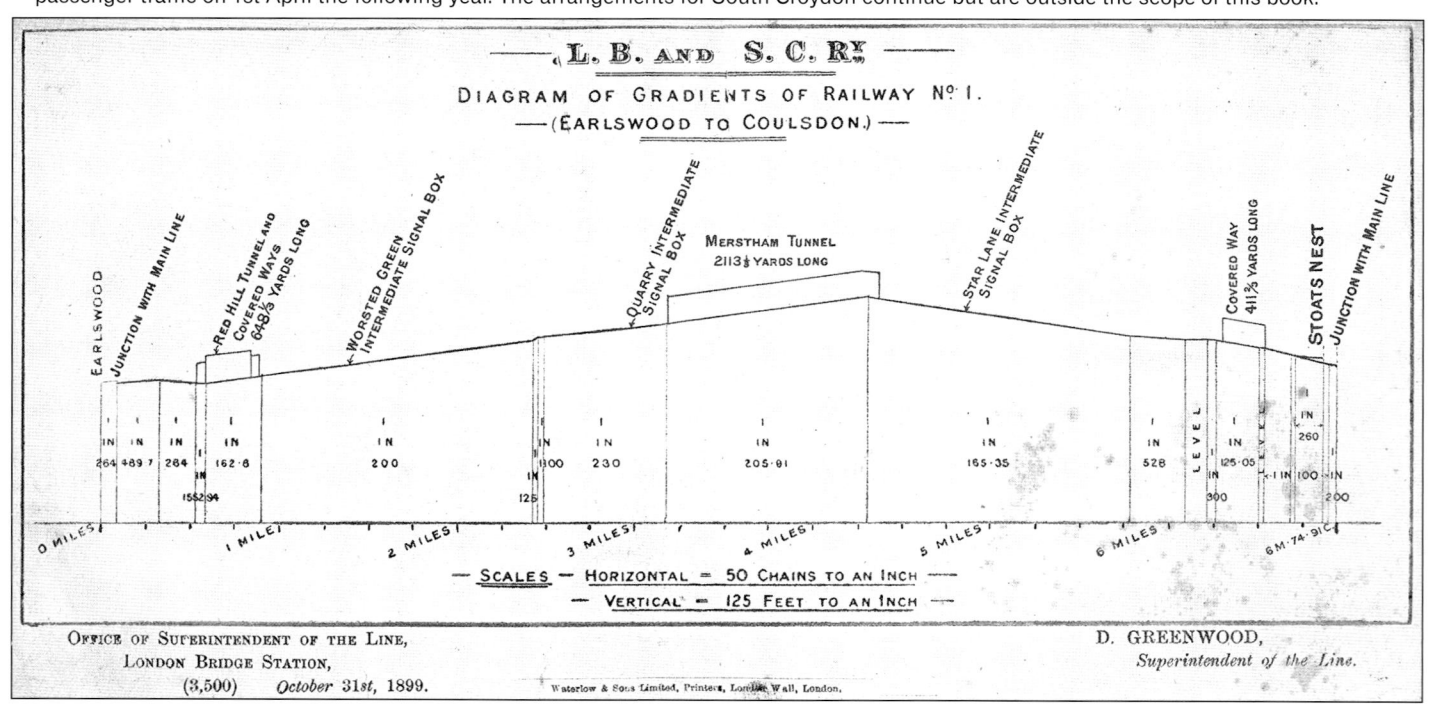

16

REDHILL GOODS BOX.—MAIN LINE SIGNALS—*continued.*

Existing Down Main Home Signal will be renewed near same site.

1. Redhill Goods Down Main Home Signal.
2. Earlswood Down Main Distant Signal.

As seen from Down Main Line Trains leaving Redhill Junction.

Existing Up Main Home Signal will be removed and a new Signal erected on Up Main side of Line, 110 yards South of Signal Box.

As seen from Up Main Line Trains leaving Earlswood Junction.

Existing Up Main Starting Signal and S. E. R. Up Distant Signals will be removed, and a new Signal erected on Up side of Line, 180 yards North of Signal Box.

1. Redhill Goods Up Main Starting Signal.
2. S. E. R. Redhill Up Main Distant Signal.
3. S. E. R. Redhill Up Loop Distant Signal.

As seen from Up Main Line Trains approaching Redhill Junction.

New Ground Disc Signal at North end of Crossing, from Up Main to Up Siding, North of Signal Box.

New Ground Disc Signal at North end of Crossing, from Up Main to Up Siding, South of Signal Box.

New Ground Disc Signal at each end of Main Crossover Road.

New Ground Disc Signal at South end of Crossing, from Down Main and Down Siding.

EARLSWOOD JUNCTION.

The Old Signal Box at Earlswood will be removed and a new Box erected at North end of Up Platform, from which the New Through Line Junction, and all Signals and Points will be worked and brought into use, together with the following New Points and Signals:—

New Crossover Road between New Down Through Line and Down Siding, with Ground Disc Signal at each end.

New Ground Disc Signal fixed at the New Junction Trailing Points will apply for Shunting from Down Main to New Down Sidings.

New Ground Disc Signal for Shunting from Up to Down Lines.

New Ground Disc Signal at each end of Crossing between Down Line and Asylum Siding.

Temporary Catch Points are laid in Up and Down New Lines North of Junction.

17

EARLSWOOD JUNCTION—*continued.*

New Down Through Line Home Signal erected between Down Through Line and Down Siding, 180 yards North of New Junction.

Existing Down Main Home Signal will be removed and a New Signal erected between Down Main and Up Through Lines, 180 yards North of New Junction.

Existing Down Starting Signal will be removed and a New Signal erected at end of Down Platform.

New Down Advanced Starting Signal erected on Down side of Line, 300 yards from Station.

Existing Up Distant Signal will be removed and a New Up Distant Signal erected on Up side of Line, 800 yards from Up Home Signal.

1. Up Main Distant Signal.
2. Up Through Distant Signal.

As seen from Up Trains approaching Earlswood Station.

Existing Up Home Signal will be removed and a New Up Home Signal erected on Up Side of Line, 100 yards South of Up Siding Points.

As seen from Up Trains approaching Earlswood Station.

Existing Up Starting Signal will be removed, and New Up Starting Signals erected at North end of New Signal Box.

1. Earlswood Up Main Starting Signal.
2. Earlswood Up Through Line Starting Signal.
3. Redhill Goods Up Main Distant Signal.
4. Redhill Goods Up Through Line Distant Signal.

As seen from Up Trains approaching Earlswood Junction,

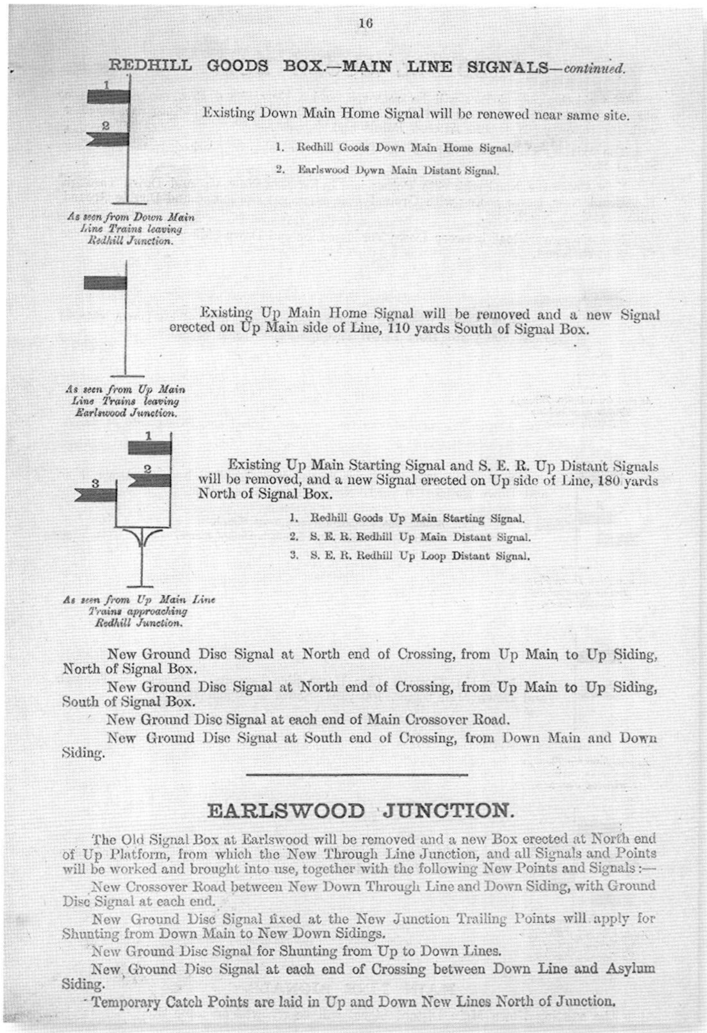

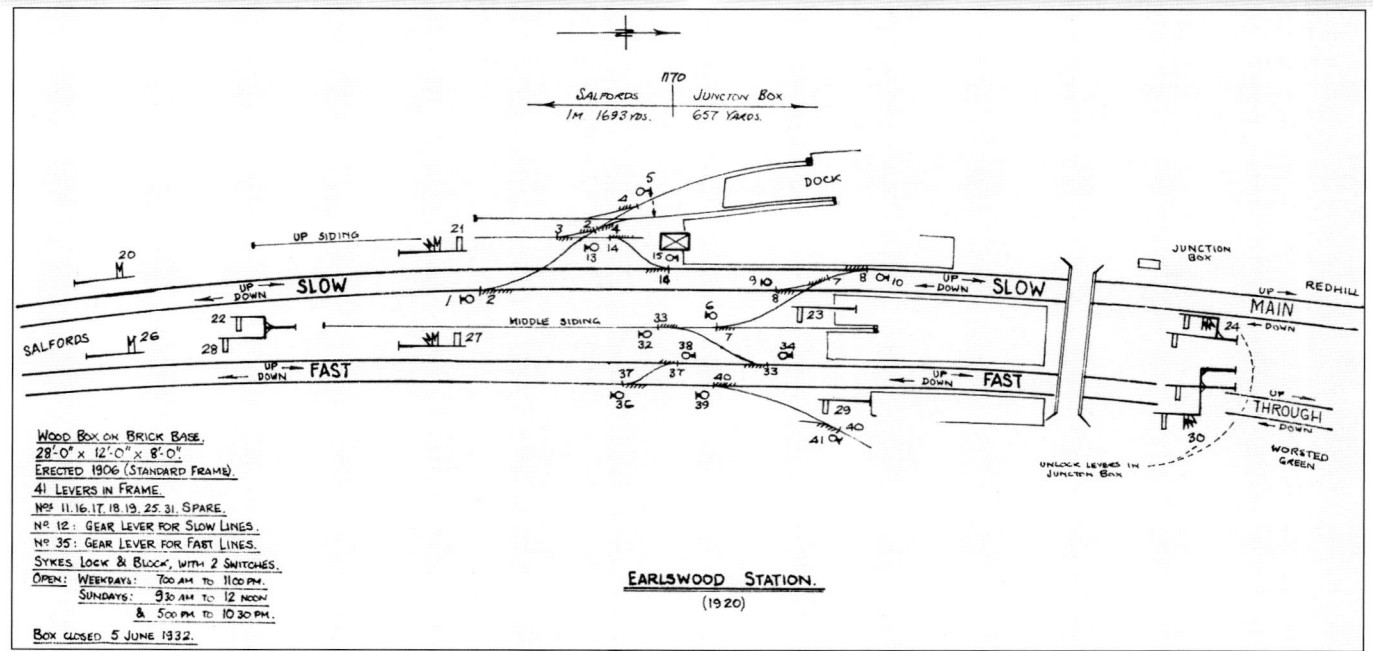

Above: Earlswood Station signal box layout in 1920.

Facing Page Bottom: Taken from the opening notice for the new Quarry Line, this is the gradient diagram for the new section of railway that opened on the 31st October 1899. This is described here as 'Railway No. 1', with 'Railway No. 2' being the onward section to South Croydon. Note the departure from the 1 in 264 ruling gradient that formed the original main line.

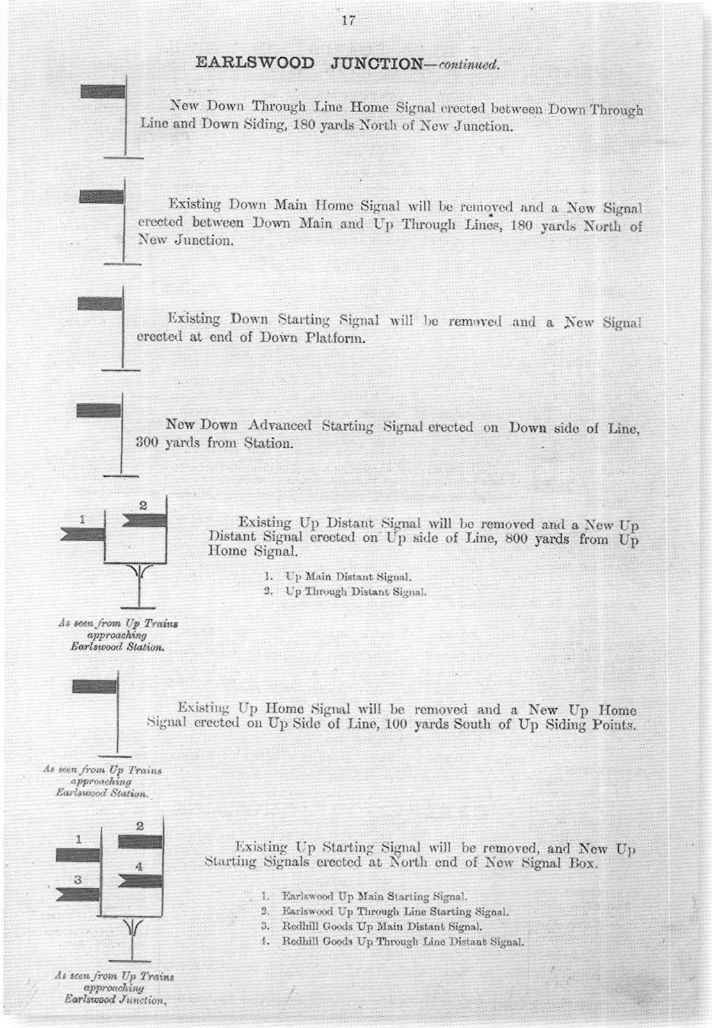

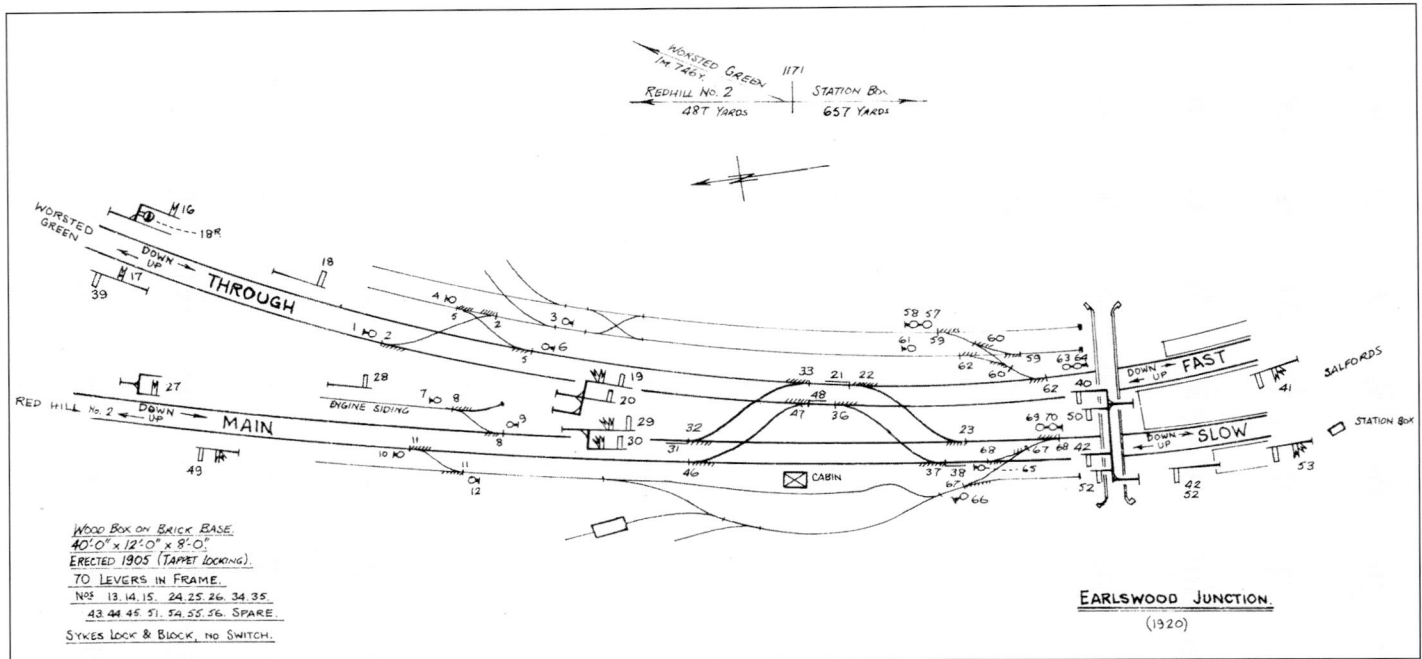

The 1905 Earlswood Junction signal box layout is seen here in 1920.

An early view of Earlswood Junction taken from St. Johns Road bridge. The through lines via Star Lane veer off to the right whilst the 'Main Line' (or 'Old Road') carries straight on towards Redhill. Some serious work is being carried out, maybe some underpinning to the large concrete retaining wall. Removal of part of the sidings has been necessary to enable the derrick to be erected (anchored to the cess rail of the Up Main and again at the top of the bank) whilst a steam boiler billows away. The magnificent LB&SCR signal structure in the centre background, carrying Earlswood Junction's home signals with Station box's distant signals below, controls Down Road moves over the junction. The two lines to the extreme right form part of the Down sidings. *John Minnis Collection*

SOUTHERN RAILWAY.

Signal Instruction No. 17, 1932.

INSTRUCTIONS TO ALL CONCERNED
AS TO THE
INTRODUCTION OF COLOUR LIGHT SIGNALS
(In place of existing Semaphore Signals)
BETWEEN COULSDON NORTH No. 2 AND BALCOMBE TUNNEL SIGNAL BOXES (VIA QUARRY LINE);

AND

ABOLITION OF EXISTING CANE HILL, QUARRY, WORSTED GREEN, EARLSWOOD STATION, TINSLEY GREEN, AND THREE BRIDGES NORTH AND SOUTH SIGNAL BOXES;

ALSO

RE-NAMING OF LINES BETWEEN EARLSWOOD JUNCTION AND BALCOMBE TUNNEL

ON A DATE TO BE ADVISED.

Rules 70, 71 and 72 to be observed. Drivers to keep a good look out for hand signals.

The existing semaphore running signals on the down and up Quarry lines between Coulsdon North No. 2 and Earlswood Junction signal boxes, and on all lines between Earlswood Junction and Balcombe Tunnel signal boxes, will be abolished, and colour light signals installed in lieu thereof.

The existing Cane Hill, Quarry, Worsted Green, Earlswood Station, Tinsley Green and Three Bridges North and South signal boxes will be abolished. Earlswood Junction and Three Bridges Central signal boxes will be known in future as Earlswood and Three Bridges respectively.

The running lines between Earlswood Junction and Balcombe Tunnel will be re-named as follows:—

Existing Name.	New Name.
Down fast.	Down through.
Up fast.	Up through.
Down slow.	Down local.
Up slow.	Up local.

A diagram showing the new signals and their location is attached to this notice, the signals being prefixed by letters to denote from which box the signals are worked, as follows:—

Prefix letters.	Signal box from which signals are operated.
C.T.	Coulsdon North No. 2.
C.S.	Star Lane.
C.R.	Earlswood.
C.Q.	Salfords (local lines only).
C.P.	Horley North.
C.N.	Horley South.
C.M.	Gatwick.
C.L.	Three Bridges.
C.K.	Balcombe Tunnel.

NOTE.—Star Lane, Salfords, Horley North, Horley South and Gatwick signal boxes will be switched out of circuit for certain periods and during the time these signal boxes are so closed the running signals will work automatically.

Automatic signals will be prefixed by the letters C.A.

Plates bearing these prefix letters and the number of the signal will be fixed to each signal post carrying running signals.

The new colour light running signals will show three, four or two aspects and will be known as automatic, semi-automatic or controlled signals, viz.:—

(a) Automatic signals are those which will not be worked from a signal box but which will be controlled by track circuit only.

(b) Semi-automatic signals are those which will be controlled from one or more signal boxes when such boxes are open, but which, when the boxes are closed, will work automatically and be controlled by track circuit only.

(c) Controlled signals are those which will always be worked from a signal box.

In certain cases 2-aspect colour light shunt signals will be provided.

Each 3-aspect running signal will consist of a group of three lamps, and the aspect exhibited at any one time will be (a) a red, or (b) one yellow, or (c) a green light.

Each 4-aspect running signal will consist of a group of four lamps, and the aspect exhibited at any one time will be (a) a red, or (b) one yellow, or (c) two yellow, or (d) a green light.

Each 2-aspect running signal (except those in tunnels) will consist of two lamps, and the aspect exhibited at any one time will be either (a) a red or (b) one yellow light.

Each 2-aspect Tunnel signal will consist of two lamps and the aspect exhibited at any one time will be either (a) one yellow or (b) a green light. (NOTE.—A red aspect will NOT be provided in Tunnel signals).

230009—1

This is the signalling notice that heralded the introduction of continuous colour light signalling on the Brighton Line, astonishingly brought into work during a mere six-hour shift.

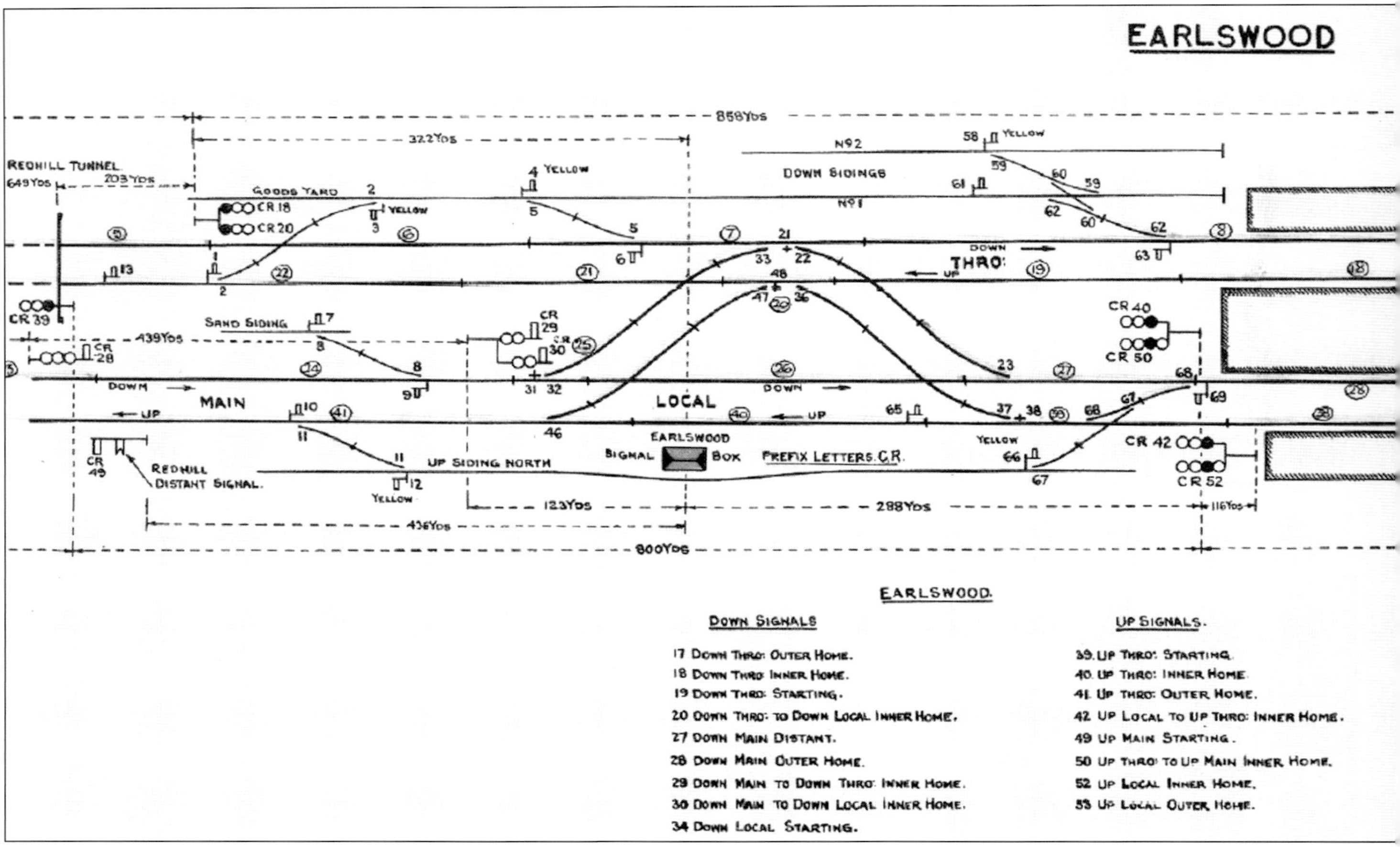
EARLSWOOD
858 YDS
322 YDS
REDHILL TUNNEL
649 YDS
203 YDS
GOODS YARD
DOWN SIDINGS
N92
N91
SAND SIDING
439 YDS
DOWN
UP
MAIN
LOCAL
THRO:
UP SIDING NORTH
EARLSWOOD SIGNAL BOX
PREFIX LETTERS. C.R.
REDHILL DISTANT SIGNAL.
123 YDS
288 YDS
116 YDS
436 YDS
800 YDS
EARLSWOOD.
DOWN SIGNALS.
17 DOWN THRO: OUTER HOME.
18 DOWN THRO: INNER HOME.
19 DOWN THRO: STARTING.
20 DOWN THRO: TO DOWN LOCAL INNER HOME.
27 DOWN MAIN DISTANT.
28 DOWN MAIN OUTER HOME.
29 DOWN MAIN TO DOWN THRO: INNER HOME.
30 DOWN MAIN TO DOWN LOCAL INNER HOME.
34 DOWN LOCAL STARTING.
UP SIGNALS.
39 UP THRO: STARTING.
40 UP THRO: INNER HOME.
41 UP THRO: OUTER HOME.
42 UP LOCAL TO UP THRO: INNER HOME.
49 UP MAIN STARTING.
50 UP THRO: TO UP MAIN INNER HOME.
52 UP LOCAL INNER HOME.
53 UP LOCAL OUTER HOME.

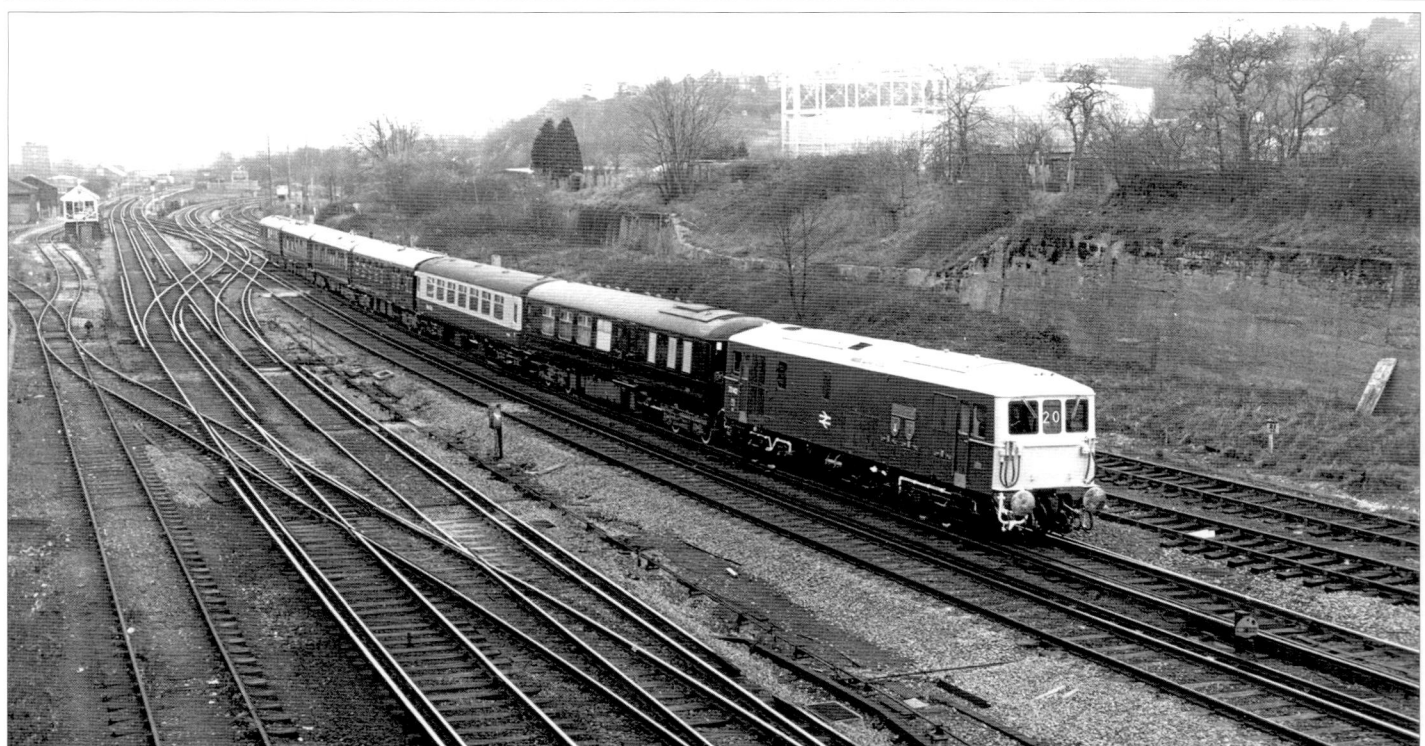

At the head the Royal Train, an immaculate Class '73' locomotive brings the President of Nigeria over the junction at Earlswood. No doubt His Excellency has just admired the fine LB&SCR 70-lever 'Type 3B' signal box, double junction and single slips on his journey to Gatwick Airport and would have been aghast if he had known that within a very short space of time all of this would be swept away, to be replaced by something far less sophisticated. Royal trains used to be a fairly common sight at Gatwick, welcoming foreign dignitaries into (or exporting them back from) the UK and it was always deemed prudent by management to have the Three Bridges S&T roster on standby near the station, in case any potential embarrassment should occur by way of an unwelcome signal failure. *17th March 1981, John Scrace*

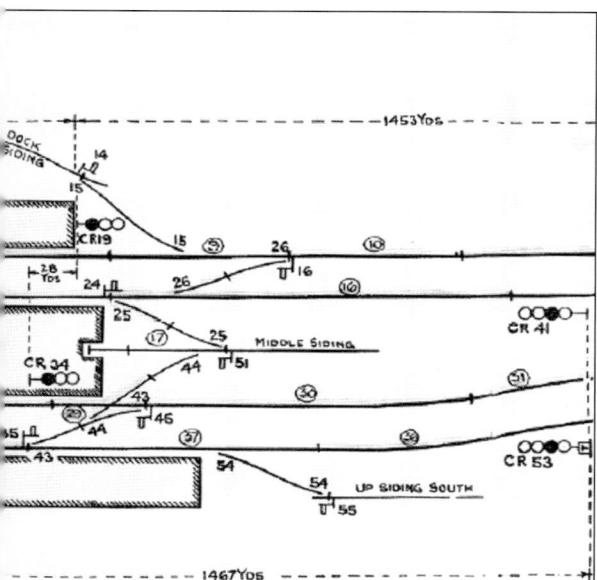

Left: Earlswood in 1933 was quite a layout. Redhill stayed purely mechanical, as can be seen, with semaphore signalling coming in on the main lines with 'approach lights' under the Up line signals for the transition from mechanical to colour light signalling. Even Earlswood's Down home signals, CR29 and CR30, were left mechanically worked, a situation that remained until 30th April 1967 when they were renewed as a single colour light signal with a Position 1 junction indicator for the Down Through line. Note the middle siding at the south end of the station, a situation not dissimilar to that at Three Bridges. At this juncture Earlswood normally worked directly to Three Bridges to the south (all intermediate boxes being switched out of use) and Coulsdon North No. 2 (with Star Lane switched out) to the north. On the 'Main Line' Earlswood fringed to Redhill No. 2 signal box.

Below: Earlswood station in all its pomp, with all four platforms provided with ornate canopies and linked by a subway. The Fast Line platforms closed in 1984 with rationalisation of the remaining buildings taking place around the same time.
Lens of Sutton Collection

Bottom: By January 1985, the Fast Line platforms are no longer in use and a 'bus shelter' contraption has been erected over the subway entrance to the Down Slow platform. The initial requirement for T205 banner repeater (the rear of which can be seen over the shelter) now becomes obvious but as the demolition of the island platform buildings brought the sighting of the main signal into full view, it was taken out of use not long afterwards.

Above: Adopting the name from its immediate predecessor, Earlswood Junction signal box opened in November 1905 but had its suffix dropped upon the 1932 resignalling, when it lost its near neighbour at the south end of the station. Looking in pristine condition, this is the view on 5th September 1968. *John Scrace*

Centre Left: The immaculate interior of Earlswood signal box, seen here during February 1980, almost as though the frame has been black-leaded in honour of the photographer's visit. The large black box nearest the camera is the 'modem' (modulator/demodulator) for the VDU screens, showing the signalman the description and whereabouts of trains within his jurisdiction. Different types of train describers share space with the three-position block instrument, to the left of the diagram working to Redhill.
Courtesy 53A Models of Hull

Left: The signal box was another casualty of the 1980s Brighton Line resignalling, closing on 2nd July 1983. Already with a rather forlorn look about it, this was the scene exactly a week after decommissioning. Interestingly (from a signal engineer's point of view), the point machine seen in the foreground is an interloper in the form of a Westinghouse '63' machine, the original 'M3' was obviously a victim of domestic renewals.

LEFT: The interior of Earlswood signal box is seen here a week after closure. The standard 'Brighton' frame of 70-levers sits below the block shelf with its single illuminated diagram, train describers and visual display units. At the time of its demise only 19 levers were classified as spare, although No. 49 lever, formerly the mechanical starting signal towards Redhill, retained its red paint and just sat in the frame minus its description plate. Anything of any value has already been removed, as can be seen by the spaces vacated under the rafters at the far end of the frame where the block bells once resided. *9th July 1983*

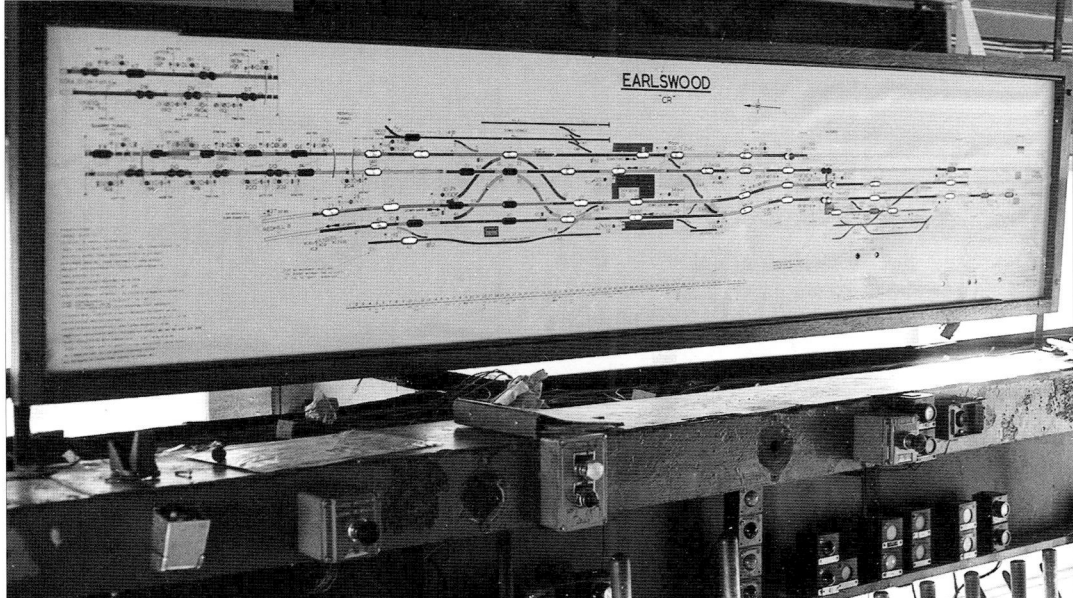

CENTRE: Looking at the number of occupied track circuits, this was not a particularly busy day for the signalman, just the box diagram post closure. Continuing on the theme of 'valuable assets' being removed, the circular scars once housed brass plungers, normally the first items to be looted. Collectors Corner was normally at the forefront of retaining anything worthy of onward sale from their premises at Euston. The 'Square D' plungers, two of which can be seen here, were always left, as they had no aesthetic qualities whatsoever. The B.R. ashtray screwed to the face of the block shelf was once an everyday sight in any smoking compartment. Salfords' Up sidings (which, as seen on page 235, was transferred on to the frame here in April 1975) can be seen towards the right-hand end of the diagram. *9th July 1983*

RIGHT: Earlswood control diagram showing the 1899 divergence of the Quarry Line and mass of sidings that once existed on the east side of the line. The southern entrance to Redhill Tunnel (sometimes called Sand Tunnel) is actually to the north of the ex-SER line to Tonbridge with a 'covered way' taking the Quarry Line under this. The official length of the tunnel, according to the LB&SCR, was 502yds, with the covered way (plus another short length at the north end) taking the total to 648⅓yds. The Southern Railway's official length was 649yds inclusive.

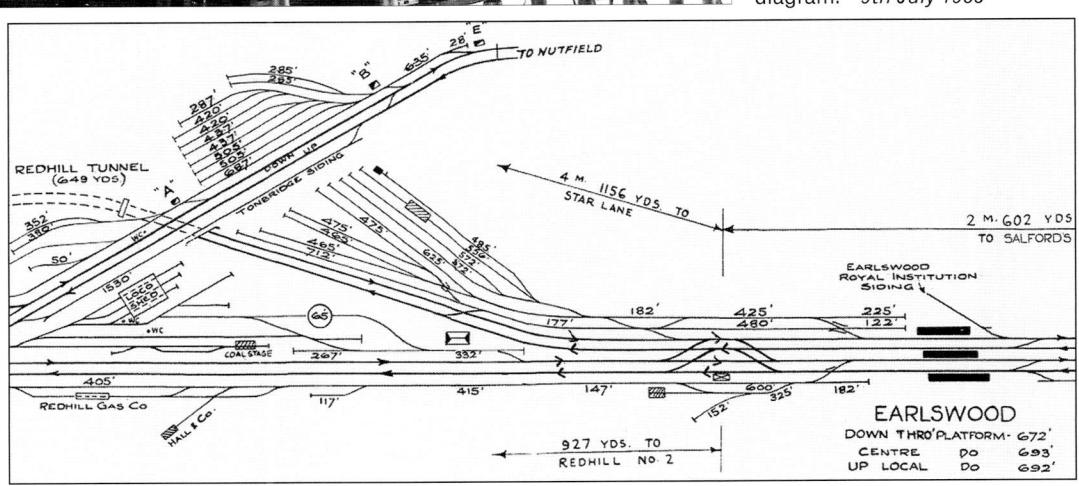

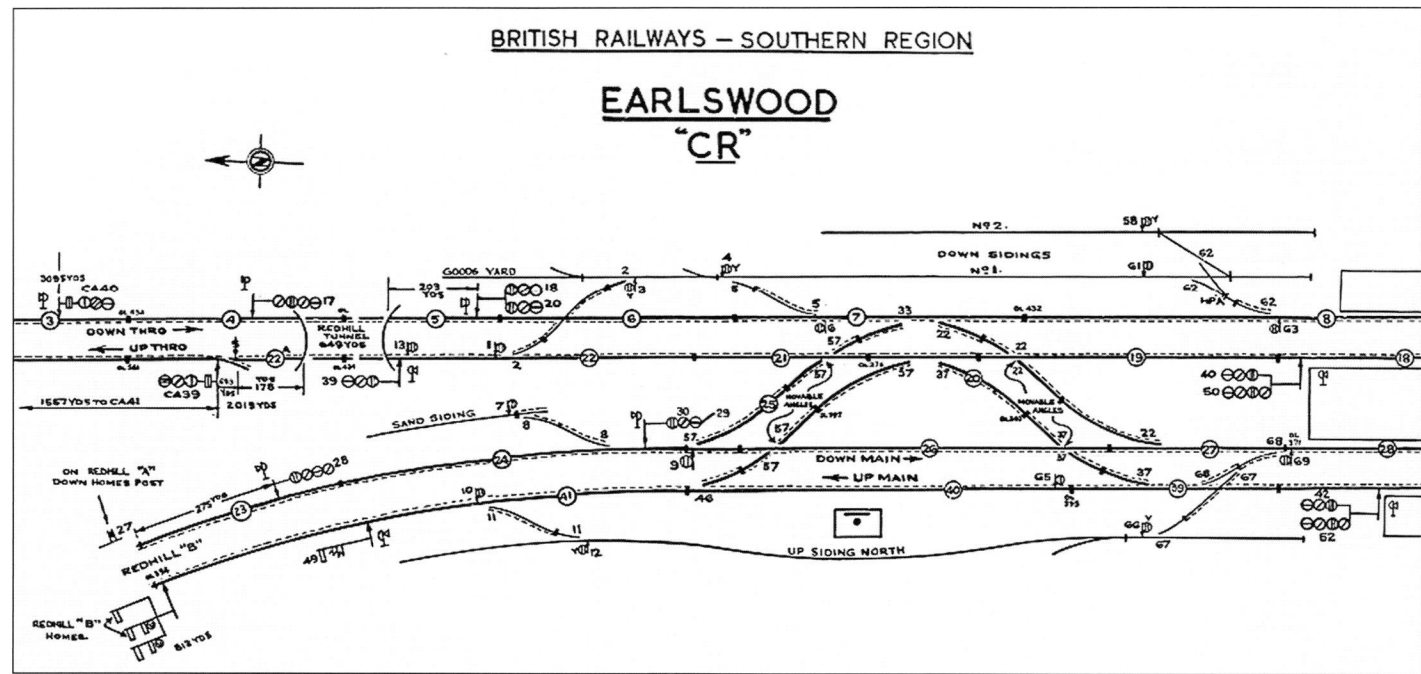

Above: This extract from the Earlswood signal box diagram (domestic copy) depicts the junction layout as of 3rd March 1975 and shows that, by this time, the fixed crossings in the parallel crossovers had been upgraded to moveable angles. The spring catch points just north of Redhill Tunnel (on a rising gradient of 162.8 lessoning to 1:200), catering for any breakaways from unfitted freight trains, seem an anachronism today but were a necessary evil even in the 1970s. The dashed lines within the diagram purely relate to the limits of track circuiting.

Earlswood's No. 49 Up starting signal is the uppermost arm in this photograph, slotted with the Up distant for Redhill 'B' below. This signal was abolished during September 1978 when the impressive array of semaphores seen in the distance was renewed as a colour light signal. Up Siding North, where the out-of-work connection once led on to Hall and Co's and Redhill Gas Company's sidings, is seen to the left of the signal whilst the sand siding veers off to the right of the picture. *March 1978*

Looking north from the end of the Up Through platform we have Earlswood's Up inner home signals, CR50 on the left applying to moves towards Redhill (Up Main) and CR40 for straight moves along the Up Through (Quarry Line). A Wickham trolley sits up against the buffer stops in the Down sidings which were gradually taken out of use, along with their main line connections, during the very early 1980s. Earlswood signal box and goods shed can be seen in the distance. *March 1978*

Seen from the end of the Up Local platform, CR52 signal gives the route towards Redhill whilst CR42 applies to moves across to the Up Through line. Although the signal heads are of differing heights, the red aspects remain parallel as the bottom aspect in CR52 is the single yellow, originally designed that way to give maximum separation between the two yellow aspects. Allegedly the red moved to the bottom because otherwise any build-up of snow on the top of the lower hood could possibly obscure the red aspect above it. Both pairs of signals were converted to a single head with route indicators on Sunday 10th September 1978, six months after these photographs were taken. *March 1978*

Running past the busy goods yard and about to enter Redhill Tunnel, Unit No. 2050 is captured forming the 09.15 semi-fast service from Brighton to London Bridge. The 1932 Earlswood sub-station sits in the vee of the junction, whilst the Down road colour light splitting signals CR18 and CR20 can be seen to the left of the last carriage. *5th September 1968, John Scrace*

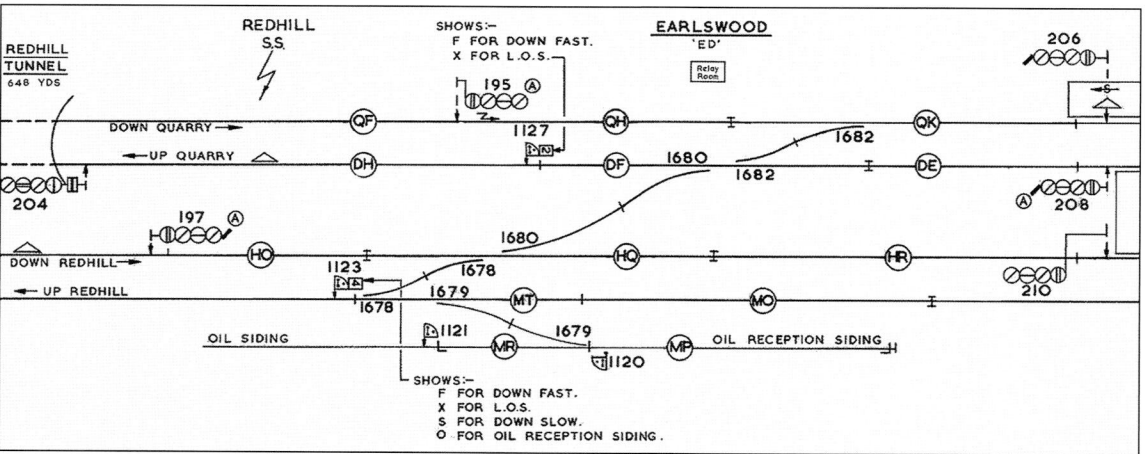

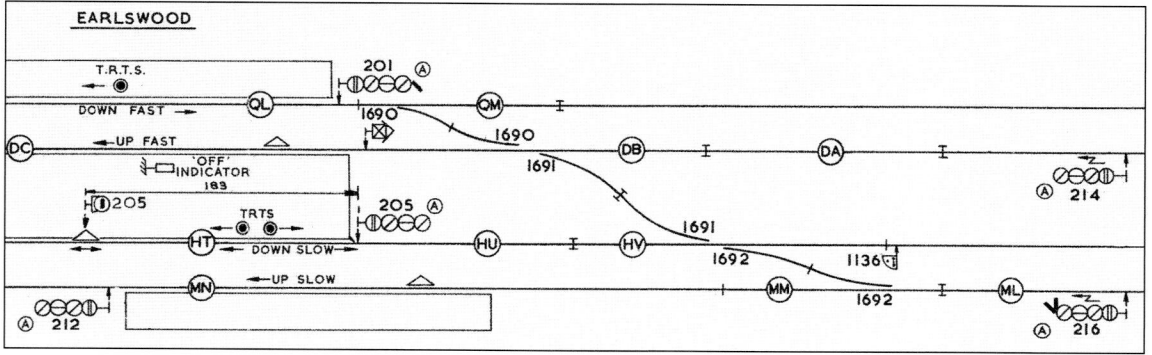

Left: The final Earlswood layout as controlled from Three Bridges panel, the north end of the station being the uppermost diagram. Although the new 'ladder' crossings at either end are of far simpler construction (and therefore maintenance), the advantages of the parallel crossovers of the old junction are gone. Since this diagram was produced, the fast line platforms have been abandoned, the T205 banner repeater has been abolished and the oil siding has been taken out of use. Redhill Tunnel seems to have shrunk by a yard compared with the earlier control diagram!

27 – Redhill

Looking south from Redhill's Down platform, this view presents a fine array of South Eastern Railway semaphore signals. The main signal bracket provides the permutations for the diverging routes towards Tonbridge on the left, the main line on to Earlswood and Brighton straight ahead, with Reigate and Guildford to the right. Redhill No. 2 signal box can be seen in the distance. Two staff crossings have been provided, with one member of staff in deep conversation and apparently in no hurry to join his colleagues on the platform, all completely indifferent to the photographer. A beautifully complete 'South Eastern' scene on the SER's main line route to Dover which remained until 1868 when the cut-off line was constructed between Sevenoaks and Tonbridge. *Laurie Marshall Collection*

Probably taken on the same day, the photographer has turned his camera northwards to record this view taking in Redhill No. 1 signal box and Up starting signals. The Up platform and main line signals are cantilevered out from the Down side, a situation that was not to last as they were later to be more conventionally positioned at the end of the Up platform. It would have taken some degree of bravery attending to the top arm of the Up through line signal. An impressive selection of advertising enamels is attached to the rear fence. *Laurie Marshall Collection*

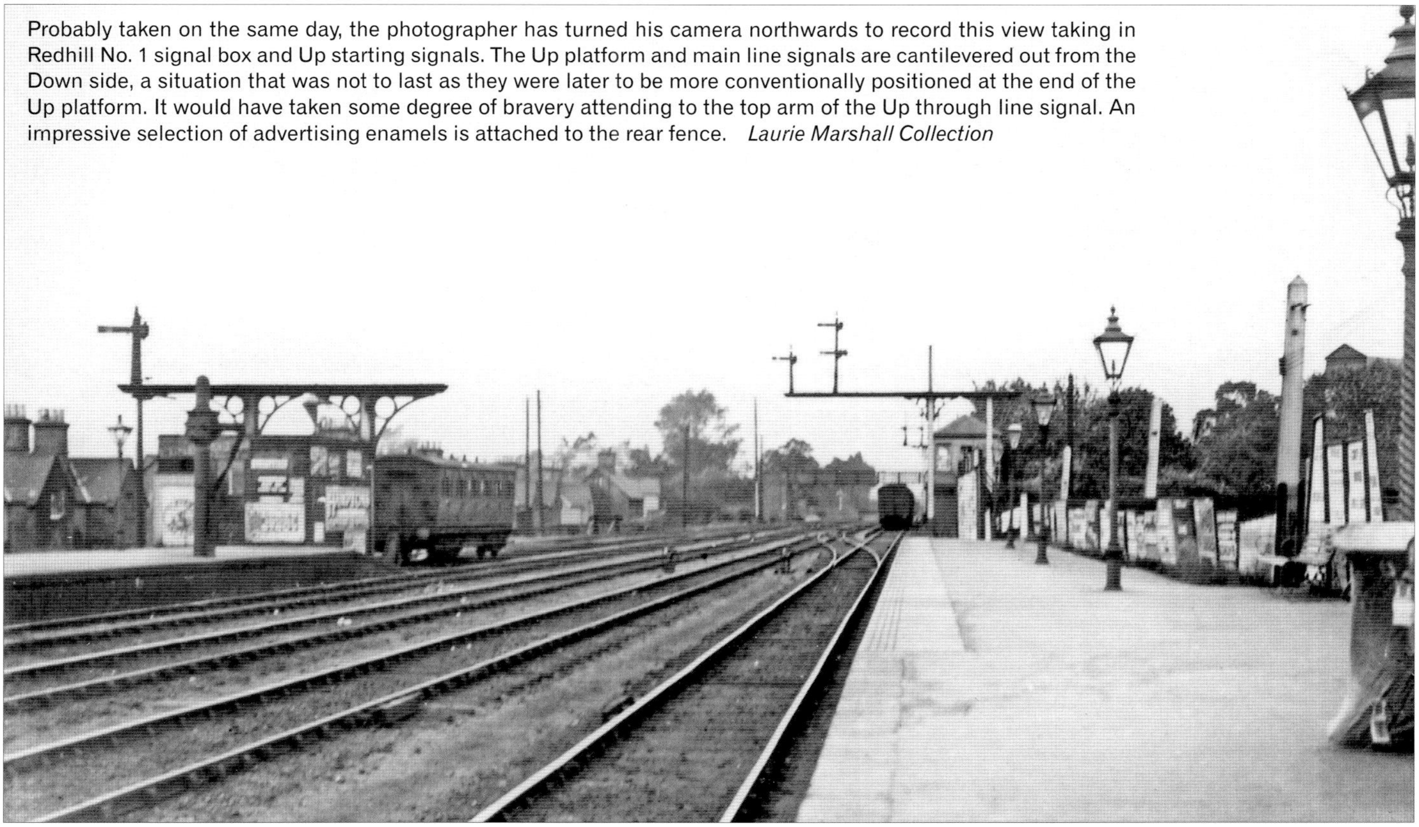

REIGATE
UP
DOWN
READING BRANCH
FIXED
TANYARD SIDING SLOT
GF 'D' 2 LEVERS
RELEASED BY 63 - GROUND FRAME POINTS INTERLOCKED WITH MID-WAY LOCK
GF 'C'
CALL ON
No. 2 SIDING
No. 1 SIDING
SELECTED BY 23
UP SIDING
UP LOCAL
UP PLAT
UP
DOWN
DOWN PL
BRIGHTON
QUARRY
ENGINE SHED
DOVER LOOP
DOWN SIDING
UP DOVER SIDING
DOVER
GF 'A' (2 LEVERS)
RELEASED BY 30.
RELEASED BY 29
G.F. 'B' (4 LEVERS)
RELEASED BY 28
NUTFIELD
83 VIA 60 NO
(WITH 60 OVER)
S.E.R. Box, 85 LEVERS IN FRAME.
Nos. 5.6.7. 13.19.27.42.45. SPARE.
WALKER'S BLOCK TO NUTFIELD.
TYER'S 3 POSITION BLOCK TO REIGATE.
SYKES LOCK & BLOCK TO No. 1 BOX & EARLSWOOD.
No CLOSING SWITCH PROVIDED.
UP HOME & CALL-ON SIGNALS 3.4.9.10.14.
15.33.36. SELECTED BY E.F. BARS IN PLATFORM ROADS. (TOP ARMS REQUIRE BARS "CLEAR" & SLOT FROM No. 1 BOX).
REIGATE 1-1291
1861
EARLSWOOD JN. 0-487
REDHILL No. 1 0-417
NUTFIELD 1-1546

1942
HOLMETHORPE 0-958
REDHILL No. 2 0-417
4 INNER SLOTTED BY No. 2 BOX.
19 SLOTTED BY No. 2 BOX FOR BACKING ON TO UP THRO OR UP LOCAL.
GPO SIDINGS
DOWN SIDING
HOLMETHORPE
UP SIDING
UP THROUGH
UP LOOP
No. 1 UP SIDING
No. 2 UP SIDING
S.E.R. BOX.
40 LEVERS IN FRAME.
Nos. 13.14.15.32.35.38.40. SPARE.
SYKES LOCK & BLOCK; NO CLOSING SWITCH.
ARMS INDICATED:- 4.4.33.36.
SLOTS INDICATED:- 36.
LIGHTS INDICATED:- (4.4).
TRACKS INDICATED:- F.J.K.M.N.U.W.
10: DOWN LOCAL BACKING CONTROL.
12: DOWN THRO. BACKING CONTROL.
35: UP THRO.
38: UP LOCAL
40: UP LOOP
NOW SPARE, BUT UNTIL 1927-1939 UNLOCKED No. 2 BOX UP INNER HOMES.
REDHILL No 1.
(1932)

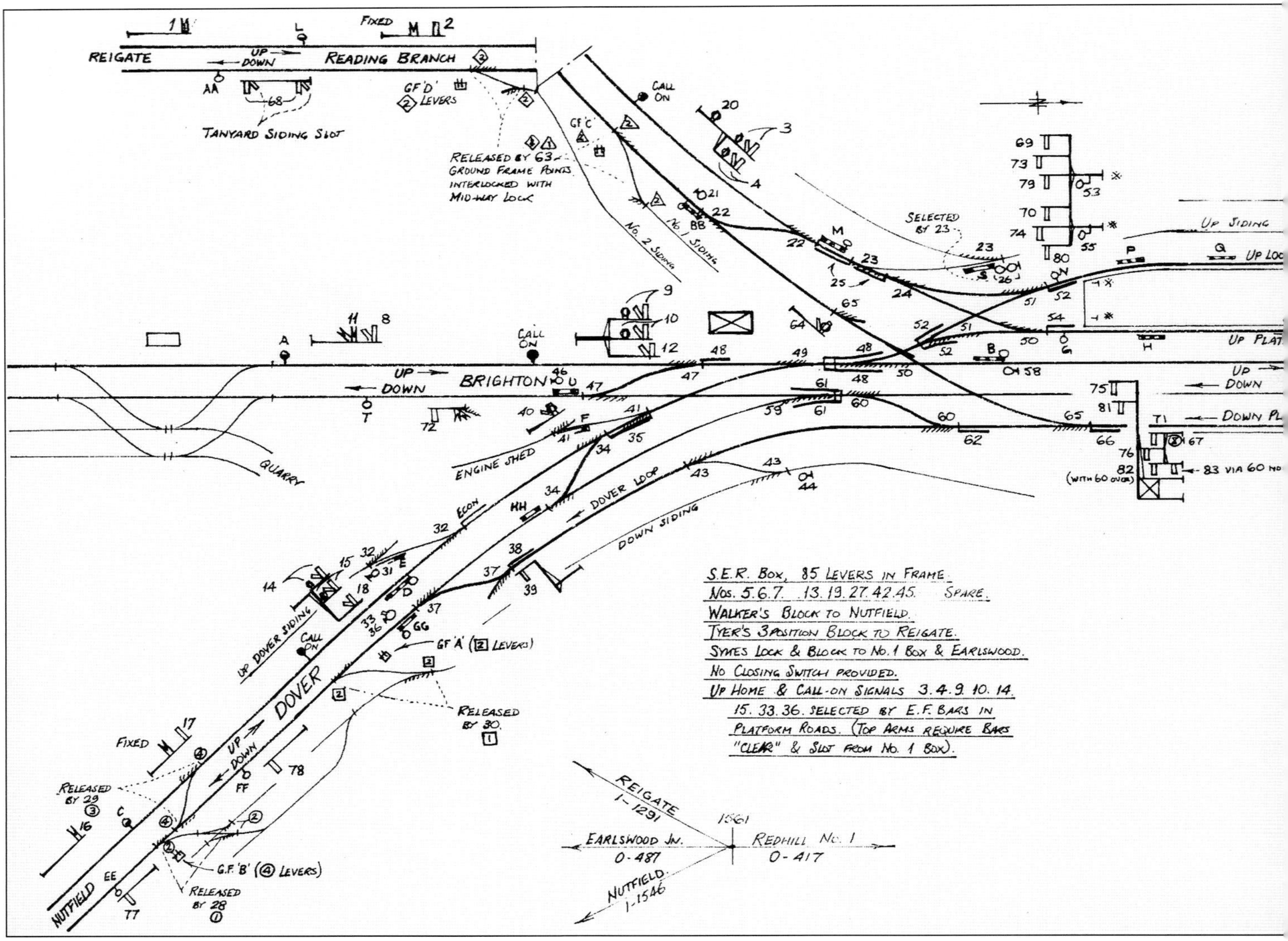

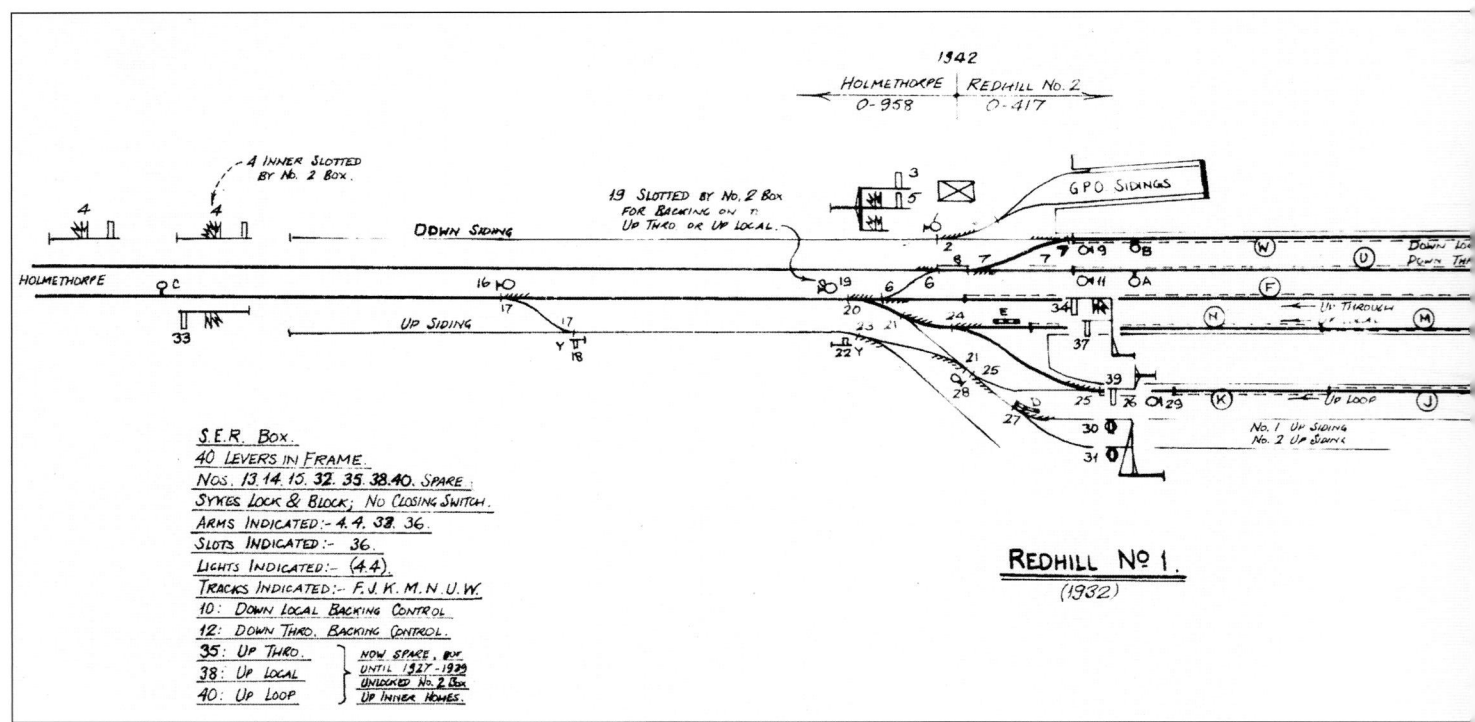

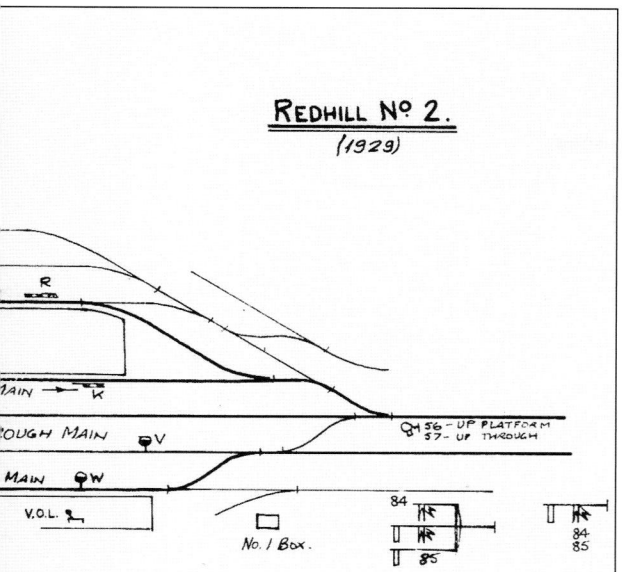

Left: Diverting off the later main line to take in the 'Old Road' via Redhill, this shows Redhill No. 2 signal box layout dated 1929, although the number of levers shown relates to the Westinghouse 'A2' replacement frame installed in 1932. Three different types of block instruments are in use, namely Walkers, Tyers and Sykes. The line designations 'Dover' and 'Brighton' are a throwback to pre-grouping days.

Above: Red Hill Junction signal box was brought into use on 5th December 1882 (along with No. 1 box), replacing an earlier structure dating from 1858. It became known as Redhill No. 2 during 1932 and received its final title of Redhill 'B' on 25th November 1956. It initially contained a 60-lever South Eastern frame which was replaced by a Westinghouse 'A2' 85-lever frame (opposite the old) on 10th April 1932, this remaining until the end. The ARP (air raid precaution) outer brick skin did little for the building's aesthetics but fortunately its structural integrity was never brought into question. *January 1978*

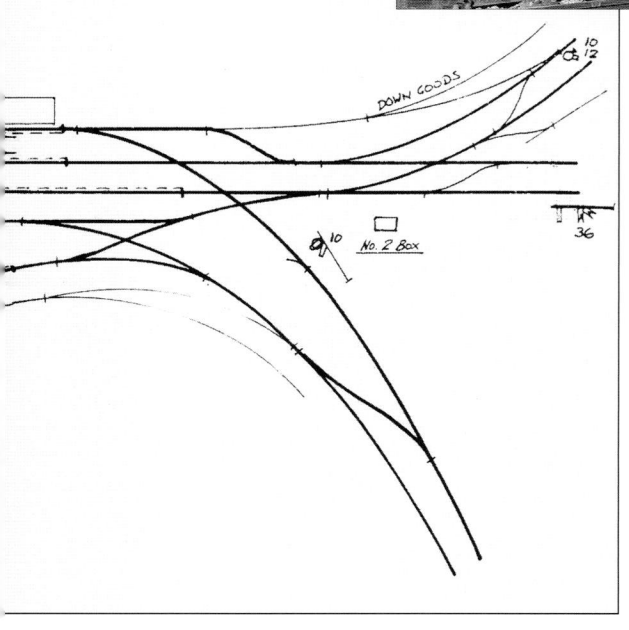

Left: Redhill No. 1 (South Eastern Railway) signal box is shown here in 1932, some nine years before it would be superseded by its Southern Railway successor. The number of levers shown again relate to the replacement SR signal box as the SER version contained a 53-lever frame.

Looking north from the top of the signal box steps, a pair of employees seem to be taking an interest in the wire run that, a little unusually, takes an elevated route to the platform starting signals. Rising up the ornately capped wooden posts (a support post taking the strain), the wires cross the running lines and continue on their lofty way to the cantilevered signals. Dominating the right background is St. Anne's Residential School, with its imposing clock tower rising to an impressive 125 feet. Bought by the Foundling Hospital in 1926 and subsequently by Surrey County Council, it inevitably became a burden rather than an asset and was demolished in 1987. *Lens of Sutton Association*

Above: A similar view to the previous photograph but from ground level – Redhill station has a decidedly weary look. Even today, the station seems to have an air of neglect although the old South Eastern canopies have been replaced and the supports have been given a coat of paint. Proving that you cannot always keep the past at bay, at the time of writing a cast-iron inspection cover on the Down platform still proclaims the initials, 'S.E.&C.&D.R.Co.'. *January 1978*

Not the best quality photograph but worthy of inclusion – this is the 'B' box diagram. Redhill 'B' received its prefix 'XC' at the same time as the new Westinghouse frame was installed. *Author's Collection*

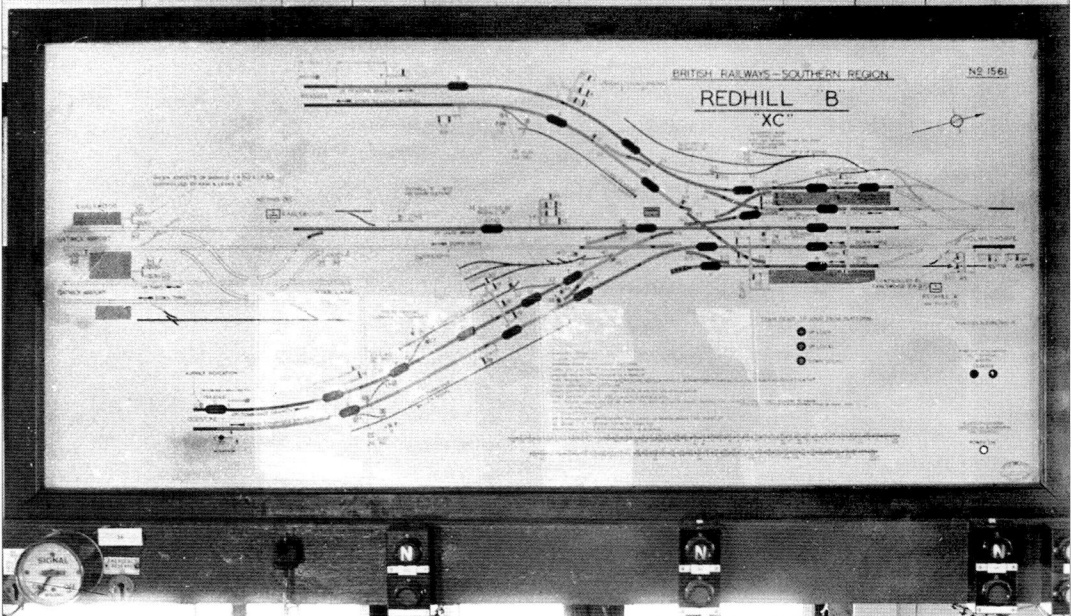

ABOVE: With Redhill 'B' signal box visible in the background, a Down London Victoria to Horsham train passes the impressive set of Up home signals. The counter-balance weight in the foreground is for 'B' box's Up distant (helping to ensure that the signal returns back 'on'), which was seen earlier beneath Earlswood's CR49 signal. *March 1978*

FACING PAGE BOTTOM: An undated photograph of the interior of Redhill 'B' signal box showing three Sykes instruments at the near end of the block shelf and two more at the far end. The author was called to attend a failure of one of the latter when covering the Redhill area from Three Bridges one late turn (cross cover being one of the unwritten laws of the local management). Having never ventured inside one before I did not really have much of a clue of how to proceed but, having touched something that had evidently got stuck, a loud 'clunk' ensued and everything returned to normal. It was recorded on the failure form as *'no cause found'*! *Author's Collection*

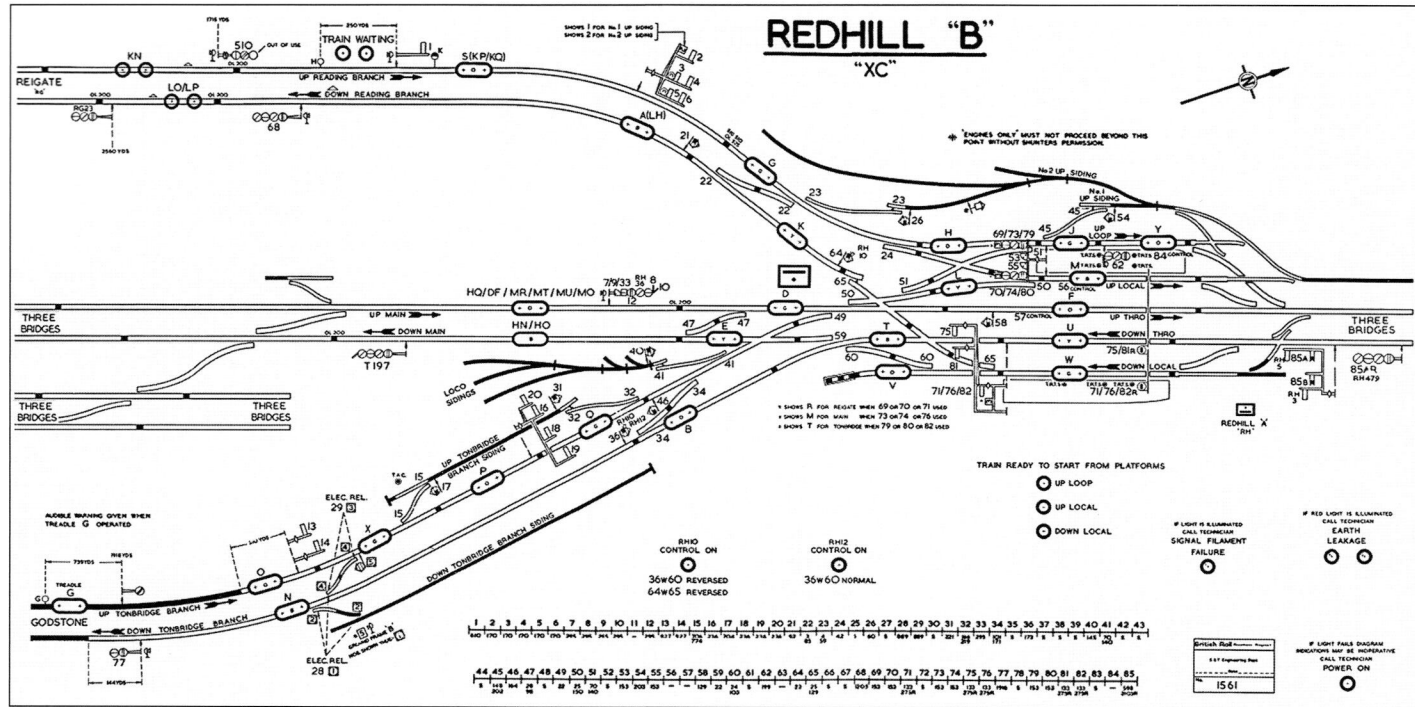

With a year and a day to go, this was the amended signal box diagram for Redhill 'B' showing it marooned as an isolated island backwater of mechanical signalling surrounded by colour light modernity. Redhill was the last area to be resignalled, not being commissioned on to the Three Bridges Area Signalling Centre until 12th May 1985. The interlocking was provided by a 'Westpac' Mk 4A geographical system as with Brighton and East Croydon. Geographical circuitry, in its most basic context, comprises standard factory-wired and pre-tested relay sets connected to their neighbours by multicore cables (with plug-couplers), efficiencies thus being achieved in the design, installation and testing of larger and more complex interlockings. *Diagram dated 11th May 1984*

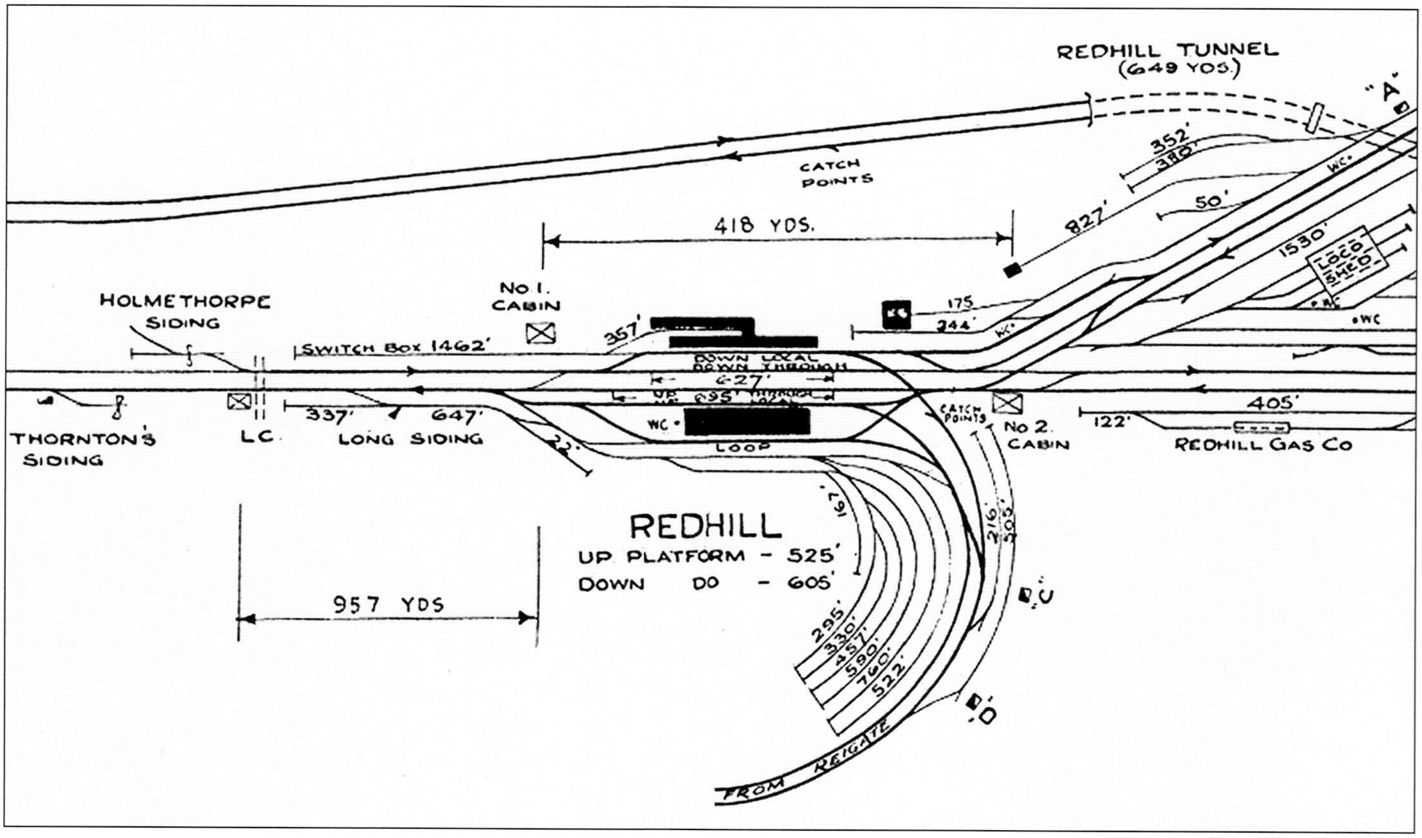

The Redhill control diagram gives the usual information regarding the length of sidings, position of water columns etc. Redhill once boasted three signal boxes as No. 3 Cabin (originally 'Red Hill Goods Yard') was once situated around the Tonbridge line; this closed on 10th April 1932 to be replaced by the ground frames more readily seen on the Earlswood control drawing (although 'A' GF can be seen at top right here).

Away from the main line but included as testament to Redhill's wholly mechanical state, which remained pretty much to the end, these are the Up inner home signals from the Reading Branch. The 'calling on' arms are lowermost along with their mechanical stencil apparatus which displayed a 'C' when the arm was 'off', the spectacles displaying a small white light for 'on' and a similar green for 'off'. The early 'theatre' type indicator adjacent to the Up Siding inner home signal showed a '1' or '2' in conjunction with the miniature (3ft 6ins) arm leading to either of those sidings. *January 1978*

Under a threatening sky, a diesel multiple unit from Tonbridge threads its way towards the Up Loop platform at Redhill. The disused cantilever structure to the left of the goods shed once carried No. 39 signal which was situated at the end of the 'Dover Loop' leading to the Down Dover line towards Tonbridge. *January 1978*

Redhill Motive Power Depot was opened by the South Eastern Railway in 1855 and, after its final allocation of eighteen BR standard tanks were moved away, it closed to steam on 13th June 1965, the final Central Division depot to do so. Coded 75B by British Railways (as a sub-shed to Brighton) it is seen here looking towards the station, with the line towards Tonbridge in the right foreground. *31st May 1959, John Scrace*

Nearly fourteen years later, the photographer returned to capture the depot after closure to steam where it remained in use as a diesel stabling point, predominantly for the Tonbridge to Guildford DMU services. For the record, the Redhill to Tonbridge line was electrified on 28th March 1994, whilst the line between Reigate and Guildford still awaits this necessary development at the time of writing. *29th March 1973, John Scrace*

Redhill 'B' XC70/74/80 and XC69/73/79 signals along with their mechanical route indicators are seen on a rainy day in January 1978; these were replaced by colour lights on 20th August 1978. The 'terrapin' huts visible between the pair housed the Redhill District S&T Department offices.

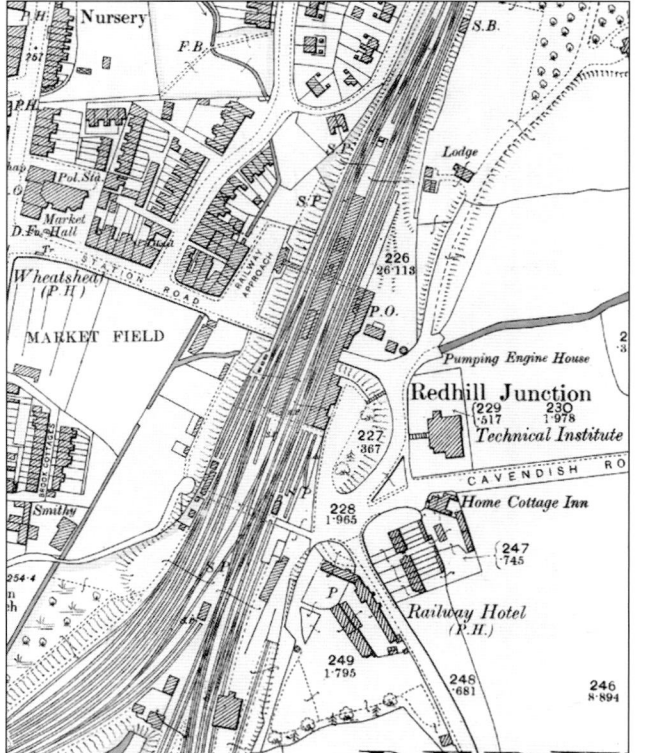
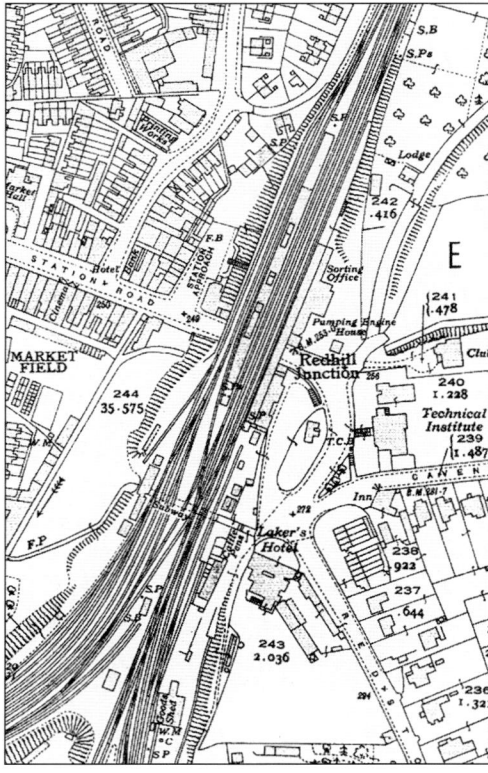

Two maps of Redhill from 1896 and 1935 respectively, the later map showing the new connection put in to facilitate moves from the Up Main to the Up Platform Loop, which was brought into work in conjunction with the installation of the new frame in 'B' box. *Reproduced by permission of the National Library of Scotland*

Is this a new signal about to brought into work, a signal recently abolished, or perhaps even a temporary 'stage work' signal waiting to be commissioned? I tend to lean towards the 'temporary' mode of thought as it is certainly a ramshackle affair and amongst Edward's collection are a few unusual photographs of temporary signals whist other work goes on. Whichever, it is a fascinating photograph (frustratingly undated) which I felt compelled to include. Taken prior to the new Westinghouse frame being installed in 'B' box in April 1932, when advantage was taken to alter the layout at the country end to allow moves into the Up Loop platform (the Up home signal only having the two routes towards the Up Platform and Up Main), this arrangement certainly has an impermanent look about it. No chances are being taken with any ambient light as the green of the spectacle plate drops into an enclosure when it returns 'on' to prevent any phantom aspect being displayed. This was not unusual where lighting from an external source was close to a mechanical signal, maybe from a nearby lamp post or even a signal box window, where the extraneous light could shine through the green glass and give a false aspect.

The circular device attached to the spindle of the signal is probably an early circuit closure to give the indication back to the signalman: the pair of insulators near the top of the post take the wires of what would be the repeater circuit. The somewhat hefty 'stop' mechanism, to prevent the arm from turning into an upper quadrant, does seem rather over engineered. On pure speculation, this may have been taken when the original cantilever (seen in the early photographs of Redhill) was being taken out of work and the changeover to the arrangement seen in the following photographs was taking place. Certainly there is some work going on as a shovel, wheelbarrow and a couple of pails can be seen. It is likely that the route indicators were reused in their new location too: part of the mechanism may be lying to the right. I do admire the immaculately dressed gentleman striding towards the camera, complete with buttonhole, although somewhat incongruously carrying what appears to be a tea caddy or a billy can. On his right are a stash of braziers, stored out of the way until they are required to prevent the water columns from freezing when winter comes round again and, standing proud over them, a SE&CR Trespass notice (giving provenance to the lines' original ownership) exhorting that, *'THE PUBLIC ARE HEREBY CAUTIONED NOT TO TRESPASS UPON THE RAILWAY. ANY PERSON SO OFFENDING WILL BE PROCEEDED AGAINST, AND WILL, ON CONVICTION, BE LIABLE UNDER THE SOUTH EASTERN & LONDON, CHATHAM & DOVER RAILWAYS ACT 1901, TO A PENALTY NOT EXCEEDING 40/-'*. All in capital letters, the only thing being that you would almost certainly have to *'trespass upon the railway'* to get close enough to read the text!
The Edward Wallis Collection

Looking south towards the junction at the country end of the Down Local platform XC71/76/82 signal can be seen nestling beneath the canopy with its three-position indicator hidden behind the arm. The Down Through signals XC81 and XC75 apply to moves towards Tonbridge or straight on towards Earlswood, there being no route available from here towards the Guildford Branch. *January 1978*

A closer view of the Down starting signals showing the double-leg construction of the cantilever bracket, the indigenous Southern Railway design ingeniously built using redundant bullhead rails. Still sitting behind the buffer stops is the post which once housed the SE&CR notice seen earlier, its replacement displayed at the top of the ramp now merely warning against crossing the line at this point and the danger of *'live rails'*. *Author's collection*

Having just exited the Up Loop platform and with No. 39 signal still in the 'off' position, a diminutive tank engine brings its lightest of loads towards the camera. The original 53-lever Red Hill No. 1 signal box, of pure South Eastern design, opened on bonfire night in 1882 and lasted until 15th June 1941 when it was replaced by its Southern Railway successor. *Laurie Marshall Collection*

Right: Looking towards 'A' box with the route set from the Up Local platform towards the Up Road. No. 37 signal on the right (applying to the Up Through line) has Holmethorpe's Up outer distant below which was repeated by a separate banner repeater on the GPO overbridge in the rear. *March 1978*

Below: A Brighton to London Victoria semi-fast via Redhill heads north past 'A' box's Down home signals with 'B' box's (motor worked) distants below. Head-codes used to be such a straightforward affair with the large, clear number denoting exactly where the train was going, in contrast to today's LED displays. *January 1978*

Facing Page Bottom: Class '47' No. 1740 brings a rake of empty hopper wagons past the stylish 'Glasshouse' Southern Railway signal box with a returning train from French's sidings at Gatwick. The background has changed considerably from the previous photograph, with the addition of the GPO siding (with the diesel shunter and associated mail vans visible) and the cross bridge for the transfer of mail from one platform to another. Michael Harvey, signalman at Redhill 'A' in the early 1970s recalls that: *"So heavy was the van traffic that it couldn't all be handled in the mail dock and had to be unloaded in the platform between trains, we even had authority to shunt into the platforms behind passenger trains and did so all the time. Redhill dealt with around 330 trains daily, but over double that number of shunt moves. Twenty van trains a weekday were normal, doubling at Christmas, which required a huge influx of extra staff. Christmastime was unbelievable, mailbags stacked to the roof and so close to the platform edge it was almost unsafe to walk along it, sometimes even blocking the doors passengers were trying to open! Indeed, I recall times when all three platforms, both through lines and the yard reception, were simultaneously occupied by freight trains – a most impressive sight".* 15th June 1973, John Scrace

The fine, clean lines of Redhill 'A' signal box seen in bright sunshine on a summer's day in June 1969. Designated as a Southern Railway 'Type 13', it contained a Westinghouse 'A2' frame of 40 levers, opening on 15th June 1941 and succumbing to the Brighton Line resignalling on 12th May 1985. *John Scrace*

The signal box interior photographed in 1978 just after the Redhill Minor Works Unit had installed BR standard three-position block instruments and converted the mechanical points to motor operation. The fibreglass point handle box (doubling as a handy storage location for the signal box shovel) contained the point handle for operating the machines in times of failure. The access to this was secured by an RKB222 padlock which could only be unlocked by a key of the same name which was issued to operating staff. The '221' key – Holy Grail access to anything signalling-wise – issued to S&T staff, would also unlock this. The two-colour blue/brown levers No's 30, 35 and 40 are the 'control' levers for the Up Through, Up Local and Up Loop respectively, effectively providing the slots to allow 'B' box to clear its signals into the platforms. *Steve Wilkins*

REDHILL

The signal box diagram with the domestic copy reproduced below for clarity. *Steve Wilkins*

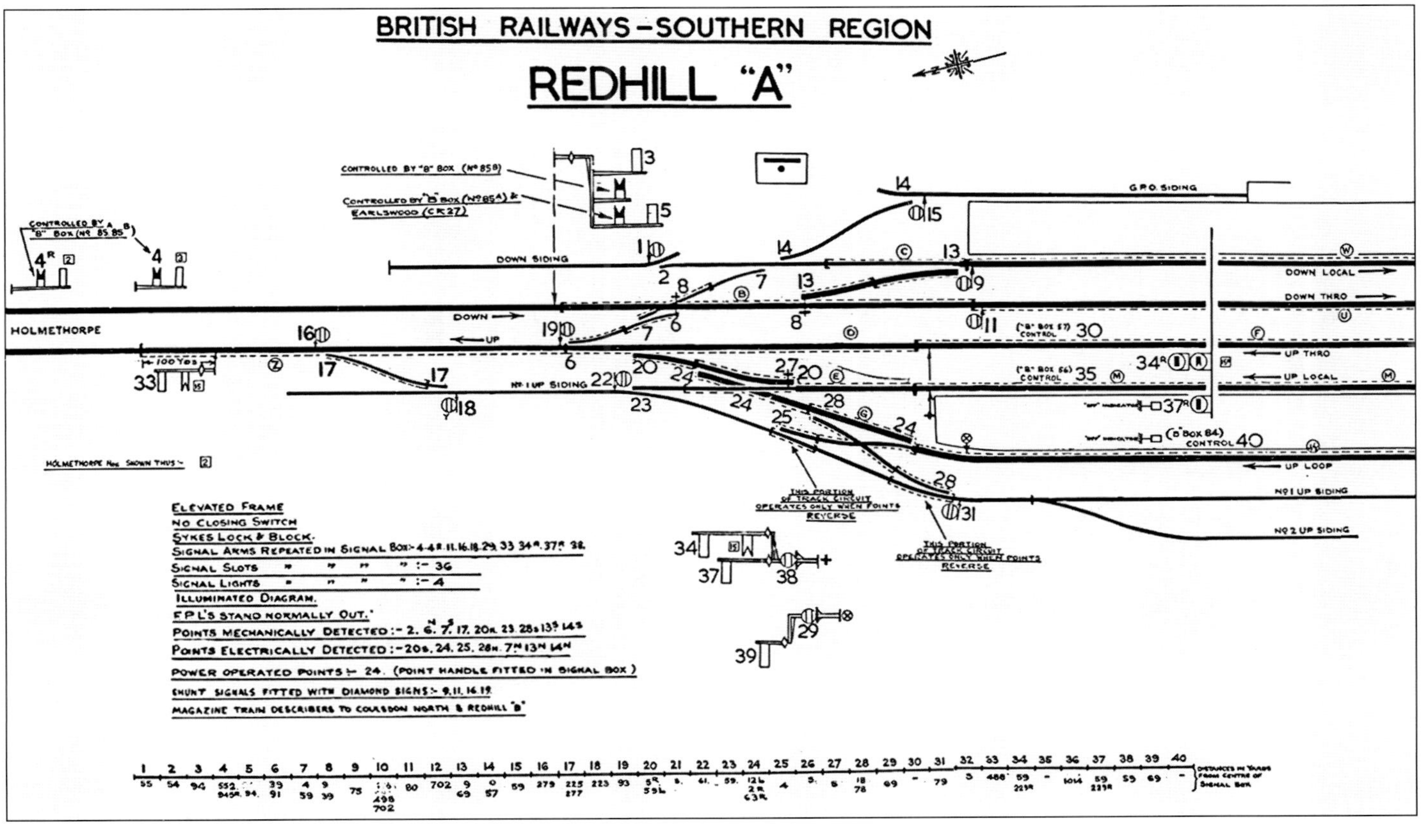

Signal Instruction No. 3 – 1985

British Rail Southern

ALTERATIONS TO SIGNALLING AND PERMANENT WAY BETWEEN COULSDON SOUTH AND EARLSWOOD/ GODSTONE/REIGATE

FRIDAY/SATURDAY/SUNDAY 10/11/12 MAY 1985

DRIVERS TO KEEP A GOOD LOOK-OUT FOR HAND SIGNALS

Commencing at 10.00 on Friday, 10 May Redhill 'A' and 'B' signal boxes will be abolished and control of the area shown on the enclosed diagram, together with the section of line between Coulsdon South and Merstham, will be transferred to Three Bridges (T) signal box.

The prefix letters of signals between Coulsdon South and Merstham will be altered from 'RH' to 'T'.

All running line signals will be provided with a telephone connected to Three Bridges signal box.

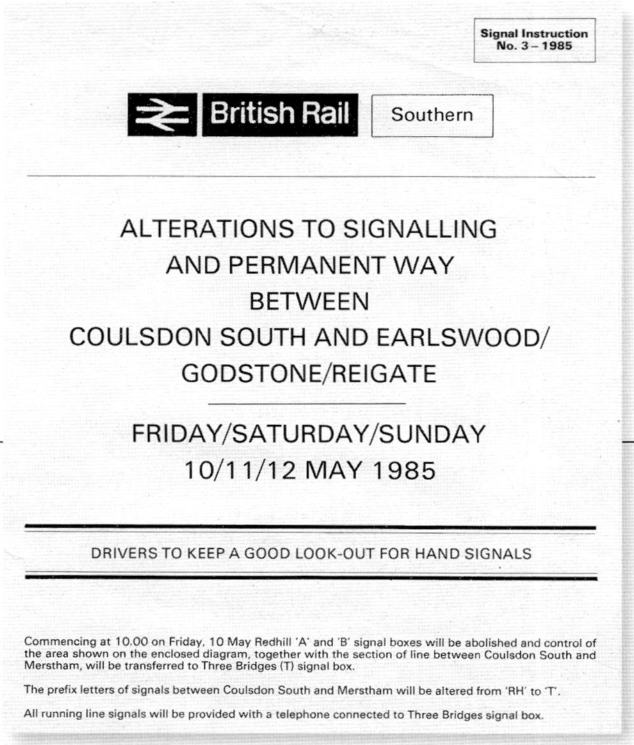

Left: Redhill was the final major commissioning of the Brighton Line resignalling scheme and the signalling notice depicting the end of both venerable signal boxes is seen here.

Below: The final Redhill arrangement commissioned on to the Three Bridges panel on 12th May 1985, the south end at the top and the north end seen below it. An element of railway 'romanticism' remained with such nomenclature as the 'GPO Siding' (although the General Post Office was actually abolished in 1969), 'Loco' (which had also ceased to exist many years previously) and 'Snow Plough Siding'. The normal enhancements came into use to increase the flexibility of the layout with the platform roads being signalled for reversible working. Note T483 signal with an impressive seven routes available.

T479 Signal positioned north of Redhill with Position 4 'feather' for moves over 1909 Points reverse.

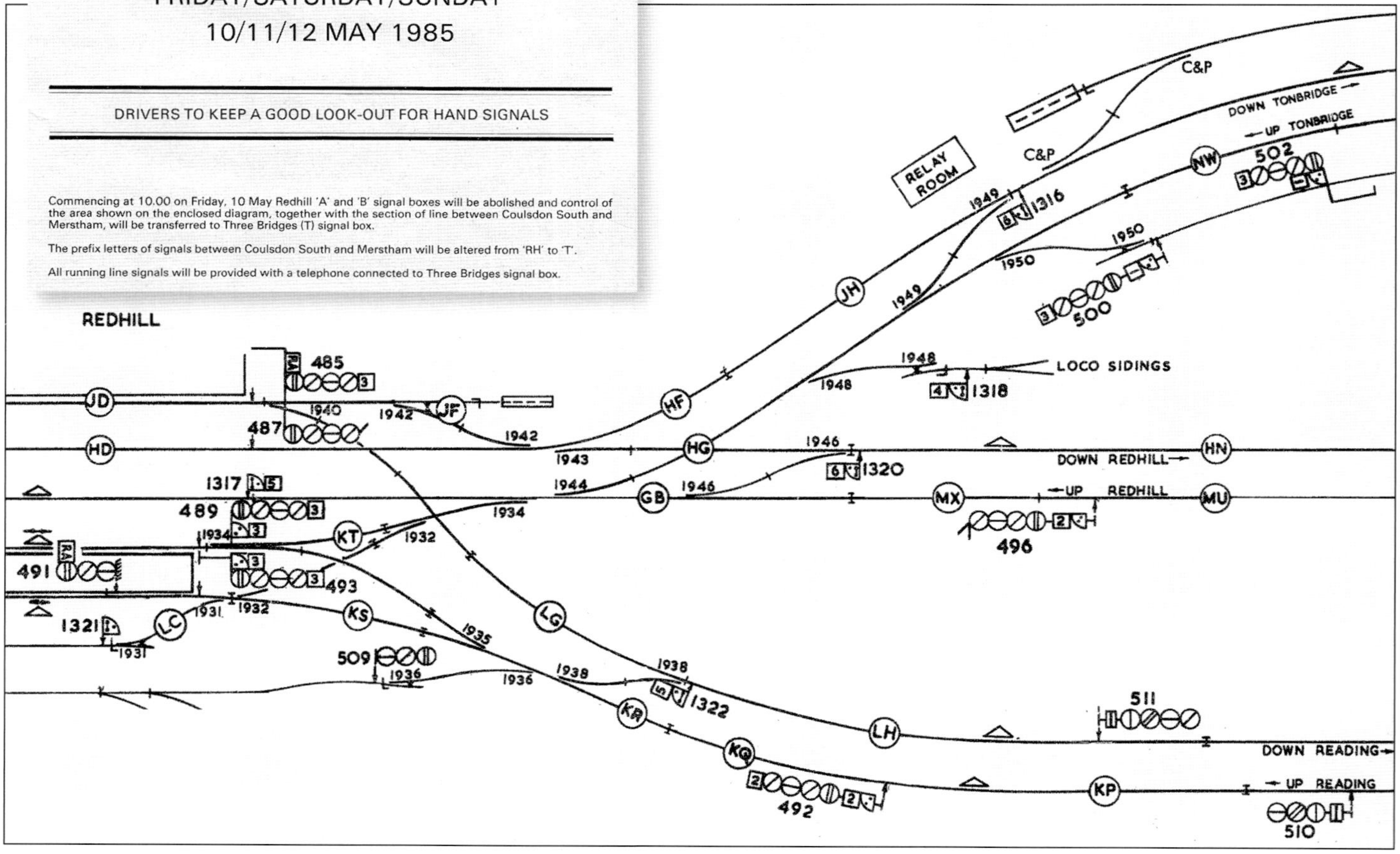

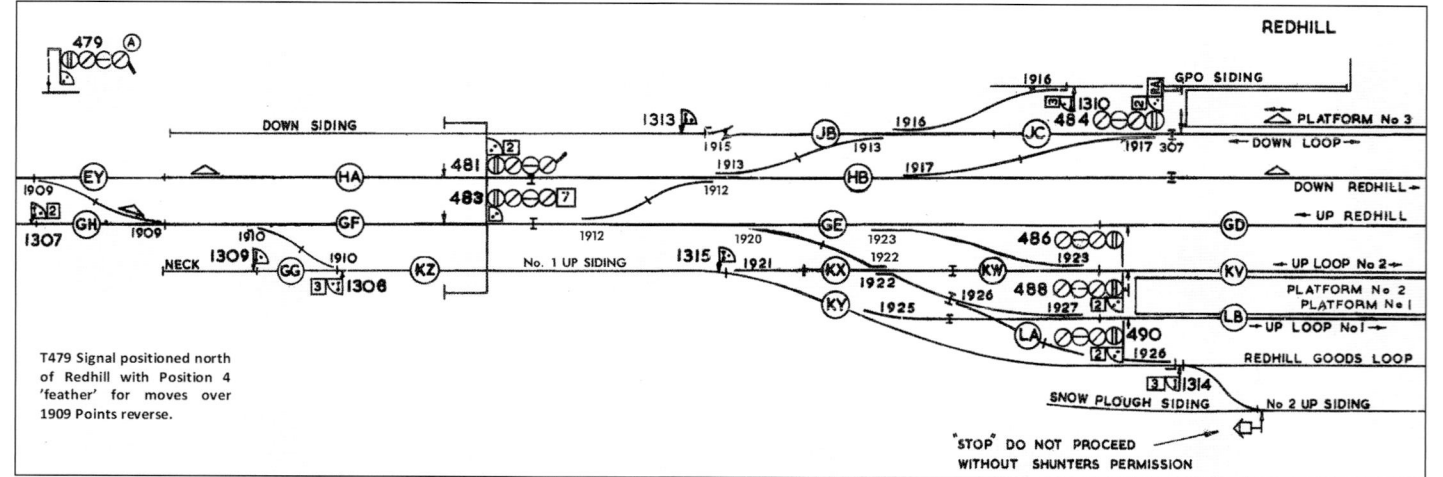

28 – Holmethorpe

Holmethorpe Siding signal box came into being on 18th February 1900 and provided sterling service for just over 83 years, being swept away by the resignalling on 26th February 1983. Of a standard SER design with its attractive vertically sliding sash windows, it housed a South Eastern tappet frame of 16 levers. Judging by the lead flashing over the nearest hip of the roof being well adrift, maybe some metal thieves had been thwarted in an attempt on some easy gain or else the Redhill area had experienced some recent strong winds. *July 1982*

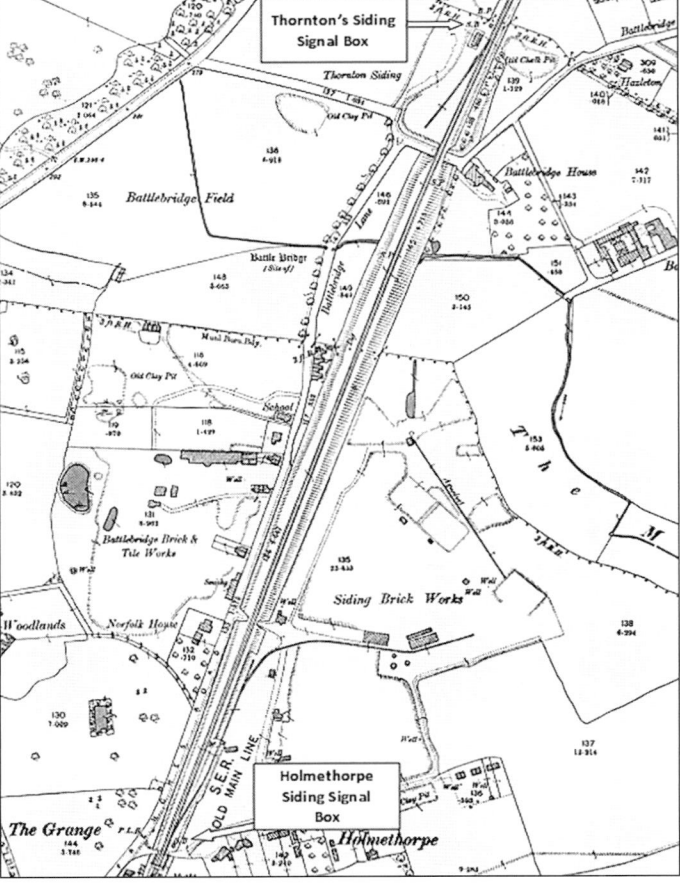

Extract from an 1896 map showing the original position of Holmethorpe siding signal box (on the Down side of the line) with Thornton's siding further to the north. Both opened in 1894 and neither were block posts. Holmethorpe closed on 18th February 1900 with the opening of the new cabin opposite. Thornton's closed on 2nd June 1940 when it was replaced by a ground frame released by the second Holmethorpe signal box, or Redhill 'A' when that box was switched out.
Reproduced by permission of the National Library of Scotland

Looking northwards from the adjacent footbridge, the signal box is either switched out or a train is soon due in each direction. 'Jim's Inn' does not seem to be inviting much patronage, whilst judging by the rust on the rails leading to the siding, that has not seen a great deal of use recently either. The new concrete cable troughing route being installed in the Down cess is complete with a UTX (under track crossing) diving beneath the siding just beyond the trap points. *July 1982*

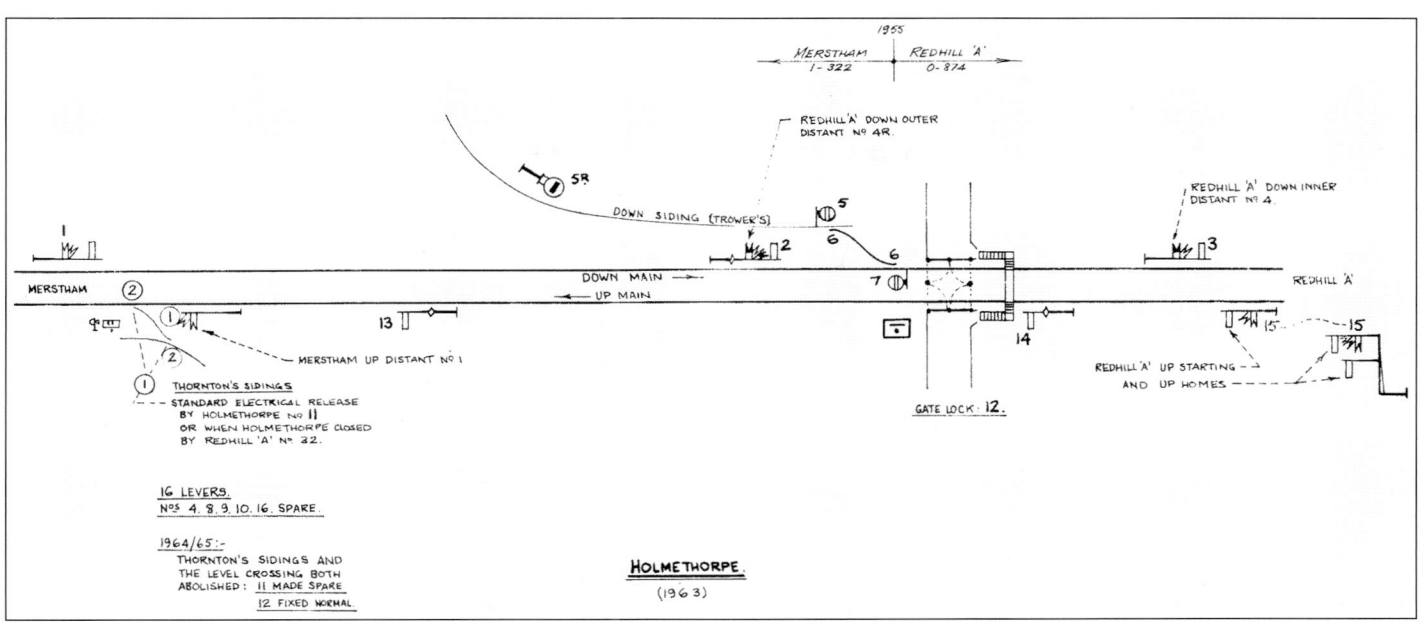

HOLMETHORPE

To be carried out on Sunday, 27th January, commencing at 8.0 am.

The 5-lever ground frame at Thornton's Siding, situated on the left-hand side of the Up line, Merstham side of signal box will be removed.

The siding and trailing connection in the Up line will be abolished.

(P/EW 4, C.D. 1963)

The layout at Holmethorpe in 1963 with the notes stating that Thornton's sidings were taken out of use in 1964/65. As seen left, this was carried out in 1963 and presumably the level crossing was abolished around the same time (although reference to it proved elusive). Trower's siding led to sand quarries and, because of the considerable gradient up to the main line, a repeater was provided to give the loaded trains a chance to breast the summit. The first Merstham station was situated in the vicinity of Thornton's siding – for all of two years.

LEFT: The attractive but basic interior of Holmethorpe signal box shows to good effect the 4½ins centres and short travel of the South Eastern Railway frame. The interlocking was housed beneath the floor with the electric lever locks, Sykes locks and associated devices housed within the wooden structure behind the frame. Enlarging the photograph reveals No. 11 lever's description plate still showing ghost lettering revealing its former function (Thornton's siding's release) while the old gate lock lever is firmly fixed in the frame by a retaining bolt. Somewhat unusual are the three repeaters at the near end of the block shelf, all repeating the same signal, namely No. 15's Up inner, outer and banner repeater distant signals, the latter mounted on the GPO overbridge at Redhill station.
February 1980, Courtesy 53A Models of Hull

BELOW: An Up freight passes the box during January 1978.

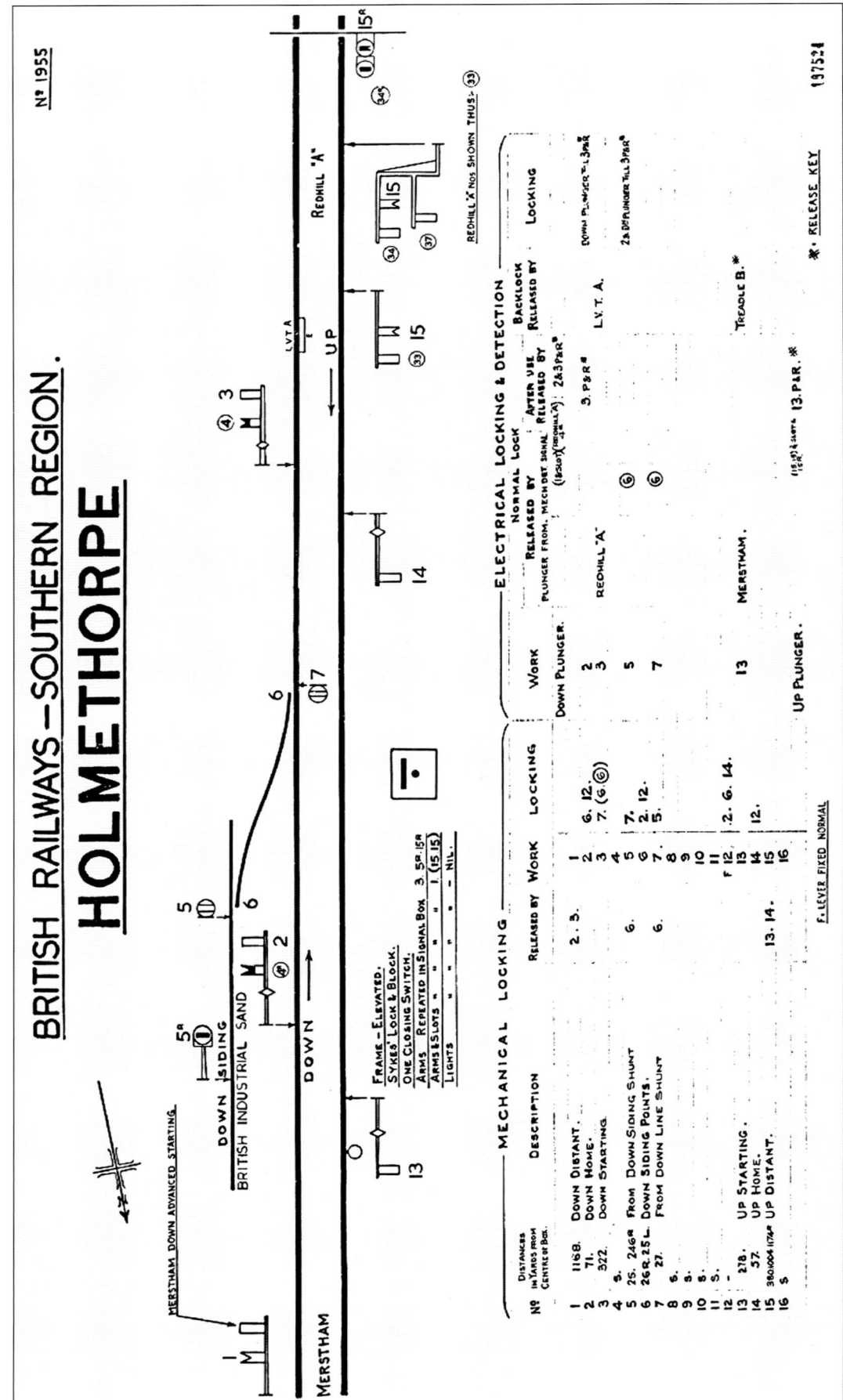

Holmethorpe signal box diagram dated 15th January 1963, produced to replace the earlier version which would have shown Thornton's sidings and the level crossing. Levers No's 11 and 12 are now shown as spare with the ex-gate lock fixed normal.

29 – Merstham

On a cold winter's day, with just a solitary passenger in view, Merstham station looks exceptionally clean and tidy along with its platform extensions that had opened just a few years previously. The station was constructed by the South Eastern Railway and opened on 4th October 1844, replacing the earlier station further to the south which had been built (with through roads, as Horley) by the London & Brighton Railway Company. *January 1961. K.G. Carr Collection, courtesy Peter Fidzcuk*

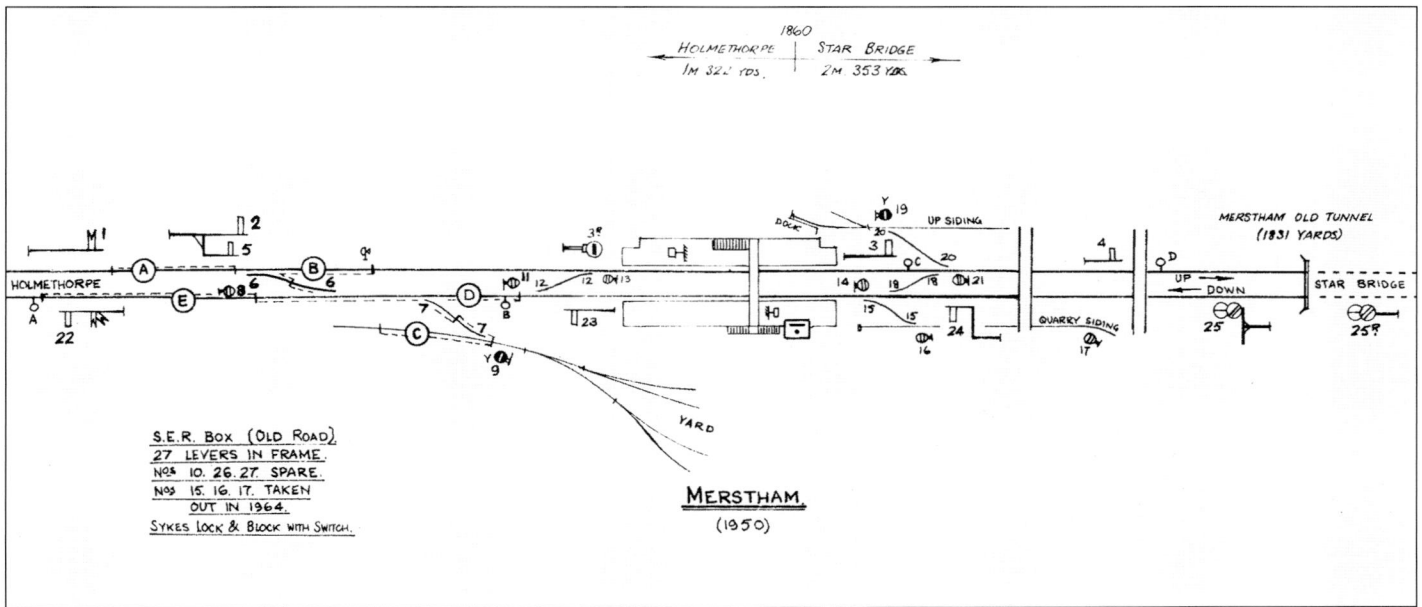

Merstham station layout depicted in 1950. The Up sidings would have coped with general freight and livestock and possessed a fixed crane of 5cwt maximum lifting power whilst the quarry siding would have dealt with the export of lime from Greystone lime quarry. This traffic ceased in 1947, but the truncated stub remained until February 1964 when it was abolished, No. 24 Down home signal being relocated on to a straight post somewhat later in October 1971. The north crossover went in April 1971 but the facing connections to the Down yard along with the south crossover remained until the resignalling. No. 25 Down distant signal is shown as a colour light on this plan but was not actually converted to such, mounted on the same offset structure as the original mechanical version, until 12th December 1955.

If you had mentioned the word 'motorway' to this photographer you would have undoubtedly received a quizzical look but, some six or seven decades later, that is what would disfigure this pastoral scene as a concrete trough would cut a swathe across the centre of the landscape. Merstham's Up sidings along with its crane and a number of wagons can be seen on the right as a passenger train makes a spectacular start away from the station. Just about visible, below the clouds of steam, is the signal box with the footbridge beyond. The underbridge seen beneath the Quarry Line carries a footpath from the station. *Laurie Marshall Collection*

Merstham station is almost obscured again in this winter view, not by steam but by flying snow blown up by Unit 7748 forming the 11.10 semi-fast service from Brighton to Victoria. The Up siding head-shunt can be seen on the right with No. 24 signal, still mounted on its cantilever bracket, carried over a non-existent siding. It was best to avoid standing line-side when a train was due to pass at speed in conditions such as these! *11th February 1969, John Scrace*

On the back of her comprehensive Eurovision Song Contest win, Sandie Shaw's *Puppet on a String* was at the top of the charts when the signalman recorded this view of Merstham station from the door of his signal box. The station footbridge also acts as a public right of way, as a footpath leads from here to cross under the Quarry Line and head up towards the North Downs. The entrance to this side was clearly out of use, however, as a new bridge (seen leading away on the left) had to be built to maintain the thoroughfare when the sidings were installed between the two main lines. When the sidings were decommissioned, the footpath was reinstated on the level and the newer bridge dismantled.
5th May 1967, Author's Collection

Another view from the signal box shows a collection of wagons and brake-vans berthed in the yard as the Brighton Belle passes by on the Up Quarry Line. The sidings, installed in 1940 to relieve congestion in the yards at Redhill and necessitating extra levers to be added to the signal box frame, were later to prove useful in the construction of the local portion of the M25 motorway, with aggregate trains making regular visits.
30th December 1968, Author's Collection

Merstham station seen looking north in September 1982, with the signal box just visible behind the Down platform. The footbridge retains its protective roof but is otherwise now open to the elements, while the Up-side canopy has been shorn of its once attractive valancing.

A fine photograph of a London Victoria to Brighton slow train entering the Down platform at Merstham. This is a relatively rare view as most photographs show the signal box after the platforms were extended (the year after this was taken), whereas this shows the structure in its entirety. This was the second signal box here as the first, situated just a short distance to the south, closed on 24th September 1906 when this opened. Originally housing a 21-lever frame, it was extended to 27 in 1940 and closed, along with the signal boxes either side of it, on 26th February 1983. *5th August 1956, E.R. Morten, Lens of Sutton Collection*

With the scar of the recently constructed M25 (opened through here in 1976) passing under the railway line in the middle distance, this is a northwards-looking view taken from the station footbridge. The Up-side siding (clipped and padlocked at this stage) runs between the two fence lines behind the platform, while the solitary mechanical shunt signal seen in the 6ft at the end of the platforms is acting as a 'Limit of Shunt' for wrong-road moves back along the Down line. *January 1978*

Above: Merstham signal box block shelf awash with brass indicators (all track circuits 'A' to 'E' indicated thus), plungers and Sykes 'Lock and Block' instruments. *6th February 1968, Author's Collection*

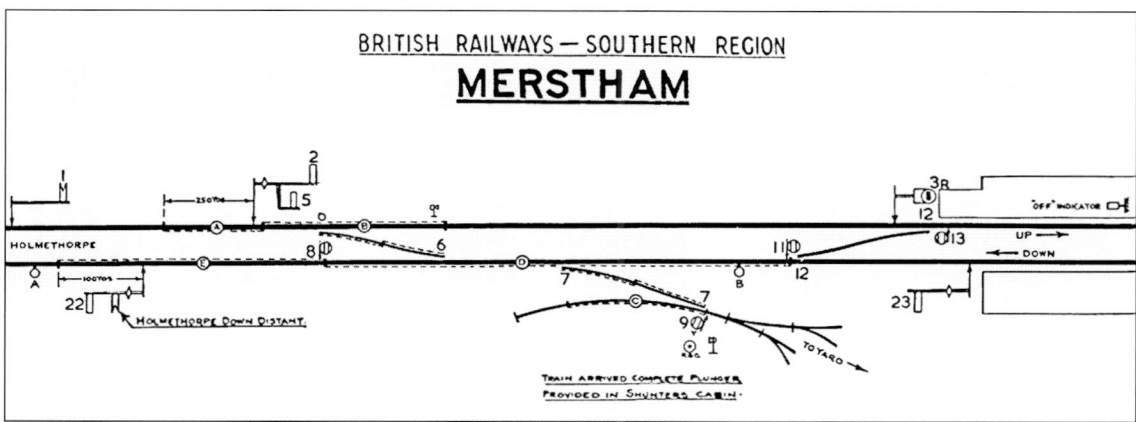

Merstham signal box diagram dating from the early 1970s.

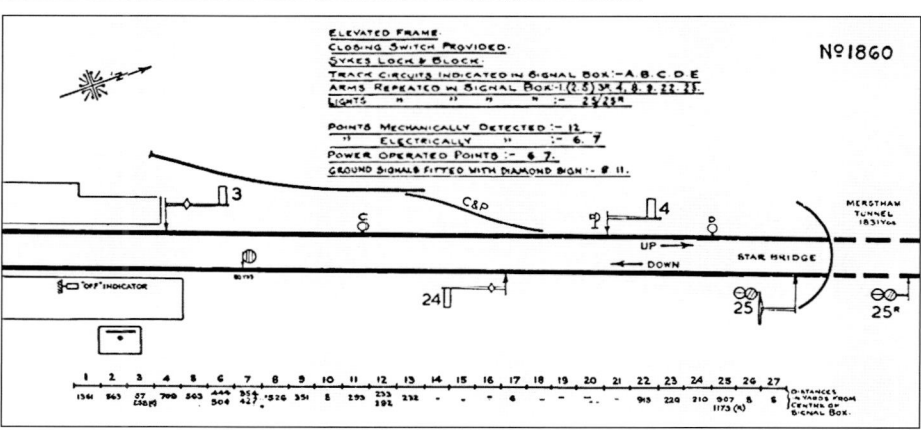

This is the immaculate signal box interior in February 1982. The Sykes instruments have been replaced by standard three-position block instruments and the illuminated diagram replaces the old track circuit indicators. The brass plungers have given way to the functional 'Square D' type but an impressive 23 levers remain in work, albeit with No. 21 fixed in the frame. The footstop gives a bit more leverage when pulling the still mechanical No. 1 Up distant, 1,361 yards away. The frame was supplied by Evans, O'Donnell who made frames for the SER at their Chippenham works, amongst other concerns and, through some complicated manoeuvres involving other manufacturers, eventually metamorphosed into the Westinghouse Company. Westinghouse bought up a large swathe of British Rail's signalling design and installation offices at the time of railway privatisation, only to be taken over by Invensys before finally being swallowed up by the giant Siemens group. *Courtesy 53A Models of Hull*

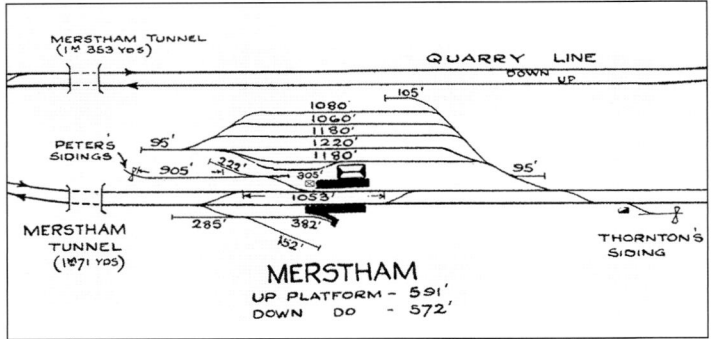

Merstham control diagram (*above*) along with the final layout commissioned on to the Three Bridges Signalling Centre (*below*). At least some modicum of respectability was retained, with one siding remaining in use.

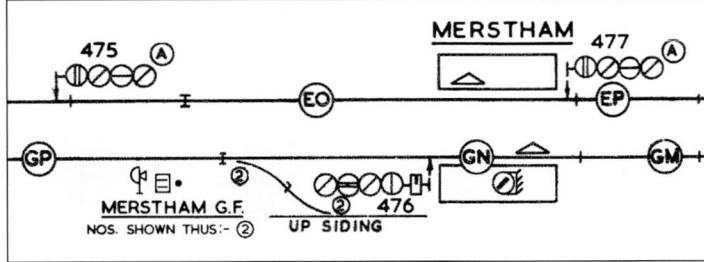

RIGHT: The title page from Signalling Instruction 35CD detailing the closure of the three remaining signal boxes on the 'Old Road' north of Redhill. For this stage the new colour light signals between Coulsdon and Redhill were controlled (although ten of them were automatics) from Redhill 'A' entailing a total of sixteen signals having to have temporary 'RH' transfers covering the 'T' of the final signal prefix plate. This situation lasted until 12th May 1985 when Redhill was commissioned and every running signal from Norwood and Selhurst to Brighton was finally prefixed with a 'T'.

Signal Instruction 35CD

British Rail Southern
CENTRAL DIVISION

ALTERATIONS TO SIGNALLING AND PERMANENT WAY BETWEEN COULSDON NORTH AND REDHILL ON SATURDAY 26 FEBRUARY 1983

DRIVERS TO KEEP A GOOD LOOK-OUT FOR HAND SIGNALS

Star Bridge, Merstham and Holmthorpe signalboxes will be abolished.
New signalling will be introduced, controlled from Redhill 'A' (RH) as shown on the enclosed diagram.
The Down Main signal RH479 will display a double yellow aspect when Redhill 'A' (RH) Down Through Home signal is in the 'OFF' position. To display a green aspect, requires Redhill 'B' Down Main Distant signal to be in the 'OFF' position.
All signal post telephones will communicate with Redhill 'A' (RH) signalbox unless otherwise shown.
Track Circuit Block working will be introduced on the Down and Up Main lines between Coulsdon North and Redhill 'A' (RH).

Essex House (R/SB43/55/31A) C. W. C. Nott
CROYDON for
 Divisional Manager
February 1983 Central Division

30 – Star Bridge

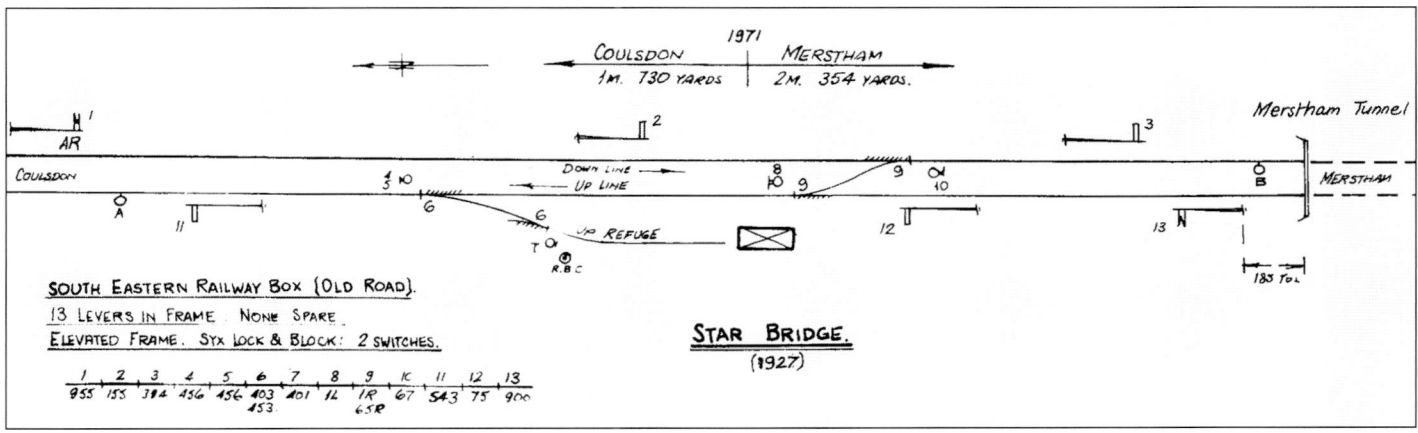

With what Edward affectionately calls the 'Grid Iron' in the background, carrying the Quarry Line over the Redhill lines (the BR Central Division Bridge Book refers to this as Star Lane *under*-bridge at 16m 40ch, this being in relation to the Quarry Line), Star Bridge signal box nestles at the bottom of the cutting. Typically for a chalk cutting, the signal wires run up the 6ft towards the bridge where the end of the refuge siding can just be seen. The telegraph route seen at the top of the cutting relates to Hooley Lane or the 'Brighton Road'.   *1931, The Edwards Wallis Collection*

Star Bridge, in its entirely mechanical state, is shown here in 1927. Along with almost every location visited on our journey the inevitable rationalisation of assets was realised here too. The Up refuge siding was taken out of use on Saturday 28th November 1953 and its associated shunt signals abolished, the crossover following in September 1972 along with its shunt signals. However, on 7th June 1957 a new signal section was provided on the Down Road. The mechanical No. 3 signal was abolished and a new intermediate home two-aspect red/green signal provided, retaining its nomenclature, 586 yards closer to Merstham. A two-aspect approach light signal was provided below No. 2 Down home signal (as required for the transition from mechanical to colour light) with a single yellow signifying a clear road towards No. 3, a green aspect to Merstham's Down home signal. Things improved even further on Sunday 26th August 1962 when a new colour light No. 2 signal was provided closer to Coulsdon, thus rendering the mechanical No's 1 and 2 home and distant redundant; see the 1969 signal box diagram for clarification. The Up road received its share of modernisation when the Up distant was renewed as a colour light signal on 16th April 1967, consequently easing the signalman's physical workload even further.

Possibly the author's favourite signal box in the book, this is Star Bridge complete with its original blue enamel South Eastern Railway nameboard. Where the Great Western Railway would extend the length of their cast iron box-boards to fit in the words 'Signal Box' as the suffix in every case, the word 'Signals' would suffice for the SER. Opened on 29th December 1895, this box did not quite make its centenary, closing, along with Merstham and Holmethorpe, on 26th February 1983. It would be nice to think that such an attractive structure could have been preserved, either on a heritage railway or even as an outbuilding in someone's garden, but regrettably it appears not to have survived the demolition gang. *September 1982*

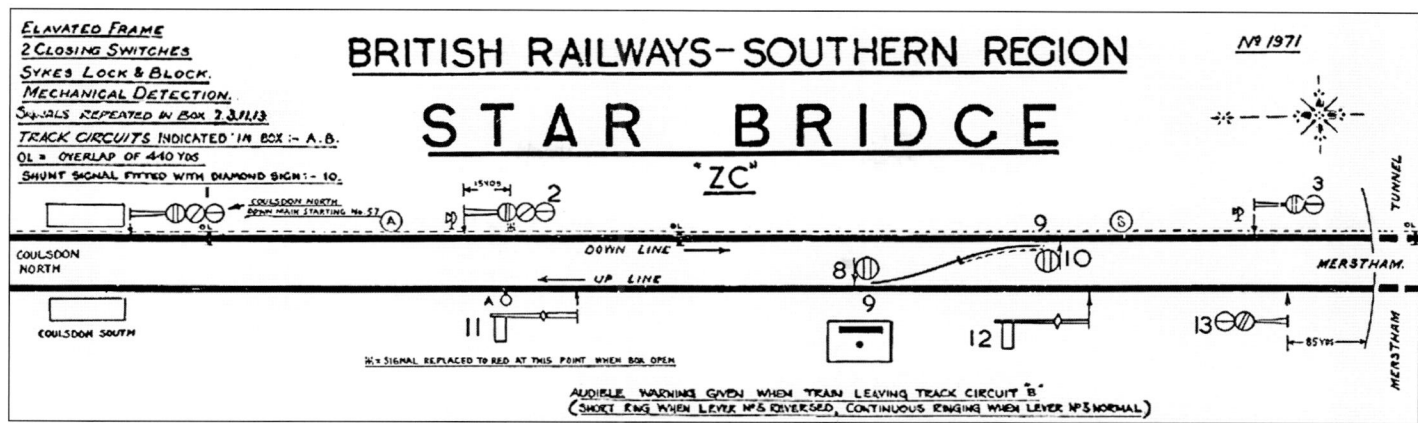

Above: The Star Bridge signal box diagram dated 15th December 1969.

Right: With its remaining brass indicators gleaming, this is the beautifully kept interior of Star Bridge signal box. The SER frame was the same as that provided at Holmethorpe but, some eight years after they were abolished, the S&T painter had obviously never been called to give a coat of white paint to the now out of use crossover and associated shunt signal levers which are still in their original colours. The alterations to the block shelf and diagram are similar to those witnessed in Merstham signal box. The signalman has given a 'line clear' to Coulsdon North, has pulled No's 1 and 2 signals in readiness, and is waiting for the same from Merstham before he can pull No. 3 signal. Both distant signals retain their mechanical repeaters even though they are now both colour lights.
February 1980,
Courtesy 53A Models of Hull

Above: Looking through the arch of Star Bridge with No. 12 signal prominent. Just visible this side of the signal is a section of flat bottom rail mounted on a block of wood; this housed a thermometer (lying in a recess hollowed out of the rail head) by which the local Permanent Way Department could measure rail temperatures. *September 1982*

Right: The 1966 signal box survey for the Central Division showing that Star Bridge took its 110V electric supply from Star Lane sub-station on the adjacent Quarry Line.

31 – Coulsdon South

'H' Class No. A546 has the road from the co-acting signals (with Coligny Welch reflectors on the distant arms) and awaits departure from the station with an Up passenger train. If only Henry Casserley had taken his camera down to the other end of the platform, he could have taken a photograph of the signal box, of which no image exists as far as the author is aware. The tall Down starter is just visible over the Up platform canopy. *28th May 1927, H.C. Casserley*

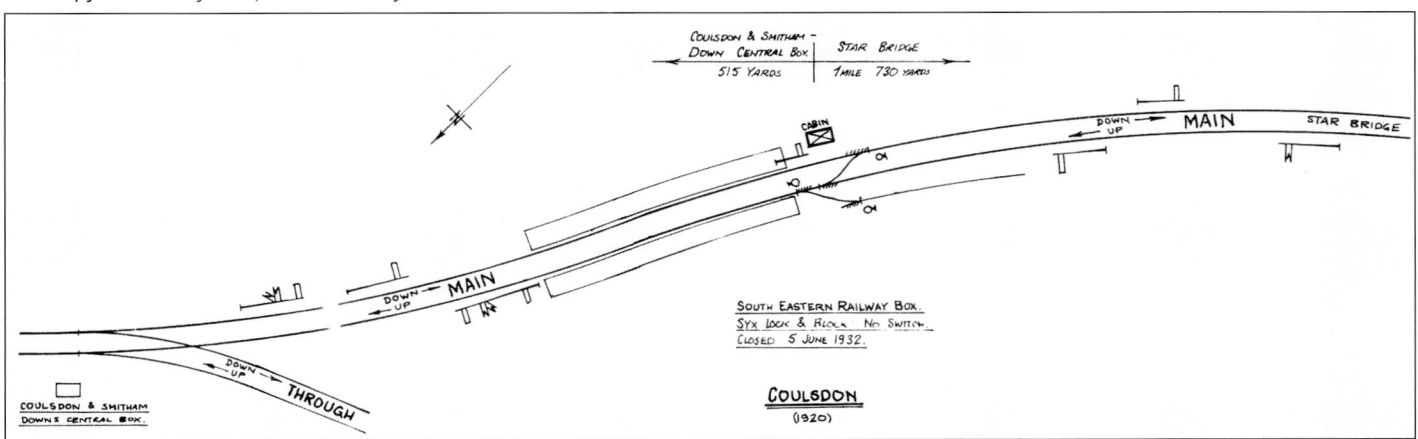

ABOVE: Coulsdon (South Eastern Railway) signal box layout in 1920 (the original drawing must have been lacking the relevant numbering sequences). A South Eastern Railway timber pattern structure opening on 1st October 1899 and closing at the same time as Coulsdon North No. 2 signal box on 2nd May 1937 (not as stated above), it housed an SER 18-lever frame.

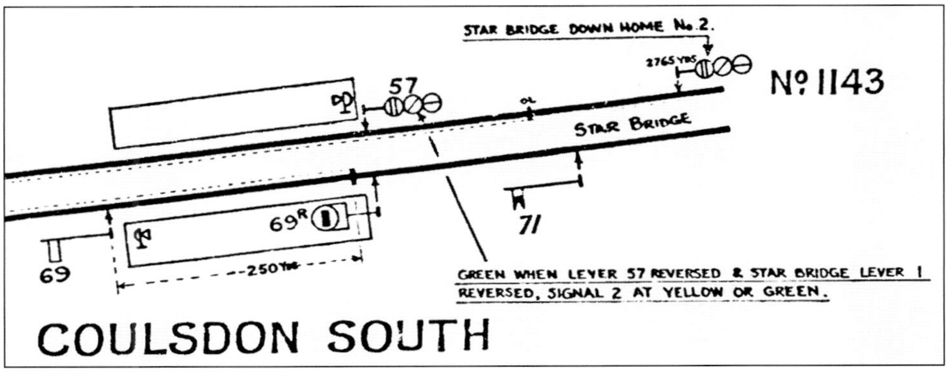

RIGHT: An extract from the Coulsdon North domestic diagram, dated 24th September 1982.

Another immaculate view of Coulsdon South station. The SER canopies, like their signal boxes, had a charm all of their own with everything aesthetically pleasing and in complete proportion. The platforms were extended at the country end (with electric lighting, while this end remains stubbornly gas lit) during late August 1957, so this photograph must date from around that time as they look very new. Just visible on the end of the nearest platform bench frame are the SER initials. *Lens of Sutton Collection*

Left: A later photograph of Coulsdon South shows a Victoria to Brighton stopping service bringing its train into the station during February 1971. No. 69 Up platform starting signal has been reduced in size and lost its distant arm, but is still mechanically worked.
Author's Collection

Below: Coulsdon South still retained its original canopies on 23rd March 1979 when this was taken. Note the destination 'finger board' slotted in position under the Down canopy, once an everyday sight. The platform benches are now of the SE&CR type with the old SER insignia absent.

32 – Worsted Green

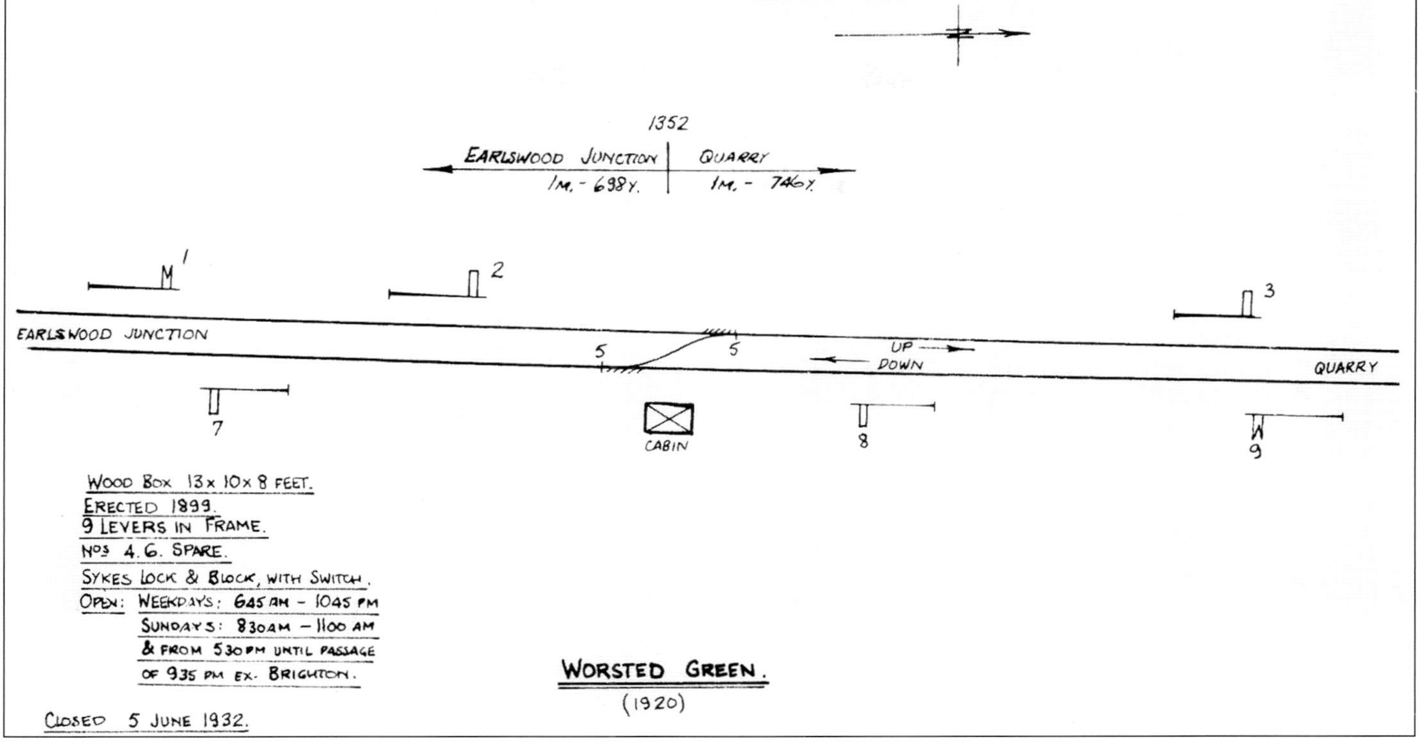

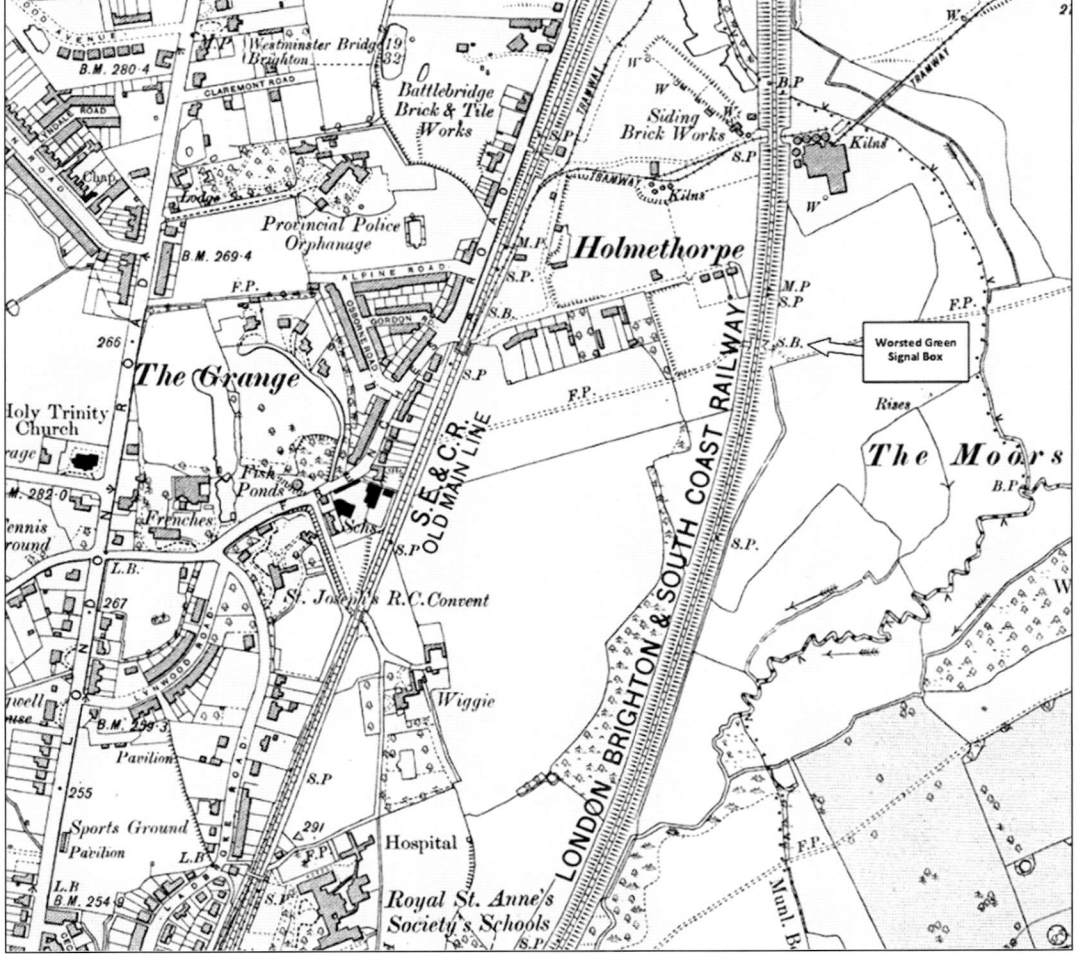

Above: As simple as it gets; this is Worsted Green's signalling layout twenty years after it opened.

Left: Three routes from London to Brighton within a half of a mile of each other: the London Road to the left, with the ex-SER main line in the centre and the new LB&SCR route to the right. Worsted Green signal box was the first intermediate cabin after leaving Earlswood and seems to have been another box that escaped the photographer's attention. This was probably due to its isolated position, although a footpath does run right next to it. However, in this extract from a 1920 map, it is possible to pinpoint its position, just a quarter of a mile directly east of Holmethorpe signal box.
Reproduced by permission of the National Library of Scotland

WORSTED GREEN INTERMEDIATE BOX.

This Signal Box and Signals are not yet completed; further notice will be given when they are ready for use.

A new Intermediate Signal Box erected on Down side of Line, 1 mile 23 chains North of Redhill Goods Box, will be brought into use, together with the following new Signals and Points :—

New Crossover Road between Up and Down Lines, laid in opposite Signal Box.

Runaway Catch Points, laid in on Up Line, 264 yards South of Up Distant Signal.

New Down Distant Signal erected on Down side of Line, 950 yards from Down Home Signal.

New Down Home Signal erected on Down side of Line, 75 yards North of Signal Box.

New Down Starting Signal erected on Down Side of Line, 275 yards South of Signal Box.

New Up Distant Signal erected on Up side of Line, 800 yards from Up Home Signal.

New Up Home Signal erected on Up side of Line, 75 yards South of Signal Box.

New Up Starting Signal erected on Up side of Line, 275 yards North of Signal Box.

The page from the 1899 opening notice detailing the signalling arrangements for Worsted Green signal box. There is an anomaly, as 'Worsted Lane' is used on the title page of the opening notice seen in the Earlswood chapter.

33 – Quarry Intermediate

Billinton Class 'B2x' 4-4-0 No. 315 brings a Down Quarry Line passenger train under Rockshaw Road bridge with the roof of Quarry Intermediate signal box just visible in the background. No. 2 Up home signal can be seen on the left.
Bluebell Railway Museum Archive, M.P. Bennett Collection

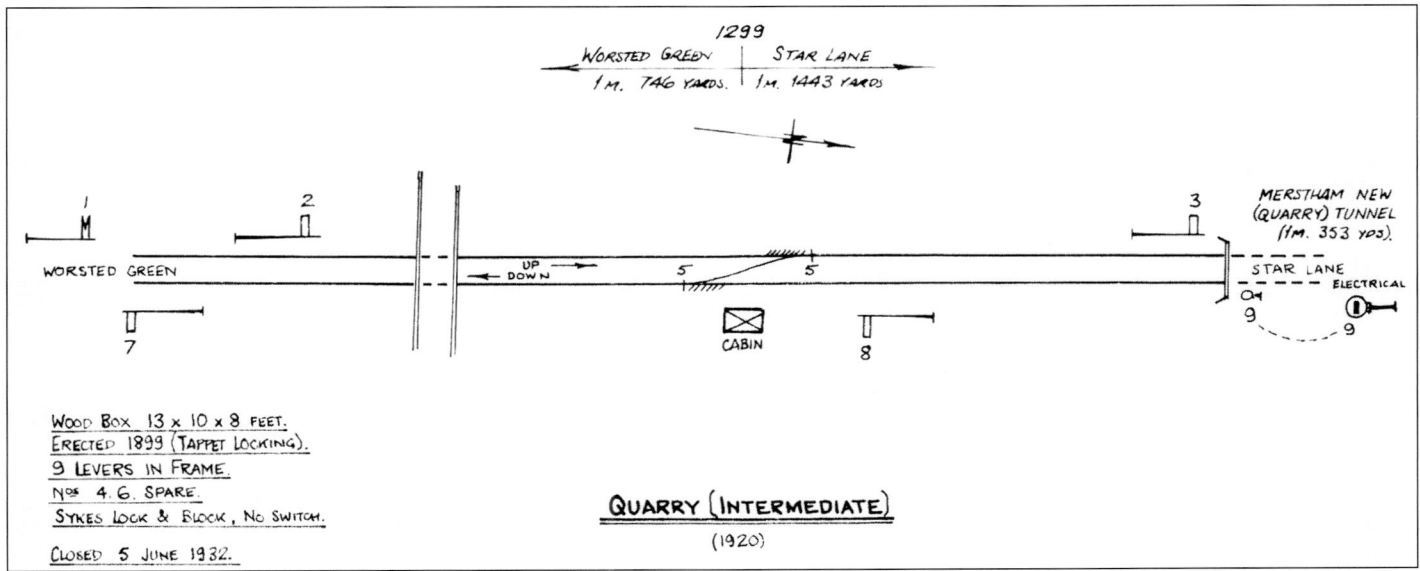

Quarry Intermediate signal box layout in 1920 with just another twelve years of its life left. Of interest is the Down road colour light distant signal within the tunnel itself, while the electrical banner repeater (with a 'fish-tail' arm) is situated on the approach to the tunnel at the northern end.

QUARRY INTERMEDIATE BOX.

This Signal Box and Signals are not yet completed; further notice will be given when they are ready for use.

A New Intermediate Signal Box erected on Down Side of Line, South end of New Tunnel, 1 mile 66 chains from Star Lane Intermediate, will be brought into use, together with the following new Points and Signals:—

New Crossover Road between Up and Down Lines, laid in opposite Signal Box.

New Down Distant Signal fixed in Tunnel between Up and Down Lines, 800 yards from Down Home Signal.

New Down Home Signal erected on Down Side of Line, 75 yards North of Signal Box.

New Down Starting Signal erected on Down Side of Line, 275 yards South of Signal Box.

New Up Distant Signal erected on Up side of Line, 800 yards from Up Home Signal.

New Up Home Signal erected on Up side of Line, 180 yards South of Signal Box.

QUARRY INTERMEDIATE BOX—*continued*.

New Up Starting Signal erected on Up side of Line, 170 yards North of Signal Box.

LEFT: The page from the 1899 opening notice detailing the forthcoming signalling arrangements for Quarry Intermediate signal box.

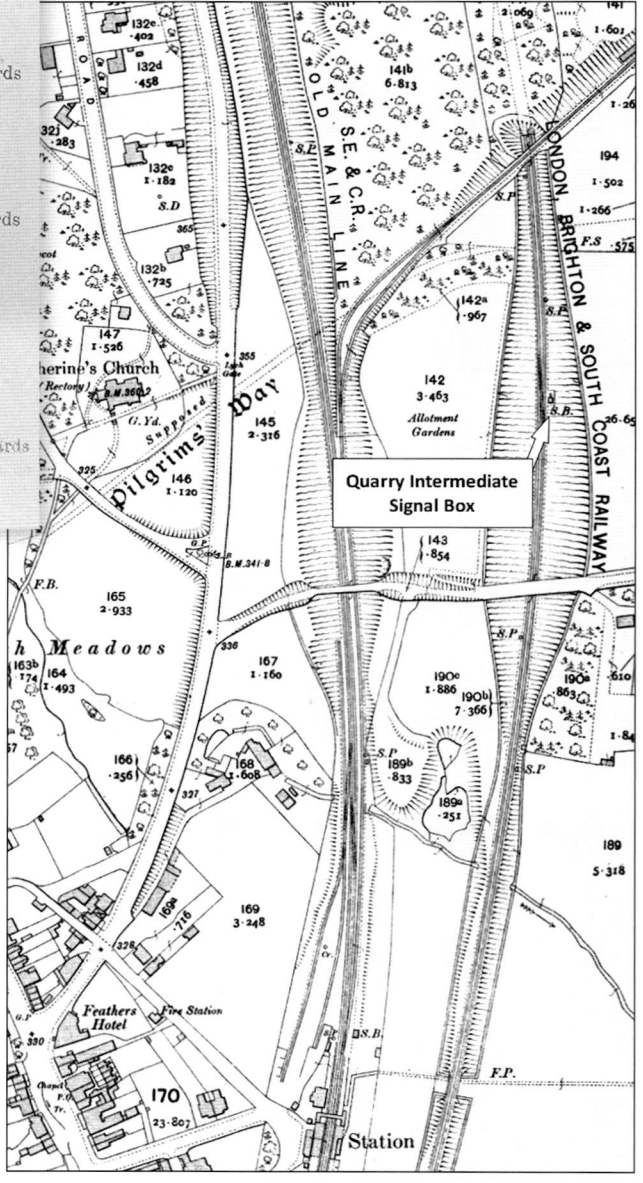

RIGHT: Quarry Intermediate signal box was situated on the Down side of the line a short distance from the south portal of Merstham New, or Quarry Tunnel. Its position with relation to Merstham station (seen bottom centre) on the old line can also be seen. The siding accessing Greystone Lime Works branches off the SE&CR route to cross the Quarry Line adjacent to the tunnel mouth. This extract is dated 1920. *Reproduced by permission of the National Library of Scotland*

Another of Maurice Bennett's beautifully composed photographs sees 'K' Class No. A790 *River Avon* hauling the 'Southern Belle' a few hundred yards south of where the previous photograph was taken. No. 7 signal remains 'off' in its wake but how insubstantial the track appears in comparison to today's standards, jointed bullhead rail fastened into chairs with oak keys but no ballast shoulder whatsoever. *Bluebell Railway Museum Archive, M.P. Bennett Collection*

Looking northwards from the bridge seen in the previous photograph, the diminutive Quarry Intermediate signal box can be seen nestling into the cutting side. Opening with the Quarry Line itself, the box contained a 9-lever frame with just two spare levers, but when this image was captured its demise must have been imminent, as can be seen here with the third rail in position, new cable route in situ and the rear of CA42 signal in the foreground. Judging by the amount of steam at the tunnel mouth, a train has just passed through whilst a lone figure can be seen walking along the 6ft towards the camera. If he was from the local Permanent Way gang he could be justifiably proud of their efforts, with an immaculate cess and finely trimmed cutting sides, worthy of any 'Prize Length' award. In the top right background can be seen Greystone Lime Works which was accessed from the long siding from Merstham seen in the previous map, the line crossing the main line on an overbridge immediately in front of the tunnel mouth.
Lens of Sutton Collection

The northern entrance to Merstham 'New' or more commonly, 'Quarry' Tunnel. The banner repeater for Quarry Intermediate's colour light No. 9 Down distant signal (situated within the tunnel itself) is seen ahead of what will become CA44 signal. Star Lane's No. 1 Up distant signal is seen with its back to the camera, with the fogging huts for that and the Down distant seen in either cess. The signal wire to the Up road signal runs, unusually, in the 6ft, which makes sense in a cutting prone to chalk falls where the wire, if it were in the usual position in the cess, could possibly give a false indication if depressed by enough of it. A retired colleague remembers that such chalk falls were a common occurrence in the chalk cuttings in the Gravesend area, necessitating renewal of wire runs where contact with the chalk had led to rusting of the wire itself.
1931, The Edward Wallis Collection

34 – Star Lane

The Star Lane Intermediate signalman poses happily for the camera just 34 days after his allegiance had changed from the London, Brighton & South Coast to the newly formed Southern Railway, although he may not have noticed many differences yet. The possibility that his job would be disappearing some nine years later had probably not crossed his mind either! The number of signalmen who lost their positions by 1932 would have been numerous although not necessarily with redundancies, as the railways were good at absorbing staff into other walks of life. In 1920, Star Lane contained a 15-lever frame with none spare. *3rd February 1923, A.W. Croughton, John Minnis Collection*

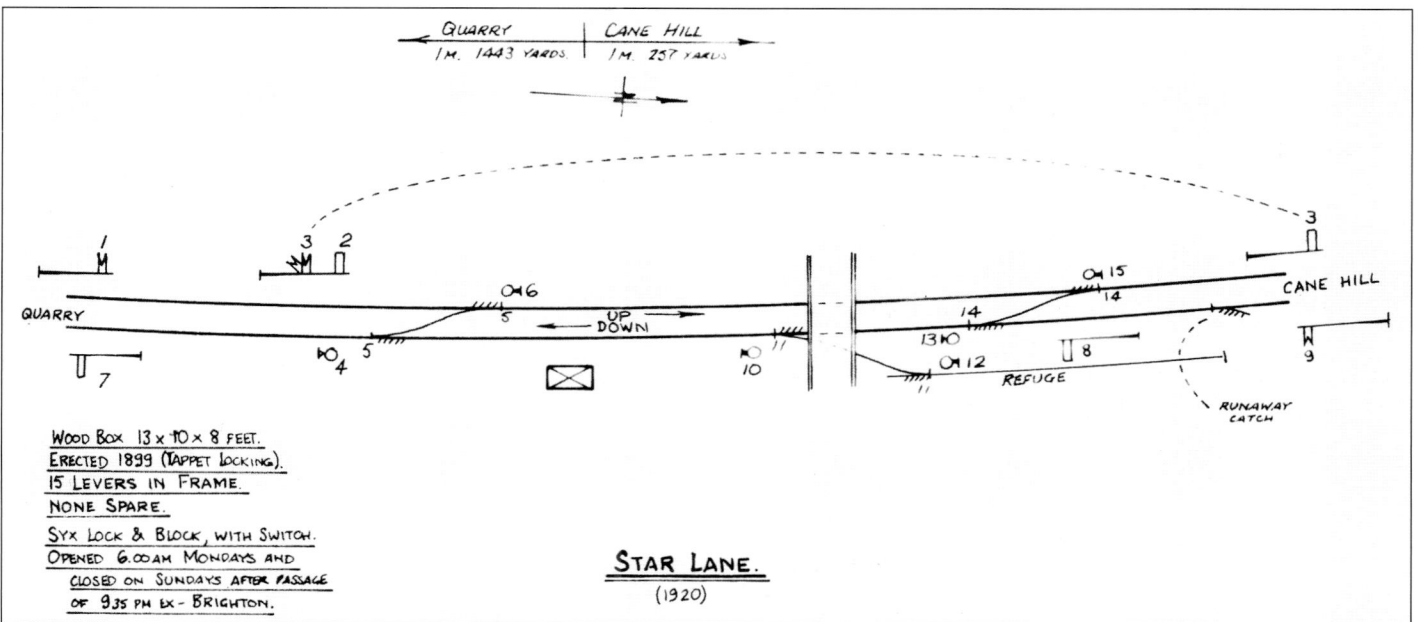

Star Lane signal box layout in 1920. With the electrification of the line in 1932 this was considered the best position for the new sub-station, thus the refuge siding was retained to serve that. No. 3 Inner distant worked from the starting signal; a similar situation was seen earlier at Patcham.

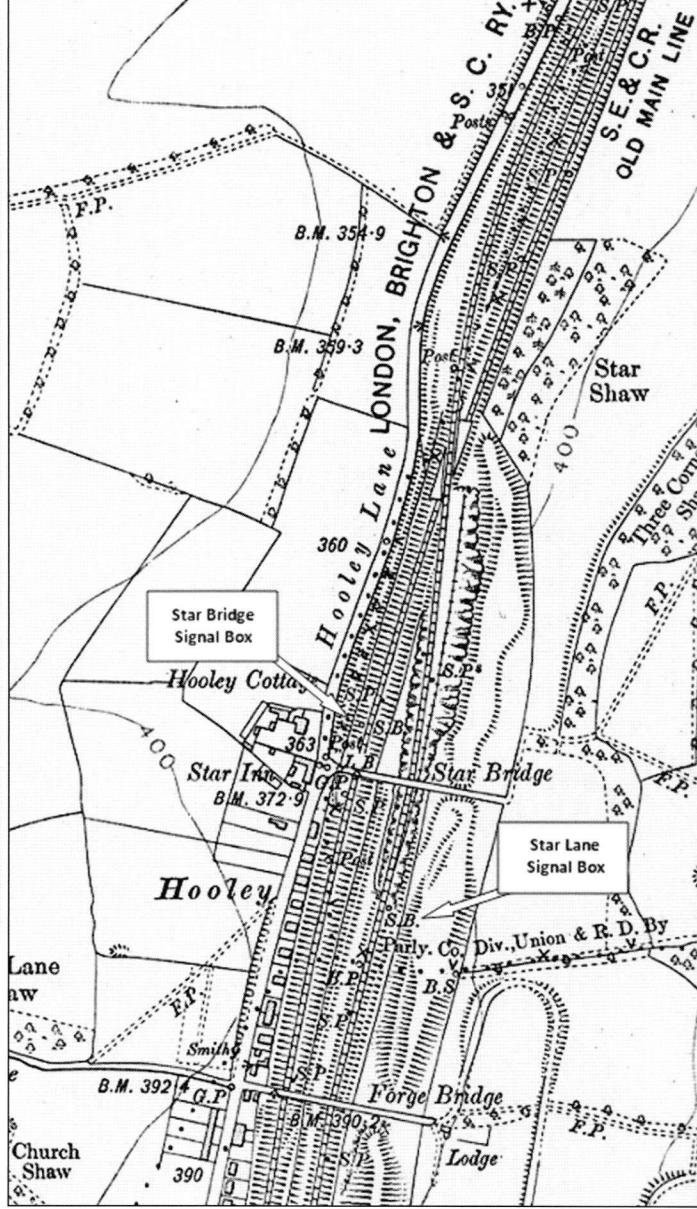

ABOVE: The page from the 1899 opening notice detailing the forthcoming signalling arrangements for Star Lane signal box. Only a single crossover was laid in initially and there is no mention of a siding.

ABOVE: Extract from a 1914 map showing the ex-SER and new LB&SCR lines running parallel to each other, the latter crossing over the former towards the top the page. Both Star Lane and its near neighbour Star Bridge are highlighted.
Reproduced by permission of the National Library of Scotland

LEFT: The Westinghouse illuminated diagram for Star Lane in 1932. Two sets of catch points are provided on the Down Line to cater for any runaways on the 1:165 rising gradient. *K.R.M.*

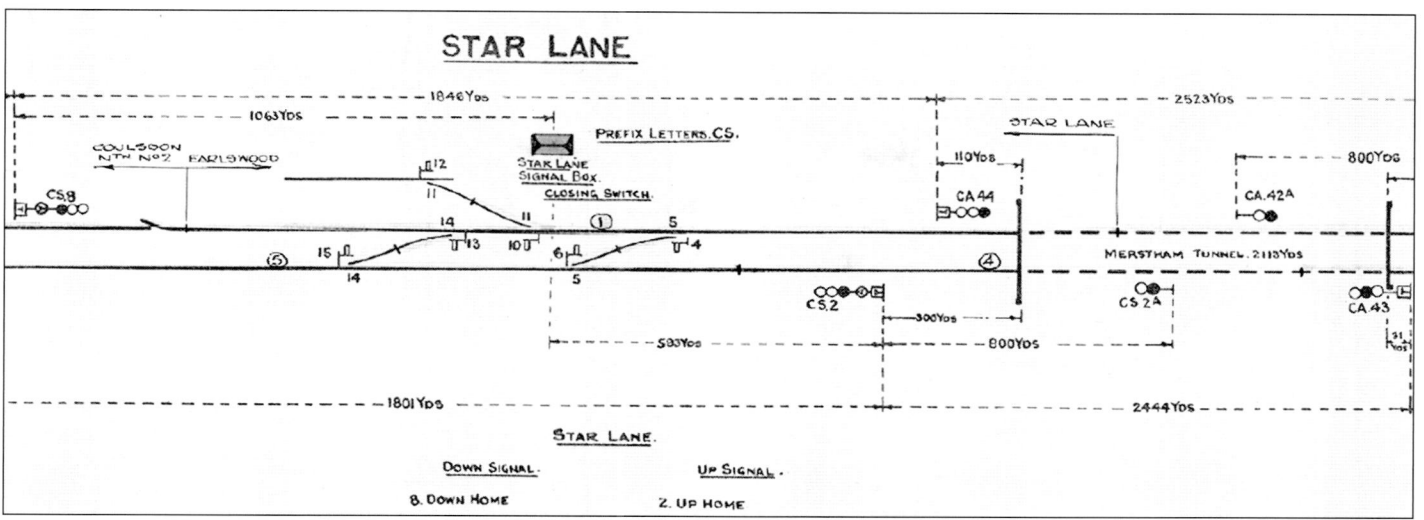

Star Lane was the only signal box that escaped the fate of the intermediate cabins that were provided with the new line as it gave access to the sub-station and, although seemingly rather extravagant, two crossovers. These would have been useful in case of emergency but also (with regard to a train accessing the siding) to enable an engine to run round its train. Inevitably, decline set in and the northernmost cross-over was an early casualty. No. 11 siding points were disconnected from the signal box on Monday 19th December 1966 and left clipped and padlocked for engineers' use only, being abolished on Sunday 28th February 1971. Similarly, No. 5 crossover was disconnected from the signal box, clipped and padlocked on Tuesday 10th June 1969 and abolished on 22nd May 1974. All shunt signals were taken out of use along with the disconnections. The signal box officially closed on 19th November 1978, but survived as an increasingly deteriorating structure into the early 1980s.

Taken from Forge Bridge looking north towards Star Bridge, Star Lane Intermediate signal box can be seen set into the steep cutting side, the signalman's route to work clearly visible. With the introduction of electrification and colour light signalling through here in 1932, problems were soon experienced with the newly installed track circuits. The electrical fouling bar seen on the cess rail of the Up Road acted as a 'back up' to this, operating as an interim arrangement to maintain the integrity of the signalling system. See the Appendix for an article on 'Early Trials with Axle Counters' which explains the situation further. *Lens of Sutton Collection*

LEFT: Looking south from Star Bridge during 1931; the conductor rails are in place but, as yet, no sign of a cable route for the signalling.
The Edward Wallis Collection

BELOW: Edward has now turned his camera northwards with the construction of the new sub-station underway at the end of the siding. With a wagon up against the buffer stops, it can be safe to say that this was the method for bringing in the building materials and even the transformers, rectifiers and switch-gear to facilitate the supply to the third rail. The Redhill lines can be seen passing beneath the Quarry Line towards the top of the photograph.
1931, The Edward Wallis Collection

```
                BRITISH RAILWAYS - SOUTHERN REGION
             DIVISIONAL SIGNAL ENGINEER'S (CTL.) OFFICE, CROYDON      TS.18.
              SIGNAL BOXES AND GATE BOXES ON THE CTL. DIVISION

 1. Place:-  STAR LANE
 2. Type of structure.   WOOD
 3. Approx. dimensions (int.)   9'-0 x 12'0
 4. Condition of S. box structure.   MEDIUM
 5. Method of illumination a) Operating floor  OIL
                           b) Ground floor     NIL
 6. Type of lever frame.   R.S.Co (15)
 7.   "   "    "    "   support.   BEAMS
 8. Method of gate operation.   -
 9. Gate stops a) Road stops   -
              b) Rail stops   -
10. Type of C.B. battery.   No 3 DRY
11. C.B. battery housed. Internal/external.
12. Leadaway a) External. Timber/Metal plate.
             b) Internal. Timber/Metal plate.
13. Date when particulars taken.   22/1/66
14. Voltage of electric supply and where from.   NIL  440V STAR LANE S/S
15. 15 tele. circuits in box.   37·39 ·SUB· CON:
16. Unusual features.         Signed....................... District Inspector
```

LEFT: The 1966 survey of Central Division signal boxes shows that whereas its neighbour on the Redhill lines had the luxury of electric lighting on the operating floor, Star Lane had to make do with oil lamps.

RIGHT: The meeting of the ways, showing to good effect how the Quarry Line sits above the lower Redhill lines and the enormous engineering works required to excavate the pair of cuttings. Star Bridge signal box can be seen below the right-hand overbridge, also giving a clear view of the new sub-station's construction with scaffold poles rising to the sky.
1931, The Edward Wallis Collection

BOTTOM RIGHT: Some forty-five years later, the 11.00am Victoria to Brighton non-stop passes Star Lane sub-station, the crossover points and siding long gone. The head-code '4' always holds a painful memory for the author. Working in Brighton signal box in the early 1970s, it was not unheard of to take the unofficial route to the station by crossing all running lines to the platform that the signalman told you was your train, in my case the 'Up stopper'. In a hurry to get home to Burgess Hill after finishing work, I mistook the platform number and without checking the head-code, boarded the train. I realised something was amiss when we flew through Preston Park. *'Oh well,'* I thought, *'we'll stop at Haywards Heath'*. Passing straight through there I vainly maintained the same hope for Gatwick and East Croydon, but no such luck as the next stop was Victoria. I was late home for dinner that night.
March 28th 1976, John Scrace

Above: This is the view of Star Lane signal box on 20th April 1976, officially still in use 'as required', although I doubt it had seen any activity for many years. *John Scrace*

Left: Although officially closed in 1978 (see notice below) the structure lingered on, as seen here in September 1982. It was demolished shortly after.

> **SUNDAY, 19 NOVEMBER – STAR LANE.** – The signal box will be abolished.
> Signal CS8 will be converted to an automatic signal and renumbered CA328. The telephone at this signal will in future communicate with Earlswood signal box.
> Signal CS2 will be converted to an automatic signal and renumbered CA327. The telephones at all signals on the Up Quarry line from signal CA39 northwards will in future communicate with Coulsdon North signal box.
> (P/EW 46 CD 1978)

35 – Cane Hill

Taken from just north of Hooley House, a Down passenger train is about to pass Cane Hill signal box. Between the fifth and sixth coaches can be seen Coulsdon & Smitham Downs South signal box's Up distant signal, the left arm of which has been removed to be replaced by splitting banners below. The telegraph poles in the distance are on the Brighton Road, whilst the Redhill lines are running parallel but out of sight in this photograph
Laurie Marshall Collection

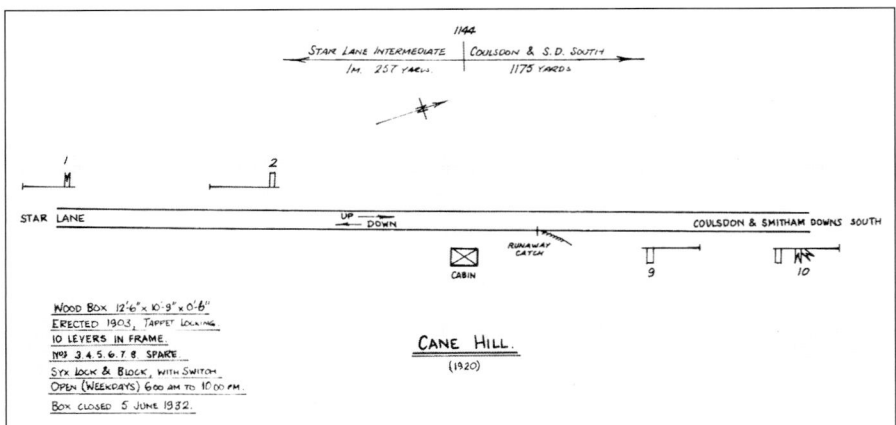

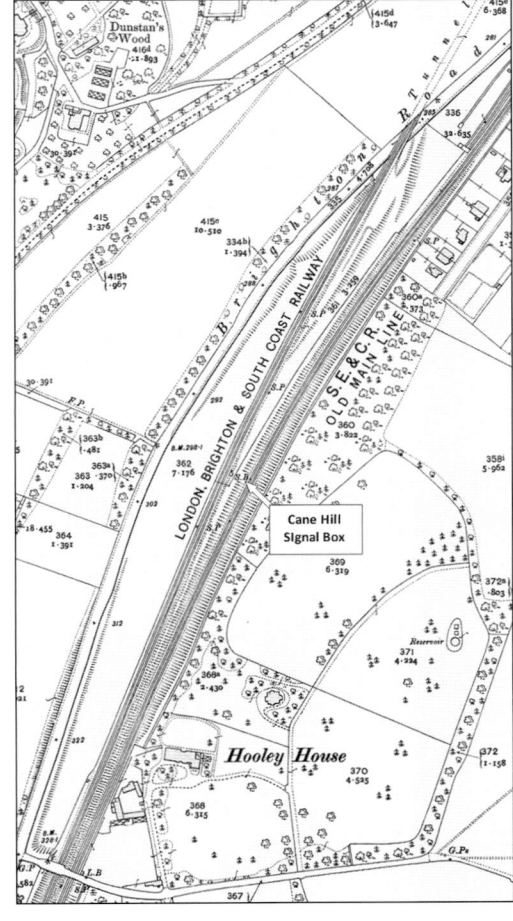

Above: Not long after the opening of the new route, it was deemed prudent to add another 'break section' cabin between Star Lane and Coulsdon, so Cane Hill arrived on the scene. Not opening until 1903, three years after the other intermediate signal boxes, it had the dubious privilege of having the lowest number of working levers in any signal box on the line, a mere 'home' and 'distant' in each direction. Being less than three quarters of a mile from Coulsdon & Smitham Downs South, its Down distant was slotted under that signal box's Down advance starting signal.

Right: From a map dated 1912, Cane Hill signal box can be seen positioned adjacent to the Down Quarry between the two main lines. For reference, Woodhouse Lane overbridge is bottom left and the 'Covered Way' (seen top right) is on the LB&SCR route and marked 'tunnel'. This ceased to be the case in 1955 when the roof was removed.
Reproduced by permission of the National Library of Scotland

Above: Taken from Woodplace Lane overbridge and with Cane Hill signal box just visible behind the fifth telegraph pole, No. 425 brings a 10-coach passenger train along the Down Quarry Line. The SE&CR line can be seen bottom right.
Bluebell Railway Museum Archive, M.P. Bennett Collection

Below: Another view from Woodplace Lane overbridge with an unidentified tank engine heading a short passenger formation along the Down Redhill line. This was a popular spot for the early photographers but it would seem that none of them ventured further along the line to get a better view of the signal box, which again can just be seen through the gloom in the distance. *7th August 1909, Laurie Marshall Collection*

36 – Coulsdon North

A photograph taken around 1912 looking from outside the shunt cabin towards the South signal box and sidings with Class 'E4' No. 492, sitting outside the engine shed. Looking along the long crossover to its turnout on to the Down Through line, four sets of double slips disappear into the distance.   *W.L. Kenning, Lens of Sutton Collection*

Coulsdon North shunting cabin is visible on the left as Class 'I3' 4-4-2T No. B24 shunts under the 6,700V overhead wires which terminated at the end of the carriage sidings. Coulsdon Shed opened in 1900 and closed in 1928.   *12th February 1928, H.C. Casserley*

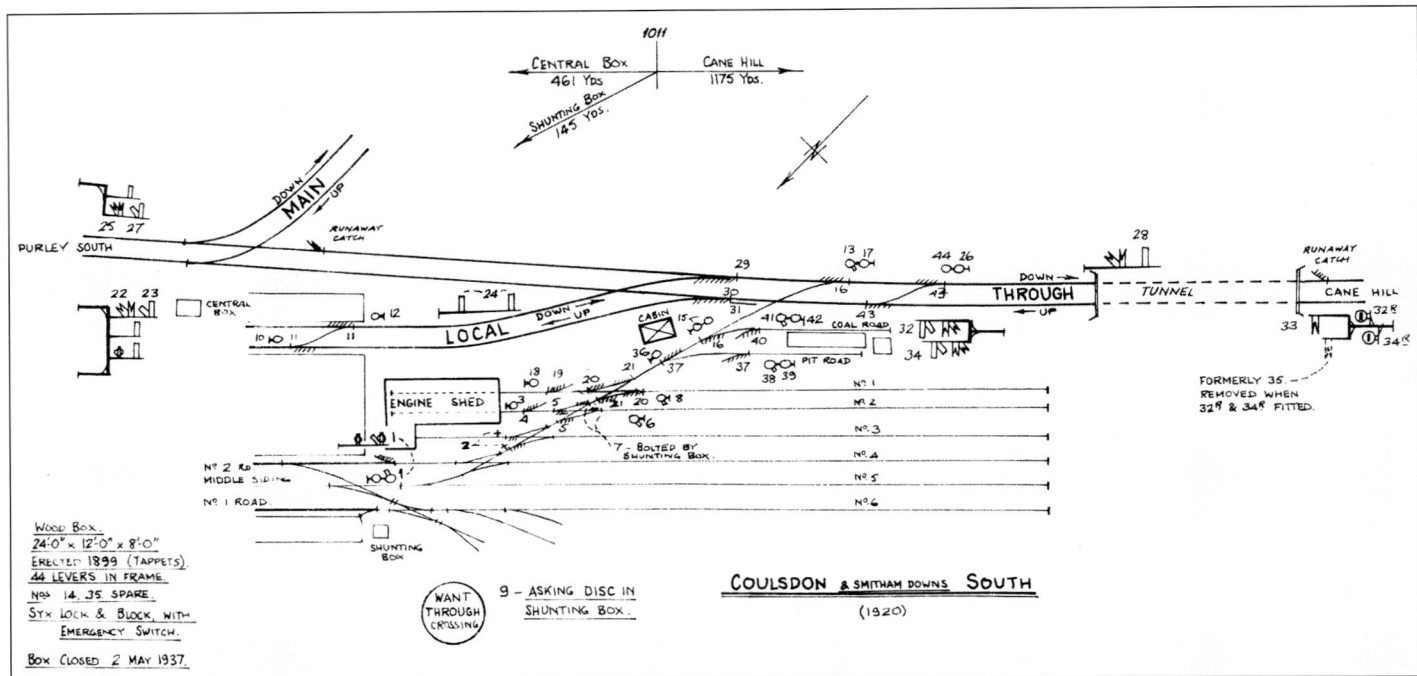

Above: Stoats Nest South signal box was the shortest lived of the three new cabins that were brought into use on 5th November 1899 and ran the gamut of name changing that must have been a popular pastime here. It became Coulsdon South in 1911 and Stoats Nest in 1918, before displaying the somewhat confusing Coulsdon West South and Coulsdon North South in 1923; pity the signalman having to repeat one of those every time the telephone rang. It became the far more sensible Coulsdon North No. 2 in December 1923 (three name changes in six months) before the Southern Railway, ever with an eye to invest to recoup the benefits, transferred the controls from here to No. 1 box. It duly closed on 2nd May 1937. Note the splitting banner repeaters below No. 33 distant signal as seen in the earlier photograph of Cane Hill.

Below: Along with Central and South cabins, Coulsdon Shunting box opened with the new avoiding line on 5th November 1899. Never a block post, it purely controlled the extensive sidings provided for terminating passenger stock along with the relevant engine moves to and from the shed. It too began life as Stoats Nest Shunting box and ran the normal name changes (Coulsdon Shunting, Coulsdon & Smitham Downs Shunting, Coulsdon West Shunting), but the 1923 name of Coulsdon North Shunting remained with it until closure on 9th October 1983.

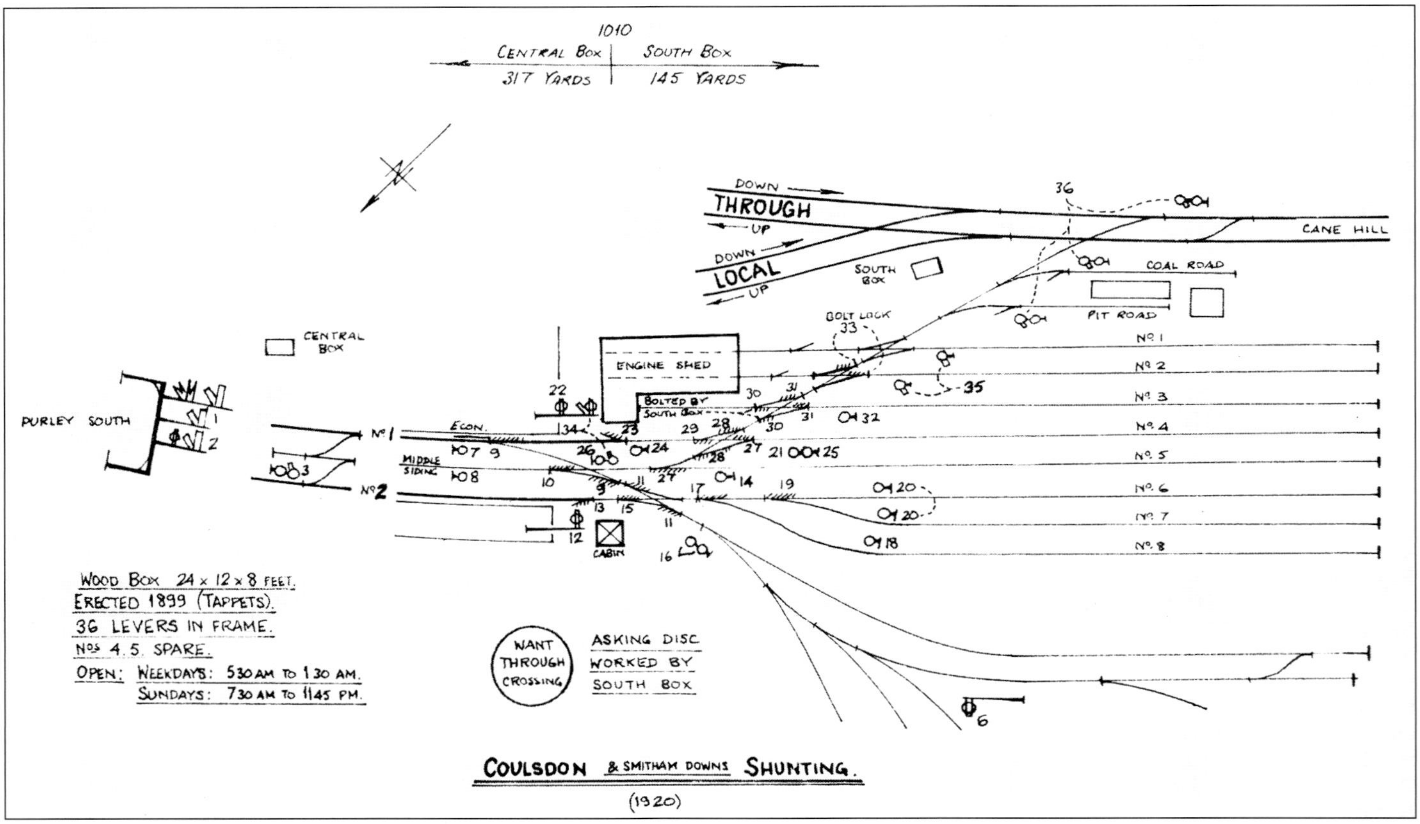

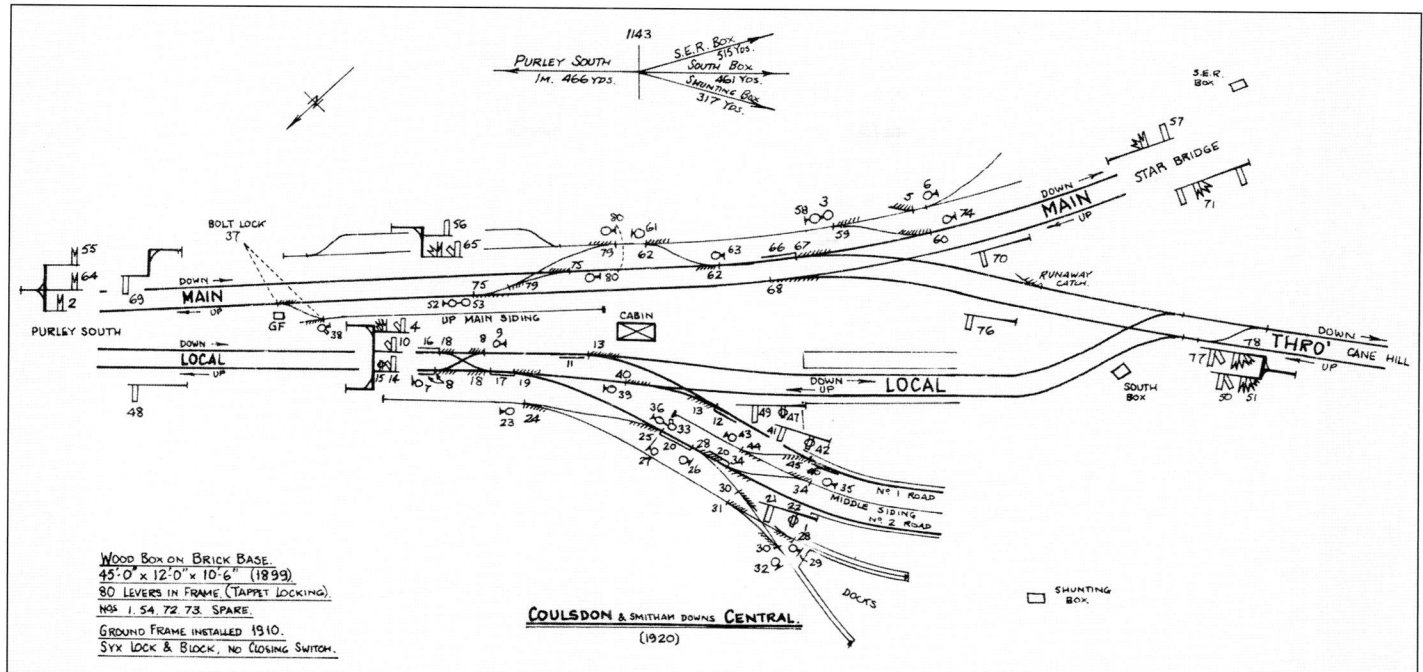

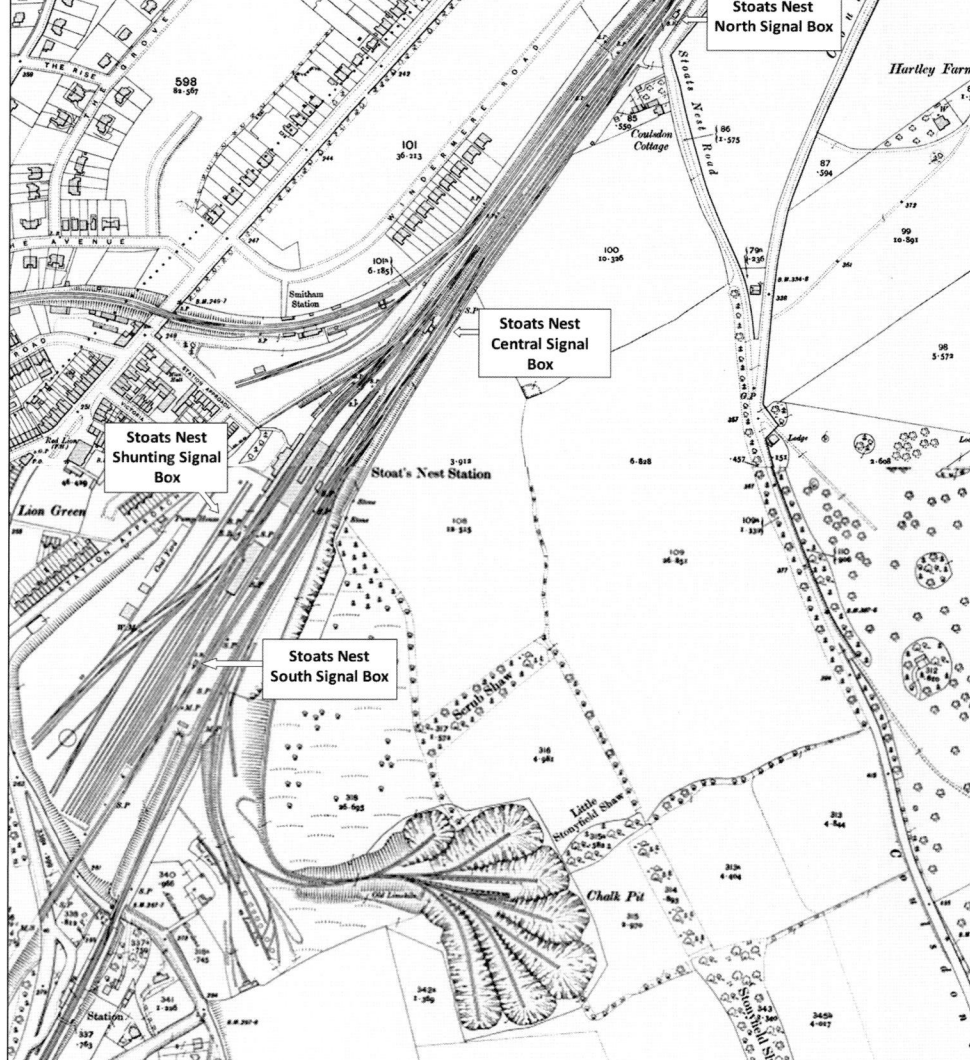

Above: Coulsdon & Smitham Downs Central was brought into use on 5th November 1899 and also enjoyed a variety of name changes during its lifetime. Christened Stoats Nest Central upon opening, its name changed to the one exhibited here on 1st June 1911, before becoming Coulsdon West Central on 9th July 1923. Coulsdon North Central followed on 1st August 1923 (so the 'West Central' suffix did not last long), then Coulsdon North No. 1 during December 1923 and finally plain Coulsdon North with the demise of its near neighbour, on 2nd May 1937. With the abolition of No. 2 signal box and its controls transferred here, Coulsdon North assumed the 'CT' signal prefix previously held by the South box. It closed on 9th October 1983.

Right: This extract from a 1910 map shows the four signal boxes that existed in the Stoats Nest area. The old South Eastern route through Coulsdon South station can be seen in the bottom left-hand corner, with the Quarry Line, only a decade old at this point in time, disappearing into the Cane Hill Covered Way just above.
Reproduced by permission of the National Library of Scotland

STOATS NEST CENTRAL BOX—MAIN LINE.

A New Junction, with Facing Points on Down Main Line laid in 10 yards North of New Local Station, and worked from the New Central Box, together with the following New Points and Signals, will be brought into use.

New Crossover Road leading from Down Siding to Down Main Line, North of New Junction, with Ground Disc Signals at each end.

New Crossover Road leading from Down Siding to Down Main Line, South of New Junction, with Ground Disc Signals at each end.

New Down Main Distant Signals fixed under Stoats Nest North Box Down Main Home Signal.

1. North Box existing Down Main Home Signal.
2. Central Box Down Main Distant Signal.
3. Central Box Down Main to Through Distant.

As seen from Down Main Line Trains approaching Stoats Nest Central Junction.

New Down Main Home Signals erected on Down Side of Line, 120 yards North of Stoats Nest New Central Junction.

1. Central Box Down Main Home Signal.
2. Central Box Down Main to Through Home Signal.
3. South Box Down Through Distant Signal.

As seen from Down Main Line Trains approaching Stoats Nest Central Junction.

New Down Main Line Starting Signal erected on Down Side of Line, 380 yards South of Stoats Nest New Central Junction.

1. Central Box Down Main Starting Signal.
2. Coulsdon Down Distant Signal.

As seen from Down Main Line Trains approaching Coulsdon Station.

Central Box New Up Main Distant Signal with high and low Arms and Lights, fixed on Coulsdon existing Up Starting Signal Post.

1, 2. Coulsdon Up Starting Signal.
3, 4. Stoats Nest Central Box Up Main Distant Signal.

As seen from Up Main Line Trains leaving Coulsdon Station.

New Up Main Home Signal erected on Up Side of Main Line, 150 yards South of Stoats Nest Central Junction.

1. Central Box Up Main Home Signal.
2. North Box Up Main Distant Signal.

As seen from Up Main Line Trains approaching Stoats Nest Junction.

STOATS NEST CENTRAL BOX—MAIN LINE.—continued.

New Through to Up Main Home Signal, erected on Up Side of Through Line, 150 yards North of Stoats Nest Central Junction.

1. Central Box, Through to Up Main Home Signal.
2. North Box, Through to Up Main Distant Signal.

As seen from Up Through Trains approaching Stoats Nest Junction.

STOATS NEST.

The New Station at Stoats Nest will have Up and Down Local Line Platforms for Trains terminating at Stoats Nest, also Platforms for Up and Down Through Line Trains running via the Local Lines only.

STOATS NEST CENTRAL BOX.—LOCAL LINE.

A new Station with Up and Down Local Lines, and Nos. 1 and 2 Bay Lines, and Middle Siding on Up Side of Line, and connected to Local Line, with Facing Points 40 yards North of new Central Box will be brought into use, together with the following Points and Signals, at the North end of the Station.

New Scissors Crossing, laid in 100 yards North of New Central Box, with Down Facing and Up Facing and Down Trailing and Up Trailing Points on Local Line, together with Ground Disc Signals at each end of Trailing Points of Scissors Crossing.

New Connection leading from Up Local to No. 2 Bay, with a Ground Disc Signal for Shunting from Up Local to No. 2 Bay.

New Crossover Road between No. 2 Bay and Middle Siding, with a Ground Disc Signal for Shunting from Middle Siding to No. 2 Bay.

New Crossover Road between No. 1 Bay and Up Siding, with Ground Disc Signal at each end.

New Crossover Road between No. 1 Bay and Middle Siding, with Ground Disc Signal at each end.

New Crossover Road between No. 1 Bay and Up Local Siding, with Slip Points leading into Horse and Carriage Dock, with Ground Disc Signals at each end.

New Down Local Distant Signal, erected on Up Local Side of Line, 800 yards from Down Local Outer Home Signal.

As seen from Down Local Line Trains approaching Stoats Nest Station.

New Down Local Outer Home Signal erected between Down Local and Up Main Lines, 400 yards from Down Local Inner Home Signal.

As seen from Down Local Line Trains approaching Stoats Nest Station.

New Down Local Inner Home Signals erected over Local Lines, 50 yards North of Down Local Facing Points.

1. Central Box Down Local Inner Home Signal to Through Line.
2. South Box Down Through Distant Signal.
3. Central Box Down Local Inner Home Signal to No. 2 Bay.
4. Central Box Down Local Inner Home Signal to No. 1 Bay.
5. Central Box Down Local Shunt to Middle Siding (stands normally blind).

As seen from Down Local Line Trains approaching Stoats Nest Station.

STOATS NEST CENTRAL BOX—LOCAL LINE.—continued.

Up Starting Signal, No. 1 Bay to Local Line, erected at the North end of the Platform.

1. Up Starting Signal from No. 1 Bay to Local Line.
2. Shunt Signal from No. 1 Bay to Up Local Line, or Up Local Siding (stands normally blind).

As seen from Up Local Line Trains leaving Stoats Nest Station.

Up Starting Signal No. 2 Bay to Local Line erected at North end of Platform.

1. Up Starting Signal to Local Line from No. 2 Bay.
2. Shunt Signal to Up Local Line or Middle Siding from No. 2 Bay (stands normally blind).

As seen from Up Local Line Trains leaving Stoats Nest Station.

New Up Local Starting Signal with high and low Arms and Lights, erected at North end of Up Through Platform.

1. Up Local Starting Signal from Through Line Platform.
2. Up Local Shunt Signal from Through Line Platform (stands normally blind).

As seen from Up Local Line Trains leaving Stoats Nest Station.

New Up Local Advanced Starting Signal, erected on Up Local side of Line, 400 yards from Central Box.

As seen from Up Local Line Trains leaving Stoats Nest Station.

Above: Billinton Class 'C2X' 0-6-0 No. B529, with a healthy loading of coal, sits in Coulsdon North sidings awaiting its next turn of duty. The 44-lever No. 2 signal box, opened on 5th November 1899 and closed on 2nd May 1937, can be seen on the right.
12th February 1928, H.C. Casserley

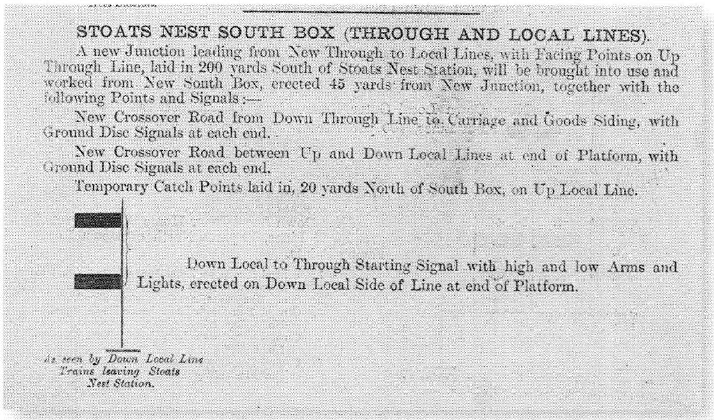

STOATS NEST SOUTH BOX (THROUGH AND LOCAL LINES).

A new Junction leading from New Through to Local Lines, with Facing Points on Up Through Line, laid in 200 yards South of Stoats Nest Station, will be brought into use and worked from New South Box, erected 45 yards from New Junction, together with the following Points and Signals:—

New Crossover Road from Down Through Line to Carriage and Goods Siding, with Ground Disc Signals at each end.

New Crossover Road between Up and Down Local Lines at end of Platform, with Ground Disc Signals at each end.

Temporary Catch Points laid in, 20 yards North of South Box, on Up Local Line.

Down Local to Through Starting Signal with high and low Arms and Lights, erected on Down Local Side of Line at end of Platform.

As seen by Down Local Line Trains leaving Stoats Nest Station.

Taken from the 1899 signalling notice for the opening of the newly quadrupled lines from South Croydon to here, these pages detail the new signalling arrangements at Stoats Nest Central and Stoats Nest South boxes.

STOATS NEST SOUTH BOX (THROUGH AND LOCAL LINES)—*contd.*

New Down Through Line Starting Signal erected on Down Side of Through Line, 110 yards South of Stoats Nest Station.

As seen from Down Through Trains leaving Main Line.

New Down Through Line Advanced Starting Signal erected on Down Side of Line, 260 yards from South Junction.

As seen from Down Through Trains approaching Star Lane Intermediate Box.

New Up Through Line Distant Signals erected on Up Side of Line, 800 yards from Up Through Home Signals.
 1. Up Through Distant Signal to Local Line.
 2. Up Through Distant Signal to Main Line.

As seen from Up Through Trains approaching Stoats Nest.

New Up Through Line Home Signals erected on Up side of Line, 140 yards from South Box Junction.
 1. South Box Up Through to Local Home Signal.
 2. South Box Up Through to Main Home Signal.
 3. Central Box Up Through to Local Distant Signal.
 4. Central Box Up Through to Main Distant Signal.

As seen from Up Trains approaching Stoats Nest.

BELOW: An extract from the Railway Signalling Company's official drawing for the front elevation of Central cabin.
Ken Bacon Collection

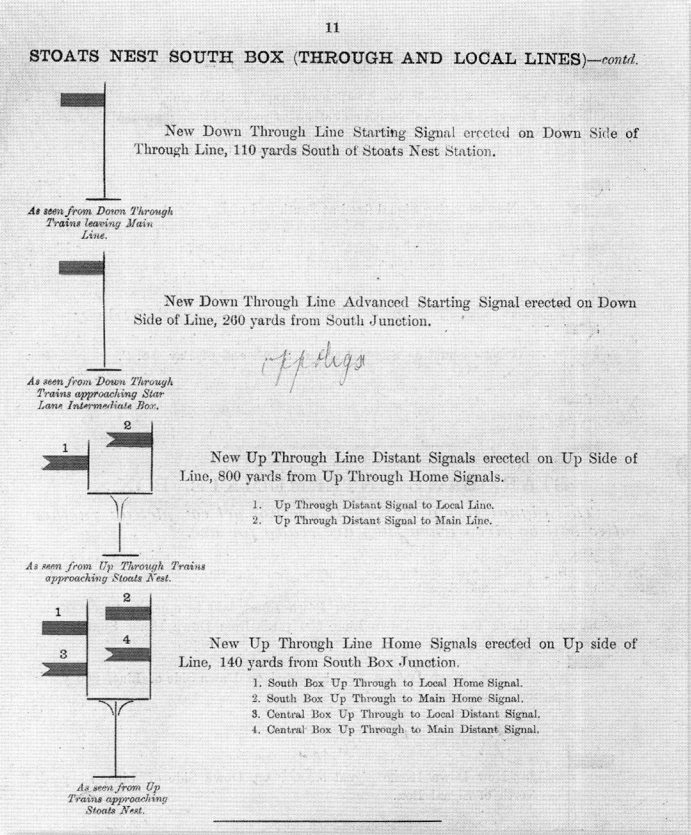

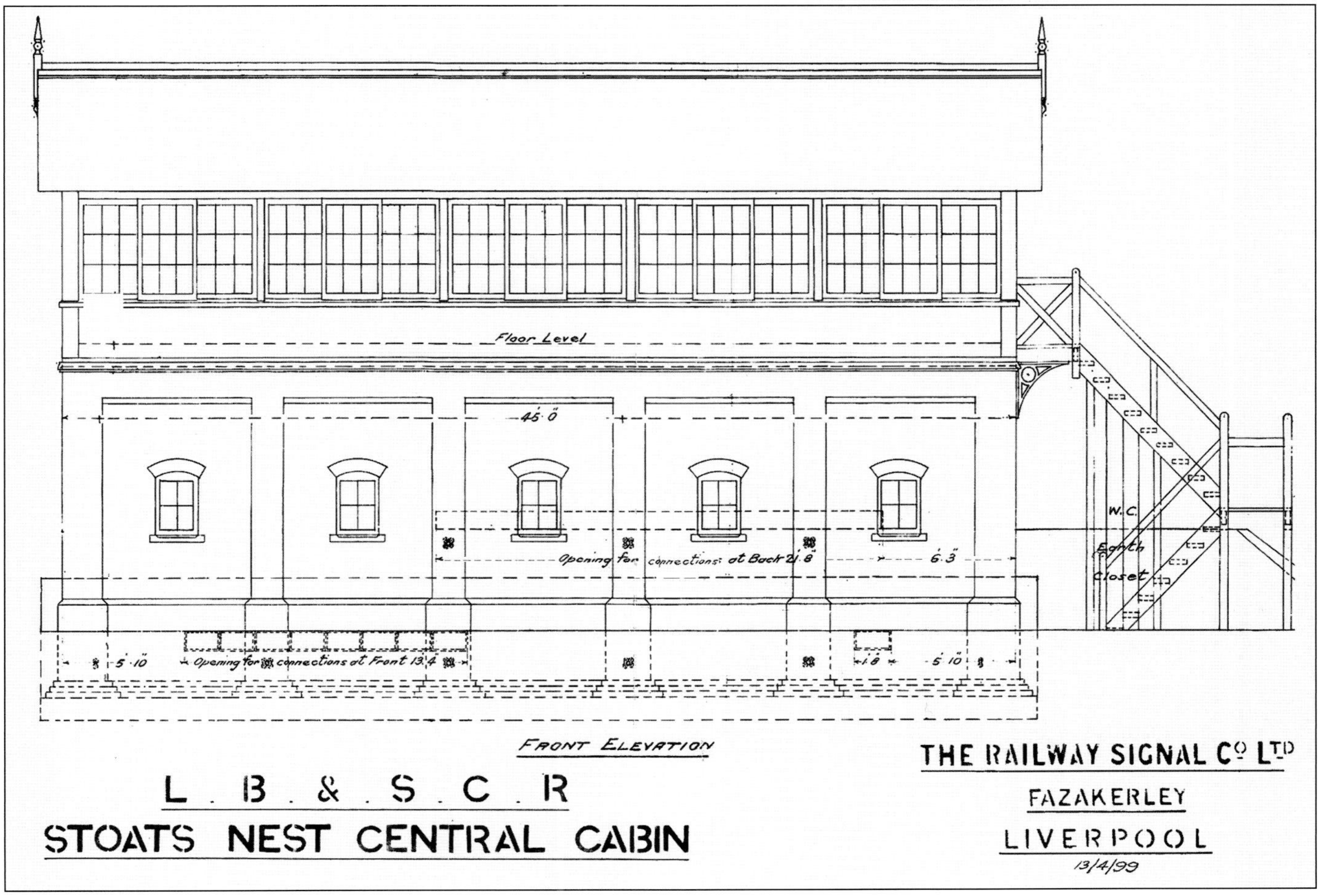

L.B. & S.C.R
STOATS NEST CENTRAL CABIN

THE RAILWAY SIGNAL Co LTD
FAZAKERLEY
LIVERPOOL
13/4/99

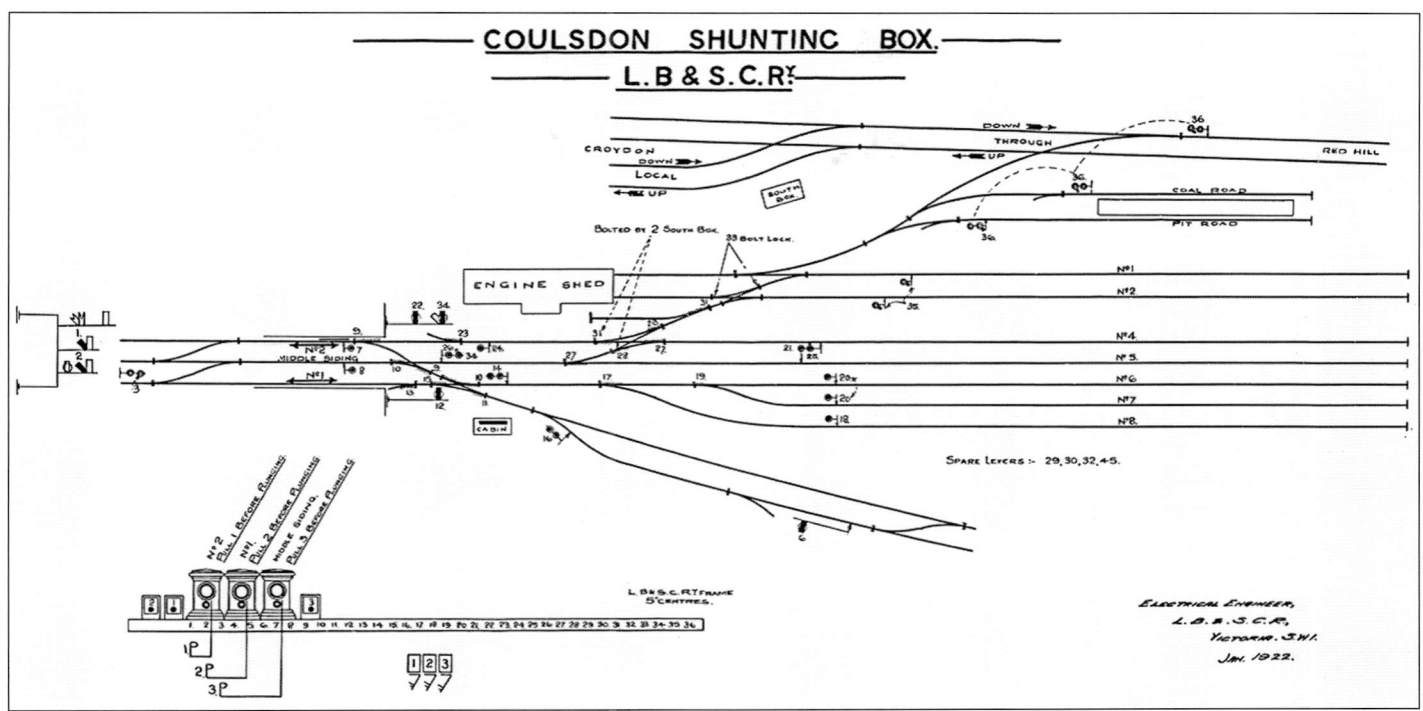

Above: The 1922 diagram for the shunting box.

Facing Page Top: Looking south towards the sidings, Unit No. 4277 waits its next turn of duty alongside Coulsdon North Shunting signal box. *27th July 1983, John Scrace*

Facing Page Bottom: The brevity of the block shelf with its solitary bell-push attests to the shunt box's status as a non-block post; this is, nevertheless, a fine photograph of the well-kept interior of the box with its 36-lever frame. *February 1980, Courtesy 53A Models of Hull*

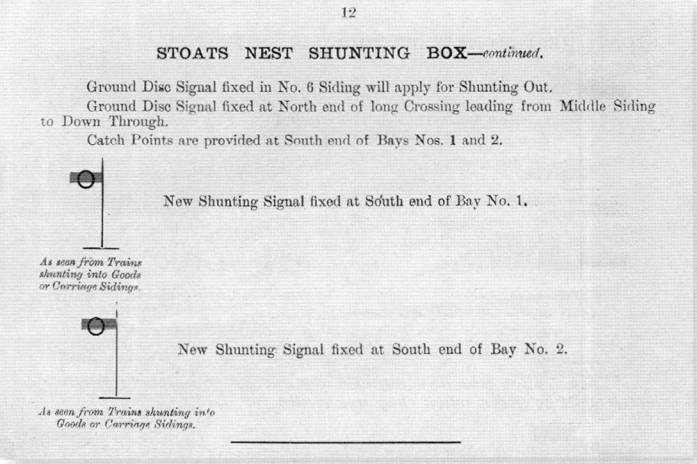

Above: Once again taken from the 1899 signalling notice for the opening of the newly quadrupled lines from South Croydon to here, these two part pages detail the new signalling arrangements at Stoats Nest Shunting box.

Left: The sad but inevitable view, taken just a few months after closure. *January 1984, Nick Catford*

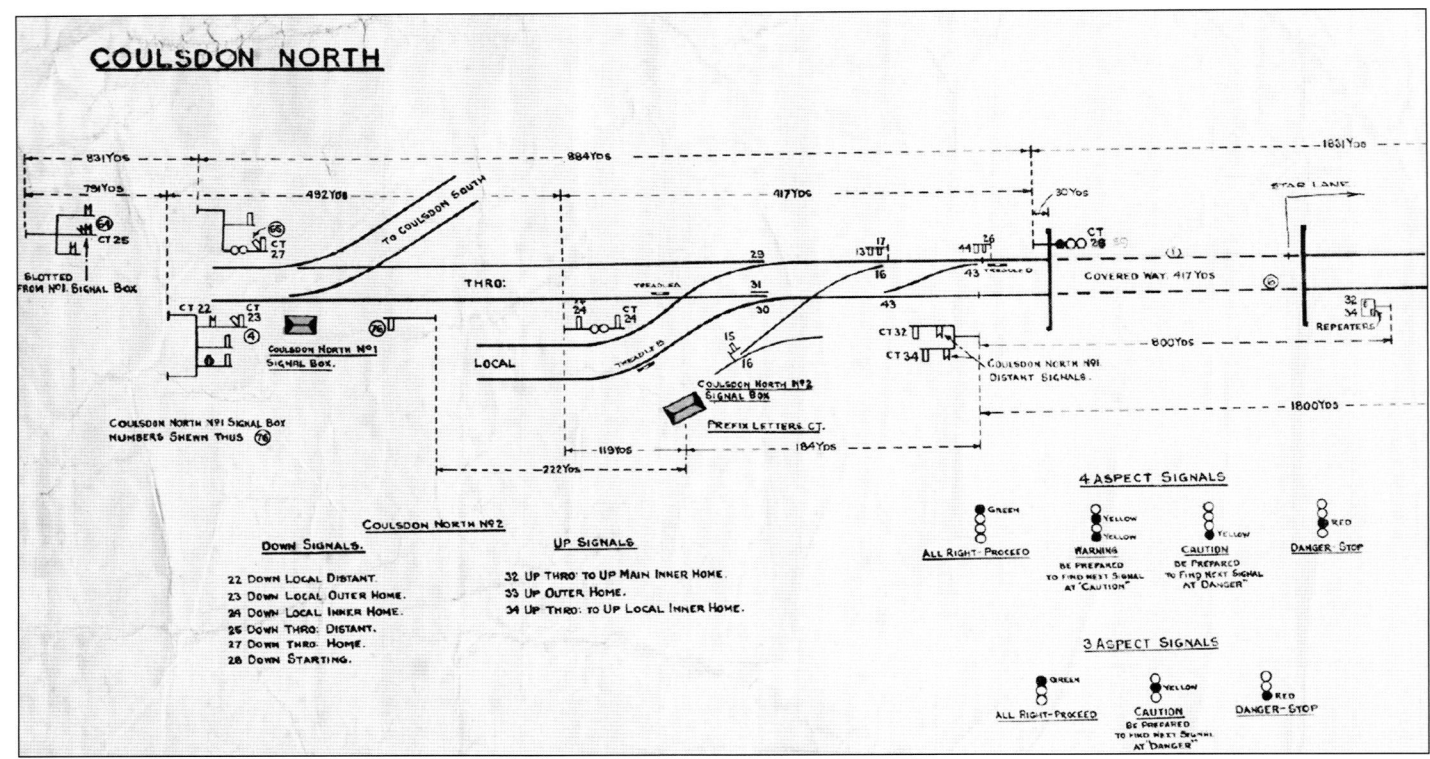

The northern end, and thus the limit, of the 1932 resignalling track plan. The first south-bound track circuit (No. 1) can be seen running through the Cane Hill Covered Way controlling CT28 signal, pencilled in as CT59 which it would become when control passed from here to No. 1 signal box.

Mechanical signalling still abounds as an electrical multiple unit brings a terminating service into Coulsdon North station. The Up starting signals are still lower quadrant whilst the Down road gantry is just visible in the distance. The transformation to colour light did not take place until 1955, with the resignalling from East Croydon to here introducing the new signal boxes at East Croydon, South Croydon and Purley. The official walkway to the signal box can be seen off the platform end, but it is not clear why the box access steps were placed at the London end, necessitating a walk adjacent to the Up Main line. *Lens of Sutton Collection*

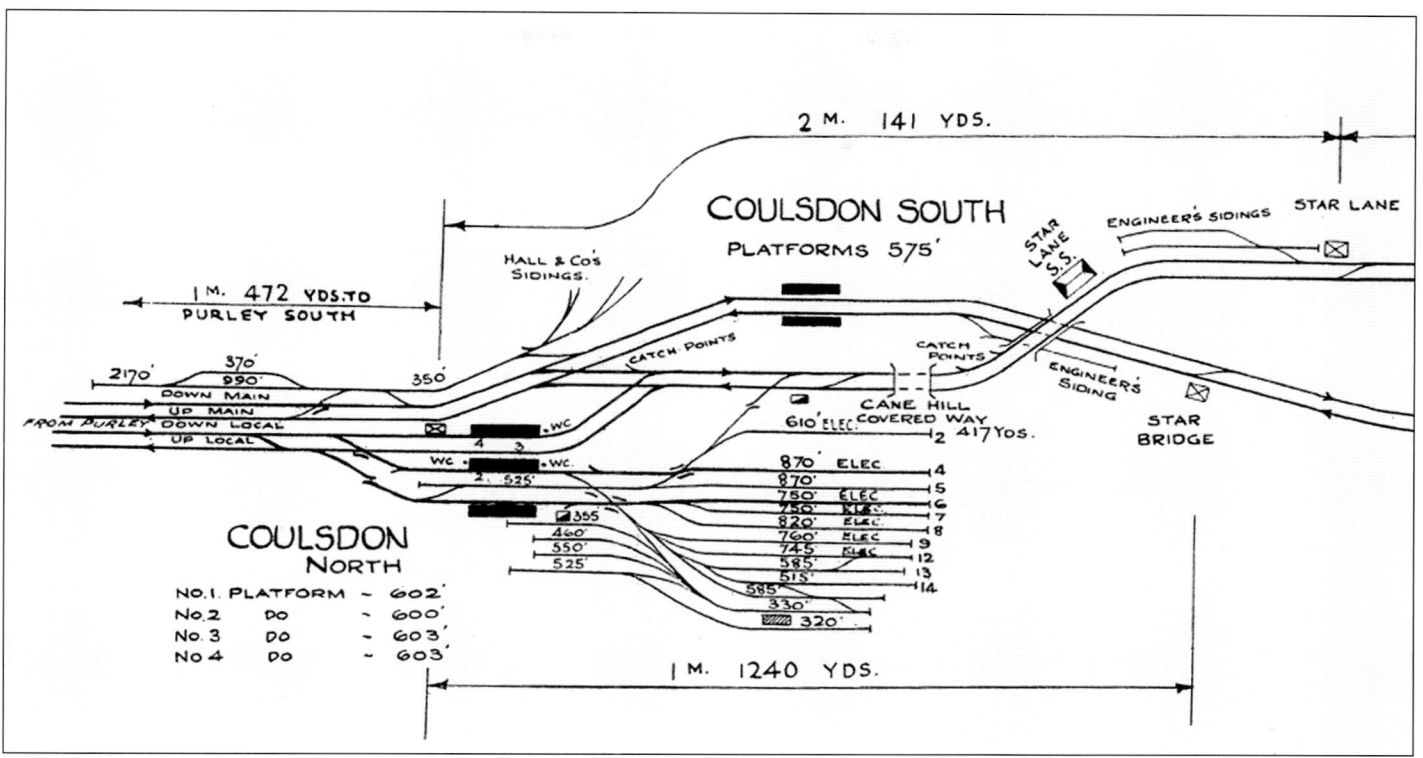

Above: The control diagram for the Coulsdon area, showing a wealth of detail. Coulsdon North No. 2 box has been replaced by a ground frame controlling just a crossover. Coulsdon Shunting box is also shown as a ground frame.

Below: Except for the two starting signals for the terminal platforms – by this time upper quadrant, their lives endangered as new signal posts can be seen in position beyond – colour light signalling has encroached and a new relay room has been built to cater for the extra circuitry required. Smitham signal box on the line towards Tattenham Corner can be seen on the left. *Lens of Sutton Collection*

SOUTHERN RAILWAY

Signal Instruction No. 20, 1937.

Instructions to all concerned as to

ABOLITION OF COULSDON NORTH No. 2 AND COULSDON SOUTH SIGNAL BOXES, ALSO INTRODUCTION OF COLOUR LIGHT SIGNALS AND NEW AND ALTERED SEMAPHORE SIGNALS BETWEEN PURLEY AND COULSDON NORTH AND SOUTH STATIONS,

On SUNDAY, 2nd MAY, 1937.

Rules 77, 78, 79 and 80 to be observed. Drivers to keep a good look-out for hand signals.

The work will be in progress from 12.5 a.m. on Sunday, 2nd May, until completed.

Coulsdon North No. 2 and Coulsdon South signal boxes will be abolished and certain new colour light signals installed. In addition, certain alterations will be made in connection with the semaphore signals between Purley and Coulsdon North and South stations. Coulsdon North No. 1 box will in future be known as Coulsdon North.

Details of the new and altered signals are shown on the diagram enclosed with this notice.

The colour light signals prefixed by the letters "C.T." will be controlled signals worked from Coulsdon North box.

Plates bearing the prefix letters and the number of the signal will be fixed on each colour light signal post.

The aspects of the new colour light signals will be the same by day as by night and the new colour light signals will be fitted with small side lights repeating the aspect exhibited by the signals to assist Drivers of trains drawn close up to such signals. Back lights will not be provided in any of the new colour light signals.

The height of the new colour light signals will vary between 10 and 18 feet above rail level.

Track circuits have been installed between Purley and Coulsdon North and the new colour light signals will be controlled by the track circuits.

Block working will not be in force between Purley South and Coulsdon North on the down lines, or between Coulsdon North and Star Lane (or other box in circuit) on the down and up through lines, except in emergency.

Telephones will be provided at certain signals as indicated on the diagram.

Fogsignalmen will not be provided at the new colour light signals.

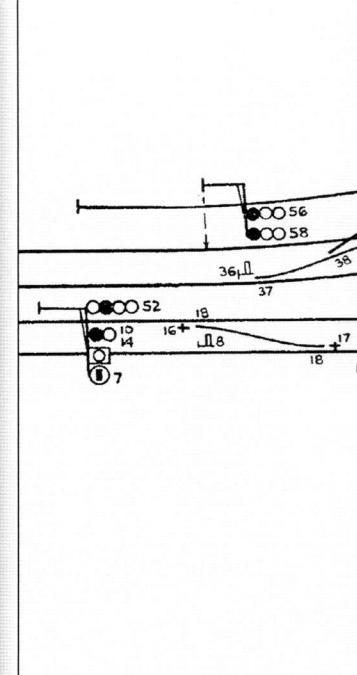

Above: Coulsdon North signal box layout (shown condensed) taken from the 1937 signalling notice.

Left: The title page from the 1937 signalling notice detailing the abolition of both Coulsdon North No. 2 and Coulsdon South signal boxes.

Facing Page: 'I3' Class 4-4-2T No. 76 brings the 11.35 ex Brighton 'Southern Belle' past Coulsdon No. 2 signal box's No. 32 signal, destined for the Up Main. No. 1 box's distant is also 'off', giving the driver a clear road towards Purley South. The electrified Up sidings, with anchor masts beyond the buffer stops, are impressively full whilst the Down cess holds the normal array of signal wires, counter-balance weights, point rodding and a compensator crank. In the distance can be seen No. 2 box's starting signal towards Cane Hill, with that box's distant signal below. The train has just exited the Cane Hill Covered Way and is crossing the Brighton Road on the skew bridge.
12th February 1928,
H.C. Casserley

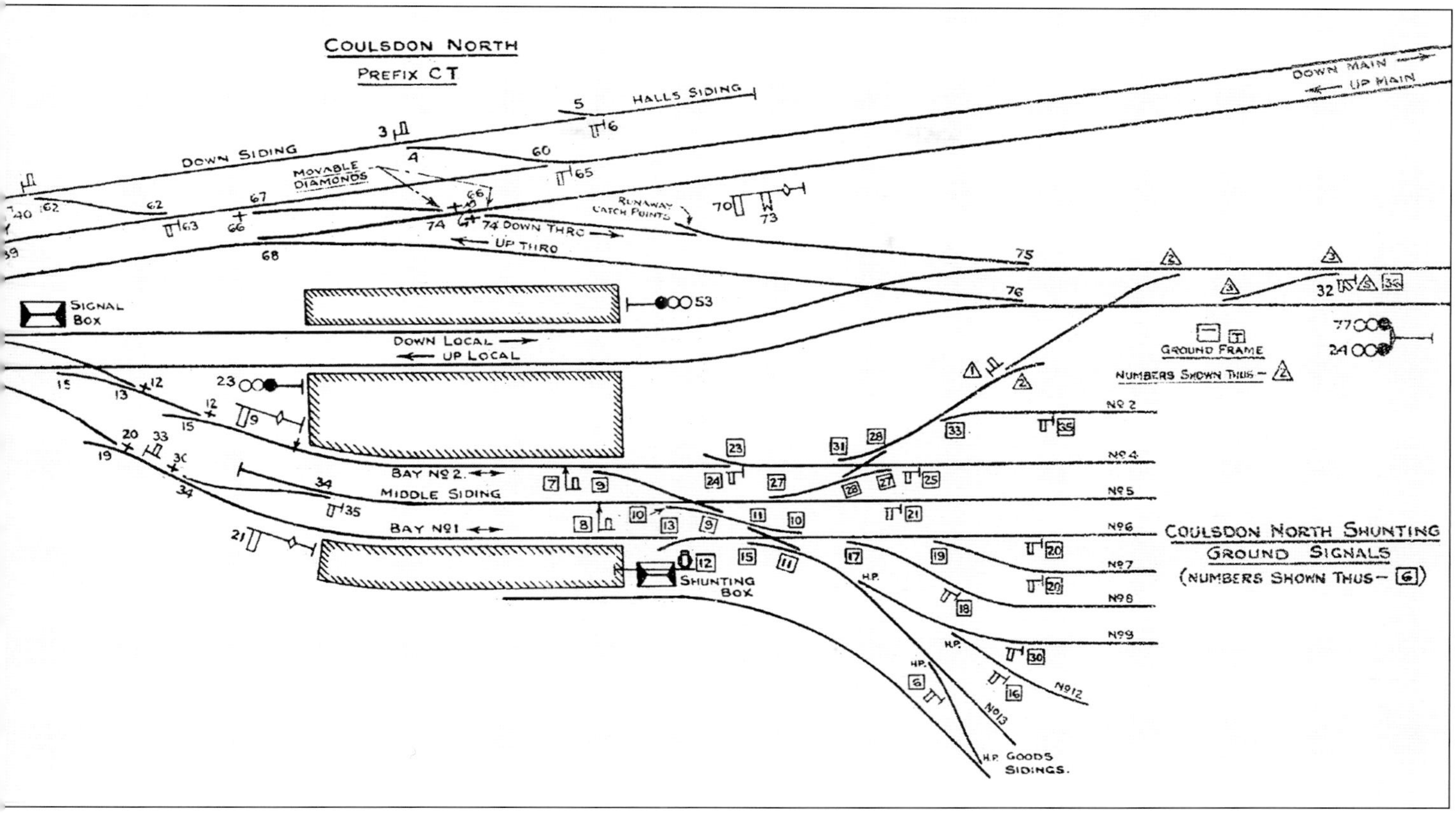
COULSDON NORTH
PREFIX CT
HALLS SIDING
DOWN SIDING
MOVABLE DIAMONDS
RUNAWAY CATCH POINTS
DOWN MAIN
UP MAIN
DOWN THRO
UP THRO
SIGNAL BOX
DOWN LOCAL
UP LOCAL
GROUND FRAME
NUMBERS SHOWN THUS –
BAY Nº 2.
MIDDLE SIDING
BAY Nº1
SHUNTING BOX
Nº 2
Nº 4
Nº 5
Nº 6
Nº 7
Nº 8
Nº 9
Nº 12
Nº 13
H.P. GOODS SIDINGS.
COULSDON NORTH SHUNTING GROUND SIGNALS
(NUMBERS SHOWN THUS – 6)

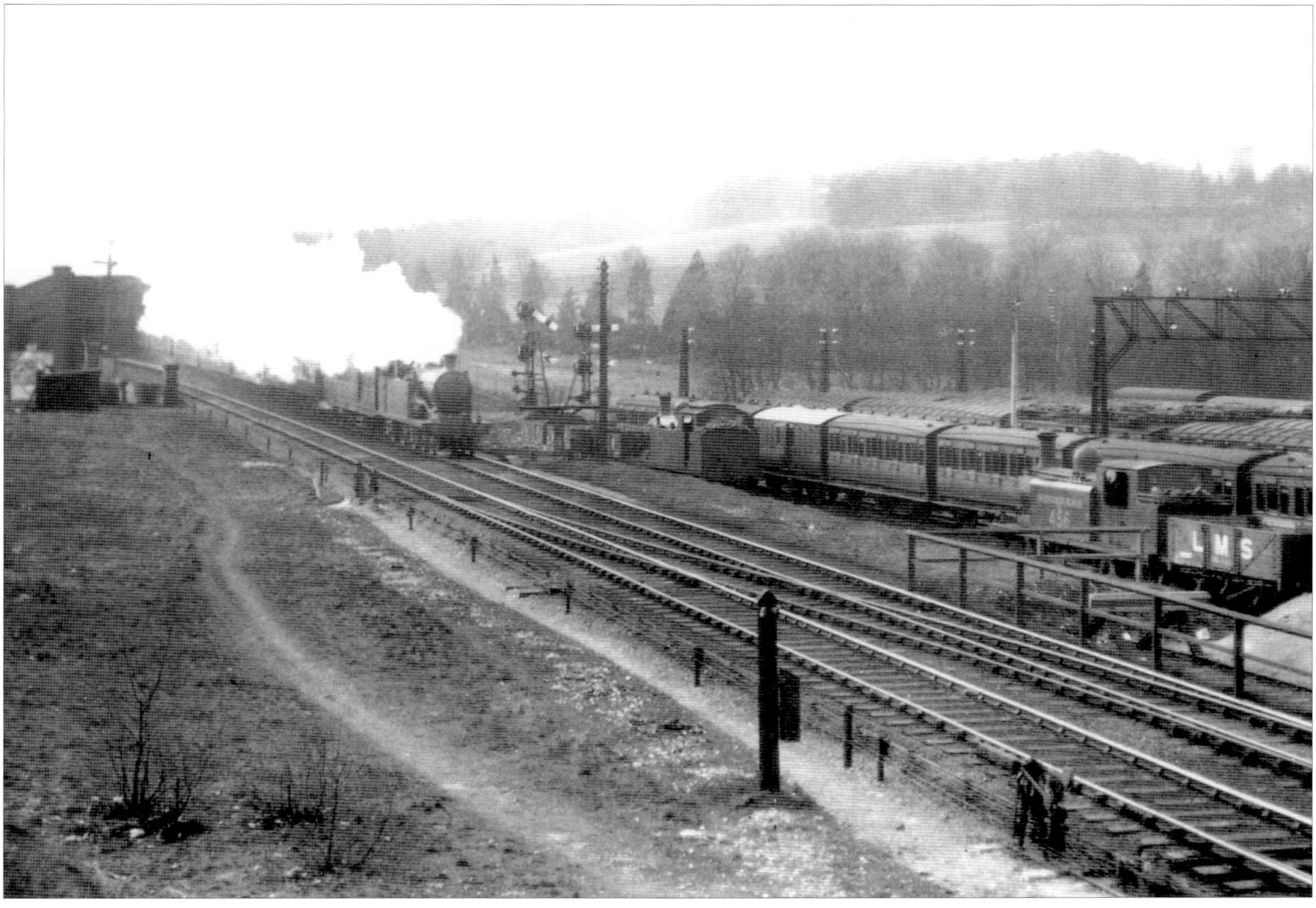
LMS

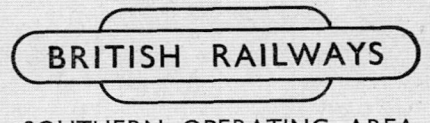

BRITISH RAILWAYS

SOUTHERN OPERATING AREA

Signal Instruction No. 1, 1955.

Instructions to all concerned as to

INTRODUCTION OF COLOUR LIGHT SIGNALS BETWEEN EAST CROYDON NORTH BOX AND COULSDON NORTH BOX

(in place of existing semaphore running signals)

and

ABOLITION OF EXISTING EAST CROYDON NORTH, EAST CROYDON SOUTH, SOUTH CROYDON STATION, SOUTH CROYDON JUNCTION, PURLEY OAKS, PURLEY NORTH AND PURLEY SOUTH SIGNAL BOXES,

also

BRINGING INTO USE NEW SIGNAL BOXES NAMED EAST CROYDON, SOUTH CROYDON AND PURLEY,

ON SUNDAY, 8th MAY, 1955

Rules 77, 78, 79 and 80 to be observed. Drivers to keep a good look-out for hand signals.

Commencing at 12.5 a.m. on Sunday, 8th May, colour light signals will be brought into use in place of the existing semaphore running signals between East Croydon North box and Coulsdon North box, linking up the existing colour light signalling at Gloucester Road Junction and Coulsdon North.

Certain semaphore signals will also be replaced by colour light signals on the branch line at South Croydon and on the Caterham and Tattenham Corner branch lines at Purley.

The existing East Croydon North and East Croydon South signal boxes, together with the North and South ground frames, will be abolished and the points at present operated therefrom will, in future, be operated from a new signal box to be known as "EAST CROYDON", situated on the up side opposite the existing East Croydon North box.

The existing South Croydon Station and South Croydon Junction signal boxes will be abolished and the points at present operated therefrom will, in future, be operated from a new signal box to be known as "SOUTH CROYDON", situated 21 yards Purley side of existing South Croydon Junction box.

The existing Purley Oaks signal box will be abolished.

The existing Purley North and Purley South signal boxes will be abolished and the points at present operated therefrom will, in future, be operated from a new signal box to be known as "PURLEY", situated in the fork between the down through and up branch lines, 94 yards Coulsdon side of existing Purley South box.

The existing down and up main lines between East Croydon and Coulsdon North will, in future, be known as the down and up through lines respectively.

A diagram showing the new and altered signals and their location is enclosed with this notice.

A plate bearing prefix letters and the number of the signal will be fixed adjacent to each colour light signal. The prefix letters will denote from which signal box the signal is operated, as follows:—

Prefix Letters.	Signal Box.
CW	East Croydon.
CV	South Croydon.
CU	Purley.
CT	Coulsdon North.

Automatic signals will be prefixed by the letters "CA".

It was another eighteen years before colour light signalling was extended northwards, this title page from the 1955 signalling notice detailing the filling in of the mechanically signalled 'hole' between Coulsdon North and Gloucester Road Junction.

FACING PAGE TOP: Looking in the same direction as the previous photograph but from further back some 26 years later, the original route via Redhill can be seen branching off to the left.
*6th November 1954,
Denis Cullum, Lens of Sutton Collection*

FACING PAGE BOTTOM: Stoats Nest (for Coulsdon and Cane Hill) station opened with the newly quadrupled line on 5th November 1899, replacing the original station that had been situated a quarter of a mile to the north. Its name changed to Coulsdon & Smitham Downs (1st June 1911) and thence, briefly, to Coulsdon West (9th July 1923) before receiving its final name of Coulsdon North on 1st August 1923. Three months to the day before the station closed its doors forever, this snapshot in time looks over the subway on platforms 2 and 3 towards the shunting cabin and the sidings. A telephone cabinet is still attached to the railings at the top of the steps and a standard pattern LB&SCR platform bench can be seen just beyond. The obligatory porter's trolley, once such an everyday sight, has probably not seen any use for years and certainly will not see any more; within a very short space of time all will be confined to memories. To cater for the still considerable commuter traffic after this station closed, improvements were made at the nearby Smitham station on the Tattenham Corner branch, though maybe not with the same grandeur.
3rd July 1983, John Scrace

Right: Coulsdon North station can be seen here in September 1982 displaying its attractive exterior with twin gables.

Three photographs depicting the slow demise of this outer suburban railway station. These poignant images were recorded during March 1979, April 1984 and January 1985 respectively.

Above: Basking in some summer sunshine, the attractive Coulsdon North signal box (the same design as the pair of its once near relations) still retained its green enamel nameboard. The 1955 relay room is beyond and the balcony for some external window cleaning was still extant, definitely a job for the box boy. *1st July 1976, John Scrace*

Below: Towards the end of its life, the well-kept interior of Coulsdon North signal box is seen here showing its 80-lever 'Brighton' tappet frame. Signalman Arthur Mansfield, minus his pipe for a change, looks the other way, while the booking lad does his best to keep out of the shot. *Ken Bacon*

Left: Two post-closure views of Coulsdon North station taken in April 1984 and January 1985 respectively; there is rarely a photograph more melancholic than that of a railway station in its death throes.

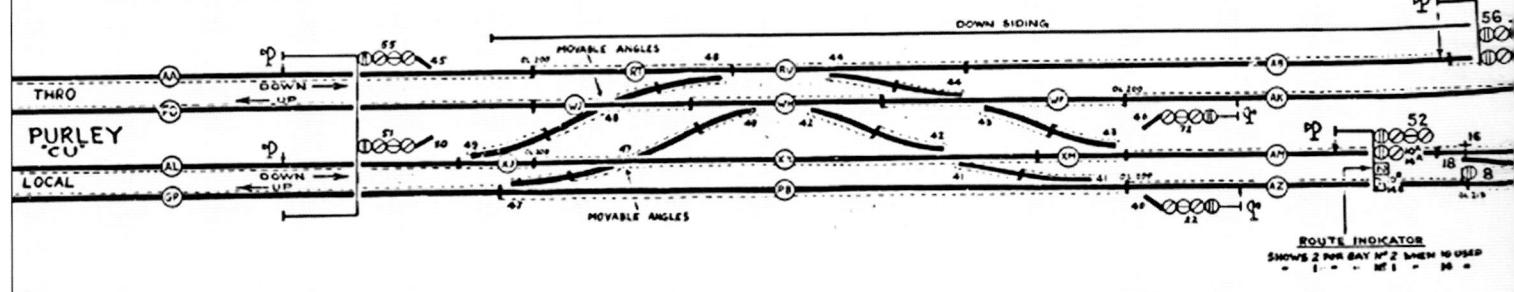
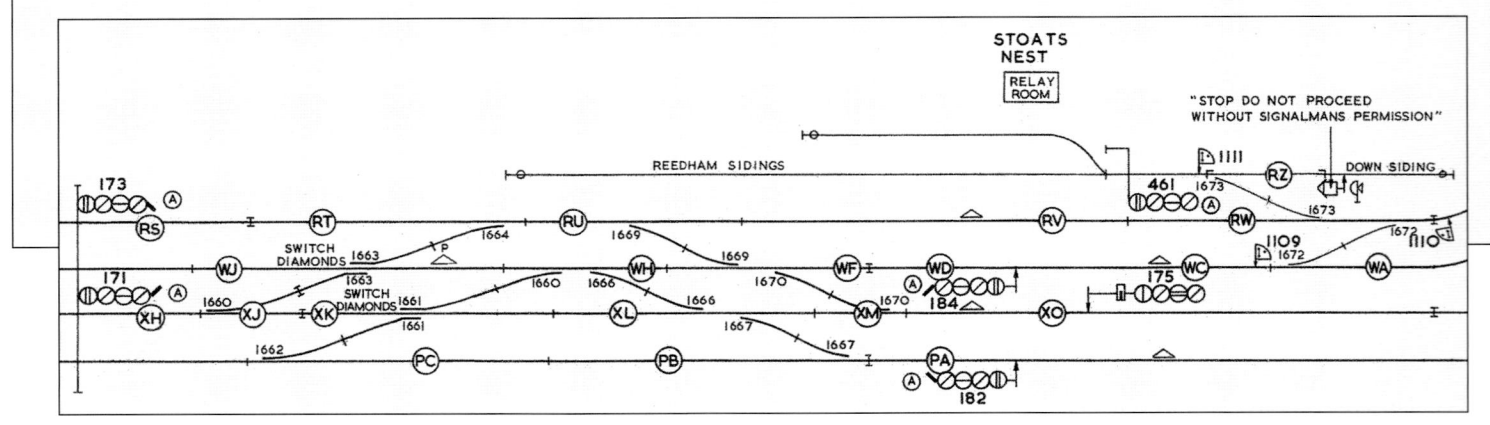

The signal box still remained in situ some six months after closure, as shown in this photograph taken in April 1984, the frame shown here with its heart ripped out.

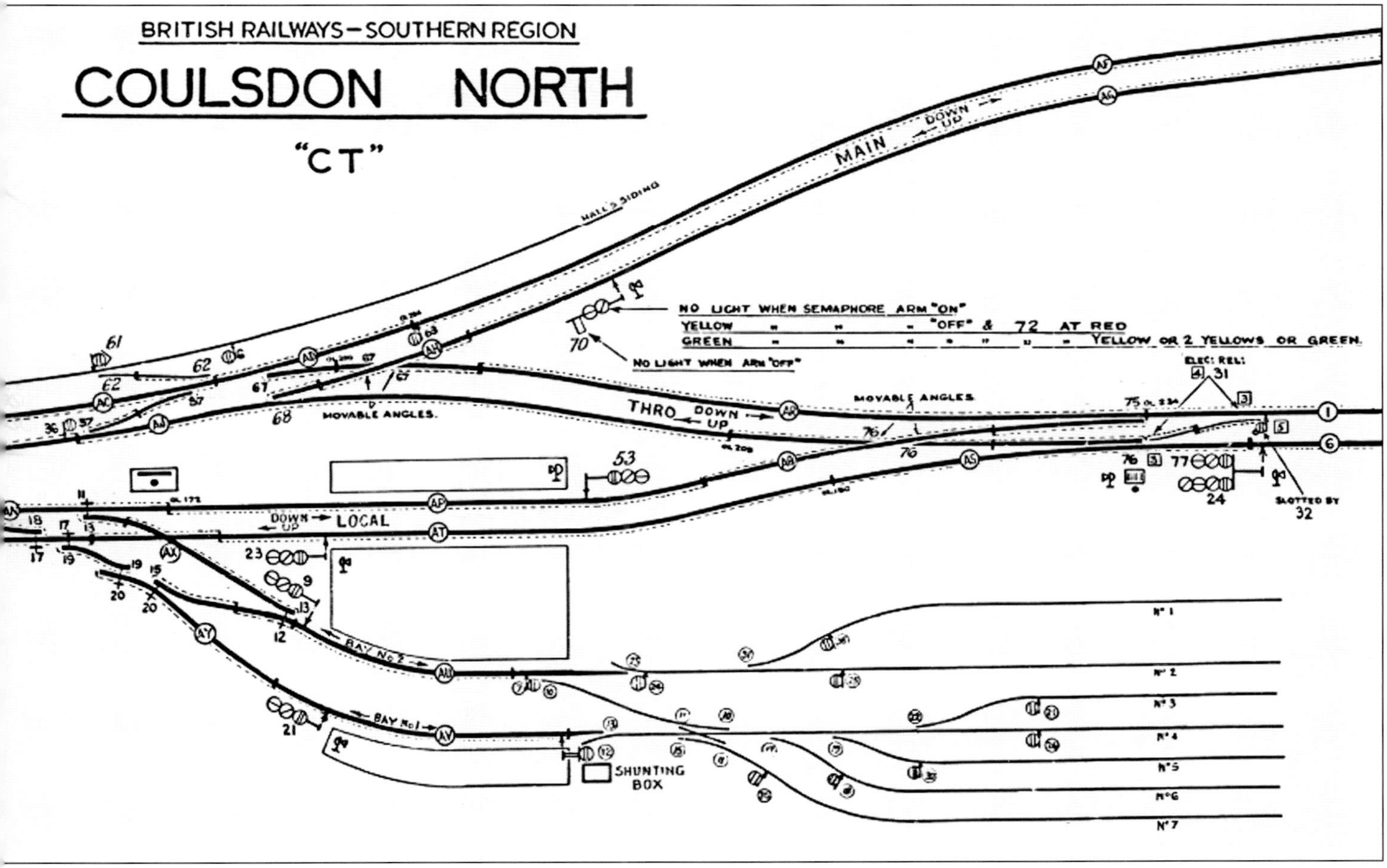

Above: Coulsdon North's area of control in 1982, the last year of its existence.

Facing Page Inset: Finally the vastly simplified Coulsdon North layout as commissioned on to the Three Bridges panel, any trace of a station's existence fully expunged.

Right: Seven months after closure and the picture tells its own story. Point stools have been uprooted, a mechanical shunt signal (still with its wire wheel attached) has been unceremoniously dumped down the bank, signal heads have been removed and, as evidenced in the near foreground, a new form of track circuit has arrived. *April 1984*

Below: Two years later the station has been flattened. The A23 was realigned through the site, so that now you would never be aware that a station ever existed here. *April 1986, Nick Catford*

Below: Finishing with a touch of nostalgia, we reach the furthest point north of the journey up from Brighton. With the electrification masts in place (albeit yet to have any hardware attached), this photograph must have been taken soon before electric services started in 1925, thus Stoats Nest North signal box seen here had been out of use for a number of years. It was the third of three signal boxes that existed at this location and received the 'North' suffix with the opening of the Central, South and Shunting boxes already discussed. Situated on the Down side of the line and opening in 1899, it housed a 24-lever frame but had a short life, closing in 1910. Suburbia has encroached along Windermere Road compared with the earlier 1910 map, as SE&CR 'J' Class No. 597 passes by on the Up Main.
Bluebell Railway Museum Archive, M.P. Bennett Collection

Appendix 1
Instructions to Signalmen and Others

This and the following pages are extracts from an LB&SCR publication, 'Instructions to Signalmen and Others' dated June 1917, all of which would have been applicable to signalmen on the Brighton line.

MISCELLANEOUS INSTRUMENTS, Etc.

TRAIN DESCRIBERS.

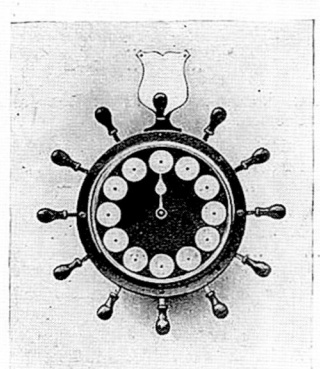

Sender Instrument.

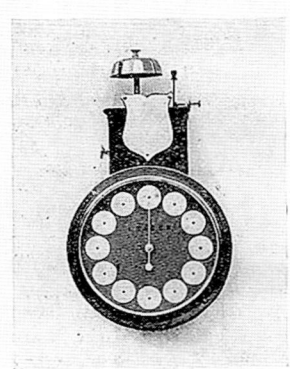

Receiver Instrument.

(a) The objects of the Train Describers are to give early information to the Box or Boxes in advance of the description and route of a Train or Engine, and to lessen the number of Rings on the Bells.

(b) Where Train Describers are in use, all Trains must be signalled on the Block Instruments, thus—

Passenger Trains and Engines	Two Beats.
Goods or Ballast Trains	Four Beats.

(c) The description and route of each Train must be given on the Describer as marked on the Dial, and the entry at once made in the Train Register Books both at the sending and receiving Signal Boxes.

(d) In the event of the Train Describers failing, the Trains must be described on Train Signalling Instruments, as per Block Signalling Codes.

(e) How to Describe a Train.—The Lever at the description required must be pulled forward, and the Lever where the Pointer is then resting put back; the Pointer will then move forward to the description required, and remain there until the next Train is described.

(f) Cancelling Signal.—If the Signalman at the sending Box gives the wrong description of a Train, he must set the Pointer to "Cancel," and then give the correct description of the Train.

(g) Winding the Sender.—The Sender Describer must be wound up every night by the Signalman on night duty. If further winding is required at any time during the day, the Signalman on duty must do what is necessary.

Note.—Some instruments are provided with 24 Tablets.

SIGNAL BOX "CLOSING" SWITCHES.

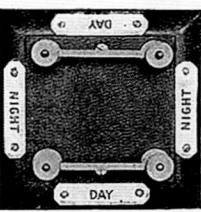

Bar Switch, showing "Day" position.

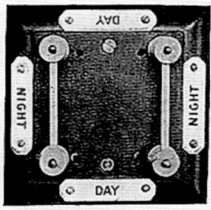

Bar Switch, showing "Night" position.

Miscellaneous Instruments, Etc.—(Continued.)

On seeing that the needle is steady in this position, the Signalman at B must insert the key in the instrument and give it one turn in the direction indicated by the arrow, which will move the indicator in the Box at A to "Key in, Starter free," when the Signalman there may let go of the "Push to Release" key, and the instrument will again be normal.

The Siding Key must not be replaced in the instrument at B until the indicator points to "Restore Key," but in the event of a mistake being made in this respect the Station Master must be called to unlock the instrument, withdraw a key, and replace it in the proper manner.

In the event of a train not proceeding from A after a key has been withdrawn, the key may be replaced in the instrument and the Cancelling Signal given in the usual way.

When six keys have been worked to B the Station Master there must unlock the instrument and take them out, then convey them personally, or send by deputy to the Signal Box at A, where they must be at once placed in the Instrument, a record of the number of keys transferred with date and time, being made in the Train Register Book at each box, and signed by the Station Master or deputy and the Signalman concerned.

SIGNAL REPEATERS.

Three-position Repeater.

Warning Signal Repeater.

Two-position Repeater.

Three-position Repeaters, round type.

Where these Electrical Repeaters are provided in Signal Boxes to repeat Signals which cannot be seen from the Signal Box, the Signalman must watch the Repeaters, especially when he moves the lever to which the Repeater applies, to satisfy himself that the Signal is working properly.

In the event of a Repeater showing that the Signal is **Off** while the lever indicates that the Signal should be at **Danger**, the Signalman must take care, until the Signal or Repeater has been put right, not to give the **Line Clear** Signal to the Signal Box in the rear until he has received the **Train out of Section** Signal from the Signal Box in advance, or, in the case of a Junction or Terminal Station, until he has first set his points so as to avoid a collision in the event of the following train over-running his Signals. If he requires to occupy the Main Line to which the defective Signal applies, he must not give the **Line Clear** Signal to the Signal Box in the rear until the operation is completed and the Main Line again clear.

NOTE.—If the Signalman can satisfy himself that it is only the Repeater that has failed, either by actual observation or is assured to that effect by some responsible person, he may give the **Line Clear** Signal in the usual way, but he must take this precaution in the case of each train.

POINT REPEATERS.

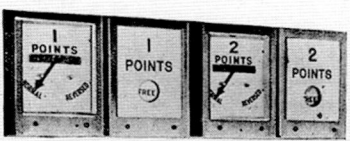

Miscellaneous Instruments, Etc.—(continued).

TRACK CIRCUIT INDICATORS.

Track Occupied.

Track Clear.

TRAIN WAITING INDICATORS.

SIGNAL BOX "CLOSING" SWITCHES.

"ON" AND "OFF" SWITCH.

Horizontal Switch.

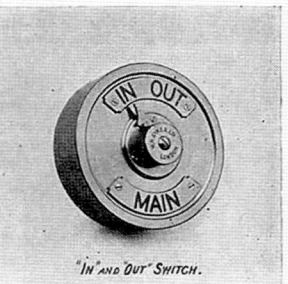
"IN" AND "OUT" SWITCH.

NOTE.—Where these switches are not in regular use, Station Masters must test them at a convenient time once a month, reporting immediately any defects that may be discovered.

INSTRUCTIONS FOR WORKING HARPER'S INSTRUMENTS.

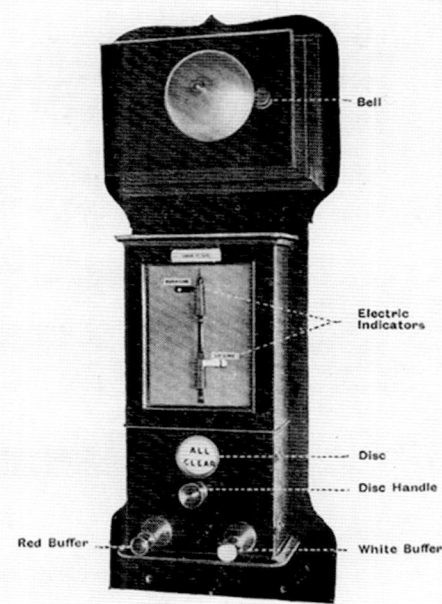

Harper's Block Signalling Instrument.

The process of signalling by Harper's Instruments is similar to that by Tyer's, with the exception that before **Line Clear** Signal can be given by B he must turn the Disc to the **All Clear** position, when the **One Beat** on the White Buffer will lower the Electric Indicator in both Boxes. When the **Train entering Section** Signal is given by A, B must turn the Disc to the **Train on Line** position and acknowledge the Signal on the Red Buffer, which will raise the Electric Indicator to **Line Blocked** in both Boxes. Before giving the **Train out of Section** Signal, the Disc must be turned to the normal position, **Train off Line but Section Blocked**, and the rings given on the Red Buffer. **Warning** Signals are also given on the Red Buffer with the Disc in the normal position.

TYER'S OR HARPER'S INSTRUMENTS ARE IN USE AS SHOWN BELOW:—

LINE.	SIGNAL BOXES BETWEEN.
Main Lines	Gatwick and Preston Park North.
Keymer Line	Keymer Junction and Cooksbridge.
East Coast Line	Lewes West and St. Leonards.
East Coast Line	Falmer and Lewes Junction.
Eastbourne Branch	Polegate and Eastbourne, Willingdon and Stonecross Junctions.
Newhaven Branch	Southerham Junction and Seaford.
West Coast Line	Hove West and Portcreek Junction.
West Coast Line	Farlington Junction and Cosham Junction.
Dorking and Horsham Line	Dorking and Horsham.
Littlehampton Branch	Ford Junction, Arundel Junction and Littlehampton.
Steyning Line	Itchingfield Junction and Shoreham Junction.
Guildford Line	Christ's Hospital North and Baynards.
Mid-Sussex Line	Three Bridges Central and Arundel Junction.
Tunbridge Wells	Tunbridge Wells and Grove Junction.
Oxted Line	South Croydon Junction and Hurst Green Junction.
Oxted & E. Grinstead Line	Hurst Green Junction and East Grinstead.
Ardingly Branch	Ardingly and Haywards Heath North.
Tunbridge Wells Line	Hurst Green Junction and Tunbridge Wells.
Uckfield Line	Redgate Mill Junction and Lewes Junction.
Epsom Downs Branch	Sutton and Epsom Downs.
Dyke Branch	Dyke Junction and the Dyke.
Hayling Island Branch	Havant and Hayling Island.

Instructions for working Sykes' Lock and Block Instruments.—(*Continued.*)

10.—SPECIAL INSTRUCTIONS AS TO THE WORKING OF SYKES' THREE-POSITION TRAIN SIGNALLING INSTRUMENTS IN USE BETWEEN LONGHEDGE JUNCTION AND LATCHMERE JUNCTION.

Sykes' Three-position Instrument.

The lower Tablet of these instruments has three positions, viz., **Blank**, **Train accepted**, and **Train on**.

The Electric Indicator has also three positions, viz., **Normal**—upright; **Line Clear**—inclined to left; and **Line Blocked**—inclined to right.

On receipt of the **Warning** Signal, provided the Line is Clear, the Signalman at B must press in the Plunger firmly, which will change his lower Tablet from **Blank** to **Train accepted**, and the Upper Tablet at A from **Locked** to **Free**, also the Electric Indicator at A from normal to **Line Clear**. B must then acknowledge the **Warning** Signal to A, who must lower his Signals for the Train to proceed to B.

On the Train passing A, the Signalman there must send the **Train entering Section** Signal to B, which must be acknowledged by B and the Switch Hook there placed over the Plunger. This will alter the lower Tablet at B from **Train accepted** to **Train on**, and put the Electric Indicator at A to the **Line Blocked** position.

The replacing of the Signals at A will leave the upper Tablet there in its normal **Locked** position.

On arrival of the train complete at B, the replacing of the Signals there will return the lower Tablet to its normal **Blank** position, and the Switch Hook must then be taken off, which will put the Electric Indicator at A to the normal position. The **Train out of Section** Signal, one beat, must then be given to A.

11.—Sykes' Electric Lock and Block Instruments are in use as shown below :—

Line.	Signal Boxes between
Main and Through Lines...	London Bridge and Earlswood Junction via Red Hill. ” ” ” ” ” via Quarry. Earlswood Junction and Gatwick. Preston Park North and Montpelier Junction. Preston Park South and Hove East.
Keymer Line	Cooksbridge Station and Lewes West.
West Coast Line ...	New England to Hove West.
East Coast Line ...	Montpelier Junction and Falmer.
South London Line ...	London Bridge and Battersea Park.
Peckham and Sutton Line and Streatham Spur ...	Peckham Rye and Sutton. Streatham and Streatham Common.
Local Line	London Bridge and Sutton Junction.
Sutton and Epsom Line ...	Sutton and Epsom Town.
Leatherhead and Dorking	Leatherhead and Dorking.
West End Line	Victoria and Balham Junction.
Croydon and Balham Lines	Balham Junction and Windmill Bridge Junction.
West End and Crystal Palace Line	Balham Junction and Norwood Junction.
Local Line...	Windmill Bridge Junction and Coulsdon and S. Downs.
Crystal Palace & Sydenham	Crystal Palace and Sydenham.
Beckenham and Norwood Joint Line	Norwood Junction and Beckenham.
West End Low Level Line	Battersea Pier Junction and Pouparts Junction.
Wimbledon and West Croydon Line	Mitcham Junction North and Mitcham.
S.E. & C. Lines ...	Longhedge Junction, Factory Junction and Stewarts Lane.
Low Level Lines	Longhedge Junction and Battersea Yard.
West London Extension Line	*Longhedge Junction and Latchmere Junction. †Latchmere and Clapham Junction North.
Oxted Line	South Croydon and Selsdon Road.

* Special Three-position instruments. † West London Extension and Sykes' combined.

PLATFORM INDICATORS.

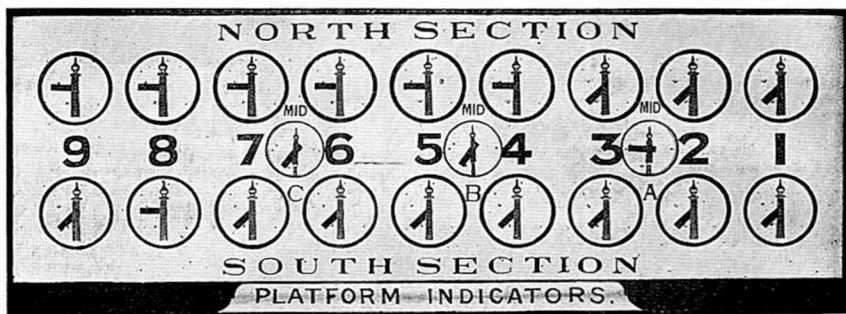

In use at Victoria South and North Signal Boxes.

These Platform Indicators are worked automatically by electrical bars, placed in the North and South sections of Victoria Station. These bars also control the Inner Home, and Swallow Tailed Signals, at the end of the platforms. If, for instance, No. 9 Platform Line is unoccupied, both the Indicators marked 9 stand at the "Clear" position, and all the Signals for that Line can be lowered. If the North Section is occupied and the South Section clear, the top Indicator stands at "Danger," and only the Inner Home Platform Signal can be lowered. If both the North and South Sections are occupied, both Indicators stand at "Danger," and the Lever of the Inner Home Signal is locked, but traffic can be allowed to enter the platform Line by "Shunt" or "Calling-on" Signal if necessary.

The Indicators go to the "Clear" position automatically as Trains leave the various Platform Lines.

The Middle A, B, and C Indicators are controlled by the track-circuits on those Roads, and show whether the Lines are occupied or clear.

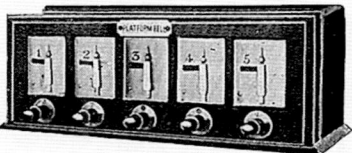

In use at London Bridge North Box.

These Indicators are lowered by the Platform Inspector pressing the Bell Keys on the different platforms when a Train is ready to start, and are put to **Danger** again by the Signalman pressing the Key on the front of the instrument when the Train has left the Platform.

8.—ELECTRIC FOULING BARS AND INDICATORS.—(*a*) These are provided at various places, and every case of failure of these appliances to work properly must be at once reported as instructed above. In addition to this, a record showing the time, &c., of the failure, must be made in the margin of the Train Register Book.

(*b*) Signalmen are warned that the provision of **Fouling Bars** does not relieve them in any way of the necessity of ascertaining by personal observation, so far as possible, whether the Lines are clear before they lower a Signal for a Train.

Electric Fouling Bar.

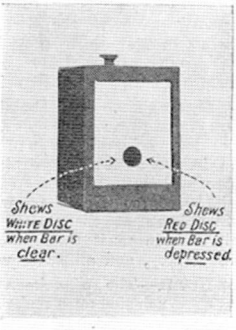

Electric Fouling Bar Indicator.

Appendix 2
Westinghouse Brake & Saxby Signal Co. Ltd

What follows is a remarkable booklet produced by the Westinghouse Brake & Saxby Signal Co. Ltd in June 1933 to publicise their role in the Brighton Line resignalling and, reproduced here, a plan of the Westinghouse works at Chippenham at around the same time when it employed some 2,700 staff.

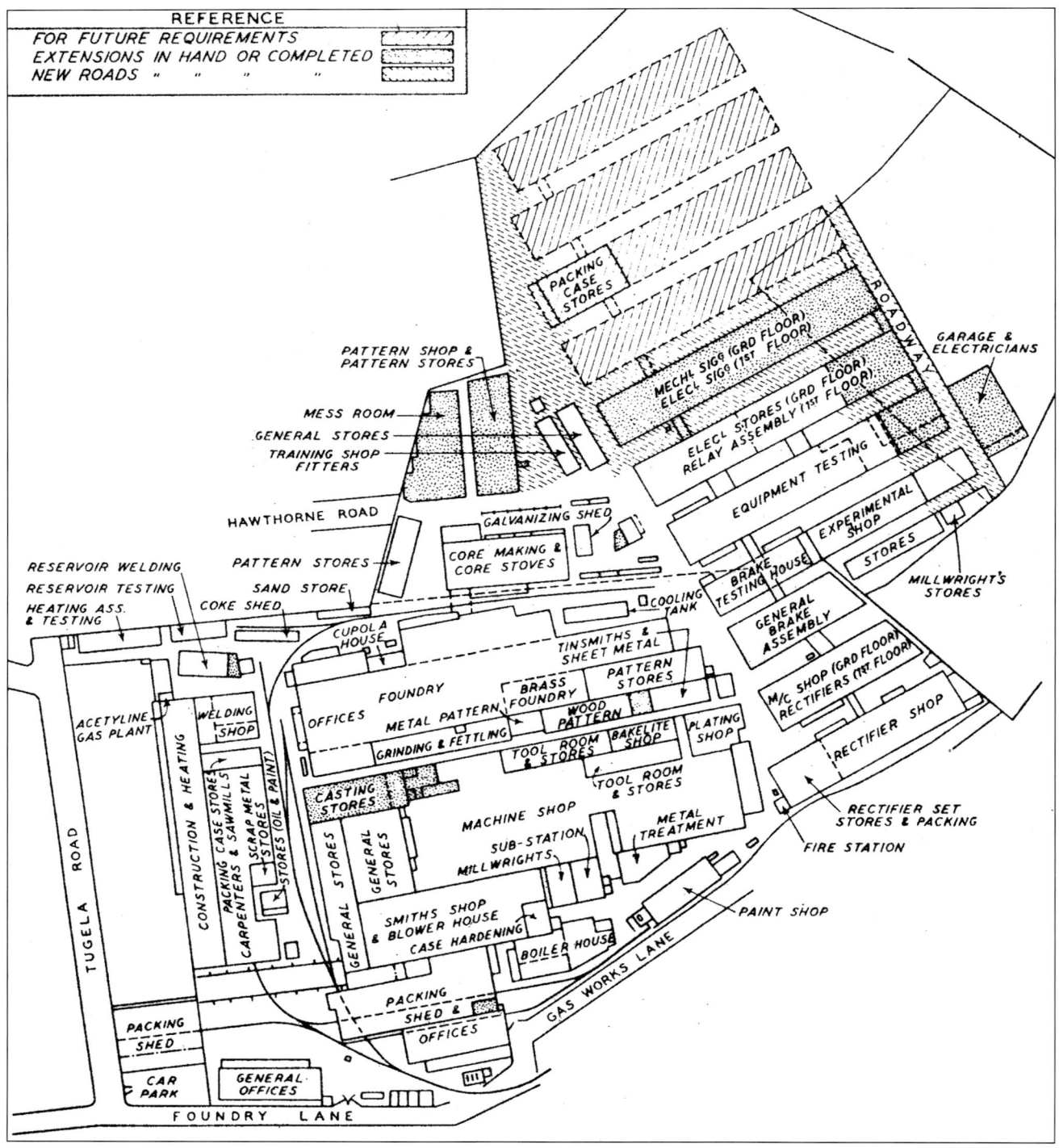

The Brighton Line Signalling

THE WESTINGHOUSE BRAKE & SAXBY SIGNAL C<u>O</u> L<u>TD</u>.
82 YORK ROAD KING'S CROSS, LONDON, N.1.

JUNE, 1933

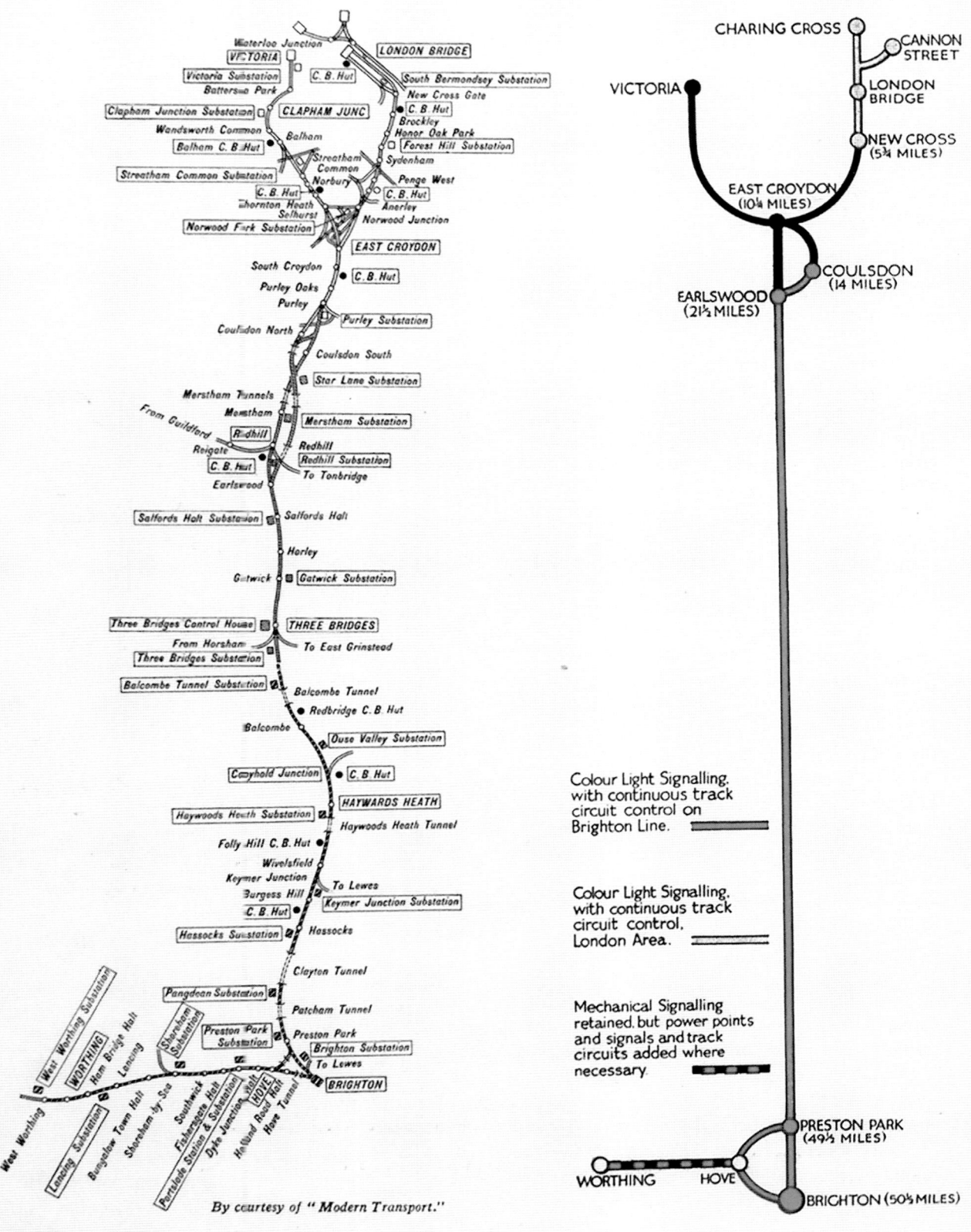

The Brighton Line Signalling

It will be recalled that between the years 1925–1929 the Southern Railway carried out an extensive programme of signalling conversion in the inner London zone and installed during that period a complete power signal system, entirely of Westinghouse manufacture, at Charing Cross, Cannon Street, Borough Market Junction, London Bridge and New Cross, and on the tracks linking up these stations. This power system covers about $47\frac{1}{2}$ track miles, carrying an extremely intense suburban traffic in addition to heavy coastal services of both passenger and goods trains.

With the extension of the Electric Service to Brighton and the resultant greatly increased train service, complete reorganisation of the signalling arrangements became a necessity. The valuable experience gained on the London power signalling showed that a similar system, modified to comply with the characteristics of the Brighton Line, would give the required facilities, and in making the decision to introduce power signalling between Coulsdon and Brighton the Railway Company have added a further 119 track miles of line which are provided throughout with colour light signals and continuous track circuits. As the electrification of the London to Brighton line constitutes the longest section of electrified railway in Great Britain, so the signalling comprises the greatest length of continuous track circuiting and complete power signalling on a British main line. Westinghouse apparatus was again selected as possessing that essential reliability necessary to withstand the severe operating conditions on the 36 miles of route, and advantage was taken of several new developments and improvements to apparatus, although, in general, the design of apparatus called for follows closely upon that which has proved equal to all the demands made on it during the previous four years.

The map and key plan opposite show the line between London and Brighton, and it will be seen that East Croydon is the Junction for all trains to and from the various London termini. The power signalling commences at Coulsdon North about 14 miles south from Victoria and continues through Earlswood Junction to Three Bridges. Three Bridges is the junction for the Horsham and Portsmouth line to the south-west, and for the East Grinstead and Tunbridge Wells line to the east; in addition, it is of importance owing to the presence of extensive goods sidings, locomotive running sheds, and the main control station for the remote control of all traction sub-stations on the Brighton line. There are four running roads between Earlswood and Balcombe Tunnel, which is about $2\frac{3}{4}$ miles south of Three Bridges, the signal cabin situated at the north end of the tunnel having the control of the junction from the four to two roads. The line diverges into four roads again between Copyhold Junction and Hayward's Heath Station, then reverts to double-road track, continuing thus to Preston Park. A branch line junction at Copyhold is controlled from Hayward's Heath Cabin, about $1\frac{1}{2}$ miles distant, crossovers being provided for the routing of trains for running into the required platforms at Hayward's Heath. Plans of the track and signal layout at Three Bridges, Copyhold Junction and Hayward's Heath, will be found at the end of this publication.

A short distance south of Hayward's Heath is Keymer Junction, where the line to Lewes and Eastbourne diverges. Preston Park is on the outskirts of Brighton, the cabin having control of all traffic to and from London, and it is here that trains running direct between London and Worthing are diverted. Brighton Station lies about $\frac{3}{4}$ mile south of Preston Park Station and besides being the terminal station of 10 platforms for London to Brighton traffic, it is also a terminal and junction for the Hastings line to the east and the Worthing and Portsmouth line to the west (the line joining that from Preston Park at Hove). There are extensive goods marshalling sidings at Brighton as well as locomotive running sheds, locomotive and carriage repair shops, large carriage sheds and washing plant for electric stock.

Hayward's Heath Cabin Interior.

Keymer Crossing Cabin Interior.

The general signalling scheme employs three-aspect colour light signals throughout for running signals and two-aspect colour light signals for shunt movements. Exceptions to the general rule are to be found in cases where it has not been possible to obtain full braking distance, and here four-aspects have been used to maintain the necessary flow of traffic. With a single exception all other types of signals, such as call-on and warning signals have been eliminated, thus adding greatly to the uniformity and simplicity of the system without interfering in any way with expeditious handling of traffic.

The system of control adopted between Coulsdon and Preston Park, a distance of approximately 31 miles, is electro-mechanical with continuous track circuiting of all running roads, and track circuit fouling protection of junctions and sidings. At Brighton the system is all-electric, controlled from a new cabin containing a 225-lever power frame. In the electro-mechanical section certain cabins were selected for retention in service and all others have been abolished. The selected cabins are those from which the routing of trains is always being carried out, or where there is at times some shunting of goods trains, or where special regulation of traffic may occasionally be necessary. Reference to the diagram on page 21 will make clear the number of cabins totally abolished, those which are normally switched out, and those, such as Earlswood, Three Bridges, Hayward's Heath, Keymer Crossing and Preston Park, which are always in service.

No distinction has been made between the two classes of cabins in the matter of equipment, except, that at Hayward's Heath and Three Bridges it was found necessary to install new Style A.2 locking frames of 54 levers and 125 levers respectively. In all cases illuminated track diagrams of the spot-light type are provided, together with illuminated indicators for colour light signals and power points. In a number of cases facing points and siding connections are situated too far from the cabin to be manually operated, and therefore high speed style M.3 point machines and colour light shunt signals have been installed, controlled from slightly shortened levers in the mechanical frames. Mechanically-worked dwarf signals are retained where distances are not too great, as also are semaphore arms on lines joining the main route. At the entrances to the colour light signalling area the semaphore distant signal arms are replaced by two-aspect colour light signals, which normally show no light, but are brought into operation by the clearing of the stop arm above them. Such a combination is illustrated on page 6.

All points in the track-circuited area, or which lead on to the running roads, are electrically detected, and all point levers are fitted with Style D lever locks and circuit controllers to track-lock the lever in the Normal and Reverse positions ; facing point bolt levers are locked in the Reverse position only. Many signal levers have electric lever locks of the Style E pattern, to lock the lever in the Normal Indication position for backlocking.

It has been possible, in the majority of cases, to house most of the apparatus in the lower compartment of the signal cabin. The apparatus to be accommodated consists of single element Style H.2 A.C. line relays for signal control, double element Style G.2 A.C. track relays, and Style G.2 three-position vane point detector relays, together with the necessary transformers, rectifiers for the point machines, and, of course, the requisite fuses, power supply switches, etc. All track feed sets are located outside the cabin in separate feed cases, and in a number of instances, the track relays are also housed outside the cabin.

Upper-quadrant Semaphore Signals, with 2-aspect Colour-light Distant Signals—Earlswood Junction.

Point Machine Crank Handles and interlocked Circuit Controllers—Earlswood Junction Cabin.

An interesting feature of the point machine control at the electro-mechanical cabins is the provision of special arrangements for hand-operating the machines. The crank-handles kept at any cabin are constructed in such a way that they are not interchangeable among the machines, but only fit their own particular point machine or group of point machines. The handles are kept normally in separate circuit controllers (see illustration opposite) whose contacts break the point control and detection circuits for the machine concerned, when the crank-handle is removed. Padlocks are placed on each controller to prevent unauthorised removal, the key being retained in the cabin behind a glass-fronted box for use in emergency, and a duplicate is in the possession of the lineman. The object of these precautions is to eliminate any possibility of confusion leading to illegitimate hand-operation of a machine in an emergency or during maintenance duties.

The apparatus outside the cabins, is uniform in design throughout the line. Track circuits at crossings and junctions are single-rail, while those for the remainder of the line are double rail. Owing to the third-rail system of traction, impedance bonds are employed on all double-rail track circuits, and in some cases additional impedance bonds are placed intermediately for cross-bonding purposes on the traction system. The average length of a double-rail track circuit is about 1,500 yards.

Impedance Bonds.

Page 7

Automatic Signals between Three Bridges and Gatwick.

The running signals are of the standard Westinghouse long-range pattern, having double filament 12-volt, 25-watt, 3-pin lamps; in addition to the auxiliary light deflecting unit in each aspect, separate sidelights have been fitted on all signals on the installation and have proved of great benefit to motormen of electric trains, which can draw up very close to a signal. All automatic signals between cabins are distinguished by an " A " light mounted just below the main signal, the " A " being illuminated only when the red aspect is showing above it. Typical automatic signal locations are illustrated on this page and page 9, those on this page showing the apparatus cases which contain the signal control relays, track feed sets, and track relays. Signals which are sometimes controlled from a cabin and at other times work as " automatics " also carry " A " lights, such " A " lights being cut out when the signal is

Automatic Signal location, Apparatus Cases with Relays, Track Feed Sets, etc.

Automatic Signals, Up Line between Three Bridges and Balcombe Tunnel.

"controlled." Exceptions to this arrangement are the fully automatic signals located at entrances to tunnels; such signals are not fitted with "A" lights, as the "one minute rule" does not apply at tunnels. The auto-signal at the entrance to Balcombe Tunnel, illustrated on the frontispiece (page 1), is an instance of this. If a train is stopped by a red aspect at one of these signals (also at any controlled signal) the driver or motorman must communicate with the nearest signal cabin by a telephone contained in a black and white striped box fixed to the signal post or nearby.

Most of the signals are mounted on pipe posts, although several bracket arrangements are to be found. The illustration of Copyhold up home signals below is an instance of a very compact structure built in our shops.

Shunt signals, one of which is illustrated on page 19, are of the globe type similar to those used at London Bridge, and display the usual Red and Green aspects with the exception of a few siding signals which have Yellow and Green aspects.

Up Home Signals, Copyhold Junction.

Three Bridges Cabin during installation of the new Locking Frame.

Before going on to describe the apparatus at Brighton, special mention must be made of a notable signal engineering feat carried out at Three Bridges. Originally there were three cabins, but under the new arrangement one cabin was to handle the whole of the work, the Central Cabin having been selected for the purpose. This cabin contained an old Saxby rocker frame of 94 levers which, it was found, could not be converted satisfactorily; it was decided therefore to install a new 125-lever Westinghouse Style A.2 frame, which was actually erected in the cabin opposite the old frame as shown above.

On the night of bringing into service of the new signalling, the new frame was connected up and the old one disconnected and eventually taken out, without any interference to traffic. The completed interior of the cabin as it now appears is illustrated below.

Referring now to the signalling at Brighton itself, it has already been mentioned that a new 225-lever

Page 10

Three Bridges Cabin, as it now appears.

Subway under the lines at Brighton Station showing old mechanical connections, now used for signal cables

power frame has been provided. The new cabin takes the place of six old cabins and the 225 power levers do the work of 562 mechanical levers.

An exterior view of the cabin is given on page 14, the windows shown being those of the main operating room, directly behind which is the relay room and linemen's mess room. Access to the cabin is by a former signal bridge now devoid of signal dolls and, in addition to being a walkway, serves to carry many of the signal cables. It may here be mentioned that, when the previous remodelling of Brighton Station in 1881, was carried out, a special subway was constructed under the running lines to accommodate point rods and signal wires. This subway, shown above, which has been extended, proved of considerable value, as it has been employed as an additional means of conducting cables from the down side across to the Worthing Branch. A general view of the interior of the cabin is given on pages 12 and 13, and clearly shows the power frame and illuminated diagrams.

Mechanical Point and Signal Connections under old cabins at Brighton, now removed.

Page 11

Interior of the new Brighton Cabin

-lever all-electric Interlocking Frame.

Reproduced by permission of " The Sphere."

Exterior of new Signal Cabin, Brighton.

Relay Room, Brighton.

Metal Rectifier Charging Plant for Point-Machine Batteries.

Page 14

The power frame is a Westinghouse Style L all-electric with no mechanical lever interlocking. Full advantage has been taken of the flexibility of the all-electric frame by dividing the levers into three sections, the two end sections being placed at an angle to the middle section. This arrangement saves a considerable amount of cabin space and at the same time increases very noticeably, the ease of co-operation between signalmen, and observation of the diagrams. Electric lever interlocking is provided on all levers and is laid out to give the same effect as mechanical lever interlocking.

All signal aspects are repeated behind the levers together with route-indicator indications, point indications, and "ground frame free" indications. Signal levers are provided with normal indication locks, but front (normal) locks are not fitted. Point levers have normal and reverse track locks, and if the track circuits are unoccupied a point lever can be pulled directly from normal to reverse, or vice versa, there being no point indication locking. Since the signal levers have no front locks and the point levers have no indication locks, it would be possible to reverse a signal lever before the points had fully responded to a previous movement of a point lever. The signal would not, however, show a "proceed" aspect in these circumstances, unless the signal lever was first put back and again pulled. In order, therefore, to assist the signalman in this respect a special indication is provided behind each signal lever consisting of an illuminated " F " which appears only when the various points in the desired route have completely responded to the movement of the lever and the requisite track circuits are clear.

The lever interlocking circuits are controlled through contact shafts on the front of the frame, while operation and selection circuits have their contacts fitted to shafts on the back of the frame. Both sets of contacts are of the high speed air break type, and can be observed, for maintenance purposes, through glass panels in the sheet steel casing surrounding each section of the power frame.

The Style M.2 Illuminated Diagrams have been specially designed for this cabin. The background of the diagrams is of pale green shade to lessen the possibility of eyestrain from constant observation, and the particular colouring of the track circuits has been chosen as being the most easily followed. Two complete diagrams are provided and, as will be noted from the illustration, are fixed above the frames and at an angle of approximately half the displacement of the power frame sections.

The cables from the power frame and diagrams, together with all cables from the track, are led into a cable compartment below the power frame floor and from there are taken through suitable ducts to the adjacent relay room, a part of which is shown opposite. The main transformers, with their switches, fuses and power distribution board, are also housed in the relay room. The cables from outside the cabin are multicore and are terminated in the relay room on porcelain terminal blocks, from which flame-proof wires connect to the relays.

A.C. relays are used for all purposes. A new type of relay has been used for point indication, viz., the Style Q. three-position vane relay, with a complement of 8N and 8R contacts, which enables a considerable economy to be obtained by the elimination of many repeater relays and relay cabinet space. Previous Southern Railway practice has been continued in the method of wiring, and in placing fuses and indication resistances close to the relays to which they refer.

The accumulator battery is housed below the relay room on track level, with the Westinghouse metal rectifier trickle charging plant and switch gear in an adjacent compartment (see opposite page). In addition to supplying the point machine current, the battery is tapped at 10-volts to supply the power frame interlocking magnets in an emergency.

Brighton Station Starting Signals, etc. Before alteration.

A plan of the track layout at Brighton showing the various signals will be found at the end of this book. The running signals are identical with those between Brighton and Coulsdon, and are supplemented in a number of cases by optical route indicators. The platform intermediate signals are not worked from levers, but repeat the starting signals. The route indicator associated with each platform intermediate

Brighton Station Starting Signals. After alteration.

Page 16

signal shows the letter " M " or " S " according to whether the main signal or shunt signal on the starting signal post is showing a " proceed " aspect.

A number of different signal arrangements are illustrated on pages 16, 17, 18 and 19. The two pictures on page 16, taken from a similar viewpoint, afford a clear comparison between the old mechanical and new colour light signalling.

Page 18

APPENDICES

Three-throw Point Layout operated by two Style M3 Point Machines.

Style M.3 D.C. point machines are employed on all power operated points. The single switch and slip layouts are of the usual design and do not require any special mention. The illustrations on this page show two power point layouts which are of considerable interest. The upper photograph shows a "three-throw" layout operated from two separate machines; while the lower one is of a movable diamond layout of which there are two sets in the yard, and which are unusual in that the diamond includes a slip connection.

Track circuits are of a similar type to those on other parts of the line; and here also, the track feed sets are located outside the cabin in separate cast-iron cases. Impedance bonds are used when there are double rail track circuits.

Movable Diamond Layout.

A diagram of the various cabins abolished is shown alongside. From this it will be noted that altogether 24 cabins involving 1,093 levers, have been totally abolished, while 9 cabins having 324 levers are normally switched out. This leaves only 8 cabins in regular service to handle the exceptionally heavy traffic, not only to Brighton, but to Worthing, Eastbourne, Portsmouth and several other branch lines.

The whole of the work (with the exception of the power frame at Brighton, which was erected by this Company) was installed by the Southern Railway and reflects the very greatest credit upon the organization and skill of the Signalling Staff, and which was further demonstrated during the various openings. The work was completed in four stages and the new signalling brought into service without any interruptions to traffic. The first section, that between Coulsdon and Balcombe, was brought into use on Sunday, June 5th, 1932, in six hours; the next, Balcombe to Copyhold Junction, on Monday, October 3rd, in fifteen minutes for each line; then followed the section Hayward's Heath to Preston Park, inclusive, on Sunday, October 6th, in one hour; and finally, Brighton Station on Sunday, October 16th, in approximately 6½ hours.

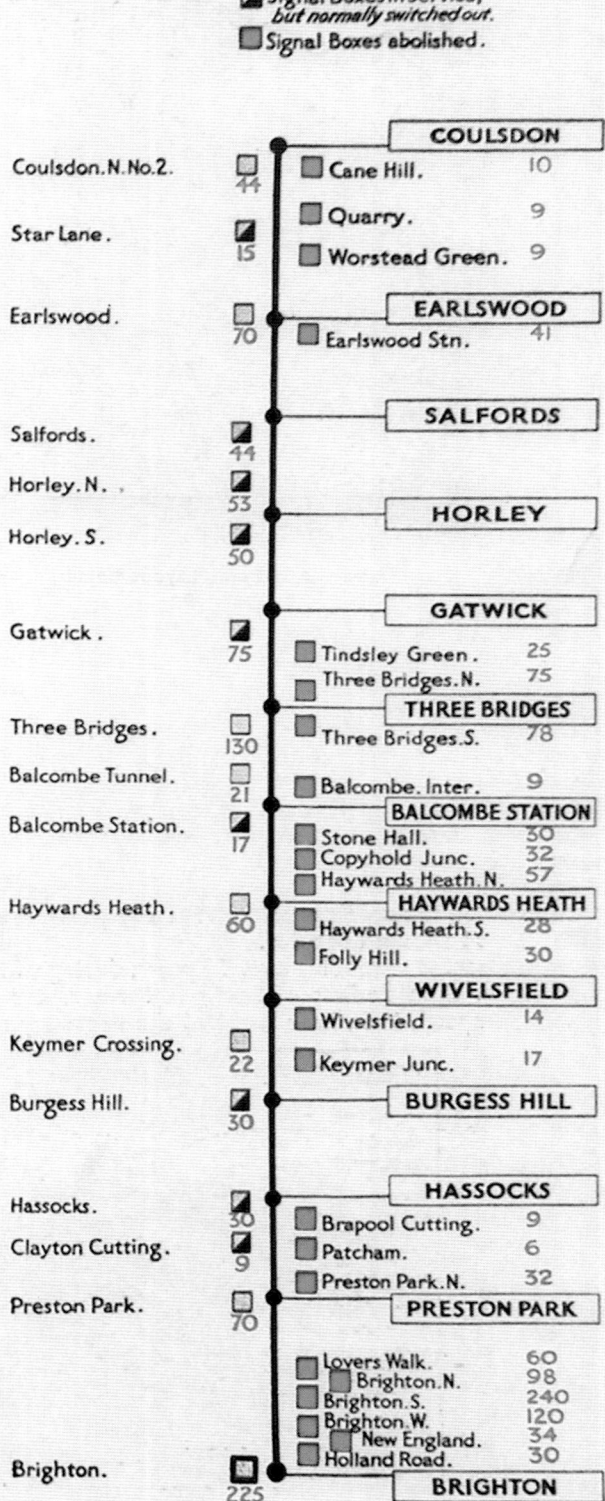

Page 21

Brighton North Cabin as first installed in 1871.

As a concluding note to this description of the latest signalling installation at Brighton some brief reference to the earlier installations may be of interest, as they constitute an outstanding and unique record of the manufacture of Railway Signalling Appliances.

The first installation was put into service about the year 1871, the materials being supplied and installed by Messrs. Saxby & Farmer. A general view of the layout is shown in the picture above. Ten years later the station was considerably extended and remodelled, and again Messrs. Saxby & Farmer were entrusted with the supply and installation of the necessary apparatus. The illustration below is a diagram of the layout of tracks and signalling at that time, while views of the largest of the three cabins are shown on the page opposite. For the purpose of comparison a view of the interior of the new cabin is also shown opposite.

Thus in a period extending over 60 years, during which three installations have been provided, the same firm, under the title first of Saxby & Farmer, and subsequently The Westinghouse Brake and Saxby Signal Company, Ltd., have supplied the necessary materials.

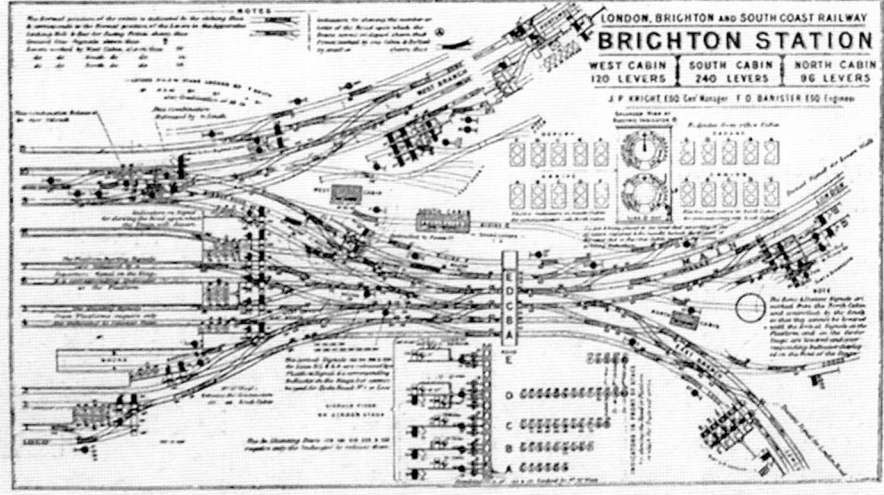

Diagram of Track Layout at Brighton as remodelled in 1881.

Brighton South Cabin. Installed 1881.

240-Lever Mechanical Frame in Brighton South Cabin. Note Mechanical Locking.

Interior of the new Cabin showing 225-Lever Power Frame with all-electric interlocking.

Appendix 3

OVER THE POINTS

A Quarterly Review of matters concerning THE SOUTHERN RAILWAY

Written by E. P. Leigh-Bennett.

No. 15. SEPTEMBER 1932

Six Anxious Hours

They were confronted with the biggest job of its kind that had ever been done; and they were given six hours in which to do it. They proposed to uproot the semaphore signalling system throughout forty-eight miles of railway track and substitute colour light signals, worked by electricity.

The Signal Engineers and their staff had, of course, been at work upon this tremendous 'change over' for some months without anyone being particularly aware of it. A little bit of work here, and a little there, on a railway track, between trains is nobody's business. Nor does officialdom want to know what is going on inside signal boxes so long as the smooth passage of trains is in no way impeded. The signal people were therefore able to carry on with their myriad preliminaries of wiring and electrical adjustments without disturbance or criticism from anyone.

But the day came when, the job having reached its climax, they had to go to the Traffic Department and ask for the free and unrestricted use of the line. This invariably creates an awkward diplomatic situation. Men deeply involved in the complex business of train movements regard it as a prime essential to peace and goodwill that 'the road' shall at no time be interfered with by what they consider quite secondary engineering necessities. The Engineer, on the other hand, says, quite frankly, that the trains are a damn nuisance at all times.

And here were the signal people wanting to commandeer a main artery of the system from Coulsdon North to Balcombe Tunnel, and have nothing move on it for a long time. Preposterous! No doubt there were suave conferences, and cups of tea, and adroit counter-suggestions. Certainly in the end there must have been compromise. For they were, in fact, given the tracks all to themselves. But only from 2 a.m. on a Sunday until 8 a.m. The traffic people affirmed that they had been obliged to make great sacrifices and difficult diversions to keep the lines clear even during that period of the weekend when trains are erroneously supposed to be at rest.

The Moving Spirit in this hazardous enterprise had given me a few technical details over the telephone a few days beforehand, and, knowing railway engineers, the careful modulation of his voice told me that something dramatic was afoot. But when he and his second-in-command joined me at 1 a.m. at Clapham Junction on that very dark Sunday morning their faces were masks of indifference and the acquired poise was perfect: for their zero hour was at hand. During the short journey to Coulsdon North they handed me a copy of the 'Operation Orders' for the night, and the printed 'Instructions To All Concerned'. Then they discussed the weather. Steady rain and a falling glass. The worst possible conditions for delicate electrical adjusting and hurried work in the open over a long stretch of road, on a time schedule of minutes with no margin possible.

To transform the train signalling over forty-eight miles of main-line track requires a coloured diagram of the job. It was thirteen feet long. We unrolled it. A maze of coloured circles containing numerals; a plethora of points. Nerve centres of the line were here exposed. They were about to probe them. The surgical operation upon the Gatwick signal box, for instance, would, it seemed, be *'tricky'*. But it was towards the Three Bridges box that their thoughts continued to stray with an obvious perturbation; for it was about to be given an entirely new frame of 130 levers, wired for power.

The Operation Orders were crisply military in tone. *'Salfords. Remove thirteen arms. Take down guy post of Up Fast starting. Ganger Burton and gang. Total eight men.'* Printed instructions sunk deep in technical waters. *'This signal will exhibit one yellow light when the Coulsdon North No. 2 Up Through to Up Main inner home and Up Through to Up Local inner home semaphore signals are in the "on" position ....'* There were sixteen pages of this sort of thing. And six hours only .... A realization of the great responsibility began to filter through me.

Coulsdon. A darkened platform. A swish of cold rain in the face. One more freight train to come through. Eight minutes to go. Two hundred and fifty-seven picked men at their posts, scattered in waiting groups over the miles ahead of us: each well aware of the consequences of his own mistake that night. Shrouded wagons clattered past us. A glance at a wrist watch: 1.59 – 'Right.' The lines were ours.

A walk on the slippery sleepers brought us very soon to some of the outlying pickets. We saw gnomes crouching in the darkness, silent, busy, sitting athwart the metals, rain dripping from cap peaks, Incomprehensible technique was the language spoken when inspecting officers addressed them. But in the rays of hand-lamps I had glimpses of their upturned faces; listened to the monosyllabic answers; heard the keenness underlying the curt speech. I knew that *they* knew that Brighton's main line was at their mercy: that they were in the act of rendering it impotent for trains; that soon after dawn broke the road would be urgently needed again; and that meanwhile the installation of a new and intricate system of power signalling devolved entirely upon them.

One may say, perhaps, that this is their job. That they are all trained men. That there had been rehearsals, and try-outs, and preparatory explanations and experiments: that nothing had been left to chance. That one must not get unduly excited about a straightforward piece of work crowded merely into a short space of time. Nevertheless, the teamwork of our railwaymen of the humble ranks (to whom bouquets are not thrown) when they are up against a stiff job, against the clock, on a filthy night, and mean to get it done, is an inspiring sight, particularly to those who have watched men of other nations in similar circumstances.

We climbed steps to a signal box. It was about to be transfigured. Nearly all its mechanical levers were to go. A posse of fitters stood by ready to act. They looked bored; but in truth they were anything but that. At a nod from a Lineman they descended into the signal-box basement; and all one could see then were fingers moving among a multitude of wires. (*'Can I borrow this lamp a minute, Fred?'* '*No. But you may as well 'ave it: 'cos you'll pinch it anyways.'*)

The testing stage began about 3 a.m. The second-in-command became vocal. He would stand in a box and call for signals; seeing if the coloured lights on the Indicator Board responded correctly. *'I want 30 track Down ... C.R. 32 Up ... Break Down 29 track ... I want to know the aspect of it ... I can't get 32 over. Why?'* (voice from the depths: *'I reckon it's skidded.'*) Whereat a well-disciplined signalman turns his head away hastily.

Gatwick platform. There is a grey smudge of dawn on the black sky. Silhouettes of men become more angular in shape. The lights of hand-lamps lose their penetration. The pallor of men's faces becomes apparent. Signal posts strew the ground. In their place big green, red, and yellow eyes of the new 25-watt colour light signals stare at us through the thinning gloom. The end of the job is in sight. A Personage of the traffic people has been with us from the start, holding a watching brief. He has been curt hitherto: his anxiety only half concealed. He has seen the hour of the first trains approaching with a grim rapidity – and the line locked against them. But now the door is ajar, and his face brightens. They look like doing it to time. *'Have a cigarette?'...*

Still, the bogy of Three Bridges looms always ahead. That is where the trouble will be, if any. There are 130 mechanical levers in that box, most of them to be transferred to power: and as for the points outside – *'Well, you'll see.'* We do. At 6.35. In the full daylight the completion of the task is exposed. They have had trouble – *'a tidy bit'.* But they have *'got over it'.* One might have known they would.

A small engine, with a saloon coach and a kitchen, has been creeping along behind us all night, is now producing breakfast, and is extremely popular. A space is cleared on the tablecloth to tot up the extent of achievement. Locking alterations made in nine signal boxes. Seven signal boxes abolished (they were working on last night's trains). One entirely new frame at Three Bridges (*urgh!*) taking over the work of three other frames. All power-working for this box connected up. One hundred and forty-one old semaphore signals disconnected and arms removed. Ninety-one new colour light signals brought into work. Electric track circuiting installed throughout the job. Traffic capacity of the line materially increased in consequence. The Personage raises a coffee cup graciously in acknowledgment of the latter fact.

'Is the first train signalled? Oh, I must *see. Excuse me.'...*

It pants heavily away from the Down Main at Three Bridges and approaches us pompously. The driver and fireman lean overside with understanding grins. A Brighton Excursion: well patronized. Faces are turned towards the track from most of the windows. The eyes record the thoughts ... *'What a lot of men hanging about on the line: Sunday morning too .... Most of them look wet through and very bedraggled, and it's a lovely morning. Curious thing ....'*

FACTS AND FIGURES

The signalling equipment of the new Electrification Extension from Coulsdon to Brighton involves:

- A new Colour-light installation over 119 miles of track, making in all 200 track-miles equipped with Colour-light Signalling by the Southern Railway, and a total of 600 Colour-light Signals.
- The provision of two new Signal Boxes and the abolition of 23 old Signal Boxes.
- 420 new Signal Levers will replace 1,187 old ones.
- 186 new Colour-light Signals will replace 393 old-pattern signals.
- 179 points will be operated by electric power.
- One new Signal Box at Brighton will replace the six present ones.

Appendix 4

Early Trials with Axle Counters on the Southern Railway

John Creed

When its main line electric passenger services opened to Brighton on 1st January 1933, the Southern Railway boasted the longest continuous stretch of colour light signalling and track circuiting in the country. Apart from the technological advances, the reduction in the number of manned signal boxes was a major economic benefit of the scheme. But such achievements were not without their teething troubles, and it is on one of these that this article will focus.[1]

The first stage of the new signalling was brought into service on 5th June 1932, between Coulsdon North, on the outskirts of London, and Balcombe Tunnel Junction, at the end of the quadruple track section, some 17 miles to the south. On this date, seven mechanical signal boxes were abolished and a further five boxes were reduced to 'Open as Required' status, with their running signals functioning automatically when the boxes were switched out. Only Coulsdon North No. 2 box, at the northern end of the scheme, Earlswood (south of Redhill), Three Bridges and Balcombe Tunnel boxes were to remain fully manned.

Among the boxes only to be opened as required in future was Star Lane, the next box south of Coulsdon North No. 2 and at the northern end of Quarry Tunnel. On 23rd May 1932, Signalman Robinson of Star Lane wrote respectfully to his station master at Coulsdon North:

<u>Electrical Fouling Bars (EFB), North and South of Quarry Tunnel</u>

Would you please obtain a ruling for me on the above, should the following position arise under Colour Light Signalling Regulations:-

In the event of a train being drawn back clear of the section after passing over or standing upon the first EFB, and before it has reached the second, what steps should be taken to put the signal and diagram indicator in order?

Could Reg. 25A(c) be made to apply with the man walking through the tunnel depressing the bar at the far end before advising the Signalman by 'phone?

The above question will arise with P.Way Trolley and Petrol cars.

Trusting you will oblige,

Yours obediently
G. H. Robinson
Signalman

Station Master Baldwin, like his staff, had doubtless read the new regulations for colour light signalling, which were to come into force in a couple of weeks' time. (These were the forerunners of the present-day track circuit block regulations.) But nowhere were EFBs mentioned. Having done a little research of his own, and discerned a more serious problem, Baldwin then wrote to Mr Latham, his Divisional Superintendent at London Bridge:

<u>Colour Light Signalling</u>

It would appear that by reason of the unreliability of track circuiting in Quarry Tunnel, as a safeguard a fouling bar has been placed at each end of the section on same lines. The first bar locks signals until released by train passing the second bar.

I attach an application from Signalmen as to how they shall release their signals

(1) if necessary to draw train back before passing 2nd bar.
(2) if trolley or petrol car does not release bars.

It would appear that no means of release is provided.

I shall be glad if you will kindly consider the point they have raised.

Personally I am more concerned with the element of danger which appears to be present in the case of a train becoming accidentally divided in tunnel. If the track is not reliable it is possible that the detached portion might come to a stand upon a faulty section and the action of the first part upon the bar would then have the effect of clearing the section for another train to enter.

Will you kindly give this possibility your consideration and oblige,

Yours truly,
J. Baldwin

---

1. The passages in this article quoted directly from the original papers, etc., have been minimally edited where necessary to clarify their meaning. This is largely a matter of style and punctuation, but in particular, the name of the tunnel referred to in the initial memo by Signalman Robinson has been standardised to 'Quarry Tunnel', its present-day official name. It was in fact referred to variously as 'Merstham Tunnel', or 'Merstham (Quarry Line) Tunnel' in some of the memoranda and letters, but the name 'Merstham' has been removed to avoid confusion for the present-day reader with the parallel tunnel on the former South Eastern line via Redhill, which carries that name today. Similarly, a reference to 'Earlswood Tunnel' has been changed to the modern name 'Redhill Tunnel'. Only in the extract from the 1934 SR Appendix and in Figures 1 and 2 have the names of the tunnels been left exactly as in the original documents.

It is probably fair to say that Baldwin's letter was not well received at London Bridge, for the very next day, Latham passed the entire correspondence up the line (literally!) to the Superintendent of Operation, E.C. Cox, at Waterloo, noting:

I may mention that I had not previously heard of the proposal to provide these fouling bars.

Four days later a reply was forthcoming from Waterloo, but sheds little light:

I understand that the Engineer intends to provide an electric fouling bar on each line near both ends of Quarry Tunnel ... These bars will afford a control similar to that of the 'Leatherhead' arrangement.

The surviving papers do not explain the Leatherhead arrangement, nor do they record what reply, if any, was given to Signalman Robinson. But they do record that the Superintendent's office pursued the Chief Engineer, or rather his Assistant for Signals & Telegraphs, former Ministry of Transport (MoT) Inspecting Officer Colonel G.L. Hall, for a further explanation, with diagram. This was duly provided (Figure 1), with the explanation that, taking the Down line as an example, Bar C depressed would open the circuit controlling CA44 signal and de-energise the relay of track TC2. Bar D depressed would then restore the circuit controlling CA44 and the relay of TC2. This was in addition to the standard control on CA44 by the occupation of track TC2.

Colonel Hall did not, at this point, explain why the bars had been provided. Perhaps he was a little reluctant to tell the whole story. But by 4th July he was confident enough to write to Cox suggesting that the men at Star Lane could be withdrawn at the end of that week. Meanwhile, however, the signalmen had not been idle, and daily reports of 'flicking' of the new track circuits were being prepared and sent up to London Bridge, and thence to Waterloo, as evidence. Thus the men remained at their posts, and on 22nd August, Hall wrote again to Cox:

I am arranging to make certain modifications in the track circuits and this is dependent upon the delivery of apparatus from the Contractors. I am afraid, therefore, that it will be necessary to retain the signalmen at Star Lane until you hear further from me.

Things had not improved by the opening of the second major stage of the colour light scheme, which included Clayton Tunnel, on 6th October; exactly the same problems were experienced. Once again, the signalmen stayed at their posts.

The cause of the problem is perhaps best explained by Hall's former colleague, Colonel Trench, who gives us a good description of the problem in his report to the MoT on the new signalling, dated 29th December 1932:

In connection with the track circuits in the long tunnels viz Quarry (2,113yds) and Clayton (2,266yds) and to a lesser extent Balcombe (1,138yds), some difficulty has been experienced in efficient maintenance owing to the formation of a black oxide on the rails which when dry is almost an insulator; when wet it becomes a conductor and it is anticipated that it can be removed by water jets.

As a temporary measure the signal boxes next to each end of Quarry and Clayton tunnels are being kept open continuously, and for all unfitted trains a 'train out of section' signal is being given to the box in rear after the signalman has observed the tail lamp in the usual manner. In addition to this, special bars have been provided at the entrance to, and about a train's length beyond the exit of both tunnels, the operation of which ensures that a train between them must correctly show 'occupation' of the track circuit and effect the locking controlled thereby. Arrangements are now under consideration in that when the full electric service commences [three days after the date of this report!] the majority of the steam engines working through the tunnels should be fitted with rail washing equipment, and it is hoped that in this manner the efficient operation of the track circuits in the tunnels can be rendered reliable, and the above-mentioned temporary measures discontinued. The company should be asked for a report on this point in say three months' time.

The provision of the rail washing equipment referred to in the MoT report was approved in December 1932, for 100 locomotives at a cost of £6 10s 0d (£6.50) each. It was simply a pipe, with valve,

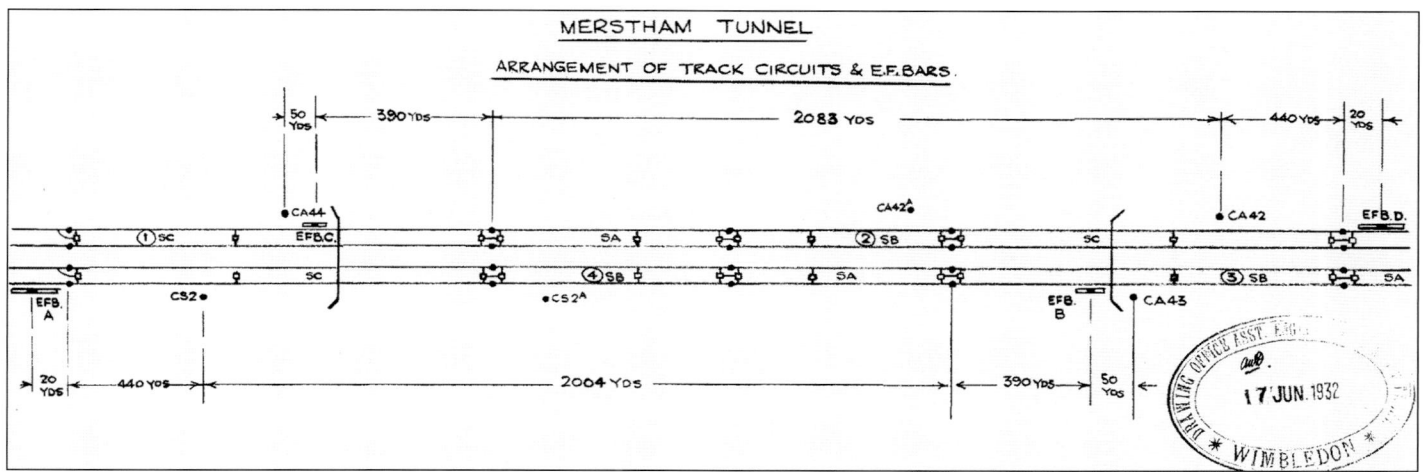

FIGURE 1: The arrangement of electric fouling bars initially installed in addition to track circuits at Quarry Tunnel, 1932. The Down road is uppermost in the sketch, London being to the left and Brighton to the right. Note how, at this early stage, the two rails of each road are drawn separately, and the impedance bonds are shown in detail. The ringed numbers are the track circuits as indicated in the relevant box; in reality each is composed of several sections, shown here as SA, SB, SC within each track.

leading directly from the boiler to discharge behind the trailing coupled wheels of the engine. Drivers were instructed to use it whether or not they had used their sanding gear, when passing through Quarry, Redhill, Balcombe, Clayton and Patcham tunnels on the main line, plus the 'Covered Way' at Cane Hill.

The initial instruction to drivers regarding rail washing was issued on 12th April 1933, and backed up with a repeat notice on 25th July. Just to make sure things were being done properly, however, some unlucky employee of the Loco Superintendent's office was stationed in the depths of Quarry Tunnel for three nights in late August. He reported that, of eleven Up and ten Down freight trains observed, only five engines had the washers in use. A gentle reminder to footplatemen was issued the following week.

By 1st November, the Chief Engineer felt that the rail-washing had been a success, and was proposing to disconnect the bars in Quarry and Clayton tunnels, leaving the signalmen in place for a while longer to watch the track circuits. He had already disconnected the bars in Balcombe Tunnel, and was proposing their recovery. A few days later he submitted a draft statement on the same lines to the General Manager, as a proposed response to the MoT's requirement for a report – which by now was almost a year earlier. Around the same time he also drafted an instruction to appear in the new Appendix due for publication in 1934, which after agreement by the Operating and Loco superintendents eventually appeared as follows:

RAIL WASHING APPARATUS FOR REMOVING SAND, ETC., FROM RAILS

A number of engines are fitted with a rail washing device for removing sand and other deposits from the rails to avoid risk of failures of track circuits. The arrangement allows a jet of hot water from the boiler to be sprayed through pipes on to the rail immediately behind the trailing coupled wheels which washes away any sand, etc., deposited on the rails.

*When sand is used to prevent slipping only, the rail washing valve must **always** be opened at the same time to ensure removal of the sand from the rail.*

When the Driver considers that the use of sand is necessary to ensure the braking of the train as well as the engine on a long gradient or when approaching a terminal, he may dispense with the use of the rail washer.

When an engine fitted with the rail washing device is passing through any of the following tunnels it is essential that the rail washing valve should be opened and kept open throughout the tunnel whether the sanding gear is used or not:-

Coulsdon Covered Way	*Redhill Tunnel*
Clayton Tunnel	*Merstham Tunnel (Quarry Line)*
Balcombe Tunnel	*Patcham Tunnel.*

By January 1934, the operators were again pressing the Chief Engineer for a definitive assurance as to the reliability of the track circuits, as they foresaw a shortage of signalmen in the approaching summer period. He was bold enough to reply:

the system of using rail washers … has, to date, proved satisfactory, and I know of no case where these track circuits have failed to shunt [i.e. show occupied] since this rail washing was introduced.

But then, in the very next paragraph, he hedged his bets:

At the same time, owing to the extreme importance of the whole question of automatic working through tunnels, I propose, before any action is taken to withdraw the Signalmen, to reinstate bar circuits and am, in the first instance, arranging to install these in Quarry Tunnel, with a view to adding this installation to Clayton Tunnel also if it proves satisfactory. As soon as the installation has been provided and is in satisfactory operation at Quarry Tunnel, I will write you in regard to the possibility of dispensing with the regular attendance of the Signalmen in Star Lane Box.

Unfortunately the response to this letter is not among the surviving papers, but we might well assume that the operators were not particularly impressed with the continued uncertainty, now almost two years after the problem initially arose.

However, we do know from a précis of the papers prepared for the Operating Superintendent in July 1934, that the bars were not in fact reinstated. It is stated that there have been no 'Danger' (i.e. wrong side) track circuit failures since November 1933, and that all 'Safety' failures have been due to broken wires, etc, and not to any problem with deposits on the rails. It concludes:

As intimated above, the Chief Engineer now thinks the Signalmen may be withdrawn but the position remains, however, that there is no guarantee that engines fitted with rail washers shall traverse Clayton and Quarry tunnels and use the washers at regular intervals and whilst with the advent of the Eastbourne and Hastings electrification the number of engines using the tunnel will be decreased, the possibility of washing the rails regularly will presumably be rendered more difficult to provide for.

Mr Ellson further advised us that he proposes to make experiments with a wheel counting device, which is an apparatus designed to take the place of track circuits, and as soon as it is delivered he proposes to test it in Quarry and Clayton Tunnels, in which case he will be asking for the Signalmen to be reinstated in order that a careful watch may be kept upon the working of the wheel counter.

On the strength of this, the whole matter was passed back to the Divisional Superintendent on 11th July, asking him if he was prepared to withdraw the signalmen at Star Lane, Hassocks and Clayton Cutting. (The fourth box, Earlswood, the next beyond the south end of Quarry tunnel, had to remain fully manned as it controlled the junction with the 'Old Road' via Redhill.) Mr Latham did not waste much time in replying – he wanted to close the boxes with effect from Monday 23rd. Unfortunately, though, the reply he received from Waterloo, on 3rd August, put the whole matter back into abeyance. The wheel counting apparatus was to be installed around the end of the month, and *'pending the result of the experiments'*, the signalmen were to be retained at all three boxes.

On 22nd August Mr Ellson provided a brief description of the proposed new arrangement, together with a diagram reproduced here as Figure 2:

In Star Lane signal box track [circuit] indicators will be fixed which will show normally clear for both Up and Down lines, and when the first wheel of a train or engine passes over the treadle 'A' on the Down line, the Down line indicator will be altered to occupied. This indicator will remain in this position until the last wheel of the train or engine has passed over treadle 'B', when the indicator will again be operated to the clear or normal position.

A similar operation on the Up line passing over treadles 'C' and 'D' will operate the Up line indicator.

At present these treadles will not operate any other signalling apparatus.

To assist Signalmen at Star Lane in noting whether these wheel counting treadles operate properly, track indicators will be fixed in Star Lane Box to indicate Section 'D' of track No. 1 and track No. 2 on the Down line and Section 'C' of track No. 3 and track No. 4 on the Up line.

These track indicators will show occupied when a train enters the track circuit and will remain so until the track circuit is clear.

The wheel counting apparatus was known as the Standard Axle Counting System, and was manufactured by Messrs Standard Telephones & Cables Ltd (ST&C), who were more widely known as suppliers to the Post Office of automatic telephone exchange equipment. The axle counter was in fact a spin-off from that industry, consisting simply of two 'uniselectors', or rotating electromagnetically-driven switches, one fed with pulses received from the 'incounting' treadle, the other with pulses from the 'outcounting' treadle. When all axles (and hence vehicles) which had entered the protected section had also left it, the two switches would be in correspondence, and this condition could be arranged to control other signalling equipment.

The equipment was a joint development between ST&C and the W.R. Sykes Interlocking Signal Co., from a suggestion by A.F. Bound, Signal & Telegraph Engineer of the LM&SR. It had already been under trial for a year, on a stretch of main line, presumably on the LM&SR system, and been found *'quite successful'*: whether 'quite' is used to mean 'fully', or 'fairly', is not stated. The Sykes company were brought into the project by Mr Bound and had particular responsibility for the development of the treadle, which was a new design. It had moving parts of very low inertia, and was designed to record accurately a number of wheels passing at high speed. It also incorporated a powerful spring to assist in preventing false impulses due to accidental physical contact during permanent way work or similar activities. The 'incounting' treadle was wired in circuit as a break contact, rather than a make contact, to provide fail-safe operation, and there were other safety features in the circuit design. The counting equipment could be mounted in a signal box locking room, or a trackside location case, and was described as requiring less space than *'a modern AC vane track relay'*; versions could be supplied to operate on a 24 or 50 Volt DC supply.

Some delay must have occurred in installing the axle counters, for it was not until 31st December that Mr Latham reported that they were in place. Eventually, on 30th April 1935, the Operating Superintendent issued the specially drafted instructions for Star Lane and Earlswood boxes:

Experimental Axle Counting apparatus has been installed at Quarry Tunnel on both the Up and Down Roads. Indicators have been provided for the area covered by the axle counting apparatus, and also for the same area covered by track circuits. This area is as follows:-

Up Road: From a point 31 yards the tunnel side of Signal CA43 to a point 440 yards the Star Lane side of Signal CS2.
Down Road: From a point 50 yards the tunnel side of Signal CA44 to a point 440 yards the Earlswood side of Signal CA42.

The function of all the apparatus is similar on both Up and Down Roads.

The indicators for the area covered by the Axle Counting apparatus and for the same area covered by track circuits should operate simultaneously, and notes should be made if this does not occur. In this connection a buzzer has been provided to operate when the Axle Counting and track circuit indicators are not in harmony. Should this buzzer operate, the Signalman should make notes as to the positions of both indicators, and also, if possible, the position of the train when the buzzer first operated, and at once send for the Signal Lineman.

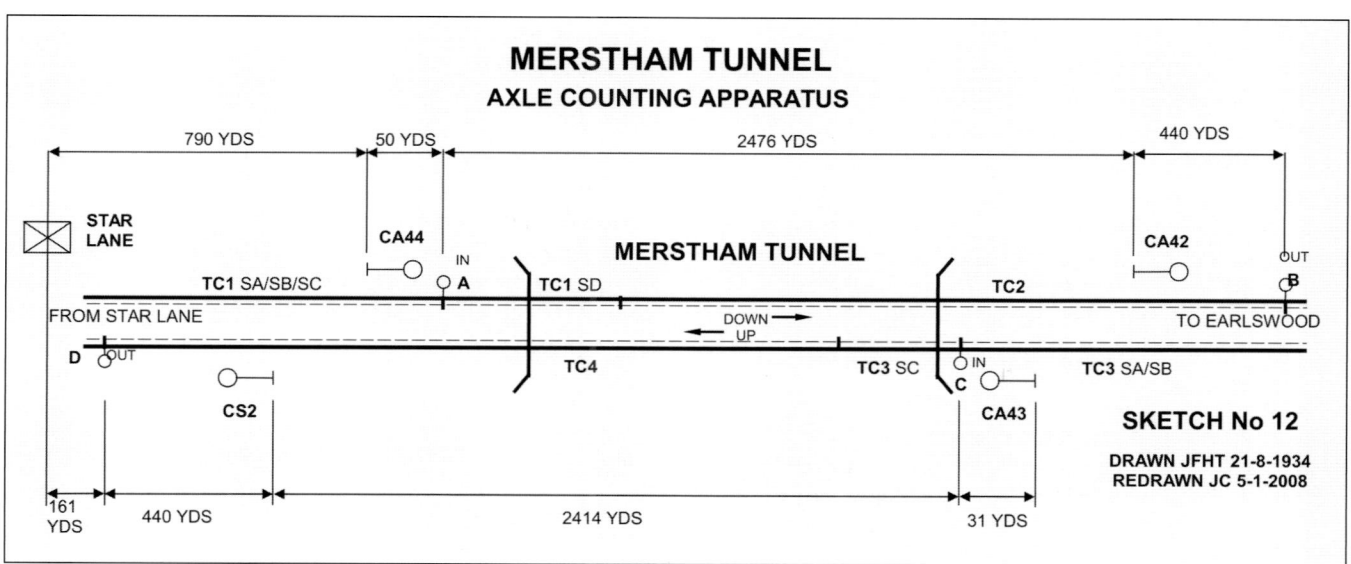

FIGURE 2: The arrangement of axle counters to achieve the same result as Figure 1, 1934. More conventional symbols are now used for both signals and track circuits. Note that additional block joints have been provided at each 'in' treadle, hence TC1 now has a Section D and TC3 has a Section C. The 'out' treadles are located at the existing running-off ends of TC2 and TC4 tracks, allowing a quarter-mile overlap, the standard distance for both semaphore and colour light signalling at that time.

> *It must be clearly understood that the whole of this Axle Counting apparatus is experimental and does not exercise any control over the signals. The track circuits and signal controls are not in any way altered, and the existing rules in regard to procedure in case of failure or suspected failure of signals or track circuits are still to be observed. No action other than that laid down in the preceding paragraph is necessary in the event of any failure of the Axle Counting apparatus, provided the track circuits, signals and signal controls operate correctly.*

Meanwhile Mr Latham was still keen to close the boxes at either end of Clayton Tunnel, where the track circuits were now behaving reliably, and had calculated that the time lost by track circuit failures would be in any case be minimal. One of the factors affecting this was that *'telephones are available* [at the signal boxes either end of the tunnel] *giving direct communication with the Gangers' houses'* and that there would therefore be no difficulty in obtaining a man to examine the tunnel at any time of day or night when this was required. He must have persuaded the Operating Superintendent this time, as a stencil notice of 28th June states:

HASSOCKS AND CLAYTON TUNNEL SIGNAL BOXES

On and from Monday next 1st July, these boxes will normally be closed except that Hassocks Box will be open for freight traffic as under:-

Weekdays		Sundays
1.30am MX)	to 4. 0am	1.30am to 4. 0am
2.30am MO)		
6. 0am	to 6.50am	
2.30pm	to 4.30pm	

also as required for van train working.

It had taken Latham almost three years to get these boxes closed. The saving, in wages costs alone, was estimated at approximately £635 p.a. For comparison, although not quoted in detail in the papers, the capital cost of a set of axle counters for one tunnel was around £200.

Meanwhile the Chief Engineer commissioned a further set of axle counters at Balcombe Tunnel on 26th August. The instructions issued to the signalmen were broadly similar to those for Quarry Tunnel, except that the buzzer was not provided. Separate indicators were provided for each line, for both the tunnel track circuit and the axle counter, and as long as these acted in sympathy, all was well. If the two indications disagreed, the lineman was to be sent for, but normal signalling of trains could continue. But, unlike at Quarry Tunnel, the axle counter was also connected to the existing indications on the illuminated diagram, in parallel with the relevant track circuit, and jointly controlling the aspect of the signal governing entrance to the tunnel. Either the axle counter or the track circuit being at clear would indicate the track circuit occupancy on the diagram – which at this period was normally all lit, with the lamp not illuminated indicating the presence of a train. It is not clear, however, from the original papers, which took precedence when one of the two systems failed, and whether the signal could still clear if the track circuit was unoccupied but the axle counter was not in its 'home' position.

Another indication that things were going well at Quarry Tunnel was the withdrawal, on and from Thursday 3rd October 1935, of the men at Star Lane box, saving the wages of three Class 4 signalmen at a total of £561 13s 2d (£561.66) p.a. But it appears that this was in fact due to improved performance of the track circuits, rather than the axle counters. Although there is no definitive statement in the surviving papers, the initial installation of axle counters may well have been disconnected by this time. It appears that the closure of Star Lane box was accepted on the grounds that the closure of the boxes at Clayton Tunnel had caused no problems. A memo written in the Operating office paraphrases a letter from the Engineer of 10th December 1935, stating:

> *the [axle counting] apparatus has been found to be fairly reliable and has run on both roads for some five or six weeks at a time without failure. [The Engineer] is not at present in a position to advise that the apparatus has been sufficiently developed to be relied upon for the signalling of a main line, but that it is a valuable standby to important track circuits, such as through tunnels. [He] adds that improvements are continually under review and it is hoped that the reliability of the apparatus will be considerably improved as time goes on.*

Further, more concrete, evidence for the ending of the initial trial is found six months later, when the papers record a completely new installation of axle counters at Quarry Tunnel. This was commissioned on Monday 13th July 1936, and was very similar to that at Balcombe Tunnel. The same instructions applied, but in the signal box the dedicated separate track circuit indication was dispensed with, that on the illuminated diagram now being deemed sufficient. This latter was not controlled by the axle counter in this case, the stated reason being a saving of several miles of wire. But we do learn in this instance that the clearing of the signal admitting trains to the tunnel was not affected by a single failure of either the track circuit or the axle counter, only a failure of both would hold the signal at red. (We must assume that Star Lane box was once again fully staffed to supervise the axle counters, but this is not mentioned in the original papers.)

At the same time as designing the new Quarry Tunnel installation, the Engineer had also prepared diagrams for providing axle counters at Clayton Tunnel. But he commented:

> *The apparatus for this, however, is not available, and I do not propose to order it until certain improvements in design, which are now under discussion with the manufacturers, have been made.*

This view of the situation is reinforced by a summary of axle counter failures between 9th August and 17th November (the year is not stated but is presumably 1936), which shows a total of thirty-four instances, eight in Balcombe Tunnel and the rest in Quarry, usually lasting for 1 to 3 hours each and with longest being 4½ hours.

In a note of 13th October, Mr Ellson mentioned that he would not at present be approaching the General Manager for funding for axle counters for Clayton Tunnel, *'in view of the comparatively unreliable character of the apparatus fitted.'*

In March 1937 an interesting note was put on file, stating that the L&NER and GWR had decided not to fit rail washers to their engines, avoiding costs of £70,923 and £43,225 respectively. The LM&SR, however, was proceeding with the work – perhaps their excursion into axle counting had also been less than wholly successful?

The treadles in Balcombe Tunnel were replaced with new models, and the equipment brought back into service on 15th April 1937. The equipment at Quarry Tunnel was still in use a month later. But in a précis of the papers prepared soon afterwards, we read:

> *intermittent failures have occurred and the Chief Engineer advises that the equipment at both tunnels were [sic] put out of service on 18th June.*

In summary, a further note states that the only real advantage that the axle counter had demonstrated was as a backup for the track circuit in the tunnel. In the event of the failure of the latter, the axle counter would continue to allow the signal to clear, and avoid delay until the track circuit could be repaired.

From this point the correspondence in the file thins out considerably. A year later, in July 1938, the Chief Engineer was asked if any progress had been made; he replied that he hoped to receive a demonstration of *'improved apparatus'* very shortly. The trial equipment was installed on the Down line at Balcombe Tunnel on 25th November 1938, but was not satisfactory. In January 1939, Mr Ellson wrote to advise that he was following up the matter with the manufacturers; his memo was marked for review on 1st July, and then again for 27th July. And there the file ends.

It seems unlikely that much effort was put into axle counters during the War, and unreliable equipment was the last thing railway operators needed at that time. But a check of the diagrams in the SRS Archive for the relevant boxes does reveal one small footnote: on a diagram for Balcombe Tunnel Junction dated 1952, an earlier note in the margin states: *'Axle counters abolished 20.4.48'*.

Now, over fifty years later, axle counters have been reintroduced to the network, although the present-day equipment uses electromagnetic detectors rather than treadles. There have been several large scale installations, for example, the West Coast Main Line resignalling controlled from the new Rugby SCC. The Rule Book was amended in 2005 to cater for the wider application of axle counters: despite the lack of track circuits, this method of working is still designated 'Track Circuit Block'.

Acknowledgements

The bulk of this article is based on a correspondence file originally held in the Rules Section at Southern Railway HQ, Waterloo. It is not a complete record, as some items are obviously missing, but it has enabled the story to be reconstructed with a reasonable degree of confidence. The material from the MoT report is taken from that file, though it can also be found at the National Archive at MT 29/87, p. 415, and is Crown copyright.

Looking through Forge Bridge towards Star Lane, this would have been the area where the 'counting out' EFB & treadle would be sited as described in the text. *1931, The Edward Wallis Collection*

Appendix 5
Signal Sighting

Although this Signal Sighting Form dates from the Railway Executive (which was a subsidiary of the British Transport Committee formed in 1948), it would have been a very similar arrangement used for the Brighton Line resignalling of 1932. Relatively simple and a far cry from today's elaborate affair, all the basic requirements are there including the make-up of the committee, although there is no signature for a civil engineer who may have to provide a base. Noting the entry for banner repeating signals, it is to the committee's credit that the only banner signals (and splitting banners at that) employed on the 1932 resignalling scheme were approaching Coulsdon North on the Up road just south of the Cane Hill covered way. These were the days before sighting distances were calculated using the line speed, requiring a sighting time in seconds; the rule of thumb back then seemed to be that with the sighting of any running signal, *'a reasonable minimum approach view can be considered to be 300 yards'*. A 1960 'Guidance Booklet' is reproduced on the following pages.

BRITISH RAILWAYS
THE RAILWAY EXECUTIVE 1872

REPORT OF SIGHTING COMMITTEE IN RESPECT OF SIGNALS AT

Name of Signal Box.. Date..................................
Signal or Signals concerned................................... Lever Nos........................
Reason for Sighting..

PROFILE   EXISTING   PROPOSED

APPROACH VIEW OF SIGNAL. Existing...........yards. Proposed...........yards.
NEW POSITION OF SIGNAL.   Existing   Proposed
Distance from Outer Rail...........ft...........ins. Distance from Box (yards)....................
Height above Rail Level...........ft...........ins.   Height above Ground Level.........ft.........ins.
If signal cannot be seen from Box, state cause..

Is Electric repeater required for
Stop Signal (a) Arm................ (b) Slot................ (c) Light................
Distant Signal (a) Arm.............. (b) Slot................ (c) Light................

IF DISTANT SIGNAL Distance from Home   Present...........yards. Proposed...........yards.
                   "   "   Signal Box "   ....yards.   "   ....yards.
                   Gradient 1 in........... * Rising/Falling between Distant and Home.
                   (Average to be given when gradient varies).

IF BANNER REPEATER REQUIRED For Stop Signal................ For Distant Signal................
Distance from Signal to Banner................yards. Height above rail.........ft.........ins,
Distance from outer rail...........ft...........ins.
Is power available for illumination ?................

IF FOG POST. Present, Fogged by * hand/machine. Proposed, To be fogged by * hand/machine.
                              Present.   Proposed.   Present.   Proposed.
Distance of, Signal post to lever....................   Lever to machine....................
    "   "   "   "   "   fog hut....................   Fog hut to detonator....................
Are electrical fog repeaters required ?....................
Conductor rail to be * cut/changed-over/remain-unchanged at fogsignalman's position.
Is protection boarding required at fogsignalman's position ?....................

IF TELEPHONE REQUIRED.
State position of telephone....................
Is protection boarding required ?.................... Does cess require to be made up ?....................

SPECIAL REMARKS....................
....
....
....

....
Operating Dept.   *Motive Power (Steam) Dept.*

                                                                       ....
                                                                       Signal & Telecommunications Engineer's Dept.
....
Motive Power (Electrical) Dept.

                    * Delete words not applicable.

Southern Region.   (WX 785) Amended.

MEMORANDUM FOR GUIDANCE OF SIGHTING COMMITTEES.

GENERAL NOTE ON SIGHTING COMMITTEE REPORT FORMS.

The sketches on these forms should shew the position of the line to which the signal applies in relation to the post, and in the case of a bracket signal or bridge the position of the signal in relation to the line to which it applies as well as all lines spanned by the bracket or bridge. Where a post is to be erected between lines, shew the lines on either side with the distance between them. The forms should be filled in entirely—it is not sufficient to leave a space blank.

Attention to be called under the heading "Special Remarks" to any proposal to erect a signal in a position where standard clearance cannot be obtained.

When trees require cutting, it must be stated whether these are on Commission's or outside property.

Signals must be referred to by their description as shewn on the signal box lever name plate and the lever number must also be quoted.

(1) **Height of signals** should be kept as low as possible consistent with giving a reasonable approach view to drivers. A reasonable minimum approach view can be considered to be 300 yards. Signals should be between 12 feet and 25 feet in height, and should rarely exceed 15 feet above rail. Duplicate arms should not be recommended if the alternative shewn in 8 (g) is practicable.

(2) **Normal position of signals** is immediately to the left of the road to which they apply, except in the following instances :—

  (a) Where an adjacent siding exists, the signal should be erected on the left of this siding if the latter cannot be slewed. (In some cases a half-bracket post may be necessary.)

  (b) Starting signals at the end of an island platform between two lines running in the same direction may both be between the two lines, either on separate posts or on a bracket post.

  (c) In the case of parallel lines separated by an ordinary 6-foot way, the signals should be, as a rule, on a bracket post to the left of the left-hand line.

  (d) Where signal bridges or gantries are recommended, the signal doll post should be 2 feet to the left of the left-hand rail of the line to which the signal applies, or as near as possible to this position.

(3) **The Spacing and Height of Signals** on bracket posts, cantilevers or gantries, should, unless the circumstances are exceptional, be in accordance with those shewn on standard Profile Drawing No. M.70-2.

4. NORMAL SPACING OF SIGNALS

  (a) Distant Signals
  The distance between a distant signal and the stop signal ahead (Home or Outer Home) should be obtained from the tables (Appendix "A") having due regard to the gradients between the distant and home signals and the maximum attainable speed of trains.

  (b) Stop Signals
  Outer home to inner home signals -
  440 yards on the level; greater spacing may be required on falling gradients.
  Starting (or Advanced Starting) Signals -
  400 yards beyond last set of trailing points, worked from the signal box on the line to which the signal applies.

Signals at a Junction, where free acceptance is required, to be 440 yards from the Junction clearance point where the line is level; greater spacing may be required on falling gradients.

When it is recommended that a signal shall be in a position different from that shewn on the signal diagram, the reason should be given on the report under the item "Special Remarks."

Signals leading over facing points should, wherever possible, be within 100 yards of the points over which they apply.

(5) **Display Boards or Sight Boards** will not be permitted under any circumstances. Where there is an overbridge or other structure immediately behind the signal, painting of the structure may be recommended—white in the case of stop signals and black for distant signals.

(6) **Distant Signals** which have to be placed under a stop signal of the box in rear must be repeated under all stop signals in advance of that signal which are worked from that box.

(7) Isolated Distant signals
Distant signals on a separate post should be substituted by colour light signals unless special local considerations, such as impossibility of obtaining an electric power supply, make this impracticable.

(7A) Marker lights will normally be white unless they are situated on the approach side of a red light, e.g. level crossing or buffer stop lamp, in which circumstances they will be yellow.

(8) **Subsidiary Signals.**

(a) For ordinary shunting movements, ground signals are to be used. In special circumstances these may be elevated either on a separate post or placed on posts carrying running signals, in which case, however, they must be bracketed out towards the direction in which they apply. Should a ground signal apply to diverging routes to the left *and* the right, this signal will be mounted centrally on the post.

(b) *Plain arms* (short) are to be provided in cases of running signals leading from the main line in the right road direction over facing points to a siding or goods line.

All running signals on non-passenger lines are to be fitted with plain arms (short).

(c) *Plain Arms* (*short*) are to be provided for "right away" movements from sidings, *i.e.*, when leading into another section or up to an Intermediate section signal.

(d) *Shunt Ahead Arms* (letter "S") are only to be provided on Section (*e.g.*, Starting or Advanced Starting) signals where shunting into the section ahead is authorised without (unless instructions are given to the contrary) the movement being put into Block.

(e) *Calling-on Signals* (letter "C") are to be provided when a movement is required to be made past a stop signal when

(i) the line between this signal and the next stop signal, or the buffer stops in the case of a terminal road, is occupied,

or

(ii) a train is required to stop at the Signal Box before reaching the next signal.

(f) WARNING SIGNALS (LETTER "W") are to be provided under stop signals only where warning acceptance is authorised, and a special warning signal is necessary.
Note – If more than one of the above functions (d), (e) or (f) is required at any one signal, a single arm is to be provided and an indicator working in conjunction with the arm is to be fixed on the post showing alternatively the letter required.

(g) *Repeater Signals* to be of the banner type with black arms illuminated at night. Banner repeating signals should not be provided if the approach view of the signal to which it would apply is 300 yards or over.

(9) **Arm Repeaters in Signal Boxes.** These are required for all distant signals and all other signals which cannot readily be seen from the Box and for the slot where such signals are slotted. Arm repeaters will also, as a rule, be necessary in the case of stop signals which are more than 400 yards from the Box, whether these stop signals are, in clear weather, within view of the Signal Box or not. A slight alteration in the position of the signal may sometimes obviate the necessity for these repeaters.

(10) Light Repeaters are required only on important lines with high speed traffic in cases where the light of the signal or banner repeater in question cannot readily be seen either by the Signalman who works the signal or by the Signalman of some other Box, but should be provided, as a rule, in all new works for distant signals that cannot readily be seen from a Signal Box that is always open.

(11) **Track Circuits, or corresponding devices,** are necessary on double lines where trains standing at signals cannot be seen by the Signalman. They will also, as a rule, be necessary in the case of stop signals which are more than 400 yards from the Box, whether these stop signals are, in clear weather, within view of the Signal Box or not.

(12) **Fog Posts.**

(a) The detonator should, whenever possible, be placed on the rail at a point 30 yards from the signal. The following distances therefore apply as a standard : signal to Fogman's Hut to be 15 yards ; Fogman's Hut to position at which detonator is placed on rail, either by hand or machine, to be 15 yards.

Some modification of the above may be necessary in cases where signals placed at the end of a platform require to be fogged. It is undesirable to place detonators on the rails in the platform as this alarms, and may injure, passengers.

Where possible, signals should be so sighted that one fog post will cover more than one signal.

(b) Fog repeaters should only be provided where signal arms cannot readily be seen by the Fogman, and as a rule should not be required for signals 20 feet high and under.

(13) Signal telephones should, normally, be positioned on the signal post. Where this is impracticable, it should be positioned 6 feet from the signal on the approach side. Where a conductor rail exists between the running line and the telephone, 80 feet single protection boarding to be provided on the approach side of the signal. A sleeper walkway 25' x 18" should be laid down leading to all telephones situated between running lines and at other places where justified by local conditions.

(14) **Position for Signal Boxes** should be selected so as to give the best possible view of the running lines and so avoid the necessity for track circuits, etc., wherever possible. The height of the floor above rail level should be given in the report.

COLOUR LIGHT AREAS.

(15) **Position of Colour Light Running Signals.** The red light of these signals to be normally 12 to 15 feet above rail level. When on a bridge or bracket over the line, the normal position to be 3 feet to left of near-side rail of line 16 feet 6 inches above rail level. A special note to be made in the report when left-hand side lights are required. Signals on straight posts to be on the left of the line to which they apply, as near to the left hand rail as practicable.

(16) **Junction Indicators.** To be above the colour light signal with the pivot light vertically in line with the lights of the colour light signal. Splitting signals are not to be installed except in the case of auxiliary running signals—*vide* next paragraph.

(17) Auxiliary signals are provided with smaller lenses than the main running signals, and are used for movements from main lines over facing points to a goods road or siding. In future, position light signals may be used. Auxiliary signals on the same post or bracket and applying to the same line as a main running signal will not show a red light. The normal spacing between running and auxiliary signals to be 2 feet 6 inches.

(18) **Subsidiary Signals in Colour Light Areas** are of the ground signal pattern without spectacles, and are floodlighted at night. Floodlit signals are not to be used except in colour light areas. Alternatively in power signalled areas they may be of the position light pattern.

(19) **Water Columns.** Where provision has to be made for water columns, at the ends of platforms, starting signals should, wherever practicable, be placed in such a position beyond the water column as will enable an engine (65 feet in length) to take water without having to pass the signal at danger.

Appendix 6
Main Line Quadrupling

As explained earlier, the original plans to continue the quadrupling of the main line were abandoned in 1912 but these were resurrected in 1963. One can only admire the confidence of the designer as he nonchalantly writes 'New Tunnel' four times and 'New Viaduct' when he reaches Ouse Valley; it is not clear whether any hard and fast plans were ever drawn up, but what would the railway have given today to have such infrastructure in place? One of the most fascinating items is at Keymer Junction where the plans for a 'flying junction' were also resurrected, along with the easing of the left-hand turn-out on to the branch and a widened level crossing.

Three sub-stations would have had to have been relocated whilst Clayton Cutting signal box would have been abolished, Balcombe Tunnel Junction presumably either being relocated or, as this is not shown, more likely put on to Three Bridges some fifteen years earlier than it actually was. How the new railway would have been incorporated into the existing signal boxes would have been interesting; again my research has not found that any plans ever materialised.

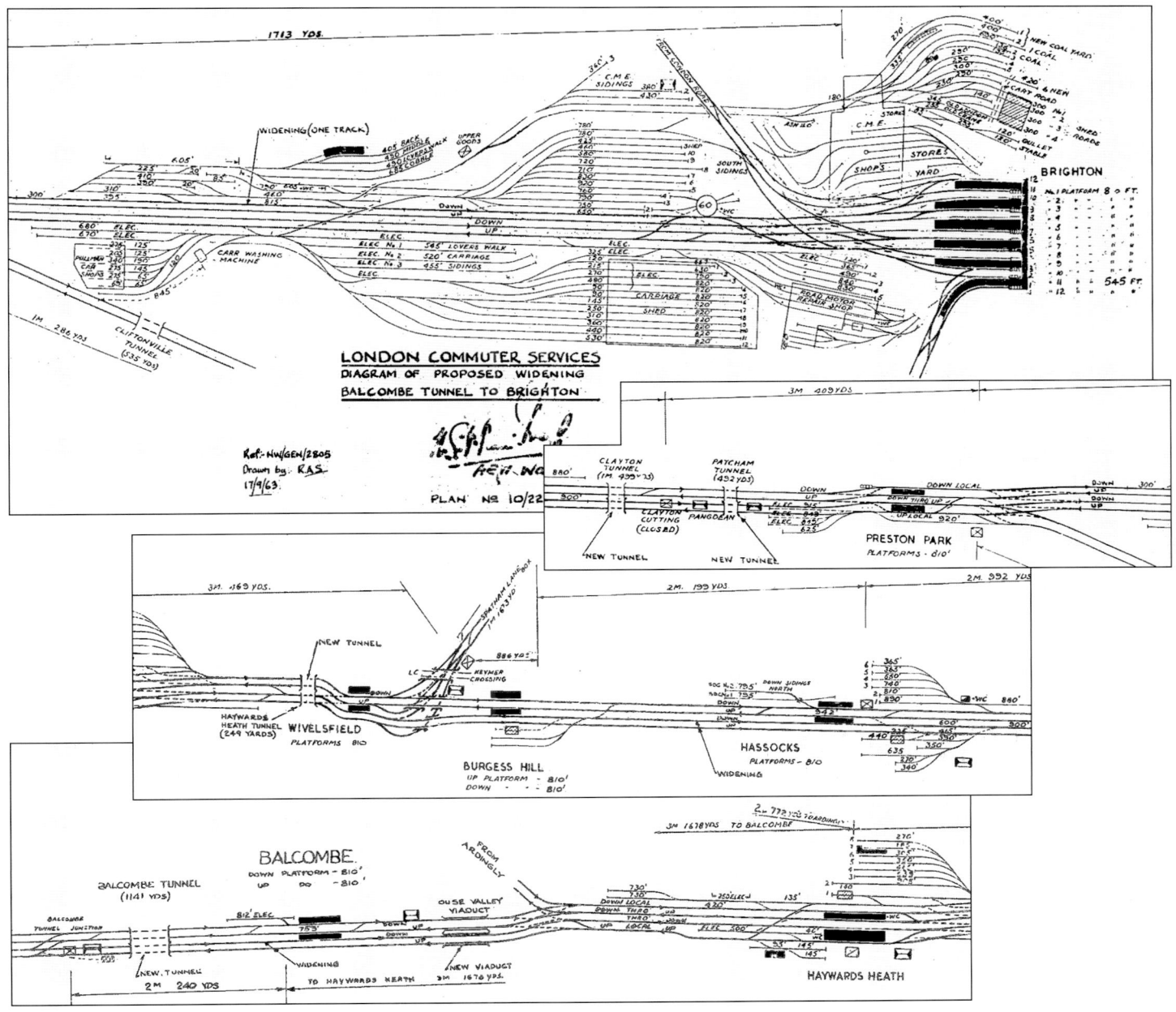

Appendix 7
The Thirteen Signal Box Scheme

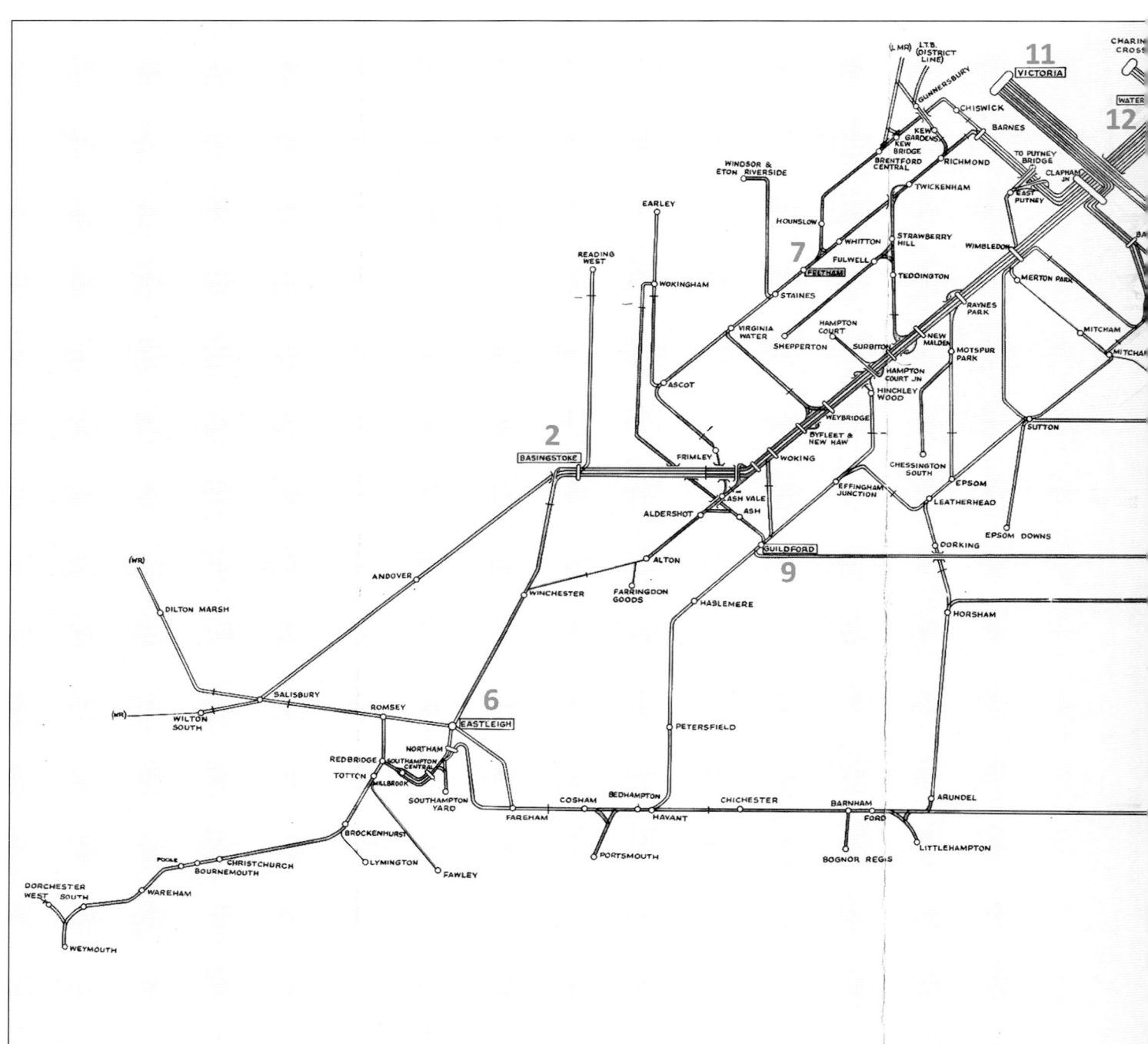

Appendices

The Thirteen Signal Box Scheme was a bold plan conceived in the late 1960s to supervise the whole of the Southern Region from that number of control centres. Dartford opened in 1970 and was seen to be the first, followed by Feltham in 1974. London Bridge opened the following year, but after this the idea was quietly dropped, although the Victoria Signalling Centre of 1980 followed a very similar area of control to that depicted here. The controlling signal boxes would have been:

1) Ashford,
2) Basingstoke,
3) Brighton,
4) Dartford,
5) East Croydon,
6) Eastleigh,
7) Feltham,
8) Gillingham,
9) Guildford,
10) London Bridge,
11) London Victoria,
12) London Waterloo,
13) Tonbridge.

The proposed area of control for Brighton signal box would have extended to a point west of Chichester and east of Hampden Park on the coastway routes, to somewhere in the Faygate region on the Mid Sussex Line via Horsham and from there to south of Dorking. On the main line Brighton would have controlled up to north of Balcombe station with East Croydon taking over from there. The controlling centres on the diagram are marked in numerical order, not in what would have been their order of construction.

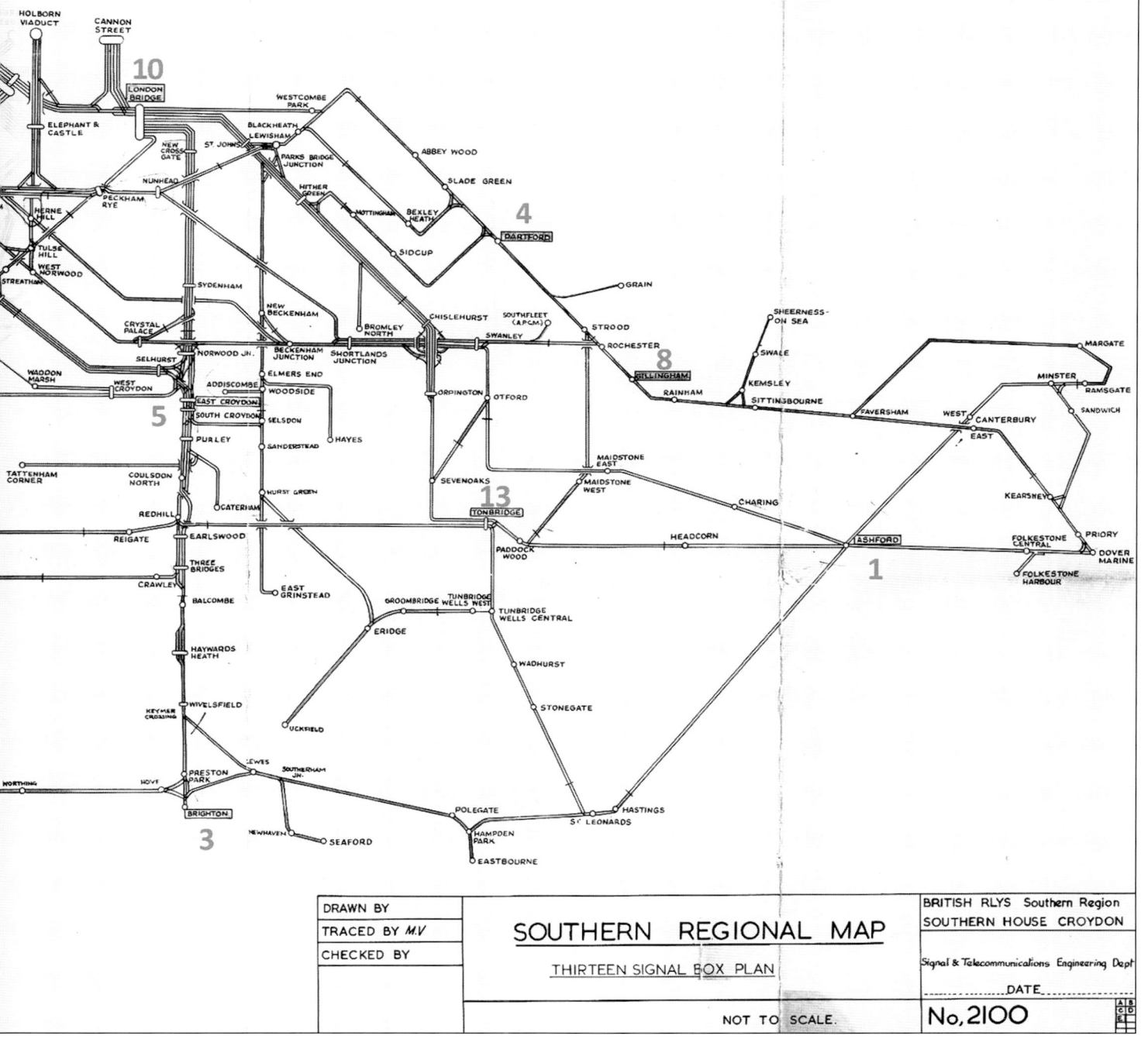

Appendix 8

Westinghouse Signals

After the beautifully produced booklet to commemorate the previous resignalling, it was somewhat disappointing that this was the best the company could manage for the much larger scheme of the 1980s.

WESTINGHOUSE SIGNALS

BRIGHTON LINE RESIGNALLING

HISTORY

Westinghouse Signals' connections with British Rail, Southern Region can be traced back to 1861 when John Saxby was employed as a foreman by the London Brighton and South Coast Railway in their workshops at Brighton. It was at this time that the Brighton Station Area was first signalled. Shortly afterwards John Saxby went into partnership with John Farmer and the company which they set up was to become one of the forebears of Westinghouse Brake and Signal Company.

In 1881 Brighton station was remodelled and new mechanical signalling equipment, supplied by Saxby and Farmer, was installed. There were six signal boxes with a total of 592 levers.

ELECTRIFICATION

In 1932, when the Brighton line was electrified, the signalling from Coulsdon to Brighton was modernised. Colour light signals and continuous track circuitry were installed. Many mechanically operated points remained but their operating levers were equipped with electric lever locks. At this time a new power signal box was built at Brighton to house a miniature lever frame. This all-electric frame had 225 levers and controlled the whole of the Brighton area including the approaches from both the East and West on the coastal lines and from Preston Park to the North.

THE BRIGHTON LINE RESIGNALLING SCHEME

The £14 million contract for the present scheme was awarded to Westinghouse in 1980 to cover design, manufacture, installation, testing and setting to work of modern four aspect colour light signalling extending from Brighton to Norwood Junction and Selhurst, just North of East Croydon. When fully commissioned in 1985, the new signal box at Three Bridges will control 180 route kilometres of railway and will have replaced 33 old signal boxes. At Norwood the new signalling connects with the London Bridge control area, completed in 1976, and at Selhurst with the Victoria control area completed last year. Thus with completion of the Brighton line scheme trains travelling between Brighton and London will do so under the control of just two signal boxes.

SUBSEQUENT DEVELOPMENTS

The Southern Region's first all relay interlocking and control panel were installed when Keymer Crossing signal box was modernised in 1959.

The development of Gatwick as London's second airport necessitated remodelling and resignalling of the station in 1978. Under the current scheme control of the signalling at Gatwick is by remote control from the new signal box at Three Bridges.

The scheme has involved extensive track remodelling. The railway in the Gloucester Road "triangle" just North of East Croydon has virtually been rebuilt and two fly-overs constructed in order to separate slow and fast services and eliminate the need for trains to cross each other's paths, thereby relieving congestion. When the scheme is completed in 1985, new track layouts will have been provided at ten other stations and junctions.

TECHNICAL AND OPERATIONAL FEATURES

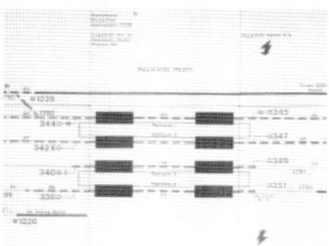

In the control room at Three Bridges are situated the control desk and separate illuminated diagram, the latter being arranged in a continuous curve to present a panoramic view of the whole control area.

Under a separate contract Westinghouse has provided a computer based train describer, which in addition to displaying train numbers on LED displays on the diagram, interfaces with the automatic route setting system. This system automatically controls the signalling in the Copyhold Junction, Haywards Heath and Keymer Junction areas. The process takes account of the state of the interlocking and information it receives from the master Timetable system to route trains automatically in accordance with their destinations in such a manner as to provide an optimum train service.

In addition to the relay interlocking at Three Bridges, there are twelve remote interlockings, controlled and indicated over Westinghouse TDM 69 data links. The largest interlockings, at Brighton, East Croydon and Redhill are geographical using the Westpac Mark IV system as used on the London Bridge scheme. The remaining interlockings are free wired.

The extensive use of the Westinghouse computer aided design facility in all phases of circuit design has speeded the production of circuits and wiring diagrams and helped to ensure their accuracy.

Override facilities, using separate FDM circuits, have been provided to enable signalmen to replace all signals to danger and thereafter institute automatic operation of certain 'preferred' routes in the event of failure of a TDM link to a remote interlocking. Local emergency panels are provided in relay rooms as further back up.

The British Rail Automatic Warning System (AWS) is being installed throughout the Brighton line.

TIMESCALE

When the contract was signed in 1980, completion had been planned for October 1986. Despite the extensive civil engineering works and the consequent signalling stage works needed, it has been possible to accelerate the programme so that the final commissioning will now take place in July 1985, sixteen months ahead of the original schedule.

BRIGHTON LINE -- FACTS AND FIGURES

Route Km	181	Relays	28,500
Track Km	451	Location cases	800
Routes	1,020	Remote Interlockings	12
Track Circuits	1,050	TDM remote control links	24
Points ends	508	Train Describer berths	608
Colour light signals	440		

WESTINGHOUSE ON THE SOUTHERN

Westinghouse Signals has a long and happy association with British Rail Southern Region, having been entrusted with many major resignalling projects which have included:

Barnes	1959	Surbiton	1969
Kent Coast Phase I — Herne Hill to Swanley	1960	Feltham	1974
Kent Coast Phase II — Hither Green to Tonbridge	1961	London Bridge	1976
		Salisbury	1981
Basingstoke	1968	Waterloo — new interlocking	1983
Tulse Hill — Crystal Palace	1968	Brighton line	1984

WESTINGHOUSE SIGNALS LIMITED
PO BOX 79, Pew Hill, Chippenham,
Wiltshire, SN15 1JD England.
Telephone (0249) 654141
Telex 44618 Telefax (0249) 652322

Bibliography

Books

Signal Box Register Volume 4: Southern Railway (Signalling Record Society, 2009)

Biddle, Gordon, *Britain's Historic Railway Buildings* (Oxford University Press, 2003)

Cooper, B.K. *Railway Centres: Brighton* (Ian Allan, 1981)

Eddols, John, *The Brighton Line* (David & Charles, 1983)

Gabe, Conway, and Wyn Ford, *The Metropolis of Mid Sussex* (Charles Clarke, 1981)

Gray, Adrian, *The London to Brighton Line* (Oakwood Press, 1977)

Hoare, John, *Sussex Railway Architecture* (Harvester Press, 1979)

Lyman, Ian P., *Railway Clocks* (Mayfield Books, 2004)

Marshall, Lawrence, *O.J. Morris's Southern Railways 1919–1959* (Middleton Press, 1997)

Marx, Klaus, *London, Brighton & South Coast Railway Album* (Ian Allan, 1982)

Marx, Klaus, *The Lewes & East Grinstead Railway* (Oxford Publishing, 2000)

Minnis, John, *The London, Brighton & South Coast Railway* (Tempus Publishing, 1999)

Mitchell, Vic, and Keith Smith, *East Croydon to Three Bridges* (Middleton Press, 1988)

Mitchell, Vic, and Keith Smith, *Three Bridges to Brighton* (Middleton Press, 1986)

Nock, O.S., *A Hundred Years of Speed with Safety: The Inception and Progress of the Westinghouse Brake & Signal Company Ltd* (Hobnob Press, 2006)

Robertson, Kevin, *Southern Infrastructure 1922–1934: Stations/Signalling/Trackwork – Photographs from the E. Wallis Collection* (Noodle Books, 2014)

Robertson, Kevin, *Southern Infrastructure 1922–1934: A Second Selection – Photographs from the E. Wallis Collection* (Noodle Books, 2014)

Tait, Geoffrey, *The Gatwick Express* (G. Tait & Associates, n.d.)

The Signalling Study Group, *The Signal Box: A Pictorial History and Guide to Designs* (Oxford Publishing Company, 1986)

Turner, J.T. Howard, *The London, Brighton & South Coast Railway*, Volumes 1-3 (Batsford, 1977/78/79)

Other Publications

BR(S) Signalling Alterations: Section 'C' WONs 1949–1985 (DVD Format, Produced by the Signalling Record Society)

SR & BR(S) Signal Diagrams (DVD Format, Produced by the Signalling Record Society)

The Signalling Record, Journal of the Signalling Record Society

Brighton Circular, Journal of the Brighton Circle

Within a wonderful panorama looking across to the London Road viaduct and beyond, the 3.15pm departure from Brighton is about to pass beneath the girder stage, while an array of locomotives musters in the foreground. *September 1903, The Laurie Marshall Collection*